MANAGERIAL

AND

INDUSTRIAL ECONOMICS

JOHN A. SHUBIN

Associate Professor of Economics
New York University

THE RONALD PRESS COMPANY • NEW YORK

2

338
S562

Library of Congress Catalog Card Number: 61-7740

Preface

This book presents a comprehensive approach for conducting an economic analysis of an industry and a firm. It demonstrates how economic concepts and analytic tools may be employed for solving industrial problems and for formulating long-range investment programs and business policies to adapt the enterprise for profitability. Throughout, the relevant principles and concepts are incorporated at that point in the book where they can be concretely employed to demonstrate economic analysis and business behavior; and the kind of knowledge and conceptual approaches is provided that leads to deeper insight into the economic nature and behavior of industry and business.

The book is written primarily from the point of view of the executive manager who employs economic concepts and analytic tools to design the enterprise and adapt the business for long-term gain, and from the point of view of the economic analyst conducting a comprehensive survey of an industry and a business, or conducting a more specialized study—for instance, a survey and analysis of structural change and productivity gains in a given industry, or the formulation of an approach for establishing an industry in an underdeveloped country.

To assure the reader sufficient grasp of the dynamic aspects of industry and business, discussions include the process of industrialization, the role of resources and technological advance, the mainsprings of productivity, and economic growth and structural change. Thus, emphasis is placed on dynamic developments as well as equilibrium tendencies in industry. The analytic framework for the economic analysis of an industry and for managerial decision making and investment planning is formulated in terms of (1) the structural design of the industry and the firm, (2) the environmental impacts on business enterprise, (3) projected economic and business trends, and (4) managerial goals and motivations.

In outlining the "structural pattern" of the composite industry and the firm, technological and economic factors that give rise to alternative patterns and behavior in industry and business enterprise are presented in some detail. Such conceptual aspects are examined as the organizational design of business and the supply and demand for productive factors within the structural and operational context found in industry, the role of technology and cost and demand factors in the growth or the maturity of an industry, and the ways in which managers adapt the enterprise to environment (cyclical fluctuations, fiscal policy, union policy) in order to stabilize operations and maximize profits.

Thus, an industry's structural pattern is outlined in terms of the particular resource, technological, production, and market aspects that characterize enterprise in a given line of business. This approach serves to clarify both internal and external aspects of business enterprise and shows why managerial decision-making problems differ from industry to industry. Such a pragmatic presentation of the theory of the firm opens up many more areas and facets for realistic analysis and quantification of managerial decision-making problems than would the presentation of a purely abstract theory of the firm. The text exposes the student to economic analysis and decision-making problems dealing with the product line, modernization of productive processes, expansion of capacity, inventory behavior, short-run adjustment of production, and long-range planning.

A large part of this book grew out of the author's teaching the course Industrial and Managerial Economics at New York University over a period of some eight years. The author acknowledges with deep appreciation the intellectual heritage of the past and is indebted to students who were the stimulus for clarifying the economic concepts and approach of the subject matter in various stages of its development. The author benefited from discussions with professional colleagues which contributed to the formulation of the scope and focus of this field of study and is grateful for the encouragement and suggestions offered. The author appreciates the kindness of the various publishers in granting permission to reproduce charts and other material in this book; numerous sources are acknowledged and special references are made in the footnotes.

JOHN A. SHUBIN

New York
January, 1961

Contents

Part I: ECONOMIC DEVELOPMENT

Part II: THE INDUSTRY

v

Part III: *THE FIRM*

Part IV:
FORECASTING AND LONG-TERM BUSINESS PLANNING

Part I

ECONOMIC DEVELOPMENT

CHAPTER 1

Resources and Industrialization

It is primarily through the growth of its productive capacity that a country attains an increase in the output of goods per man-hour. If there is to be an improvement in living standards, the growth in national income must be greater than the growth in population. Economic growth is, therefore, the long-term increase in output of goods and services per capita—the increase must be in terms of real income per capita.[1]

The economic development of each country is shaped by its particular geographical setting and resource endowments and by the development of its cultural, as well as economic, institutions. As the institutional environment in the Western countries evolved, conditions became more conducive to economic growth. The *process of economic growth* in the United States and Western Europe occurred through a series of interrelated evolutionary developments and structural transformations in the economy which may be briefly summarized.

The gradual unification and integration of the national economy increased the size of markets and enlarged the scope of geographical specialization which led to increased efficiency in the utilization of resources and labor and a rise in the level of output. Thus in the

---

[1] "Real" income is generally measured in dollars of constant purchasing power: the money expression of national income must be corrected by a price index which adjusts for changes in the price level of goods and services. An increase in real income per capita understates somewhat the improvement in the level of living, since an increase in income does not fully reflect the improvement in the quality and durability of goods and the social value of greater leisure resulting from the long-run trend toward a shorter work week. Though it is not measurable, the ultimate output of an economy is the amount of "utility" created and enjoyed by society.

3

early agrarian economy the transition from self-sufficient agriculture to commercial agriculture raised the level of production through the more effective allocation and exploitation of resources. The rise of trade and the development of private enterprise and a favorable environment for business facilitated the expansion of commerce and the growth of an entrepreneurial class which accumulated capital for the development of industry.

Once economic growth starts, it tends to become cumulative— growth is sustained by the greater availability of natural resources, the expansion of population and labor force, larger savings from rising national income, and technological progress. The development of transportation and the discovery of new resources and improved methods for their exploitation enlarged the resource base and the availability of materials for industry. The growth of population increased the size of the labor force and the market for goods, stimulated investment in industry, and increased the degree of flexibility in the economy. Savings accrued from earnings in business and from growing national income; and investment was stimulated by the profit prospects created by growth in markets, the discovery of rich resources, and advances in technology.

Entrepreneurs, on the basis of a series of early technological innovations, increasingly industrialized production by establishing mechanized factories for the low-cost output of goods. This progressively displaced the high-cost handicraft method of output in the supply of growing markets. Through plow-back investment industrialization spread and new industries grew out of technological advances in the form of new products, processes, materials, and energy sources. Simultaneously industrial efficiency increased through improved organization of production and distribution of goods. The rise of big business ushered in large-scale research which accelerated the creation of technological innovations. These opened up new fields for business and, in turn, stimulated investment.

The growth of mass-production industry increased the efficiency of production; and the growth of industrial centers comprised of specialized producers led to additional economies which lowered the input prices of productive factors. Technological advances and internal and external economies lowered the cost of production and the input prices of materials and labor, giving rise to long-term gains in productivity.

An analysis of the process of economic growth and industrialization outlines the structural evolution and the moving forces of economic development which offer insights into the nature and growth of industry and into the managerial problem of planning investment in business enterprise. The process of economic growth and the development of business enterprise are traced in the pages following.

Development of a National Economy

The emergence of the national economy and the transition to capitalism induced early economic growth through gradual transformation of the agrarian economy. As trade widened, regional specialization of economic activity increasingly took over. The early village produced at a subsistence level and was virtually self-sufficient. Households and manorial estates turned out agricultural goods and handicraft products for direct consumption, though some goods were exchanged locally. In market towns and larger villages handicraft output was somewhat more specialized. The economy, based on hand methods of production, was unable to increase output per capita.

The gradual growth of commerce, however, created a merchant class and a group of enterprising master craftsmen who were able to see and exploit economic opportunities. Commerce was hampered, however, by regional and local restrictions (tolls, tariffs, local money systems) of the independent and semiautonomous principalities. Merchants and traders recognized the business opportunities and economic benefits that would accrue from a central government which would remove the internal restrictions to trade, create large national markets, unify the economy, and promote foreign trade. Hence, the growing merchant class supported the monarch against the feudal barons (and their local restrictions) who stood in the path of the creation of a strong central state and an integrated national economy.

Once established, the centralized autocratic state pursued nationalistic economic policies (i.e., the mercantilist philosophy) designed primarily to strengthen the power of the state through the fostering of trade, chartering of monopoly companies, acquisition of colonies, and other measures. Their effect was incidentally to improve business and enrich the merchants.

The national state enlarged the scope of commerce, encouraging a limited expansion of industry (primarily on the basis of handicraft production) and fostering a measure of economic growth through greater geographical specialization. So the Western European countries gradually evolved from their predominantly self-sufficient village pattern to national economies oriented to regional and international markets.[2] Because of their early transition to comparatively cen-

---

[2] By the late eighteenth century economic life had become less static. As a consequence mercantilist regulations became antiquated and inoperative.

tralized states and their advantageous geographical and economic orientation, England, France, and Holland developed viable nationalistic-commercial empires that have continued into the twentieth century. The transition to a national economy opened up lucrative internal trade and profitable commercial opportunities throughout the world.

However, the growing entrepreneurial class felt increasingly hampered by the restraints of governmental mercantilist policies. Businessmen were at first unable to secure removal of the restraints which limited the scope and opportunity for enterprise. Thus, there ensued a conflict between the merchant middle class and the aristocracy for the domination of the state. In England the revolution of 1688 led to a government dominated by large merchants and landlords and friendly to business interests. In America the revolution of 1776 opened the way to economic liberalism—the Constitution of the United States removed the commercial barriers among the member states and thereby forged a national economy. By mid-nineteenth century in Western Europe the increasingly influential middle class (merchants, bankers, and industrialists) attained sufficient political influence to remove governmental restraints progressively on business and thereby establish the institutional environment that permitted capitalist enterprise to flourish. The legal system, too, became geared to the needs and interests of the middle class and private enterprise.

Industrialization initially took hold in England in mid-eighteenth century because of a favorable combination of geographical, political, and economic factors which permitted uninterrupted evolution of economic development. Beginning about 1760, a series of inventions were made that in time completely revolutionized the existing methods of producing goods.

The transition to a capitalist economy involved a greater legal recognition and protection of property rights, the elimination of certain restraints on trade, the curtailment of government intervention in economic affairs, and the reservation of a large area for private initiative and enterprise for profits. Stimulated by the profit motive, business enterprise flourished in a favorable environment which included freedom of contract and increased mobility of the productive factors, thus allowing a greater play of the market forces in the allocation of resources for the output of the goods and services. The growth of capitalism and the expansion of industry were accompanied and facilitated by the development of a sounder money and banking system, stock exchanges, and the modern corporate form of enterprise. The advent of effective and comparatively stable governments in the nineteenth century preserved business institutions and insured the maintenance of the domestic tranquility required for economic expansion on the basis of the growth in the supply of labor, capital, and other resources.

NATURAL RESOURCES, LABOR, AND CAPITAL FORMATION

Once economic growth had begun through a greater volume of trade and geographical specialization and the emergence of a favorable institutional environment, economic growth was sustained by the expansion of markets and the increase in the quantity of productive factors and technological development. Rising national income and purchasing power, coupled with technological progress, created investment outlets which induced further savings and capital accumulation. This led to still further growth in national income. The development of transportation progressively increased the scope of the market and the scale of production.

Development of Transportation and Markets

Improvements in ocean shipping and the extension of foreign trade led to increased overseas settlement and the acquisition of colonies which were more or less integrated with the growing economies as suppliers of raw materials and as markets for products. Throughout the nineteenth century markets were growing not only because of improved transportation but because of the increase in demand stemming from population growth and rising income. The expansion of overseas trade augmented specialization and raised productivity. The level of earnings and the accumulation of capital were thereby promoted.

Western governments fostered the improvement of transportation and communication because of their desire to encourage trade and economic development. Revolutionary improvements in transportation were an essential factor in the development of national economies. During the nineteenth century transportation (railway, road, inland water, and ocean shipping) expanded. Service improved in speed and reliability and became less expensive. Railroads provided direct, fast, and continuous service not offered by other transportation media. Because of their capital-intensive nature and large potential capacity, transportation networks absorbed large amounts of investment, the return from which extended into the future as the carrying capacity became more fully utilized. The provision of quick transportation opened up geographical areas and accelerated the development of resources.

The spreading transportation network linked a multitude of small isolated trading and producing centers. The enlarged scope of economic activity and markets encouraged the adoption of mass-production methods in the output of a greater volume and variety of goods. By increasing the mobility of productive factors and by enlarging the area over which resources could be used in production, transportation networks widened geographical specialization and increased efficiency in the use of human as well as natural resources.

Development of Natural Resources

The possession of rich natural resources by no means guarantees that a country will undergo rapid economic development, for resources may lie unused. Until economic and technological development reveals their use-value, resources may even remain undiscovered. It is the level of technology and the state of industrial arts that, in fact, determine what constitutes a natural resource. In the process of economic development, technological advance opens up new possibilities for the exploitation of resources, and as population grows and markets widen, resources provide a base for a more specialized organization of production. A country's industrial development is, of course, influenced by the particular resources it possesses.

Industrial growth depends on the availability of such metallic resources as iron, manganese, copper, zinc, tin, and bauxite and on the availability of such fuel resources as coal, petroleum, gas, and hydroelectric sites. Natural resources are brought into effective use especially quickly when complementary resources and population and market centers are located in close proximity. Shortages in some resources can usually be made up through imports.

The rapid expansion of transportation in the United States, especially after 1860, opened up rich areas and accelerated the development of the economy. Agricultural development supported the expansion of manufacturing industry and commerce by supplying industry with low-priced raw materials (fibers, oils, etc.) and by providing workers with abundant food. The development of agricultural resources involved changes such as those in landholdings and the introduction of new and improved crops and techniques of cultivation.[3]

[3] In Europe the gradual transition to commercial agriculture increased production through the consolidation of small parcels of land (i.e., through the inclosure movement) and through an expansion of acreage attained by drainage and other methods

The increasing demand for agricultural products was met by more intensified and improved output generally. The United States, for example, added 50,000,000 acres to its cultivated area during 1870–90. With the development of transportation and the growth of urban and overseas markets, American agriculture was transformed from self-sufficient farming to commercial farming. The relative scarcity of labor induced the American farmer to use more machinery. The increased output in America and other areas of the world lowered the price of farm products. This stimulated the search for improved methods of output and encouraged further specialization.

The contributors to agricultural progress have been varied—private societies, government agencies, and publicly supported agricultural schools. Progress has come along a number of lines: (1) Output was increased by bringing additional land into production through improved reclamation and conservation practices. (2) Agricultural yield per acre was increased through improvement of soil fertility made possible by a better system of crop rotation, the study of soil chemistry and plant nutritional requirements, and the use of chemical fertilizers. (3) Agricultural yield and the quality of crops have been improved through new and better varieties of plants, the breeding of higher-yielding and stronger "disease-resistant" plants, and through the control of plant diseases. (4) Output of livestock was increased and quality improved through selective breeding, control of diseases, and the development of more nutritional and cheaper feeds. (5) Output was increased and costs reduced through mechanization—the development and more extensive use of equipment permits better methods of cultivation and savings in labor time.

Long-term productivity gains in agriculture, mining, and other extractive industries increase the output of materials needed by industry and release an immense amount of labor for industrial employment. Thus growth and progress in agriculture and mining smooth the way for industrialization to increase output in the manufacturing and service sectors of the economy.

Progress in agriculture and other extractive industries is obviously aided by manufacturing which shoulders some of the work of the extractive industries by supplying such items as equipment, fuel, and chemical fertilizers. Long-term growth in one sector of the economy tends to promote directly growth in other sectors. In the short run, however, growth in one sector may entail competition for labor and other productive factors with other sectors of the economy.

of reclamation of wasteland. The growth of urban markets in turn led to greater specialization and efficiency in agriculture.

Growth of Population and Labor Force

Since the start of the nineteenth century, the population and labor force in the United States and Europe have grown tremendously. This growth was made possible in the first instance by an increase in the production of food, clothing, and other necessities. Past and projected growth trends of the population of the United States are indicated in Table 1-1. Rate of growth stems directly from the annual natural increase plus net immigration (i.e., the annual number of births minus the annual number of deaths, plus the annual number of immigrants minus the annual number of

TABLE 1-1
Population of the United States: Actual, 1900-58,
and Projected, 1965 and 1975

Year	Population (thousands)			Average Annual Increase in Total Population	
	Total	Male	Female	Period	Per Cent
Actual					
1900	76,094	38,869	37,226		
1910	92,407	47,554	44,852	1900-10	2.0
1920	106,466	54,295	52,171	1910-20	1.4
1930	123,077	62,297	60,780	1920-30	1.5
1940	132,122	66,352	65,770	1930-40	0.7
1950	151,683	75,530	76,153	1940-50	1.4
1955	165,248	82,001	83,245	1950-55	1.7
1958	174,064	86,207	87,858	1955-58	1.7
Projected					
1965	193,643	95,562	98,081	1958-65	1.5
1975	225,552	111,113	114,439	1965-75	1.5

Source: U.S. Department of Commerce, Bureau of the Census.

emigrants). Both economic and non-economic factors affect the rate of population growth. Improvements in medicine, nutrition, and living standards lower infant mortality and increase the life span of people. Population growth in Western countries enabled greater specialization in production and more effective development and use of natural resources—expansion in production was closely related to the rapid increase in population.

Since the labor force is made up of a portion of the population, a growing population means an increase in the absolute size of the labor force. Because of the comparatively high rate of population increase during the period of its expansion, the United States had a "young" population. The young population in terms of age-mix (i.e., the proportion of people found in various age groups) enlarged the labor-force ratio (the ratio of labor force to population). Young workers were generally more productive, particularly during the period of industrialization when the necessary physical effort was still considerable in production. The adaptability of the labor force was enhanced by the fact that young people entering the labor market were comparatively mobile. Because labor mobility permits better matching of worker skills to jobs, it improves the productiveness of workers in industry. Continued mechanization and technological progress in agriculture, manufacturing, mining, and transportation displace manual labor and enlarge the supply of manpower

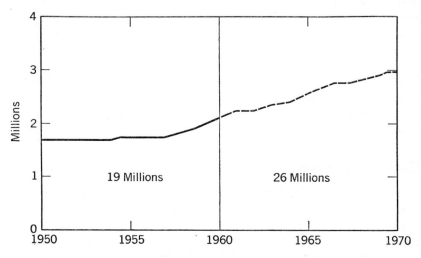

Fig. 1–1. New young workers entering the American labor force 1950 to 1970. (U.S. Department of Labor, *Manpower Challenge to the 1960s.* Washington, D.C.: Government Printing Office, 1960, p. 14.)

for economic growth. Steady growth of the labor force facilitates the flow of manpower to the expanding sectors of the economy.

Though the increasing number of entrants into the labor market swells the size of a labor force, this has been partially offset historically by the gradual shortening of the workweek. The industrial worker put in 75–80 hours a week a century ago; today the American worker puts in less than 40 hours. Because long working hours result in considerable fatigue and inefficiency, this gradual cut in the workweek has tended to raise the output per man-hour. Except for the most strenuous occupations, continuing reduction of the workweek below 40 hours may possibly lower the weekly output per worker.

The trend toward the earlier retirement of older workers and the withdrawal of younger adolescents (prompted by child labor laws and the spread of compulsory education) was an additional factor operating to reduce the labor-force ratio. This also changes the composition of the labor force so as to make the more vigorous and productive young a larger proportion of the whole. Economic development changes the industrial and occupational composition of the labor force (i.e., the distribution of the labor force among various industries and occupations). Industrialization also changes the spatial distribution of labor with respect to its allocation among geographical regions, rural and urban categories, and cities of various sizes. The growing national income and higher living standards in the advanced countries improve the quality and effectiveness of labor through education and training, better diets, and improved medical service. With the secular growth of the economy, continued expansion and improvement in education lead to additional gains in labor productivity. But it is essentially through capital formation that a country increases the long-term productiveness of labor and natural resources.

Capital Formation

Economic growth depends on savings and capital formation—investment in plant and equipment to establish factories and other productive facilities. If an economy is to save, it must produce more than it consumes. In the process of saving and investment, the economy shifts resources from the production of goods for current consumption to the production of capital goods (the creation of productive capacity) to be used for enlarging the future output of goods.

The initial economic surplus required for capital accumulation came from early increases in production above the subsistence level. This increased production came from greater geographical specialization and more effective exploitation of resources. In the earlier period of economic development, capital accumulated as a result of the growing commerce and trade that preceded the Industrial Revolution. It was accumulated by merchants who made profits from trade and commercial transactions and by landlords who received rent and earnings from their agricultural estates. The early industrial entrepreneurs and promoters of factory enterprise came largely from the prosperous merchants, landlords, and proprietors of handicraft shops, who had amassed private savings for investment in profitable business ventures.

Entrepreneurial capital accumulation was stimulated by the prospect of high profits from the adoption of more efficient production technology (from the adoption of mechanized factory output in place of handicraft output) to turn out goods for growing markets. As industrialization spread, capital formation became more self-generating: More capital was accumulated through the use of the retained earnings of business for plow-back investment. Internal financing was a primary means of financing industry up to the mid-nineteenth century.

The long-term growth in national income permitted larger personal as well as business savings. Business enterprise began to supplement plow-back financing with external financing which tapped those pools. The financing of business expansion through the use of external funds was facilitated by the growing adoption after 1850 of the modern corporate form of enterprise. The development of large-scale industry and the introduction of capital-intensive production processes called for an amassing of capital which an individual or several partners were usually not able to accumulate—hence the growing adoption of the modern corporate form of enterprise with its external financing through the public sale of securities to private investors. Further, the corporate form of enterprise stepped up domestic and international mobility of investment capital. In the second half of the nineteenth century, private investors and financial institutions in the advanced industrial and commercial countries (Britain, Belgium, and the Netherlands) supplied large amounts of capital to the rapidly growing industrial economies of Germany and the United States. Developing central-banking and commercial-banking systems in the advancing countries also supplied considerable amounts of funds. Long-term financing and credit creation through banking systems played an increasingly important role in the accumulation of capital required for industrialization and exploitation of technological innovations.

INDUSTRIALIZATION: TECHNOLOGICAL ADVANCE IN INDUSTRY

The growing volume of savings and widening markets with large potential demand created the economic pressure for greater output and the need for cost reduction through improvements in production technology. The search for new production methods stimulated the application of knowledge for the improvement of the industrial arts. Imaginative shopmen continued to invent and design production machines and to employ the steam engine as the source of power to operate the equipment. As man gradually reduced primary reliance

on human effort for increased output, he removed the historical bottleneck to increased productivity. Man was able to multiply im-
mensely his own productive effort by subdividing the production
process and designing power-driven machines as substitutes for manpower to carry out the series of operations necessary for the conversion of materials into final products. The power-driven mechanized
process housed in a building became the primary physical facility of
the factory system.

By mid-nineteenth century the United States had the requisites
for accelerated growth. Rapid industrialization did not take place
until 1860 when the western territories were being opened up and
the population grew rapidly. By that time production technology
and industrial organization suited to the United States had been
worked out in England and needed only to be adapted to American
conditions. The big upsurge in the industrialization of the United
States, Germany, and England came largely after 1870 when mass-
production technology and the railway, steel, coal, power, and ma-
chine-tool industries grew rapidly.

Thus, the process of industrialization started through the introduction of power-driven machinery and the factory system; the era
of industrialism began when the factory system of production supplemented commerce as the prime force of economic life in Western
Europe and the United States. The factory system was successively
introduced to new fields of production, spreading from industry to
industry and country to country as the requisite conditions for its
adoption came into existence. The Industrial Revolution of the
eighteenth century set in motion a process which attained greater
momentum as it proceeded through the nineteenth and into the
twentieth century.

The progressive evolution to an integrated economy and spread
of the factory system promoted economical output through greater
division of labor and the use of specialized mass-production processes which efficiently combined productive factors and lowered the
input of labor and materials per unit of output of goods. In the
process of industrialization, *new manufacturing industries originated*
or evolved from these sources: (1) The initial factory industries
grew through the displacement of the early handicraft production
of such consumer goods as textiles. (2) Additional consumer industries came into existence as household production (food canning,
bread baking, garment making) was taken over by factories for output on a commercial basis. (3) Many industries found their origin
directly in technological innovation—the electric power, automobile,
and plastics industries put out goods or services that displaced or

supplemented the output of older industries. (4) New industries putting out wholly new or novel products (motion pictures, television sets, air-conditioning units) also found their direct origin in technological progress. (The industries turning out novel products created a new consumer utility and market.) (5) The producer's goods industries, such as machine manufacturing, had their origin in derived demand—that is, from the growth of industry as a whole. As consumer-goods manufacture, transportation, and mechanized agriculture expanded, the growing demand for producer's goods led to the rapid development of the capital-goods industry. The capital-goods industry was among the fastest growing branches of manufacturing.

Once started, economic development tends to become cumulative: given the initial savings and a large market potential, the economic base for self-sustaining growth is created by the adoption of improved technology which increases output and savings and permits the further accumulation of capital and the adoption of new techniques and facilities of higher productivity. Hence, the introduction of the factory system as the vehicle of industrialization established an essentially self-expanding production technology in place of the earlier comparatively static system.

Technological innovations were a primary basis for, and stimulant to, industrialization. The scope and variations in scientific discovery and in the development of technology are immense. Though technological innovation stems from a wide and intricate combination of scientific developments, from an economic point of view progress in technology takes shape as, and is reducible to, certain primary *forms of advance*. Technological progress develops with these primary types of advance:

1. The development of products—creation of new products and the improvement of existing products
2. The development of materials—the discovery of new materials and the adaptation of existing materials to new uses
3. The development of power—innovations in mechanical power and the discovery of new types of energy
4. The development of chemical and electrical processes—discovery of new processing techniques and the improvement of existing techniques
5. The development of mechanical processes—discovery of new mechanical production techniques and the improvement of existing machinery
6. The development of mass-production methods and improvements in managerial practices—the rationalization of industry.

Technological progress in a given industry typically proceeds with the above forms of advance, but significant progress may be concentrated in one form. Not infrequently a given development in technology involves two or more forms of advance that are closely interrelated. The development of a new process, for instance, may produce a new material that may go into the making of a wholly new product. Progress in technology is both cause and effect—advances in technology stimulate capital formation and the accumulation of capital accelerates technological research. Technological progress and capital accumulation have been primary conditions and requirements for economic growth, and historically they have occurred in sufficient magnitude to offset diminishing returns in production. The primary forms of advance outlined below will indicate how technology has created new industries, led to enormous gains in productivity, and significantly changed the structure of the economy.

Development of Products

Producers have made notable progress in the art of designing products for increased consumer utility and for greater economy in manufacture. Progress in the design and improvement of products has, in part, been made possible by the development of better production techniques, more effective technical control of processes, and improvements in materials.

In general the durability and the life of both consumer goods and capital goods are extended, with greater durability gains in capital goods. Producers strive for a better balance in the wearability and life of the components that make up the final product. Progressively they have eliminated flaws and weaknesses in products, thus forestalling the premature wearing out of individual components. Because of the greater durability and reliability of products, expense for repair and maintenance tends to be lowered. Since fewer units of the product are required to satisfy the replacement demand of the market, resources are conserved, and materials, labor, and capital are released for other uses. Important also are the improvements which add new features and qualities to products, thus increasing their utility to consumers. Research and development introduce new products (e.g., household appliances, antibiotics) which not only enlarge the scope of consumer satisfaction but give rise to new industries.

Moreover, significant gains in industrial productivity are attained through industry-wide standardization and simplification programs, which eliminate excess variety in products and reduce the number of model sizes, and through redesigning of products for use of more economical production methods and more economical materials that are newly developed.

Development of Materials

Technological advances widen and enlarge the material resources base of industry through innovations that permit more complete and fuller utilization of raw materials and through the development of new and improved materials. The creation of new materials as well as the improvement of existing materials often grows out of the development and adoption of new processes and techniques.

Technological progress increases the supply of materials through improvements in processes that make for more effective and more thorough extraction of ore deposits, use of lower grades of raw materials, beneficiation to enrich lean ores, and use of smelting methods that conserve and "stretch out" mineral deposits. Through chemical and physical treatment, new processes have enabled industry to convert such cheap resources as coal, petroleum, cotton, wood, salt, sulfur, and gases into new materials with distinctive properties that widen their use. Every waste item, in fact, is considered a potential starting point for a new material. Chemical technology created synthetic materials and products in the fields of plastics, pharmaceuticals, detergents, and insecticides, for example.

Modern chemistry not only duplicates nature but creates materials with entirely new properties. It is possible not only to make the same material from different bases but also different materials from the same base. The development of a wide variety of materials has enlarged the possibilities of substitution. Production processes are adapted or new ones are developed to permit the use of cheaper materials in the manufacture of existing types of products. All this makes for keener competition among materials in general. Research widens the supply and increases the substitution and competition among energy materials—coal, lignite, petroleum, natural and artificial gas, hydroelectric power, and nuclear materials.

Development of Power

Technological advances in the field of industrial power played an integral role in the mechanization of production. The invention of the steam engine in the eighteenth century was the initial advance in the provision of industrial power. This early engine was the prime mover that powered the production machines and equipment in the textile mills, flour mills, breweries, and mines. The supply of steam power improved through the development of high-pressure steam engines and more effective methods of transmitting power from engines to machines. New prime movers (the electric dynamo, steam turbine, gasoline engine, diesel engine) evolved in the years from 1865 to 1900 to compete with the reciprocating steam engine and to promote new technological advances.

Faraday's work early in the nineteenth century eventually led to momentous advances in the provision of electric power for industry. The development of the dynamo (1873) ushered in a supply of electric power to industry, and the development of the transformer (after 1883) allowed for the transmission of electricity over longer distances. The invention of the steam turbine in 1884 provided a more efficient means for turning large dynamos and supplying power. As the range of transmission of electricity is extended, the erection of the economical "super-stations" makes available service in ever-wider areas, and the development of the "grid" system for distribution improves the reliability of electric power and lowers the cost of supplying it.

Electricity accelerated the mechanization of industry and increased the automatic character of machinery. Electric power, having the advantages of divisibility and flexibility in use, has facilitated the more general application of power in industry. The supply of power was made divisible and adaptable through the use of individual electric motors to drive each machine and through the use of small motors in the machine to turn its separate mechanisms (pumps, spindles). The use of electric power and motors led to the gradual revision and modernization of the layout of plant equipment along more rational and effective patterns that made possible more efficient flow of work through the process and prompted lower costs of production. Moreover, improvements in electric power prompted additional improvements in mechanical production processes as well as in non-mechanical processes.

Development of Non-mechanical Processes

The mid-nineteenth century witnessed an acceleration in technological advances in the form of new chemical and electrical processes—processes for producing ferrous and non-ferrous metals and for refining and converting petroleum, coal, natural chemicals, and other raw materials into a host of products.

By 1850 malleable iron and cast iron were produced cheaply by the puddling process, but the conversion of iron into steel was expensive. Little steel was produced until the development of the Bessemer process (1856), in which a cold blast of air injected at the bottom of a molten mass of iron in a furnace creates intense combustion that burns out carbon; the process substantially reduced the time required to convert pig iron into ingot steel. But the Bessemer process for making steel was difficult to control, and the steel was not of high quality. The adoption of the Siemens open-hearth converter in 1866 enabled the ironmasters to put out a higher-quality steel. In this process a hot stream of air and a flame of gas play on top of a mass of molten iron and slowly burn out the carbon. Though the method was somewhat slower, it permitted the use of scrap iron and produced more steel from a given charge in the converter.

In 1878 Thomas and Gilchrist introduced the practice of lining the Bessemer and the open-hearth furnace with magnesium limestone to permit the use of phosphoric iron ore which previously had been useless for steelmaking. The phosphorus combined with the limestone which, with other impurities, was run off as slag.[4] New innovations in processing further advanced steelmaking. The duplex process combined the Bessemer and the open-hearth process to speed up and reduce the cost of output. The electric furnace was introduced to put out high-quality steel alloys. The adding of manganese, tungsten, vanadium, chromium, or other ingredient metals to the molten charge in the furnace produced steel alloys of the desired hardness, tenacity, ductility, and resistance to rust.

The availability of rich iron and coal deposits in Western Europe and the United States and advances in processes, coupled with mechanization of metal fabrication (rolling, forging, pressing, and machining), led to an enormous expansion in the output of low-cost ingot steel and steel products. The growing supply of ferrous metals was supplemented by the increased output of non-ferrous metals made possible by innovations in the form of new processes—chemical and electrochemical refining of copper, aluminum, lead, zinc, etc. The expanding output of lower-priced metal alloys stepped up industrialization by providing higher-quality metals for the design of improved productive facilities—sturdier and better machinery, steam boilers, electric equipment, railroad rolling stock, and numerous other capital goods. Advances in chemical processes improved oil refining and allowed the breakdown and conversion of coal and

---

[4] The Thomas and Gilchrist innovations converted the large phosphoric iron ore deposits of Lorraine, France, into a rich resource which, together with Ruhr coal, enabled Germany to develop a great steel industry that contributed to her rapid industrialization before World War I.

natural chemicals (sulfur, potash) into a multitude of new materials and by-products. The "cracking" process in the distillation of oil improved the quality of petroleum products. The petrochemical industry derives synthetic organic chemicals from oil and gas. The distillation of coal for coke produces dyestuffs, drugs, solvents, and the like. The liquefaction of coal produces raw materials for plastics, synthetic rubber, and textile fibers.

Development of Mechanical Processes

The past hundred years have witnessed immense progress in the techniques and art of mechanizing operations in manufacturing, mining, agriculture, and transportation. Industrial mechanization is the process of developing and applying power-driven equipment for the performance of productive operations in the output of goods.

Initially the innovator designed equipment that was basically a device that mechanized existing tools and smaller devices to reproduce manual operations in the performance of such basic tasks as cutting, twisting, crushing and pulverizing, and grinding. When he acquired greater mechanical experience and knowledge, the innovator was able to apply mechanical principles and combine devices in his machine design to perform a wide variety of operations for manipulating or transforming material into useful products. His machine designs became more intricate and effective and found wider application in industry as he was able to build machines with improved alloys and such new prime movers as electric motors, hydraulic devices, and pneumatic devices.

EXTENSIVE MECHANIZATION. The first stage in industrialization was the extension and spread of mechanization (capital widening). Though the spread of mechanization varied in speed from industry to industry, the new production technology progressively extended its application until it came to embrace industries producing capital goods as well as consumer goods. The spread of mechanization to various fields of production roughly ran a similar course in all regions that became ripe for industrialization. In America, however, the abundance of natural resources and the relative scarcity of labor led to the development and greater utilization of the laborsaving type of machinery.

Industrialization entered an advanced stage of development after 1870 when important technological advances were more widely introduced in the fabrication of metal products. The mechanization of the metalworking trades was based on the development of "machine tools." Machine tools are the devices (lathes, planers, shapers, boring mills) that use mechanical power to drill, turn, mill, or otherwise cut and shape metal. They employ mechanical power to drive and control the cutting tool or the metal to be shaped and fabricated.[5] Progress in metalworking trades significantly reduces the cost of fabricating metal products. Though machine tools emerged as the "master tool" of practically all industry, they largely make up the production equipment of the metalworking industries.

A growing demand for machine tools and for producer's goods in general derives from the increasing pace of industrialization and from the mechanization of agriculture, mining, and transportation. The manufacture of machine tools has emerged as the very foundation of industrialization, and the ability to make plant machinery was a key feature of industrialization wherever it spread. The "capital-goods" stage of industrialization was the mark of an advanced industrial economy. By the turn of the century, the large industrial countries (the United States, Germany, and England) had attained a well-developed capital-goods industry which produced plant machinery for the overseas as well as the domestic market.

INTENSIVE MECHANIZATION. Since mid-nineteenth century, industrial output had expanded in Western Europe and the United States not only through the spread of machine methods to new fields of production but through the more intensive mechanization of the industries already producing on a factory basis. This "deepening" of capital progressively reduces the input of labor and increases the output per man hour with a consequent rise in productivity. The increased mechanization of factory production, however, called for greater managerial emphasis on the task of coordinating the productive factors, a problem that was a natural consequence of the intricacy of processes and specialization of functions.

In "perfecting" the factory and "deepening" the capital input, managers successively replaced older machines in the production line with improved and more automatic equipment and with more "tooled-up" machines. Jigs, fixtures, and other tooling were built and installed in production machines to hold parts in place, thus eliminating manual preparatory activity and hand finishing of work,

---

[5] Many men had contributed to the development of the early versions of the machine tools in the years from 1770 to 1800. Henry Maudslay in 1797, for example, had improved the metal-turning lathe by inventing the slide rest which made it easier to achieve precision metal cutting. Technicians, particularly after the mid-nineteenth century, further advanced the art of designing machine tools in a number of diversified and specialized forms.

while at the same time improving accuracy and workmanship. Attachments were designed and installed on machines to attain the automatic feeding and ejection of work. Plant managers also introduced mechanical devices to carry out inspection and quality control, the handling and storing of materials, and plant maintenance and other supporting activities that serve and facilitate the production line in its fabrication and assembly of a product.

The early method of transmitting power to machines (the overhead shafting, pulleys, and belts) was gradually replaced by the more efficient electric-motor drive for each machine or for a group of machines. Machinery and equipment of improved design and built of better metal alloys were sturdier, more durable, and capable of turning out work of greater uniformity and precision. Machines, too, were improved in terms of greater power and speed—this enlarged the machine output capacity.

The adoption of improved measuring instruments and gauges enabled the production worker and the inspector to do better work. In time, fully mechanized inspection devices and machines were used to control the quality of work and also to displace inspectors. Improvements in the handling and storing of materials, especially after World War I, achieved substantial laborsavings. Manual handling methods are increasingly being displaced by conveyor belts, monorails, fork-lift trucks, and adaptable overhead cranes.

MASS-PRODUCTION TECHNOLOGY AND SPECIALIZED PRODUCTION

Intensive mechanization was accelerated by the steady transition to the mass-production method of manufacture. This method of production was increasingly employed for the output of agricultural machinery, typewriters, automobiles, and other products for which there were extensive markets and a large potential demand. The mass-production method of output employs *repetitive* processes and specialized facilities to put out a large volume of standard products. The economic feasibility of employing mass-production processes depends on a large market and the standardization of the product. The larger the output of uniform products, the greater the division and specialization of processes and operations possible. The mass production of uniform products in turn calls for the standardization of the materials, the production facilities and processes, and the level of workmanship. This means that quality, performance, and other required norms for the productive factors must be specified, established, and maintained. Hence, standardization underlies mass-production technology and makes possible large-scale output and distribution.

But how does modern mass-production industry, in fact, achieve efficiency and economy in output? It achieves a low-cost combination of productive factors because a large volume of output permits the division of the process into comparatively simple steps and tasks that can be highly mechanized on an economical basis. Since each step in the process is simple, efficient special-purpose equipment (production machines, tools, handling and inspection devices) can readily be designed and built. Recent technological advances in mechanization (automation), moreover, make it economically feasible to design facilities that (1) automatically perform a series of different operations on a given component part or (2) simultaneously perform a series of different operations on a given part or piece of work.

Thus, the mid-twentieth century witnessed the further perfection of the factory. Electronically controlled "transfer" machines are being adopted in increasing numbers. These facilities automatically move and position parts from one machine to the next. Machines are being designed with automatic control devices; the devices employ the "feedback" principle (the feedback of information as to the condition and state of the operation) for the self-regulating control of the machine process. The self-correcting feedback control facilities are introduced only when they are economical and suited to the industrial process.[6]

It is fundamentally the intensive utilization of specialized machinery and speed in production that attains low labor costs and low capital costs per unit of output of product. Through the adoption of mass-production methods, producers essentially substitute specialized facilities for high-priced labor. Division of labor and the use of specialized facilities transfer the "work effort" and the skill from the operator to the machine, making the quantity and quality of output more dependent upon the machine process than upon the operator. Thus, mass-production facilities permit the employment of semiskilled workers for the output of goods that require a relatively close uniformity in the quality of workmanship. Moreover, highly intricate facilities can perform technical operations and do work that cannot otherwise be carried out. The uninterrupted op-

---

[6] When the industrial conditions made it economically feasible, electronic computers were introduced. These devices are used for data processing in inventory control, quality control, production planning, accounting (accounts receivable and payable), financial records, etc. Information and instructions are fed on punched cards or tape, and mathematical operations and solutions are quickly put out by the computer on magnetic tape or recorded on cards or rolls of paper.

eration of such integrated manufacturing processes is, of course, essential in keeping production costs at a minimum.

Ideally, to realize the full economic benefit from the mass-production method calls for a comparative fixity (the "freezing") of the design of the product and the manufacturing process for the duration of the productive life of the facilities. Because of the inflexibility of many types of special-purpose equipment and because the equipment is often susceptible to rapid obsolescence, producers attempt to anticipate radical changes in the product design and in the techniques of production in order that they may plan for their systematic adoption with a minimum of obsolescence. This conversion can often be timed to coincide with periodic plant modernization and machine replacement.

Mass-production methods have been introduced in those industries in which the product and the process can be standardized and the facilities employed intensively for a large volume of output. An up-to-date bituminous coal mine, for example, uses specially designed facilities for cutting, loading, and rapid transit of the product to the surface. The cigarette industry employs specially built facilities in its carefully controlled repetitive process for aging, handling, blending, shredding, and rolling of the tobacco and for packaging of the product. The large bakery uses mass-production facilities for the blending, sifting, and mixing of flour, proofing of dough, and for the baking and wrapping of bread. The cannery employs specialized mass-production equipment for cleaning and trimming, blanching, filling, preheating, sealing, cooking, cooling, labeling, and packing of the product.

A more elaborate mass-production system, however, is required for the manufacture of the "assembled type" of durable goods, as in the case of the automobile, appliance, radio, and watch industries. The same production method, though less complex, is employed in the output of such soft goods as shoes and ready-to-wear clothing. For the output of the assembled type of product, mass-production technology employs the principle of interchangeability of parts— standard interchangeable components go into the final assembly of the product. The mass assembly of the product requires that the component parts and the subassemblies be manufactured in advance of the final assembly stage of the process. The completed product is the final assembly made up of a number of parts and subassemblies that are put together in a planned sequence on a moving platform or other conveyor. At appropriate points in the process, subassembly lines feed components to the final assembly line where they are installed to complete the product. The mechanical pacing of the assembly lines (on which the product is gradually built up) coordinates the flow of production and sets the rate of output.

To achieve effective interchangeable-parts manufacture, component parts must be fabricated within the prescribed specification limits of size so that any one part selected at random from a large number of the same kind of parts will fit in assembly and function satisfactorily with any one of a large number of mating parts. Thus, we find that the parts made for one sewing machine or tractor will fit all others of the same model. The mass output of highly engineered products (automobiles, radios) calls for rigid adherence to stipulated limits of size and other specifications by a large number of suppliers who manufacture hundreds of parts and subassemblies (transmissions, generators, electric motors, electronic controls). Errors in the interpretation of specifications or the output of substandard units results in large financial losses and delay or shutdown of assembly lines. Depending on the nature and the design of the product, the tolerance limits of the specifications may be wide or narrow. The more liberal the "specs" (i.e., the wider the limits), the greater the speed and economy of output.[7]

For economy of output, the items that make up a line of products are designed for maximum interchangeability of components among the various models. Through analysis and ingenuity, designers and production engineers often create a wide diversity of products from common component parts and subassemblies. Their product specifications stipulate the manufacture of component units to be used in common for the various products in the line, and they also stipulate the purchase from outside producers of standard supply items (bolts, tubings, pipe fittings) and assembled units (ball bearings, gear-reduction sets, pumps, valves, instruments). These mass-produced components are then built up on the assembly lines that put out the stipulated line of products. Hence, a minimum number of manufactured components are designed to assemble into a maximum number of end products. By extending the application of the principle of interchangeability in the above manner, engineers attain a

---

[7] When close precision fitting of parts is necessary, costly fabrication of these parts can be avoided through the use of broader tolerances and "selective assembly." Under this method companion parts going into the product are gauged and sorted into classes according to size. During assembly the units of each class are selected for installation with mating parts of the corresponding class or size bracket. The economic applicability of the selective-assembly method is determined by balancing the savings gained in manufacturing against the difficulty and cost of replacing the parts when the product later comes up for repair.

large volume output of components, increase the repetitiveness of processes, and thus widen the scope of the mass-production system.[8] This conserves resources by permitting longer production runs, which reduce the total amount of capital facilities required for a given output and reduce inventory levels by stepping up their turnover.

Though modern production is predominantly repetitive production (plants are specially designed to put out a large volume of standard products), a small portion of the output in the manufacturing sector of the economy is devoted to non-repetitive production —products manufactured to customers' specifications. Such production is essentially single-unit or small-order work put out by adaptable plant facilities. Since each order is distinct and different, production is handled on an individual-order basis. Many of the components and subassemblies that go into the special-order products are, however, standard items mass-produced on a repetitive basis. The job shops turning out special-order products are found in a number of industries that undertake custom type of production, viz., shipbuilding, special machinery and equipment, foundry products, and experimental or prototype products. Fundamentally, these producers "sell" their manufacturing capacity—the backlog of diverse orders make up the "effective demand" against the comparatively adaptable plant capacity.

The construction industry erects on a non-repetitive basis many of its structures (commercial buildings, plant buildings, industrial installations, public works). Though the industry erects each project according to stipulated specifications, the fabricated steel, structural sections, plumbing, and other items erected or installed are standard items turned out by the mass-production industries. The non-repetitive phase of construction work is the unique assembly of components and sections to the special design. The construction industry does, however, put up many standard structures: low-income dwellings, certain kinds of commercial buildings (chain stores, gasoline stations), and some plants of horizontally combined firms that have duplicate establishments. In the mass-production of such structures, not only are the components (sections, equipment, and fixtures) standard and mass-produced, but the entire design of the structure itself is largely standard. This permits the extension of standard processes to the final erection phase of the project. The foregoing innovations in production processes and technology ulti-

---

[8] Even a small country such as Sweden or Belgium can competitively attain the economies of mass production if it supplements its home market with an adequate volume of steady exports and if its producers establish specialized chains of plants, each concentrating in a narrow line of production.

mately derive from the general progress in industrial research and the inventive process, as outlined in the pages following.

RESEARCH AND DEVELOPMENT

Because communication and dissemination of scientific and technological knowledge is wide and because the needs and problems of industry are more or less common to all industrial societies, a given discovery is often simultaneously made by two or more people or organizations in different places. Technically, the discoveries may be duplicate inventions, or they may be equivalent inventions, i.e., serving the same purpose. The state of arts, inventions, and technological progress is, in a sense, the result of the industrial and economic process; in the broader perspective it can be viewed as a social process influenced by the cultural traits and values of society. Economic development fundamentally depends upon the growth of technological and scientific knowledge.[9]

In the second half of the nineteenth century, as a result of progress in the physical sciences, independent scientists and engineers produced an increasing number of commercially important inventions. The choice of subject depended on the inventor's background, interest, and abilities, as well as on his estimate of the profitability of a discovery. Their detachment from industry permitted them to embark on original research (often in an improvised laboratory) which in outstanding cases led to major new discoveries.

In carrying out the inventive process, the innovator thinks up, contrives, or discovers by study and experiment some technique or item. The professional inventor draws upon the accumulated knowledge and the results of technical experiments of his day. During the inventive process he may rearrange or combine in a new pattern the existing techniques and devices to make something new; or he may apply scientific principles in a practical manner for some pro-

[9] From the time of early industrialization, inventors and practical shopmen were motivated in their creative effort to improve the techniques of production by the profits that can be made by introducing new or improved products to supply growing markets and by reducing costs through the development of more economical prime movers, materials and fuels, and mechanical techniques and processes for production of goods. They were also, of course, motivated by the psychological reward and social recognition of their creativeness. The inventions of the eighteenth and much of the nineteenth century (the steam engine, devices for spinning and weaving, machine tools, new methods for smelting ore) were not made by scientists in laboratories who applied the discoveries of pure research. The inventions were made primarily by shopmen and imaginative artisans who were close to the practical problems of production and who knew very little science. These innovators applied their practical knowledge and mechanical experience to the solution of the technical problems of production and to overcoming obvious deficiencies in processes and products.

ductive purpose. The innovator makes the invention patentable [10] by embodying it in a drawing, model, or in some other physical form which achieves complete and accurate disclosure of his idea.

The pattern of technological advance in industry typically consists of successive accretions to, and modifications of, the existing practice in the industrial arts and technological knowledge. Engineers and practitioners in industrial plants encountering a production problem develop in time a method or a device to solve or circumvent the problem. Moreover, individuals working in one art or technical field not infrequently make unanticipated inventions in another field. The great developments in industrial technology (the internal-combustion engine, airplane, nuclear energy) are primarily the result of long-run cumulative increments of discovery and improvement rather than the creations of individual geniuses.

Thus, man enlarges and advances scientific knowledge through the research process whereby he hypothesizes and manipulates concepts and applies principles and experiments to extend, verify, or refine knowledge. The knowledge he gains may lead to the formulation of a theory, or it may facilitate the practice of an art. Progress, therefore, calls for two broad categories of research effort: (1) Basic research explores the fields of pure science (mathematics, physics, etc.) to gain greater knowledge of, and new insights into, nature. (2) Applied research and development translate the findings of pure research into production or some practical use.

Basic research is concerned with exploring the unknown and with learning more accurately the characteristics of known facts, all without any particular thought of their immediate, practical utility. Because it explores the unknown without definite goals, basic (fundamental) research is the ultimate source of scientific knowledge, the pacemaker of progress in technology. Basic research is unpredictable—there is no way of telling where new discoveries will be found or what observations will be made. Discoveries often result from experiments undertaken with very different purposes in mind and from accidental findings.

The growth of pure science cannot be forced. Knowledge in pure science is stimulated by an intellectual environment conducive to creativeness, and its growth depends upon wide dissemination of scientific findings, communications, open discussions, and the sharing of ideas. European governments early established the tradition of fostering scientific progress through direct financial support to universities and other centers of scientific learning. Throughout the

---

[10] A patent is a contract, dealing with an invention, between the government and the inventor.

nineteenth century the United States depended on Europe as a source of scientific capital. American advances in the applied technical arts were built upon the basic discoveries of European scientists.[11] In the last decade of the nineteenth century, however, American governmental financial support and private endowments for scientific research in colleges and non-profit institutions were developed. Since basic research contributes invaluable knowledge to society, it is obvious that a relatively small investment in basic research can, over a period of time, yield considerable returns, though a clear distinction cannot always be made between pure and applied research. "There is a perverse law governing research: Under the pressure for immediate results, and unless deliberate policies are set up to guard against this, *applied research invariably drives out pure.*"[12] Pure science has flourished when basic research has been carried out in a favorable intellectual climate with adequate financial support and social recognition.

Applied research aims to translate the accumulated knowledge and the abstract discoveries of pure science into practical use. A broad division of labor has evolved among applied scientists responsible for putting basic research to practical use: The discoveries in the life sciences are applied by physicians and agricultural scientists; the discoveries in the physical sciences are applied largely by engineers. The pure scientist effectively works on his own—guided by his curiosity about nature, he freely moves from one problem to another as his results warrant and as his interest shifts. The work of applied scientists and engineers, however, can be outlined in advance and organized as a group effort to attain rather specific results and particular technological goals. Applied research can be more or less directed in its translation of pure science into new and improved products, materials, and processes. In contrast to basic research, applied research can be somewhat stepped up through accelerated programs but at higher cost. Applied research must feed on a constant flow of new basic knowledge if it is to attain long-term technological advance. Basic scientific discovery and technological advance tend to become increasingly inseparable.

Thus, technological progress is attained through the application of scientific knowledge and the use of the analytical methods of science for the improvement of the industrial arts. Industrial technology is essentially the result of the application of accumulated knowledge and techniques for the designing of products and mech-

[11] Vannevar Bush, *Science, The Endless Frontier* (Washington, D.C.: Government Printing Office, 1945), pp. 2, 14.
[12] *Ibid.*, p. 77.

anisms and for developing production processes that efficiently use productive factors. Technology is, then, a primary resource of society; without it natural resources, in the economic sense, would be non-existent. The growth of science accelerates progress in industrial technology and has significant economic and social effects as well. The achievement of progress in industrial technology means that men engaged in basic and applied research must be educated in the broad areas of science and in its specialized fields and that men engaged in the technical phases of industry must be trained in the various fields of engineering and technology.

Progress in industrial technology increasingly depends upon a division of labor and performance along three levels of endeavor: (1) pure research and discovery in fundamental science, carried out by universities and other centers of science and by independent pure scientists; and (2) applied research, carried out (for optimum effectiveness) in expensively equipped and well-financed laboratories by a staff of scientists whose organized effort is directed toward particular problems, goals, or fields of technology; and (3) development, design, and testing of the results (the products, materials, or processes) of the research laboratory, carried out by the engineering staff in preparation for output or operation of the prototype on a production or commercial basis. The foregoing stages in the creation of advanced technology are used for entrepreneurial profit-making purposes, military purposes, and such social purposes as the advancement of medicine and health and conservation of natural resources.

Applied industrial research developed gradually. The inventive contributions by independent scientists and by engineers employed in industry promoted growth in such fields as the electrical and chemical industries; inventors translated the basic discoveries of science into such innovations as the incandescent lamp, the telephone, and the electrolysis of aluminum. Though industry increasingly relied on the systematic application of science to attain progress in production technology, the inventive work of scientists and technicians was hampered because they were financed on a meager basis and worked in improvised laboratories. Moreover, it became somewhat more difficult for the individual scientist or engineer to maintain an adequate flow of inventions and improvements because of the growth in the volume of scientific knowledge and because of the increasing complexity of processes.

Many of the newer industries found it necessary to organize large research laboratories in order to maintain an adequate flow of new technology. German producers in the chemical and electric fields, early recognizing the vital role of organized research, had established research laboratories in the last decades of the nineteenth century. In the United States the larger firms in the newer industries had established, by the beginning of the twentieth century, research laboratories for the systematic exploitation of new scientific discoveries.

Such large and rich corporations as Bell Telephone, Du Pont, General Electric, and Eastman Kodak established large-scale research organizations and developed them to a high level of effectiveness. The practice spread as the big producers in the fields of radio, petroleum, chemical, and automobile production adopted organized research as a competitive policy. Because they had more rationally integrated their organized research effort with the company manufacturing program, these firms were able to gear more closely their research effort and the flow of technological innovations to the needs of their businesses.

Though the independent inventor and the research scientist with a few aides in the small firm continued to secure a large number of patents, their contribution to technological advance became proportionately smaller; large-scale specialized research went far beyond their physical capacities and surely beyond the financial resources available to them. They were handicapped by the high expense of developing new ideas and of testing and trying out advanced technology. Often, too, they were involved in costly law suits to protect their patents against infringements.

By the mid-twentieth century the large industrial countries had attained a high, in fact revolutionary, level in industrial technology on the basis of accelerated research. The impetus for the adoption of large-scale research by American industry came from a number of sources. The big firms (especially those in the "science-based" industries) had long come to realize the limitations of individual scientific research in the output of technological developments. The emergence of large corporations made it commercially feasible to allocate immense funds for research and development as a competitive practice. Profitable firms are, moreover, stimulated by tax inducements to undertake costly research. They are, for instance, allowed to deduct research and development outlays as a current expense against earnings. Because of the role of technology in defense preparedness, major industrial powers had adopted the policy of appropriating enormous sums for research and development. The by-products of progress in such technology were often adaptable to

commercial exploitation. Technological innovations and the development of new industries, moreover, bring about important structural changes in the economy.

QUESTIONS FOR REVIEW AND APPLICATION

1. Identify and briefly discuss the evolutionary developments and structural transformations in the economy that established the "self-generating"
process of economic growth. In your discussion indicate (a) the developments
that lowered the input of productive factors in the output of goods (i.e., reduced costs) and (b) the developments that enlarged the quantity of productive
factors available for economic growth.

2. (a) What long-term changes increased the absolute size of the American labor force? (b) What changes tended to offset partially the growth in the
size of the labor force in terms of effective man-hours per year?

3. Identify and explain the factors that must be taken into account in projecting the size of the labor force (in terms of man-hours) into the next decade.

4. What were the different origins of the various manufacturing industries?

5. "The richness of a country's natural endowment partly depends on the
state of industrial arts—the level of applied technology." Explain.

6. Illustrate how progress in technology widens and enlarges a nation's
resource base.

7. (a) Identify six types or forms of technological advance. (b) Illustrate
how two or more types of technological advance may be embodied in a single
technological innovation. (c) Distinguish between intensive and extensive
mechanization and between capital-saving, laborsaving, and cost-saving types
of technological advance.

8. Distinguish between (and illustrate) direct and indirect technological
displacement of labor.

9. "Some types of technical advances break down skilled crafts, displacing
the skilled craftsman with semiskilled operators; while other technical advances
call for technicians with new types of skills." Explain and illustrate.

10. Explain how research and technological advance may not only change
production processes and modify the composition of a firm's occupational structure but change the composition of its product line and the location of its plants.

11. Show how technological advance, through capital savings and increased
labor productivity, releases manpower and other resources from one sector of
the economy for employment in the expanding sectors of the economy.

12. (a) What are the main features of the mass-production method of output? (b) "Mass production is limited by the extent of the market and the
engineer's ingenuity in designing a line of products comprised of components
common to the various models that make up a product line." Explain.

13. Explain the relationship between social investment, cultural capital, and
progress in science and technology.

14. Distinguish between pure research and applied research. What is the
nature of their relationship?

15. How does the function of the inventor and the technologist in the economy differ from that of the entrepreneur?

CHAPTER 2

Economic Growth and Structural Change

STRUCTURAL CHANGE IN THE ECONOMY

The process of economic growth involves shifts in economic sectors and in the direction of investment. It occurs through the growth of large industrial centers which augment geographical division of labor and the rise of big enterprise and large combinations which obtain economies of scale. Industrial expansion occurs through the incessant emergence of new industries which more than offset the retarded growth of some mature industries.

With respect to *over-all structural change,* the process of economic growth involves: (1) the lengthening and the specialization of the vertical stages of production and (2) shifts in the structural composition of the economy, that is, changes in the contributive share to the gross national product (GNP) among the various economic sectors—agriculture, mining, transportation, manufacturing, and service industries. These two structural changes evolve more or less concurrently. The development of the vertical structure of production creates greater "roundaboutness" in the over-all production process: the extraction and transformation of raw materials into final products occur through a series of specialized stages employing appropriate capital facilities. Though the system of specialized stages and establishments lengthens the over-all productive process, such an industrial system puts out a larger volume of goods at lower unit cost. Depending on its size and degree of self-sufficiency, a highly industrialized economy has comparatively more specialized stages than a less industrialized economy.

The main vertical stages of production in an industrial economy include (1) generic and extractive production, (2) early-stage manufacture, (3) late-stage manufacture, and (4) distribution through specialized market channels. From their initial extractive stage, raw materials flow through successive specialized stages and processes of production and gradually ripen into final products.

Generic production and extractive production take material resources directly from nature. The generic industries (principally agriculture and forestry) grow their products. The natural resource can be preserved: it can be replaced or reproduced, and in many cases it can be increased through the application of capital. Capital outlay for drainage of swamps and for the construction of fertilizer plants, for example, increases the "quantity" of productive land and enlarges the output capacity. Generic industries supply manufacturing industries with such basic raw materials as timber, fibers, livestock, and food crops.

The extractive industries are those whose raw material exists in nature but whose resources are exhaustible. These industries mine natural deposits of, for example, ore, petroleum, chemicals, and asbestos. The material is taken from nature without replacement; the supply gradually diminishes. Even though the deposit may be worked slowly, the industry is temporary. The extractive and generic production processes usually involve the breakdown, withdrawal, and handling of materials. Some extractive industries extend their operations to include a preparatory process, the separation of minerals and the preliminary refining and beneficiation of ores to reduce bulk and lower the cost of shipping.

Manufacturing industries employ mechanical, chemical, and electrochemical processes to transform organic and inorganic materials into products. These industries may be classed as early-stage, intermediate-stage, and late-stage manufacturing.

Early-stage manufacturing converts the raw materials supplied by extractive and generic production into primary products (such standard materials as metal alloys, lumber, cement, flour) and into many secondary products. Some early-stage manufacturing employs transforming processes (metallurgical and chemical processes) to convert materials from one state to a more useful state (e.g., ores to metal, silicon to glass); while other early-stage manufacturing employs analytical or disassembly-type processes to break down and transform a raw material into a primary product and a number of secondary (by-product) materials (e.g., coal to coke and its by-products). These production processes put out primary and secondary products in comparatively fixed proportions.

In many cases additional processing converts primary materials into intermediate products or semimanufactured goods. Rolling mills, for example, process steel ingots and aluminum ingots into standard sizes of plate, channels, beams, angles, bars, and other shapes which are procured by a large number of industries for manufacture into a variety of final products. The output of some primary materials (aluminum and copper alloys) requires a long production interval and a number of separate and distinct processes; while the output of other primary materials (cement and flour) calls for a short production interval and fewer processes.

Late-stage manufacturing converts homogeneous primary materials and intermediate materials into final products. Chemical processes, for example, combine refined materials and ingredients into final products. Fabrication processes convert primary materials (metal, rubber, pulp) directly into end products; and they also convert primary materials into component parts. Assembly processes then join the parts into subassembly units. These in turn are brought together and installed in final assembly processes that turn out completed products.

A lengthy over-all production interval, one involving many different processes (often housed in separate plants), is generally required for the output of intricate, assembled products of high-unit value (medical equipment, diesel engines, ships). A short over-all production interval and fewer separate distinct processes are usually typical for the output of such low-unit-value products as foods, clothing, and many household furnishings. The degree to which a given process can be specialized (i.e., the extent to which mass-production methods can be applied) depends on the size of the market and the volume of demand for standard-type goods or homogeneous commodities.

During periods of high-level production, some stages in the vertical structure of production may have inadequate capacity (bottlenecks), while other stages may have ample or even excess capacity. When economic planners (whether planners for defense production or for economic development) analyze an industrial subsector (e.g., mining or metallurgical industries) in the vertical structure of production, they can identify and anticipate stages of potential bottlenecks, stages of ample capacity, stages that may rely on imports, stages that are highly integrated, and others. They can, therefore, plan for rational and balanced development consistent with their objectives.

The process of industrialization and economic growth brings about significant *shifts in the composition of the economy.* The output of all major sectors in the economy grows but at different rates so that their proportionate contribution to national income is substantially altered. Agricultural and mineral production (i.e., the primary industries) in the American economy, as in most advanced industrial countries, grows but at much less than the average rate. Production in manufacturing (the secondary industries) has shown greater growth. The output in the service industries, including transportation and utilities (the tertiary industries), has expanded most of all.

The distribution of total employment has tended to follow the contributive share of each sector to the national income. The employment of labor shifted away from agriculture to manufacturing, trade, and services, with a somewhat greater proportion to services. As the economy became more industrialized and mechanized and as production technology improved, it became possible to provide a greater volume of food, clothing, housing, and manufactured goods with the employment of a smaller proportion of the labor force. Productive factors were thus released for employment in other fields of economic activity.

Though in absolute terms (measured in value added) agriculture grew enormously, its proportionate contribution to national income fell from about 27 per cent in 1870 to about 8 per cent in recent years.[1] Significant, too, is the fact that food processing over the decades has moved away from the farm to the factory. Output in mining fluctuated between 2 and 4 per cent of national income; its share of contribution to national income averaged about 3 per cent. The somewhat lower rate of growth in the output of mining in the past two decades is partly attributable to the increasing use of oil and natural gas in place of coal.

The somewhat higher-than-average rate of growth for manufacturing enabled it to increase its contributive share from about 15 per cent to about 31 per cent of the national income in the period from 1870 to 1950. Important shifts occurred within the manufacturing sector. Such early industries as textiles, leather, and forest products declined in relative importance, while such newer industries as metal-producing and metal-using industries, petroleum re-

---

[1] Data for trends in the economic sectors are partly based on two sources: Simon Kuznets and Raymond Goldsmith, *Income and Wealth of the United States—Trends and Structure* (London: Bowes & Bowes Publishers, Ltd., 1952), and Arthur F. Burns, *Production Trends in the United States Since 1870* (New York: National Bureau of Economic Research, Inc., 1934).

fining, and chemicals increased in relative importance. The share of the producer's goods industries has tended to increase, as is to be expected, during rapid industrialization. Durable-goods and non-durable-goods industries have kept about the same relative production in recent decades.

TABLE 2-1
Per Cent of Total Change in Manufacturing Output
Contributed by Various Industries

	Relative Impor- tance, 1948	Per Cent of Total Change		
		1948–53	1953–56	1948–56
Total manufacturing		100.0	100.0	100.0
Durables.	51.0	71.7	36.6	62.2
Primary metals	8.0	5.8	3.5	5.2
Fabricated metal products, ordnance.	6.4	9.6	−6.2	5.4
Non-electrical machinery. . .	10.0	10.3	3.5	8.5
Electrical machinery.	5.2	12.4	9.8	11.7
Transportation equipment . . .	8.9	25.1	8.2	20.5
Stone, clay, and glass products	3.1	2.2	5.2	3.0
Lumber and products	3.8	1.1	1.6	1.2
Furniture and fixtures	1.7	0.8	3.8	1.6
Miscellaneous manufacturing	2.6	1.7	5.0	2.6
Instruments	1.4	2.7	2.3	2.6
Non-durables.	49.0	28.3	63.4	37.8
Textile mill products	7.3	0.5	2.7	1.1
Apparel.	4.9	2.0	3.9	2.5
Rubber products	1.6	1.4	1.0	1.3
Leather and leather products	1.7	0.2	1.5	0.6
Paper and allied products . . .	3.4	3.4	8.5	4.8
Printing and publishing.	4.6	2.3	8.5	4.0
Chemicals and allied products	6.3	10.5	20.7	13.2
Petroleum and coal products .	4.0	2.9	3.5	3.1
Food and kindred products . .	12.8	4.3	13.0	6.7
Tobacco manufactures	2.4	0.8	0.2	0.6

Source: See footnote 2.

Schulze and Tryon, in their discussion of the output pattern of manufacturing in the years following World War II, tabulated the percentage of change during the years 1948–56 (Table 2–1) and pointed out the probable trend for the immediate future:

Some of the major features of the shift in output patterns during the postwar period can be explained by two major factors: the increase and subsequent cutback in the demand for military hard goods and the continuation of the long-run trend toward greater fabrication per unit of materials input. Barring any major shifts in the proportion of output taken by defense, the years immediately ahead should probably witness a more even distribution of output

TABLE 2-2
United States National Income by Industry, 1956-59
(millions of dollars)

	1956	1957	1958	1959
All industries, total	350,836	366,943	367,686	399,648
Agriculture, forestry, and fisheries	16,087	16,365	18,798	16,813
Mining	6,243	6,238	5,357	5,471
Metal mining	1,092	951	757	716
Anthracite mining	170	162	130	113
Bituminous and other soft coal mining	1,543	1,569	1,223	1,198
Crude petroleum and natural gas	2,602	2,767	2,476	2,600
Non-metallic mining and quarrying	836	789	771	844
Contract construction	19,515	20,247	20,034	21,685
Manufacturing	109,268	112,476	104,125	119,400
Food and kindred products	8,799	9,075	9,313	10,030
Tobacco manufactures	747	807	879	969
Textile-mill products	4,382	4,157	3,967	4,641
Apparel and other finished fabric products	4,410	4,381	4,323	4,728
Lumber and furniture products	5,138	4,718	4,516	5,344
Lumber and wood products, except furniture	3,245	2,825	2,757	3,321
Furniture and fixtures	1,893	1,893	1,759	2,023
Paper and allied products	4,186	4,016	3,952	4,452
Printing, publishing, and allied industries	5,436	5,700	5,687	6,180
Chemicals and allied products	7,739	8,100	7,945	9,211
Products of petroleum and coal	4,344	3,957	4,037	4,543
Rubber products	1,895	1,914	1,809	2,132
Leather and leather products	1,461	1,480	1,373	1,539
Stone, clay, and glass products	3,920	3,871	3,775	4,492
Metals, metal products, and miscellaneous	23,486	24,377	21,559	24,423
Primary metal industries	10,891	11,293	9,052	10,326
Fabricated metal products, including ordnance	7,719	8,089	7,647	8,624
Instruments	2,325	2,409	2,343	2,727
Miscellaneous manufacturing	2,551	2,586	2,517	2,746
Machinery, except electrical	12,182	12,333	10,611	12,501
Electrical machinery	7,521	8,358	7,936	9,589
Transportation equipment, except automobiles	6,395	7,539	7,034	7,052
Automobiles and automobile equipment	7,227	7,693	5,409	7,574
Wholesale and retail trade	58,192	60,350	61,094	66,909
Finance, insurance, and real estate	32,367	35,276	37,415	40,518
Transportation	16,841	17,208	16,331	17,462
Railroads	7,619	7,503	6,799	6,926
Local and highway passenger transportation	1,415	1,452	1,409	1,462

TABLE 2-2 (Continued)

	1956	1957	1958	1959
Highway freight transportation and warehousing	4,647	4,885	4,907	5,585
Water transportation	1,012	1,101	920	941
Air transportation (common carriers)	877	910	974	1,140
Pipe-line transportation	305	315	312	323
Services allied to transportation	966	1,042	1,010	1,085
Communications and public utilities	12,658	13,405	14,087	15,286
Services	37,252	39,978	41,741	45,090
Hotels and other lodging places	1,749	1,810	1,774	1,928
Personal services	3,929	4,159	4,185	4,391
Private households	7,839	8,383	8,723	9,251
Commercial and trade schools and employment agencies	215	235	229	243
Business services, n.e.c.	4,189	4,627	4,874	5,431
Miscellaneous repair services and hand trades	1,457	1,532	1,482	1,630
Motion pictures	891	841	783	821
Amusement and recreation, except motion pictures	1,279	1,326	1,420	1,542
Medical and other health services	7,564	8,187	8,935	9,749
Legal services	1,965	2,115	2,192	2,351
Engineering and other professional services, n.e.c.	1,866	2,036	2,005	2,162
Educational services, n.e.c.	1,767	1,948	2,127	2,362
Non-profit membership organizations, n.e.c.	2,542	2,779	3,012	3,229
Government and government enterprises	40,401	43,155	46,605	48,840
Rest of the world	2,012	2,245	2,099	2,174

Source: U.S. Department of Commerce, Survey of Current Business, vol. 40 (July, 1960), Table 8.

increases between durable and non-durable goods. There is no reason to believe, however, that there will be any cessation of the long-term trend toward a more rapid increase in the output of finished goods industries relative to raw materials industries.[2]

The service sector has experienced enormous growth (Table 2–2). Broadly defined the group includes trade, banking, and finance; personal and government services; and transportation and public utilities. It excludes the goods-producing industries—manufacturing, mining, construction, and agriculture. Measured in terms of share of national income or share of labor force, the service sector

[2] C. L. Schulze and J. L. Tryon, *Prices and Costs in Manufacturing Industry*, Study Paper No. 17, prepared for Joint Economic Committee, Congress of the United States (Washington, D.C.: Government Printing Office, 1960), p. 14.

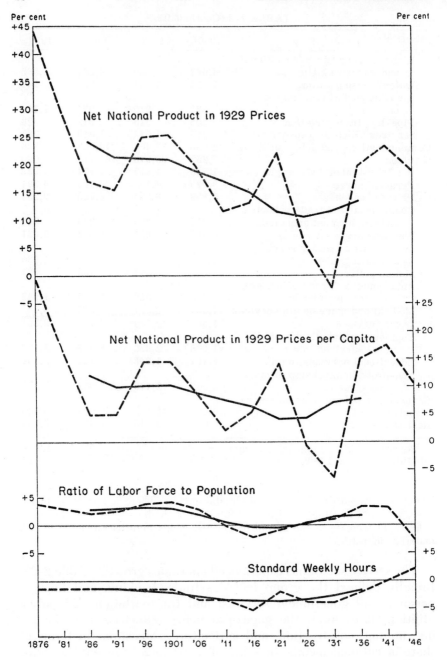

Fig. 2–1. (See next page for caption.)

has increased from roughly one-fifth in 1870 to about one-half in the 1950's.[3] Having accounted for virtually all the growth in employment since 1953, the service industries may be considered as the "growth" sector of the American economy. Among the factors contributing to the growth of services are urbanization, rising national income, increased availability of higher education, and a higher percentage of married women in the labor force. We see that the rise of new industries contributes to the shift among economic sectors as well as to economic growth.

RISE OF NEW INDUSTRIES AND ECONOMIC GROWTH

The American economy from 1876 to approximately 1950 grew at an annual rate of 3.5 per cent in terms of net national product in constant prices. This is roughly a thirteenfold increase for the eighty-year period. Since the population more than tripled during the same period, the net national product per capita grew at an annual rate of 1.9 per cent. During the period, moreover, the workweek declined from approximately 65 hours to 40 hours, while the labor-force ratio increased about 25 per cent. (Fig. 2–1.)

Because a number of economic changes invariably take place in any long time span, estimates of the long-term growth of national product and output per man-hour are, at best, statistical approximations. The estimated growth in national income is somewhat overstated (shows an upward bias), since it neglects to include adequately earlier household production (e.g., bread baking and garment making) which in recent decades are included in factory production. On the other hand, the estimated growth trend and the improvement in living standard also are somewhat understated (show a downward bias), since they do not take into account such benefits as increased leisure from the shorter workweek and improvements in working conditions. If an industrial index of production is

[3] George J. Stigler, *Trends in Employment in the Service Industries,* a study by the National Bureau of Economic Research, Inc. (Princeton: Princeton University Press, 1956), pp. 5, 6.

Fig. 2–1. Trends in growth rates of American economic expansion. Broken lines indicate percentage rates of change since preceding overlapping decade, plotted at decade centers. Solid lines show five-item moving average with end items weighted one-half. (Moses Abramovitz, *Resources and Output Trends in the United States Since 1870,* Occasional Paper 52. New York: National Bureau of Economic Research, Inc., 1956, p. 16.)

used for long-term measurement, it has additional deficiencies. It does not, for instance, adequately represent the contribution of many new products which initially are put out in small volume and the contribution of by-products put out by the further processing of residual materials.

The total production of an economy is, at any time, the sum of the outputs (value-added in production) of all industries, while the growth of the economy is measured by the long-term increase in total production. The rate of increase in total production is made up of the rates of output of established industries augmented by the rates of output of industries newly introduced into the economy.

In their development and life span, industries tend to pass through a series of stages in a common pattern of growth and maturation. An industry ordinarily takes root after a period of technological development and experimentation. It then enters a stage of rapid growth and later enters another stage at which it tends to grow at a declining rate. Eventually the industry experiences a decline in its level of output.[4] Industries, of course, differ with respect to the duration and the intensity of the various stages in their development pattern. Retardation in the growth of an industry, for instance, may for a time be offset by a major technical improvement or by a structural change which invigorates the industry.

If the total production of the economy depended solely on the rate of output of the established (the "old") industries, there would have been an appreciable retardation in the growth of total output and national income. The maintenance of economic growth depends more or less upon the continual introduction of new products and new industries. The contribution to total production by the new industries depends on the number of new industries that come into existence and on the rate and magnitude of their output in terms of value-added. Since the process of industrialization and the progress of technology create new industries, total production in the economy expands at a rate greater than that of the growth of established industries.

The nature and life history of a factory industry tend to be characterized by the industry's "source of origin," e.g., the industry may have grown out of the conversion of early handicraft production to factory production or out of the invention of a new product and process. The various sources of industry origin also indicate the kinds of structural changes that take place in an economy undergoing industrial development. As earlier indicated, in the process

---

[4] Arthur F. Burns, *Production Trends in the United States Since 1870* (New York: National Bureau of Economic Research, Inc., 1934), pp. xv, xvii.

of industrialization manufacturing industries "originated" from the displacement of handicraft production, from the absorption of household production, from technological innovations that created substitute or supplementary products, from industrial research that created wholly new products, and from the growth of capital-goods industries based on derived demand.

The origin and development of industries took place over a long span of time that made up the various phases in the historical process of industrialization. In the process of economic growth, new industries obviously contribute a varying proportion or share to the increase of total national income. Their contribution to total production would be less in an economy which is in the mature stage of development as compared to an economy which is in the early stage of industrialization.[5]

To explain why individual industries experience retardation in growth and why some industries experience a decline in the absolute level of production, we must look to the reasons why certain industries take root in a given region or in a given economy. The kind of industries that eventually take root and grow in a given economy is determined by the factors that make for geographical specialization. Certain industries develop in a given region because they can produce economically and profitably there. Economic factors in the region favor these industries, that is, give these industries a comparative advantage and a higher return in the use of the productive factors over other industries that may conceivably take root in the same region. The factors that make for geographical specialization of industry include: (1) the kind and richness of natural resources, (2) population density and size of the labor force, (3) the magnitude of capital accumulation, (4) the stage of industrialization of the economy, (5) the size of the domestic market and accessibility to world markets, and (6) government policy with respect to promotion of specific industries. Because these factors are subject to secular change, the relative growth and size of industries also are subject to change.

The various developments that take place during secular change can be identified as the specific causes of retardation in the growth of an individual industry. The output of an industry tends to reach a saturation point in the market, particularly when the demand is relatively inelastic. The rate of population growth may decline and

[5] Because its industry need not gradually evolve from the "historical origins" of industry, we can readily see why a country, industrializing in the mid-twentieth century on the basis of the latest technology, can, if it attains a sufficient rate of capital accumulation and possesses adequate resources, achieve an impressive rate of industrial growth.

thus adversely affect demand. The gradual depletion of resources leads to rising costs and prices which lower sales and output volume. Technological advance (e.g., improvements that increase product durability or otherwise make for economy in use) may call for a smaller volume of output to satisfy the market. Technological advances create substitute products and services (oil for coal, trucking for rail hauling) that reduce the demand for an industry's product. A growing overseas competition from a foreign industry with a superior economic base for industrialization may check the growth of an industry. A rise of profitable new industries with a superior capability for attracting labor, materials, and capital (i.e., for bidding up the input prices for existing industries) can retard the growth of an established industry.

The decline in the percentage rate of growth of established industries tends to be more or less offset by the rise and growth of new industries. The over-all rate of growth in national income is thus made up of the aggregate output of existing industries augmented by the output of new products and services that come from the incessant introduction of new industries.

But what are the underlying forces for the long-run growth in national income? The process of growth (as we have traced it earlier) involves the evolution and development of favorable social and economic institutions, the expansion of commerce, the spread of the factory system and industrialization, and other transformations and economic developments. The increase in total production grows directly out of technological-organizational progress, the accumulation of capital, the exploitation of natural resources, and the growth of the population and labor force. The utilization of these interrelated productive factors is stimulated by the over-all development and expansion of the economy itself. The growth of population, for instance, was increased by improvements in living standards, including medical services. Population growth and rising income continually enlarge the market for goods as well as stimulate investment in such capital-intensive facilities as public utilities and housing. Investment for the expansion of capital facilities increases the output and the flow of income, and the rise in income in turn augments the growth in capital facilities. Capital stock accumulates faster than the growth in the labor force (in terms of annual man-hours of work), particularly when affected by investments in such economic overhead establishments as schools, hospitals, highways, and other public productive facilities.

Even though the capital stock in the American economy increased at a faster rate than the supply of other productive factors, there has been no tendency for output per unit of capital (the average productivity of capital) to decline. The expansion of applied research and technological-organizational progress maintains the productiveness of capital and also enlarges the resource base and the supply of materials. Technological-organizational progress, in fact, tends to increase the productivity of both capital and labor and influences the trend in investment and the capital-output ratio.

TRENDS IN INVESTMENT AND CAPITAL-OUTPUT RATIOS

The capital-output ratio measures the capital intensiveness of production, the ratio of capital to output. The amount of capital required to establish productive capacity in an economy varies over time. Variations in an economy's capital-output ratio stem from variations in the growth rate of the labor force relative to the abundance of natural resources and capital, from technological change associated with the transition from early-stage to advanced-stage industrialization, and from shifts among the sectors of the economy. Because of the variations in an economy's capital-output ratio, the growth of an economy would call for varying amounts of investment to maintain a given rate of increase in national income and employment.

During an economy's early stage of growth and industrialization, large amounts of capital are required to mechanize and expand the various fields of production. The amount of capital required per unit of output depends on the field of production and the degree of mass-production technology applicable. The advanced stage of economic growth requires capital for industrial adjustments as well as for continued growth. The demand for investment comes from industry's need to modify or to enlarge capacity to meet shifts or increases in demand, to establish new enterprise or convert existing plants for the output of new products or services, and to carry out research to obtain technological advances that provide low-cost capacity and improve the competitive position of the enterprise. As compared with early-stage growth, mature-stage development tends to require less incremental capital per unit of output of goods. This is due to the fact that industry is comparatively well developed, the economy applies more capital-savings types of technological advances, and to other structural changes in industry discussed below.

The nature of an industry's production technology and the size and peculiarities of its market determine the level and trend of the industry's capital-output ratio. Such "economic overhead" facilities as railroads, pipelines, hydroelectric power, and other public utilities typically absorb large amounts of investment per unit of output. Their high capital-output ratio (their capital intensiveness) is due to the wide geographical dispersal of the market for their services, the extensiveness of their facilities, and the relative indivisibility of their plant. Their high capital-capacity ratio also derives from the fact that they tend to be built ahead of demand and are somewhat underutilized in earlier years. As the economy grows and population increases, the economic-overhead industries become more fully utilized, and the capital-output ratio declines. Technological-organizational advances introduced through the replacement of equipment and modernization of plant produce a further decline in the capital-output ratio.

Capital-output ratios differ among manufacturing industries. The textile and apparel industries, for example, have a low capital-output ratio, because their production technology calls for a comparatively small proportion of capital relative to labor and because their facilities are divisible. The primary metals and the chemical industries have a high capital-output ratio because their production technology requires capital-intensive processes and because their integrated processes are less divisible.

The capital-output ratio in the manufacturing sector of the American economy has varied over the past century. From 1880 to 1919 the capital-output ratio rose in manufacturing; since 1919 the capital-output ratio has declined and seems to have leveled off. Since World War II the trend in the capital-output ratio for mining has roughly paralleled that of manufacturing. In 1880 the capital-output ratio for manufacturing stood at .547. This means that it took $547 (in 1929 dollars) in fixed capital and working capital to produce $1,000 in goods. By 1919 the capital-output ratio rose to 1.022; it took $1,022 in total capital to put out $1,000 in goods.[6]

The rise in the capital-output ratio in the earlier decades meant that more capital was employed per unit of output. The increase in the capital-output ratio included, of course, some excess capacity. The rising trend in the ratio was primarily due to greater mechanization of industry. In the process of industrialization, capital-widening augmented by capital-deepening called for higher investment per unit of output. Mechanical and chemical processes and facilities were continually introduced in place of manual methods of production. In the process of perfecting the factory, the creation of plant

[6] Daniel Creamer, "Postwar Trends in the Relation of Capital to Output in Manufactures," *American Economic Review*, vol. 47 (May, 1958): 250.

capacity called for increasing amounts of capital inputs (in place of labor inputs) as mechanical methods spread not only throughout the whole of the production process but to such factory service activities as material handling and testing and inspection. New facilities purchased for plant expansion or plant improvement essentially introduced laborsaving technology, reducing the input of labor per unit of output.

The decline in the capital-output ratio (the capital coefficient) in manufacturing since 1919 meant that, on balance, less capital was employed per unit of output. In 1919 $1,022 in real capital turned out $1,000 in real income.[7] Important forces were at work to lower the capital-output ratio in the manufacturing sector. These forces were sufficient after 1919 to more than offset certain developments which worked to increase the capital-output ratio. Let us first inquire into the forces that worked to raise the capital-output ratio (and which were more than offset by other forces at work).

The continued spread of mechanization throughout manufacturing processes and into many additional factory service activities and clerical activities called for greater investment in machinery and equipment. Machines continued to displace labor. Changes and improvements in products called for greater outlays for equipment. Products, particularly since the 1920's, became more complex and elaborate, embodying new features, embellishments, and such superfluities as attractive packaging. All this tended to lengthen the fabrication, machining, and assembling processes. Moreover, the greater frequency of product improvements and restyling (to some extent spreading to producer's goods) called for periodic revision in plant facilities and outlays for equipment and retooling. Industry, because of competitive necessity, increasingly turned to modernization programs for cost reduction. But modernization of production processes and clerical activities entails outlays for engineering, plant revision, and purchases and installations of new equipment, including computers and other business machines.

A number of developments were at work to offset the above forces, causing a decline in the over-all capital-output ratio in manufacturing. The decline in the capital-output ratio after 1919 was due to the greater shift to mass-production methods of output, to increasing adoption of capital-saving innovations, and to improvements in the organization and layout of plant facilities to conserve factory floor space and lower investment in plant buildings per unit of output.

[7] *Ibid.*, p. 250.

The increased standardization of products and the greater shift to mass-production processes (the shift was augmented by the expansion of such industries as the automobile and appliance industries) permitted greater specialization of plants and the utilization of special-purpose, high-capacity production facilities. The use of specialized, high-speed machines lowers the capital input (as well as the labor input) per unit of output. Since mass production depends on the large markets which are typical of bigger countries, the decline in the capital-output ratio is partly a consequence of economic growth and rising national income.[8]

Capital-savings technological advances introduced through equipment replacement and plant additions also work to lower the over-all capital-output ratio. The adoption of the more automatic types of machines (and to some extent "automated" processes) make for greater speed and volume of output, thus lowering the amount of producer's goods required per unit of output. Savings in capital also occur through the adoption of new chemical and electrochemical processes in place of capital-intensive mechanical processes.

Advances in the art of industrial engineering since the 1920's enabled plant-layout experts to design and install rational factory-layout schemes. Significant savings in capital were attained through the increased conversion to the line-flow type of production (i.e., line layout) and to vertical integration of processes and plants and through the development of efficient over-all layout of plants at industrial sites. The rational layout of processes and allocation of factory floor areas speeds up the production cycle, reduces handling and inspection activities, and conserves factory floor space. A greater output volume from a given-size building and factory floor area (i.e., greater "production density") is also attained through the use of mezzanine floors; adoption of overhead monorails, high-stacking storage methods, effective inventory-control systems; and elimination of temporary storage areas and aisle space.[9]

Revisions and improvements in processes and in plant layout are often made within existing buildings or structures. Since buildings are adapted and reworked to fit changes in layout and modernization of facilities, they are less subject to obsolescence as compared to equipment. The increased conversion to mass-production processes and to rational plant layout since the 1920's has called for less outlay

---

[8] Because they specialize in industries that mass-produce goods for world markets, such small countries as Belgium and Switzerland attain relatively low capital-output ratios for the respective industries.

[9] John A. Shubin and Huxley Madeheim, *Plant Layout* (Englewood Cliffs, N.J.: Prentice-Hall, Inc., 1951), pp. 312–315.

for plant buildings as compared to outlay for equipment. Since the 1920's the relative importance of outlays for equipment and structures has changed. Equipment in the mid-1950's accounted for more than two-thirds of total purchases as compared with less than half of total purchases in the earlier period. Investment in equipment per person engaged in manufacturing increased from $1,300 in 1929 to $2,100 in 1955; investments in structures per person engaged decreased from $2,900 to $2,300.[10] The long-term growth of manufacturing inventories roughly paralleled the growth of equipment.

The adaptability of production and the mobility of capital have improved because of the decline in the capital-output ratio in manufacturing, mining, and public utilities and because of the shift in the composition of fixed capital in manufacturing. As the capital-output ratio declines, depreciation charges on fixed capital make up a smaller part of the unit cost of production. When capital as a "sunk" cost is a smaller percentage of total costs, industrial production is more adaptable. Business enterprise can shift its field of production with a smaller loss in terms of capital obsolescence or misdirected investment. (The high burden of excess capacity during periods of low business volume, of course, remains.)

The long-run mobility of capital, particularly in manufacturing, has improved. Since the share of equipment in total fixed capital has increased, a bigger share of fixed capital is annually written off as a depreciation charge than in earlier years. Equipment depreciates faster and can be written off more quickly than plant buildings. The quicker conversion of fixed capital to cash means that business recoups its investment sooner. The greater availability of funds from depreciation allowances enables business to shift its investment more easily to new fields. Capital thus becomes more mobile.

Since 1946 corporations have generated an increasing share of their internal funds from depreciation allowances. The steady rise in funds from depreciation allowances is partly due to the shift of investment to equipment. The rise in depreciation funds in absolute terms is also due to the growth in total investment in plant and equipment. At the end of 1945, the book value of corporate gross fixed assets was $138 billion; by 1955 it had grown to $300 billion.[11] As a short-run factor the emergency provisions of the 1950 Revenue Act were influential in enlarging depreciation funds. The act per-

[10] Donald G. Wooden and Robert C. Wasson, "Manufacturing Investment Since 1929," *Survey of Current Business,* vol. 36 (November, 1956): 9–10.

[11] Loughlin F. McHugh, "Financing Corporate Expansion in 1956," *Survey of Current Business,* vol. 36 (October, 1956): 13.

mitted business to write off over a five-year period, for tax purposes, approximately three-fifths of the outlay for production facilities certified as necessary for defense purposes. In 1954 an accelerated write-off was allowed on a permanent basis for business as a whole. The revenue law of 1954 permits the use of the "declining-balance" method, as an alternative to the "straight-line" method, for writing off facilities. The new method charges off a larger portion of depreciation faster than the old method. An enlarged flow of depreciation funds accelerates both the replacement and mobility of capital which in turn increase industrial productivity.

TREND AND MAINSPRINGS OF PRODUCTIVITY

Long-term gain in productivity is evidence of economic progress. Progress in terms of economic expansion and rise in living standards had its physical basis in the increased productiveness of resources, as well as in the quantitative growth of total productive factors. Though the increase in productivity has a number of economic consequences, a significant consequence is that a gain in productivity releases resources which can be allocated to maintain economic growth and improve living standards.

The concept of *productivity* refers to the ratio of output of goods or services obtained from the input of a single productive factor or from the input of all productive factors. Productivity may be broadly defined as the rise in output obtained from resources expended. A gain in productivity essentially means an increase in output from a given input of productive factors, that is, a higher ratio of output to input. A productivity gain is registered when the same quantity of output is obtained from a smaller input of resources.

A *productivity measure* can be any measure that relates output to the input of one or more factors of production. Output per man-hour is one type of measure of productivity, for example, the output of steel or coal per man-hour worked. Hence, output per man-hour measures the relationship between labor time consumed and the number of products put out, or the ratio of the quantity of output to man-hours worked. Labor productivity can be measured by comparing the quantity produced by a given number of man-hours (or workers) with the output by the same number of man-hours at another time. Productivity can also be measured in terms of capital input (i.e., investment in plant and equipment) or in terms of total factor input.

There are, of course, problems in measuring productivity. The output of a product, for instance, cannot always be measured adequately. Output measures, moreover, do not ordinarily reflect improvements in the quality of the product turned out. Quality tends to improve over time, but the change is not easily measurable and seldom is it measured. Thus, quality improvement in goods is generally ignored in the preparation of production indexes for measuring productivity. Moreover, productivity gain has little meaning or usefulness in those fields of production in which output is difficult to define or gauge. For instance, it is difficult to gauge the physical volume of construction activity and to measure "production" in the fields of trade, insurance, and banking.

Measuring productivity in terms of man-hours is generally a matter of convenience. Labor productivity as a measure usually takes total production workers or total wage earners as the input factor and excludes the service employees. But so long as the ratio of the production force and the service staff is constant, as is usually the case in the short run, labor productivity as a measure is not appreciably impaired. Output per man-hour is, nonetheless, a significant measure of productivity because it relates human resources to physical production; the effectiveness in the utilization of human resources is of paramount significance. In labor-intensive fields of economic activity and industries, output per man-hour obviously tends to be a comparatively accurate index of productivity. A particular productivity index may, of course, be more useful for one purpose than for another. The output per man-hour of the nation's total labor force employed tends to be a more accurate gauge of long-run productivity for the economy as a whole than output per man-hour as a gauge of productivity in a specific industry.

Changes in output per man-hour should not be confused with changes in efficiency. An increase in output per man-hour in a given industry is not per se an efficiency objective of productive effort; it is rather the net savings in the cost of total factors which indicate improved productive efficiency. Ideally, in order to measure long-run productivity in a given industry, output must be related to the input of all productive factors or cost elements. The measurement of productivity in terms of output per unit of net capital input or in terms of capital and labor input (i.e., "total factor" productivity), however, involves difficult problems in the quantifying of the actual input of productive capital.[12]

---

[12] Net fixed-capital input is gross fixed capital less depreciation charges (this includes a contingency allowance for obsolescence), which is an accounting measure of capital consumption used for computing net income for tax purposes. An "accounting" net fixed-capital stock tends to understate the actual productive capacity in industry as a whole since the depreciated portion of capital does not correspond to the actual

Output per man-hour does not measure the specific contribution of labor, capital, or any other input factor, for the volume of output derived from the input of resources into a productive effort depends on many factors. Because of changes in production technology and changes in the relative prices of factors, the proportion in which factors are combined changes over time. As the proportions in factor combinations vary in a given industry, changes in the ratio of output to input reflect factor substitution as well as a change in the over-all productivity of the total effort. The substitution of capital for labor creates, in a sense, an upward bias in output per man-hour as a productivity measure, but factor substitution is also a source of over-all productivity.

The problem of obtaining a precise measure of over-all productivity is indicated by studies of the rate of gain in productivity. Output per man-hour in the United States has increased 1.9 per cent as an annual average during 1899–1953, according to one study.[13] The economy's gain in productivity differed among the economic sectors and varied over time (Table 2–3). The rate of productivity gain since World War I appears to be greater than the rate in the two decades prior to the war. The gain in the service sector during 1899–1953 was less than average, while in manufacturing and mining the gain in labor productivity was above average. The rate of productivity gain among manufacturing industries differs widely, and there seems to be greater variability in the rates of change among industries than for the economy as a whole or for individual sectors of the economy (Table 2–4).

Data on productivity trends can serve a number of purposes. If analysis indicates a steady rise in productivity, economic projections are more useful for indicating probable trends. The index of out-

---

deterioration and retirement of productive facilities. (To compute the capital input in terms of gross capital less actual deterioration and retirement would, indeed, be a difficult problem of measurement.) To keep older facilities at an adequate level of operating effectiveness often requires more maintenance and repair and greater workmanship and effort by the operator on the production line. The increased maintenance and worker effort is a labor input that stretches or sustains, for a time, the productiveness of capital. Plant productiveness can thus be partially maintained by a substitution of labor for capital.

A firm need not use all the available depreciation funds to replace and maintain the productiveness of the original plants. It may use depreciation funds to erect an additional plant in a new location to serve a new market, or it may erect a plant to put out a new product. Such "creation" of capacity is possible because in the long run the increased productiveness of new facilities (which embodies capital-savings technology) often requires a smaller outlay (sometimes a modest outlay for modernization) to maintain the capacity of the original plant.

[13] John W. Kendrick, *Productivity Trends: Capital and Labor,* Occasional Paper 53 (New York: National Bureau of Economic Research, Inc., 1956), pp. 9–11.

put per man-hour, for example, can be useful for estimating labor requirements. Interregional comparisons of productivity can point to some of the active forces or conditions that account for differences. The level of, and changes in, productivity affect the rate of economic growth and involve problems in the division of income

TABLE 2-3

Indexes of Real Product per Man-hour for the Private Economy
in the United States, 1947-58

(1947-49 = 100)

Year	Man-hour Estimates Based Primarily on Data From							
	Bureau of Labor Statistics					Bureau of the Census		
			Non-agricultural Industries					Non-agricultural Industries
	Total	Agri-culture	Total	Manu-facturing	Non-manu-facturing	Total	Agri-culture	Non-agri-cultural Industries
1947	96.7	90.5	97.5	97.6	97.3	97.4	90.6	98.4
1948	100.2	107.1	99.4	100.1	98.9	100.3	107.5	99.4
1949	103.1	102.2	103.3	102.6	103.9	102.2	101.6	102.4
1950	110.4	116.2	108.8	109.5	108.4	110.3	116.1	108.5
1951	113.2	114.6	110.6	111.2	110.0	115.2	114.1	112.8
1952	115.7	124.5	112.0	113.0	111.3	118.9	124.0	115.5
1953	120.4	138.6	115.1	118.3	112.8	123.9	138.0	119.0
1954	122.6	148.3	116.9	117.4	116.7	127.0	147.9	121.8
1955	128.0	153.3	121.9	125.6	120.0	133.1	152.9	127.5
1956	128.8	160.7	121.8	127.1	119.1	134.2	160.2	127.7
1957	132.3	168.6	124.4	127.7	122.9	137.8	168.6	130.0
1958[1]	133.4	190.1	124.3	([2])	([2])	137.6	190.1	128.6

Source: U.S. Department of Labor, Bureau of Labor Statistics.

[1] Preliminary, subject to revision.

[2] Not available.

NOTE: These indexes were computed by the U.S. Department of Labor, Bureau of Labor Statistics, from estimates of real product and man-hours. The real product estimates, referring to 1954 prices, are based primarily on national product statistics of the Department of Commerce, Office of Business Economics, except for the manufacturing real product estimates which were developed by the Bureau of Labor Statistics.

Output per man-hour estimates, based primarily on Bureau of Labor Statistics man-hour data, relate, in concept, to man-hours paid; whereas estimates based primarily on Bureau of the Census labor-force data relate, in concept, to hours worked. The former include, the latter exclude, paid vacations, sick leave, and holidays. The difference between the two measures may, however, be due in part to statistical as well as conceptual differences. Both sets of man-hour estimates cover the man-hours of wage and salary workers, the self-employed, and unpaid family workers.

from productivity gains and choice of method for dealing with such dislocations as inflation and economic instability.

The *mainsprings of productivity* are many. The long-term gain in productivity (as in economic growth itself) is brought about by more thoroughgoing industrialization, technological advance, capital accumulation and replacement, discovery of rich resources, improve-

TABLE 2-4
Indexes of Output per Man-hour for Selected Industries, 1929-58
(1947 = 100)

Industry	1929	1935	1939	1945	1950	1954	1955	1956	1957	1958 (prel.)
Non-manufacturing										
All mining[1,2]	62.9	76.4	90.0	95.5	105.7	....	....	....	....	....
Anthracite[1]	....	87.8	110.6	98.6	95.4	127.2	132.9	157.5	148.0	....
Bituminous coal[1]	....	76.1	89.1	94.2	114.5	149.2	159.9	164.3	166.9	178.3
Copper (recoverable metal)[1]	....	88.2	90.2	102.8	114.3	106.7	120.4	116.1	125.7	139.1
Iron (usable ore)[1]	....	82.6	94.2	104.1	102.5	92.0	117.1	109.8	107.9	97.8
Lead and zinc (recoverable metal)[1]	....	131.0	132.3	103.4	127.0	114.6	116.6	117.1	123.0	....
Railroad transportation (revenue traffic)[3]	..	66.2	74.4	103.6	110.5	124.0	137.2	143.5	146.4	155.2
Telegraph[4]	56.7	71.8	83.1	97.3	112.4	94.0	96.0	92.1	89.0	....
Manufacturing										
Beet-sugar refining[5,6]	....	88.7	107.4	85.5	123.2	137.9	....	....	....	....
Canning and preserving group[1]	61.6	90.4	90.0	102.5	118.3	140.0	145.3	154.9	159.9	....
Cement[7]	64.3	72.6	89.7	80.9	116.0	144.0	150.7	162.0	155.0	....
Clay construction products[5,6]	82.9	79.5	94.3	82.9	115.0	123.5	135.8	138.8	130.8	....
Coke group[7]	87.0	79.7	92.9	93.7	99.2	100.4	115.6	118.7	119.4	....
Confectionery[5,6]	48.1	79.2	89.4	100.4	102.5	118.4	127.0	131.5	144.3	....
Flour and other grain-mill products[3,6]	95.3	99.5	109.5	99.0	100.0	122.1	127.1	132.2	142.6	....
Glass containers[5,6]	....	....	77.2	91.4	100.2	101.4	105.2	105.8	105.5	....
Hosiery total[5,6]	....	....	87.0	114.4	115.4	129.9	126.0	125.8	129.4	....
Full-fashioned[5,6]	....	....	81.0	116.5	122.0	141.4	139.9	146.5	148.2	....
Seamless[5,6]	....	....	95.3	111.9	109.9	121.1	115.5	111.2	115.7	....
Malt liquors[5,6]	....	....	85.5	101.9	120.4	130.9	134.5	137.5	142.6	....
Paper and pulp[5,6]	80.8	95.5	109.2	95.6	118.9	129.1	137.5	144.9	146.2	....
Rayon and other synthetic fibers[5,6]	14.2	31.8	46.9	81.1	151.6	186.6	224.8	233.3	267.9	....

54

Steel, basic[1],[6]	57.8	62.9	79.3	.....	111.9	115.9	129.4	130.4	128.9	126.6
Primary smelting and refining of										
copper, lead, and zinc[5],[6]	87.8	74.7	98.0	95.0	122.1	142.4	151.1	150.0	155.7	.....
Tobacco products group[1],[6]	52.5	69.4	80.0	96.5	119.3	125.5	126.2	131.8	141.4	152.4
Cigars[1],[6]	50.4	75.8	91.3	106.9	122.5	137.8	141.8	155.4	168.6	199.1
Cigarettes, chewing and smoking										
tobacco, and snuff[1],[6]	55.4	62.8	69.6	86.3	115.6	113.2	111.5	111.2	118.2	119.0

[1] Production worker hours paid.

[2] For 1929, covers almost all industries; for 1935 to 1950, represents 6 principal industries (bituminous coal; anthracite; crude petroleum, natural gas, and natural gasoline; iron; copper; and lead and zinc), representing 80 per cent of total employment.

[3] Refers to Class I line-haul railroads; in terms of hours worked plus constructive allowances, for all hourly-basis employees.

[4] Output per employee. Covers principal wire-telephone and ocean-cable carriers.

[5] Production worker hours paid prior to 1947, and worked since 1947.

[6] Adjusted to levels indicated by 1947 and 1954 Censuses of Manufactures.

[7] Production worker hours worked.

Source: U.S. Department of Commerce, Bureau of the Census, Statistical Abstract of the United States, 1959 (Washington, D.C.: Government Printing Office, 1959), Table 286, p. 226.

55

ment in the quality of labor, increase in the size of markets and in use of mass-production methods, internal and external economies, and certain shifts in the composition of the economy and industry. The upward trend in productivity grew out of the interaction of the foregoing economic developments and conditions that take place in the process of industrialization, that is, in the gradual transition to the more advanced forms of production and organization.

Over-all productivity increases as the more highly mechanized factory progressively displaces the less efficient earlier forms of production and as the more effectively organized plants competitively eliminate the less efficient plants. Productivity gains and economic growth in turn provide the means for a higher level of capital accumulation and the adoption of more advanced types of processes that combine productive factors more economically. The gradual expansion of research and development accelerates the flow of innovations and tends to maintain the upward trend in productivity. Because improvements in production technology are essentially embodied in new capital formation and in capital replacement and plant modernization, gross capital formation serves to offset, or at least to put off, the tendency to diminishing returns that inheres in mere quantitative growth of productive facilities. An increase in capital per worker increases the productive effectiveness of worker effort. The upward trend in output per man-hour thus more or less parallels the upward trend in capital per worker.

Improvements in production facilities and processes are augmented by the discovery and exploitation of rich resources and by the improvements in the quality of materials. The speed of processing and fabricating materials is accelerated and the level of productivity stepped up as industry progressively adopts new or improved standard materials in place of earlier types of materials (sometimes lacking in uniformity) that are more difficult to process. The fuller utilization of raw materials in the form of by-product output increases the value-added in industrial output. Productivity, too, is augmented by improved regularity and reliability in the supply of materials, speed in transportation, more effective inventory-control practices, and the relatively smaller amounts of inventory required to sustain a given level of output and sales.

The quality and effectiveness of labor improve with the greater mobility of workers, more effective compensation plans, and better placement and labor-relations practices. In the turnover of generations, better-trained young workers gradually replace the initially less-trained older workers. Higher productivity is achieved in expanding industries as young workers enter growing industries.

The increase in the size of markets (stemming from growth of population and purchasing power) permits adoption of efficient large-scale methods in the distribution of goods. Thus, productivity tends to increase with the growth in the size of the economy. The level of technology and productivity is improved through the development of product designs that make for low-cost processing. Early- and intermediate-stage industries can, through the reduction of excessive variety in their end products, employ more specialized plants. Fabrication and assembly industries are able to increase their productivity through greater standardization of final products and the use of interchangeable components that permit greater plant specialization and longer production runs.

Productivity gains grow out of *internal economies* that arise from technological advances in processing which reduce the quantity of input factors required per unit of output, organization along lines of rational specialization and integration of plants, logical layout of plant facilities, employment of specialized professional personnel and managerial methods that achieve an efficiently operating organization, and use of production-planning systems that obtain speed in output. Productivity gains also, of course, grow out of *external economies* (which essentially reduce the input price of productive factors and lower the cost of distribution) that arise from greater geographical specialization (e.g., the development of industrial centers comprised of highly specialized producers) and increasing returns which accrue from the improvement and more intensive use of such "economic overhead" services as transportation, communication, utilities, and education and health facilities. Private and public investment in fields that accelerate the gain in productivity obviously step up the rate of economic growth.

The economy's over-all gain in productivity is augmented when substantial efficiency gains are registered in very large industries (e.g., steel, automobile, petroleum, cement, power) that put out billions of dollars in net value of goods as compared to increases in efficiency in smaller industries whose value-added in production is relatively unimportant. Productivity gains in big industries release immense resources available for the expansion of the growing sectors of the economy.

The effect of productivity gain in a given industry on the allocation of productive factors among industries depends partly on the elasticity of demand for the industry's products. Technological and productivity improvements in industries putting out products of relatively elastic demand lead to expansion of the industry and to its greater absorption of materials and labor. Productivity gains in industries putting out goods of inelastic demand generally lead to a shift of resources to other branches of the economy.

The upward trend in productivity stemming from the foregoing long-term factors is conditioned by certain developments that tend to retard the rate of gain in productivity and cause short-term variations in its trend. When an industry puts out an excessive variety of products, productivity gain is slowed because of the reduced opportunity for the utilization of mass-production methods. The over-all productivity gain may be slowed by a shift in economic sectors. The relatively more rapid expansion of the service sector (trade, insurance, personal services) of the economy means that a sector with a relatively low-rate productivity gain is "displacing" a sector of a relatively high rate in productivity gain (e.g., manufacturing).

The downturns of the business cycle and the accompanying lower rate of investment in improved facilities tend to slow the growth of productivity. There is a certain correlation between changes in the rate of production and changes in the trend of productivity. A drop in the rate of output relative to available capacity tends to affect the productivity level adversely. Though production workers may be released when an industry operates at a low level of capacity, certain service employees and overhead activities cannot ordinarily be cut back to the same proportion, with the result that the labor requirement per unit of output is increased. This short-term drop in productivity may be offset by industries that shut down marginal plants and concentrate production in the more efficient plants. During periods of boom and peak-business volume, the recruitment of marginal workers, the utilization of marginal facilities, material shortages, and the increased delays in production tend to retard the "gain" in productivity. Both shifts in the rate of gain in productivity and cyclical fluctuations are, moreover, among the factors that give rise to variations in long-term economic growth.

VARIATIONS IN LONG-TERM ECONOMIC GROWTH

The secular growth of an economy tends to be uneven because of variations in and interaction of certain long- and short-term factors. Among the factors that make for an uneven rate of economic growth are: (1) the shifts in the composition of the sectors that comprise the economy, (2) variations in productivity gains, (3) variations in capital accumulation and the capital-output ratio, (4) variations in the growth of the population and labor force, (5) variations in the availability of material resources, and (6) variations in the magnitude of cyclical fluctuations. It is the mutually interrelated impact of changes in these factors which accounts for uneven economic growth (see Fig. 2–1). Long-run variations in economic growth would exist even if an economy maintained a high level of employment and the cost and dislocations of heavy military expenditures were absent.

Long-term shifts in the relative size of economic sectors (changes in the sector-mix) tend to make for uneven economic growth because the pace of technological progress and capital-output ratios differ among sectors. Though progress in agriculture increased output per farm worker and released labor in large numbers for economic expansion, it was essentially the expansion in the manufacturing sector that stepped up the rate of economic growth. The growth of the industrial sector was accelerated by the development of large mass-production industries (steel, automobile, petroleum, power, chemicals) in which big gains in efficiency accrued from technology and economies of scale. Periodic technological breakthroughs and the rise of new industries cause some irregularity in economic growth. The expansion of the service sector in recent decades tended to lower the over-all rate of economic growth because of the fewer opportunities for substantial technological progress in the personal-service sector as compared with the manufacturing and agricultural sectors.

The uneven growth of the economy is also due to variations in research and development effort and in the rate of over-all productivity gain. Over-all growth in productivity is affected not only by shifts in the relative size of the economic sectors but by the magnitude and direction of the research and development effort which, in part, depends on the relative profitability of industries and the amount of retained earnings available for investment in technology. Long-term structural and technological changes give rise to internal and external economies which contribute to secular growth. The magnitude of internal and external economies undoubtedly varies over time and thus affects the pace of economic growth.

Variations in capital accumulation make for a discontinuous growth of the economy. The rate of savings and capital accumulation affects the rate of growth in national income, and this in turn affects the volume of savings and investment. An economy may experience a drop in the rate of savings because of a decline in the propensity to save, a fall in per capita income caused by a drop in the rate of productivity gain or by a cyclical decline in business, or because of a diversion of resources for "non-productive" government services and defense purposes financed by tax revenue. An economy can, on the other hand, accumulate increased savings when there is a rise in the propensity to save, a rise in per capita income because of rapid gains in productivity, or a cyclical upswing in national income.

Savings and capital accumulation are stimulated by profitable investment opportunities. To the extent that industry is competitive, prospective profits induce an expansion of capacity, and lower prices increase effective demand which makes for a high utilization of productive capacity. Investment opportunities tend to be affected adversely by the rise of oligopolies and monopolistic pricing practices which lower sales volume and tend to retard the expansion of industry. Savings and capital accumulation may expand because of a growth in investment opportunities which more than offset the retarding effect of market imperfections. Investment opportunities and economic expansion derive from, and are stimulated by, such factors as accelerated technological development and the discovery of new, rich resources, an increase in aggregate demand stemming from population growth and a rise in the propensity to consume, and lower interest rates and expansion of bank credit.

Variations in the growth rate of the population and labor force influence the rate of investment and economic development. A decline in population growth will tend to lower the aggregate demand for goods and retard the rate of investment. The decline in investment may, however, be offset by expenditures for other purposes (e.g., research, social welfare, defense). An increase in the growth rate of the population and labor force enlarges the aggregate demand for goods (e.g., dwellings, consumer durables), stimulates investment, and induces economic growth—assuming, of course, the adequacy of resources. But the increase in population is as much a consequence of economic growth as it is a condition for growth.

The growth in the labor force parallels the growth in population only if the ratio of the labor force to population is constant and the length of the workweek is constant. In the second half of the nineteenth century, for example, the American population grew at a rapid rate, but the labor force grew at a slightly higher rate because of the increase in the ratio of the labor force to population. In the first half of the twentieth century, the population tended to grow less rapidly. The labor force grew at a somewhat slower rate than the growth of population because the ratio of labor force to population (in terms of man-hours) tended to decline until the decade of the forties largely due to a steady reduction in the length of the workweek. Since the forties, however, population growth increased, and the ratio of the labor force to population also increased somewhat because a higher proportion of women joined the labor force, while the length of the workweek declined only slowly. The growth rate of the American labor force (in the decade of the sixties, at least) will tend to be somewhat proportionate to the growth of population; the anticipated small reduction in the length of the workweek will be offset by the increase in the proportion of women entering the labor force. The increased supply of labor in the mid-sixties and beyond will derive from the higher rate of population growth of the forties and fifties and from the continued displacement of industrial labor through laborsaving advances. An economy must grow at a rate sufficient to absorb the increase in its supply of labor. Insufficient absorption of the new entrants into the labor force may adversely affect the marriage rate, family formations, and the future growth of population. (See Fig. 1–1.)

Economic growth depends on the availability of natural resources. The discovery of rich resources and the development of low-cost substitute materials tend to stimulate economic growth. The depletion or a growing scarcity of such key resources as iron ore, coal, oil, timber, and agricultural land handicaps or slows economic growth. A developing scarcity in many types of materials can be and has been offset by greater research effort and by investment in new types of facilities which can economically process and exploit leaner (or marginal) resources or can put out substitute materials. The allocation of research effort and capital to the job of offsetting scarcity in materials of course diverts research and capital from other productive uses. But a large, rich economy can offset the depletion of many types of resources through research and investment as well as maintain long-term growth.

Business cycles involve a number of economic dislocations and imbalances which are essentially of a self-generating nature. Cyclical fluctuations contribute to variations in the secular growth of the economy. Uneven economic growth is partly due to the fact that cyclical fluctuations take place in a long-term or secular setting of economic growth. The secular setting is essentially comprised of the quantitative and qualitative trend in productive factors and technology and of the structural change in the economy. It is not only the magnitude and duration of the boom and the depression which shapes the trend of secular growth; it is also the secular trend which affects the magnitude and duration of the boom and the depression. Thus, short-term and long-term factors interact. Cyclical fluctuations, especially severe depressions, tend to retard secular economic growth because they adversely affect the level of investment, the growth in productive capacity, the rate of technological progress, and the size and effectiveness of the labor force.

Capital accumulation takes place in an environment of cyclical fluctuations; boomtime investment and depressiontime investment determine the level of capital formation and the level of productive capacity in the long run. Cyclical changes in investment derive from variations in profit expectations, in the size of retained earnings, and in the cost of external financing (i.e., the rate of interest and the availability of funds). Investment in productive capacity is largely based on the growth of derived demand. Investment is, thus, induced by the rate of increase in sales and output during the upswing in business. But before induced investment can take place, industry must operate at high-capacity levels, the stepup in demand and output must be appraised as being based on long-run factors (it must be considered non-temporary), and investment funds must be available. Thus, a comparatively broad pickup in output may give rise to induced investment, and the cumulative expansion accelerates the growth in capacity during prosperity and boom.

The rate of growth in productive capacity during the prosperity and boom period often tends to exceed the rate of growth of long-run aggregate demand, and the overexpansion of industry relative to current demand (excess capacity) contributes to a drop in profit levels and in profit expectations. And, unless offsetting forces develop (or are introduced), the contraction in business volume and the drop in the level of investment tend to become cumulative. The magnitude and pattern of investment differ markedly from one boom to the next because of structural changes in the economy, changes in capital-output ratios, techniques in demand promotion, the role of government, and other reasons.

Pronounced cyclical fluctuations tend to retard the rate of economic growth because the irregularity of business volume limits the effectiveness with which industry can plan its long-range investment programs and expand productive capacity. Boomtime capital expenditures and additions of highly productive facilities may not fit the product-mix or the regional sales requirements of the market that prevails in a longer time period. Cutbacks in expansion projects at the onset of a recession result in a certain amount of misdirected capital in terms of properly engineered productive capacity. The overexpansion in time of prosperity and the low level of capital formation and replacement in recession and depression mean that productive capacity is technologically less up to date than would have been the case if expansion had been more evenly geared to the long-run increase in demand and output. The shutdown of mines and other productive units in the extractive industries results in some impairment of capacity and loss of resources.

The shortage of investment funds from retained earnings during times of recession may limit the effectiveness with which industry can carry out its long-range projects in research and development. Productivity gains also tend to be uneven over the business cycle, as has been indicated earlier. The loss in skill among the unemployed during a depression and the curtailment in training and apprentice programs and in technical schools reduce the long-run productiveness of the labor force. Because of the tendency of producers during recession times to shift to "economy" types of models and products that can be cheaply turned out by processes that do not require capital-intensive facilities, the amount of funds needed to replace facilities is reduced.

The tendency toward secular retardation is likely to be greater if an economy is allowed to slip periodically into a severe recession. A depression may be prolonged and recovery slowed by the coincidence of such retardation factors as a decline in family formations, in the propensity to consume, in the pace of technological developments, and in the incremental capital-output ratio (i.e., the relative absence of profitable investment opportunities that call for capital-intensive facilities).

In an advanced economy the long-term actual growth of output (i.e., growth of GNP in constant dollars) may fall below the secular growth of the economy's productive capability, or potential GNP. The growth of actual GNP at a pace slower than the growth of an economy's potential capacity and the resulting underemployment of resources is generally interpreted as an evidence of secular retardation. This means that, though the economy is growing, the long-term actual growth of output is slower than the secular growth of the economy's productive potential, that is, less than the full-employment level of growth. The continued increase in the size of the labor force may lead to an intermittent increase in unemployment. The gap between the trend of actual growth and potential growth would be reflected in a more or less chronic underemployment of productive resources. Hence, if the growth in output should continue to fall below the secular growth of the productive potential, underemployment would tend to increase secularly.

In monetary terms secular retardation is reflected in the inability of an economy to invest its savings. Since the secular growth of an economy enlarges the quantity of productive resources and potential capacity, savings in "real" terms (i.e., the potential output above current consumption) are greater than the savings in financial terms. But if profit opportunities exist, the expansion of bank credit can provide the necessary funds needed for investment. Because savings (investment funds) are not absorbed due to a low-incremental capital-output ratio and the inadequacy of profitable investment outlets, the contraction in the volume of output results in a less than full-employment level of economic activity. A decline in the volume of profitable investment outlets and in the rate of capital accumulation retards the trend of actual economic growth relative to the growth of potential capacity. A retardation in economic growth will occur when profitable investment opportunities (i.e., net investment) at full employment develop more slowly than the available funds or net savings at full employment.

In the economically advanced countries a comparatively steady growth in productive potential and in actual output is possible when there is a balanced increase in the quantity of productive factors and expenditures for research and development and when there is an absence of pronounced cyclical fluctuations. A decline in the growth of one or more of the productive factors (labor, capital, and material supply) or in the research and development effort will tend to make for retardation in the rate of economic expansion, unless there is an offsetting increase in the growth of other factors that can serve as effective substitutes.

A country experiencing a decline in the growth of its population and labor force or a growing scarcity in material resources can nonetheless maintain economic growth through heavier capital accumulation and accelerated research which lower the input of scarce productive factors per unit of output. Technological progress can be made in terms of laborsavings, material-savings, as well as capital-savings improvements. Economic growth can be maintained by investment for improvement of the economic overhead facilities which augment external economies. The stepup of investment for technological progress and for improvement of economic overhead will not only increase the gain in productivity and lower the input of variable factors per unit of output but will create additional new investment opportunities as well as offset inflation.

A comparatively high level of employment in the American economy in the late forties and in the fifties was largely maintained by population growth, increasing outlays for technological development, a high level of investment, defense expenditures, "automatic stabilizers" provided by the public budget and fiscal practices, and by such measures as unemployment insurance and price support of farm products.

If long-run growth is to be achieved, an economy must maintain balanced growth. This means that the level of investment must be sufficient to absorb the growth in the labor force. A given level of investment generates a certain increase in national income and demand, but it creates a varying amount of productive capacity because of changes in the incremental capital-output ratio. The capital-output ratio varies over time but in the long run tends to decline. The incremental capital-output ratio (i.e., the investment required to attain a given increase in output capacity) depends not only on the direction of investment but on the developments in pro-

TABLE 2-5

Selected Indicators of Economic Growth Potentials, 1959-75[1]

(per cent increase per year[2])

Indicator	Rate of Growth, 1909-58	Projected Potential Growth Rates, 1959-75		
		A	B	C
Total labor force	1.4	1.9	1.7	1.5
Total employment, including the Armed Forces	1.4	1.9[3]	1.7[4]	1.5[5]
Average annual hours of work. .	−0.6	−0.4	−0.5	−0.6
Total man-hours	0.9	1.6	1.2	0.9
Stock of private plant and equipment in constant prices	2.4	3.2	2.7	2.2
Average age of capital stock. . .	0.3	−0.2	−0.1	0.0
Composition of demand	0.1	0.015	0.001	−0.005
Gross national product in constant prices	2.9	---	---	---
From 1959, actual (preliminary estimate)	---	5.2	4.7	4.2
From 1959, potential	---	4.6	4.0	3.5

[1]Some rates of change in this table vary slightly from those given in the similar Table 4-1, p. 101 of the "Staff Report on Employment Growth and Price Levels," because of the incorporation of later data and refinements of analysis not then available.

[2]Computed by compound interest formula, using initial and terminal years.

[3]Assumes 97 per cent of the labor force employed in 1975.

[4]Assumes 96 per cent of the labor force employed in 1975.

[5]Assumes 95 per cent of the labor force employed in 1975.

Source: See footnote 14.

duction technology. (See pp. 13–26.) To maintain full-employment growth, the rate or level of investment must therefore vary. A given constant rate of investment may at times overexpand capacity relative to the amount of income and demand it generates; and at other times the same investment level may not create sufficient capacity to satisfy the current aggregate demand. To maintain full-employment growth means that the rate of savings (including bank credit) and investment must vary with changes in the incremental capital-output ratio and changes in the growth of complementary productive factors if it is to be sufficient to employ available pro-

ductive capacity and labor, that is, sufficient to realize an economy's
potential productive capability.

Any projection of economic growth must obviously be based on
certain assumptions with respect to the availability of productive
factors. Some forecasters deal with this problem by formulating
alternative projections (Table 2–5):

Three alternative projections of potential output and of its rate of growth to
1975 were prepared [by Knowles and Warden]: high (labeled A), medium
(B) and low (C). These projections reflect trends of population, participation
in the labor force, unemployment, hours of work, changes in the stock, and the
average level of prosperity. These projections, which, of course, are subject
to some error, are designed to indicate a realistic range of potential growth
rates that our economy might experience over the next decade.[14]

TABLE 2–6

Range of Estimates of Gross National Product and Underlying Factors,
1959, 1980, and 2000

	1959	1980			2000		
		Low	Medium	High	Low	Medium	High
Population (million persons)	177	226	245	279	268	331	433
Civilian labor force (millions)	69.3	93	99	108	116	138	173
Civilian employment (millions)	65.7	88	95	105	110	132	168
Average hours per week Agricultural employment	45.2	36.3	40.2	45.6	29.6	36.3	45.6
Private non-agricultural employment	40.6	34.2	37.4	40.5	29.2	34.8	40.5
Productivity (per cent yearly increase in output per man-hour)							
Agricultural	5.2 *	3.8	4.2	4.8	3.6	4.2	4.9
Private non-agricultural	1.9	1.7	2.3	3.2	1.7	2.5	3.6
GNP (billions 1959 dollars)	484	933	1,030	1,220	1,630	2,140	3,210
GNP per capita (1959 dollars)	2,730	4,130	4,200	4,370	6,080	6,470	7,410

* Long-term average.
SOURCE: See footnote 15.

The economy and resources of the future were projected (Table
2–6) by Fisher and Boorstein in 1959:

It may readily be admitted that the size and shape of the future economy cannot be known with any exactness now. However, it may be projected on the

[14] James W. Knowles, with the assistance of Charles B. Warden, Jr., *The Potential
Economic Growth in the United States*, Study Paper No. 20, prepared for Joint Eco-
nomic Committee, Congress of the United States (Washington, D.C.: Government
Printing Office, 1960), pp. 38, 40.

basis of past trends and other factors. [Table 2–6] indicates tentatively a range of possibilities for 1980 and 2000 depending on the number employed, the number of hours they work, and how productively they work. Incorporated in assumptions about productivity are notions about the future availability of raw materials, among other things.[15]

Economic growth depends not only on certain over-all structural developments in the economy but on the structural pattern and developments in specific industries, which is the primary concern of the three chapters of Part II following.

QUESTIONS FOR REVIEW AND APPLICATION

1. Compare individual research with the large-scale research of big firms.
2. In what way has the emergence of the large corporation (including the big holding company) contributed to the acceleration of technological progress?
3. What structural changes in the economy may be expected to take place during the process of growth and development of a comparatively large underdeveloped country with diversified resources?
4. Explain what is meant by the capital-output ratio. Does an increase in an economy's capital-output ratio mean that the economy is becoming less efficient, or does it necessarily mean that investment opportunities are increasing? Explain.
5. Identify and briefly discuss (a) the developments in an advanced economy that tend to increase the capital-output ratio in industry and (b) the developments that tend to lower the capital-output ratio.
6. (a) Explain and illustrate how productivity can be measured. (b) "Output per man-hour is a better index of the economy's productivity gain than it is a measure of productivity of a single industry." Explain.
7. What are the main sources of productivity gains?
8. How might public outlays for certain types of capital projects and social services (expansion and improvement of transportation, technical schools, public health, and the like) that augment external economies step up the rate of productivity gain? Will cost reduction from such public outlays work to offset partially whatever inflationary pressures may exist?
9. Explain how laborsaving and capital-saving technological advances can enlarge the quantity of productive factors available for economic growth in a country whose population is stationary as to size.
10. "Economic growth, in physical terms, partly depends on the continued emergence of new industries—the introduction of new products, by-products, and services." Explain.
11. Why does economic growth, notably in terms of GNP, not proceed in a straight line upward?
12. Do some governmental short-term remedial actions sometimes clash with long-term objectives in maintaining economic growth and stability? Explain.

[15] J. L. Fisher and E. Boorstein, *The Adequacy of Resources for Economic Growth in the United States*, Study Paper No. 13, prepared for Joint Economic Committee, Congress of the United States (Washington, D.C.: Government Printing Office, 1959), p. 47.

References and Supplementary Readings
for Part I

*ABRAMOWITZ, M. "Economics of Growth." In B. F. Haley (ed.). *A Survey of Contemporary Economics.* Homewood, Ill.: Richard D. Irwin, Inc., 1952, vol. II, pp. 132-182.

BURNS, A. F. *Production Trends in the United States Since 1870.* New York: National Bureau of Economic Research, 1934.

CARTER, C. F., and WILLIAMS, B. R. *Industry and Technical Progress; Factors Governing the Speed and Application of Science.* (On behalf of the Science and Industry Committee, London.) London: Oxford University Press, 1957.

CLARK, COLIN. *The Conditions of Economic Progress.* London: Macmillan & Co., Ltd., 1951.

CONFERENCE ON RESEARCH IN INCOME AND WEALTH. *Problems of Capital Formation.* New York: National Bureau of Economic Research, Inc., 1957.

DEWHURST, J. F., and associates. *America's Needs and Resources.* New York: Twentieth Century Fund, 1955.

DOMAR, EVSEY. *Essays in the Theory of Economic Growth.* New York: Oxford University Press, 1957.

Entrepreneurship and Economic Growth. Conference: Social Science Research Council and Harvard University Research Center in Entrepreneurial History, Cambridge, Mass., Nov., 1954. Cambridge: Harvard University Press, 1954.

FABRICANT, S. *The Output of Manufacturing Industries, 1899–1937.* New York: National Bureau of Economic Research, Inc., 1940.

GALESON, WALTER (ed.). *Labor and Economic Development.* New York: John Wiley & Sons, Inc., 1959.

HIGGINS, BENJAMIN. *Economic Development.* New York: W. W. Norton & Co., Inc., 1959.

HIRSCHMAN, ALBERT O. *The Strategy of Economic Development.* New Haven: Yale University Press, 1958.

KEIRSTEAD, BURTON. *The Theory of Economic Change.* Toronto: Macmillan Co. of Canada, Ltd., 1948.

KINDELBERGER, CHARLES P. *Economic Development.* New York: McGraw-Hill Book Co., Inc., 1958.

KRUTILLA, JOHN V., and ECKSTEIN, OTTO. *Multiple Purpose River Development; Studies in Applied Economic Analysis.* Baltimore: Johns Hopkins Press, 1958.

*KUZNETS, SIMON S. *Lectures on Economic Growth.* Glencoe, Ill.: Free Press, 1959.

LEIBENSTEIN, HARVEY. *Economic Backwardness and Economic Growth.* New York: John Wiley & Sons, Inc., 1957.

LEWIS, W. ARTHUR. *The Theory of Economic Growth.* London: George Allen & Unwin, 1955.

* Suggested reading.

MEIR, G. M., and BALDWIN, R. E. *Economic Development: Theory, History, Policy.* New York: John Wiley & Sons., Inc., 1957.

MOORE, WILBERT E. *Industrialization and Labor.* Ithaca, N.Y.: Cornell University Press, 1951.

NURSKE, RAGNAR. *Problems of Capital Formation in Underdeveloped Countries.* Oxford: Basil Blackwell & Mott, Ltd., 1953.

REDER, MELVIN W. *Labor in a Growing Economy.* New York: John Wiley & Sons, Inc., 1957.

SCHUMPETER, JOSEPH. *History of Economic Analysis.* New York: Oxford University Press, 1954.

SVENNILSSON, I. *Growth and Stagnation in the European Economy.* Geneva: United Nations Economic Commission for Europe, 1954.

WILLIAMSON, HAROLD F., and BUTTRICK, JOHN A. *Economic Development: Principles and Patterns.* Englewood Cliffs, N.J.: Prentice-Hall, Inc., 1954.

Part II
THE INDUSTRY

CHAPTER 3

Structural Pattern:
Location, Labor, and Material

SCOPE OF ANALYSIS AND QUANTIFICATION

Businessmen and production managers generally consider firms in the same line of business or field of economic activity to be in the same industry. For instance, they regard the textile industry as consisting of producers of cloth, the shoe industry as producers of footwear, the pharmaceutical industry as producers of drugs and medicines. Thus, the term "industry" customarily denotes all firms and plants devoted to the output of a single product or a closely related group of products. The industry grouping of firms and establishments serves a number of purposes. Executives appraise their business situations in terms of their market share of the industry's total sales. The industry "group" functions as an agency for trade-association activities and for industry-wide collective bargaining. Public policy designates certain industries for tariff protection or subsidies; governmental legislation is often enacted to cover certain industries, such as public utilities, the bituminous-coal industry, and the maritime industry.

Pragmatic economic analysis must rest on the formulation of a realistic concept of an industry. The Census of Manufacturing defines an industry as a group of plants or establishments producing the same or closely related products or services. Establishments that comprise an industry are the plants (factories, mills, mines, distribution and other service facilities) engaged in the same type of productive activity. Auxiliary establishments are grouped with the productive plants that they support. An auxiliary unit is devoted to a non-manufacturing service activity (power generation, warehousing, maintenance, research and development) to facilitate the principal productive activity of plants of the same firm. An industry's establishments and firms are, of course, not static. Firms may give up old productive activities and take on new activities, thus branching off into different industries.

Though a plant may produce two or more related products in different quantities, it is its primary products that classify the establishment in a particular industry. Most industries are comprised of plants with a high degree of concentration (specialization) of output in a particular product or a group of very closely related products (Census estimates 90 per cent). Similarity in products and in productive processes is a meaningful and useful criterion for grouping establishments into specific industries (into homogeneous production segments of the economy) and for placing firms into one or more industries. Firms in a given industry typically buy or employ the same kind of materials, labor, and production technology to put out similar products. Thus, industries are designated and identified on the basis of their technology and homogeneity of production (on the basis of the supply side of economic activity) rather than on the basis of close substitutability of demand for products. Many industries turn out products that have no close substitutes, while a number of industries put out products that have close substitute items turned out by other industries.

Some types of economic analysis (e.g., market studies and demand analysis and estimating) would, obviously, require the grouping of productive enterprise on the basis of establishments putting out products that are close substitutes sold to buyers in the same markets. Traditional economic theory, for instance, employs a concept of "an industry" to group firms and buyers so as to permit formulation of aggregate supply and demand functions or schedules and hypothesizes the movement of the industry toward "equilibrium," and therein an economic allocation of productive factors for maximum consumer satisfaction. Because it assumes that firms in an industry are single-product enterprises turning out identical goods, this concept of an industry is of limited value for realistic supply and demand analysis in the manufacturing and service sectors of the economy. Price theory based on imperfect competition is more realistic since it recognizes that firms typically produce differentiated (distinctive) products or services. Such price analysis identifies its industry as a group of firms producing closely substitutable products and as being closely engaged in the competitive process. However, this conceptualization of an industry lacks some realism since many firms are multiple-product as well as multiple-plant enterprises. Firms are often engaged in the output of products classified in different industries, and they often include plants located in widely separate areas and producing for local markets.

An economist may define and delineate an industry in any way that best suits the purpose of his analysis. He also prunes away data irrelevant to the structure and behavior of the industry and the respective firms. He may, for instance, limit his study to the steel industry or he may undertake a broad study of the metallurgical industry. He may include producers of substitute products or include producers of complementary products. In a study of the container industry, he would include producers of tin cans and producers of glass, paper, and plastic containers.

Conceived as a comparatively narrow, homogeneous economic segment, the industry concept thus provides a realistic approach to an industry-by-industry study of the economy and to the study of individual industries and their structure. Industries, however, differ with respect to the degree of structural homogeneity. A highly homogeneous industry is one that consists of establishments that employ the same kind of processes and materials for the output of identical or closely similar products. The shoe and meat industries are, for instance, more homogeneous than the chemical and rubber industries. The more heterogeneous the industry and the more diversified the firms, the more difficult is the industry to analyze. The electronics industry is obviously more difficult to study than the flour-milling industry.

An economic analyst may undertake an *industry study* for one or more purposes. He may aim (1) to compile the data necessary for planning the scope and structure of a firm and for providing the guides for managerial policy and decision making; (2) to provide a basis for pending legislative measures (tax levies, antitrust action, etc.) dealing with an industry and to predict the economic impact and consequences of such measures; (3) to formulate an approach for establishing an industry in an underdeveloped area; and (4) to appraise an industry's structural logic and performance with respect to pricing and resource allocation, adaptability, growth, productivity, and profitability.

The economist must look to the structure of the industry and to the organization of business enterprise if he is to analyze and predict the interaction and behavior of industrial and business operations.

An industry's particular structural pattern derives from the confluence of the production technology, resource utilization, and organizational designs of the constituent plants and firms and from business adaptation to the configurations of the market, cyclical fluctuations, governmental policy, and other external factors.

In making an industry survey, an analyst essentially characterizes and, wherever useful, quantifies in economic terms the structural features and behavior of an industry and a representative firm, as will be discussed in Parts II and III. He characterizes *an industry's structural pattern* in terms of input-output relations, location pattern, labor and material supply conditions, product coverage, cost and supply behavior, growth trend and demand behavior, market structure, and pricing practice. He characterizes *a firm's structural design* in terms of the product line and scope of business, type of multiple-plant system and economies of scale, break-even analysis, and competitive position. He analyzes special problems of short-run business operations (e.g., seasonality) that occur in a given industry. The analyst also ascertains how external impacts (unionism, taxation, cyclical fluctuations, for example) influence the structure of an industry and business operations (see Chap. 9).

Because decision making and policy formulation must be based on future economic developments, business analysts find it necessary to project economic trends and to forecast the course of general business activity. In order that they may adequately formulate their short- and long-range plans, business executives, for instance, find it necessary to forecast labor and material prices, market demand, and monetary and fiscal policies, as outlined in Chapter 10.

Executives generally employ *capital budgeting* to plan business investments for maximum economic advantage in the fulfillment of their long-range program. Through the capital-budgeting procedure, executives allocate funds among competing investment proposals on the basis of relative profitability and contribution to the achievement of long-term goals, as discussed in Chapters 11 and 12.

A business analyst generally finds it necessary to estimate and project production cost and sales volume and revenue for long-term investment decisions as well as for short-term operating decisions. An analyst finds the *break-even chart* particularly useful for such purposes. A break-even chart presents the relationship between total cost and total revenue for various volumes of output within the limits of the firm's productive capacity (see Fig. 3–2).[1]

---

[1] In preparing a meaningful break-even chart for a future period, an analyst plots the total-cost curve and the total-revenue curve on the basis of the capacity, costs, and selling prices that will prevail in the future period of business operations. Such a

In addition to break-even analysis, an analyst employs such techniques and approaches (discussed in standard statistics textbooks) as sample surveys, scatter diagrams, time series and trends, correlation analysis, and ratios to quantify an industry's structural features and to facilitate the formulation of long-term plans. An analyst finds the ratio an especially useful method for measuring certain structural aspects of an industry and business behavior. In analyzing short-run business operations, for instance, he uses operating and financial ratios, such as the inventory-sales ratio which can indicate the adequacy or excessiveness of stock levels for anticipated business conditions. In gauging the capital intensiveness of an industry's production process, he uses the capital-output ratio which essentially measures the capital input required for a given volume of goods. In measuring an industry's gain in productivity (the increase in output per man-hour), the analyst generally uses the change in the ratio of output of goods for a given input of labor. In gauging an industry's production concentration and characterizing its market structure, he uses the concentration ratio which measures the percentage of the total output of a product that was produced by the four largest or by the eight largest producers in the industry.

An analyst often uses a *scatter diagram* to ascertain the relationship between variables in industrial and business behavior. His scatter diagram plots a distribution of items, measuring one variable on the x axis and the other variable on the y axis. If there is a relationship between two variables (e.g., a relationship between business investment and GNP over a period of years), the points plotted will tend to follow a diagonal line; this line (the line of regression) indicates the average relationship between the two variables. (See

---

chart will show how the level of profits will be affected by anticipated changes in production technology, input prices, and selling prices.

An analyst may estimate the total-cost curve on the basis of an accounting, statistical, or engineering approach. Because the accounting and statistical approaches are based on past data (past operations), he would generally find these approaches not useful for projecting a total-cost curve for a future period when not only input prices (wage rates and the purchase prices of materials) but production processes and the organization of the physical plant are likely to be changed by plant expansion, replacement, and modernization. To prepare a useful break-even chart for a future period, an analyst generally finds it necessary to use the engineering approach, whereby he projects the cost-output relationship for future output and production technology by converting the estimated physical inputs of materials and labor into production costs and by converting the physical-product output to sales revenue on the basis of anticipated selling prices. (For discussion, see pages 305–308.) An analyst would find engineering estimates of costs and revenue and break-even analysis particularly useful for managerial decisions dealing with selection of processes, plant size, and the computation of estimated return on investment.

Fig. 10–10). A regression equation would describe the nature of the relationship among variables.

When he desires to show relative rather than absolute change in industrial development, the analyst uses a *ratio chart*. A common type of ratio chart is the semilog chart for the time series, scaled logarithmically on the y axis and arithmetically on the x axis.

When he desires to present statistical data graphically with reference to time of occurrence, the analyst employs a *time-series chart* which presents data along the horizontal axis in accordance with its time of occurrence. The values of the dependent variable (e.g., size of the labor force or employment), shown along the vertical axis and plotted at various intervals of time, are connected by a straight line to form a continuous curve extending over the entire period covered by the chart (see Fig. 10–1).

The analyst may fit a trend line to a time series as a freehand line or as a mathematical equation. In plotting the trend of a time series, he would often use the moving average as a method for smoothing out cyclical movements and random fluctuations (see Fig. 2–1). The trend of a time series (e.g., secular growth of GNP) derives from such long-term forces as population growth, capital formation, and technological advance. An analyst would sometimes project a trend into future years on the basis of past time-series data, as in the case of demand for steel in Figure 4–10. In undertaking time-series analysis, an analyst would essentially measure and interpret various changes or movements as they appear in the series over a period of time. This is illustrated in Figures 4–9 and 4–10 which show the past trend in the output of specific products and in Table 3–2 which presents the trend of estimated demand for selected key materials.

An analyst notes that when two related variables plotted on a scatter diagram involve a definite relationship, the plotted points tend to follow a definite path or line of movement. A correlation would thus exist when there is a close relationship between two groups of data—the closer the relationship, the higher the degree of correlation. An analyst uses *correlation analysis* when he desires to establish the interdependency between two or more variables in numerical terms. The coefficient of correlation is the measure of the degree of association between two variables.

The essential purpose of correlation analysis is to formulate a graphic presentation or a mathematical equation that best expresses the relationship between variables in order to facilitate forecasting. In many cases graphic methods are as suitable as mathematical methods. The graphic method uses a curve to explain the relationship. Changes in the demand for a product, for instance, may be graphically projected on the basis of changes in population, income, and other variables (the independent variables). On the basis of economic analysis, the independent variables are considered to be controlling. The statistical analysis is known as "simple correlation" when only one independent variable is involved and as "multiple correlation" when two or more variables are involved. The dependent variable (e.g., demand) can be forecast once the independent variables (e.g., population, consumer income) have been forecast for a given period and the nature of the functional relationship is known. In cases in which the effect of a given event occurs later in time, the introduction of an appropriate time lag improves the accuracy of forecasting.

The appropriate statistical and analytical tools, economic principles, and conceptual approaches are, in fact, employed throughout this book at the point at which they are required and can be concretely applied for analyzing an industry and business enterprise and for formulating long-range investment plans and business policy to adapt the enterprise for profitability.[2] A broad-gauge industry study, however, would at the outset appraise the role and size of an industry in the economy.

INDUSTRY SIZE. An industry's size and contribution to the economy are indicated by the type of products it puts out (whether consumer necessities, consumer durables, services, or capital goods) and its volume of output. An industry's size and growth trend may be measured in terms of capital invested, number of people employed, material input, physical output, value of output, and value-added in production. Some of these measuring rods are more appropriate than others. Net capital invested as a measure of an industry's size and growth, for instance, is obscured by the problem of realistically gauging capital consumption (understatement or overstatement of depreciation in real economic terms is difficult to avoid) and by the capital-saving technological advances that increase the productivity of capital and lower the capital-output ratio. Industry size and trend of output measured in terms of the number of workers employed does not take into account variations in the length of the workweek and in the number of shifts in plant operation, and it neglects gains in labor productivity (in output per man-hour). Industry size measured in terms of raw-material input (e.g., barrels of oil absorbed by a refinery, tons of grain absorbed by a

[2] See Quantification in the index for the scope and breakdown of economic measurement.

distillery) may be suitable in some cases, but it does not allow for changes in the quality of material or in the quantity of material required per unit of the various products put out, and it overlooks the more thorough utilization of raw materials for the output of by-products.

An industry's size and growth may be appropriately measured in terms of physical units of output when the goods are comparatively uniform over time (e.g., kilowatt-hours of electricity, tons of copper, gallons of wine). But since new features are added to many products and the quality of most goods improves over time (for instance, when color television sets displace black-and-white sets or when a new-model washing machine is introduced), physical output as a criterion of growth lacks sufficient precision. Physical output also does not indicate the full measure of an industry's real growth when two products are combined into one, for example, when a new-model earth-moving machine is designed to do excavation work formerly done by two different types of machines.

Industry size indicated in terms of gross sales or value of output (in real terms) takes into account changes in product-mix and the addition of new items, but it does not reflect an industry's actual productive contribution since it generally includes the material and service inputs from other industries and neglects quality improvement in the product. Value-added (in real terms) is generally the most appropriate and useful index for measuring an industry's size and growth trend, since it takes into account changes in product-mix and the addition of new items and excludes the material and service inputs from other industries. (For a discussion of output measured by an index of production and a man-hour index, see page 134.)

Because of their size, structure, productivity gains, and other developments, big industries (meat, textiles and clothing, power, steel, automobile, chemical and petroleum industries) have a significant influence on the economy. But many smaller industries (pharmaceuticals, for example) make a notable contribution to economic and social progress. The market structure and degree of competition in the bigger industries have a decided influence on inflation or deflation, on the over-all price structure in quantitative terms, and on efficiency in the allocation of resources. Variations in output and in the growth of big industries have a significant impact on national income and on employment, especially when the industries are geographically concentrated. Variations in the volume of their production also have a significant impact on input-output relations with other industries.

INPUT-OUTPUT RELATIONS

Production in each industry involves the input of materials, labor, and other resources for a given output of goods. The materials, fuel, and other inputs come from a number of industries, and an industry's output is sold and distributed to a number of industries as well as to the household and government sectors. Input-output analysis is the study of such interindustry relations, and the input-output relations of an industry are identified as its "production function."

Economists have compiled input-output tables to show an economy's quantitative interrelations among industries.[3] An input-output table lists an economy's industries (or economic sectors if industries are grouped) along the left-hand side of the table to show output quantities along horizontal rows and lists the same industries across the top of the table to show each industry's inputs in the vertical columns (Table 3–1). The industries listed on the left side show along the horizontal row how each industry's (or each sector's) output and sales (in monetary value) for a given year are distributed to other sectors, including the household, export, and government sectors. The horizontal row for the rubber industry, for instance, would show the output and the amount of rubber products distributed (sold) to agriculture, apparel, motor vehicle, and other industries. An industry's vertical column would show how it obtains its needed inputs of materials and other goods from the industries listed on the left side of the table. The vertical column for the motor-vehicle industry would show the inputs purchased from the textile, rubber, metal, and other industries that are required for the given output level of vehicles. Thus, the horizontal rows in the table show the outputs and sales of each economic sector to other sectors, and the vertical columns show the purchases and inputs of each sector from other sectors. Input-output data may be presented in relatively minute detail (tables have been compiled for some four hundred industries of the United States economy), or the data may be compiled or summarized in more aggregate terms and classified into coarser economic sectors (the 1947 table for the American economy shows forty-two economic sectors, for example).

The input-output table or model essentially shows the interdependent economic activities and the flow pattern of productive factors among economic sectors for a past year. A definite relation-

---

[3] See Wassily W. Leontief *et al.*, *Studies in the Structure of the American Economy* (New York: Oxford University Press, 1953), pp. 3–52.

TABLE

Input-Output Table: The Quantitative Flow

INDUSTRY

INDUSTRY PRODUCING	1 AGRICULTURE AND FISHERIES	2 FOOD AND KINDRED PRODUCTS	3 TEXTILE MILL PRODUCTS	4 APPAREL	5 LUMBER AND WOOD PRODUCTS	6 FURNITURE AND FIXTURES	7 PAPER AND ALLIED PRODUCTS	8 PRINTING AND PUBLISHING	9 CHEMICALS	10 PRODUCTS OF PETROLEUM AND COAL	11 RUBBER PRODUCTS	12 LEATHER AND LEATHER PRODUCTS	13 STONE, CLAY AND GLASS PRODUCTS	14 PRIMARY METALS	15 FABRICATED METAL PRODUCTS	16 MACHINERY (EXCEPT ELECTRIC)	17 ELECTRICAL MACHINERY	18 MOTOR VEHICLES
1 AGRICULTURE AND FISHERIES	10.86	15.70	2.16	0.02	0.19	—	0.01	—	1.21	—	—	0.05	*	0.01	—	—	—	—
2 FOOD AND KINDRED PRODUCTS	2.38	5.75	0.06	0.01	*	*	0.03	*	-0.79	*	—	0.44	*	*	*	*	*	*
3 TEXTILE MILL PRODUCTS	0.06	*	1.30	3.88	*	0.29	0.04	0.03	0.01	*	0.44	0.09	0.03	—	0.01	0.02	0.0	
4 APPAREL	0.04	0.20	—	1.96	—	0.01	0.02	—	0.03	—	—	*	*	—	*	*		
5 LUMBER AND WOOD-PRODUCTS	0.15	0.10	0.02	*	1.09	0.39	0.27	*	0.04	0.01	—	0.02	0.02	0.06	0.06	0.09	0.0	
6 FURNITURE AND FIXTURES	—	—	0.01	—	—	0.01	0.01	—	—	—	—	—	—	—	—	*	0.01	0.
7 PAPER AND ALLIED PRODUCTS	*	0.52	0.08	0.02	*	0.02	2.60	1.08	0.33	0.11	0.02	0.05	0.18	*	0.09	0.04	0.	
8 PRINTING AND PUBLISHING	—	0.04	*	—	—	—	—	0.77	0.02	—	—	—	—	—	0.01	0.01	0.0	
9 CHEMICALS	0.83	1.48	0.80	0.14	0.03	0.06	0.18	0.10	2.58	0.21	0.60	0.13	0.12	0.18	0.13	0.08	0.	
10 PRODUCTS OF PETROLEUM AND COAL	0.46	0.06	0.03	*	0.07	*	0.06	*	0.32	4.83	0.01	*	0.05	0.90	0.02	0.04	0.	
11 RUBBER PRODUCTS	0.12	0.01	0.01	0.02	0.01	0.01	0.01	*	*	*	*	0.04	0.05	0.01	*	0.01	0.13	0.
12 LEATHER AND LEATHER PRODUCTS	—	—	*	0.05	*	—	0.01	—	*	—	—	—	1.04	—	—	*	0.02	*
13 STONE, CLAY AND GLASS PRODUCTS	0.06	0.25	*	*	0.01	0.03	0.03	—	0.26	0.05	0.01	0.01	0.43	0.21	0.07	0.07	0.	
14 PRIMARY METALS	0.01	*	—	*	0.01	0.11	—	0.01	0.19	0.01	0.01	*	0.04	6.90	2.53	2.02	1.0	
15 FABRICATED METAL PRODUCTS	0.08	0.61	*	0.01	0.04	0.14	0.02	*	0.13	0.08	0.01	0.02	*	0.05	0.43	0.62	0.	
16 MACHINERY (EXCEPT ELECTRIC)	0.06	0.01	0.04	0.02	0.01	0.01	0.01	0.04	*	0.01	—	—	0.01	0.07	0.28	1.15	0.	
17 ELECTRICAL MACHINERY	—	—	—	—	—	—	—	—	*	—	—	—	0.01	0.05	0.24	0.58	0.	
18 MOTOR VEHICLES	0.11	*	—	*	—	*	—	—	—	*	—	—	*	*	0.03	0.03	0.	
19 OTHER TRANSPORTATION EQUIPMENT	0.01		—	—	—	—	*	—	*	*	&	—	*	*	*			
20 PROFESSIONAL AND SCIENTIFIC EQUIPMENT	—	—	—	—	—	*	0.01	0.03	0.01	—	—	—	*	*	0.04	0.04	0.	
21 MISCELLANEOUS MANUFACTURING INDUSTRIES	*	0.01	*	0.26	*	0.02	0.01	—	0.03	—	*	0.02	0.01	*	0.02	0.05	0.1	
22 COAL, GAS AND ELECTRIC POWER	0.06	0.20	0.11	0.04	0.02	0.02	0.12	0.03	0.19	0.56	0.04	0.02	0.20	0.35	0.08	0.10	0.	
23 RAILROAD TRANSPORTATION	0.44	0.57	0.09	0.06	0.14	0.05	0.22	0.07	0.29	0.27	0.04	0.04	0.15	0.52	0.13	0.16	0.	
24 OCEAN TRANSPORTATION	0.07	0.13	0.01	0.01	0.01	*	0.02	*	0.04	0.09	*	*	0.01	0.08	*	*	*	
25 OTHER TRANSPORTATION	0.55	0.38	0.08	0.03	0.14	0.04	0.12	0.03	0.10	0.47	0.01	0.02	0.07	0.16	0.03	0.04	0.	
26 TRADE	1.36	0.46	0.23	0.37	0.06	0.06	0.18	0.03	0.17	0.02	0.05	0.06	0.05	0.36	0.20	0.26	0.	
27 COMMUNICATIONS	*	0.04	0.01	0.02	0.01	0.01	0.01	0.04	0.02	0.01	0.01	*	0.01	0.02	0.02	0.03	0.	
28 FINANCE AND INSURANCE	0.24	0.15	0.02	0.02	0.08	0.02	0.02	0.02	0.02	0.02	0.13	0.01	0.01	0.05	0.06	0.04	0.05	0.
29 REAL ESTATE AND RENTALS	2.39	0.09	0.03	0.10	0.02	0.02	0.03	0.06	0.03	—	0.01	0.02	0.02	0.06	0.03	0.04	0.	
30 BUSINESS SERVICES	0.01	0.63	0.07	0.10	0.02	0.06	0.02	0.06	0.42	0.04	0.02	0.05	0.01	0.03	0.05	0.09	0.	
31 PERSONAL AND REPAIR SERVICES	0.37	0.12	*	*	0.04	*	*	0.02	0.01	0.01	*	*	0.03	0.01	0.01	0.01	*	
32 NON-PROFIT ORGANIZATIONS	—	—	—	—	—	—	—	—	—	—	—	—	—	—	—	—	—	—
33 AMUSEMENTS	—	—	—	—	—	—	—	—	—	—	—	—	—	—	—	—	—	—
34 SCRAP AND MISCELLANEOUS INDUSTRIES	—	—	0.02	—	—	—	0.25	—	0.01	—	0.01	—	0.01	1.11	0.02	0.05	*	
35 EATING AND DRINKING PLACES	—	—	—	—	—	—	—	—	*	—	—	—	—	—	—	—		
36 NEW CONSTRUCTION AND MAINTENANCE	0.20	0.12	0.04	0.02	0.01	0.01	0.04	0.01	0.04	0.03	0.01	0.02	0.03	0.10	0.03	0.05	0.	
37 UNDISTRIBUTED	—	1.87	0.30	1.08	0.73	0.27	0.17	0.50	1.49	0.65	0.27	0.27	0.47	0.32	1.14	1.71	0.	
38 INVENTORY CHANGE (DEPLETIONS)	2.66	0.40	0.12	0.19	*	0.01	0.09	0.03	0.14	0.01	*	0.03	*	0.11	*	*	*	
39 FOREIGN COUNTRIES (IMPORTS FROM)	0.69	2.11	0.21	0.28	0.18	0.01	0.62	0.01	0.59	0.26	*	0.04	0.14	0.62	0.01	0.05	*	
40 GOVERNMENT	0.81	1.24	0.64	0.38	0.34	0.11	0.50	0.34	0.76	0.78	0.11	0.14	0.32	0.82	0.48	0.77	0.	
41 PRIVATE CAPITAL FORMATION (GROSS)	DEPRECIATION AND OTHER CAPITAL CONSUMPTION ALLOWANCES ARE INCLUDED IN HOUSEHOLD ROW																	
42 HOUSEHOLDS	19.17	7.05	3.34	4.24	2.72	1.12	2.20	3.14	3.75	5.04	1.08	1.20	2.35	5.53	4.14	6.80	3.4	
TOTAL GROSS OUTLAYS	44.26	40.30	9.84	13.32	6.00	2.89	7.90	6.45	14.05	13.67	2.82	3.81	4.84	18.69	10.40	15.22	8.3	

NOTE: Each number in the body of the table represents billions of 1947 dollars. Asterisks stand for sums less than $5 million. Totals may not check due to rounding.

3–1

of Goods and Services Among Industries

PURCHASING — **FINAL DEMAND**

Column legend:

- 26 TRADE
- 27 TRANSPORTATION
- 28 (… TRANSPORTATION)
- 29 COMMUNICATIONS
- 30 FINANCE AND INSURANCE
- 31 REAL ESTATE AND RENTALS
- 32 BUSINESS SERVICES
- 33 PERSONAL AND REPAIR SERVICES
- 34 NON-PROFIT ORGANIZATIONS
- 35 AMUSEMENTS
- 36 SCRAP AND MISCELLANEOUS INDUSTRIES
- 37 EATING AND DRINKING PLACES
- 38 NEW CONSTRUCTION AND MAINTENANCE
- 39 UNDISTRIBUTED
- 40 INVENTORY CHANGE (ADDITIONS)
- 41 FOREIGN COUNTRIES (EXPORTS TO)
- 42 GOVERNMENT
- PCF = PRIVATE CAPITAL FORMATION (GROSS)
- HH = HOUSEHOLDS
- TOTAL GROSS OUTPUT

26	27	28	29	30	31	32	33	34	35	36	37	38	39	40	41	42	PCF	HH	TOTAL
*	0.01	—	*	—	—	—	—	0.12	—	—	0.87	0.09	0.17	1.01	1.28	0.57	0.02	9.92	44.26
0.01	0.03	0.07	0.01	—	—	—	*	0.25	*	0.02	3.47	*	0.42	0.88	1.80	0.73	—	23.03	40.30
0.01	0.01	0.03	*	—	—	*	0.03	*	—	0.01	—	0.05	0.52	0.06	0.92	0.10	0.02	1.47	9.84
*	*	0.02	*	—	—	—	0.02	0.02	*	0.01	0.02	*	0.15	0.21	0.30	0.28	*	9.90	13.32
0.01	*	0.03	*	—	0.14	*	*	*	—	0.11	0.01	2.33	0.35	0.17	0.17	0.01	0.04	0.07	6.00
—	—	*	0.04	0.08	—	—	—	*	—	—	—	0.20	0.20	0.08	0.03	0.05	0.57	1.46	2.89
—	—	*	0.57	*	*	—	*	0.06	0.03	—	0.68	0.06	0.17	0.04	0.15	0.06	—	0.34	7.90
*	0.02	0.10	0.03	0.21	—	2.45	0.03	0.17	0.01	0.01	0.03	—	0.68	*	0.07	0.16	0.09	1.49	6.45
0.01	0.02	0.07	*	*	—	0.01	0.20	0.22	*	0.03	0.04	0.64	1.25	0.30	0.81	0.19	—	1.96	14.05
0.09	0.45	0.20	*	0.01	0.78	*	0.06	0.06	*	0.01	0.01	0.62	0.36	0.06	0.68	0.18	*	2.44	13.67
—	0.13	0.06	*	0.01	—	—	0.07	*	—	*	*	0.06	0.47	0.09	0.17	0.02	0.01	0.71	2.82
—	*	*	—	—	—	—	0.03	0.01	—	0.01	—	*	0.29	0.11	0.08	0.03	0.02	2.03	3.81
*	*	0.04	—	—	—	—	0.02	0.01	—	*	0.06	1.74	0.36	0.10	0.21	0.02	0.01	0.34	4.84
—	0.01	—	*	—	—	—	—	*	—	0.15	*	1.19	1.24	0.16	0.77	0.02	—	0.02	18.69
*	0.01	0.06	*	—	—	*	0.03	0.01	—	0.06	0.02	3.09	1.44	0.21	0.39	0.05	0.28	0.95	10.40
—	0.01	0.01	—	0.02	—	—	0.15	*	—	0.07	—	0.51	2.24	0.37	1.76	0.18	5.82	1.22	15.22
—	0.01	0.01	0.05	—	—	0.01	0.09	*	—	0.04	—	0.77	1.27	0.25	0.44	0.17	1.75	0.93	8.38
—	0.13	0.02	*	—	*	—	1.05	*	—	0.07	*	0.04	0.67	0.40	1.02	0.15	2.98	3.13	14.27
0.08	0.13	—	—	—	—	—	*	—	—	0.01	—	*	0.46	0.02	0.32	1.25	1.20	0.17	4.00
—	*	—	*	—	—	0.01	0.05	0.18	—	0.01	—	0.02	0.24	0.03	0.18	0.08	0.26	0.62	2.12
*	*	0.01	*	—	—	0.15	0.16	0.05	0.05	0.11	0.02	0.03	0.68	0.04	0.19	0.08	0.51	1.89	4.76
*	0.09	0.49	0.01	0.06	3.15	*	0.31	0.16	0.05	—	0.22	0.03	0.02	0.03	0.35	0.20	—	—	9.21
*	0.06	0.08	*	0.01	0.42	0.03	0.03	0.05	*	0.03	0.25	0.71	0.30	0.08	0.59	0.33	0.27	2.53	9.95
0.22	—	—	—	—	—	—	—	—	—	*	—	—	*	1.16	0.31	—	—	0.10	2.29
0.04	0.25	0.31	*	*	0.13	0.03	0.01	0.02	*	0.02	0.10	0.57	0.17	0.04	0.32	0.35	0.10	4.77	9.86
0.01	0.42	0.20	0.01	0.04	0.75	0.14	0.37	0.29	0.01	0.09	1.06	2.52	1.01	0.20	1.00	0.05	2.34	26.82	41.66
*	0.04	0.33	0.06	0.09	0.06	0.43	0.12	0.07	0.01	—	0.01	0.04	0.08	—	0.04	0.15	—	1.27	3.17
0.12	0.30	1.00	*	1.85	0.56	0.02	0.12	0.09	0.03	—	0.07	0.40	—	—	0.14	0.03	—	6.99	12.81
0.01	0.15	1.96	0.05	0.21	0.21	0.06	0.71	0.40	0.18	—	0.39	0.08	—	—	—	0.22	0.80	20.29	28.86
*	0.03	1.71	0.09	0.14	0.04	0.06	0.12	0.02	0.10	—	0.06	0.13	0.42	—	*	0.04	—	0.18	5.10
0.01	0.26	1.42	0.02	0.11	0.03	0.07	0.56	0.08	0.02	0.03	0.23	0.82	1.17	—	—	0.08	0.27	8.35	14.30
*	*	—	—	0.02	—	—	—	0.09	—	—	—	—	0.16	—	—	5.08	—	—	8.04
—	—	—	—	—	—	—	—	0.01	0.39	—	—	—	0.01	—	0.13	—	—	—	2.94
—	0.04	0.39	0.01	0.11	0.03	0.02	*	*	0.01	—	—	*	0.01	—	0.03	*	—	—	2.13
—	0.01	—	—	—	—	—	—	0.15	—	—	—	—	—	—	—	—	—	13.11	13.27
*	0.13	0.18	0.18	0.03	4.08	*	0.06	0.34	0.02	—	0.07	0.01	—	—	—	5.26	15.70	0.15	28.49
0.04	0.03	2.59	0.01	0.71	0.36	0.31	1.13	0.91	0.22	—	0.59	0.43	—	—	—	—	—	—	21.60
—	—	—	—	—	—	—	—	—	—	0.40	—	—	—	—	0.02	—	—	—	4.43
0.50	0.08	—	0.03	0.10	—	—	—	—	*	0.07	—	—	0.01	—	—	1.31	—	1.32	9.52
0.26	0.77	3.30	0.44	1.11	4.00	0.21	0.50	0.17	0.32	0.07	1.41	0.47	2.19	0.34	0.83	3.46	0.22	31.55	63.69
0.90	6.20	26.42	2.15	7.93	14.06	1.08	8.20	9.41	1.50	—	4.20	10.73	2.27	—	0.85	30.06	—	2.12	223.58
2.29	9.86	41.66	3.17	12.81	28.86	5.10	14.30	13.39	2.94	2.13	13.27	28.49	21.60	5.28	17.21	51.29	33.29	194.12	

SOURCE: Wassily W. Leontief, "Input-Output Economics," *Scientific American,* vol. 185 (October, 1951): 16–17.

ship exists, particularly in the short run, between the amount of inputs absorbed by an industry and its level of output. Input-output analysis rests on the central concept that an industry's production function (the relationship between the volume of output and the size of inputs) is relatively stable. Since all industries do not undergo rapid technological change and a complete re-equipping of plants in any short period of a few years, it may be assumed that for many industries the input-output structure (and the production function) is relatively stable for a given future period.

To attain a given level of output, each industry (e.g., motor vehicles, footwear) requires a certain quantity of inputs or purchases from other industries or economic sectors. An industry's inputs and purchase requirements can be expressed as "input ratios." Though the input requirements (the input absorption from various economic sectors) would tend to be relatively constant for a large number of industries (canned foods, beverages, dairy products, paints), the input ratios for some industries may change appreciably over time. A realistic estimate of the input needs from input ratios for a given future output of motor vehicles must, for instance, take into account changes in product-mix, changes in product design and material specifications and substitutions (e.g., aluminum for steel, synthetic leather for other materials), the trend in the capital-output ratio, and the trend in labor productivity. The input estimates for some industries (electrical goods) would have to take into account the introduction of new products and the extent to which these may displace old products. Estimates also take into account the amount of excess productive capacity that may exist as well as the extent to which technological advances in products and processes will induce obsolescence in facilities and capital replacement. Estimates of input ratios also must be based on whatever innovations and structural changes may occur in industry, for instance, the adoption of annual product re-styling or greater plant dispersal in the industry. If relatively accurate estimates or adjustments in input ratios can be made for changes in products, technology, and the like, input ratios may be realistically projected for a period of several years. Adjusted input-output data may, therefore, provide relatively accurate cost ratios which show dollars of given inputs per dollar of given output for an industry. Thus, for a given or assumed level of "final bill of goods" to be produced in a future year, a relatively accurate input-output table or structure among industries may then be projected. An industry's input-output pattern together with the regional distribution of resources in an economy underlies an industry's location pattern.

LOCATION PATTERN

The kind of products an industry puts out and its volume of output generally determine its production technology and the kind of labor and materials required; this in turn more or less determines its location pattern. In many cases a number of specific factors also influence an industry's location pattern. Cost factors as well as historical accidents play a part.

The ideal location of a business establishment is one that attains the lowest combined cost of procuring materials and labor and producing and shipping the most profitable volume to the market. Businessmen do not always select an economically rational location. They may have selected the location for the personal convenience of the company officers, or they may have selected the location on the basis of an inadequate cost-and-profit computation. The location may be unsuitable in terms of long-term costs and profitability. Earnings may not have been estimated for the proper time horizon. The location, for instance, may have become obsolete because of the early depletion of raw-material resources or shifts in the market for the products.

Because industries differ with respect to production technology and input factors, the unit-cost method for selecting location is the most logical since it takes into account and weighs all factors and cost elements of conducting business. In selecting locations for its establishments, management must investigate and weigh the relative advantages of possible locations on the basis of the cost of procuring labor, materials, and utilities and of the cost of producing and distributing the goods to customers. Thus, selection of location must take into account the present and future size of market; the present and future cost of input factors, transportation, taxes, and legal restrictions; and the proximity to service and allied industries. The primary objective is to align the location and size of plants and distribution outlets in that combination which attains the most profitable sales volume, economical plant size, and efficient production.

In some industries the source of raw materials is the most important location factor; in others, the market; and in still others, labor or one or more other factors are important. Industries can be identified as labor-oriented, material-oriented, or market-oriented when one of these factors is a primary location consideration. In labor-oriented industries the locational pull may stem from a geographical concentration of skilled and efficient labor or from the fact that labor is plentiful and cheap. Because labor costs make up a sizable proportion of the unit cost of the product, the textile industry tends to be labor-oriented. The cotton-textile industry migrated southward mainly because labor in the South is cheaper and more tractable.

Proximity to the source of raw materials and fuel or the availability of an economical means of transportation is a key location consideration for industries using materials of such bulk or of such perishability that they are expensive to transport. Because the conversion of the materials to the finished product results in a substantial weight loss which reduces the cost of transportation, paper mills locate in timber-growing areas, and sugar refineries and fruit canneries locate in areas that grow their respective crops. Location at a cheap source of power is important to industries that employ electroprocessing and electrochemical reactions as in the output of aluminum and ferroalloys.

Proximity to market is emphasized by industries in which the transporting of the final product is more costly than the transporting of the raw material. Ordinarily, it costs more to ship glass products to the consumer than it does to ship silicon sand in bulk to the factory. Sand is subject to lower freight rates than glass products. Market-oriented location is also characteristic of industries that cater to a large central market which sets the pattern for style changes (as in the case of producers of women's apparel) and of industries that provide technical advice and servicing (as in the case of tool and die shops).

Where the market and the source of materials are both significant location considerations, production plants may locate at both ends —at raw materials and at the market. For example, oil refineries are found at the oil fields and at large urban markets. Unless there are special considerations, industries do not ordinarily locate at some mid-point between raw materials and the market. To do so would involve a costly break in carriage between the market and the materials. Moreover, the producers may not have an adequate contact with the market nor would they be able to integrate their plant operations with the output of materials at the source.

Some industries are widely dispersed while others are geographically concentrated in certain areas. Extractive industries are, of course, scattered to the extent that mining and agricultural resources are geographically dispersed. Many service industries tend to be scattered in comparatively small plants because of the need for personal contact in selling, for example, job-printing and laundries.

It is sometimes economical to concentrate manufacture geographically in a few large plants, whereas in other cases it is economical to disperse production in a large number of smaller plants.

Where, because of bulk, weight, or perishability, widely consumed products are costly to ship and the products are manufactured from materials widely available, the geographical concentration of production is likely to be low. Bakeries, breweries, brickyards, and cement plants are widely dispersed. In the case of labor-oriented industries, as skilled and other grades of labor become more and more mobile and spread through the country, some formerly concentrated industries tended to migrate to other areas. Thus, the degree of dispersal (or degree of concentration) in many manufacturing industries tends to be determined by the equilibrium between opposing forces: the extra cost of transportation balanced against the economies of large-scale production. When the material or the product is costly to ship, manufacture will tend to be rooted near the scattered material or markets. When the economies of scale are appreciable and the cost of transportation is low relative to the value of the product, plant production tends to be concentrated.

Thus, the establishment of a few large plants designed to produce for national and international markets is advantageous when the economies of scale are appreciable and the shipping cost is a relatively small part of the over-all cost of production and distribution, as is the case with watches, instruments, and drugs. When production is concentrated at some distance from raw materials and markets, the industry must create sufficient value-added in production from the use of skilled or other labor and from plant facilities, and it must obtain sufficient economies from large-scale operations to offset some of the double transportation cost of shipping materials from the source and shipping the products to broad markets.

Plants, particularly of the metal-using industries, find it profitable to locate in industrial centers. Industries tend to locate in relation to industries to which they are linked with respect to supply of materials and components, capital facilities and tooling, and a pool of labor. The growth of specialized industrial centers is sometimes due to historical circumstance but more often stems from the external economies accruing to plants producing in the area. The gradual development of cheap and fast long-distance transportation by waterways, railways, and trucks has been influential in the trend toward geographical concentration of many manufacturing industries. Concentrated production in specialized industrial centers develops a pool of skilled labor. The attracting of immigrant labor, for example, furthered the growth of the clothing industry in New York City and the shoe industry in New England. Moreover, the development of specialized auxiliary, service, and marketing enterprises in a given area furthers the development of cumulative specialization along certain lines of business. The geographical specialization of an area tends to generate advantages which attract additional industries to the area.

The concentration of certain types of plants and establishments in an industrial center gives rise to external economies. In the case of large establishments, external economies augment internal economies. The gradual development of a pool of skilled labor and technicians is a continuing asset. Industrial centers attain a high degree of division of labor among plants and service enterprises of interdependent producers. The specialized plants of firms attain varying degrees of local integration with the establishments of other firms. Medium- and small-sized establishments as specialized producers linked to related industries also enjoy the benefits of external economies. Functioning as suppliers and subcontractors, such establishments operate at low cost because they enjoy a sufficient volume of business to enable the fuller utilization of their specialized capacity.

Moreover, industrial firms located in specialized areas benefit from the ready availability of service from construction and repair firms, tool and die shops, foundries, and other technical and expert-service establishments. Firms are able to benefit from small inventories and hand-to-mouth purchasing, since they can procure materials and supplies on short notice. Low costs are obtained through the use of common transport terminals and warehouses and economical services from power and other public utilities. By enabling purchasers to "shop around" on the spot, specialized industrial centers also make for efficient distribution.

The location of industry and the specializations of industrial centers, of course, change over time because of secular developments. Plants migrate and industries change their location patterns because of regional shifts in markets, depletion of resources or the discovery of resources in new areas, development of new or substitute materials and fuels, development of new processes that call for new input factors, development of low-cost transportation (pipelines, specialized tankers, and air transport), and shifts in the labor force and in the supply of required occupational skills.

THE LABOR FORCE AND THE OCCUPATION STRUCTURE

The labor force as a productive factor is more important in some industries than in others. Both internal and external factors determine the importance and the character of an industry's work force and the behavior of wages. The *internal factors* that affect the role of an industry's work force and the complexity of the occupation structure include the proportion of labor cost in the total cost of production, the nature of the production process, and the extent of technological change in the industry. The role of the work force is greater when labor costs make up a high proportion of the unit cost of the product. For instance, because of the comparatively long processing interval, intricacy of operations, and diversity of skills employed, industries producing finished capital goods require more labor input and create greater value-added in the product than most industries turning out consumer non-durable goods. The availability of qualified labor is obviously more crucial to labor-intensive industries, especially when plants are located in outlying regions away from large labor markets. Expanding industries and those undergoing rapid technological progress usually experience considerable change in their occupation structure and have an acute recruitment problem during periods of business expansion, particularly when plants are located in smaller labor markets.

The character of the labor market and the degree of industrial concentration, unionization, and production stability are among the *external influences* that affect an industry's work force and wage structure. Industries subject to shifts in market demand for products or to strong seasonal and cyclical fluctuations in output must deal with the problem of labor turnover, layoffs and rehiring, and the maintenance of a core of skilled workers. Highly concentrated industries often have a strong position in the recruitment of labor, considerable influence on the labor market, and some discretion in wage payment, particularly if the industry is not unionized. Highly unionized industries must, of course, bargain and negotiate with organized labor on matters dealing with the design of the wage structure, compensation, conditions of employment, and the supply of labor.

Occupation Structure of an Industry

An industry employs various types of factory, clerical, and professional labor that make up the occupational structure of its work force. The composition of an industry's occupation structure is determined by the nature of its processes and diversity of operations, the size of the industry, and the degree of mass-production technology employed. An occupation structure may consist of a comparatively wide range of job grades and skills, as in the case of metalworking industries, or it may consist of a narrow range of occupations as in the case of the bread-baking and the liquor industries. The occupational structure may be comparatively stable, as in the shoe and textile industries, or it may undergo change stemming from technological developments in processes that call for new skills.

An industry's occupational structure typically consists of an *ascending hierarchy of job grades*. Most industries, notably those in unionized fields and governmental agencies, have developed "formal" occupation structures. Experts employing job-evaluation techniques have rated and ranked the occupations of various industries to arrive at comparatively consistent occupational differentials from the lowest to the highest job grade. The gradation of occupations reflects job differentials based on a composite of factors that usually include the degree of skill, effort, responsibility, and favorability of working conditions. Such formal occupational structures facilitate the determination of occupational wage differentials considered by management and labor to be a rational and sound basis for establishing a scale of wage rates for various job grades in the occupational structure.

Jobs are ordinarily grouped into unskilled, semiskilled, skilled, clerical, and technical and professional categories, each of which makes up a separate occupational labor market. Mass-production industries employ a relatively high percentage of semiskilled workers who perform various specialized, routine tasks that are usually learned on the job and mastered in a relatively short time. Skilled labor is made up of such craftsmen as machinists, toolmakers, welders, and electricians. The proportion of skilled workers tends to be higher in durable-goods than in non-durable-goods industries. Technical workers include various types of engineers, designers, laboratory aides, statisticians, and the like; professional workers include purchasing agents, public-relations men, and various managerial personnel.

Some occupations are specialized to certain industries, that is, a portion of the labor force is occupationally tied to a particular industry. Skilled and technical occupations often tend to be specialized to certain industries, though many types of skilled and technical workers are common to a number of industries. Labor specialized to particular industries is obviously less mobile with respect to employment among industries than labor that is not so specialized. Many of the unskilled, clerical, professional, and managerial personnel are not specialized to particular industries. Since these categories are common to many industries, they can enjoy considerable industrial mobility, especially when located in large urban or industrial areas.

Continued technological progress in industry has created a demand for a greater number of engineers and craftsmen—men to design and develop new products and processes and men to control and maintain the new equipment. Thus the ratio of engineers, scientists, and technicians has been on the increase. The ratio is higher in industries employing diverse processes and emphasizing research and development (e.g., petroleum, electrical-equipment,

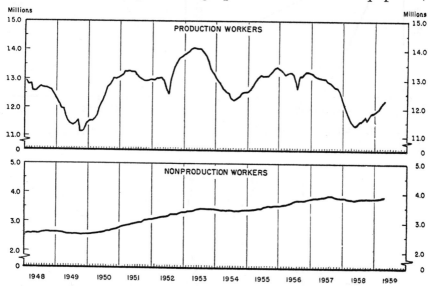

Fig. 3–1. Numbers of production and non-production workers in American manufacturing, seasonally adjusted, January, 1948, to April, 1959. (U.S. Department of Labor, Bureau of Labor Statistics.)

and chemical industries). The occupational trend has also been in the direction of a higher proportion of salaried personnel (Fig. 3–1). Because of the greater marketing and clerical activities involved, the proportion of salaried workers is somewhat higher in late-stage manufacturing, particularly in the consumer-goods industries, than in other industries.

Demand for Labor

An industry's demand for labor depends on the production volume required to meet the market demand for goods or services. Hence, the demand for labor derives from consumer demand for goods.

The demand for, and the supply of, each grade of labor influences the rate of wages prevailing in the labor market (Fig. 3–2). When there is a surplus of a given grade of labor relative to job openings, wages tend to fall. When there is a scarcity of labor relative to job

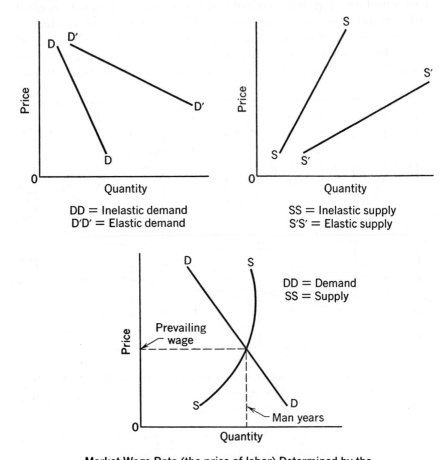

DD = Inelastic demand
D′D′ = Elastic demand

SS = Inelastic supply
S′S′ = Elastic supply

DD = Demand
SS = Supply

Market Wage Rate (the price of labor) Determined by the Equilibrium of Supply and Demand

Fig. 3–2. Demand and supply curves *(top)*. The market price of labor as determined by supply and demand *(bottom)*.

openings, wages tend to rise. A number of imperfections (both on the demand and supply side) in the labor market, however, limit the automatic operation of the law of supply and demand in determining wage rates. To the extent that there is competition, wage rates in a given labor market tend to move toward that level at which the quantity of workers seeking jobs equals the demand for workers.

The amount of labor of each type that an industry employs depends on the level of wages it must pay for the grade of labor. If wages are comparatively high, an industry ordinarily employs less labor; if wages are low, an industry finds it profitable to employ more labor. Hence, the amount of labor that producers employ varies inversely with the rate of wages, that is, the typical demand curve for labor slopes downward and to the right. For each level of output, an industry employs that quantity of various types of labor that is required to fill the various positions in its production process and organization. Producers strive for that complement of various classes of labor needed to maintain the desired balance in its production processes and operations.

According to the marginal-productivity theory of wages, producers hire labor of various grades up to that point at which the marginal product obtained from the last unit of each type of labor is equal to the wage paid. Hiring workers beyond this point would be unprofitable. But the marginal product of labor depends not alone on the skill and effort of labor; it also depends on the effectiveness of plant organization, production techniques employed, and the price of the product. Moreover, the marginal cost of labor may be lower than its contribution if productivity gains increase the contribution of labor while wages remain unchanged or rise more slowly. Producers typically do not compute cost and revenue data in such form as to be able to determine the precise point at which the last unit of a particular class of labor hired just pays for itself. It is obvious, of course, that producers will strive to avoid overstaffing their organization with unproductive labor, and there is no doubt that they will comb their organization and lay off superfluous personnel when profits begin to drop off sharply. The marginal-productivity theory of wages lacks some practical realism in that it implies that wages are set in a market of free competition between the buyers and sellers of labor services, that labor is informed on wage rates and is highly mobile, and that the economy continually operates at a high level with work for all job-seekers.

Changes in an industry's demand for labor come from cyclical and seasonal changes in the demand for an industry's product, shifts in consumer tastes for products, and secular rise in national income. During periods of peak-business volume, when there is a scarcity of certain skilled and professional labor, producers at times hoard scarce grades of labor and engineers in anticipation of further shortages in labor. During periods of business decline and layoffs, producers are ordinarily obliged (because of seniority rights) to reassign some workers to different jobs. Difficulty in filling positions with qualified workers sometimes makes for some redundancy of labor in certain operating departments. Changes in the demand for labor by a given industry also come from changes in the length of the workweek, changes in the rate of labor turnover and absenteeism (which determine the number of "extra" workers needed to man the production process properly), changes in the method of wage payment (time payment or incentive payment), and changes in the rate of productivity gain in the industry.

The *elasticity of demand for labor* differs among industries. The elasticity of demand for labor generally reflects the elasticity of demand for the industry's products. If the consumer demand for the product is elastic, the industry's demand will also be elastic. The demand for labor, however, tends to be less elastic if the labor cost comprises a small proportion of the unit cost of the product. Since monopolistic producers tend to restrict output in order to hold up prices, the demand for labor by a monopolistic industry would ordinarily be less elastic than the demand for labor by a highly competitive industry.

Because of the comparative fixity of production technology, the short-run demand for labor tends to be less elastic than the long-run demand. An increase in the wage rates of millwrights or inspectors, for instance, will not appreciably lower the number employed, and certainly not by as large a percentage as the increase in the hourly rates. Because of the opportunities for changes in production technology and increased mechanization that occur over time, the long-run demand for labor tends to be more elastic than the short-run demand.

The long-run elasticity of demand for labor also depends on changes in the prices of other productive factors. If an industry can employ alternative processes that take different proportions of labor input relative to other factors, the flexibility in production technology makes for greater long-run elasticity of demand for labor. The slope of the long-run demand curve for labor thus reflects the substitutability of capital for labor. At high-wage rates an industry is induced to adopt laborsaving devices in order to cut down the input of labor. This change in the proportion of labor input per unit of output takes place through the adoption of new processes that occur when plant facilities are replaced or when new plants are built to expand capacity.

Supply of Labor

The availability of labor for a given industry depends on the industry's location pattern and a number of underlying factors in the market that determine the conditions and behavior of the supply of labor. Instead of a single homogeneous labor market, there are, of course, many regional and local labor markets in the economy. Local labor markets exist because of the relative immobility of labor between areas. The regional immobility of labor largely accounts for geographical wage differentials and is due to the cost of moving, home-ownership, personal ties to a particular community, and ignorance of job opportunities in other areas. Geographical, as well as industrial, immobility of labor is also due to the prevalence of pensions, insurance, and seniority provisions in labor-management contracts.

A given labor-market area is made up of a number of occupational groups. To the extent that there is occupational immobility, each comparatively homogeneous occupational group makes up a separate labor market. The geographical area within which individual workers are willing to take employment makes up their "normal employment preference area." The limits of a labor market generally extend beyond the built-up area of a city or town, and the limits tend to differ for each occupational group. With the increase in the use of automobiles and the expansion of superhighways, labor markets have generally expanded. In addition to the choice of jobs in the preferred area of employment, workers also, of course, have preferences with respect to particular industries, employers, pay levels, and steadiness of work. Workers will, for instance, extend the boundaries of their employment area and will commute over greater distances for jobs that pay well or offer opportunities for advancement.

An industry's location pattern tends to determine its labor recruitment problem. Industries that are adaptable with respect to location can advantageously select plant and business sites near large or desirable labor markets. Geographically concentrated industries can generally attract workers and develop a pool of specialized labor. Allied industries (those based on a similar production technology) located in the same region tend to develop and draw on a common pool of skilled and technical labor. When large establishments locate in smaller communities, they generally find it necessary to attract a labor force through housing projects, training programs, favorable wage levels, good working conditions, and the like. Large producers, moreover, often undertake state-wide and national recruitment for technical and managerial personnel, particularly when the labor market is tight.

The quantity of labor services offered by a particular occupational group tends to vary directly with wage rates. The labor-supply curve slopes upward and to the right—at higher-wage rates more labor services are offered. Usually it is only after a lapse of time that workers respond to a change in wage rates and that industry adapts its combination of productive factors to changes in the market price of labor. At higher wages people are ordinarily willing to work longer hours. But if wages rise above a certain level so that their income far exceeds the level to which they have been accustomed, some workers are less inclined to work longer hours or to work regularly; some people prefer increased leisure to added income. Their withdrawal of labor services often takes the form of absenteeism.

The *short-run supply of labor* for an industry depends on a number of factors. An industry can to some extent increase the availability of labor by lengthening the workweek and can hire the unemployed workers. Since most workers are actively employed, the available supply of labor is obviously smaller than the total labor force. An industry can attract workers from other industries if it offers higher wages or such other inducements as overtime or steady work. During recession times many workers will take jobs at lower pay because of the worsening of employment opportunities. When industries in the fields of capital goods, consumer durable goods, and construction, for instance, lay off labor, these workers are available to industries less susceptible to cyclical fluctuations and to industries in their rapid-growth stage. The latter industries, having their pick of skilled and technical labor, can accelerate their productivity gains and improve their competitive position relative to other industries.

An industry's labor supply also consists of new entrants into the labor market, workers who move into an area from other regions, and people who are not ordinarily in the labor market except when job opportunities are very good. When the labor market is tight and wages attractive, an increasing number of women, older people, and adolescents join the labor force. An industry's labor supply also depends on the effectiveness of its recruiting practice, the effectiveness of public-employment exchanges in notifying people of job opportunities and in placing people, and the extent to which unions control the availability of certain grades of labor. The long-run supply of labor, especially the supply of a given type of labor, is obviously more elastic than the short-run supply.

The *long-run supply of labor* depends on a number of factors that underlie the labor market. Though the availability of labor for a given industry depends on the ease with which it can locate near a suitable labor market, the long-run supply in a given market area stems from the growth in population, the movement of people into the area, and the trend in the length of the workweek and number of days worked per year.

Changes in the supply of various grades of labor occur through retraining for new occupations, retirement of old workers, and the occupational selections of the new entrants into the labor force. A gradual improvement in the quality and productiveness of the labor force occurs through the normal turnover in the labor force: as older workers retire, they are ordinarily replaced by better-trained, more productive younger workers.

In general, the more limited the supply of a given grade of labor, the higher will be the wage paid for the grade as compared to other grades of labor. Occupational- and industrial-wage differentials provide the primary incentive for workers to shift from low-wage jobs; pay differentials thus serve as a primary manpower-allocative mechanism. People tend to select or shift into those occupations that appear to offer greater income, opportunity for advancement, steady employment, desirable working conditions, and prestige.

People qualify for various occupations on the basis of their native abilities and the amount of training they have had. The supply of skilled, technical, and professional labor thus depends on the distribution of native abilities among people, the motivation for training and preparation, and the availability and cost of training or education. The higher the abilities required and the more expensive and lengthy the training, the smaller the increase in the supply of the given grade of labor. When the "cost of entry" is high for a given occupation, the rate of pay and other advantages must be large enough to justify the cost as compared with other occupations.

Thus, the extent to which an industry can increase its supply of skilled and professional labor depends on the special aptitudes required, the cost of training, the location of its establishments, compensation offered, the social status of the occupation and industry, and the comparative attractiveness of alternative occupations. Most large producers ordinarily secure a flow of trained labor from apprentice training programs and technical institutions. Though some pick up their trade while working or gain the required qualification along the line of normal occupational progression, many workers qualify for skilled jobs primarily through technical schools and apprentice training. Large producers often offer a wide training program on company time and on the employees' own time. Producers usually anticipate the scarcity of a given type of labor and provide for its supply through their own training programs.

Industries that enjoy the advantages of a young, vigorous work force are typically the newer, rapidly growing industries. Growing industries ordinarily hire many of the new entrants into the labor force. Such industries usually secure a high-quality work force with many key and technical positions staffed by well-trained, high-caliber personnel. Young people are attracted to expanding industries because of the opportunities for advancement.

An industry's supply of, and demand for, labor also depend on its rate of gain in productivity. An average annual increase of 3 per cent in output per man-hour means that the industry can produce the same volume of output with a 3 per cent smaller work force. How effectively an industry employs and conserves labor also determines its supply of available labor services. An industry conserves its labor by stabilizing production and by providing steadier employment. Seasonal layoffs may be minimized by producing for stock, by introducing supplementary products for output during the dull season, and by scheduling plant-maintenance work and vacations for the slack season. Labor may be conserved by training and placing workers in positions that fit their skills and aptitudes, by reducing production delays, excessive absenteeism, labor turnover, and accidents, and by avoiding premature retirement of older workers. Some industries, however, follow the wasteful practice of hiring no one over forty-five years of age and retiring workers in their mid-sixties. Some producers feel that older workers are less adaptable to changes in work patterns and that the financing of pensions and medical insurance would be higher if older workers are hired.

Occupational-Wage Differentials

Occupational-wage differentials reflect differences in the degrees of skill, effort, and attractiveness of jobs, in the relative scarcity of various types of labor, and in the extent of labor-market imperfections and monopolistic controls that may exist (Fig. 3–3).

Occupational-wage differentials arise, in part, out of the fact that occupations call for different types and degrees of skill. The more exacting an occupation with respect to skill and training and the smaller the supply of qualified workers, the higher the wage tends to be. The relative scarcity of various grades of labor thus stems from the restrictions on entry into various occupations. The restric-

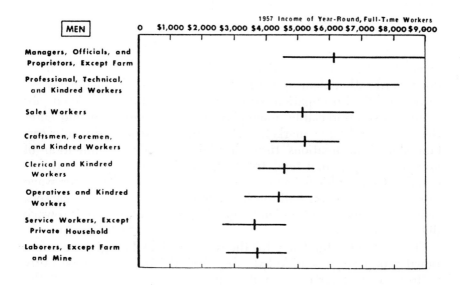

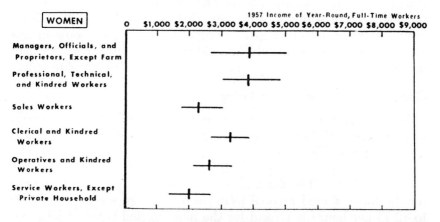

Note: The mark on each bar indicates the median (average) income of the workers in the given occupational group: Half made more and half less than this amount.
The length of the bar shows the income range of the middle half of the workers in the occupational group. One-fourth earned less than the amount indicated by the left end of the bar, and one-fourth earned more than the amount indicated by the right end.

Fig. 3–3. Wage or salary for middle half of workers in major occupational groups. (U.S. Department of Labor, Bureau of Labor Statistics, *Occupational Outlook Handbook*, 1959 ed. Washington, D.C.: Government Printing Office, 1959, p. 29.)

tions are due to the unequal distribution of native ability, unequal opportunity for training, and social prejudice in job opportunities.

Occupational and geographical immobility also restricts the supply of labor and thereby accentuates wage differentials. To the extent that there is occupational mobility, such mobility tends to be downward rather than upward. For example, if job openings were fewer in skilled occupations or if the wage level of semiskilled jobs were to rise appreciably, unemployed skilled workers would enter the semiskilled labor market. When unions restrict entry into certain skilled occupations through such methods as limitation of apprenticeships, they tend to maintain occupational wage differentials. Geographical immobility forestalls the tendency for wage rates to move toward uniform levels among regional labor markets, though, to some extent, union bargaining reduces geographical wage differentials.

There is some tendency for the wages of jobs in a given occupational group (e.g., semiskilled jobs, clerical jobs) to become fairly uniform, except for compensating differences. In order to fill the less attractive jobs, industry finds it necessary to compensate workers for unattractive features or aspects, that is, "to equalize the differences" between jobs in a given occupational group. People in less attractive occupations would be paid somewhat higher wages than people in the more attractive occupations, other things being equal.

Compensation Plans in Industry

The commonest method of compensation in industry is time payment whereby the basic wage is computed on a time basis, such as a wage rate per hour or day, or a salary per week or month. The time-payment plan is applied either on a flat-rate basis or on the rate-range basis. The flat-rate wage (e.g., $1.50 per hour) prevails for the lower-skilled manual jobs; the rate-range wage (e.g., $2.00 to $2.25 per hour) is typical for the more skilled types of jobs and for most salaried jobs. In addition to this base pay, industries typically offer a variety of supplementary payments (overtime rates, vacation pay, shift differentials).

Such industries as the garment, shoe, cigar, and rubber-tire industries satisfactorily use the incentive wage or a piece-rate plan to compensate production workers largely because the processing conditions in these industries are suitable to the use of incentive payment.[4] Incentive plans for individual output or for group output

[4] In addition to compensating employees on the basis of measured output, incentive plans are used to reward foremen on the basis of material savings and labor savings and to compensate salesmen on the basis of sales volume, for example.

may be computed on a straight piece-rate basis or on the basis of a guaranteed hourly rate plus a bonus that varies with extra output above a certain level (the standard task). The incentive-payment plan is suited to those industries in which the worker's production is measurable in terms of units of output and standard tasks can be established, in which there is a sufficiently direct relationship between the worker's effort and output, in which the quality of the product does not decline because of the incentive stimulus, and in which interruptions to the flow of work are not excessive. Workers accomplish more when they are given definite production goals and are paid according to the quantity of output. Job for job, incentive compensation generally provides higher earnings than time-rate compensation.

Industries find that time payment is satisfactory (and incentive payment not very practical) when the rate of output is mechanically paced by the process or by an automatic handling system, when quality may be sacrificed under the spur of a wage incentive, and when work is not sufficiently standardized and the production process is subject to excessive unavoidable interruptions.

Industry Wage Differentials

The average wage level is higher in some industries than in others. An industry's level of average wages depends on the types of labor employed, location, unionism, proportion of labor costs in total costs, and degree of monopoly in the industry (Fig. 3–4).

Industries characterized by high average wages would tend to be those that have a high proportion of skilled and technical jobs in their occupation structure, are located in high-wage regions, bargain with strong labor unions, have a small proportion of labor costs in the total cost of production (wage increases would not bulk large in increased cost of production), are profitable growth industries actively recruiting and bidding for labor, are able to maintain steady gains in productivity, or have sufficient monopolistic control over the product marketed to be able to pass on wage increases to consumers in the form of higher prices.

Industries characterized by low average wages would tend to be those that have a high proportion of low-skilled jobs and a high proportion of women or immigrant labor in the work force, are located in low-wage regions, offer steady employment and considerable overtime work, are in their mature or declining stage of development, or are in a non-unionized field of production. As in the case of labor cost per unit of output, an industry's material

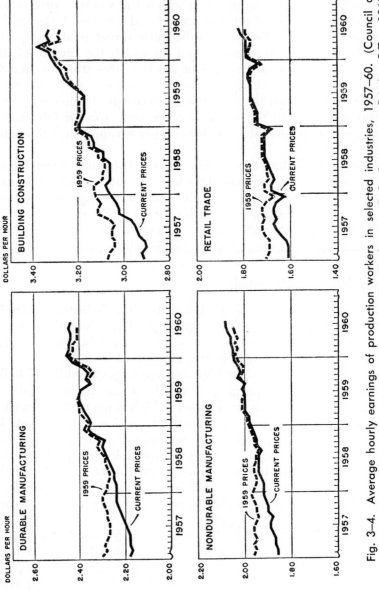

Fig. 3–4. Average hourly earnings of production workers in selected industries, 1957–60. (Council of Economic Advisers, *Economic Indicators, August 1960.* Washington, D.C.: Government Printing Office, 1960, p. 14.)

cost per unit depends on the type of product put out, supply conditions, and on other factors analyzed in the pages following.

MATERIALS AND INVENTORY BEHAVIOR

Raw materials are specified materials, components, and supplies an industry purchases for further processing into finished goods.[5] The trend of material costs and the adequacy of supply can appreciably influence the growth and development of an industry. An industry's material problem and the importance of its inventories are indicated by the proportion of material cost in the unit cost of the product, the magnitude of investment in inventories relative to sales volume (the inventory-sales ratio), the diversity of items making up the materials input, and the extent of price fluctuations in materials. The role of materials in industrial operations can be outlined through an analysis of the factors underlying the demand for, and supply of, materials.

Demand for Materials and Inventory Behavior

An industry buys raw materials and components for their inherent properties. The kinds of materials an industry absorbs are determined by the types of products it makes. The product design and material specifications determine the kind and quantity and influence the cost of materials per unit of output. The degree of standardization in materials and the extent to which product simplification is attained by the industry also influence the material cost per unit of output. Total material cost will vary directly with the purchase price, with changes in the amount of material required per unit, and with the volume of output.

The demand for materials is essentially a derived demand; it stems from the market demand for the industry's finished goods. An industry's long-term material requirements depend largely on the growth trend of the industry. (See Table 4–1.) In order to ascertain the role of materials in an industry and the economic behavior of inventories, we must look to the long- and short-run factors underlying the demand for materials and the stability of inventory levels.

LONG-RUN DEMAND FOR MATERIALS. An industry's long-run demand for materials depends on the growth of market demand for the

[5] Raw materials are the materials an industry absorbs for further processing and transformation; the term "raw materials" is not used to indicate the degree of processing that materials have undergone.

finished goods, new products introduced by the industry, reduction in selling prices, and the trend of material-input prices. When materials are cheaper to buy, they are substituted for other input factors. The long-run demand for materials and the level of material inventory are also influenced by the availability of substitute materials, the kind of production technology employed, and the degree of vertical integration in the industry. These and other factors underlying the demand for materials are discussed in the pages below.

The projection of estimated demands for certain key materials are discussed in the following quotation from Fisher and Boorstein, and presented in Table 3–2.

More recent tentative estimates of demand for selected raw materials in 1980 and 2000 are indicated in the following table. Low, medium, and high estimates are derived from a variety of assumptions regarding over-all trends in the economy (population, households, labor force and employment, technology and productivity, investment and consumption, Government expenditures, etc.), as well as more specific assumptions about trends in those end product and service categories making large use of resources (construction, heat and power, food, clothing and apparel, hard goods, transportation, etc.).

TABLE 3–2

Estimated Demand for Selected Key Materials, 1980 and 2000 [1]

		1980			2000		
	Current	Low	Medium	High	Low	Medium	High
Timber (billion board feet)	34.6 (1957)	44	66	103	49	100	215
Wheat (million bushels)	934 (1958)	930	1,120	1,310	1,110	1,480	1,880
Feed grains [2] (billion feed grain units) ..	245 (1956)	267	310	410	310	410	660
Cotton (million bales)	13.0 (1959)	11.9	16.7	23.2	12.7	23.2	44.9
Oil (billion barrels)..	2.97 (1957)	4.65	5.94	7.43	6.92	11.13	17.90
Coal (million tons)..	385 (1958)	497	756	1,071	383	978	1,921
Iron ore (do)	140 (1957)	132	197	330	125	270	690
Aluminum (do)	1.9 (1958)	4.1	10.6	23.9	6.7	24.3	77.0
Copper (do)	1.56 (1958)	2.1	4.1	7.6	2.9	8.9	23.9
Fresh water withdrawals (trillion gallons per year) ..	71.8 (1954)	120.5	125.7	149.0	162	178.8	263.6

[1] Estimated export demand is included for wheat, feed grains, and cotton. Export demand for the other items is insignificant, except for coal for which exports in recent years have been around 10 per cent of total production.

[2] Includes corn, oats, barley, and grain sorghum. 1 feed grain unit has feed value of 1 pound of corn.

SOURCE: See footnote 6.

On the basis of the over-all projections for the growth of the economy and population cited above, the total demand for oil in the United States has been projected to rise from about 3.4 billion barrels in 1960 to 4.7–7.4 billion barrels in 1980 to 6.9–17.9 billion barrels in 2000. The medium, or most probable projection, is for a demand of about 5.9 billion barrels by 1980 and 11.1 by 2000. Aggregate demand during the whole 40-year period between 1960 and 2000 would be about 193 billion barrels on the low projection, 258 billion on the medium projection, and 348 billion on the high projection.

These projections are of course subject to considerable uncertainties and what actually occurs may deviate even from the broad range covered by the projections. A major change, for example, in the method of powering automobiles, trucks, and locomotives could reduce the demand even below the lower limits indicated by the projections.

Despite the uncertainties, however, the projections do give a reasonable indication of the range within which the demand for oil is likely to fall.[6]

When close substitute materials are available, the industry's demand for a given material will tend to be somewhat elastic. Producers will select the best-suited material on the basis of comparative cost. The cost comparison takes into account the relative cost of processing the product as well as the material cost per unit of output.

The frequency of product restyling and model changeovers influences material specifications as well as inventory levels. Before model changeovers can be economically made, raw materials, semifabricated items, and components that are unsuited to the new models must be used up in production or disposed of in a manner that avoids serious loss. Poor inventory-control practices can lead to considerable obsolescence in materials. An industry's inventory level and demand for materials depend on the effectiveness in forecasting material prices and estimating the market demand for finished goods and on the effectiveness of the inventory-control systems employed in the industry.

Both internal and external factors determine the over-all level of inventory (raw-material stocks, goods in process, and finished goods) and the inventory-sales ratio. In short, the amount required for raw-material stocks is determined by the procurement lead-time, carrying charges, and the need to maintain the rate of output; the amount necessary for goods in process is determined by the production interval and the rate of output; and the amount needed for finished stock depends on the quantity required to meet satisfactorily the delivery needs of sales. The inventory-sales ratio in

[6] J. L. Fisher and E. Boorstein, *The Adequacy of Resources for Economic Growth in the United States*, Study Paper No. 13, prepared for Joint Economic Committee, Congress of the United States (Washington, D.C.: Government Printing Office, 1959), pp. 48, 55.

many industries has, in fact, gradually declined because of improvements in transportation, greater vertical integration, adoption of improved inventory-control systems, and greater use of the hand-to-mouth buying practices.

An industry requires a certain stock of raw materials so that production can be planned and scheduled in advance of the actual output of goods. The raw-material stock must be of sufficient size to feed the production process without interruption and to permit continuity of production, even though the output rate is increased or delays occur in material deliveries because of transportation interruptions and work stoppages. Too large a stock, however, is costly to hold and involves a sacrifice of liquidity. Many industries hold a stock adequate for a reasonable number of weeks of production. Producers generally aim to adjust stock levels to anticipated changes in the product-mix and in the rate of output and sales.

The time required for procurement affects the quantity of materials that must be held in storage for production scheduling. The stock must be of sufficient size not only to permit effective scheduling of production but adequate enough to provide time for the replenishment of raw-material stock without pressure. Thus, purchasing agents in placing orders take into account the procurement lead-time, that is, the interval between the placing of an order and the receipt of material at the plant. The more uncertain the delivery of materials, the longer the time allowed for procurement; the longer the procurement lead-time, the larger must be the stock of raw materials to assure continuity of production. When there are numerous sources of supply and when suitable substitute materials are available, the short-run supply is relatively elastic, and the industry's procurement lead-time tends to be shorter and more certain.

Producers and distributors design inventory-control systems and employ control ratios to routinize procurement and regulate inventory levels on a rational basis. The industry's trade association generally provides inventory ratios which often serve as useful bench marks for inventory-control purposes. A firm's inventory-control system generally stipulates the reorder point for procurement and the reorder quantity for the economical purchase of each raw-material item and component. The *reorder-point quantity* is the quantity necessary to fulfill production schedules during the replenishment period, including a safety allowance (a reserve balance) which protects and guards against stock depletion that may result from an abrupt stepup in output and sales. Hence, the reorder point is established on the basis of the quantity necessary for uninterrupted production and on the basis of the procurement lead-time, which takes into account supply conditions.

The reorder quantity plus the reserve stock establishes the maximum current stock level of material. Hence, the stock-output ratio for raw materials provides for stock variation within a given range. The *reorder quantity* (the economical quantity to purchase at one time) is established on the basis of two opposing considerations: the economies obtainable through bulk buying (e.g., quantity discounts and low transport costs per unit) and the inventory-carrying charges (interest, storage, spoilage). Bulk buying makes for economies, but larger stocks involve higher carrying charges. Through inventory-control analysis production men establish an optimum purchase quantity which strikes an economical balance between the savings from bulk buying and the cost of holding inventories. During comparatively stable business conditions, each industry tends to have a typical inventory-sales ratio.

In order that they may maintain efficient operations, businessmen endeavor to keep the over-all inventory stock at a certain desired level (Table 3–3). In selecting a desirable or optimum inventory-sales ratio, producers generally take into account the procurement lead-time, the level of purchase prices, the quantity of material necessary to feed production for efficient flow of work, the economical purchase quantity, and the cost of funds tied up in inventory relative to the return from alternative investment opportunities. The actual inventory-sales ratio often differs or deviates from the optimum level because of miscalculation of supply conditions, unanticipated fluctuations in output and sales volume, and difficulty in accurately predicting sales. In short, the impact of external factors gives rise to inventory dislocations whereby stocks may be either short or in excess. Thus, businessmen are often involved with the problem of adjusting inventory levels to changes in supply conditions and material prices, cash position and the need for liquidity, and sales estimates. During a business upswing and rising prices, businessmen typically accumulate and build up inventory levels; at the onset of a recession (or any period of declining sales and prices), businessmen liquidate excess inventory.

SHORT-RUN DEMAND FOR RAW MATERIALS. Changes in the rate of output are generally the major determinant of changes in raw-material stock and goods-in-process inventory. Since businessmen hold inventories in order that they may support their production rate and sales, the anticipated sales and planned output volume in-

TABLE 3-3

Manufacturing and Trade: Sales, Inventories, and Orders, 1940-59

(In billions of dollars. Data comprise all companies, both corporate and non-corporate, major activities of which are in manufacturing or trade. Farm and other non-farm businesses not included. Beginning in 1954, retail trade estimates based on a new method of estimation adopted by Bureau of the Census. Wholesale trade estimates beginning 1950 are adjusted to the scope of the 1954 Census of Wholesale Trade and are not strictly comparable with data for prior years which were adjusted to the 1948 Census of Wholesale Trade.)

Item	1940	1945	1950	1954	1955	1956	1957	1958 Total	1958 April	1959 April
MANUFACTURING AND TRADE										
Sales	145.6	286.2	476.1	568.3	627.3	657.6	675.8	648.3	52.2	60.7
Manufacturing	70.3	154.5	231.4	282.4	316.1	332.5	340.6	314.7	25.2	30.8
Durable goods	29.7	75.2	105.6	134.8	156.9	165.7	169.9	148.6	11.9	15.8
Non-durable goods	40.6	79.3	125.8	147.5	159.1	166.9	170.7	166.1	13.3	15.1
Wholesale trade	28.9	53.7	101.0	116.8	127.4	135.3	135.1	133.1	10.7	12.2
Durable goods	7.5	10.9	35.4	40.0	48.2	52.8	50.4	47.3	3.7	4.7
Non-durable goods	21.4	42.8	65.6	76.8	79.2	82.5	84.8	85.8	7.0	7.6
Retail trade	46.4	78.0	143.7	169.1	183.9	189.7	200.0	200.4	16.3	17.6
Durable goods	13.6	16.0	52.9	58.2	67.0	65.8	68.5	63.4	5.3	6.2
Non-durable goods	32.8	62.0	90.8	111.0	116.9	123.9	131.5	136.9	11.0	11.4
Inventories (seasonally adjusted) book value[1]	22.2	30.9	63.4	75.5	81.7	89.1	90.7	85.2	87.6	87.3
Manufacturing	12.8	18.4	34.3	43.0	46.4	52.3	53.5	49.2	51.5	50.8
Durable goods	6.3	8.8	16.8	24.1	26.7	30.7	31.1	27.9	29.4	29.2
Non-durable goods	6.5	9.6	17.5	18.9	19.7	21.6	22.4	21.3	22.1	21.7
Wholesale trade	3.2	4.6	9.1	10.4	11.4	13.0	12.7	12.0	12.2	12.1
Durable goods	1.1	1.5	4.3	5.1	5.8	6.6	6.6	6.3	6.3	6.4
Non-durable goods	2.1	3.1	4.8	5.3	5.6	6.4	6.1	5.7	5.9	5.7
Retail trade	6.1	7.9	19.9	22.1	23.9	23.9	24.5	24.0	23.9	24.4
Durable goods	2.5	2.4	8.8	10.1	11.2	10.7	11.4	10.8	10.8	11.3
Non-durable goods	3.6	5.5	11.1	12.0	12.7	13.2	13.1	13.2	13.2	13.1
Ratio of inventories to sales[2]										
Manufacturing	2.06	1.48	1.57	1.86	1.68	1.79	1.89	1.93	2.07	1.67
Durable goods	2.29	1.58	1.68	2.19	1.90	2.08	2.21	2.34	2.57	1.92
Non-durable goods	1.88	1.39	1.48	1.55	1.46	1.49	1.56	1.57	1.65	1.43
Wholesale trade	1.30	0.91	0.96	1.07	1.02	1.08	1.14	1.10	1.15	0.97
Durable goods	1.70	1.40	1.27	1.52	1.34	1.41	1.57	1.60	1.73	1.36
Non-durable goods	1.16	0.78	0.80	0.84	0.83	0.88	0.88	0.83	0.85	0.73

...	1.35	1.46	1.44	1.44	1.50	1.50	1.55	1.46	1.21	1.46
Durable goods	1.83	2.11	2.04	1.91	1.97	1.91	2.13	1.61	1.74	1.97
Non-durable goods	1.11	1.16	1.15	1.20	1.26	1.27	1.31	1.27	1.07	1.29
MANUFACTURING										
Inventories, by stages of fabrication (seasonally adjusted)[1]	50.8	51.5	49.2	53.5	52.3	46.4	43.0	34.3	18.4	12.8
Purchased materials	16.9	16.7	16.1	17.1	17.2	15.5	14.4	14.5	8.1	4.7
Goods in process	14.6	14.7	14.3	15.8	15.7	13.9	12.4	8.5	5.0	2.9
Finished goods	19.4	20.1	18.8	20.6	19.4	17.0	16.2	11.3	5.3	5.2
Durable goods	29.2	29.4	27.9	31.1	30.7	26.7	24.1	16.8	8.8	6.3
Purchased materials	8.3	8.0	7.5	8.3	8.7	7.4	6.5	6.1	3.2	2.1
Goods in process	11.5	11.8	11.3	12.7	12.8	11.1	9.8	6.0	3.5	2.0
Finished goods	9.3	9.7	9.0	10.1	9.2	8.2	7.7	4.7	2.1	2.2
Non-durable goods	21.7	22.1	21.3	22.4	21.6	19.7	18.9	17.5	9.6	6.5
Purchased materials	8.6	8.8	8.5	8.8	8.5	8.1	7.9	8.4	4.9	2.6
Goods in process	3.0	2.9	3.0	3.1	3.0	2.8	2.6	2.5	1.5	0.9
Finished goods[2]	10.0	10.4	9.8	10.5	10.1	8.8	8.4	6.6	3.2	3.0
Ratio of inventories to sales[2]										
Durable goods										
Purchased materials	0.54	0.70	0.63	0.60	0.59	0.52	0.62	0.58	0.52	0.74
Goods in process	0.76	1.03	0.94	0.93	0.87	0.78	0.88	0.58	0.72	0.67
Finished goods	0.62	0.85	0.77	0.68	0.63	0.60	0.69	0.52	0.34	0.88
Non-durable goods										
Purchased materials	0.57	0.66	0.63	0.62	0.60	0.60	0.65	0.65	0.73	0.74
Goods in process	0.20	0.22	0.21	0.21	0.21	0.21	0.21	0.22	0.22	0.24
Finished goods	0.66	0.77	0.73	0.73	0.69	0.65	0.69	0.61	0.44	0.90
New orders	30.7	24.3	310.8	327.1	339.9	326.0	269.8	251.8	126.4	81.7
Durable goods	15.6	10.9	144.5	157.0	173.3	166.2	121.9	123.8	47.3	40.5
Non-durable goods	15.1	13.4	166.4	170.1	166.6	159.8	147.9	128.0	79.1	41.2
Unfilled orders[1]	50.2	46.5	46.8	50.7	64.2	56.9	46.9	41.1	20.9	18.4
Durable goods	47.1	44.0	44.0	48.1	61.0	53.4	44.1	36.6	18.0	16.5
Non-durable goods	3.2	2.5	2.8	2.6	3.2	3.5	2.8	4.6	2.9	1.8

[1] End of period.

[2] Ratio of average inventories to average monthly sales; average inventories based on weighted averages of end of month figures.

Source: U.S. Department of Commerce, Bureau of the Census, Statistical Abstract of the United States, 1959 (Washington. D.C.: Government Printing Office, 1959), p. 498.

fluences the rate of procurement and inventory levels. Thus, the trend of output and sales generally determines whether producers build up or liquidate inventories. When sales rise by a larger quantity in one period (e.g., in one month) than in a preceding one, businessmen generally increase the rate of inventory accumulation.

Seasonal variations in production or in sales generally give rise to changes in stock levels. The size of raw-material stock is also influenced by seasonality in the supply of materials—producers sometimes must acquire material when it is available, as in the case of some agricultural materials and iron ore deliveries in some areas. But when supply conditions permit, businessmen adjust their raw-material stocks in line with changes in the rate of output and sales. Because of the procurement interval, changes in raw-material inventory levels tend to lag somewhat behind changes in the rate of production and sales (Fig. 3–5). The lag may be increased by errors in sales forecasting.

Producers use inventory-output and inventory-sales ratios to gauge the adequacy of stock levels. But they do not maintain the same inventory ratios for every business situation, as earlier indicated. Producers generally aim to maintain the inventory-sales ratio they consider desirable or "optimum" for the prevailing and anticipated business conditions. The short-run demand for raw materials and the desired level of inventories depend, therefore, not only on the variations in the rate of output and sales but also on the rate of interest, trend of material prices, procurement lead-time, and on the need for liquidity. Producers, for instance, would tend to set higher inventory-sales ratios and accumulate inventories when interest rates decline, material prices move upward, or when procurement lead-time lengthens.

Producers would, on the other hand, tend to set lower inventory-sales ratios and liquidate inventories if opposite conditions prevail. Businessmen tend to hold smaller inventories if they must borrow at higher rates of interest or to place a higher rate of interest as the "cost" of internal funds they invest in inventories; they liquidate material stocks and adopt hand-to-mouth purchasing in periods of declining material prices; and they keep smaller raw-material inventories when they can quickly replenish their stocks because of shorter procurement lead-time. During periods of considerable idle capacity in the material-producing industry, purchasers hold smaller inventories because suppliers vie for sales through quicker deliveries. During periods of peak business activity, rising prices, and tight capacity among suppliers, purchasers strive to accumulate and hold higher material stocks because of the longer procurement lead-time and the possibility of material scarcity, particularly when suppliers and unions are in dispute. If sales decline and the industry has over-produced at the onset of a business downturn, producers cut back

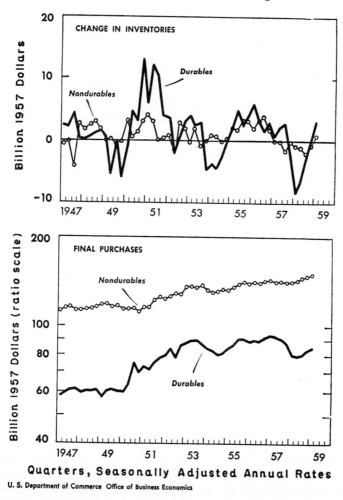

U. S. Department of Commerce Office of Business Economics

Fig. 3–5. Wider changes in inventories of durable goods *(top)* reflected the greater volatility in their demand *(bottom)*. The cyclical fluctuations in inventories occurred mainly in durable goods. (U.S. Department of Commerce, *Survey of Current Business*, vol. 39 [April, 1959]: p. 3.)

the rate of output and procurement of materials and gradually liquidate excess stocks. The downward adjustment of inventory levels generally lags behind the trend of sales a number of months, depending on the industry.

GOODS-IN-PROCESS INVENTORY. Goods in process are partially converted or fabricated materials (items on which labor has been expended) but are not yet completed, finished goods ready for shipment. The size of an industry's work-in-process inventory (including semifinished stocks) relative to output is determined by the stability of production, the effectiveness of production planning, the number of stages (including in-process storage) in the over-all production cycle and the degree of vertical integration, and the level of production relative to plant capacity. These determinants of in-process stock-output ratio are explained below.

The degree of production stability and the effectiveness of the technical control of processes affect the quantity of inventory required for work in process. More material is absorbed by an uneven production process wherein irregularities and delays result from machine failures and frequent job changeovers and short production runs. The effectiveness of an industry's production-planning practice also influences the amount of in-process material required. The tighter the over-all production cycle and the control system, the more rapid the turnover of work and the smaller the work-in-process inventory relative to output. Except for seasonal variations in production and periods of inventory adjustment, an industry's short-run stock-output ratio for goods in process tends to be comparatively stable for a given level of output.

The long-run stock-output ratio for work in process depends on the types and combination of processes (e.g., continuous or intermittent processes; repetitive or non-repetitive production) employed in the industry and the length of the over-all production cycle from raw materials to final products. The over-all in-process inventory also depends on the number of stages or plants (which determine the need for in-process stock storage) in the entire production cycle, the degree of vertical integration in the industry, and the degree of mass-production technology employed. In short, it is an industry's production technology and multiple-plant system which essentially determine the amount of raw material absorbed (the in-process inventory) in the over-all production cycle.

To the extent that an industry employs continuous processes, work-in-process inventory is relatively constant for a given rate of output. Semifinished stocks between stages or plants can, however, be built up or worked down. To the degree that an industry employs repetitive intermittent processes (i.e., goods are put out in lots or batches), work-in-process inventory is less rigidly tied to the rate of production. In assembly-type production, for instance, stocks of semifinished material and components are typically produced in advance of assembly, accumulating as in-process stores in parts depots at various stages in production and held ready to feed the next process, as in the case of farm equipment and automobile manufacture.

The bigger the lot size or batch of components and subassembly units processed at one time, the larger is the inventory of work in process, including in-process storage. Production planners compute the *economical lot size* (an optimum quantity of work to process at one time) by balancing the "preparation costs" of a production order against its "carry charges." In repetitive multiproduct manufacture and in processes by which similar types of components are put out alternately on the same production facilities, optimum lot size can be established through cost analysis. The larger the lot size processed at one time (the longer the production run), the lower the preparation costs (down time, machine set-up cost, and other plant services) but the higher the carrying charges (interest on funds tied up in inventory, storage cost, insurance, and deterioration). Hence, the optimum lot size for a production order is that quantity for which the sum of preparation costs and carrying charges are at a minimum. Since the over-all production cycle in intermittent manufacture is broken down into stages (e.g., fabrication processes and assembly processes), in-process stocks can pile up between stages or plants when production and sales slump (i.e., when the output rate is cut back); and stocks can be drawn down and depleted when production is quickly stepped up. The stock-output ratio for in-process inventory can, therefore, vary with short-term fluctuations in output as well as with the frequency of model changeovers and the seasonality in production.

In jobbing production to customers' specifications, manufacturing orders are typically put out intermittently in batches. In contrast to repetitive production, work in process in job-order production usually requires a *shrinkage allowance*, that is, an extra quantity of components must be included in the production order to compensate for the anticipated "normal" spoilage and scrap caused by fabrication errors and substandard work. In job-order production large orders and groups of identical orders are usually written up to comprise individual manufacturing orders which approach the optimum lot size. When customers' orders differ in specifications and fabrication, the size of a customer's order must of necessity be the lot size. Willingness to take small orders and sharp competition among producers on the basis of quick delivery also lead to smaller lot sizes in the industry.

Changes in the rate of output, especially in intermittent production (both repetitive and non-repetitive output), make for changes in the quantity of goods in process. When production is stepped up, the rise in in-process inventory will obviously precede (occur earlier than) the rise in the volume of output of finished goods currently being completed. Thus, changes in the quantitative level of work-in-process inventory somewhat lead the rate of output, but it cannot lead longer than the interval of one production cycle. When an industry produces at capacity level, in-process inventory relative to output (the stock-output ratio) rises because of the utilization of older and less efficient facilities, difficulty in production planning, and higher idle time due to more frequent temporary production bottlenecks. In multiple-shift production maintenance crews have less time and opportunity to repair facilities. Further, with respect to the impact of changes in the rate production on inventory ratios, if an industry produces at a low level relative to capacity (say, a twenty-five-hour workweek), the in-process inventory relative to output will tend to rise for the period (assuming no need for inventory adjustment).

The over-all inventory-sales ratio tends to rise at lower levels of output because the larger finished stock-sales ratio generally more than offsets the lower raw-material inventories (lower because of the shorter procurement lead-time). Hence, it is largely in this middle range of production capacity that the total inventory is more or less tied to the rate of production and the inventory-sales ratio relatively constant, that is, except for periods of overaccumulation and underaccumulation of inventories when stocks must be adjusted.

FINISHED-GOODS INVENTORY. A stock of finished goods (completed items ready for shipment) is necessary in repetitive production because completed goods flow off the production line continuously, while sales and shipments to customers are somewhat irregular. In multiproduct industries a *replenishment* (*reorder*) *point* is ordinarily established for each product at that level which will allow sufficient time for production to restock finished goods so as to supply the average needs of customers. Inventory carrying charges are taken into account in determining the size of the reserve finished stock economical to hold. The carrying charges are balanced against the gain (and the competitive advantage) realized by having a comfortable inventory margin which permits shipments of any size on short notice. Thus, the optimum level for the finished-goods inventory can be determined on the basis of marginal analysis.

In order that they may keep the stock-sales ratio in line with anticipated business conditions, producers aim to adjust the rate of output to anticipated changes in sales volume and competitive conditions. Because of the inability to predict sales accurately and to adjust instantaneously the rate of output, finished goods may continue to be liquidated for some time after sales have increased. The threat of stock depletion below prudent levels leads to an appropriate stepup in output. Producers may continue to accumulate finished stock for some time after sales have turned down, because they are not able to forecast sales with sufficient accuracy to adjust finished stocks to changes in sales and because they are reluctant to cut back production until they are certain that business is falling off. Thus, the size of the reserve stock depends on the timeliness of decisions to adjust production to changes in sales and on the speed with which the rate of production can be changed. The speed of building up finished stocks is determined by the length of the production interval and the time needed to increase the rate of output. Overtime production can be quickly inaugurated, while the time required for hiring workers to man available production facilities or to staff an additional shift depends on the supply of labor.

A high stock-sales ratio in industries supplying materials and semifinished goods does not necessarily call for a reduction in output. Because middlemen and producers of finished goods resort to greater hand-to-mouth purchasing during periods of slack sales, suppliers of primary materials and parts are obliged to compete on the basis of fast deliveries as well as on price. They, therefore, assume the burden of carrying larger inventories of finished goods, and as a consequence investment in inventories may increase sharply in earlier-stage manufacturing industries.

In industries characterized by seasonality in sales, the plan producers employ to deal with seasonal variations influences the level of finished-goods inventory. The industry may stabilize output at a relatively constant rate which builds up inventory levels during periods of slack sales, while the peak sales period draws down the stock. The industry may, on the other hand, synchronize the rate of output to current sales volume.

An industry's over-all inventory level also depends on the length of its distribution channel, the number of middlemen, and the type of marketing system employed—for example, whether selective marketing or general marketing is employed. Finished-inventory levels likewise depend on the extent of forward integration in the industry. Late-stage consumer-goods industries tend to have a higher stock-sales ratio for finished goods than the earlier-stage industries.

Supply of Materials

The long-run supply of materials for an industry depends on the adequacy and richness of the resource, the availability of substitute materials, the cost of expanding the capacity for producing material, and the technological developments affecting the material and its output.

The supply depends also on the nature of the material. Some materials are easily storable, others quickly deteriorate or are costly to store. The resource may be renewable or exhaustible in nature. If the resource is renewable (e.g., stands of timber and crop land) and adequate in quantity, the cost of material tends to decline in the long run, and the material supply is not likely to make for instability in the industry. An exhaustible resource (e.g., oil and mineral deposits) poses problems of another sort. Unless the resource is extensive or technological advances have developed adequate substitutes, an exhaustible resource leads to rising costs and the possible decline of the industry.

The investment and time required for the exploration and discovery of resources often place limits on the development of an adequate supply. High depletion allowances in the petroleum and in some mineral industries encourage the exploration and discovery of commercial deposits. It is the commercially exploitable (the proved) reserves that are relevant to the immediate growth of an industry rather than the potential reserves. Though the proved reserves may be adequate for an industry as a whole, some producers may own small reserves, while others may hold large reserves. When an industry is favored by an abundant and cheap material source, it is likely to grow and have a strong competitive position in the world market. A large, profitable industry can also develop new products and uses from its materials. As the richer and more accessible resources approach depletion, the costs of materials tend to rise and the industry is compelled to push a vigorous search for new domestic and foreign deposits. Producers may find it necessary to rely more heavily on foreign sources of supply, with the attendant uncertainties.

The supply of materials is at times enlarged through the development of improved methods for the discovery and extraction of the resource. The industry may find it necessary to invest heavily in the development of new processes designed to exploit commercially leaner or inferior deposits. New techniques often permit the economical utilization of lower-grade deposits. Various beneficiation processes, for example, are employed to remove undesirable ingredients and to improve the quality of lean ores. The resulting weight reduction in the material lowers the shipping cost and often facilitates the conversion of the material. These savings tend to offset the extra cost involved in utilizing lean ores.

Gradual improvements in the quality and uniformity of materials facilitate the workability of the material in the plant, speeding up processing and lowering the percentage of the product scrapped. The use of higher-quality material often improves the durability or performance of the final product. Newly developed materials may serve as suitable substitutes for depleting resources. Faster and cheaper transportation and communication and more efficient preservation and handling conserve materials and thereby enlarge the available supply. Thus, the long-run supply of many types of materials tends to increase through technological advances that directly or indirectly "enlarge" the resource base.

Conservation practices can enlarge the effective supply of raw materials in a number of ways. "Conservation" essentially means the complete and thorough utilization of natural resources without waste or damage to existing resources. Crude materials are increasingly being converted into by-products. The multiple-use approach in the development of resources achieves a more thorough utilization of natural resources and creates two or more economical sources of material supply—for example, petroleum and gas from oil wells and hydroelectric power, irrigation water, and nitrates from river-valley projects. Final products may be redesigned to effect a switch from scarce materials to abundant materials (e.g., plastics and fibers in place of expensive metals), and products may be redesigned to eliminate "over-specification" which wastefully absorbs excess amounts of high-priced materials. An economical supply of raw materials can come from various types of commercial scrap or waste. The metal industries, for instance, draw on the scrap-metal market. Supplies of various types of scrap material arise from rolling mills, foundries, and other metalworking processes in industry, from the junking of old automobiles, railroad rolling stock, and farm machinery, and from the wrecking of buildings and other structures.

The long-run elasticity of material supply depends on the lead-time required to open up resources and to expand capacity, on the amount of investment (the incremental capital-output ratio) required to enlarge capacity, and on the trend of average unit cost of output. When comparatively inaccessible resources are to be opened up, it may take two or more years to enlarge capacity and build the necessary transportation facilities, as in the case of expanding the output of bauxite and hydroelectric power for the production of aluminum ingots. When plantations for output of rubber, coffee, or pulp must be renewed or expanded, it may take a number of years to enlarge capacity. The expansion of materials supply from agricultural output, however, may be obtained by the next harvesting season.

Hence, if the enlargement of output capacity involves considerable time, investment, and higher unit cost of output, the long-run supply will be comparatively inelastic; in the face of strong demand, the price in the short run will rise sharply. If output capacity can be quickly enlarged at low investment and if unit cost tends to decline because of economies of scale, the long-run supply tends to be relatively elastic. When, because of abnormally high demand or miscalculation of long-run material requirements, capacity is over-expanded, the excess output capability results in a relatively elastic short-run supply. In the absence of price maintenance or output restrictions, earnings in the material-producing industry may be low, and the shortage of internal investment funds tends to impede modernization and cost reduction in the output of materials.

Because of the general tendency to create excess capacity, the volume output of many domestically produced non-agricultural materials can ordinarily be increased quickly. Hence, the short-run supply of non-farm raw materials generally responds somewhat directly with changes in the demand for such materials.

The supply of agricultural raw materials, however, usually does not respond in elastic fashion to short-run changes in demand. Since the current supply of agricultural raw materials depends on the weather, plant disease, and other production conditions, the supply is largely determined by the volume of current output and is, therefore, somewhat independent of the demand for the final products. The short-run supply of agricultural materials, thus, tends to rise and fall independently of the demand changes for the final goods produced.

An industry's supply of raw materials also depends on, and is influenced by, the degree of competition among the suppliers of the materials. When there are many independent suppliers of comparatively homogeneous and uniform materials, the market will be competitive, and material prices will tend to be lower. If, in addition, there are close substitute materials, the supply will tend to be more elastic and prices comparatively low. Materials tend to be produced under monopolistic conditions and sold at higher prices when the material resource is limited or is geographically concentrated. Even when material resources are adequate and geographically dispersed, single ownership and coordinated production can result in commensurate monopoly control of material supply. Unstable supply conditions and monopolistic control of raw materials tend to encourage backward integration by the material-using industry. Such vertical integration is also encouraged when economies can be derived from the linking of extraction, processing, and fabrication of the material. Thus, an industry may be substantially integrated backward to the source of material supply, as in the case of the petroleum, aluminum, and steel industries, or it may be non-integrated and rely on many independent and competitive suppliers of the material.

QUESTIONS FOR REVIEW AND APPLICATION

1. What are the purposes or value of industry studies? Identify narrower-type industry studies and illustrate.

2. (a) Define an industry. (b) Explain what is meant by a "homogeneous" industry. (c) "The products put out by different industries differ with respect to product coverage, homogeneity, technical stability, and the number of market segments supplied." Explain.

3. (a) Identify and briefly explain the salient structural features of an industry. (b) Explain why the value-added method rather than the gross-value method more correctly measures the output (and the size) of an industry's producers when they include both integrated and non-integrated firms.

4. (a) What is meant by interindustry input-output relations? (b) Are input-output tables useful for projective purposes? Explain.

5. Discuss the factors that determine an industry's location pattern.

6. Identify and briefly explain the factors that make for geographical concentration and the factors that make for dispersal of an industry's establishments.

7. Explain why a big automobile producer will tend to concentrate geographically the production of many of his components and subassemblies in one area, while regionally dispersing his final-assembly plants.

8. Discuss the factors that determine an industry's occupational structure and influence its occupational-wage differentials.

9. "Problems related to manpower utilization are usually crucial to industries that employ labor-intensive processes, require specialized skills peculiar to the industry, and are comprised of scattered plants, many of which are located at a distance from sizable labor markets." Explain.

10. (a) How do changes in the relative scarcity of productive factors (i.e., changes in their purchase cost) influence the proportion of factors combined in the productive process? (b) How does the short-run change in the input of labor take place as compared to the long-run change in the input of labor?

11. (a) Identify and briefly explain the various factors that determine an industry's long-term demand for labor. (b) Show how these factors may be used to project an industry's demand for labor.

12. (a) Identify an industry's sources of short-run supply of labor and of long-run supply of labor. (b) What problems are involved in projecting an industry's long-run supply of labor in both qualitative and quantitative terms?

13. What factors make the material supply and inventory problem more crucial to efficiency and profitable operations in some industries than in other

industries? For instance, what inventory problems occur in industries confronted by seasonality in sales, annual product restyling, and rapid technological developments affecting materials?

14. What effects have the seasonality of supply and the length of the production cycle in the cigarette and the leather industries on inventory requirements and on the risk in the purchase of raw materials (hides and tobacco), the prices of which tend to be volatile?

15. How did the shift from natural to synthetic rubber influence the structure and competitive pattern in the rubber industry?

16. (a) Explain what is meant by the optimum sales-stock ratio. (b) What short-term changes affect the optimum sales-stock ratio and prompt an industry to accumulate or to liquidate inventories?

17. Under what cyclical and other external conditions will an industry shift from hand-to-mouth buying to foreward buying in the procurement of materials?

18. What long-term factors influence the trend in an industry's stock-sales ratio?

19. Discuss the factors that determine an industry's long-run demand for materials.

CHAPTER 4

Structural Pattern:
Supply and Demand Behavior

PRODUCT COVERAGE AND MARKET

An industry's field of economic activity is identified and characterized by the kind of products it puts out and the markets it supplies. An industry's field of production may be characterized with respect to the kind of materials utilized; for example, there are metalworking industries, woodworking industries, leather industries, and ceramic industries. An industry's field of economic activity may also be characterized by the stage or stages of production involved. For example, early-stage industry turns out primary materials (steel, lumber), intermediate-stage industry turns out semimanufactured goods, and late-stage production turns out final consumer's goods or producer's goods.

Range of Product Coverage

The productive effort of a given industry is typically concentrated in the output of a group of closely related products (generally identified as the primary products); a smaller portion of its productive effort is ordinarily devoted to the output of certain secondary products. The primary products of the meat industry, for instance, are beef, pork, and lamb, which are distributed to a rather specific consumer market; the secondary products are hides, bristles, and other by-products which are distributed in a number of separate markets. Because of the considerable economies that accrue from the specialization of production, plants are typically set up to put out a specific product or a limited number of products that are closely related on the basis of production technology.

Certain technological and economic factors determine the composition and the range of an industry's product coverage. A broad product coverage, for instance, is usually typical of industries that employ analytic-type processes. In the processing of raw materials, many early-stage industries employing analytic-type processes break down crude materials into a number of primary and secondary products. In such industries the various "joint products" are put out in more or less fixed proportions.

A narrow product coverage is generally typical of industries that employ synthetic-type processes. In such industries specialized plants are set up to fabricate components or to put out ingredient materials that come together in subsequent assembly to make up the finished product. The existence of large markets for certain complex products (automobiles, appliances, agricultural implements) makes it economically feasible to apply a high degree of division of labor, i.e., to employ specialized plants for the output of parts and materials and other specialized plants for the assembly of a few related products. A comparatively broad product coverage is, however, not uncommon in industries that utilize synthetic-type processes. The fabrication phase of manufacturing (foundry and machining operations) can be designed and engineered for the adaptability (and for ease in retooling and changeover) necessary for comparatively efficient output of components that can go into the assembly of various final products, as in the case of instrument-making and machine-manufacturing industries.

Degree of Product Differentiation

A given product in an industry's product coverage may be comparatively homogeneous, or it may be highly differentiated. From an economic point of view, product differences and the physical characteristics of products are not relevant unless buyers believe the features to be significant to the value or utility of the product. Products are, of course, considered to be different if they serve different end uses and markets and, particularly, if they require different materials and processes for their output. The degree of product differentiation in an industry depends on the number of producers in the industry, the extent to which producers find it profitable to put out products of their own distinctive design, and the extent to which alternative designs in products are technically possible. Products tend to become more easily differentiated as technological progress creates new materials and new methods and devices for obtaining a given effect. (Technological progress also increases the possibility and ease of substitution among products.) Late-stage industries (particularly those in the field of consumer goods) tend to put out highly differentiated products; while early-stage and intermediate-stage industries tend to put out somewhat homogeneous products which are usually graded and standardized.

The standards developed and adopted by an industry ordinarily stipulate specifications and tests for the various products and for various grades of materials. Standards are important for producers as well as consumers. Basically the aim of standards for consumers is to assure buyers that the product will uniformly measure up to a given level of performance or quality. The standardization of product design and materials is, of course, a prerequisite for the utilization of mass-production methods of output.

Industries differ with respect to the technical stability of products—the degree to which their products change over time. The products put out by extractive industries and early-stage industries tend to be more stable (less susceptible to change) than the products put out by late-stage industries. Product design changes, and the adoption of new products for output in late-stage industries is generally considerable because of product innovations, shifts in consumer tastes, and the competitive practice of periodic product remodeling.

Product changes affect processes in a number of ways. They generally call for retooling and revisions in processes and facilities. If product changes involve the addition of new features and if they become more intricate in their design, the revisions require a changeover in production and generally tend to increase the length of the production interval. The opportunity for cutting costs is somewhat lessened—unit costs may even rise in the short term. Product displacement and changes in the product-mix tend to create imbalances in capacity; some plants or production lines develop excess capacity while others have a shortage of capacity.

The adoption of the practice of annual product restyling initially increases the replacement demand for goods because it accelerates obsolescence and depreciates the value of products in the hands of consumers. The continuation of annual remodeling, however, does not further increase the replacement demand.

The *market demand* for a product refers to the quantities consumers will buy at various prices at any given time. Market demand can be portrayed as a demand schedule or as a curve showing the quantities that will be purchased at each of a series of prices (see *DD* in Fig. 3–2). The demand curve essentially shows the price-quantity relationship. The quantity of the product or service the market will buy at any time varies inversely with price: the lower the price, the larger the quantity the market will buy; the higher the price, the less the market will buy. Effective demand for a product is the quantity consumers will buy at a given price.

A *change in demand* means that consumers will buy more or buy less of a product at a given price. A decrease in demand is graphically indicated by a shift of the demand curve downward and to the left; an increase in demand is graphically indicated by a shift of the curve upward and to the right. The demand for a product may increase (i.e., the market buys larger quantities at a specific price than previously) because of an increase in individual income, a shift in consumer tastes toward the product, or a rise in the prices of substitute products.

Market and Distribution Channels

An industry's market area is the area of demand to which it supplies products. The size of the market determines the extent to which specialization in industry can economically take place. The scope of the market (whether local or embracing a wide area) depends on several factors. Wide markets tend to be found in industries that put out products inexpensive to ship, usually non-perishable goods whose value is considerable relative to their bulk (e.g., watches and drugs), and in industries that are geographically concentrated. Narrower markets exist for products that are highly perishable or are bulky and expensive to ship. Narrow markets are often supplied by the local plants of industries that have a widely dispersed location pattern. The improvement and cost reduction in transportation and the lowering of tariffs and other trade restrictions widen the market for products, thus providing the basis for increased specialization in production and distribution.

An *industry's marketing function* includes transportation, grading and storing, selling, and financing. These activities are dispersed throughout the distribution system, from the factory to retail outlets and final consumers. The attainment of a large volume of sales at a low marketing cost is the underlying factor that influences the kind of distribution channel an industry employs. Some industries find it profitable to sell through a single channel; others use a multiple-channel system, e.g., selling directly to users, directly to retailers, and to wholesalers who resell to retailers. The type of distribution method that achieves a large sales volume at low distribution cost depends upon the nature of the industry's market (i.e., scope, type of consumers, buying habits, size of average sale) and the nature of the product (technical, stylish, perishable, for instance). By contrasting industries that sell in the industrial markets with industries that sell in consumer (household) markets, we can illustrate how the nature of the market and the nature of the product determine the kind of channel system generally utilized by an industry.

The *industrial* (*or business*) *market* is composed of commercial establishments that buy materials, fabricated parts, supplies, and equipment used for producing goods and services. In contrast to purchasers of consumer goods, the buyers for business firms tend to be geographically more concentrated, fewer in number, and often expert purchasing agents who buy on a comparatively rational basis. They make large-volume purchases, usually on the basis of specifications and performance, competitive bidding, and speed of delivery; they often call for functional packaging. Industrial purchasing typically originates in derived demand; the kind and quantities of materials to be procured depends on production requirements based on anticipated changes in market demand for finished goods.

Producers who supply goods to the industrial market find it most profitable either to distribute goods directly to the users from their factory or sales branches, or to distribute through wholesale middlemen who sell to users. The industrial market is generally characterized by comparatively short distribution channels. Most producers of industrial goods find it economical to sell directly to users of machinery and equipment because of the high unit value of the products, the geographical concentration of their market, minimum physical handling of the goods, or the need to provide for technical servicing and installation of equipment. Manufacturers of steel, locomotives and cars, electrical equipment, and special machinery typically sell directly to users.

Producers distribute industrial goods through wholesale channels when they sell standard goods (building materials, office supplies) to markets comprised of a comparatively large number of customers who generally buy in relatively small quantities. The wholesalers carry a broad line of goods which they purchase in bulk and, through economies in buying and storage, efficiently serve as "purchasing specialists" for their customers. Steel companies, for example, sell part of their output to steel warehouses (the wholesalers) where small orders for many firms are filled.

The *consumer* (*household*) *market* is composed of a mass of comparatively unskilled buyers (the consuming public) who make frequent, small-quantity purchases. Their untrained purchasing is influenced by advertising and sales-promotion schemes and is generally done on a trial-and-error basis. Producers who supply consumer goods generally distribute through one or more of the following channels: wholesalers or jobbers who sell to retailers, middlemen who sell to wholesalers or large retailers, and retailers directly. Most producers of consumer goods find it economical to distribute through wholesalers (the traditional channel); they also sell to large retailers and to associations of small retailers. The wholesaler achieves economies through specialization in his stage of distribution: he buys in big quantities a large variety of goods and thereby benefits from quantity discounts, bargaining power in price negotiations and terms of purchase, and from low-cost transportation, assembly, and storage. His specialized operation enables him to make quick deliveries and sell more economically in his market area than producers can if they sell their comparatively narrow lines of goods in small quantities to a multitude of retailers in scattered areas. The canned-food industry, for example, sells largely through brokers; it also markets a portion to wholesalers and chain stores.

Producers who find it profitable to distribute consumer goods directly to retailers are those who deal in fashion and style goods, those who sell to a comparatively concentrated market, and those who produce goods of high unit value. The women's-wear and the men's-clothing industries, for instance, distribute much of their product directly to retail stores. Producers of women's wear emphasize the direct-to-retail channel because their market and sales are concentrated in the large shopping centers, demand is seasonal, goods are vulnerable to rapid style obsolescence, and the garments which can be produced quickly permit rapid adjustment to shifts in market demand. The meat industry distributes the bulk of its product directly to retail stores from plants and branch houses. The meat packers sell a smaller percentage of their output to wholesalers, institutions, and other large ultimate consumers. The automobile industry, because it puts out a product of high unit value, distributes passenger cars and trucks directly to dealers. The automobile industry integrates its wholesaling function with the operation of regional assembly plants and district sales offices. Storage is split between the manufacturer and the dealer.

Producers in some industries have integrated "forward" into the distribution function. They own or control distribution establishments (e.g., branch warehouses and wholesaling organizations and/or retail outlets) as in the automobile, farm-implement, and women's-apparel industries. Rubber-tire and shoe manufacturers, for instance, largely sell directly to consumers through their own retail chains. Department stores to some extent integrate retailing with wholesaling and sometimes with production. When it is economically suited to the industry, integrated distribution achieves effective marketing and sales promotion and better control over pricing and customer servicing.

Industry's Market Segments

A "single" market exists when an industry's product is purchased primarily by a group of consumers who largely use the product for the same purpose, as in the case of footwear, meat, and home furniture. In such homogeneous markets demand analysis is simpler to conduct, and greater statistical reliability can be attained in estimating sales for the product.

An industry often puts out several related items that make up its product coverage. The aggregate demand for an industry's total output (i.e., the total demand for all items in the product coverage) is the amount purchased by the industry's aggregate market which may be made up of several market segments for each of its products. Thus, when an industry's product has separate groups of buyers who use the product for different purposes or who differ in demand elasticity, the over-all market may be broken down into distinct, homogeneous market segments. A market segment for a given product may thus be defined as a separate group of buyers who use the product for the same purpose and who have similar demand characteristics. Market segments also derive their identity from the fact that producers typically design or adapt their product for specialized uses.

The petroleum industry's aggregate market, for instance, consists of the market segments for each of its products: gasoline, kerosene, diesel oil, etc. The market for diesel oil is made up of the truck-market segment, the farm-market segment, the railroad segment, and the marine-shipping segment. The automobile industry's aggregate market for passenger cars is made up of buyers, for example, from the household-market segment, the commercial-market segment, the government-market segment, and the foreign-market segment. An industry may sell its primary products in one major market and each of its secondary products in a number of widely separate market segments. The meat-packing industry, to illustrate, sells its primary products (beef, pork, and lamb) to the food market, but it sells each of its secondary products (hides, bristles, fertilizer, and organic chemicals) in a number of separate markets.

When the product is costly to ship and the industry's plants are geographically dispersed to supply regional markets, market segments may be broken down regionally. Each market segment for a product may require a special distribution channel through which the product moves in a long or short series of sales transactions, though two or more kinds of products may be distributed through the same channel.

Each of the several market segments for a given product may differ with respect to the length of the distribution channel, method of demand promotion, type and degree of competition, pricing practice, cyclical demand, and seasonal demand. The seasonal demand for a product in one market segment may offset the seasonal demand for the product in another segment. The demand determinants and the long-run growth in demand among the market segments often differ. When the market segments exhibit similar trend characteristics, the respective segments may be combined for statistical analysis. Some market segments may have no near substitute products; other market segments may have close substitutes. When a market segment has close substitutes (as in the case of the market segments for containers or for fibers), the substitute goods may be included in a broadened definition of the "product" for purposes of sales forecasting and demand analysis. The magnitude and trend of demand are among the factors that influence the type of production technology an industry employs and the level and trend of long-run costs. These aspects of industry behavior are analyzed in the next section.

PRODUCTION: COST AND SUPPLY ANALYSIS

Broadly construed, an industry's productive activities are those activities that add utilities (want-satisfying attributes) to goods. The productive activities of mining and manufacturing add "form utility" by transforming materials into a more useful form. Transportation adds "place utility" to goods by moving them to the market; warehousing adds "time utility" by storing goods from the time of plenty to the time of relative scarcity when their value to consumers is greater.

Modern industry produces goods and services through a system of interdependent, specialized productive activities. The degree of specialization depends on the size of the market which in turn is governed by transportation costs and purchasing power in the market area. Specialization in productive activities takes place on a number of levels: geographical specialization, industrial and plant specialization, and labor or occupational specialization (professional, craft, semiskilled, and other categories).

Specialization has its economic disadvantages as well as advantages. When an area is highly specialized in its productive activity, industry in that area sacrifices some adaptive capability for adjusting to shifts in demand and to rapid changes in business conditions. Specialized semiskilled tasks are not only monotonous but offer little opportunity for individual expression through workmanship. In the final analysis, however, specialized industry provides more personal income and, through the shorter workweek, leisure time which enables people to participate in cultural and recreational activities. The specialization of productive activities means that industry and labor channel their productive efforts to those lines of output that efficiently exploit a region's natural endowments in terms of material and human resources. Because specialization involves the organization and concentration of resources for the output of certain types of products, it leads to the subdivision of the processes into simple tasks which permit the design and use of highly mechanized special-purpose machinery which obtains economies of mass production and augments productivity.

Production Structure and Specialization

When managers and technicians design the product and plant facilities, they seek to employ the latest processes to attain the least-cost combination of productive factors. It is essentially the productive process embodied in capital facilities, however, which combines factors for the output of goods. The physical nature of the process may be mechanical, chemical, electric, or a combination of these. The process may be repetitive and highly continuous as in oil refineries, or it may be non-repetitive and intermittent as in the manufacturer of special-purpose equipment.

In a coordinated series of operations, the production process employs energy in various forms (mechanical, electrical, chemical, thermal) to convert or transform materials into finished goods. Labor, as the active agent, operates the machines, handling devices, and other facilities that apply the energy in the productive process to convert materials into a more useful state. Operationally, therefore, the interrelated productive factors going into the output of goods include material and energy inputs, facilities embodying the process and applying the energy, and labor which operates or regulates the process. In the process of transforming goods into a more useful state, the value-added derives from the conversion of materials and their absorption of energy, plant facilities, and labor.

Since each industry's structural pattern differs from that of other industries—each industry being more or less unique—industries differ in terms of technological change, economic behavior, and types of business problems confronting management. The nature of an industry's structural pattern and production technology cannot be considered as given data from which economists formulate concepts and evolve theory. Production technology is itself a fundamental factor accounting for an industry's unique behavior with respect to capital mobility, adaptability, output performance, supply behavior, growth potential, and other such aspects. Managerial planning, business forecasting, and decision making must obviously take into account the industry's particular structural pattern, business behavior, and production behavior. (For further discussion of these topics, see Plant Production: Factor Proportionality; Capacity in Chap. 7.)

An *industry's production structure* can be characterized in terms of product coverage, type of processes and degree of specialization, degree of vertical integration, processing interval, capital intensiveness, degree of adaptability, and location pattern.

An industry's product coverage, for instance, may be broad or narrow, and the products put out may be technical items of high unit value or non-technical and of low unit value. Typically, standardized products are put out by specialized plants which employ repetitive, mass-production technology. Production is generally carried out through a vertical pattern of successive stages of specialized processes from the extraction of materials to the completion of the final product. The over-all production cycle may involve a long series of sequential stages and an extended or lengthy processing interval (as in shipbuilding), or it may involve a few stages and a short processing interval (as in fruit canning). Production may employ capital-intensive processes and require a long lead-time for expansion of capacity (as in the output of aluminum ingots), or it may employ labor-intensive processes and require a short lead-time for expansion (as in the making of garments). Processes and facilities may be highly specialized, or they may be adaptable and convertible to the output of other types of technically related products. An industry's location pattern (whether concentrated or dispersed) is largely determined by its particular production processes and input requirements, multiple-plant system, and the kinds of markets supplied.

Modern industries are typically comprised of plants that specialize according to product or according to a given kind of process.

Product specialization of plant means that each plant devotes its effort to the output of one kind of product or to the output of a few closely related products. In the shoe industry, for instance, some plants concentrate on the output of low-priced women's shoes while other plants concentrate on high-priced shoes. Some plants in the rubber industry specialize in the production of tires, while others specialize in the output of conveyor belts. Industries with a narrow product coverage (cement, beet sugar) typically consist of a large number of duplicate plants engaged in the output of the same kind of product. Industries with a broad product coverage (machine- and food-producing industries) can be segmented into "sub-industry" groups or "product divisions" comprised of plants engaged in a narrow field of production. The prevalence of a high degree of plant specialization in the output of a "single product" is statistically indicated by the *product-concentration ratio*—the ratio averages 90 per cent for all manufacturing establishments, according to the Census of Manufacturing (1957). Plant specialization is, of course, not solely confined to manufacturing. It extends to service establishments such as repair shops and stores.

Plant specialization according to type of process or stage of production is typical of large-scale industries comprised of a long series of separate stages or distinct processes in the over-all production cycle from raw materials to the finished product. In such industries separate plants are set up to carry out each stage or phase of the over-all process. Production in an industry may thus extend vertically over a long series of stages or distinct processes, or it may range over a short series. Each stage is generally housed in a separate plant. The number of plants in a vertical chain depends, of course, on the field of production. Food-processing industries consist of a few stages or plants in the chain, while metalworking industries generally consist of a number of stages and plants in the vertical chain. In a metalworking industry, for instance, early-stage production may be comprised of blast furnaces, conversion mills, rolling mills, foundry plants, and forging plants (see Fig. 3–1); intermediate-stage production may be comprised of light-machining plants and heavy-machining plants; and late-stage production may be comprised of subassembly plants and final assembly plants.

The number of stages and plants in an industry's over-all production cycle depends on (1) the volume of output, (2) the length and divisibility of the over-all process into distinct and separate stages, and (3) the requirements of location. The larger the volume of output, the greater the division of production into separate stages that can logically be organized into individual specialized plants.

Each plant would carry out a given process up to a certain point, and the following plant would take over the product for further processing. The sequential series of operations within a given plant generally terminates at the completion of the fabrication of a part, at the completion of the conversion of materials, or at the completion of an assembly.

In the case of a small volume of output of a product, the separate stages (or processes) in the over-all cycle of production would be set up within a single plant as individual departments (foundry department, machining department, assembly department). Because of the small-scale output, the processing facilities would not be highly specialized nor highly mechanized. But, as the volume of output increases, the individual production departments are split off and set up as separate plants, specializing in a given process or stage. Auxiliary departments, too, may be set up as separate auxiliary plants, e.g., a by-product or waste-disposal plant, a maintenance shop, and a power plant. Hence, industries that produce a large volume of output are able to utilize a high degree of mass-production technology by subdividing the over-all process and setting up separate plants that specialize according to process stage and setting up plants that specialize according to type of product.

Large-scale production by means of a series of separate specialized plants permits greater flexibility with respect to location; plants may be geographically dispersed as well as geographically concentrated. Each specialized plant can be located in the area and at the site that obtains low-unit cost processing: plants processing bulky materials or products may be located at the source of raw materials, and labor-intensive plants may be located at large labor markets. Plants may be located at points of "bulk-breaking" and transshipment of goods by another media of transportation. Thus, we can see that when a given location obtains low-cost output for a given phase in the over-all production process, the particular phase can be established as a separate plant at the most favorable location or site.

A homogeneous industry, as indicated earlier, is one in which the constituent plants employ the same or very similar kinds of processes and materials to produce a given type of goods. Early-stage industries tend to be more homogeneous than late-stage industries. Though the constituent plants of an industry may be similar in the sense that they produce the same kind of goods, an industry's plants often differ with respect to size, modernity (up-to-dateness), physical organization, adaptability, and so on.

Differences among plants in a given industry derive from a number of sources. An industry's production technology may be comparatively new and constantly undergoing development as in the case of the output of antibiotics, or the technology may be long established and somewhat stable as in the weaving of textiles or in the distilling of whiskey. Because new plants are typically erected on the basis of the latest production technology, rapidly growing industries generally have a higher proportion of modern plants using up-to-date technology than slow-growing industries. Older and less profitable industries often include plants that differ markedly in production technology, depth of processing, adaptability, and efficiency. These variations may be due not only to the slow addition of new plants but to the inadequate replacement of facilities, outmoded locations, and tradition-bound and ineffective managerial practices found among some producers.

Since technicians can choose from among alternative engineering approaches and methods, an industry's plants and production tend to differ with respect to product design, processes, and material input. But, because many early-stage industries typically use industry-wide specifications or standards for the products they put out, plants in these industries produce more or less identical products and employ somewhat more identical processes than do the plants of late-stage manufacturing industries.

Product and process uniformity tend to be greater in highly concentrated industries (i.e., those comprised of comparatively few producers). On the other hand, because successful product differentiation is a means of securing a strong competitive position, product and process differences, especially in late-stage industries, are greater than would be the case if technical factors alone were operative.

The application of industrial research for the development of many new and substitute materials has increased the variety of materials used by plants to produce the same kind of products. Tire plants may use synthetic or natural rubber, textile mills may weave cloth of synthetic fibers or natural fibers, and shoes may be made of leather or composition materials. The adoption of a substitute material generally requires modifications in processes and sometimes calls for a distinctly different type of process.

Plants often differ with respect to the length (depth) of the process employed to turn out similar products. Plants located in highly developed industrial centers can shorten their production process by purchasing from suppliers fabricated parts, power, maintenance services, and other necessities. Plants located in less-developed areas find it necessary to carry out more of the production process within their establishments. Differences in the depth of the process, moreover, make for larger variations in capital-output ratios, plant organization, and size than would otherwise be the case. Plants in the same industry differ in size (in terms of investment and in output capacity) not only because of differences in the length of production processes and production technology employed, but because of differences in the market share and size of the local market supplied and differences in managerial policies concerning geographical dispersal of production.

Measurement of an industry's output or size (as explained earlier on pages 79–80) may be obtained in a number of ways. Production may be measured by means of an index number as illustrated in Figure 9–1. The industry's index of production may be based on physical units of output, such as tons, barrels, and yardage; and output may be broken down by the type of products that make up the product coverage. Long-term changes in the industry's product coverage and product-mix would, however, make the foregoing index unsuitable for intertemporal comparisons. Comparability of data between periods can be approached by expressing the physical output of the various items in terms of a key product. The output volume of each product would be converted into a standard unit of measure (man-hours for the key product) on the basis of man-hour input required to produce the item. The ratio of an industry's output (in terms of value-added) to man-hour input would measure the "gain in output per man-hour," that is, the productivity gain.

An industry's output is sometimes measured in terms of a man-hour index. Output would be measured by multiplying the industry's man-hour input by the estimated change in output per man-hour of productivity. The man-hour index of output is a useful measure of production in industries that put out a great variety of items whose range in price is wide, as in the case of machine manufacturing, tool making, and other special-order production. An industry's output may also be expressed in terms of the percentage of capacity utilized. Output measured as a percentage of "rated capacity" is sometimes misleading because of the gradual accretions to an industry's capacity.

An analyst can summarize an *industry's output and over-all production status* in terms of percentage of capacity utilization, two or more indexes of production adjusted for seasonal variations, inventory levels, backlog and new orders, size of labor force employed, length of the workweek, and others.

At any given time each industry has a certain fixed capacity which can put out the product in a given number of varieties, sizes, or models (e.g., pianos produced in a number of models). An industry's *effective supply* is the quantity of the product that firms are turning out at any given time and are willing to sell at the going price. Thus, effective supply at any given time ordinarily consists of the industry's current rate of output and the quantity of finished goods in the distribution system. When expressed as a percentage of rated capacity, an industry's current output indicates the extent to which it can increase its rate of production by taking up available capacity without expanding or adding new capacity. An industry's supply of a product may be indicated as a schedule (or curve) showing the relationship of output quantities to a series of prices. (See Fig. 3–2.)

A supply schedule or supply curve shows the total volume of output of the product that firms will turn out or offer for sale at each of a series of prices. At higher prices firms in the industry tend to produce and offer larger quantities of the product. The typical supply curve indicates that the quantities the industry will produce and offer for sale vary directly with price. The quantity supplied and price move in the same direction primarily because the industry's cost of production (including the price of input factors) tends to rise in the short run as more is produced within the limits of existing capacity. Hence, supply is generally determined by the costs of production; the higher the price, the greater the inducement to produce.

The *elasticity of supply* refers to the extent to which the amount produced or offered varies with changes in price. Elasticity is essentially the responsiveness of output volume to changes in price, and this would be indicated by the slope of the supply curve. An industry's supply schedule or curve may be relatively elastic or inelastic. Supply is elastic if a given change in price (say, 5 per cent) results in a more than proportional change (e.g., 10 per cent) in the amount firms will produce or offer for sale. Variations in price are thus accompanied by proportionately greater variations in the amounts offered. Supply is inelastic if a given change in price (5 per cent) results in a less than proportional change (2 per cent) in the amount that will be produced or offered; a higher price will not induce producers to turn out very much more than they have turned out at a lower price.

A change in an industry's supply means a change in the position of its supply curve. A *decrease in supply* would mean that producers offer smaller amounts at each of a series of prices than they had previously—the supply curve has shifted to the left. A decrease in supply generally results from a rise in the cost of production. An *increase in supply* would mean that the industry offers larger amounts at each of a series of prices than it had previously—the supply curve has shifted to the right. An increase in supply generally results from cost reductions stemming from improvements in production technology, more rational organization in industry (e.g., more effective specialization and integration of production), and lower prices for input factors. Thus, changes in the supply of goods are caused by changes in the cost of production.

Cost Determinants in Production: Short-Run Costs

Goods have value and command a price on the market because they have utility and are scarce; they are scarce because the productive factors required to put out goods are limited in supply and involve a procurement cost. In economic analysis the term "costs" has a number of related meanings. When individuals, for instance, produce goods or repair them (e.g., furniture and garments) for their own use, costs represent the effort and sacrifice in producing or renewing the goods. When firms put out goods, the cost of production consists of the payments and entrepreneurial sacrifices necessary to obtain all the productive factors required to turn out the goods.

Economists distinguish between accounting costs and economic costs. Accounting costs are the actual business costs and outlays for a past period of operation. These costs go into the preparation of balance sheets and income statements which show the firm's financial status and the earnings for a past period. Accounting costs and financial statements are necessary for determining tax obligations, depreciation funds, and the earnings available for investment or dividend distribution by the firm. Because accounting costs are essentially the costs of past operations designed to serve a comparatively narrow purpose, they do not reflect the scope of economic forces that operate in productive enterprise and all the cost influences that bear on business decisions; they do not indicate the relevant cost concepts that managers must consider when they plan future business operations and investments. Accounting costs, moreover, are inadequate for decision making for future business operations because accounting costs are not conceptually consistent. Interest on borrowed capital, for instance, is included as an accounting cost, but imputed interest on shareholders' investment is not included in accounting costs.

From the economic viewpoint the economic costs of production include not only payments for materials, labor, and interest on borrowed funds (i.e., the explicit costs) but also the cost of productive factors used but not directly paid for (the implicit costs), such as imputed interest on the owners' investment and the unpaid salaries of owner-managers. The imputed costs based on the alternative return to factors (the opportunity cost) do not show up in accounting records and financial statements but are nonetheless essential economic costs (a necessary return to productive factors) that must be covered if a firm is to stay in a given line of business. The economic costs of production, therefore, include the compensation, at their respective market value, for all productive factors required in the output of goods. In the analysis of the organization of productive operations and investment, the economist employs such cost concepts as the opportunity cost, incremental cost, long-run costs, and short-run costs.

Because productive factors have alternative uses and employment opportunities, a businessman must pay as much for a factor as is bid or paid by other firms which can profitably employ the factor. The employment of any productive factor thus involves a cost which is equal to the competitive price offered for that factor in its alternative productive uses. To employ a productive factor, a firm therefore pays or estimates in its decision calculation the *opportunity cost* for the factor, which is the higher return obtainable by the factor in its alternative uses. When businessmen invest funds in a particular venture or capital project, they must compare the estimated return with that from alternative fields of investment. The opportunity cost of using capital for a particular purpose would thus be the return foregone from the alternative uses of the funds, e.g., savings from investment in plant modernization may be compared with income foregone by passing up an opportunity for gain through adoption and sale of a new product.

To compute the investment outlay required for enlarging a plant, remodeling a product, and changing over production or for converting idle machines for the production of items formerly purchased, businessmen take into account and compute the *incremental cost* (the added outlay needed as compared to the "sunk" investment). In computing the outlay, businessmen must, of course, estimate the *future cost* of the incremental investment, and this calls for estimating the price level (cost) of input factors that will be used.

To analyze an industry's cost behavior and supply pattern, we must differentiate between long-run and short-run costs. An industry's *long-run costs* (and long-run supply) are based on, and are the result of, changes in output capacity, the relative scarcity of productive factors, economies of scale, and technological advance. "Long run" is the time period or lead-time required to erect new plants and commence regular production; it is also considered the time required to wear out and retire existing capacity. Thus, long run is the period long enough for all productive factors to be freely variable and all costs to be variable.

An industry's *short-run costs* are based on the rate of output (utilization of productive capacity), and its short-run supply is the output capability based on the capacity of existing productive establishments and the price of input factors. Whereas in the long run producers are able to vary capacity and plant size and to select different processing technology, in the short run they are only able to vary the rate of output within the limits of existing capacity. The short-run period, therefore, is an interval long enough for producers to vary the output rate, but it is not of sufficient duration to permit expansion of capacity or retirement of worn facilities without loss. The short period serves to conceptualize short-run costs (fixed costs, variable costs, total average costs, marginal costs) which are useful for economic analysis of cost behavior in a going concern, for break-even analysis, and for planning and budgeting short-term business operations.

On the basis of the foregoing discussion of cost concepts and cost behavior, we can see that a comprehensive grasp of economic costs requires that they be defined in economic terms. The meaning and role of economic costs can be operationally defined by outlining their origin in terms of the alternative uses of scarce resources (on the basis of their relative or marginal productivity), the influence of current technology and future developments, and the short- and long-run use of productive factors in business enterprise. By seeking out the factors that determine production costs and by analyzing the behavior of costs, we can more effectively identify and characterize (1) the economic and technological forces that underlie the efficient use of resources and (2) the cost concepts that businessmen must take into account when they plan their short- and long-range programs and investments and when they make decisions dealing with the composition of the product line, selection of processes and location, multiple-plant organization and plant size, the operating budget and pricing problems, sales promotion, plant mergers, and other questions.

The *cost determinants* for producing a product or a line of products (a line of refrigerators) include such interrelated factors as the design of the product, production technology, size of plant and rate of output, the price of input factors, managerial efficiency, and economies of scale. The general level of the cost of producing a product would obviously depend on the type of product. Locomotives and similar large, intricate goods are more costly to produce than such simpler products as motorcycles and sporting goods.

The determinants of the cost of production may be conceptually classified as follows:

The *current technology and processes* employed in plants determine the level of unit cost of production through (1) the technical effectiveness of the present design of the product, (2) the kind of production technology used and the size and organization of plants, and (3) the price and combination of input factors absorbed in production.

The *short-run determinants* of production costs include (4) the rate of output (percentage of capacity utilized) and the continuity and stability of production and (5) managerial efficiency.

The *long-run determinants* of the cost of production include (6) the extent to which technological advances reduce costs and (7) the extent to which economies of scale (increasing returns) accrue and the output capacity at which tendencies toward diminishing returns develop in the industry.

Though the foregoing cost determinants (amplified in the pages following) are conceptually classified into current, short-run, and long-run categories to show the origin and nature of their influence, in actuality they operate concurrently in determining the output costs in productive establishments. The long-run cost determinants, for instance, operate continually through technological progress and capital replacement, the restructuring of plant specialization, the development of improved or cheaper materials, and production improvements that cut costs or enlarge capacity.

PRODUCT DESIGN AS A COST DETERMINANT. The cost of production is to some extent predetermined by the effectiveness with which engineers design the product for economical processing and for use of cheaper factors. The design of the product and the cost in producing it also depend on the volume that can be sold at a selected range of prices, the relative cost of input factors, and the type of production technology that is available for use.

Businessmen (and their production engineers) generally aim to design products for output and sale at a certain volume and range of prices. The volume of goods to be put out determines the extent to which efficient mass-production processes are economically feasible. Engineers can develop or adapt processes for the use of cheaper input factors—whether labor, materials, or capital. The processes and materials to be used influence in turn the design of the product; engineers can to some extent design the product so that it can be put out by the more economical processes available and be made of lower-priced, though adequate, materials. The relationship and logic in the over-all design of a product line also affect the cost of producing and distributing goods. The above technical-economic aspects and the alternative methods available for achieving low-cost factor proportionality are discussed in the section of Chapter 7 dealing with Plant Production: Factor Proportionality; Capacity.

TECHNOLOGY AS A COST DETERMINANT. The unit cost of turning out a product depends partly on the amount of research and engineering effort devoted to the development of low-cost production processes. The larger the volume of the product to be put out, the greater the research and development effort that can be absorbed to economic advantage. Engineers achieve cost reduction from advances which increase plant productivity through the development of more economical processes, development of product designs which permit faster production processing (e.g., attainment of greater interchangeability of components among models and related products), development of materials which are cheaper or can be fabricated more economically, and other means. Since a considerable development interval generally elapses from the time of an initial discovery or invention to its commercial applicability, the length of this lead-time can in many cases be estimated and cost savings roughly projected. Since new facilities embody the latest technical improvements in processing methods, technological advances in the relatively mature industries are adopted by producers largely through the replacement of older or obsolete machines. Big advances in technology, of course, accelerate the replacement of facilities.

A study of technological progress in a given industry can yield rough estimates of the probable cost reduction that can be attained. The actual cost reduction obtainable in a given case can be estimated only by a careful comparative-cost study of a proposed plant-modernization program. In cases in which firms have both new and old branch plants devoted to the output of the same kind of product, potential cost reduction through plant replacement can be approximated by comparing the processing costs between old and new plants with an allowance for anticipated cost-reduction gain from the use of latest technological improvements. The pace of technological advance in an industry partly depends on the size of expenditures for research and development. Technological and productivity gains in a given industry are, of course, augmented by cost-reduction and technical improvements that are acquired and absorbed from machine-supplying industries such as those that develop and sell office machinery, data processing machines, electronic control devices, mechanized handling facilities, etc.

PRICE OF INPUT FACTORS. Changes in material prices and wages influence the unit cost of production over time. Because different processes absorb input factors in different proportions and because changes in the prices of input factors affect the proportionality in the combination of factors for least-cost production, changes in the price of input factors influence the choice of production processes from among alternatives. The choice of production processes and facilities comes up when plant facilities are to be replaced or capacity expanded. Changes in the prices of input factors affect the relative economy of different processes and influence the choice of processes for replacement of plant facilities and for use in new plants to be erected to expand capacity. A rising trend in the level of wages promotes the development and the adoption of laborsaving types of facilities; a rising trend in the level of material prices encourages the use of processes that conserve materials, prompts the revamping of the product design to reduce the quantity of material required per unit of product, and stimulates the search for, and the development of, cheaper materials.

SHORT-RUN COST DETERMINANTS—THE RATE OF OUTPUT. For most plants the short-run total-cost curve (illustrated as *TC* in Fig. 4–1) increases at a varying rate with changes in the volume of output. In the typical short-run cost pattern, the total-cost curve first moves upward at a decreasing rate and then begins to rise at an increasing rate as production reaches capacity. The total-cost curve essentially reflects the law of diminishing returns in the use of a fixed factor.

The short-run total-cost curve (the *TC* curve in Fig. 4–1) shows the total cost on the vertical line for the various rates of plant output which are measured on the horizontal line. A firm's total revenue in the sale of the goods produced may be represented by the *TR* curve. Revenue increases proportionately if we assume constant prices for the various rates of output and sale. If output is *OP*, total revenue and total cost are equal. The firm incurs a loss if its output and sales are below the break-even point *OP*, where total costs and total revenue are equal. If the firm is to make a profit, it must produce and sell beyond the break-even point *OP* but it must not exceed *OL*.

Short-run production costs, when broken down as to the degree to which they vary with changes in the rate of output, essentially consist of fixed costs, variable costs, and average total cost per unit.

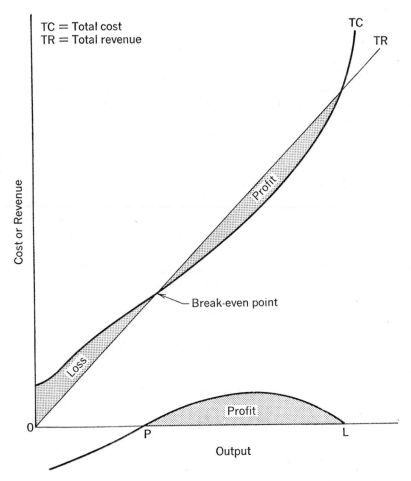

TC = Total cost
TR = Total revenue

Cost or Revenue

Profit

Break-even point

Loss

Profit

Output

Fig. 4-1. Short-run production costs illustrated on a break-even chart.

This classification of costs is useful for budgeting short-term business operations, for break-even analysis, and for the economic analysis of short-run behavior of costs. *Fixed costs* are those expenses (e.g., depreciation charges, interest on funds used to acquire facilities, insurance) which in total remain constant regardless of the rate of output of goods or services. Total fixed costs must be met or absorbed regardless of whether the plant is running at half capacity or at full capacity. Total fixed costs, though constant in the short run, would, of course, increase in the long run if plant capacity were enlarged through extension of floor space and purchase of additional productive facilities. The longer the time period for which decisions dealing with production processes and facilities are made, the fewer the cost items that are fixed. In the short run, though fixed costs remain constant as a total, they vary per unit with changes in the rate of output. Fixed cost per unit declines as output increases; the bigger the output, the smaller the fixed cost per unit.

Variable costs are payments for direct labor, material, and other variable agents required for plant output of goods. Variable costs are those which vary in total with changes in the rate of output, but are not necessarily proportionate to the change in the volume of output. (See Fig. 4–2.) The variable cost per unit of output in a given plant typically declines to a certain level and then rises again as the limits of productive capacity are reached. This is because as variable factors are applied to a fixed factor, the marginal physical output per input of variable factors tends to increase and then later to decrease. The relative change in unit variable cost for different rates of output more or less depends on the kind of productive processes employed by a plant. In some cases unit variable cost may be relatively constant for the middle range of plant output capacity; in other cases unit variable cost may change very slightly for much of the range of plant output capacity.

It is sometimes useful in economic analysis to segregate or identify in total costs those expense items that are semivariable. Semivariable costs (e.g., plant maintenance and utilities) vary in total amount but not directly with the rate of output.

At any given rate of output, average total cost per unit is obtained by dividing total cost by the number of units produced; average unit cost is the sum of unit variable cost and unit fixed cost. The change in the level of average total cost depends on the rate of plant operation. Thus, short-run costs are fundamentally a function of the rate of output. But, as earlier indicated, the level of unit cost also depends on product design and technology, the price of input factors, managerial efficiency, and the size and organization of plant and economies of scale in the industry.

Since variable factors (direct labor and direct materials, primarily) are inputs added to fixed plant, the average total cost per unit varies with the degree of utilization of plant because of the law of increasing and diminishing returns. With an increase in the rate of output, the average unit cost declines because of the fuller and more intensive utilization of plant and other fixed factors and the consequent spreading and allocation of fixed cost over more units of output. As full plant capacity is approached, however, average unit cost rises because of diminishing returns on the variable agents in the use of a fixed factor (plant). Thus, as plant output

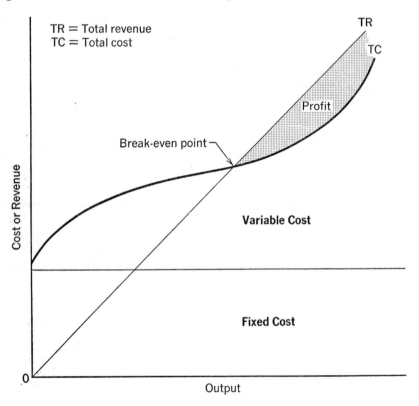

Fig. 4–2. Short-run production costs presented on a break-even chart showing fixed cost, variable cost, and total cost.

increases, the short-run cost curve tends to assume a U-shaped form of one pattern or another. The plant output volume at which the average unit cost is at its lowest point (that is, at optimum capacity) is the production volume at which profit per unit would be the highest. But the output volume yielding the largest total profit may be at a higher volume, where marginal revenue (the addition to total revenue gained from the sale of an additional unit) equals marginal cost. Insofar as marginal revenue is higher than marginal cost, the sale of extra units adds more to total revenue than to total cost.

As variable factors are added to a plant of a given size, the marginal product (the change in total output resulting from successive inputs of variable factors) first tends to increase and then to decrease. The *marginal cost* would be the increase in the total cost (i.e., the additional cost) resulting from an output increase of one unit or batch.

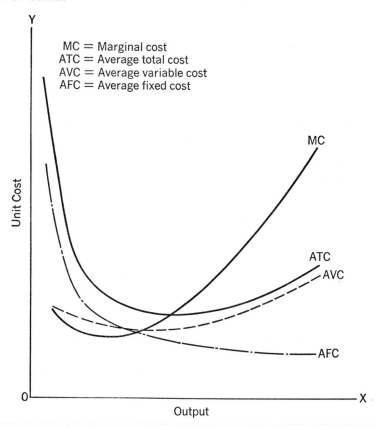

Fig. 4–3. Short-run cost structure of a plant (or of a single-plant firm) showing cost components.

The cost curves in Figure 4–3 graphically illustrate the behavior of various classes of short-run costs. Output in units is measured along the horizontal axis (*OX*) and costs along the vertical axis (*OY*). Figure 4–3 illustrates the behavior of average fixed cost (*AFC*), average variable cost (*AVC*), average total cost (*ATC*), and marginal cost (*MC*).

The marginal-cost curve represents the addition to total cost resulting from successive units of output. Since total fixed costs are constant for a given plant, the incremental cost for putting out successive units consists of variable costs. Average variable cost per unit will continue to fall so long as marginal cost is less than unit variable cost. As full capacity is approached and larger incremental inputs are required for successive outputs, the marginal cost exceeds the average variable cost. Thus, marginal cost generally falls and rises more steeply than unit variable cost because, in the calculation of average variable cost per unit, the marginal cost for each successive unit put out is distributed among the previous units through the allocation of total variable cost to the total output per day or other production period.

The marginal cost generally declines over a range of output until it approaches optimum capacity and then it rises sharply. In the initial range of plant capacity, the marginal cost (which is included in the computation of average total cost per unit) has the effect of lowering the average unit cost. When the output rate reaches a point at which the incremental cost for an additional unit is the same as average unit cost (marginal cost neither raising nor lowering unit cost), average total cost per unit is at its lowest point (i.e., at optimum). When production is pushed beyond optimum to a higher rate of output, marginal cost has the effect of raising average total cost per unit.

Joint products and joint costs exist when an increase in the output of one product gives rise to an increase in the output of another product. Joint products from the same raw material may be put out in fixed proportions (beef and hides) or produced in more or less variable proportions (gasoline and kerosene; ice cream and milk). Since most plants are highly specialized in the output of a given type of product, the problem of prorating the production cost in a given plant among joint products occurs somewhat infrequently. After its "split-off" point from a common material, the cost of labor and machine and factory burden for a joint product is computed and allocated in the same manner as for any product. The problem of prorating costs among joint products largely involves the allocation of the cost of the common raw material, common initial processing, and administrative expense. A method not infrequently used to allocate the latter costs is to prorate the costs on the basis of the relative values (prices) or sales revenue gained from each of the joint products. The managerial problem in joint-product output often involves the relative incremental expense and revenue associated with an increase in the output of one joint product in response to a rise in the demand for the item. If over-all profitability is to be maintained, the marginal revenue gained from the stepped-up sale of one joint product must be sufficient to cover not only revenue losses that may be incurred from the need to dispose of the overproduced joint product at a lower price but also to cover the incremental cost for both items.

Factors Influencing the Shape of the Short-Run Cost Curve

The particular shape a short-run cost curve assumes differs among industries and often among plants in the same industry. The shape of the short-run average cost curve is determined by such technological and operating aspects as (1) the proportion of variable cost to fixed cost, (2) the divisibility of plant facilities, (3) plant adaptability to overtime and multiple-shift operation, and (4) plant adaptability to variations in the amount of subcontracting of production of components and adaptability to changes in the product-mix. Thus, the shape of the short-run cost curve reflects a composite of various technological, organizational, and operating aspects.

In industries in which variable factors (labor, materials, and fuel or power) comprise a high proportion of unit cost at optimum capacity, the pattern of variation in the unit variable-cost curve will dominate the pattern of the short-run cost curve. If the material cost comprises a high proportion of unit cost, average variable cost will, within the broad range of output capacity, tend to decline to the extent that economies are obtainable through larger material procurement. In most cases in which fixed costs are a small proportion of unit cost, average variable cost tends to be relatively constant within the limits of capacity, and the marginal-cost curve gradually slopes downward before turning upward as it approaches optimum capacity. The resulting flat-bottomed, saucer-shaped unit-cost curve means that plant output could be varied widely with only moderate variations in unit costs.

In industries in which fixed cost comprises a high proportion of total cost, the fall in unit fixed cost associated with increases in output dominates the pattern of the unit-cost curve. The downward pull of unit fixed cost overshadows any tendency for unit variable cost to rise until full capacity is approached. Thus, the spreading of a large overhead cost results in a relatively sharp downward movement of unit cost within the broad range of output capacity.

The degree of divisibility in productive facilities and their adaptability to variations in labor and material input influence the shape of short-run cost curves, particularly the degree of linearity in unit variable cost and in marginal cost. Plant facilities and process are divisible when the plant is organized according to a process-layout pattern (i.e., process specialization), wherein the constituent production departments or shops (or whole plants) are comprised of identical or similar machines (as in a press shop, welding shop, tire-molding shop, machine shop). Since plant facilities and operations are vertically divisible, output can be easily varied by operating a varying number of machines in each of the production departments or in each of the plants in a multiple-plant system. Because each machine or a group of machines is manned by one operator or by a crew of a given size and an economical input of direct labor and material to production machines can be maintained for each level of output (though this is not necessarily true for factory indirect or service labor), average variable cost and marginal cost will be relatively constant for a wide range of output within the limits of capacity. Thus, when fixed cost is high, plant divisible, and the ratio of labor to plant facilities invariant for each level of output within the limits of capacity, unit cost declines uniformly, and the total-cost curve tends to be linear up to capacity. When duplicate machines in a plant (or duplicate plants in a system) vary in age and efficiency and when production is scheduled and facilities are put into operation in the order of decreasing efficiency, average variable cost will rise as less efficient machines are put into use, and unit cost will rise earlier than otherwise.

A plant is indivisible when the product is turned out by a single, large facility (e.g., a distillery) or by a technically integrated production line comprised of machines and work stations physically linked in the process by a mechanically paced handling system. When such a physically indivisible plant must be operated continuously round the clock (or is operated a fixed number of hours per week, say, a forty-hour week), output can generally vary only within certain narrow limits above and below optimum capacity (e.g., plus or minus 10 per cent of the optimum rate), with the result that the unit-cost curve and the average variable-cost curve assume a steep U shape. The comparatively small variation in the rate of output is not infrequently obtainable by varying the operating speed of the equipment or process and by varying somewhat the input of labor and material.

When an industry's plants (and multiple-plant units) are comprised of expensive, relatively indivisible equipment (i.e., only partially divisible facilities, as in a metallurgical plant with several stands of rolling mills or large extrusion presses or in a printing plant with several stands of large presses), an increase in the rate of output through the hiring of more labor and the scheduling of production on successive units or stands of the big equipment results in a discontinuous (kinky), downward-sloping unit-cost curve and a staircaselike upward path in the total-cost curve.

Since many plants often include both divisible and indivisible facilities, producers ordinarily vary the rate of output through a combination of methods best suited to the processes of the various plants and production departments: the output rate of divisible facilities would be adjusted by varying the degree of plant utilization through starting up or shutting down of machines and increasing or decreasing the input of variable factors; and the output rate of indivisible facilities would be adjusted by varying the intensity of plant utilization in the time dimension, i.e., by varying the length of the workweek and number of shifts (Fig. 4-4).

In much of mass-production industry, wherein production involves indivisible continuous processes and mechanically paced (or automated) fabrication lines and assembly lines comprised of an integrated series of machines and work stations, plants must generally be operated as a unit with a more or less full complement of labor at any one time. During plant production at any one time, the physical ratio of material and labor to fixed plant is comparatively inflexible. Variations in output are generally attained by varying the number of hours worked per day, number of days per week, and the number of shifts of plant operation. As the intensity in plant utilization increases in the time dimension (i.e., more hours per week), the unit-cost curve slopes downward, and the average-variable-cost and marginal-cost curves are more or less constant or linear for a wide range of output (depending, of course, on the magnitude of total fixed cost).

Process engineers may not only design plants for ease of inaugurating overtime and multiple-shift operation for higher output levels but for ease of increasing the rate of output beyond capacity through plant adaptation for a bigger input of components purchased from subcontractors. Heavier reliance on outside suppliers tends to make for constancy in average total cost. By virtue of the above type of plant adaptability, even though a firm's sales decline, plant-layout design can provide for operation at high plant capacity and high company employment through the "pulling in" of outside (subcontracted) work—i.e., through cutting back of procurement of components from suppliers. Moreover, when plant is designed to accommodate changes in product-mix, such production adaptability tends to lower total fixed cost (investment in plant) but somewhat raises unit variable cost (and changeover cost), thus making for greater linearity in average total cost per unit. The inability to stabilize short-term variations in output also tends to raise the level

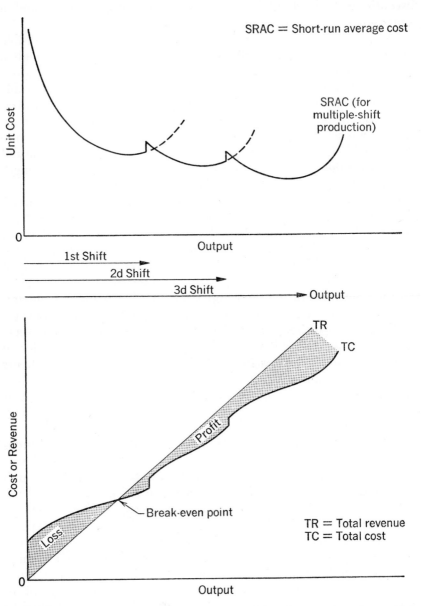

Fig. 4–4. Short-run average-cost curve and break-even chart for multiple-shift production.

of unit cost. Difficulty or errors in estimating sales may, of course, be at the root of irregularity in production and in unit cost. Plant adaptability and variability in operations can, therefore, result in somewhat different short-run cost curves in the operation of the same plant or multiple-plant establishment at different times, excluding the influence of changes in input prices. The impact of differences in production technology, plant divisibility, plant adaptability for varying subcontracting and product-mix, and alternative methods for varying the rate of output do not, of course, occur in isolation. The short-run cost curve reflects the composite influence of these and other factors.

An industry adjusts its output rate and influences unit cost of production by varying the length of the workweek and the number of shifts of plant operation and by putting into operation or by withdrawing idle and high-cost facilities. Short-run cost curves among producers in a given industry would differ to the extent that plants and multiple-plant units differ in type and degree of specialization, depth of production and scope of operations, production technology and divisibility, modernity, and adaptability.

Certain generalizations can nonetheless be made with reference to the *factors influencing the shape of an industry's short-run cost curve.* As an industry, in response to rising demand and selling prices, increases its rate of output through inauguration of a longer workweek and pays overtime wages, the downward-sloping average unit-cost curve will have an angle or kink at the transition to overtime output; and as the industry increases output by putting less efficient facilities into operation, unit average costs move upward (Fig. 4–4). If, in the absence of reserve or idle plant capacity, the industry further increases the rate of output through adoption of second-shift and third-shift operation, the short-run cost curve will again have a small upward angle or kink as the industry pays shift differentials and hires additional supervisory and service personnel (indirect labor for maintenance, inspection, and clerical work) which raise plant overhead expense. When an industry produces at high capacity on a multiple-shift basis, average variable cost per unit in some industries generally moves upward because of an increase in the percentage of the product rejected or scrapped, greater difficulty and expense in coordinating "tight" plant production, a rise in production delays and bottlenecks and in maintenance costs, some rise in input prices as producers bid up the prices of scarce factors, and a rise in inventory-carrying charges if stock-sales ratios increase for whatever reason.

In industry short-term production, rising-cost tendencies and declining-cost tendencies work simultaneously. The spread of high fixed costs in capital-intensive industries often appreciably offsets the rise in variable costs, tending to make for linearity in average unit cost for a wide range of output. Because producers can often anticipate a relatively permanent increase in demand and a rise in price, they generally build plant in advance of increases in demand. This permits regular single-shift operation, usually at a lower-cost level. Thus, except for peak seasonal levels of output, the short-run tendencies toward higher costs and kinks in the short-run cost curve are forestalled by provision of reserve capacity. Productivity gains in industry (usually through equipment replacement and plant modernization) work to lower the level of costs and may wholly or partially offset whatever rise in wages and material prices that may occur.

Short-Run Production and Supply in the Industry

The volume of goods that an industry can supply in the short run largely depends on the size of its productive capacity, that is, on the size of an industry's "over-all plant." The volume of output also depends on the unit cost of output. Unit cost tends to be higher when the volume of business fluctuates appreciably or when production is irregular. Production in the short run is sometimes irregular or unstable, especially in the durable-goods industries. Production may be irregular because of periodic product restyling and remodeling which involve curtailment of output and model changeover. Short-run production may vary because of shift in consumer demand for products and because of seasonality in market demand or in the supply (availability) of raw materials, as in the case of the fishing, wine, and sugar beet industries. Producers in seasonal fields occasionally build up a large finished stock (e.g., automobiles, apparel, air-conditioning units) in the expectation of a strong seasonal surge in demand. If the expected surge fails to materialize, producers cut back output to liquidate excess inventories.

An industry's output is at times pushed to peak capacity because of the development of anticipatory demand. In such cases a large temporary demand develops because buyers anticipate shortages that may result from work stoppages or from interruption of imports and because buyers anticipate a rise in prices. Induced by an expected price rise, customers engage in "forward" buying or "hedge" buying in order to beat an expected price rise. If the work stoppage fails to materialize or if the price hike is smaller than anticipated, buyers, caught with excess inventories, curtail purchases to work off excess stock. During the ensuing period of slack business volume, producers vie for sales by offering quick deliveries, and, because of the short procurement lead-time, buyers find that they can safely cut their material inventory to a low level, thereby conserving working capital. An industry's output and sales may be irregular and unstable because of overexpansion in a competing industry and sharp price competition from substitute products. Synthetic fibers, for example, may compete with natural fibers, television with motion pictures, plastic containers with paper containers, and so on.

The rapidity with which an industry can vary its current rate of output and the lead-time required for expanding plant capacity determines the ease with which an industry can adjust supply. The speed with which an industry can increase or decrease its production determines its ability to adapt to changes in market demand, i.e., its ability to work off a backlog of orders or to build up or to liquidate finished inventories. The ease of varying the rate of output affects an industry's competitive position in cases in which substitute products are closely competitive, for example, when aluminum cables compete with copper cables, when glass containers compete with plastic containers, and when oil and gas compete with coal as a fuel for generating electric power or for heating dwellings and commercial establishments.

The *factors that underlie an industry's short-run elasticity of supply* and determine the speed of varying the rate of output are (1) the amount of unsold finished goods in the distribution pipe line, (2) the adaptability of the production process to quantitative changes in the product-mix, (3) the length of the production interval and the ease of sales forecasting, (4) the ease of varying the length of the workweek, (5) the adaptability of the production process to variations in the input of labor, (6) the amount of available or unused capacity, (7) the ease of increasing output through multiple-shift production and the ease of cutting back output, and (8) the lead-time for procuring materials and labor and the trend of input prices. The foregoing factors (amplified below) influence the shape of the short-run cost curve, and the short-run costs fundamentally underlie short-run elasticity of supply.

The *current supply of goods* depends on the size of the unsold finished stock in the distribution pipeline (i.e., on the current stock-sales ratio). This depends in part on the storability (perishability and physical deterioration) and style obsolescence of goods. Stocks of garments and automobiles, for example, are subject to deterioration or obsolescence, whereas stocks of liquor, coal, cement, and grain are less subject to deterioration. The size of finished stock in the distribution channel is also determined by inventory-carrying charges, economies of bulk buying, the need to make deliveries from stock, and price trends (inflation or deflation). Inflation induces inventory accumulation, and deflation induces inventory liquidation. Occasionally an industry overproduces; it accumulates unsold finished goods in its factories, warehouses, and marketing outlets. Overproduction in the economic sense means that an industry cannot sell its finished goods at prices sufficient to cover costs and yield a normal profit.

Short-run supply and output behavior is influenced by the degree of production adaptability, and this in part depends on the nature of the industry's production technology. Industries that employ analytical processes (processes that break down and transform raw materials into a number of different products) often put out goods in relatively fixed proportions; an increase in the output of one product will give rise to an increase in the output of the joint product in a certain fixed ratio. Industries that employ synthetic processes (processes that assemble components) can, within limits, vary the output quantity of the different items that make up the product-mix. Production facilities in such industries (e.g., wood-working, leather-working, cloth-cutting facilities) are somewhat adaptable to quantitative *changes in the product-mix*. Production lines can be designed to fabricate two or more kinds of components, and assembly lines can be adapted to turn out two or more related products or models. Strip mills in steel-fabricating plants, for example, are generally adaptable to the output of sheet metal as well as light plate metal. Textile mills can generally weave cloth from natural fibers or synthetic fibers. The foregoing features of an industry's production technology permit considerable variation (elasticity) in the output of specific products.

An industry's *production interval* (the time needed to complete a product or a batch from beginning to end) and the ease of production planning and control affect the speed of varying the volume of output and adjusting the supply of finished goods; and they also influence the size of finished stock that must be held and the carrying charges (cost) of holding inventories. Industries with a long production interval can begin to build up finished stocks only after the increased rate of output has reached the end of the production cycle with the enlarged flow of goods. Industries with a short production interval can readily increase or decrease the output of finished goods in order to build up or to deplete finished stock; a shortage or an oversupply of stock can be quickly rectified. The length of an industry's production interval reflects the depth of its over-all production process. A long production interval is generally found in industries turning out high-value intricate products made up of many components that call for time-consuming fabrication and assembly. The production interval is, of course, lengthy in the job-order production of such items as turbines, generators, and ships.

The ease and reliability of forecasting an industry's near-term sales volume facilitate the adjustment of short-run supply. Effective forecasting provides time for better inventory control and production budgeting, permits more economical adjustment of output to sales requirements, and promotes a steadier, more efficient rate of production.

The ease with which an industry can vary the *length of the workweek* affects its ability to adjust output, i.e., affects the elasticity of supply. Most industries adjust the rate of output by varying the length of the workweek. Cutting back production by reducing the length of the workweek (say, from forty to thirty-five hours), rather than by laying off workers, minimizes the disruption of a balanced and trained work force. The inauguration of overtime work is often the fastest way of increasing the input of labor and enlarging output. Increasing output through overtime work rather than through the recruitment of new workers minimizes the dilution of trained supervisory and technical personnel (usually a scarce resource) and avoids the cost of recruiting and training new workers. During the period of a tight labor market, overtime production is often the only alternative to recruiting untrained or marginal labor. But the prospect of continued reliance on overtime operation at premium pay induces an industry to train new workers.

Managers may also vary the rate of output by increasing or decreasing the *input of labor* through hiring or laying off of workers. The ease and cost of varying the rate of output through hirings or layoffs depend upon the degree to which the production process is adaptable to variations in the input of labor, i.e., whether the size of the work force can be varied by small additions and reductions or whether the work force must be varied by large additions or reductions. The rate of operations can be varied in small increments when the production facilities and capacity are divisible, consisting of individual machines or small groups of complementary machines, as is often the case in machine shops, foundries, and press shops. Production in this case can be economically varied by shutting down individual machines or a small group of related machines and laying off workers or by hiring workers and starting up machines. When the production process is indivisible, as in the case of an integrated facility, the rate of output (aside from the overtime method) must be varied in large increments which entail the hiring or layoff of a comparatively large crew of workers. The resulting irregularity in production tends to raise the unit cost of output.

If there is considerable *unused capacity* in the industry, short-run supply tends to be relatively elastic, particularly when output can be increased with only a small rise in average unit costs (more precisely, marginal costs). Under such conditions an increase in market demand and a rise in price will induce a substantial increase in the volume of output through a fuller utilization of available capacity, that is, through overtime operations and the hiring of new workers to man idle facilities and to staff multiple-shift output schedules. The extent to which the volume of output can be increased after overtime and multiple-shift operations have been introduced depends on the amount of available stand-by and marginal capacity. *Increased plant capacity* can sometimes be temporarily achieved by postponing long-term maintenance work, that is, by putting off scheduled overhaul of key facilities. When the industry is operating at peak capacity, short-run supply at the high ranges of output will be comparatively inelastic; even a sharp rise in price will not induce much increase in output. An industry can sometimes draw in additional output capacity (usually at a higher production cost) by subcontracting work to producers with available capacity who are normally "outside" the industry but who can readily tool up for the required production.

The *lead-time for procuring materials* from suppliers influences the speed of increasing the rate of output. Production planners prepare output schedules and stipulate the required forward buying on the basis of the lead-time for procuring materials as well as on the basis of the production interval and the sales-forecasting period. The procurement lead-time often depends on the general level of business. During periods of low business activity, suppliers make quick deliveries. Because of the faster procurement and replenishment of raw-material stocks, producers buy on a hand-to-mouth basis and carry smaller inventories. Thus, when there is an ample supply of raw materials and available capacity, output and supply of finished goods in manufacturing industries tend to be comparatively sensitive to changes in demand and in price. During periods of peak business activity, procurement lead-time is longer, and raw-material inventory levels tend to be proportionately higher. Inventory-carrying charges are also higher.

When an industry pushes its production rate to a high level through overtime and multiple-shift operations, it is often confronted by one or more bottlenecks that cause delays and a rise in the unit cost of output. The production delay may be due to capacity limitation at some particular stage or operation in processing, to machine failures at key operations, to a shortage of certain grades of skilled labor, to a shortage in material or components because of their scarcity, or to delays in transportation.

After operating at a peak level of output for a time, an industry may find a *reduction in rate of output* necessary in order to liquidate finished stocks which have been built up in anticipation of a heavy demand that failed to materialize. Producers may successively cut the volume of output by shutting down equipment, by eliminating the second (or third) shift, by eliminating overtime and reducing the length of the workweek, or by closing down high-cost plants and concentrating production in the more efficient plants. The method used for cutting back output of course affects the unit cost of production.

If capacity has been enlarged in a highly competitive industry and prices have declined, production will continue at a relatively high level so long as sales receipts cover the variable cost of doing business. A competitive industry with sizable excess capacity will thus tend to have a highly elastic short-run supply schedule. A fall in demand and price will not result in a decline in capacity until older plant facilities wear out. The short-run supply curve in monopolistic industries tends to be somewhat elastic in the sense that firms tend to hold back production in order that they may not depress prices or accumulate excess finished goods.

Thus, the shape of the short-run cost curve (the change in the average unit cost) is determined by the principle of increasing and diminishing returns in the utilization of fixed plant, the productivity of plant facilities over the range of output, the trend of input prices, and other factors that underlie the elasticity of supply outlined above. Average cost per unit declines as plant capacity is put to productive use because fixed costs are spread over a larger number of units. As output is increased beyond the optimum volume of production, average cost per unit rises largely because the additional labor employed is combined with smaller amounts of productive capacity; the higher variable cost (particularly labor cost) per unit more than offsets the lower fixed cost per unit.

Long-Run Cost for the Representative Firm

Managers in their long-range planning for plant expansion and other capital projects find that all productive factors are variable and that there are no fixed costs. When managers build successively larger plants and produce at capacity, unit cost declines because of economies of scale; long-run average cost varies with the size or scale of plant capacity. But once a plant of a given size is established, unit cost will vary with changes in the rate of output. Thus,

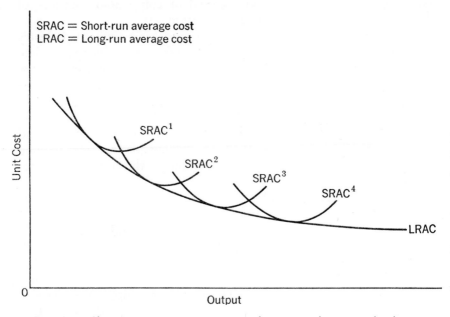

Fig. 4–5. Short-run average-cost curves shown in relation to the long-run average-cost curve.

for the operational counterpart to the short-period cost-output relation or function, we have the long-period cost-size relationship which reflects the economies of scale.

The short-run average-cost curves ($SRAC^1$, $SRAC^2$, etc.) in Figure 4–5 show how average cost varies with rate of output for plants (or multiplant units) of alternative size or capacity. In Figure 4–5 the broad long-run average-cost curve ($LRAC$) (drawn tangent to each of the $SRAC$ curves) envelops a succession of short-run curves and shows how the theoretical long-run average cost (i.e., unit cost at its lowest point for each scale of plant or multiplant combination) declines with increases in the size or scale of productive capacity.

In Figure 4–5 a small-scale plant with high unit-cost capacity is represented by the short-run-cost curve $SRAC^1$; an optimum-sized plant or multiplant combination, with its low unit-cost capacity range stemming from the full exploitation of economies of scale inherent in production technology, is represented by the short-run cost curve $SRAC^4$. With successive increases in productive capacity (single-plant followed by multiplant capacity), long-run average cost declines, and then the average cost tends to level off and become more or less linear for the range of capacity that is likely to be built (assuming no changes in technology and price of input factors). The long-run average cost turns upward only to the extent

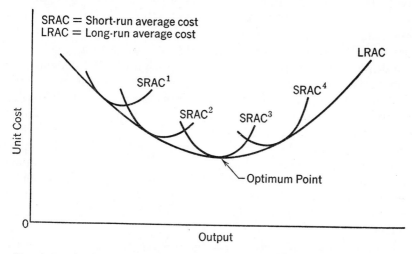

Fig. 4–6. The long-run average-cost curve, the hypothetical **U**-shaped long-run planning curve, enveloping the short-run average-cost curves.

that diseconomies in the management of plant production are permitted to develop.

Since it is generally assumed that a capacity beyond the optimum size leads to higher long-run average cost because of the rise of diseconomies in production management, the shape of the LRAC curve is usually hypothesized as a **U**-shaped curve (Fig. 4–6). The **U**-shaped curve is generally designated as a "planning curve" because it is assumed to serve as a guide for the selection of plant size, and it cautions against and forestalls selection of a plant scale that results in higher long-run average costs due to diseconomies in management.

A **U**-shaped planning curve may be hypothesized if we assume that a larger-scale capacity is provided only through the erection of a bigger single plant or through the successive enlargement of a single plant, and that an increase in scale is not accompanied by any restructuring in the organization of the managerial function. This, of course, is usually not the case for capacity scale beyond optimum-sized plant as it would occur in actuality, assuming other things being equal. In actual experience, when managers are at any given time selecting a capacity scale (the size of a production unit) from among alternative sizes of capacity, they select the size of capacity on the basis of anticipated production technology and the price of input factors.

When executive managers stipulate the provision of a comparatively large output capacity for particular products or when they successively increase the scale of productive capacity in large increments, industrial engineers find that they can provide efficiently managed low-cost productive capacity by designing and setting up a multiplant combination and by setting up a parallel decentralized managerial organization which forestalls the emergence of diseconomies from ill coordination of the specialized functions involved in production operations. A *decentralized managerial organization* provides for managerial division of labor in terms of the level of managerial responsibility. Thus, operating managers, such as plant superintendents (who head more or less autonomous plant-management units), devote their efforts exclusively to the management of single plants; while the top executive group assumes responsibility for formulating long-range investment plans and over-all company policy.

If we assume that a firm's production is largely confined to that of a single industry, the general shape of its LRAC curve depends on whether the industry produces under conditions of decreasing, constant, or increasing long-run average costs. The LRAC curve for a big oligopoly firm will tend to correspond more or less to the industry's long-run cost curve. But the concept of long-run average costs rules for the hypothesized static situation. A big oligopoly producer in an increasing-cost industry may, for instance, have a broad saucer-shaped SRAC curve. Market demand, however, may not be of a size at which the firm produces in the rising-cost range of capacity. In actual business operations over time (i.e., in the dynamic situation), a producer is generally able to lower his unit cost for a given volume of output through adoption of technological improvements and other methods that achieve a gain in productivity.

A big oligopoly producer in a decreasing-cost industry may have a LRAC curve which slopes downward for a wide range of capacity before it becomes somewhat linear. Long-run average costs, however, may decline for any range of scale that is likely to be built. The size of firms and the scale of productive capacity are limited by "the scope of the market." When markets are relatively small, the scale of plants may not achieve the size at which considerable economies obtain. In industries characterized by a comparatively small optimum size for the firm, the percentage of firms of optimum size (or larger) would obviously be proportionately greater. When producers sell in large markets, a bigger percentage of the firms and plants will be of optimum size than when producers sell in small markets.

When the optimum size for the firm is larger than that for productive capacity (which is often the case when the product sells in a large national market), economies of scale for the firm lower the level of the LRAC curve. In this case a big firm may be comprised of a large chain of duplicate plants, or it may be comprised of two or more multiplant combinations (groups of related plants), each selling in a separate regional market.

Economies of scale for the firm essentially stem from the use of managerial and business specialists, from large-quantity procurement which lowers input prices for materials and contractual services, from large-scale low-cost financing, from extensive research which attains big technological gains, and from large-scale marketing which lowers distribution and promotion cost per unit of output.

Scale economies in distribution are proportionately larger when a firm sells a demand-related product line. In such cases managers must balance the diseconomies from scale in production against the relatively big economies from scale in distribution as well as against the competitive advantages gained from marketing demand-related goods.

An increase in the size of the firm brings about *economies in research* which accelerate the pace of technological advance. Large firms spread the cost of big outlays for research over a large volume of output. At any given time a large enterprise would generally employ technology of higher productivity than a smaller firm not only because of economies and greater mechanization by virtue of bigger scale in production but also because of technological advances created in large laboratories by virtue of scale in the firm. Moreover, if we assume the dynamic (the "real") situation, as technological improvements are introduced in production over time (through capital replacement, modernization, and expansion), the level of unit cost of production drops. Progress in technology tends also to increase the scale of the optimum-sized plant and the optimum-sized multiplant combination through development of more productive facilities and a fall in the capital-output ratio. The cost-reduction impacts of technological progress over time would be indicated by the successive lowering of the static *LRAC* curve for the range of capacity, as shown in Figure 4–7.

Diseconomies in the firm tend to grow largely out of excessive or illogical product diversification and overextended scope of business activity. Though a diversified firm's volume of dollar sales may be large, its sales may be comprised of products and services in widely different industries, a high proportion of which may be produced in relatively small quantities at comparatively high unit cost.

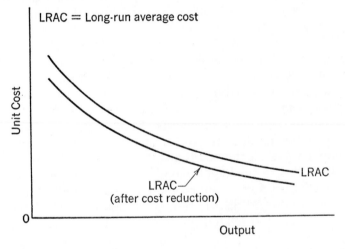

Fig. 4–7. A drop in the long-run average-cost curve obtained through adoption of cost-reducing technological improvements.

As a consequence the immense diversity in the range of top-management problems and in the scope of decision making may exceed executive capacity and wisdom in formulating long-range plans and in investing company funds in the fields of highest return. But the firm's gain from large-scale research may, however, offset these managerial diseconomies.

The overspecialization of an enterprise also can result in a waste of resources and high-cost operation. An overspecialized enterprise is vulnerable to sharp shifts in market demand and to technological obsolescence of products and processes. The utilization of narrowly specialized processing methods and the resulting absence of an adequate degree of adaptability often make it uneconomical to introduce some types of technical improvements. The indivisibility in the facilities of highly integrated processes tends to forestall piecemeal plant modernization and adoption of improved processing facilities.

STRUCTURAL FACTORS INFLUENCING THE LONG-RUN COST CURVE FOR PRODUCTION AND THE MEASUREMENT OF COST. In the long-run growth and development of an enterprise, the relevant cost-size relationship is essentially an anticipated (estimated) relationship. Managers find little occasion for need to measure empirically the cost-size function for current and past conditions. The projection of a cost-size relationship on the basis of historical data would be a measurement which excludes changes in production technology, changes in the price of input factors, changes in the product-mix, changes in the design of the multiplant system, and so on.

A realistic measurement projecting long-run cost is based on the *engineering method.* The engineering method for computing the empirical cost-size function is a measurement of the anticipated physical input-output relationship which, in turn, is expressed in monetary terms. The measurement and projection of the cost-size relationship for future conditions involves an estimate of the anticipated product-mix, production technology, price of input factors, scale of output, and multiplant combination. The engineering estimate of future cost-size relationship would thus take into account technological and structural changes in the organization of production and in the multiple-plant system that are associated with successive increases in the scale of output in the given industry.

The *structural factors that shape the long-run production-cost curve* include (1) economies of scale from production technology and efficient combination of factors, (2) degree of divisibility in plant facilities, (3) economies from vertical integration, (4) degree of physical adaptability in plant, (5) organizational adaptation to changes in the multiple-plant combination, and (6) ease of plant dispersal. These factors which structure the long-run cost curve for an enterprise are traced below.

Economies of scale from production technology and capital obtain so long as successively larger capacity permits greater division of labor and more extensive use of specialized production methods and highly mechanized facilities which reduce the input of productive factors. Successive increases in scale typically permit utilization of the more efficient methods and techniques available in the existing state of technological art.

The optimum size of the plant and the multiplant combination is determined by the scale of output required to utilize fully and economically relatively indivisible productive factors. Optimum size tends to be larger when production involves the use of specialized high-priced technicians and specialized high-capacity equipment. Because of the comparative indivisibility and high productivity of plant facilities in many fields of modern manufacturing, mining, and transportation, increases in scale can only be made in relatively large increments. The capacity balance among indivisible production and service facilities is more economically obtained in the higher ranges of multiplant capacity.

In selecting processes and in designing a plant or a multiplant combination, engineers provide the kind and degree of plant and production adaptability required to meet anticipated shifts in output and sales. Though plant adaptability tends to ward off partially the impact of obsolescence and to lower the cost of plant revisions, it does so at the sacrifice of somewhat greater economies that would obtain from more extensive specialization in production. The tendency toward economies of scale is thus somewhat lessened when plants are designed for greater adaptability to changes in product-mix and adaptability to changeover or conversion of facilities to new model or new product output. On the other hand, the design of capital-intensive plants for ease in accelerating the rate of output through multiple-shift production lowers the short-run unit cost of output for the higher reaches of output capacity.

With increases in the scale of productive capacity and volume of output of given products, managers generally find it profitable to produce a larger proportion of their component parts, material needs, utilities, and other services within their own establishments rather than to buy these items from outside suppliers. Thus, with increases in scale, managers find that an increase in the depth of production obtains economies from vertical integration. As the depth of production in a multiple-plant system increases, output in terms of value-added grows faster than output in physical units. This change in the physical structure of production tends to obscure somewhat the measurement of the cost-size relationship.

If economies of scale from an increase in capacity occur when production shifts from a small shop to a large plant, economies of scale from the same "state of technological art" (which includes the managerial-organizational art) achieve lower long-run average cost when a larger rationally designed multiplant combination is set up. When management stipulates the establishment of large output capacity to put out a given product, industrial engineers would usually design and erect a multiplant combination rather than a single giant plant, because their comparative cost study (which includes the expense and effectiveness of plant management) would generally indicate the former to be more efficient for the anticipated operating conditions. In designing a multiplant system, production managers are guided by comparative-cost analysis in the selection of the most appropriate and efficient multiplant combination from among alternatives.

Engineers design a multiple-plant system by breaking down the over-all production process into logical subdivisions and allocating the various phases of production to separate plants. The larger the scale of capacity to be provided, the more readily can the over-all process be subdivided into phases and set up as specialized optimum-sized plants. The constituent plants in a multiplant system may be specialized according to stage of processing (particularly when the over-all process is lengthy and consists of well-defined, easily separable phases), according to finished product (when the product line consists of technically distinct items), or, as is often the case, according to some economical combination of the foregoing.

An increase in the scale of production and in the multiplicity of plants gives rise to certain *economies that derive from flexibility in locating plants*. Because multiple-plant production is segmented into plants embodying different phases of production, constituent plants can be located in areas and at sites where the price of input factors and the cost of distributing finished goods are the lowest. By permitting greater geographical dispersal of plants, multiple-plant production obtains greater mobility in physical facilities and more efficient use of productive factors as a whole. Appropriately designed multiple-plant combinations also make for ease of expansion in capacity.

Because the geographical size and density of an industry's market influence the organization pattern of a multiplant combination for a given scale of output, they influence the level of its LRAC curve. A geographically broad market, because it encourages the erection and dispersal of smaller duplicate branch plants (particularly for the output of finished products costly to ship), tends to make for higher long-run average costs. A market of the same size within the confines of a smaller geographical area (i.e., a denser market), because it permits concentration of output in fewer but larger plants serviced by large auxiliary facilities, tends to make for lower long-run average costs.

Decreasing-cost industries which produce for large markets tend to be comprised of large multiplant firms. In selecting the appropriate scale of capacity for their market, oligopolistic producers in such industries take into account the lower unit cost obtained from larger-scale output, and they take into account the size of effective demand at different price levels (i.e., they consider the elasticity of demand). On the basis of the anticipated trend of long-run unit cost relative to the range of likely selling prices, producers can roughly gauge the range of capacity that will be most profitable to establish. To the extent that the market is price competitive, producers will tend to select larger-scale capacity, so long as unit cost declines as capacity is increased and the lowering of price expands sales and enlarges total profits on the basis of a large volume of business.

Because in a decreasing-cost industry a bigger plant or multiplant combination produces at lower costs, managers often find it more profitable to erect a larger plant. Managers, instead of selecting a smaller plant which they would utilize at near capacity, can often profitably select a larger-scale plant or multiplant combination with lower unit-cost capacity and "underuse" the plant in the output of goods. A large, new plant that is to replace a smaller, older plant or is to compete with older establishments can produce at lower unit cost not only because of the economies of scale but because new production facilities embody the latest technological improvements and cost-reduction techniques and because they are typically designed to process improved or cheaper materials.

In the dynamic, long-run situation managers must deal with the problem of revising and adjusting productive capacity. The restructuring of a going concern's multiplant system (or some part of the system) for the output of a forward-looking product line calls for varying degrees of plant conversion and re-equipping, disposal, or abandonment of certain facilities and for the addition and integration of new plants and equipment at various points in the system. Plant capacity may be added through erection, purchase of an existing plant, leasing, or the acquisition of a subsidiary through the purchase of a controlling interest.

Long-Run Cost and Supply in the Industry

The long-run cost curve essentially underlies long-run supply. The long-run average-cost curve (like the short-run cost curve) is not an entity in itself. As previously indicated, it is largely determined by (1) the effectiveness of product design, (2) the productivity of the technology employed, (3) the proportionality in the combination of productive factors, and (4) the emergence of internal and external economies and tendencies toward decreasing cost.

As an industry expands its output capacity, tendencies toward decreasing costs and toward increasing costs are simultaneously at work, assuming no change in technology. In all industries the forces working toward decreasing costs and those working toward increasing costs are in some kind of balance. Whether long-run costs decline or increase depends on the relative strength of the two tendencies. Decreasing-cost tendencies may dominate for a given range of capacity and output, and increasing-cost tendencies may dominate for the following range of capacity. In some cases the two tendencies are somewhat in balance so as to result in constant long-run average costs over a wide range of output capacity.

If the rising-cost tendencies prevail, as is often the case in extractive industries, the field of production is designated an "increasing-cost industry." If the declining-cost tendencies prevail, the field of production is called a "decreasing-cost industry." Manufacturing industries are generally characterized by declining costs for a wide range of capacity, but if capacity is extended far enough, tendencies toward rising costs develop. The concept of the LRAC curve, of course, assumes technology to be constant. But, as discussed later, advances in technology can and do drop the level of the long-run average-cost curve.

Internal and external economies that develop as a result of expansion of industry lower the long-run average cost of production. The extent to which these economies lower long-run costs varies with the industry. *Internal economies* are those that arise within a firm's plants or multiple-plant system. As a firm expands its plants or its multiple-plant system, it can more extensively employ mass-production methods of output. Internal economies essentially derive from specialization and efficiencies that inhere in large-scale operations and in vertical integration of production. Internal economies also accrue from large-scale distribution.[1]

External economies are those that arise from developments outside the individual firm and can generally be reaped by all producers in the industry. As the industry expands, its large demand for plant equipment leads to the growth of specialized producers of machines who supply equipment at lower cost. Improvement and greater standardization in materials reduce input prices for the industry as a whole. Subcontractors and specialized producers generally arise

---

[1] Internal economies from large-scale operations tend to reduce the number of firms in the industry. If the industry did not grow beyond a few large efficient plants, there would be a strong tendency toward oligopoly or monopoly, because new firms entering the industry must, of necessity, begin by producing on a small scale at comparatively high costs. This would be particularly true when economies accrue from vertical integration and when output based on subcontracting for the supply of semifabricated materials and components is not readily available.

to supply components and accessories economically to the industry. External economies thus stem from the general development of an industry and an industrial area as a whole. Greater increasing returns, for instance, derive from the intensive utilization of well-developed, economic-overhead industries in an area—e.g., transportation, utilities, specialized banking services, industrial hospitals, and other service establishments.

The increasing returns from large-scale operations are subject to certain countertendencies. As an industry expands beyond a certain size, tendencies toward rising long-run cost become more pronounced. The greater bureaucratic red tape that tends to develop in large, highly centralized firms lowers efficiency. The practice of "building ahead of demand" by capital-intensive industries creates at times a considerable amount of idle capacity which raises the overhead cost per unit of output. Producers may find it necessary to increase expenditures for advertising and promotion in order to expand sales and utilize productive capacity.

Because input prices of productive factors affect the cost of the final product, the elasticity in the supply of materials and labor influences the cost of production. Industries using large amounts of scarce materials are often directly or indirectly subject to increasing-cost tendencies. In agriculture and other extractive industries expansion beyond a certain point tends to result in rising long-run average costs because the required productive agents are limited in quantity (assuming, of course, no change in technology). Thus, if expansion is carried far enough, particularly in industries heavily dependent on scarce resources, increasing pressure on natural resources tends to raise long-run costs.

In manufacturing industries in which materials account for a high proportion of the unit cost of the product (e.g., meat packing, beet sugar refining), rising material-input prices partially offset the tendency toward decreasing cost. But capital-intensive industries that expand rapidly during depression years or periods of considerable unemployment (e.g., the chemical and the frozen-food industries in the 1930's) can often obtain a low long-run cost curve for the period because of the low investment outlays for acquisition of plant and equipment and because of low material and labor costs. The expansion of an industry during periods of full employment and a tight economy can only be accomplished by drawing productive agents away from other industries or by bringing into use poor resources. Hence, the utilization of marginal factors and the bidding away of factors from other uses raise input prices, tending to increase costs.

In an advanced economy the foregoing forces working to raise long-run costs are often directly or indirectly offset by *progress in technology*. When an industry reduces production and material costs through technological advances, it successively lowers the level of long-run costs. Progress in agriculture, for instance, lowers the long-run costs through improved seed and plants, improved chemical fertilizers, and improved methods of cultivation and mechanization. The resulting increase in the output per acre as well as in output per man-hour involves greater capital input and, as a consequence, an increase in the marginal productivity of land. This increase in marginal productivity also occurs indirectly: the development and expansion in the output of synthetic fiber displaces cotton fiber and releases land for other types of agricultural output.

Technological progress can also work to offset the rise in the cost of material from resources that tend toward scarcity. An industry's material supply may be increased and input prices lowered through improved methods of discovery and extraction, as in the case of the oil industry. The improvement of, and greater uniformity in, the quality of materials reduce the processing cost per unit of output. When scarce materials become costly, an industry is not infrequently successful in developing a cheaper substitute material. It is often through the shift to a material produced under conditions of increasing returns that an industry changes the slope of its long-run cost curve. Industries processing crude materials can often lower input prices through greater by-product output. Cost reduction in the chemical industry, for instance, is obtained not only through the development and use of larger stills, evaporators, and filter processes but also through the greater yield in total product output from the same raw materials.

Rapid advances in an industry's production technology often sharply lower the long-run cost curve. The introduction of the automatic loom in the textile industry, the rotary kiln in the cement industry, the continuous rolling mill in the steel industry, and automated processes in the automobile industry are illustrative of rapid advances that lower the long-run cost curve. The continued process of "perfecting the factory" also obtains a successive lowering of long-run average costs. Long-run costs also tend to decline when the competitive process eliminates marginal producers in the industry and when producers introduce industry-wide rationalization measures.

RATIONALIZATION IN THE INDUSTRY. A "rationalized" industry is one that has evolved the type of industry structure and organizational arrangements and practices that fully attain the technological and economic potential inherent in the industry. The rationalization of an industry is advanced by economic analysis and by a specialized application of scientific management to the industry-wide structural aspects and practices. A "rationalization movement" attains industry-wide technological efficiency and economies through a logical extension of vertical integration and horizontal combinations of plants, through the adoption of a well-designed standardization program for all producers, and through the development of auxiliary establishments that serve the industry as a whole. The steel, automobile, and petroleum industries have, through mergers, expansion, and interfirm cooperation, achieved rationalization to varying degrees.

Extensive *vertical integration* is possible in industries comprised of a long sequential series of plants that process materials to final completion of the product. The larger the scale of production and the more extensive the application of mass-production technology, the greater is the amount of vertical integration possible. When it is feasible, vertical integration among plants attains economies by permitting greater specialization of plants, by eliminating some terminal operations and inventory stocks which are superfluous when processes are integrated, and by permitting more effective over-all planning and coordination of production. Because of the need for production adaptability, producers sometimes limit the degree of vertical integration. Large-scale producers of consumer durable goods who periodically remodel and restyle their products often prefer to purchase parts and assembled units from outside suppliers rather than produce these items in their own plants. In this way they avoid the cost and problem of revising processes and retooling when new-model components are to be manufactured.

When it is economically feasible, *horizontal combinations* attain control over duplicate branch plants engaged in the same processing stage of production. Centralized home-office departments can often efficiently perform many of the service functions (purchasing, selling, market research, promotion) for the combination as a whole. Horizontal combinations attain greater stability in over-all sales, ease of cutting back or increasing the production volume, quick adaptability to regional shifts in demand, and in other aspects.

A rationalization trend in the industry leads to the growth of highly *specialized producers* of machinery and tooling who concentrate in the output of the type of equipment that meets the specific needs of the industry. The industry acquires specialized suppliers who produce on a large scale standard items, components, or services purchased in comparatively small quantities by the many producers in the industry. The latter producers would be unable to turn out these items economically since they consume the items in limited amounts.

Monopolistic "cooperative" arrangements and cartels have been agencies for the promotion of industry rationalization. But cartels typically go beyond the rational structuring of the industry for long-run economic gain. They often "rationalize" the market and competition in a manner that controls the market (e.g., through market pools and sales-allocation schemes), regulates and administers prices on an industry-wide basis, limits the availability of the latest technology only to members, and restricts entry of new producers into the industry. Cartels generally assure the "competitive position" of member producers. Their monopolistic objectives lead to excessive trade restrictions and government export subsidies. In their net effect they stifle the growth of the industry itself and accentuate cyclical fluctuations. The subtle nature of their arrangements sometimes makes it difficult to distinguish between "economic" rationalization and "cartelized" rationalization, which have somewhat opposite effects on the trend of long-run supply.

LONG-RUN SUPPLY. An industry's long-run supply schedule is essentially based on its long-run cost trend associated with changes in output capacity. An industry's long-run cost curve reflects the relationship between cost and increases in productive capacity, given sufficient time for expansion of capacity and organization of productive factors. Changes in an industry's output capacity and long-run supply are induced by the trend of long-run costs and by changes in market demand and selling prices. A persistent fall in the price of goods will divert resources away from the output of unprofitable goods (resulting in a shrinkage of the industry's capacity) to the output of goods that are profitable to produce and sell. In the long run an industry's capacity and supply of goods tend to increase gradually because of productivity gains stemming from internal and external economies.

The *factors that underlie an industry's long-run elasticity of supply* include (1) the effectiveness of long-range forecasting of demand, (2) the adaptability (convertibility) of productive facilities, (3) the lead-time for expansion of capacity, (4) the relative scarcity of productive factors, (5) the extent to which the industry tends to hold excess capacity, and (6) the degree of rationalization in the industry. The foregoing factors also, of course, influence an industry's long-run cost of production, as has been earlier indicated.

The longer the time period and the more remote the delivery date, the greater the opportunity for adjusting output and capacity to changes in demand and price and to changes in costs, and the greater, generally, is the elasticity of supply. The long-run elasticity of supply (the ease of varying productive capacity) thus depends on the ease and reliability of long-range forecasting of demand. Utilities, on the basis of population growth and building permits, are generally able to make comparatively reliable forecasts of long-run demand. Such forecasts provide ample time for orderly and more economical expansion of capacity.

The elasticity of long-run supply also depends on the adaptability of productive facilities—the ease of converting plant to other productive uses. Because of the similarity of production technology among certain industries, capacity in one industry may be cut back by converting idle facilities to the output of products of an industry in which there is a shortage of capacity. Late-stage manufacturing industries that put out assembled products usually have a greater degree of production convertibility than early-stage industries.

Many late-stage industries can convert their facilities and processes to the manufacture of other types of final products that are made from the same kinds of materials. A metalworking plant or a garment plant can often convert to the output of many kinds of end products made from the same types of materials. Chemical plants and oil refineries, on the other hand, can usually produce only the kind of products for which they were designed. In many cases, however, a certain amount of plant adaptability can be provided for in the initial design and selection of processes without much sacrifice in the level of productivity.

An industry's long-run supply would tend to be inelastic if existing capacity is not readily adaptable to the output of other types of products, if capital and labor cannot readily enter the industry, or if it is time-consuming or costly for producers to expand capacity. The long-run elasticity of supply thus depends on the ease or difficulty with which capacity can be expanded and additional raw materials and labor drawn into the industry and on the time required for existing plant to wear out or be converted to other productive uses. Producers can draw capital out of the industry (disinvest) by not replacing productive facilities which are fully depreciated. An industry's long-run elasticity of supply would thus be influenced by the magnitude of investment required to create capacity (i.e., by the capital-output ratio) and by the length of time required to expand capacity. The lead-time for plant expansion in "competing" industries producing close substitute products would also influence the long-run elasticity of supply.

An industry's lead-time involves the interval required to design, locate, and erect new plants and to commence production. The lead-time depends on the complexity of processes, the amount of special-purpose equipment that must be built to specification, the time required to lay out and erect the plant, and the time required to break in the work force and eliminate the flaws in the process before the plant can produce on a commercial basis. The lead-time for dairies, bakeries, and printing plants would be comparatively short because the structures are comparatively simple and equipment is of standard make and available from manufacturers' stock. The lead-time for pulp plants, ore beneficiation and reduction plants, blast furnaces, and other capital-intensive facilities would generally be comparatively long.

Long-run supply thus tends to be more elastic when plant expansion does not rely on heavy investment in productive facilities and on scarce productive factors (e.g., highly technical, special-purpose equipment and skilled labor). An industry's elasticity of supply is sometimes influenced by the lead-time required to expand the output of the raw materials it uses. The elasticity of material supply depends on such factors as the size of proved reserve of resource deposits, the availability of suitable substitute materials, the extent of governmental support or stabilization of raw-material prices, and the amount of excess capacity in the supply industries.

CAPACITY UTILIZATION. Idle or excess capacity exists when an industry over time does not produce and sell as large a volume of goods as its mines, plants, or distributive outlets are equipped to supply. Excess output capacity tends to grow out of certain technological developments and frictional changes in industry and certain structural characteristics of industry.

Rapid technological advances sometimes increase productive capacity more quickly than the growth of demand for goods. The development of processes to put out new substitute products that displace older products can quickly enlarge over-all productive capacity. The development of processes to put out synthetic fibers and plastics, for instance, partially displaced cotton textiles and natural leather, giving rise to short-term idle capacity in the industries producing the latter products. When innovations and capital-savings improvements call for comparatively small investment outlays for their commercial exploitation, producers are quick to adopt the improved methods and facilities because of the cost savings and profit opportunities they offer. Though the new facilities and processes generally render obsolete older capacity, old facilities, rather than being discarded, are sometimes held as stand-by facilities and are sometimes converted to other productive uses. When demand and selling prices are low, the less efficient (or marginal) facilities lie idle. But if production costs fall because of a drop in input prices or if selling prices and demand turn up, producers find that they can put idle marginal facilities to profitable use.

Technical improvements that increase a product's durability and life span not only tend to reduce replacement demand but proportionately increase an industry's capacity in terms of "product utility" produced. The life span of tires, radios, and many household appliances, for instance, has tended to increase over time.

Certain frictional and secular changes in industry at times give rise to idle capacity. Pronounced shifts in market demand from one product to another can create idle capacity. The shift in consumer demand from coal to oil and natural gas has added to the coal industry's unused capacity occasioned by wartime expansion. The erection of new plants in more favorable locations and in regions of growing population and demand may, for a time, render capacity idle in the older areas. Regional shifts of population create some idle capacity in older emigrating areas, and the movement of population to suburban areas often causes idle capacity in urban distributive and service enterprises. Unused capacity from the above types of sources is generally absorbed by the long-term rise in aggregate demand stemming from growth of population and purchasing power.

Idle capacity tends to develop out of monopolistic pricing practices; firms in oligopolistic industries would likely hold back their output volume in order to maintain profitable prices or prevent prices from declining. Oligopolistic market situations tend to forestall the long-run movement of an industry toward a "position of equilibrium" wherein firms would operate closer to the optimum rate of output. During periods of sharp advances in demand, however, a firm typically increases its production rate to a point beyond optimum capacity, that is, unless the firm has provided for "extra" capacity in anticipation of such an increase in demand. As a competitive policy many producers (notably those in fields involving a long lead-time for expansion), in fact, do provide for a planned reserve capacity as a contingency in anticipation of demand increases.

Producers, ever intent on increasing their market shares, do not like to be handicapped in the race for increased sales volume and new markets. They therefore often "build ahead of demand" and acquire some extra or reserve capacity for competitive purposes. Instead of building a smaller plant which they would use at near capacity, producers not infrequently build and only partially use a larger-scale plant which produces at lower cost and also provides desired reserve capacity. Reserve capacity is sometimes provided through a plant-layout design (including some stand-by equipment) that permits quick inauguration of multiple-shift production, with anticipated bottlenecks removed in advance. Producers generally acquire planned excess capacity in anticipation of a demand up-swing that may arise from a rapid cyclical increase in general business, inflation-induced business expansion, and the like. Through their ability to maintain quick delivery on the basis of ample capacity in all lines of output, oligopolistic firms aim not only to beat their rivals to new demand and to the demand that crops up when marginal producers drop out but to prevent new competitors from getting a foothold in the industry. Though every firm may not hold excess capacity or carry the same amount of extra capacity, planned excess capacity may exist in an industry as a whole. There is, of course, no practical basis or yardstick for identifying or measuring what portion of capacity is "undesired" excess capacity and what portion is "planned" excess capacity.

Because of the comparative indivisibility of plant facilities in many industries and the durability (longevity) of equipment, producers cannot always expand plant capacity in small increments or stages. In expanding a plant they must for technical reasons add equipment of certain minimum size, and in building an additional branch plant, they must erect a plant of a minimum economic size to obtain the available level of productivity. In order that they may be in a position to capture their share of the anticipated increase in demand, each producer, in adding plant equipment, must of necessity create capacity in excess of his immediate requirements. Since many producers tend to build ahead of demand, the total amount of "duplicated" extra capacity may at times be considerable. Moreover, when firms build branch plants or distribution establishments in suburban areas and in regions of expanding markets or build plants to penetrate new markets, they are generally obliged to carry idle capacity for a certain period, since it takes time to promote sales and become established.

In some cases unused capacity continues to mount beyond the point where an industry has ample reserve capacity to meet anticipated demand. If desirable alternative investment opportunities are comparatively absent, large firms may find it profitable to invest internal funds in vertical expansion, whereby new capacity is created through greater forward or backward integration. These firms can then put their newly added facilities into operation by pulling in (not renewing) subcontracted work performed by supplier-firms that produce materials or components. Automobile producers, large department stores, and certain chain food stores sometimes build plants to meet some of their supply needs. If the former supplier-firms cannot find adequate markets or cannot convert their production capability to the output of products with expanding markets, their production capability adds to the industry's idle capacity.

During prosperity and boom times overoptimistic producers tend to expand capacity in anticipation of greater increases in demand. When the anticipated demand fails to measure up to expectations, producers cut back expansion plans and stretch out capital projects. But, because of the long lead-time in some industries, a substantial amount of the capacity under construction in these fields is generally carried to completion. Hence, some industries tend to be caught with an expanded production capability greater than that of their usual planned reserve capacity. Higher total fixed cost adds to unit costs during a period when sales volume and revenue begin to decline.

The maintenance of high prices in the face of shrinking demand during periods of recession tends to further the decline in sales volume and add to idle capacity. Industries with low break-even points are generally able to maintain earnings. Firms operating below their break-even points can stay in business so long as they are able to cover their variable costs. Capacity reduction and disinvestment in overexpanded industries are usually very slow so that idle capacity can persist for a long period of time. The retirement of overextended capacity tends to be delayed in instances in which large diversified firms sustain or subsidize for a time their low-volume unprofitable lines of business from the earnings of their more profitable lines.[2] The extent of unused capacity in a given industry depends on the magnitude and shifts in the growth factors (expansion of population and aggregate demand, technological advance, etc.) which, more or less, account for different rates of growth among industries. An analysis of the factors underlying an industry's growth trend follows.

INDUSTRY GROWTH TREND: DEMAND ANALYSIS

An industry's evolutionary development is reflected by its growth trend as well as by the changes in its structural pattern. Industry

---

[2] High fixed costs incident to widespread excess capacity in an era of improved methods for administering prices may be a factor in inflation.

growth is best measured by the trend in volume of output in terms of value added in production computed in constant dollars. Even though value-added as a yardstick of output neglects product improvement, value-added is generally the most suitable available gauge of growth because it takes into account changes in the product-mix and the addition of new items to an industry's product cov-

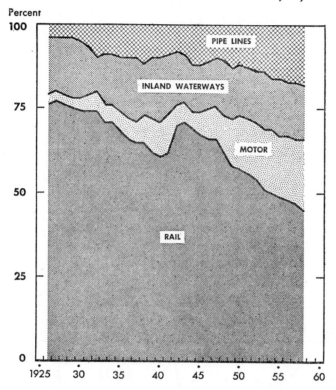

Fig. 4–8. Shifts in relative standing within an industry group illustrated by intercity ton-miles by all carriers. (U.S. Department of Commerce, *Survey of Current Business,* vol. 39 [June, 1959]: p. 5.)

erage. The growth trend of an industry can be expressed in annual percentage increases in output. An *industry's relative growth* can be indicated by comparing its average annual rate of increase in output with the long-term 3.5 per cent growth of real GNP in the American economy. A growing industry would then be one that is expanding capacity and output at a rate greater than the economy's growth trend. A mature industry may be identified as one that is growing at a rate approximating that of the economy's rate, a declining industry as one falling behind the growth of GNP.

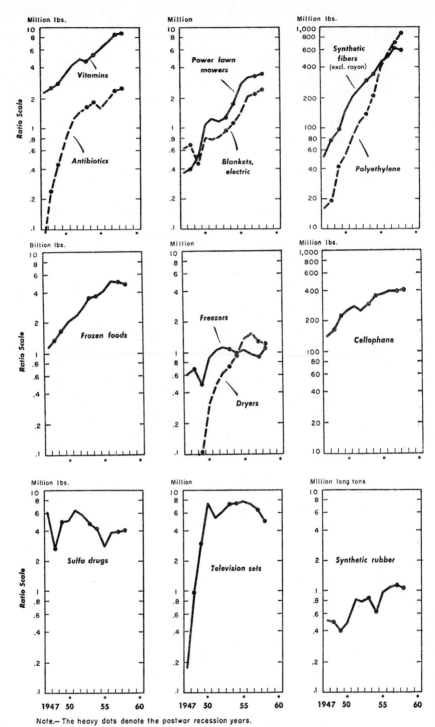

Note.— The heavy dots denote the postwar recession years.

U. S. Department of Commerce, Office of Business Economics

Fig. 4–9. (See next page for caption.)

178

Broad industry groups (e.g., the transportation, the fuel, and the food-processing groups) generally grow at a relatively moderate rate; shift in the relative standing among individual industries, however, often occurs within the group (Fig. 4–8). Though the transportation industry, for instance, has been growing at a moderate rate, the expansion of air transport and motor trucking has tended to displace railroad transportation. Generally the primary factor accounting for the expansion of a broad industry group is the growth trend of the economy as a whole; and the economy's growth in turn depends on the growth of population, technological advance, capital accumulation, and other factors discussed earlier in Chapter 1. For some individual industries the economy's growth trend is less controlling. The impact of GNP on the growth of an individual industry may, in fact, be relatively negligible, particularly in the short run. Some long-established industries (electricity and chemicals) have grown in output at times when GNP has leveled off or has declined.

Individual industries in their development and life pattern generally pass through stages of growth and maturity: After a period of initial technological experimentation and market adaptation, an industry takes root and enters a stage of rapid growth (e.g., the farm-machinery industry); it then enters a period of diminished growth and finally a period of slow growth or gradual decline, as in the piano and coal industries. Industries, of course, differ with respect to the intensity and duration of the various stages in their development pattern (Fig. 4–9). If, for instance, a new industry's market potential is large and producers adopt a low-price, high-volume policy, the initial expansion usually gives rise to economies of scale. Cost reduction and price competition lower price, broadening the market and increasing effective demand. Thus, when the potential market for a new product of relatively elastic demand is large, a new industry in an advanced economy can often quickly grow to large size. High-profit prospects will attract venture capital, and the resources required for the expansion of a new industry are often widely available in a large advanced economy. The availability of resources is at times indicated by the fact that many semi-fabricated materials and components required for the output of a

---

Fig. 4–9. Variations in development patterns of selected fast-growing products in postwar years. Some products have maintained their strong uptrend *(top)*, growth has slowed in others *(middle)*, and for some growth has been checked *(bottom)*. (U.S. Department of Commerce, *Survey of Current Business*, vol. 39 [May, 1959]: p. 22.)

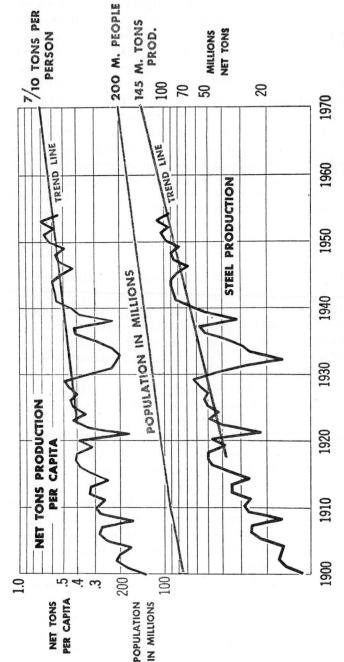

Fig. 4–10. Growth trend of the steel industry shown in relation to population increase, 1900–70. (U.S. Senate Subcommittee on Antitrust and Monopoly, Hearings during 1957, *Administered Prices—Steel*. Washington, D.C.: Government Printing Office, 1958, p. 606.)

new product can be supplied by subcontractors at a reasonable cost. When available industrial capacity is readily convertible to the output of new products, as in the case of the output of room air-conditioners, the capital-output ratio for the expansion of the industry would be low and growth can be rapid.

The rapidity and the extent to which a new industry may grow also depend on the kind of product put out (Table 4–1; Fig. 4–10). If the industry is to supply a luxury product or capital goods that can be used by only a limited number of producers, the industry will probably not grow to large size. But if the industry is to supply staple, non-durable goods (frozen food) or consumer durable goods (home freezers) purchased by broad income brackets, the industry will generally experience rapid and extensive growth in a large country of relatively high income per capita and in cases in which a large export potential exists. The speed of expansion of an industry in its early growth stage, of course, depends on consumer acceptance and the cost of distribution and market penetration. In the case of radio and television sets, market acceptance was very rapid during the industry's initial growth stage. After the initial potential market was "filled," sales tended to level off (Fig. 4–9). Consumer acceptance may, on the other hand, be gradual. The broadening and expansion of sales may take many years, as has been the case for aluminum and air travel and transport. An industry's period of rapid growth may, therefore, be of relatively short duration, and the industry may quickly move into a stage of maturity; or an industry's period of rapid growth may extend over many years and gradually shade into the stage of diminished growth or decline. The growth of an industry partly depends on the shape of the long-run cost curve and the trend and behavior of demand. The behavior of demand depends not only on the kinds of products put out, the size of the potential market, and the price elasticity of demand but on producers' demand analysis and policies and actions in product improvement and demand promotion through various methods indicated in the pages following.

The Interrelationship of Demand

The demand for an industry's product may be comparatively independent of the demand for other goods, or it may be more or less related to the demand for other products or services. An industry's product in a given market segment may have a competing substitute product which serves the same purpose. Power plants, for instance, are often set up to use either fuel oil or natural gas, whichever is

TABLE 4–1

Growth Trend in Output of Products

Production of Selected Products and Services, 1948, 1957, and 1958

Product or Service	Unit of Measure	Production		
		1948	1957	1958 (preliminary)

Rapidly Growing Products—Increases at an Average Annual Rate of $7\frac{1}{2}$ Per Cent or More

40 Per Cent and over				
Transistors	Thous.	1,318[1]	28,738	47,051
Antibiotics	Thous. lb	240	2,373	2,500
Television sets	Thous.	975	6,399	4,920
Polyethylene	Mil. lb	19	708	880
Styrene plastics and resins	Mil. lb	165	776	720
Vitamins	Thous. lb	2,566	8,569	8,700
Helicopters, non-military	Units	71	310	186
Rubber, synthetic, all types	Thous. lg. tons	488	1,118	1,053
Detergents, synthetic	Mil. lb	636	3,507	3,594
30 to 40 Per Cent				
TV broadcasting stations	Number	50	521	546
Air ton-miles flown	Mil. miles	223	601	613
Fibers, synthetic, except rayon	Mil. lb	75	626	592
Dryers	Thous.	92	1,294	1,211
Coffee makers, automatic	Thous.	600	4,365	4,200
Argon	Mil. cu. ft.	30	397	372
Air-conditioners, room	Thous.	74	1,586	1,550
Rubber or latex core mattresses	Thous.	34[4]	577	620
Tape recorders, home use	Thous.	100[2]	500	410
Carpets and rugs, tufted	Mil. sq. yd	21[2]	100	110
Shavers	Thous.	1,650	6,650	6,400
20 to 30 Per Cent				
Effervescent wines, withdrawals	Thous. wine gal.	1,063	2,238	2,502
Tractors, off-highway type	Units	414	5,133	4,086
Jet fuel	Mil. bbl	21[3]	63	74
Air revenue passenger-miles flown	Bil. miles	6	25	26
Blankets, electric	Thous.	675	2,200	2,410
DDT	Mil. lb	20	124	n.a.
Lawn mowers, power	Thous.	397	3,300	3,452
Ammonium sulfate, synthetic	Thous. sh. tons	264	1,040	1,094
15 to 20 Per Cent				
Locomotives, diesel-electric	Units	2,254	1,312	434
Disposals, food	Thous.	175	550	616
Plastics and resin materials, total	Mil. lb	1,485	4,340	4,600

TABLE 4-1 (Continued)

Product or Service	Unit of Measure	Production		
		1948	1957	1958 (preliminary)
Distilled spirits, withdrawals	Mil. gal.	108	158	155
Magnesium.	Thous. sh. tons	10	81	30
Trailer coaches, mobile-home type	Thous.	85	143	132
Skirts, separate	Mil.	35	88	84
Frozen foods	Mil. lbs.	1,347	5,000	4,765
Mixers, food, std. and portable	Thous.	1,570	3,600	2,765
Methanol, synthetic	Mil. gal.	156	229	226
Canned fruit juices	Mil. lbs.	2,458	2,121	1,819
Phonographs, single.	Thous.	351	3,718	3,212
10 to 15 Per Cent				
Freezers, farm and home.	Thous.	690	925	1,101
Waists, blouses, and shirts	Mil.	94	181	177
Aircraft, civilian, airframe weight	Mil. lbs.	10	22	17
Garden tractors	Thous.	185	178	170
Fibre drums.	Mil.	18	27	27
Aviation gasoline.	Mil. bbls.	46	112	113
Sulfa drugs.	Thous. lbs.	2,660	3,843	4,040
Dishwashers, motor-driven	Thous.	225	390	425
Formaldehyde.	Mil. lbs.	617	1,351	1,390
Phenol, natural and synthetic	Mil. lbs.	297	556	510
Transparent film for packaging	Mil. lbs.	205	590	627
Ammonia, synthetic anhydrous	Thous. sh. tons	1,375	3,734	3,831
Clocks.	Thous.	9,995	8,400	8,100
Repairs, household durables	1940=100	331	629	638
Nitric acid.	Thous. sh. tons	1,133	2,843	2,698
Chlorine gas.	Thous. sh. tons	1,640	3,948	3,600
Motor truck transportation	Bil. ton-miles	116	261	260
Cellophane.	Mil. lbs.	165	390	403
Douglas fir (softwood plywood).	Mil. sq. ft.	1,871	5,413	6,136
Aluminum, primary ingots	Thous. sh. tons	623	1,648	1,564
Water heaters, electric	Thous.	1,040	800	824
Fermented malt liquor (beer)	Thous. bbls.	91,291	89,882	89,011
$7\frac{1}{2}$ to 10 Per Cent				
Still wines, withdrawals	Mil. wine gal.	110	140	143
Insulating board and hardboard.	Thous. sh. tons	1,270	1,563	1,630
Acetylene.	Mil. cu. ft.	5,144	10,525	10,696
Oil burners, residential	Thous.	420	674	578

TABLE 4-1 (Continued)

Product or Service	Unit of Measure	Production		
		1948	1957	1958 (preliminary)
Oxygen	Bil. cu. ft.	16	33	38
Rayon and acetate	Mil. lbs.	1,124	1,139	1,014
Distillate fuel oil.	Mil. bbls.	381	669	631
Ranges, electric	Thous.	1,600	1,365	1,355
Pipelines, oil (transported)	Bil. ton-miles	120	233	223
Power sprayers and dusters	Thous.	131	98	102

Moderately Growing Products—Increases at an Average Annual Rate
of Less than $7\frac{1}{2}$ Per Cent

6 to $7\frac{1}{2}$ Per Cent

Coats, separate, men's. . .	Thous.	4,900	9,043	8,440
Fans.	Thous.	3,795	5,303	4,332
Acetylsalicylic (aspirin) .	Thous. lbs.	11,016	18,054	21,003
Fabricated structural steel	Thous. sh. tons . . .	2,718	4,180	3,664
Repairs, passenger cars and trucks.	1940=100	262	317	322
Electric power, total	Bil. kw.-hr.	337	716	724
Acetic acid.	Mil. lbs.	422	544	570
Gypsum wallboard, incl. lath	Mil. sq. ft.	5,035	6,514	7,117
Suits, women's	Mil.	15	10	10
Merchant ship construction, del.	Thous. gr. tons . . .	164	320	564
Radio broadcasting stations	Number	2,662	3,717	3,889
Natural gas, marketed . . .	Bil. cu. ft.	5,148	10,680	11,015
Sanitary and tissue	Thous. sh. tons . . .	1,188	1,912	1,961
Glass containers.	Mil. gross.	99	148	145
Cleaning and dyeing.	1940=100	247	256	252
Pulpwood consumption . . .	Mil. cords.	21	36	35
Corn pickers, field	Thous.	79	41	42
Woodpulp.	Mil. sh. tons	13	22	22

5 Per Cent

Refrigerators, electric. . .	Thous.	4,766	3,350	3,117
Lamps, bulbs and tubes. . .	Mil.	1,837	2,683	2,605
Trailers, truck.	Thous.	45	61	49
Oleomargarine	Mil. lbs.	908	1,463	1,573
Cigarettes, production . . .	Bil.	387	442	470
Washing machines, electric and gas.	Thous.	4,196	3,791	3,692
Printing paper	Thous. sh. tons . . .	3,151	4,051	4,031
Radios, incl. auto	Thous.	16,500	15,428	12,577
Toasters	Thous.	4,850	4,000	3,400

4 Per Cent

Cans, metal, steel consumed	Thous. sh. tons . . .	3,245	4,595	4,761
Superphosphate	Thous. sh. tons . . .	1,900	2,455	2,415

TABLE 4-1 (Continued)

Product or Service	Unit of Measure	Production		
		1948	1957	1958 (preliminary)
Aniline	Mil. lbs.	92	113	100
Motor fuel, all types	Mil. bbls.	922	1,438	1,423
Heating pads	Thous.	1,600	2,055	1,920
Innerspring mattresses, except crib	Thous.	6,226[4]	8,018	7,986
Telephones in service	Mil.	38	64	67
Sulphuric acid	Thous. sh. tons	11,456	16,388	15,852
Work pants	Thous. doz.	3,500	6,047	5,900
Trousers, separate, dress and sport	Mil.	38	71	73
Cheese	Mil. lbs.	1,098	1,404	1,408
Fertilizers, commercial.	Thous. sh. tons	17,596	22,650	22,900
Canned fruits	Mil. lbs.	2,500	3,443	3,327
Benzene, chemical and motor grade	Mil. gal.	184	332	290
Crude petroleum	Mil. bbls.	2,020	2,617	2,448
Aircraft engines, civilian	Thous. hp	2,799	7,231	3,850
3 Per Cent				
High explosives, industrial	Mil. lbs.	639	919	816
Vacuum cleaners	Thous.	3,361	3,190	3,295
Irons	Thous.	6,660	7,625	5,550
Beef	Mil. lbs.	9,075	14,211	13,350
Ice cream	Mil. lbs.	2,721	3,119	3,183
Wax petroleum	Mil. bbls.	4	6	5
Sulphur, crude	Thous. long tons.	4,869	5,491	4,645
Truck and bus tires	Mil.	15	13	13
Canned vegetables (commercial pack)	Mil. lbs.	5,917	7,748	8,150
Coarse paper	Thous. sh. tons	3,027	3,663	3,631
2 Per Cent				
Kerosene	Mil. bbls.	122	109	110
Bathtubs, total	Thous.	1,948	1,873	2,114
Shirts, dress, sport, business, utility	Mil. doz	17	20	21
Steel ingots and steel for castings	Mil. sh. tons	89	113	85
Newsprint consumption	Thous. sh. tons	4,010	5,149	4,950
Automotive replacement batteries	Mil.	25	26	25
Cement, portland	Mil. bbls.	205	298	311
Finished steel products, total	Mil. sh. tons	66	80	60
Pig iron	Mil. sh. tons	61	79	57
Meats, total	Mil. lbs.	21,300	26,928	25,760
Shoes and slippers	Mil. prs.	480	598	582
Dresses, women's	Mil.	227	251	241

TABLE 4-1 (Continued)

Product or Service	Unit of Measure	Production		
		1948	1957	1958 (preliminary)
Condensed and evaporated milk.	Mil. lbs.	3,755	2,880	2,721
Typewriters, std. includ. portables	Thous.	969	1,497	1,226
0 to 2 Per Cent				
Confectionery sales.	Mil. lbs.	2,673	2,769	2,824
Paint, varnish, and lacquer	Mil. gal.	272	313	338
Residual fuel oil	Mil. bbls.	466	416	363
Passenger car tires.	Mil.	67	94	84
Railroad revenue freight ton-miles	Bil. miles	641	622	555
Passenger cars.	Thous.	3,909	6,113	4,258
Cattle hide and side kip . .	Thous.	26,070	25,511	23,790
Newsprint	Thous. sh. tons . . .	876	1,797	1,723
Book publications	Number of editions .	9,897	13,142	13,462
Sugar, refined.	Thous. sh. tons . . .	6,971	8,785	9,172
Hosiery, shipments, total .	Mil. doz. prs.	144	147	146
Tractors, wheel type, ex. garden type.	Thous.	530	236	224
Truck and buses	Thous.	1,376	1,107	877
Cooking stoves, gas, domestic	Thous.	2,750	1,969	2,050
Combines (harvesterthreshers)	Thous.	91	45	46
Pork, ex. lard.	Mil. lbs.	10,055	10,482	10,525
Railroad freight cars. . . .	Thous.	115	100	44
Cotton broad woven goods .	Mil. linear yds. . . .	9,640	9,539	8,975
Machine tools, metal, cutting type.	Thous.	50	54	27
Flour, wheat.	Mil. bbls.	142	122	126
Products Showing Declining Trends				
Up to 2 Per Cent				
Cigars, production.	Mil.	5,645	5,903	6,210
Lumber, total	Bil. bd. ft	37	34	33
Bituminous coal	Mil. sh. tons	600	493	405
Woolen and worsted woven goods	Mil. linear yds. . . .	498	291	273
Suits, men's	Mil.	23	20	18
Overcoats and topcoats, men's.	Thous.	6,200	5,516	5,050
Railroad revenue passengermiles	Bil. miles	41	26	23
Work shirts	Thous. doz.	4,600	4,121	3,620
Carpets and rugs, wool type	Mil. sq. yds.	90	56	49
Textile bags, burlap.	Index 1940-49=100 .	108	94	93
Creamery butter	Mil. lbs.	1,504	1,549	1,510

TABLE 4-1 (Continued)

Product or Service	Unit of Measure	Production		
		1948	1957	1958 (preliminary)
Lead, refined	Thous. sh. tons . . .	407	537	472
2 to 5 Per Cent				
Sheep and lamb skins	Thous.	33,492	25,565	25,726
Local transit, passengers carried.	Bil.	17	8	8
Inner tubes, pass. truck and bus.	Mil.	70	40	41
Rails and accessories . . .	Thous. sh. tons . . .	3,517	2,265	989
Lead, mine.	Thous. sh. tons . . .	390	338	266
Manufactured tobacco. . . .	Mil. lbs.	245	179	180
Soap, natural	Mil. lbs.	3,180	1,433	1,338
Railroad passenger cars. .	Units	946	841	130
Ironers	Thous.	477	44	35
Anthracite	Mil. sh. tons	57	25	22
Range boilers	Thous.	536	163	n.a.
5 Per Cent and Over				
Textile bags, cotton.	Index 1940-49 = 100 .	68	31	28
Silk consumption.	Mil. lbs.	7	8	5
Locomotives, electric . . .	Units	8	4	0
Black blasting powder . . .	Mil. lbs.	33	4	3
Locomotives, steam.	Units	86	0	0

n.a., Not available.
[1]Data are for 1954.
[2]Data are for 1951.
[3]Data are for 1952.
[4]Data are for 1947.
Note: The average annual rates of growth shown are based upon the change in output from 1929 to 1957 or from first year production data are available.
Source: U.S. Department of Commerce, Survey of Current Business, vol. 39 (May, 1959); 23-24.

cheaper; cement blocks are substitutes for brick in the erection of certain types of structures; aluminum cables substitute for copper cables in the transmission of electricity; and aluminum window sashes are often used in place of wood ones. When two products are substitutive, an increase in the sale of one tends to decrease the demand for the other.

The demand for an industry's product (e.g., butter) that has a substitute (margarine) in a given market segment will be affected by price changes in the substitute product. A price reduction in the substitute will result in a shift of demand away from the industry's product; a price rise in the substitute will result in a shift of demand toward the industry's product, all other demand factors being held constant. Such demand behavior is designated as *cross elasticity of demand*, which may be conceptually stated as the percentage change in quantity demanded of product A which would result from a 1 per cent change in the price of product B, other things being equal. When two products are close substitutes, the cross elasticity of demand will be high; if they are not near substitutes, it will be low.

The demand for an industry's product may be complementary to that of the demand for another product. Two or more products or services are complementary when they are used jointly (e.g., batteries and automobiles). The demand for one product is derived from the demand for the complementary product. Because complementary products have a joint demand, an increase in the consumption of one product increases the demand for the other. When the sales of products jointly demanded involve a consistent time lag of the "dependent" product relative to the "parent" product, the derived-demand relationship of the products often permits comparatively reliable forecasting of sales.

The demand for complementary products (electric ranges and electricity) also involves cross elasticity of demand. A sharp reduction in the price of electricity will in some areas lead to an increase in the sale of electric ranges and air-conditioners, and an increase in the price of electricity will lead to a decrease in the demand for these products.

A derived-demand relationship also exists between producer's goods and consumer's goods. But it is essentially in the long run that an industry's demand for productive facilities and other capital goods derives from the consumer demand for the industry's products. An industry also demands and consumes various types of materials, components, and supplies in relatively fixed proportions, particularly in the short run. In the long run, however, an industry's derived demand for materials shifts to cheaper substitute materials when their use involves no appreciable increase in processing costs.

The effective demand for an industry's output (the sales volume at any time) depends on the *price elasticity of demand* for its products. Price elasticity of demand refers to the degree of change in the amount purchased relative to a given change in price, that is, the degree of responsiveness of buyer purchases to changes in price. Demand is inelastic if the proportional change in the amount purchased is smaller than the proportional change in price. Demand is elastic if the proportional change in quantity purchased is greater than the proportional change in price.

Thus, depending on the elasticity of demand, a change in price for a product may cause the total sales revenue to decrease, increase, or remain the same. A product in some price ranges may have a greater elasticity of demand than in other price ranges. The elasticity of demand over a given price range can be roughly measured by the effect of a price change on total sales revenue received by sellers of the product. If a lowering or a raising of price results in no change in total sales revenue, the demand in that price range has an elasticity of "unity." If a lowering of price reduces total sales revenue, the demand in that price range is inelastic. Consumer demand is ordinarily inelastic for a product that is considered somewhat of a necessity or is habitually used (e.g., salt and cigarettes) and for a product used jointly with a more expensive product (e.g., electricity consumed by home appliances and gasoline consumed by automobiles).

If a lowering of price increases total sales revenue or a raising of price reduces total sales revenue, the demand in that price range is elastic. Demand tends to be relatively elastic for products that are not urgently needed, products that have many adequate substitutes, products that are costly (i.e., high unit value), and products whose replacement is postponable (e.g., durable goods). A drop in price for products with a relatively elastic demand would substantially increase sales revenue; a rise in price would drastically reduce sales revenue.

A major factor influencing the demand for nearly all classes of goods and services is the level and trend of national income. Though national income and aggregate demand largely move together, the close relationship does not necessarily carry over to the demand for specific types of goods. Consumer choice on what to buy depends not only on income but on habitual consumption patterns, adequacy of stocks held by consumers, relative prices of goods and diminishing marginal utility, and on sellers' effectiveness in stimulating demand through product improvements and other methods. Changes in total disposable personal income bring about some change in the demand for all goods and services, but the change is not uniform for all classes of goods. The amount spent for particular items depends on the sensitivity of sales to changes in the level of income.[3]

Elasticity is essentially the percentage change in sales or in effective demand (the dependent variable) resulting from a 1 per cent change in an independent variable such as a 1 per cent change in consumer income or in price. The income elasticity of demand for a given class of goods is measured by the percentage change in

---

[3] For estimates of sensitivity of sales to changes in disposable personal income, see the study made by the U.S. Department of Commerce presented in Chapter 10.

quantity demanded, divided by the percentage change in the level of income.

If the consumer demand for a class of goods is not very sensitive to changes in income, the coefficient is usually less than 1 and the demand is therefore inelastic with respect to changes in income. If sales of a certain type of goods are very sensitive to changes in income, the coefficient is greater than 1, and demand is elastic. The demand for the products put out by an industry thus depends on the income elasticity of demand as well as on price elasticity of demand. Income elasticity of demand is, of course, influenced by the time element, that is, whether a rise or a decline in the income level has just been reached or has prevailed for some time. A study of income elasticity of demand for various types of products is presented at the end of Chapter 10.

Demand analysis may be employed (1) to identify the factors influencing the behavior of demand for particular products, (2) to appraise the demand determinants and estimate shifts in demand, (3) to develop approaches and methods for promoting demand and consumption of given products, and (4) to formulate pricing policies. The projection of long-term changes in demand provides a basis for product planning and for adapting or adjusting plant capacity for anticipated production requirements. *An analysis of the trend and behavior of the demand for an industry's products and of the factors underlying an industry's growth trend serves to exemplify the factors influencing demand and the problem of estimating long-term demand.*

The continued growth of many consumer-goods industries depends on such factors as the price elasticity of demand, the trend of long-run average costs, the degree of competition and the trend of prices in the industry, and the rise in income and population. If demand is relatively elastic and producers compete on the basis of price, declining long-run cost in production and marketing and declining prices open up new markets, and the increased effective demand induces expansion of the industry. If the demand is inelastic and long-run costs tend to rise, the industry's growth is generally more limited.

The Declining Industry and the Trend of Demand

Though an industry as a whole may be experiencing a decline in volume of output, certain firms may be enlarging their market share. The competitively stronger firms generally gain a dominant position in the more expanding (or less stagnant) market segments and cut production costs; they may also, of course, increase their volume of business by diversifying their product lines to include products that sell in markets of growing long-run demand, that is, by expanding into the fields of growing industries. Notwithstanding a drop in long-term demand and sales, a declining industry can nonetheless be a progressive industry if it improves its products, reduces costs, and lowers prices. It would contribute to over-all economic growth by employing resources efficiently and by releasing productive factors for profitable employment in other fields. Growth in an advanced economy essentially stems from the development of new industries and new products or services and from the quality improvement of end products. The over-all growth and progress of the economy therefore does not depend on the uniform growth of all industries.

Old industries in the declining stage of development are generally characterized by a stationary or a falling level of output, chronic overcapacity, low employment levels, and low or declining prices and profits. Though capital equipment may be largely depreciated in the accounting sense, plant facilities are relatively durable, and machines can last many years before they are discarded or scrapped. Producers in a declining industry can continue to operate and sell domestically and on the world market because old plant and equipment can, while they last, continue to compete on the basis of prices which do not cover replacement costs.

Declining demand and excess capacity tend to retard capital replacement. A rapidly declining industry often becomes a depressed industry, and the physical stagnation of an industry is generally accompanied by increasing costs and deterioration of its financial position. The financial inability to renew capital equipment and modernize plant is generally an important factor accounting for the continued decline of an industry. Because of low profitability, deficits, and the inability to attract investment funds, a declining industry often cannot make an adequate research and development effort to improve processing technology and cut costs, uncover and promote new uses for its products, or to develop new products.

Because of the location of its plants and the unadaptability of its production facilities, an industry (e.g., shipbuilding and copper refining) may be unable to convert its facilities readily to other productive uses. Though it is the economic logic of a competitive market system to produce an adjustment and shrinkage in the capacity of a declining industry to long-term shifts in demand, the movement of an industry toward such a point of equilibrium may be a long-drawn-out process. Structural rigidity, factor immobility, and lack of financial resources may forestall effective reorganization and adjustment to long-run market conditions. The structural rehabilitation of a stagnating industry may not only call for plant modernization, cost reduction, and technological development but for the relocation of plants and the reorganization of the industry.

The leveling-off or the decline in demand for an industry's output may be due to a number of factors. Unless offsetting forces develop, an industry is generally subject to a leveling-off or a declining trend in production when its long-run costs are constant (or rising) and when the demand is relatively inelastic or is declining. The demand may be adversely affected by the fact that an industry's hard goods tend to become more durable as their longevity is extended through the use of improved materials, technical improvements in components, and superior product design generally. Thus, as typewriters and home appliances, for instance, become more durable, the replacement demand for them tends to decline to a lower level. Excise taxes levied on products of a relatively elastic demand also tend to lower the level of sales.

The demand for an industry's output may gradually fall off because of the loss of export markets. The development of a competing overseas industry may be based on superior resources, the protection of a customs union, currency devaluation, and economic advantages that accrue from the secular development of a country. Export markets may also decline because importing countries impose higher tariffs or other trade restrictions. In some cases a domestic industry may shift part of its production to its expanding overseas branches. American industries, intent on circumventing tariff walls, establish overseas plants in order that they may competitively sell in a large "common market." American motion-picture producers, for instance, have often made films abroad because of lower labor costs, authentic locale, blocked currencies, and subsidies.

A mature industry may experience a gradual decline in demand for its products because of the rise of a new industry that puts out a lower-priced (or superior) substitute product or service. Shifts in consumer tastes, wants, and buying patterns may adversely affect the long-run demand for an industry's products. The motion-picture industry has felt the competitive impact of television. New types of building materials have made inroads into the market for lumber. Competition from the use of home washing machines and other appliances has been a retarding factor affecting the volume of business for commercial laundries.

The Mature Industry: Demand Analysis and Growth

Since the individual oligopolist puts out a significant share of the industry's output, he must, if he is to estimate his demand, take into account changes in industry demand and the probable change in his market share. In estimating the level of demand for his product and market share, the oligopolist must therefore first estimate industry demand and then take into account the effect of his price policy and plans for product improvement and sales promotion and the effect of his rivals' price policies and promotion practices on his market share, that is, he must take into account the element of cross elasticity of demand as well as the demand determinants for the type of products he sells.

The demand determinants for producer's goods differ from those for consumer goods. The major *demand determinants for producer's goods* include (1) the level and trend of industrial output and national income (the cyclical turn), (2) businessmen's estimate of the trend of future sales and the need for new capacity, (3) the amount of investment fund available from retained earnings and depreciation allowances and the ease (cost) of external financing, (4) the pace of technological advance in creating cost-reduction opportunities through plant modernization and in stimulating adoption of new products requiring new facilities, and (5) the average annual replacement requirements (which depend on the current rate of plant utilization, the stock of productive capital, and the amount of excess capacity).

The major *demand determinants for consumer durable goods* (automobiles, appliances, furnishings) are (1) the trend of disposable personal income and population growth, (2) buyer's optimism regarding future income and employment, (3) the level and adequacy of the stock of durable goods held by consumers, (4) prices relative to all consumer prices, (5) the trend of installment credit and financing terms, and (6) the frequency and effectiveness of product improvement and restyling and sales promotion.

The demand for most consumer non-durables, however, is more closely geared to the trend of population growth, the level of disposable income, and the extent of product improvement.

If the demand for the products of a mature industry is relatively elastic, declining long-run cost and price competition will usually induce at least a moderate rate of growth. If, however, the demand is relatively inelastic and the decline in long-run cost is not appreciable, the industry's expansion of output will tend to level off. But the tendency for the leveling off of an industry's demand and expansion may be more or less offset by the long-term rise in consumer income and population and by the promotion of demand through product improvement, more intensive advertising and selling efforts, introduction of new products, and so forth. These and other factors underlying the trend of demand and trend of growth of a mature industry are discussed below.

For most industries population growth and the trend of national income underpin the growth of demand for products. After its initial growth stage, an industry in the mature stage of development often gains a further increase in sales through market research and the introduction of additional product varieties or models for better adaptation to the consumption needs of different income brackets and market segments. Both high-priced and low-priced models, for instance, are introduced, and various models and sizes are offered to buyers to induce purchases of more than one model. Large profitable firms accumulate retained earnings and employ the financial resources to maintain sales revenue and to stimulate growth in output. Big producers typically appropriate large sums for aggressive research programs to develop new products, uncover new uses for products, as well as to cut costs through the improvement of processes.

Industries putting out products that respond to sales promotion (cigarettes, beverages, many luxury goods) have generally managed to increase (or at least maintain) their share of the consumer's dollar expenditures. Big producers in such industries typically make heavy outlays for advertising. The high tax on profits, moreover, tends to induce larger expenditures for market development and sales promotion and the provision of larger expense accounts for the conditioning of purchasing agents to product receptiveness. Some fields of business organize joint programs and approaches for the promotion of greater consumer acceptance of their products and for the stimulation of industry demand.

An industry, particularly one in the field of durable goods output, gains a moderate expansion in its market when it initially adopts the practice of providing installment credit or liberalizes credit terms (e.g., introduces the "revolving" credit plan) and when it adopts trade-in discounts and promotes the development of a used-product market (Fig. 4–11). The development of establishments for the sale of used products (both consumer and producer durables) widens consumption and the fuller utilization of goods through the "trickling down" of products to marginal purchasers and lower-income groups. It is, however, the initial introduction of installment sales and trade-in discounts that enlarges the over-all market for an industry's products. When the limits are reached, demand cannot be further increased on the basis of the consumer's future income. Installment-selling practices tend to make for somewhat greater cyclical (and sometimes seasonal) instability in demand, and the extra carrying charges, of course, raise the level of the prices actually paid by buyers.

The long-term dollar sales volume and demand for an industry's goods are influenced by the extent to which products can be improved or upgraded into higher-priced items. The practice of up-

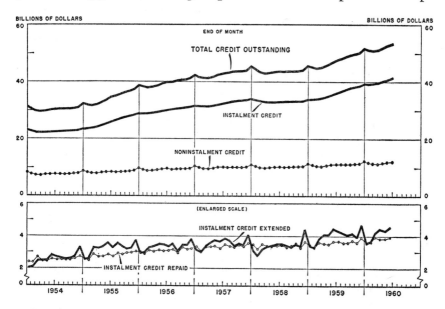

Fig. 4–11. Consumer credit as a demand determinant for consumer goods. (Council of Economic Advisers, *Economic Indicators, August 1960.* Washington, D.C.: Government Printing Office, 1960, p. 28.)

grading products is more typically available to industries producing final consumer goods (processed foods, clothing, appliances, and other consumer durables) than to the early- or intermediate-stage industries producing primary materials and semifabricated products. The upgrading of products and the introduction of higher-priced brands and models do not increase the physical volume of sales so much as they increase the dollar volume of sales.

Industries producing final consumer goods add quality to upgraded goods by using materials with better finishes, adding extra features, and using luxury packaging to embellish and enrich the products. The industry aims to gain adoption of the luxury features as standard equipment and pushes the sale of higher-priced lines in place of the low-priced lines. The upgrading of products sometimes increases the cost of production more than the intrinsic value added for consumers. During prosperity and boom times buyers generally respond to upgraded goods, "trading up" for more expensive lines of goods and higher quality; many customers become somewhat indifferent to higher prices. In the upswing of business, the dollar volume of sales increases faster than the physical volume of sales (aside from the inflationary influence). Some low-priced items tend to be dropped from production during periods of extended prosperity, and the trading-up behavior tends to simulate an inflationary effect. The trading-up phenomenon characteristic of boom times tends to be replaced by the "trading-down" behavior during recession and depression times as shoppers look for bargains and sale merchandise. Because competitive industry during recession and depression times introduces more low-priced brands and economy models and because many more used goods are rebuilt for resale rather than scrapped, the dollar volume of sales falls more than the physical volume of sales.

As compared to the sale of non-durables, the sale of durables adds to the stock of existing goods which provide services and utility over a number of years. The demand for durables thus consists of a "replacement" demand and a "new" demand. In the mature industry the replacement demand (for automobiles, appliances, as well as for producer's goods) becomes a larger part of total demand. Because the services of durable goods are embodied in a large stock of existing goods held by users and because of the ease of postponing the replacement purchase of durables, small changes in the demand for the services of durable goods (both producer's and consumer's durables) create big changes in the current demand for durable goods of all sorts.

Industries producing consumer durables have, notably since World War II, been able to increase somewhat the replacement demand by adopting the practice of annual restyling of products in order to more quickly render obsolete the products held by consumers. Because the initial introduction of the practice of annual product remodeling has tended to enlarge the late-model portion in the over-all stock of consumer durables, the postponability of replacement can be greater and the shrinkage of sales more abrupt than would otherwise be the case. If a recession develops into a depression, consumers not only delay replacement longer, but when they do buy, a greater number trade down for economy brands and models in the low-price range. The *dollar* demand, particularly for durables, thus often tends to fall cyclically and rise more rapidly than the physical volume of sales. Notwithstanding their cyclical influence, the adoption of the practices of product upgrading and annual remodeling and restyling nonetheless tends to increase the level of the long-run demand.

When a durable-goods industry successfully develops and introduces a radically new model or machine which markedly renders obsolete the existing stock of durable goods, it eliminates the distinction between replacement demand and new demand. Market anticipation of the availability of a radically new model often abruptly shrinks current demand and generally plays havoc with inventories and production schedules of current models. The superiority of genuinely novel new models raises demand and output to new levels, and the industry earns a new lease on life and reverts to the growth stage.

Some mature industries have enlarged the long-run demand by developing new uses for their established products and penetrating new markets. Through lower prices and the development of low-cost fabrication methods, the paper and aluminum industries have, for instance, been able to open new markets for their products and thereby enlarge the demand.

An industry's enlargement of the demand for its output may be based on the more or less continual introduction of new products, as in the case of antibiotics and electric appliances. The chemical industry also has maintained growth in the demand for its output through the development of new products such as plastics, synthetic rubber, synthetic fiber, and detergents. The new items have been penetrating the market of, and displacing the demand for, older types of materials. Plastics, for instance, are now used as an alternative material to metal, wood, and leather in many products. Synthetic rubber accounts for more than one-half of the rubber consumption by American industry in the 1950's. Synthetic fibers are supplementing cotton and wool and actively competing with them.

The interaction of a multitude of economic factors gives rise to *shifts in consumer-spending patterns* and influences the demand for an industry's output. The spending of an individual consumer generally increases less than proportionately as income rises; savings are relatively large in the high-income brackets, while consumers at the bottom of the income scale generally spend all their income. If the rise in income were the only factor involved, it might be expected that as personal disposable income (in real terms) moved upward, there would tend to be a less than proportionate rise in consumer expenditures. Various economic changes accruing over time, however, affect the distribution of personal income and savings and influence the composition of consumer expenditures for different types of goods and services.

The long-term factors influencing the distribution of personal income and the demand for an industry's output include both institutional and economic changes that modify consumers' spending and savings patterns and affect the level of demand for different types of goods and services. Governmental expenditures, for instance, have a varying impact on the demand for different types of goods and on the level of employment and distribution of income by industries in different areas. Changes in the tax structure, in minimum-wage laws, in unemployment insurance, and in pension plans influence the distribution of disposable personal income and affect consumption patterns. Shifts in population and changes in the ownership of different types of assets (liquid holdings, corporate securities, homes, and automobiles) influence consumption patterns.

In contrast with the investment market, a significant feature of the consumer market is its greater relative stability over the business cycle. Aggregate consumer demand (particularly for nondurables and services) is less sensitive to changes in national income than is the aggregate business demand for capital goods. But because of the magnitude of aggregate consumer demand, the fluctuations in consumer expenditures can exceed the total expenditures in all other markets combined.

The long-term *consumer spending-income ratio* (i.e., the consumption function) is influenced by the continual introduction of new or improved products and services, the development of new uses for products, and other demand stimulants discussed earlier. The spending-income ratio is also influenced by previous peak income levels. Past high-income levels influence for a time current spending-income ratio because of the desire of consumers to maintain their standards of living. Thus, even though consumer-spending patterns change and consumer spending typically increases and decreases with income, total consumer expenditure tends to have a somewhat fixed relation to the level of disposable income (generally approximating 94 per cent).

An industry's growth depends not only on the trend of demand, product innovations, and costs but on the type and degree of competition, that is, on the industry's market structure, which is characterized in Chapter 5.

QUESTIONS FOR REVIEW AND APPLICATION

1. Explain what is meant by an industry's production function.

2. (*a*) Explain why the nature of the production technology and the low capital-output ratio in the clothing industry tends to make for many small-scale producers. (*b*) How do the above structural features and the aspects of fashion and seasonality of demand contribute to the intensity of competition in the clothing industry?

3. (*a*) What are the various ways in which an industry's plants differ? (*b*) Is an industry's optimum-sized plant the same for all locations? Explain.

4. Are the opportunities for economies from vertical integration of production the same for all industries? Explain.

5. (*a*) In what way do an industry's production technology and type and design of product influence costs? (*b*) Identify and briefly explain the underlying factors that determine or influence a producer's short-run costs.

6. Cite an example of an industry (or a productive process) that has a high ratio of fixed costs to total costs. Cite one with a low ratio. Explain the disparity.

7. Explain why the marginal cost per unit differs from the average variable cost per unit.

8. Identify and briefly explain the factors that influence the shape of a producer's short-run cost curve in a given industry.

9. Identify and briefly explain the factors that determine or influence the elasticity of an industry's short-run supply.

10. (*a*) Distinguish between short-run costs and long-run costs. (*b*) Explain what is meant by cost as a function of the rate of output and cost as a function of size.

11. (*a*) Explain the long-term relationship between changes in wage rates, technological improvements, and changes in the unit cost of production. (*b*) How does a change in factor proportionality take place in the long run? Do outlays for equipment replacement facilitate a desired change in the proportionality of productive factors?

12. Identify and briefly explain the factors and developments that determine or influence an industry's long-run costs of production.

13. What are the factors that underlie or influence the elasticity of an industry's long-run supply?

14. (*a*) What are the problems or difficulties in using the statistical method and the accounting method for conducting empirical cost studies for use in business planning? (*b*) What are the limitations in using statistical or accounting empirical cost studies (i.e., historical cost trends) for business planning and decision making?

15. Why is the engineering method for estimating costs more useful for decision-making purposes than the statistical or the accounting method?

16. (*a*) Explain the limitations in the use of "accounting" costs for managerial decision making. (*b*) Identify, explain, and illustrate several decision-making costs that may be used in decisions concerned with expansion of plant capacity, adoption of cost-cutting innovation, introduction of a new product, and the like.

17. Distinguish between direct and derived demand. Illustrate.

18. (*a*) Distinguish among price elasticity, income elasticity, cross elasticity, and promotion elasticity of demand. (*b*) Would promotion elasticity tend to be greater in a pure oligopoly or in a differentiated oligopoly? Explain.

19. What are the factors that determine or influence the demand for producer's goods? For agricultural machinery?

20. (*a*) Does the durability of a consumer good affect the behavior of the demand for it? Explain. (*b*) What are the demand determinants for consumer durable goods? Discuss.

21. How does the demand for television sets differ from the demand for automobile radios?

22. How do the two major segments of the tire market (the replacement demand and the original-equipment demand of automobile makers) differ?

23. What kind of data would you need to indicate the growth trend of an industry? Distinguish between a mature industry and a growth industry.

24. What factors tend to lower production cost per unit of output as an industry expands capacity over time? Discuss.

25. Discuss the cost factors, demand characteristics, market promotion practices, and product innovations that influence the growth of an industry.

26. What factors would you say accounted for the growth of the aluminum industry since 1940? For the growth of the antibiotic industry?

CHAPTER 5

Structural Pattern:
Market Structure and Pricing

MARKET STRUCTURE:
CONCENTRATION; PRICE BEHAVIOR

Industries differ with respect to the type and extent of competition among producers, that is, with respect to *market structure,* which refers to the competitive relationship among producers in the sale of products in given markets. An industry's market structure determines the relative effectiveness of price changes and price trends in regulating the level of output of a product and in allocating productive factors for the output of goods and services of maximum consumer utility. An industry's particular market structure (the extent of price competition among producers) is determined by the number of sellers and buyers, the ease of entry of new producers, the extent to which products are differentiated, and the closeness of substitute products put out by other industries. Although the degree of competition obviously cannot be precisely measured, economists, nonetheless, theoretically classify market structures as pure competition, pure monopoly, monopolistic competition, and oligopoly.

Pure Competition and Pure Monopoly

A purely competitive industry is one in which there is no restriction of entry and in which a large number of producers and sellers offer identical products, with no producer offering a large enough quantity to influence the market price. Since the products are identical and consumers buy on the basis of price and have no preference as to sellers, no firm would have any influence over the price of the industry's product. At the opposite extreme is pure monopoly. An industry is a monopoly when a single producer or a group of sellers acting in concert controls the entire supply of a product and has the power to determine the price. But because more or less close substitutes exist for most products, a monopolist's price-fixing power is generally limited. Few industries approach the concept of pure competition, and monopolies as such are seldom left unregulated. Thus, an industry rarely fits the rigid definition of pure competition or monopoly. In most industries the competitive situation is between the two extremes; aside from agriculture, most industries include elements of both competition and monopoly. Producers or sellers generally have some measure of control over the prices of their products so that competition is somewhat imperfect. The theoretical models of pure competition and pure monopoly essentially serve as frames of reference for conceptualizing and structuring imperfect competition.

Imperfect competition exists when a firm controls a large enough supply of a product or when it sells sufficiently differentiated products to influence the selling price. Industries under imperfect competition are of two general types of market structure: oligopoly (characterized by fewness of firms and significant restriction to entry) and monopolistic competition (characterized by firms putting out differentiated products).

Monopolistic Competition

An industry in monopolistic competition consists of a considerable number of competitors who sell similar but differentiated products. Monopolistic competition is characteristic of many industries putting out final products. Firms in the apparel and shoe industries, for instance, produce similar products, but each firm puts out its own brand, model, or trade-marked product. When a firm competing with many rivals successfully differentiates products (whether real or fancied) or the conditions of sale (e.g., exclusive distribution outlets and particularized service), it can exercise some degree of control over its selling price.

Monopolistic competition is distinguished from oligopoly by the fact that there is no significant restriction to entry of new firms and by the presence of a relatively large number of firms, each selling differentiated products to a small proportion of the total market. A firm's product line is often comprised of some highly differentiated items which sell to customers who buy on the basis of quality or style and of some low-priced brands and models designed to sell to customers who generally buy on the basis of price. A firm may also differentiate its business and sales by offering credit and various types of customer services.

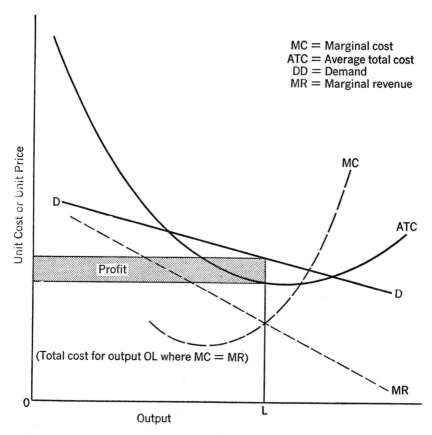

Fig. 5–1. Theoretical price-output adjustment for a firm's short-run profit maximization under conditions of imperfect competition.

Since firms doing business under conditions of monopolistic competition sell similar (though not identical) types of products, the demand curve facing a firm tends to be quite elastic because of the ease of substitution among brands and models (Fig. 5–1). To the extent that a firm successfully maintains or promotes its demand

and sales through effective product differentiation, it enjoys a limited degree of monopoly; its demand curve is somewhat more inelastic than that of a firm selling under pure competition. Because of the relatively large number of sellers in the market, a firm selling a differentiated product has a degree of independence in setting price without much concern of possible retaliation. The firm can, within limits, set its price and need not accept the prevailing price.

A firm's independence in setting price is, in the final analysis, limited by the fact that competitors sell similar products (competing brands and models) which are essentially close substitutes. Successful product differentiation, however, tends to avoid some of the hazards of losing business when competitors cut prices. A firm also may be able to raise prices somewhat without an appreciable decline in its sales volume. Effective product differentiation permits a firm to raise prices but only within the limits set by competitive brands or models that may be readily substitutable if the firm overprices its products. Thus, a firm's independent price-fixing power is monopolistic only up to the point at which significant brand or model substitution occurs; beyond this point the firm must be price competitive. If a firm cuts prices to take some business away from competitors, there is little likelihood of retaliation since, because there are many firms in the market, each feels only a slight loss in sales. Moreover, since demand for many consumer goods generally increases when consumer income rises (or when the market expands for other reasons), the expansion of sales through effective product differentiation often means that the successful firm gains a larger share of the growing demand relative to its competitors.

Though under monopolistic competition each producer sets his prices and there is no industry-wide prevailing price, the prices of most firms are closely related because of the ease of substitution. If firms produce a larger volume, they lower unit costs as they approach optimum capacity (the point of lowest unit cost), but they may lower total profits because they can only sell a larger volume at a lower price—marginal revenue will be less than marginal cost for selling extra units. Theoretically, the price-output policy under monopolistic competition results in a production rate at which unit costs are somewhat higher than minimum average unit cost, which tends more often to obtain under pure competition (Fig. 5–1). Firms under monopolistic competition and differentiated oligopolists can enlarge profits not only through price administration but through the cost-cutting improvements and various demand-promotion methods discussed earlier.

Oligopoly

An oligopoly is an industry in which the entry of new firms is significantly restricted and which typically consists of a few firms that supply the market. An oligopolistic industry may supply a local or a regional market, or it may supply a national or international market. In an oligopolistic market structure there is no definite agreement among firms concerning price or output. An oligopoly may also consist of a few big firms that supply a large proportion of the market (say, 75 per cent) and a substantial number of smaller firms (the "competitive fringe") that sell the balance of the market. A producer may be an oligopolist for one or a few products he sells but not for other items. (A variant of oligopoly is *duopoly* in which there are only two firms.)

An industry is a *pure oligopoly* when the relatively few firms in the line of business sell identical (or nearly identical) products. Because it is commercially less practical to differentiate products in the fields of earlier-stage production, the pure-oligopoly market structure is generally more characteristic of early-stage industries. Such products are typically graded and are produced under standard (or very similar) industry-wide specifications as in the case of metals, plate glass, lumber, and meat. When an industry consists of a few firms, each firm's sales influence the price and the competitive behavior of its rivals. Because a price reduction or a price increase affects sales volume and earnings, a firm must anticipate the retaliation of rivals before changing price. In planning its price and rate of production, a firm in an industry of pure oligopoly must therefore take into account the reaction of rival firms. Firms under pure oligopoly often charge the same price, with the result that firm's market shares are relatively stable in the short run.

An industry is a *differentiated oligopoly* when it consists of relatively few firms that sell differentiated products, as such final-stage industries as the automobile, cigarette, soap, coffee, and liquor industries. Elements of both oligopoly (fewness of firms) and product differentiation exist in this type of market structure. As the number of firms in an industry declines through mergers and through the elimination of marginal producers, monopolistic competition shades into differentiated oligopoly.

Under differentiated oligopoly moderate price differences generally exist among rival firms. The independent price-fixing power of each oligopolist increases to the extent that they successfully differentiate their products. Because buyers for business firms generally purchase on the basis of specifications or performance, producers of capital goods (machinery and equipment) differentiate their goods primarily through product improvement and through better delivery performance, service, credit availability, and other terms of sale. In estimating demand for his product, the oligopolist must first estimate industry demand and then take into account the effect of his price policy and plans for product improvement and the price policies and product plans of his competitors in order to estimate his market share.

Industry Concentration and Producers' Market Position

The concentration of a large percentage of the output of a product in a few firms contributes to oligopoly power and administered prices (managerial discretion in pricing). The degree of oligopoly in an industry can be indicated by the *concentration ratio,* which is the percentage of the total value of output of a product turned out by the four largest or by the eight largest producers (Table 5–1). The concentration of production may also be indicated by the number of the largest producers (or by the percentage of all producers) that among them turn out a designated percentage of the industry's total output. If an industry's concentration ratio is measured in terms of total assets or in terms of the number of people employed rather than in terms of value of output, concentration (i.e., producers' market share or market domination) may be exaggerated because certain firms may be more vertically integrated than others. Concentration when measured in assets would tend to be overstated because bigger producers (by virtue of their large volume) generally find it economically feasible to use capital-intensive types of processes to a greater degree than do smaller producers. Since concentration ratios have been computed for domestic production, industry concentration and producers' market shares are overstated for products that are partly imported, for instance, wine, pulp, and watches.

Of the industries classed in the high concentration-ratio category (industries in which 75 per cent or more of the production is concentrated in the four largest firms), the four biggest producers of locomotives and parts supplied 90 per cent of the product in 1950; while, of the industries classed in the low concentration-ratio status, the four largest producers of women's suits and coats produced 5 per cent of the value of the product in 1947.

Since the concentration ratio is compiled in terms of national output, it understates the degree of oligopoly for products regionally or locally produced and distributed, for instance, cement, creamery products, bread, and certain lines of clothing and home furniture. For a concentration ratio to be meaningful in the "measurement" of oligopoly, it must be computed on the basis of appropriately delineated geographical boundaries of the market for products put out for local distribution because of high transportation costs. Certain producers in industries classed as low concentration on the national basis may actually enjoy considerable market dominance in regional and local areas.

The different items that make up the "product" for concentration-ratio analysis generally include the output of specialized firms that produce certain varieties or narrowly specified items for particular market segments. The concentration ratio, therefore, would not adequately indicate market dominance for firms that successfully maintain an exclusive position by specially adapting their product output for sale to comparatively narrow market segments.

The compilation of meaningful concentration ratios for industries thus involves solution of the classificatory problem of realistically delineating the range of items to be included in a "product," and it calls for an appropriate geographical delineation of the market. Even if a concentration ratio were appropriately designed for the relevant product group and market, the correlation between concentration and monopolistic consequences and price discretion may be weakened by the existence of potential substitutes and other factors. Concentration ratios would overstate oligopoly power for industries confronted by high cross elasticity of demand—many products have a chain of potential substitutes at various prices. Moreover, since producers strive to adapt products to new uses and since new products spring up in various fields of output, market and product boundaries in many fields of production are in a continuous state of change, tending to render obsolete any previously computed concentration ratio. Thus, a static concentration ratio may provide only a glimpse of the actual market structure and competitive situation for highly dynamic industries.

Company concentration of output generally differs from plant concentration of output. *Plant concentration of production* may be measured by the percentage of an industry's output produced by a designated number of plants. (The average plant size—and also the efficient plant size or optimum plant—would, of course, vary from industry to industry.) High plant concentration of production would, for instance, be indicated if the five largest cigarette-producing plants turn out 30 per cent of the industry's output; while low plant concentration of production would be indicated if the five largest shoe plants (or cement plants) turn out 6 per cent of the

TABLE 5-1.
Concentration of Production: Per Cent of Total Shipments Made by Large Manufacturing Companies
in Selected Industries, 1947-54

[First 45 industries as determined by value of shipments in 1954. A "company" comprises all manufacturing establishments owned by the company plus those of subsidiaries or affiliates over which the company has acknowledged control. Per cents were computed by adding together all establishments classified in the specified industry under common ownership; selecting the largest 4, largest 8, and largest 20 companies in each industry on basis of value of shipments of all products made by these establishments; and using these values of shipments of the companies as numerator, and total value of shipments of the industry as denominator. Top 4, 8, and 20 companies not necessarily identical for each year. Value of shipments includes transfers of products between manufacturing establishments of same company (interplant transfers). "N.e.c." means not elsewhere classified.]

Industry	Census Year	Number of Companies	Value of Shipments[1] ($1,000)	Percentage of Total Value of Shipments Accounted for by			Primary Product Specialization Ratio[2]	Coverage Ratio[3]
				Four Largest Companies	Eight Largest Companies	Twenty Largest Companies		
Motor vehicles and parts	1947	779	3,544,924[4]	56[4]	64[4]	78[4]	(5)	(5)
	1954	991	6,111,479[4]	75[4]	80[4]	87[4]	(5)	(5)
Petroleum refining	1947	227	6,623,708	37	59	83	0.99	0.97
	1954	253	11,757,218	33	56	84	.99	.98
Steelworks and rolling mills	1947	111	2,275,697[4]	48[4]	63[4]	81[4]	(5)	(5)
	1954	102	4,020,264[4]	54[4]	70[4]	85[4]	(5)	(5)
Meat-packing plants	1947	1,999	977,144[4]	41[4]	54[4]	63[4]	.96[6]	.99[6]
	1954	2,228	1,394,486[4]	39[4]	51[4]	60[4]	.98	.87
Aircraft	1947	47	605,983[4]	53[4]	75[4]	97[4]	(7)	(7)
	1954	46	3,348,876[4]	47[4]	76[4]	96[4]	.89	.99
Radios and related products	1947	709	773,233[4]	26[4]	35[4]	54[4]	(5)	(5)
	1954	1,612	2,130,207[4]	24[4]	35[4]	53[4]	(5)	(5)

Industry	Year	No. of companies	Value of shipments	(4)	(8)	(20)		
Fluid milk and other products[8]	1954	4,572	4,233,983	23	29	36	.82	.94
Paper and paperboard mills	1947	·[9]	2,589,114	19	31	48	.99	1.00
	1954	391	3,792,810	33	42	55	.94	.86
Food preparations, n.e.c.[10]	1947	2,357[11]	1,592,324	5	7	11	.97	.81
	1954	19,223	3,255,967	7	11	18	.90	.95
Sawmills and planing mills	1947	16,594	2,519,453					
	1954	54	3,247,200					
Aircraft engines	1947	202	464,623	72	88	98	.97	.81
	1954	8,115	3,188,950	62	81	93	.90	.95
Newspapers	1947	8,445	1,891,252	21	26	36	.93	.91
	1954	5,985	3,091,027	18	24	34	.94	1.00
Bread and related products[12]	1947	5,470	2,403,589	16	26	36	.95	1.00
	1954	413	3,067,017	20	31	40	.98	.99
Cotton broad-woven fabrics	1947	33[11]	2,912,651	18	29	49	.98	.99
	1954	34	2,789,621					
Blast furnaces	1947	2,372	1,713,945	67	82	96	.94	.84
	1954	2,037	2,753,998	65	82	96	1.00	1.00
Prepared animal feeds	1947	201	2,112,241	19	27	40	.98	1.00
	1954	1,054	2,702,267	21	29	43	.95	.89
Aircraft equipment, n.e.c.	1947	542	105,327	37	58	75	.95	.90
	1954	561	2,342,536	20	32	52	.82	.38
Refrigeration machinery	1947	1,856	587,928[4]	39	55	72	.86	.66
	1954	1,461	1,006,193[4]	36	51	69		
Canned fruits and vegetables	1947	11,810	1,640,754	27	35	46	.91	.94
	1954	11,970	2,228,947	28	39	52	.90	.94
Commercial printing	1947	202[13]	1,513,136	9	13	20	.86	.86
	1954	1,323	2,202,074	10	16	24	.85	.86
Organic chemicals, n.e.c.	1947	1,433	973,044	59	73	87	.77	.80
	1954	294[15]	2,198,687				.97	.98
Paperboard boxes	1947	1,084	1,474,743	18	27	41	.96	.98
	1954	692	2,179,580	16	26	41		
Inorganic chemicals, n.e.c.[14]	1947		562,426	36	51	74	.87	.78
	1954		1,859,372	29	41	57	.92	.92
Flour and meal	1947		2,526,646	40	52	68	.94	.84
	1954		1,858,888					

[1] Footnotes on pages 211–212.

TABLE 5-1 (Continued)

Industry	Census Year	Number of Companies	Value of Shipments[1] ($1,000)	Four Largest Companies	Eight Largest Companies	Twenty Largest Companies	Primary Product Specialization Ratio[2]	Coverage Ratio[3]
				Percentage of Total Value of Shipments Accounted for by				
Beer and ale	1947	404	1,316,085	21	30	44	1.00	.99
	1954	263	1,857,053	27	41	60	1.00	1.00
Tires and inner tubes	1947	35	1,547,040	77	90	99	.90	.95
	1954	27	1,841,732	79	91	99+	.88	.99
Structural and ornamental work	1947	1,600	855,101	23	27	37	.86	.88
	1954	2,829	1,809,971	18	23	31	.89	.88
Footwear, except rubber	1947	1,077	1,726,609	28	35	45	.99	1.00
	1954	970	1,790,717	30	36	45	.99	.99
Metal stampings	1947	1,954	1,177,396	17	25	37	.86	.81
	1954	2,215	1,727,544	14	21	33	.82	.83
Rubber industries, n.e.c.	1947	733	945,257	30	38	53	.85	.81
	1954	1,152	1,677,072	28	37	50	.88	.78
Pharmaceutical preparations	1947	1,123	941,290	28	44	64	.91	.98
	1954	1,128	1,643,140	25	44	68	.91	.94
Cigarettes	1947	19	1,131,891	90	99+	100	.96	1.00
	1954	12	1,640,950	82	99+	100	.99	1.00
Pulp mills	1947	132	939,604	28	39	59	.99	1.00
	1954	141	1,577,291	29	42	61	.99	1.00
Paints and varnishes	1947	1,154	1,248,841	27	36	48	.94	.96
	1954	1,337	1,494,399	27	37	50	.95	.97
Dresses, unit price	1947	4,165	1,359,030	3	5	9	.95	.97
	1954	4,072	1,455,080	4	7	12	.96	.95
Periodicals	1947	2,106	1,059,566	34	43	58	.94	.98
	1954	2,012	1,440,961	29	40	54	.95	.97

Industry	Year							
Paper and board products, n.e.c.	1947	676	786,917	15	25	43	.86	.86
	1954	770	1,427,622	25	39	58	.90	.89
Gray-iron foundries[16]	1947	1,554	1,173,039	16	24	35	.92	.87
	1954	1,321	1,418,947	26	34	46	.94	.87
Prepared meats[17]	1947	(11)	234,758[4]	(11)	(11)	(11)	(11)	(11)
	1954	1,254	330,312[4]	16[4]	24[4]	35[4]	.83	.28
Motors and generators	1947	224	995,640	59	66	80	.81	.92
	1954	266	1,389,078	50	59	75	.82	.84
Tin cans and other tinware	1947	102	678,924	78	86	94	.97	.99
	1954	109	1,366,766	80	88	96	.98	.99
Copper rolling and drawing	1947	56	1,064,033	60	77	92	(7)	.92
	1954	64	1,320,608	53	71	90	.95	.90
Wire drawing	1947	103	912,891	45	62	82	.96	.37
	1954	150	1,266,436	36	54	74	.95	.39
Women's suits, coats, and skirts[18]	1954	3,178	1,261,320	3	6	11	.94	.93
Poultry-dressing plants	1947	330	478,993	32	40	58	.88	.88
	1954	1,189	1,257,892	17	23	33	.96	.97

[1] Comprises for all manufacturing establishments classified in an industry (a) value of products "primary" to the industry, (b) value of "secondary" products, which are primary to other industries, and (c) "miscellaneous receipts," such as those for contract and commission work on materials owned by others, scrap and salable refuse, repair, etc. Excludes sales of products bought and resold in same condition. 1947 figures for some industries reflect minor revisions.

[2] Measures extent to which establishments classified in an industry "specialize" in making products regarded as primary to the industry. That is, value of shipments of primary products of establishments in the industry is expressed as a ratio of total shipments of all products made by these establishments (excluding "miscellaneous receipts," such as those for contract and commission work on materials owned by others, scrap and salable refuse, repair, etc.). 1947 ratios for some industries reflect minor revisions.

[3] Measures extent to which all shipments of primary products of an industry are made by plants classified in the industry, as distinguished from secondary producers elsewhere. That is, value of shipments of primary products made by plants classified in the industry is expressed as a ratio of total shipments of primary products made by all producers, both in and out of the specified industry. 1947 ratios for some industries reflect minor revisions.

[4] Value added by manufacture used as basis for making calculations because of large amount of duplication resulting from use of products of some establishments in the industry as materials by other establishments in the same industry.

[5] Not shown because total value of primary products shipped includes large amount of duplication.

TABLE 5-1 (Continued)

6 Based on combined figures for Meat-packing plants and Prepared meats.

7 Not available.

8 Excluded from 1947 census.

9 Comparable data not available. In 1947, Building paper and board mills combined with Paper and board mills.

10 Includes Vinegar and cider mills, Liquid, frozen, and Dried eggs processors, for which figures were published separately in 1947.

11 Comparable data not available due to significant revisions in 1947 classification of plants or products.

12 For 1947, includes multiunit bakeries producing baked goods at each location for sale through a retail outlet at the same location; excluded for 1954.

13 Comparable data not available. In 1947, Organic chemicals, n.e.c., included Intermediate coal-tar products.

14 Includes government-owned privately operated plants.

15 In 1947, Sulfuric acid combined with Inorganic chemicals, n.e.c.; separate figures tabulated for 1954. Specialization ratio and coverage ratio for combined industries for 1947 were 87 and 80, respectively.

16 Gray-iron foundries includes in addition to commercial (jobbing) foundries "captive" foundries at separate locations producing gray-iron castings for other plants of the same company. Accordingly, the ratios do not reflect market shares in the commercial foundry industry.

17 Includes data for Sausage casings.

18 Includes data for Women's suits and coats and Women's skirts; shown separately in 1947 and therefore comparable data not available.

Source: U.S. Department of Commerce, Bureau of Census, Statistical Abstract of the United States, 1959 (Washington, D.C.: Government Printing Office, 1959), pp. 792-793.

industry's output. An industry would be more competitive (less oligopolistic) when it has low firm concentration and low plant concentration, that is, when the divergency between company and plant concentration of output is relatively small. But for the measurement to be meaningful, company and plant concentration must be expressed in terms of the appropriate market supplied (whether local or national). An industry with high firm concentration of production and high plant concentration of production (e.g., several large firms, each owning one or more large plants) would have considerable oligopoly power, particularly if firms typically produced and distributed locally. But since, in the latter case, economies of scale presumably derive from the large plants, the existence of high firm concentration of production would be economically logical, and antitrust action would therefore be illogical.

A considerable amount of monopoly would presumably be indicated if an industry is comprised of a few big firms, each owning many plants (i.e., high firm concentration of production and low plant concentration). Though the divergency between company and plant concentration would be relatively large, the firms' process-related plants and auxiliary plants may be rationally linked to form large production systems. Economies of scale also, of course, derive from a group of interrelated and vertically linked plants organized to form a large multiple-plant system or an industrial complex. If, on the other hand, an industry is primarily comprised of large firms, each owning or controlling many duplicate plants (a horizontal combination), economies may derive from large-scale research and development, distribution and sales promotion, and purchasing. If economies from the foregoing sources are not appreciable or if the inherent economies are not realized, the concentration of economic power in horizontal combinations would be largely for monopolistic gains.

The characterization and the analysis of oligopolistic markets must take into account the essentially heterogeneous nature of the industrial structure, market behavior, and the competitive process. Approaches for gauging oligopoly are more meaningful when they seek to characterize the nature of the actual competitive process rather than a theoretical state of monopoly. A pragmatic study of monopolistic market behavior thus calls for individual analysis and appraisal of industries.

A realistic analysis of oligopolistic industry and producers' market dominance must not only be based on a properly designed concentration index, but it must also cover such features as the type and degree of product differentiation, whether the industry sells to business buyers or to ultimate consumers, the extent of bilateral oligopoly, the degree of vertical integration, the pace of technological advance, the ease of entry of new competitors, and the industry's stage of development (i.e., whether it is in the early-growth, the mature, or the declining stage). Some multiple-product firms, for instance, may put out complementary products and items that tend to stabilize sales revenue over time; others may use the sales revenue from their profitable lines of business to sustain or revitalize their declining lines of business through product remodeling and aggressive sales promotion. The competitive process, of course, differs for different economic sectors and fields of production. As compared to late-stage producers, early-stage producers often do not have the same latitude for product differentiation and sell to the industrial market comprised of more rational buyers rather than to the consumer market comprised of purchasers who are generally more receptive to sales promotion.

The movement of a product from raw material to completion along the chain of producers and distributors and the repeated profit-margin additions are important factors accounting for the final price level of a product. Monopolistic competition in non-integrated industries comprised of a long series of production stages may result in high ultimate prices as materials and goods pass through successive markets and a series of price markups at customary margins. When economically feasible, the integration of a number of production stages by one firm can circumvent whatever restrictive market controls exist over transfer of goods, substituting for them intra-firm transfers at cost. Vertical integration may, of course, be based on the production-cost savings that can be realized in certain industrial processes rather than on market-restriction considerations.

Oligopolistic industry develops from scale economies in production and distribution, bargaining power in the purchase of input factors, successful product differentiation, and big outlays for research and sales promotion. Monopolistic price increases by oligopoly industry, however, tend to be somewhat limited by *potential competition* including closeness of substitutes. Potential competition depends on the ease of entry of new producers into the industry. If there is considerable difficulty of entry by new competitors, established firms can maintain a high price level (considerably above that of the competitive level) without attracting new entrants to the industry. If entry is easier, established firms will have commensurately less latitude in maintaining prices above the competitive level. Entry is easier when new producers can establish their business without need of large amounts of investment capital and when the new entrants can gain an adequate volume of sales and produce at costs comparable to those of established firms.

Impediments or barriers to the entry of new firms derive primarily from the advantage of established producers over new entrants with respect to volume of sales and customer acceptance of well-known brands and trade-marked products and with respect to lower production and distribution costs. New producers entering an industry generally have difficulty in attaining an adequate volume of sales because big firms have established their product and sales volume with the market and enjoy considerable buyer allegiance for their goods as a result of successful product differentiation, company reputation, and years of advertising. Existing firms, moreover, often have the additional marketing advantages of well-established status with distributors, exclusive outlets, and company-controlled dealer-service organizations.

Entry into new fields of business is somewhat less difficult for big firms than for independent promoters and potential entrepreneurs. Large established firms can overcome the impediments to entry (particularly if they are not too great) because of their status as going concerns and the availability of research facilities and retained earnings. Large diversified firms can exploit promising innovations in products and technical developments in new fields more effectively than newly organized firms or small businesses, because they can direct their capital resources, technical and managerial personnel, and promotional resources (their total "concentrated economic power") to the exploitation of new ventures. Their financial losses in new fields can be written off against the earnings from their well-established lines of business. Big firms also, of course, penetrate new fields through the acquisition of smaller firms and through mergers. The impact of the economic power of big corporations on the competitive process and on the market structure thus consists of both the concentration of production of a given product and the concentration of ownership or control of a large share of the economy's productive resources (i.e., the absolute size of big business).

INDUSTRY'S PRICE POLICIES AND PRACTICES

The degree of imperfect competition in an oligopolistic industry depends, as previously indicated, on the fewness of producers, the extent of restriction to entry of new firms, and the relative absence of close substitute products. If there are no near substitutes and restrictions to entry are substantial, the industry's price-fixing power can be considerable—approaching that of monopoly. If demand grows over time and there is no increase in the number of firms in the industry, the oligopoly market structure takes on bigger dimensions. In a relatively pure oligopoly the prevailing price in the industry is determined by the market demand for the product in relation to the industry supply—the quantities that the few producers are willing to sell at each of a series of prices.

Because each firm in a pure oligopoly offers a product that is identical (or very similar) to that of its rivals, the demand facing an individual oligopolist is highly elastic. The demand curve for the output of a firm is more horizontal (more elastic) than that for an industry. A firm may, however, be a dominant oligopolist in the sale of one or a few products in certain market segments, but in other markets or for other items in its product line, the firm may meet considerable price competition from rival firms.

In formulating price policy or in planning a price change, an oligopolist takes into account the price policies and practices of his competitors. Thus, under pure oligopoly, if a firm raises price, its business will largely shift to competitors. The oligopolist may not be able to count on other firms' "going along" with a price increase, with the result that his rivals may take over some of his sales at their lower price. If, on the other hand, a firm lowers price and its rivals do not, its sales will increase substantially, since the firm will attract buyers from rival firms. But a price-cutter would ordinarily expect rival producers to follow suit, and, as a result, all producers would incur a loss in income.

Although an oligopolist's price policy and initiation of price changes take into account his competitors' price policies, he cannot be certain what their reaction to his price change will be. Ordinarily, if an oligopolist changes his price, others are likely to follow, though they may not make an identical change. If he raises his price, competitors may not follow his lead, but if he lowers his price, he can usually assume that competitors will. A differentiated oligopolist, of course, has greater latitude in setting price, since the demand curve for his output is more inelastic than that under pure oligopoly. Because of cost differences among the firms, price under oligopoly tends to be a compromise. The prevailing price may be one that more or less maximizes the profits of many of the firms. Since their output costs differ, each producer would likely set a different price if he could act independently. Theoretically, an "independent" oligopolist would maximize his profits by producing at that rate of output capacity at which marginal revenue equals marginal costs, as indicated in Figure 5–1. As compared to that which would prevail in highly competitive industries, prices under oligopoly are generally above minimum average total cost.

A firm that is able to cut costs does not always feel free to lower prices and pass on the savings to consumers. Unlike that in a highly competitive industry, cost reduction in an oligopolistic industry does not typically (at least in the short run) lead to price reduction. Each producer tends to retain the prevailing price. Price changes in an oligopoly do occur over time, but they are infrequent. Thus, under oligopoly there is a tendency toward price rigidity or price inflexibility. Though competition between oligopolists and big firms is keen, it does not usually take the form of price competition but rather *non-price competition*—product improvement and periodic restyling, promotion and advertising, and favorable terms of sale and customer services, for example.

Price Stability and Price Leadership

Price inflexibility is generally a common feature of oligopoly. Oligopolists hesitate to cut prices for fear of retaliatory price cutting and the possible outbreak of cutthroat competition and a price war. Oligopolistic prices, moreover, tend to be somewhat stable because producers, particularly those in early-stage production, generally believe that demand is somewhat inelastic, that a price cut will not lead to any appreciable increase in sales volume. Producers of consumer durables and capital goods feel that an increase in sales essentially stems from growth in consumer income, population, and other non-price considerations and that a price cut therefore would induce little expansion in sales in the long run. By building capacity ahead of demand and thereby attaining elasticity in supply, oligopolists can better maintain an orderly long-run price structure, i.e., they can avoid short-term price variations. Many producers, moreover, feel that widespread consumer expectation of general price changes affects short-term sales and that price-cutting often merely results in postponement rather than in an increase in purchases.

In the face of declining demand during a cyclical downturn in business volume, oligopolistic industry, in contrast with competitive industry, generally cuts back production instead of lowering price. Though oligopoly industries do maintain more or less stable prices, their product output and employment generally fluctuate widely over the business cycle, particularly in the durable-goods industries. In order to maintain their market share during a downswing, oligopolists find that they must lower or adjust their price to meet any price cuts of competing substitute products. Unfavorable experiences with price instability and price "dislocations" by oligopolies have generally led to efforts (tacit or formal) for stabilization of prices through price-maintenance laws or arrangements, price leadership, and interfirm (trade association) cooperation in the provision of statistics and information on output, prices, costs, accounting practices, and other marketing aspects.

Many states have enacted resale *price-maintenance laws* ("fair trade" laws); and Congress, through the Miller-Tydings Act (1937) and the McGuire Act (1952), sanctioned these laws when interstate commerce is involved. The resale price-maintenance laws were designed to protect a manufacturer who desires to control the selling price of brand products and to protect small merchants against the price-cutting competition of the large-scale, efficient retailer who markets the same goods. The laws give manufacturers the legal right to make a contract with a retailer to fix the minimum price at which brand-name or trade-marked products may be sold in the state. In cases in which price-maintenance laws are effective, manufacturers, by making a contract with one merchant, can bind all retailers. Since manufacturers can refuse to sell to price-cutters, merchants are not free to compete for business by lowering price.

Price leadership can readily exist without explicit agreements, particularly in industries in which oligopolistic market structure is prominent and the products more homogeneous. Price adjustments and stabilization through price leadership exist when most firms set their prices at the level of (or at a somewhat consistent relationship to) prices set by the leading firm in the industry. The largest oligopolist thus often assumes leadership in setting prices that others follow. When a price-leader announces his new price level or schedule of price differentials for his products, all other firms generally follow suit. Instead of engaging in aggressive price competition, smaller firms learn (i.e., assume a price policy) to shelter themselves under the "price umbrella" established by the dominant firm. Price leadership tends to be less influential and less effective during depression and boom times. When the supply is scarce during boom times, some firms take premiums above the list price. During periods of depression, weaker firms make price concessions in an effort to capture sales and stay in business.

Leadership in pricing obtains stabler prices in the long run when the leader takes into account the interests of his competitors, market shifts, and industry-wide factors in adjusting prices to business conditions. Because of structural changes in the industry, shifts in the market, and technological change, a price-leader generally employs an adaptive pricing procedure or policy. Price leadership nonetheless essentially derives from the oligopolistic market structure with its ever-present threat of price retaliation and the desire of firms to avoid the hazards of price instability and cutthroat competition.

A well-established large firm (usually the largest oligopolist) assumes price leadership because of its bigger role and influence in the market, greater economic stake in the welfare of the industry, effectiveness in assessing and forecasting the market, and its economic power to impose its will, if necessary. The biggest firm is generally able to estimate more effectively the market because of larger outlays for market research and forecasting, contact and familiarity with a wider sector of the market, and greater knowledge of future demands, particularly since market share is sometimes materially influenced by a firm's own promotion and product plans and marketing policies. Because of the foregoing factors and his appreciation of the influence of price and profit potential in inducing entry of new producers, a price-leader can make somewhat feasible price changes and price policy that firms in the industry are likely to follow. In adjusting prices or in formulating policy, leaders in many industries often aim for a profit level at a desired long-run rate of return on investment and a predetermined share of the market.

When a producer adopts a new product, he generally sets the price at a level that he feels will effectively compete with a commercially established substitute product. Some businessmen are reluctant to undertake *experimental pricing* because of the great expense involved and the need for skilled researchers and because they fear that the testing of different prices may "spoil" the market. To determine the price of a wholly new product, one with no near substitutes, businessmen sometimes find that they must undertake experimental pricing, a procedure whereby they test buyer or consumer response to different prices in selected markets and use the results to determine the appropriate price or pricing approach. In order to tap the discretionary demand for his product by buyers in high-income brackets, a businessman may initially set a comparatively high price, particularly when demand is relatively inelastic with respect to price but elastic with respect to demand promotion. He may, on the other hand, develop a low-cost design and set a relatively low price for a new product in order to ward off potential competitors, to penetrate the market quickly, and to accelerate the development of a large demand which will permit use of efficient, mass-production methods of output.

Pricing Methods: Cost-Plus and Flexible Markup

In pricing commercially established goods and services, business-men use such methods (or a combination of methods) as cost-plus-a-fair-profit, flexible markup, and the imitation of prices set by a price-leader in the industry. A businessman may use the cost-plus method to arrive at a preliminary price and then adjust the price to anticipated competitive conditions, market demand, and trend of wages and material costs.

In many industries in which firms have some discretion in setting price, most businessmen tend to use the *cost-plus method* for pricing, that is, they set price by adding to unit cost a fixed percentage markup or margin (a margin they consider to be a "fair" profit). Cost-plus pricing tends to be used universally in the distributive trades and is not uncommon in manufacturing. A distributor generally adds his customary markup to the procurement cost of goods (the invoice cost of merchandise). If a distributor, for instance, pays $10.00 for an item and takes 30 per cent for his margin, he quotes his price at $13.00. A manufacturer using cost-plus pricing would add his markup to the "full cost" of producing a unit of the product. This would include unit cost of direct labor, direct material, and overhead. The "full cost" per unit of output may be based on the actual cost in a recent or in the current production period, it may be based on the anticipated actual cost for the next (future) production period, or it may be based on "standard costs" derived, for example, from an engineering cost estimate for direct material and labor and for overhead at a selected rate of capacity utilization.

Profit margins on unit cost differ among industries and firms. Margins tend to be lower in industries with a high inventory turn-over and in more competitive industries. Profit margins are generally higher in industries with a low inventory turnover, in those in which risk and uncertainty are greater, and in industries of oligopolistic market structure. The firm that is more effective in product differentiation and innovation and the firm that attains lower unit cost would obviously be able to take a higher profit margin than most of its competitors.

Businessmen are inclined to adopt a cost-plus pricing approach for various reasons. The cost-plus method seems to be a practical and comparatively simple system to apply. It provides for adequate ("fair") profits; it offers a practical pricing method (particularly when based on the appropriate "standard costs") for attaining a desired industry-wide price stability; and it does not require an estimate of the demand for a firm's goods. Businessmen, moreover, are inclined to the view that the demand for most products is comparatively inelastic with respect to price and that a firm's sales volume depends on such factors as its competitive position, consumer income, and employment prospects.

Cost-plus pricing, especially when it is rigidly applied, has a number of deficiencies. Cost-plus pricing uses the wrong cost when it takes past or current cost as a basis for setting future prices. The appropriate cost is future cost, particularly the estimate of the incremental cost of future output. Moreover, in cases in which a firm puts out two or more different items (joint products) from a given material or process, the arbitrary allocation of joint-processing costs among products may lead to price rigidity which limits the firm's capability for adapting to new competitive or demand conditions. A rigid cost-plus pricing policy based on industry-wide "standard cost" data would generally mean that an efficient firm which successively reduces costs would not undersell competitors and expand its sales volume.

Cost-plus pricing cannot be slavishly applied by firms that must adapt to changing business conditions. Shifts in demand and economic fluctuations generally compel firms in the more competitive industries to use an adaptive pricing method. Businessmen who use *flexible-markup pricing* (i.e., periodical adjustment of margins to changes in business conditions) presumably take into account competitive conditions, seasonal variations in demand, changes in consumer income and demand, elasticity of demand, and the influence of the volume of output on unit cost. A firm would tend to apply a larger markup on its highly differentiated products and on products that have been improved and to apply smaller margins on products that are meeting increased competition and have to be carried by the more profitable lines. Businessmen generally find that they can raise price margins during a business upswing and are somewhat obliged to mark down prices when business gets bad; they at times find it necessary to slash prices to move excess inventories or to liquidate existing stocks in preparation for a changeover to a new model.

Product-Line Influence on Pricing—Complementary and Substitute Products

Scope, composition, and interdependence of items in a product line affect pricing practice. Industry pricing tends to be more standardized when member firms put out comparatively homogeneous products. But since firms often put out somewhat diverse products as well as related products and since many firms put out items classed in other industries, the product-line aspect of production and marketing influences pricing. If he is to price products for maximum effectiveness and profitability, a seller would not apply a uniform percentage markup (or some other arbitrary markup) on all the items in the product line.

The product-line influence on the pricing of products depends on the kind and degree of interdependence among the items that comprise a firm's product line. The nature of the relationship of a product to other items in the product line often affects the pricing of a given product. When a seller prices products on the basis of economic analysis, he would take into account the demand relationships and the cost relationships among the items in the product line, the degree of market maturity of each product (the degree of market acceptance as compared to potential demand), and the competitive conditions for each product and his over-all marketing strategy.

A firm's marketing strategy, for instance, may call for the periodic use of the time-worn *loss leaders,* wherein a product (or a group of products) is priced below the customary price or at cost in order to draw customers who will buy other goods. A producer putting out a comparatively broad product line and selling in different markets can often manipulate his price structure for market promotion purposes or for competitive purposes. He may direct his selling effort to high-margin products, the earnings from which offset the below-average margins on some other products in his line. A producer may have considerable discretion in pricing his distinctive, highly differentiated products at a substantial markup, while he may price competitively other products which he carries to complete a market-related line in order to accommodate buyers who find it advantageous to group and place their orders with a single supplier.

A producer who limits his output to one segment of a complete product line (i.e., a specialized producer) sometimes has greater flexibility in pricing as compared to a full-line producer. A producer putting out a full line of demand-related products for sale to the same or similar markets often finds it necessary to maintain internally logical price differentials among the various product sizes or models. If he is to adjust the price level of one product model or size, he must consider the effect on the over-all price structure of his line of products.

In certain industries producers put out goods that are closely related in demand (complementary or substitutive products) or closely related in supply (joint-cost products). Producers putting out such *demand-related* products endeavor to find a profitable (or the optimum) price relationship for the respective items in the product line. In economic terms the optimum price relationship for demand-related products is one that yields the largest total profit for the group —the greatest differential between total cost and total revenue. When demand-relatedness among products involves *complementarity*, the items are used in combination or together in providing an integral service, for example, cameras and film, razors and blades, ski equipment and ski togs, and automobiles and automobile insurance. A price cut for one item may lead to an increase in demand for its complementary item. A seller thus sometimes finds it profitable to set a low price for one item in order to enjoy an above-average markup in the sale of the complementary item. A producer essentially aims to price complementary items in that relationship that maximizes profits from the sale of all the demand-related goods. Producers often look to the long-run effects in determining the relative prices for complementary products. Many consumers tend to take up a bargain now, even though they may find supplies (or repairs) relatively expensive in the future. A producer sometimes prices equipment fairly low, with the aim of selling supplies and genuine replacement parts at a higher than average margin. When a producer of complementary products is confronted by a new rival interloper who puts out only one (or a portion) of the complementary items (e.g., supplies or components), the producer loses his opportunity to offset the earnings foregone on the sale of equipment at a low price with the big earnings gained from the sale of supplies and components at a high price.

Producers in some industries put out *substitute products* that fill the same consumer need or market. A firm's substitute or competing items in its product line may differ in form, quality, or size. Fields of business in which the product line includes substitute or competing items are exemplified by producers of material-handling equipment (belt conveyors, monorails, overhead cranes), producers of containers (glass, tin cans, paper containers), producers of fruit juices, and meat packers turning out dressed beef, pork, and lamb. Substitutions also occur in product lines that include different sizes and quality of the same product. The demand interdependence and the substitutive nature of such product lines make for cross-elasticity of demand: a price change (increase or decrease) in one item will generally lead to a rise or a fall in the demand for the substitute items. Thus, when a producer or distributor sells more of one item or brand, he sells less of another.

If a producer or seller of similar or substitute products applied the same markup formula (a markup on full cost or on the cost of converting purchased materials into finished goods) to price the products, he would be ignoring differences in the demand behavior among market segments, in competitive conditions, or in the degree of market maturity of each item. If the seller is to design a price structure that maximizes return, he should take into account the particular market and demand factors that govern the sale of each item and promotion of consumption.

A producer can design his product line and price structure for demand-related items to maximize total sales and earnings by offering products priced at those levels that appeal to buyers of different income brackets or consumption patterns, while appropriately limiting the number of product varieties or sizes so as to achieve economies in production and distribution. Thus, in formulating his product-line and marketing strategy, a manufacturer often finds it profitable to design products to sell at a certain final selling price. This "inverted pricing" approach essentially starts with a selling price that certain income brackets or market segments will pay and works back by designing a product that can be produced and distributed at the necessary cost level that will yield the desired profit margin.

Product differentiation through variation in styling and use of brand names and appropriate distribution channels, particularly for technical or intricate products for which rational comparisons are difficult, can often segment the market so that skillful product-line pricing can profitably exploit differences in demand elasticity among various buyer groups. By offering a "stripped" model and a deluxe model of the same product, for instance, a producer can offer not only a wider price range for customers but can apply different profit margins to the models. If he feels that the demand for the deluxe model is relatively inelastic, he may apply a bigger percentage markup on the deluxe model as compared to other models. He may market high-priced, chrome-trimmed items through exclusive distributors who appeal to affluent buyers who customarily purchase the "best" or the well-established brands, and he may market his low-priced models or varieties under different brand names through discount houses and other channels to compete with rival low-priced products that appeal to people who buy on the basis of the lowest price.

"Price lining" for each level of quality and style of the same product, moreover, can establish two or three customary price levels (or price zones) for each brand to fit the various income brackets and demand elasticities. For certain types of goods, this pricing and product-design approach permits the maintenance of stable prices by varying the quality and composition (and sometimes the size) of a product to accommodate changes in the cost of production and in the price of input factors. Producers often find it necessary to establish price differentials for items in a product line that differ only in size. Price differentials based on size are rational from a demand and cost standpoint when the benefit or value to consumers differs or when the cost of production differs for each size. Trade custom sometimes compels uniformity in the pricing of items of different size even though production costs differ appreciably. In selecting the price relationship for different sizes of an item, producers must consider the extent to which typical buyers will substitute one size for another size of the same product. If buyers tend to substitute smaller sizes for larger sizes, sellers may apply a lower markup on the larger size (offer an economy size) to induce buyers to shift to the purchase and consumption of the large size.

In industries in which such factors as the design of the product, promotion methods, and distribution channels are variables (subject to manipulation) and in which opportunities exist for changes in technology and production cost, price policy and price decisions are an integral part of the over-all production and marketing strategy, and price cannot readily be isolated from other managerial considerations. Many firms in the same industry or in the same specialized field of business tend to have similar price patterns and policies because of a common frame of reference in terms of type of products, technology and cost structure, competitive environment and market structure, and methods of non-price competition. It is essentially from its market structure and market segments that an industry derives its price pattern and price differentials (discount structure).

Differential Pricing: Price Discrimination Based on Market Segmentation

In theory *price discrimination* refers to the practice of using a different markup above marginal cost to price different units of essentially the same product, that is, the practice of charging a different price to different (or the same) customers for the same product-service bundle. (*Price discrimination* may also be defined as the differential treatment of each class of customers in terms of price and service not attributable to differences in the cost of supplying them with the product.) Discriminatory pricing (differential pricing) is possible because the market for an industry's product is comprised of more or less homogeneous customer groupings (market segments) which differ in the intensity of demand, that is, in the price elasticity of demand.

Through differential pricing a producer gains by exploiting the differences in demand elasticity among buyer groups. He enlarges his earnings by breaking down the over-all market into homogeneous segments and applying that price differential for each buyer group that yields the largest total earnings, either by setting a higher price for customers with inelastic demand or by setting a lower price for customers with an elastic demand which swells sales and permits volume production at low unit cost.

But if he is to use differential pricing successfully, the producer must effectively separate and sufficiently seal off the various market segments to keep the product from moving through resale from low- to high-price market segments. Differential pricing thus requires adequate market segmentation so that customers cannot escape a higher price through procurement in the market where the price is lower. Producers can sometimes sharpen market segmentation and reduce leakage between segments by modifying and adapting the product and the conditions of sale to fit the particular requirements of each market subgroup. When it is commercially feasible, they design two or more versions of the product to facilitate differential pricing. In addition to the technique of varying the design of the product, producers sharpen market segmentation through appropriate packaging, branding, choice of distribution channel, and advertising. For differential pricing to be profitable, a producer's incremental cost of segmenting the market must not exceed his incremental gain in revenue.

Thus, producers find it profitable to use differential pricing when demand elasticity differs among buyer groups, when methods can be found or devised to segment the market sufficiently to prevent any appreciable leakage between segments, and when there are no legal or social inhibitions to discriminatory pricing. Hence, the practical application of differential pricing essentially calls for appropriate market segmentation, the breakdown or subdivision of the over-all market into homogeneous subgroups according to degree of demand elasticity. Market segments, moreover, may differ not only in demand elasticity but in the degree of competition and in the degree of cyclical sensitivity of demand.

When a producer uses the differential pricing approach to design his scale of prices, he essentially adapts his prices to the demand elasticity of each buyer group. Producers in many industries use differential pricing to tailor selling prices and services to the purchasing circumstances and demand characteristics of homogeneous customer groupings segmented on such bases as the trade status of the customer (e.g., wholesaler versus retailer), the size of his purchase, and his geographical location. Differential pricing is thus possible when markets are (1) separable by selection of distribution channels (for distributors' discounts), (2) separable by size of customer or amount of purchase (for quantity discounts), (3) separable by distance (for geographical differentials), (4) separable in time (for off-season discounts), and (5) separable on the basis of different uses of the product (for product-use differentials). By means of effective market segmentation producers can use differential pricing not only to exploit demand elasticity for a gain in sales revenue but to penetrate new markets and expand sales, to improve the effectiveness of market promotion, and to reduce the cost of production and distribution.

CASH DISCOUNTS. These discounts are price reductions based on promptness of payment, typically 2 per cent off if paid in 10 days with full invoice due in 30 days. By means of cash discounts, firms reduce their need for working capital as well as expedite collections which lower the cost of selling.

TIME DIFFERENTIAL PRICING. Such pricing is used when price elasticity of demand varies over the course of a season, a week, or a day. Through price discounts for off-season buyers, such industries increase the utilization of available productive capacity, lower the fixed cost per unit of output over time, and often find it possible to charge somewhat lower prices for customers who delay and concentrate their purchases for slack periods or who consume more during slack periods. Firms in the clothing, meat-packing, anthracite coal, recreation and resort, and other seasonal industries vary their prices over the year. Utilities and show business, for instance, vary their rates throughout the day or week.

PRODUCT-USE DIFFERENTIAL PRICING. This applies in industries putting out products for which the market is separable into segments comprised of customers (e.g., commercial purchasers, household purchasers) who use the product for different purposes and who therefore often differ in demand elasticity. Producers who put out materials (aluminum, plywood, rubber, asbestos cloth) that go into the fabrication of different types of products generally quote prices that are competitive with substitute materials. Producers of tires and producers of automobile parts offer one price discount to manufacturers who install the items on new cars and another discount to distributors who sell the items for replacement purposes. The telephone, gas, and power industries charge different rates for the commercial and domestic use of their services.

Distributors' Discounts (Functional Discounts). Distributors' discounts are essentially designed to induce each type of middleman (wholesalers and retailers, for example) to carry out his respective marketing function. Ideally, an industry's trade-channel discount structure consists of a scale of price deductions which correspond to each middleman's function and position in the distribution system. An industry's distribution channels sometimes include market segments that consist of somewhat homogeneous demand characteristics (e.g., as in the meat-packing industry) which provide a means for differential pricing based on demand elasticity.

When trade-channel discounts are set at margins that cover the operating costs and normal profits of the average or bulk-line distributor, the industry's over-all marketing function is generally maintained at a level of stability and performance which contributes to the growth and adaptability of the industry. If discounts are too low, the distribution system will tend to thin with the result that over-all sales will be sluggish; if discounts are too high, the distributive capacity will tend to be overextended, and prices for ultimate consumers will be proportionately higher. Functional discounts may be somewhat ineffective in cases in which distributors cannot be neatly classified as to type. Some distributors, for instance, perform both wholesaler's and retailer's functions to varying degrees. Since a producer's cost of selling goods to each type of distributor (e.g., wholesaler versus retailer) differs, the level of trade-channel discounts must more or less correspond to the cost savings attained through different outlets if a producer is to be assured of legal sanction by the Federal Trade Commission.

Producers favor and generally offer generous discounts to that class of distributors whose function in the over-all marketing system is well adapted for economical marketing. Some producers occasionally aim to induce a distributor to push the sale of his products by offering a larger discount. A well-established manufacturer with successful product differentiation, however, will generally be able to maintain his market with no special concessions to distributors. In most industries the distributors' discount structure is more or less competitively determined. Discounts offered by one producer are generally matched by another.

Quantity Discounts. Producers are sometimes under pressure to offer secret price cuts to big customers in order to retain their business. Such price concessions, however, are aside from discounts offered on the basis of a systematic quantity-discount scheme. When producers sell goods to buyers with elastic demand, they are able to sell proportionately larger quantities at lower prices. To enlarge his revenue, a producer need only enlarge his quantity discounts to the amount necessary to attract larger sales. Moreover, by designing an economy model or a stripped version of the product to sell to buyers whose demand is relatively elastic, a producer is often able to penetrate new mass markets.

Producers sometimes offer a cumulative discount to buyers who purchase steadily throughout the year or a longer period. Producers are inclined to offer such price discounts when they gain economies from more effective production planning, steady output, and lower inventory investment. Generally, however, quantity discounts are the regular price concessions producers offer to buyers who purchase a larger quantity at one time; the producer usually varies the price of the product according to the amount purchased. In most industries, for instance, carload prices are lower than less-than-carload prices. Producers sometimes grant quantity discounts to utilize excess capacity and thereby further reduce the unit cost of output. Quantity discounts that induce buyers to purchase a larger amount at one time, however, generally attain savings only in selling and distribution expense.

In granting quantity discounts producers aim to induce customers not only to place orders in larger lots so as to displace some of the expensive small-order sales but to secure a larger share of the customers' total purchases and thus to increase the producer's market share. Unless they are justified by cost saving in manufacturing, selling, and delivery or by the seller's bona fide efforts to counter competitors' price reductions, quantity discounts are generally considered illegal.

GEOGRAPHICAL PRICE DIFFERENTIALS. Geographical discrimination in pricing exists when producers quote prices for different regions of the market that do not reflect differences in transportation cost. The extent and the manner in which an industry applies geographical differential pricing depends on (1) the location pattern of the industry and the proportion of transportation costs to the unit cost of the product, (2) the degree to which the product is uniform among producers in the industry, (3) the extent to which the industry seeks resale-price maintenance, (4) the extent to which an established geographical price practice has become customary in the industry, and (5) the extent to which a given geographical price discrimination practice is legally permissible. A customary geographical pricing practice tends to persist in an industry because new entrants generally find it necessary to adopt the competitors' geographical pricing method.

The quotation of a *uniform delivered price* to all customers who buy similar quantities regardless of location (i.e., postage-stamp pricing) is generally found in industries in which the cost of transporting the product is slight relative to the value of the product, as in the case of drugs, cosmetics, watches, etc. Postage-stamp pricing permits sellers of differentiated and branded products to advertise nationally and seek to maintain a uniform resale price in all areas.

Under *uniform f.o.b. mill pricing* producers quote the same price at their plant to all customers who buy a similar quantity, and the customer pays the freight cost to his location. Such pricing is not discriminatory since the delivered price to a customer differs only to the extent of differences in shipping cost to each buyer. When the transportation cost is high relative to the value of the product, a sole producer in a given area will enjoy a natural competitive advantage in his local market, particularly if the industry's product is comparatively uniform. In cases in which producers in capital-intensive industries have unused capacity, such producers are inclined to absorb some of the freight cost of sales to customers in the more distant regions. Such partial freight absorption (which is somewhat akin to zone pricing) permits a producer to penetrate the more distant and somewhat exclusive market areas of other producers, thus enabling him to utilize capacity more fully.

Under *freight-equalization pricing* a producer computes his delivered price by adding to his factory price the transportation cost for a sales order from the nearest competing plant to the customer. By absorbing some of the freight (i.e., by equalizing freight cost), a producer aims to meet the price competition of the rival firm nearest to the customer. Freight-equalization pricing tends to be adopted by high fixed-cost industries that turn out a homogeneous product which has a high transportation cost relative to the value of the product. When it is not used continually and systematically by the industry, freight-equalization pricing is generally not found to be illegal.

Under *zone pricing* a producer geographically subdivides the over-all market into zones and charges a uniform delivered price for each zone but different delivered prices between zones. In computing the delivered price for each zone, the producer presumably adds to his factory price the average transportation cost to each zone. Industries that are likely to use zone pricing are those that put out products that involve somewhat high transportation cost in the shipment of the product. Zone pricing results in geographical price discrimination to the extent that producers reap a higher profit margin on sales made to nearer zones or on sales to nearer customers in a given zone as compared to the more distant customers in the zone. When zone pricing which involves appreciable price discrimination is systematically used by an industry, its legality is open to doubt.

Under *single basing-point pricing* an industry's producers compute the delivered price, irrespective of the customer's location, by adding to the factory price the transportation cost from a single geographical point or producing base, as in the case of "Pittsburgh-plus" formerly used in the steel industry. Industries that sell goods to other producers have tended to use the basing-point system for computing delivered price. A phantom freight charge (essentially an extra profit margin) is included in the delivered price of sellers located at considerable distance from the basing point who sell to local customers. The price discrimination resulting from the use of the single basing-point system has been held to be illegal by the FTC, particularly for industries with a dispersed plant-location pattern which turn out products that involve high transportation cost relative to the value of the product.

Under the *multiple basing-point system* producers compute delivered prices by adding to factory price a freight charge to the customer from any one of two or more basing points customarily used by the industry, regardless of the producer's actual cost of transportation to the customer. Such geographical price differentials involve some phantom freight in certain cases and some freight absorption in other cases. Though the multiple basing-point system is employed in some industries, there is doubt as to its legality in cases in which geographical price discrimination is considerable.

Firms in a given line of business are interrelated not only through more or less common pricing practices, as outlined above, but through organized interfirm relations set up for mutual advantage.

INTERFIRM RELATIONS

Firms in the same industry or in similar line of business set up trade associations as non-profit organizations for mutual benefit. There are over ten thousand national, state, and local associations of business firms and professions. Trade-association membership, which is of course voluntary, may be horizontal or vertical. A horizontal association is comprised of firms in the same stage of production or business activity, that is, they are competitors. A vertical association is comprised of firms in successive stages in the production or marketing of similar products. Firms cooperate through their trade associations to advance mutual interests by providing such services as traffic information, credit information, joint advertising, market surveys, industry standardization programs, cost-accounting procedures, and statistics on industry operations, prices, and terms in contracts.

Trade associations, notably in industries processing bulky materials and products (lumber, canned food), cooperate in dealing with such traffic problems as freight classification and changes in freight rates. Many associations provide members with information pertaining to the credit standings of dealers with whom the industry does business. Joint advertising is commoner in industries comprised of small producers selling in wide markets and in industries putting out products that are comparatively uniform (e.g., specialized agricultural products). Cooperative advertising may be designed to increase the general consumption of the product, to ward off competition from substitute products, and to introduce a new type of product put out by the industry.

Standardization and product simplification are common joint undertakings by trade associations. Associations have been instrumental in formulating standard specifications for raw materials and stipulating standard grades, sizes, and specifications for certain types of products. In some cases standardization has extended to stipulation of terms in commercial contracts including discount scales. Through product-simplification programs associations have reduced excess variety in sizes of containers and in certain types of goods. Standardization and product simplification reduce processing cost and inventory levels, lessen waste, contribute to conveniences of benefit to buyers and sellers alike. But when standardization and product simplification eliminate the availability of cheaper grades, they limit a buyer's range of choice in that he is obliged to purchase a more expensive item.

Producers in many industries employ (sometimes through the trade association) patent pools for the interchange of patent rights through a system of cross-licensing among firms. A patent pool avoids some of the expensive litigation between patent-holders over conflicting or overlapping patent grants. The use of an efficient new process or improved product designs and components often requires the availability of a number of patents. Broad cross-licensing agreements tend to increase the degree of competition among the member producers in the industry. Because they have a number of important patents to contribute, patent pools are often limited to big firms. Hence, a big producer can use the large number of the pooled patents in return for the limited number he owns and contributes to the pool. Small producers sometimes have a patent-exchange arrangement with some one large firm. Because of the relatively limited patent exchange with one big producer, a small producer can enjoy only a small segment of the total patented technology available to big producers. When members of a patent pool exclude certain rival firms, the production costs of the latter producers may be relatively high with the result that competition in the industry is lessened. If the pool refuses licensing privileges to outsiders, it stands as a considerable barrier to the entry of new producers into the industry, and this, too, weakens competition. Some cross-licensing arrangements of certain firms have, particularly in the past, extended to the international field and were to some extent used for cartelistic market allocation and restriction of competition.

The statistical reporting to members of trade associations generally covers the industry's rate of production, inventory levels, sales and shipments, unfilled orders or backlog, cancellation of orders, and capacity. The industry's volume of output may be shown as a percentage of rated capacity, and production may be broken down according to product. The rate of output may be expressed as a ratio of shipments, and finished inventories may be indicated as stock-sales ratio. Output, shipments, and inventory levels may be compared with a past period as well as forecast. Producers' projection of sales and GNP can indicate "balanced" production, "underproduction," or "overproduction." High stock levels with considerable idle capacity would indicate pressure on prices and may foreshadow price cuts (or off-season discounts) to liquidate stock, particularly if the industry annually puts out new models or styles.

Since much plant production is relatively homogeneous in a given industry and since the cost-accounting problem and approach are similar for many producers, it is natural for trade associations to provide an accounting service. It partly derives from the precedent set for the use of a uniform cost-accounting method by the utility commissions and the Interstate Commerce Commission in their rate-regulation problems. Many associations have designed and advanced the use of a uniform cost-accounting system suited to the industry; their service ranges to the provision of a standard cost-accounting system. The use of a well-designed uniform cost-accounting system insures that producers have accurate cost data for tax purposes and for informed and intelligent pricing. The availability of industry cost information and cost ratios (which may be presented as industry averages) enables producers to make comparisons and to seek out cost-reduction measures when their costs are out of line. The dissemination of industry cost figures can lead to an appropriate minimum price (one sufficient to cover cost) and to a greater uniform cost figure. Since membership in an association is voluntary, compliance with industry standard-practice proposals should not be assumed.

Besides promoting the use of uniform cost-accounting methods which aid in forestalling price cutting due to producers' ignorance of their true costs, associations have tended to influence price through *open price reporting* carried out by the exchange of price lists or by reporting through the association or publicly. The dissemination of price statistics by the association places firms in a better position to meet the tactics of purchasing agents intent on playing one producer against another. A compilation of price data can indicate the range of prices at which products are being sold. The availability of average prices over a period of time indicates the price trend. Price information aids firms in setting their prices with respect to the average price, if not at the average level. Timely price information tends to better stabilize prices and limit fluctuations to a smaller range. Bona fide price reporting limits secret price cutting and, in the case of an oligopoly, tends to facilitate price leadership.

In addition to joint activities through trade associations and patent pools, firms sometimes develop interindustry relations in the form of *reciprocal business dealings* whereby independent concerns make mutual concessions to promote the commercial interests of each. A well-known form is reciprocal buying whereby one firm buys the products or services of another with an assurance that the other firm will make reciprocal purchases. Thus, a firm can sometimes use its buying power to promote its sales. The kinds of structural features and relations in industry conducive to the development of reciprocal buying are situations in which a large firm (particularly a diversified company) produces products for sale to industrial firms to whom it is a potential customer. A firm can seek out among its suppliers those who are potential customers. Firms in the field of transportation and producers of machinery, industrial materials, and electrical supplies, for example, would likely engage in reciprocal buying. Since a railroad buys steel and coal, it can induce producers of these products to use its transportation service in exchange for reciprocal purchases of steel and coal. A large diversified firm producing locomotives or other rolling stock can induce railways to buy its products in exchange for the purchase of their transportation service. Since tight reciprocal-buying arrangements can ward off rival firms from certain markets, reciprocity tends to secure a firm's position in the market, expand its sales, and enlarge the firm's size. Reciprocity is economically significant when producers can gain sales that they would not otherwise acquire in ordinary market situations. Thus, reciprocal buying derives from imperfectly competitive markets and accentuates market imperfections.

Interfirm cooperation may take the form of *joint ownership* and use of a facility (a power plant or transportation facilities) or the *joint development* of a new type of production process. A joint venture for large construction undertakings often involves a number of corporations which contribute the different specializations required for the completion of the engineering project. Usually the major interest in the joint undertaking is held by a sponsoring company which works out the role of all participating firms. Upon completion the "partners" generally share the final return on the bases of capital contributed. The scope and pattern of interfirm relations differ, of course, for each line of business, as any industry study would indicate. Since a firm is an operating unit in a given line of business, an economic analysis of a firm in a given field is an extension of the study of an industry. Chapter 6 is devoted to an analysis of the structural design and behavior of a firm.

QUESTIONS FOR REVIEW AND APPLICATION

1. What are the factors that determine an industry's market structure—the competitive relationship among producers in the sale of products in given markets? Discuss.

2. Why is pure oligopoly commoner in early-stage industries than in industries engaged in final-product output?

3. What is the competitive fringe of an oligopolistic industry?

4. Do pure oligopolies have greater discretion in setting price than do differentiated oligopolies, other things being equal? Explain.

5. Can a differentiated oligopolist more readily estimate his market share from a projected industry demand than a pure oligopolist? Explain.

6. (a) What is meant by an industry's concentration ratio of production? (b) Does industry concentration of production contribute to oligopoly? Explain.

7. (a) How may the concentration of production in a given industry be measured? What are the problems in measuring such concentration? (b) Distinguish between an industry's company concentration ratio of production and its plant concentration ratio of production. Is there necessarily a direct correlation between the two?

8. Explain how a patent pool arrangement among big producers can step up the pace of technological advance in an industry. Can such a pool impede entry of new producers into the industry? Explain.

9. What are the principal types of barriers that tend to impede entry of new producers into a highly concentrated oligopolistic industry?

10. How does an oligopolistic market structure contribute to price stability?

11. (a) Explain what is meant by price leadership. (b) What aspects of an oligopolistic market structure permit a producer to assume price leadership?

12. Explain why price followership tends to be less common during boom and depression times.

13. Why do firms in the same line of business (industry) tend to follow the same or similar pricing practices?

14. Will producers find it advantageous to make the same percentage change in selling prices for all models in a product line? Explain.

15. "When a producer consistently uses cost-plus pricing (i.e., always adds the same markup), he ignores elasticity of demand and the influence of the rate of output on unit cost." Explain.

16. Explain why producers who use flexible markup pricing would likely take into account differences in demand elasticity among the various market segments.

17. What market and demand conditions are necessary before discriminatory price (differential pricing) can be successfully employed by sellers?

18. What are the principal types of market segmentation that permit producers to use differential pricing?

19. Explain how effective differential pricing by an industry can be a means for enlarging total sales volume and for increasing total earnings.

20. Distinguish between functional discounts, quantity discounts, geographical price differentials, and the multiple basing-point system of pricing.

21. How does the single basing-point system of pricing affect expansion of an industry's capacity in different areas of the country?

22. (a) "Though producers in certain industries may not actually compete on the basis of price, they usually strive for an increase in market share on the basis of non-price competition." Explain. (b) What are the principal forms of non-price competition?

23. What are the important forms of interfirm relations in industry?

References and Supplementary Readings for Part II

Input-Output Relations

*CHENERY, H. B., and CLARK, P. G. *Interindustry Economics.* New York: John Wiley & Sons, Inc., 1959.
LEONTIEF, WASSILY. *Studies in the Structure of the American Economy; Theoretical and Empirical Explorations in Input-Output Analysis.* New York: Oxford University Press, 1953.

Location

GREINHUT, M. L. *Plant Location in Theory and in Practice; The Economics of Space.* Chapel Hill: University of North Carolina Press, 1956.
HOOVER, E. M. *The Location of Economic Activity.* New York: McGraw-Hill Book Co., Inc., 1948.
LOSCH, AUGUST. *The Economics of Location.* New Haven: Yale University Press, 1954.

Labor Force

DAVIS, PEARCE, and MATCHETT, GERALD J. *Modern Labor Economics.* New York: The Ronald Press Co., 1954.
SHISTER, J. *Economics of the Labor Market.* Philadelphia: J. B. Lippincott Co., 1956.
SLICHTER, S. H. *Union Policies and Industrial Management.* Washington, D.C.: The Brookings Institution, 1941.
STIEBER, JACK W. *The Steel Industry Wage Structure; A Study of the Joint Union-Management Job Evaluation Program in the Basic Steel Industry.* Cambridge: Harvard University Press, 1959.
VITELES, MORRIS. *Motivation and Morale in Industry.* New York: W. W. Norton & Co., Inc., 1953.
WOYTINSKY, W. S., and associates. *Employment and Wages in the United States.* New York: Twentieth Century Fund, 1953.

Materials and Inventory

ABRAMOVITZ, MOSES. *Inventories and Business Cycles, with Special Reference to Manufacturing Inventories.* New York: National Bureau of Economic Research, Inc., 1950.

Cost, Demand, Market Structure, and Pricing

ANDREWS, P. W. S. *Manufacturing Business.* London: Macmillan & Co., Ltd., 1949. Chaps. 3-7.

* Suggested reading.

*BACKMAN, JULES. *Pricing Practices and Price Policies.* New York: The Ronald Press Co., 1953. Chaps. 5, 12.
*BAIN, JOE S. *Pricing, Distribution and Employment.* New York: Henry Holt & Co., Inc., 1948. Chaps. 2-3, 5-8.
*BAIN, JOE S. *Industrial Organization.* New York: John Wiley & Sons, Inc., 1959. Chaps. 2, 4-11.
*BERGFELD, ALBERT J., et al. *Pricing for Profit and Growth.* New York: McGraw-Hill Book Co., Inc., 1957.
*CLARK, J. M. *Economics of Overhead Costs.* Chicago: University of Chicago Press, 1923. Chap. 3.
*COLBERG, M. R., BRADFORD, W. C., and ALT, R. M. *Business Economics; Principles and Cases.* Rev. ed.; Homewood, Ill.: Richard D. Irwin, Inc., 1957. Chaps. 3-6, 9.
*DEAN, JOEL, and Joel Dean Associates. *Managerial Economics.* Englewood Cliffs, N.J.: Prentice-Hall, Inc., 1951. Chaps. 2, 4-5, 7-9.
*DOYLE, LEONARD H. *Economics of Business Enterprise.* New York: McGraw-Hill Book Co., Inc., 1952. Chaps. 2, 4, 8-9, 11-13.
*KAPLAN, A. D. H., DIRLAM, JOEL B., and LANZILOTTI, ROBERT F. *Pricing in Big Business.* Washington, D.C.: The Brookings Institution, 1958.
*OWENS, RICHARD N. *Business Management and Public Policy.* Homewood, Ill.: Richard D. Irwin, Inc., 1958. Chaps. 20-23.
*OXENFELDT, A. R. *Industrial Pricing and Market Practice.* Englewood Cliffs, N.J.: Prentice-Hall, Inc., 1951. Chaps. 4-5.
RICHMOND, SAMUEL B. *Principles of Statistical Analysis.* New York: The Ronald Press Co., 1957.
*SPENCER, MILTON, and SIEGELMAN, LOUIS. *Managerial Economics.* Homewood, Ill.: Richard D. Irwin, Inc., 1959. Chaps. 3, 5, 7, 8.
*STIGLER, GEORGE J. *The Theory of Price.* New York: The Macmillan Co., 1946. Chap. 16.
*WEINTRAUB, SIDNEY. *Price Theory.* New York: Pitman Publishing Corp., 1949. Chap. 14.

Rationalization in Industry

BRADY, R. A. *The Rationalization Movement in German Industry.* Berkeley: University of California Press, 1933.
FLORENCE, SARGENT P. *The Logic of American and British Industry.* Chapel Hill: University of North Carolina Press, 1954.
NELSON, RALPH L. *Merger Movements in American Industry 1895–1956.* Princeton: Princeton University Press (National Bureau of Economic Research, Inc.), 1959.
URWICK, LYNDALL. *The Meaning of Rationalization.* London: Nisbet & Co., Ltd., 1929.

Cases and Problems

MILLER, S. S. *Manufacturing Policy; A Casebook of Major Production Problems in Six Selected Industries.* Homewood, Ill.: Richard D. Irwin, Inc., 1957.

Industry Studies—General

*ADAMS, WALTER (ed.). *The Structure of American Industry.* Rev. ed.; New York: The Macmillan Co., 1954.
ALDEFER, E. B., and MICHL, H. E. *Economics of American Industry.* 3d ed.; New York: McGraw-Hill Book Co., Inc., 1957.

* Suggested reading.

ALLEN, EDWARD L. *Economics of American Manufacturing.* New York: Henry Holt & Co., Inc., 1952.

ALLEN, G. C. *British Industries and Their Organization.* London: Longmans, Green & Co., Ltd., 1945.

GLOVER, J. G., and CORNELL, W. B. *The Development of American Industries.* 3d ed.; Englewood Cliffs, N.J.: Prentice-Hall, Inc., 1951.

VANCE, STANLEY. *American Industries.* Englewood Cliffs, N.J.: Prentice-Hall, Inc., 1955.

*ZIMMERMANN, ERICH W. *World Resources and Industries.* Rev. ed.; New York: Harper & Brothers, 1951.

Industry Studies—Specific

ANDREWS, PHILIP W. S., and BRUNNER, ELIZABETH. *Capital Development in Steel: A Study of United States Steel Companies, Ltd.* Oxford: Basil Blackwell, 1951.

BACKMAN, JULES, and GAINSBURGH, M. R. *The Economics of the Cotton Textile Industry.* New York: National Industrial Conference Board, 1946.

BAIN, JOE S. *The Pacific Coast Petroleum Industry.* Berkeley: University of California Press, 1944–1947. (3 vols.)

BARGER, H., and SCHURR, S. H. *The Mining Industries, 1899–1939: A Study of Output, Employment and Productivity.* New York: National Bureau of Economic Research, Inc., 1944.

BRIGHT, ARTHUR AARON. *The Electric Lamp Industry: Technological Change and Economic Development from 1800 to 1947.* New York: The Macmillan Co., 1947.

CARR, C. C. *Alcoa, an American Enterprise.* New York: Rinehart & Co., Inc., 1952.

DAUGHERTY, C. R., de CHAZEAU, M. G., and STRATTON, S. S. *Economics of the Iron and Steel Industry.* New York: McGraw-Hill Book Co., Inc., 1937. (2 vols.)

DAVIS, H. S., and associates. *Vertical Integration in the Textile Industries.* Washington, D.C.: The Textile Foundation, 1938.

FEDERAL RESERVE BANK OF CHICAGO. *A Financial and Economic Survey of the Meat Packing Industry.* Chicago: The Federal Reserve Bank of Chicago, 1946.

FEDERAL TRADE COMMISSION. *The Copper Industry.* Washington, D.C.: Government Printing Office, March, 1947.

FEDERAL TRADE COMMISSION. *Report on the Motor Vehicle Industry.* Washington, D.C.: Government Printing Office, 1939.

GLAISER, MARTIN G. *Public Utilities in American Capitalism.* New York: The Macmillan Company, 1957.

HAIGH, R. W., and McLEAN, J. G. *The Growth of Integrated Oil Companies.* Cambridge: Harvard University Press, 1954.

HAYNES, W. *Chemical Economics.* New York: D. Van Nostrand Co., Inc., 1933.

HEMPEL, E. H. *The Economics of Chemical Industries.* New York: John Wiley & Sons, Inc., 1939.

HUETTIG, M. D. *Economic Control of the Motion Picture Industry.* Philadelphia: University of Pennsylvania Press, 1944.

SCHRAEDER, GERTRUDE. *The Growth of Major Steel Companies.* Baltimore: Johns Hopkins Press, 1953.

SEIDMAN, J. I. *The Needle Trades.* New York: Rinehart & Co., Inc., 1942.

SMITH, T. R. *The Cotton Textile Industry of Fall River.* New York: King's Crown Press, 1944.

SUBCOMMITTEE ON THE STUDY OF MONOPOLY POWER, HOUSE JUDICIARY COMMITTEE. *The Iron and Steel Industry.* Washington, D.C.: Government Printing Office, 1950.

TENNANT, R. B. *The American Cigarette Industry.* New Haven: Yale University Press, 1950.

* Suggested reading.

United Nations Department of Economic Affairs. *European Steel Trends in Setting of the World Markets.* (Prepared by the Steel Division, United Nations Economic Commission for Europe.) Geneva: United Nations, 1949.

U.S. Department of Agriculture. *Technological Progress in the Meat Packing Industry.* Marketing Research Report 29. Washington, D.C.: Government Printing Office, 1945.

U.S. Department of Agriculture and Colorado A.&M. College. *The Economics of Sugar Beet Mechanization.* Washington, D.C.: Government Printing Office, 1953.

U.S. Department of Commerce, Office of Domestic Commerce. *U.S. Petroleum Refining—War and Postwar.* Washington, D.C.: Government Printing Office, 1947.

U.S. Department of Labor. *Capital Requirements and Operating Ratios, Men's Shirt Industry.* Washington, D.C.: Government Printing Office, 1952.

U.S. Department of Labor. *The Paperboard Industry: Capital Requirements and Operating Ratios.* Washington, D.C.: Government Printing Office, 1953.

Part III

THE FIRM

CHAPTER 6

Structural Design: Organization and Scope of Enterprise

Managerial and industrial economics deals with the nature of the firm, particularly the corporate firm, as the principal productive unit in the capitalistic economy. The firm typically functions as a specialized productive unit which is integrated with other business and consuming units in the economic process through numerous market transactions. The firm performs its economic function through the production of goods and the distribution of income to labor and other factors and through the accumulation of retained earnings and external funds for capital formation. The economics of business enterprise largely analyzes the central role of the executive entrepreneur in combining productive factors and in designing the scope and structure of the enterprise. It also conducts an analysis of the firm's short-run productive function and adjustment to market demand and its long-run structural adaptation to changes in technology and input prices of productive factors and to shifts in market demands. It is primarily through firms and their plant establishments that economic growth and progress take place. The firm's economic and technological organization and the effectiveness of managerial direction essentially determine productive efficiency and the volume of goods that can be produced with available resources.

An economist may study the structural design of a business in a given field for one of a number of *analytic purposes*. He may wish

(1) to seek out those structural features of the firm that provide insight into the nature and behavior of the operating enterprise as compared to the simplified theoretical model hypothesized by conventional economic theory, (2) to show how environmental impacts (shifts in demand, cyclical fluctuations, taxation) influence the structure of business enterprise, (3) to identify the mainsprings of productivity and economic growth on the enterprise level, and (4) to provide a basis for forecasting, decision making, and long-range business planning and investment. Since the firm is a producing unit in an industry, the economic analysis of business enterprise is an extension of the study of an industry.

A comprehensive study of business enterprise and its behavior essentially involves an analysis of the structure of the firm as presented in Part III. The structural design of a firm is comprised of a given pattern of managerial organization, scope of business and line of products, plant specialization and factor proportionability, the multiple-plant system, break-even and cost pattern, competitive situation, and sources of profitability.

The Corporate Firm

The firm as a business unit consists of capital facilities and other resources devoted to a profit-making venture under unified managerial control. Comprised of one or more establishments, the firm buys labor services and various material resources in one set of markets, transforms the material through a productive process (adds value), and then sells the goods or services in another set of markets with the purpose of making a profit. The firm's business operations and productive process are characterized by interdependence of functions and division of labor. A business enterprise relies on a central controlling authority to integrate and coordinate the specialized activities and commercial transactions of the enterprise. The firm is primarily the governing agency exercising control over commercial transactions and plant establishments producing and distributing goods and services for a profit. The authority and entrepreneurial direction inherent in the firm derives from its particular form of ownership—whether that of the proprietorship, partnership, corporation, holding company, or other form.

The corporation is the most prominent ownership form of enterprise in the medium and large enterprise and in many fields of small business. The prominence of the corporation derives from the fact that the corporate form facilitates the raising of large amounts of capital necessary to exploit modern highly mechanized production technology and large-scale organization structure, whether in the field of transportation, public utilities, trade and distribution, or manufacturing. The features of the corporation which appeal to and attract investors and thereby facilitate the amassing of capital are: the availability of various classes of ownership shares which differ with respect to risk, income, and control; the availability of either a small or a large ownership share (permitting investors to diversify their holdings and reduce risk); limited liability in stock ownership and ease of sale or transferability of ownership; and the comparative stability and continuous existence of the corporation which enable it to borrow funds more easily. Business corporations differ in many ways. Significant from the economic point of view are those which differ with respect to (1) ownership and control and (2) scale and adaptability of organization.

A *private or closed corporation* is one whose stock is held by a few individuals or by a family who as actual owners generally exercise their prerogatives of ownership and control of the enterprise. The closed corporation, like the individual proprietorship and the partnership, is essentially owner-manager dominated. Most large business enterprises, however, are *public corporations,* so designated because stock ownership is scattered and widely held by the general public. Large corporations are ordinarily multiple-plant enterprises. Some of their divisional plants and establishments may have been financed and built by the company, while others of their establishments may have been acquired through mergers or are controlled as subsidiaries. Some firms have come into existence through consolidation, a process whereby a new corporation is formed when two or more companies combine to succeed themselves.

A *holding company* is generally organized to gain control of other corporations through the purchase of a controlling bloc of their voting stock. (The controlled subsidiary company retains its legal identity.) The holding-company device has often been used as a step toward merger or consolidation: after securing control of a number of corporations, the holding company merges the subsidiaries (e.g., through issuing stock in exchange for securities of the subsidiaries) into a single corporation comprised of many divisional units. Most corporations in the United States are operating-holding companies. Such holding companies are directly engaged in business through their own establishments and, as "parent" corporations, also control subsidiary companies. Less prominent is the pure holding company. This is a non-operating corporation which simply acquires a sufficient amount of voting stock in other corporations and controls the subsidiaries through the voting privilege of its owned stock.

In its growth through acquisition of subsidiaries, a holding company aims to gain control of desired operating companies by means of a small outlay in cash. It need only acquire a bare majority of the voting stock (which is usually a small percentage of total capitalization) of an operating company to obtain control. Sometimes only "working" control is sufficient if ownership of the common stock of the operating company is broadly scattered. The holding company may purchase the controlling interest of an operating company with the proceeds from the public sale of the holding company's securities, such as bonds and preferred stock. The holding company may also obtain funds by floating collateral trust bonds secured by the stock of the controlled subsidiary companies. Sometimes a holding company can induce shareholders of the operating company to take the securities of the holding company in exchange for their voting stock.

The holding-company device has been used to obtain pyramided control of immense business empires. After the initial empire-building stage, a holding company tends to simplify its over-all system by merging one subsidiary with another and by eliminating some intermediate holding companies. Most parent corporations provide their subsidiaries with managerial and professional services (on a fee basis, of course) in areas of accounting, finance, advertising and promotion, and engineering and research. Such services may be economically justified when subsidiaries are small, are largely in the same field of business, or are mainly engaged in production and distribution. Financing is often an important service to subsidiaries; a holding company may, for instance, purchase for resale the securities of a subsidiary, or it may advance funds directly on a subsidiary's note.

Because of its ease of organization, the holding-company form of enterprise enjoys considerable flexibility with respect to financing, expansion, and development of business. The managers of a holding company may quietly acquire the controlling stock of desired operating companies without consulting the corporation whose stock is being purchased. The parent corporation may use its subsidiaries (or organize new ones) to handle such phases of business as transportation, the supplying of components, or overseas business. The holding-company device permits the parent corporation to acquire control of an operating company for the purpose of penetrating new fields of business or, sometimes, for acquiring available plant capacity and more business volume more cheaply than it would be to build a new plant and organize an establishment from scratch. A parent corporation may use the holding-company device for both vertical and horizontal expansion. The parent corporation may also divert business from one subsidiary to another in line with an over-all plan for the allocation of production; it may more widely use the trade name of a successful subsidiary corporation for promotion of sales or for the introduction of a new product.

Since subsidiaries operate as separate legal entities, a parent corporation can minimize its loss in an unprofitable subsidiary or venture by merely liquidating its stock investment through the sale of the controlling shares. A parent corporation can thus use the holding-company device to reduce risk in the undertaking of a new venture. Damage suits and claims against a single subsidiary generally do not seriously injure other subsidiaries or the holding company itself.

In addition to income from fees for managerial and other services rendered to subsidiaries, the holding company derives income in the form of dividends and interest on the stock and bonds it holds in the subsidiaries. The equity earnings of the holding company can be high because of the pyramided control of many subsidiaries, though such pyramiding can also multiply losses in similar proportion. Holding companies have at times abused subsidiaries by charging excessive fees for services, exacting large cash dividends, securing substantial "upstream loans," and by other measures.

As compared to a multiple-plant corporation or to a consolidated company, a holding company is not without its disadvantages. High administrative costs occur from the maintenance of many corporate structures which involves outlays for franchise taxes, salaries and expense accounts for officers, boards of directors, and the like. Though the tax burden is somewhat lowered because the parent corporation's earnings from one subsidiary are offset by the losses in another subsidiary, corporate income taxes must be paid as profits pass from one subsidiary to another up the pyramided system. The tax burden against the constituent subsidiaries sometimes induces the holding company to merge the subsidiaries into a single corporation comprised of many divisions.

ROLE OF EXECUTIVE MANAGEMENT

The actual management of many larger public business corporations (especially those in the holding-company class) has tended to pass into the hands of the "management group" (top officers and "inside" directors) who are relatively free to operate the business and pursue policies without much interference from the bulk of the stock-owners. Investors generally play a passive role in company management because stock ownership in a large corporation is widely dispersed (individual investors typically diversify their holdings among corporations) and because many shareholders, lacking interest or knowledge, are unable to appraise adequately or express an intelligent opinion on company policies. The "management control" or the "separation of ownership and control" feature of many large corporations also derives from the fact that generally only a small proportion of the total securities issued by a corporation is voting stock, and, at most, a 51 per cent holding of voting stock is often sufficient to secure control. The management group may insure its position through the availability of unissued voting stock which may, if necessary, be issued to the appropriate control group. But management's "trusteeship" position, need for profitable operations and steady dividend payments, and company reputation more or less insure the over-all direction of the enterprise in the interest of stock-owners.

In the typical large corporation the board of directors, as a separate body, does not ordinarily assume an important role in the leadership function, particularly with reference to initiation of decision making.[1] In the management-controlled corporation the board of directors, as an independent body, often tends to be somewhat passive. Through its control of proxy machinery, moreover, the executive group itself selects many of the board members. A study of 535 manufacturing corporations showed that executives as inside members occupied from 40 to 50 per cent of the seats on the board of directors.[2] Inside directors include presidents, vice-presidents, sales executives, financial vice-presidents and treasurers, and plant and works managers. If the board of directors is largely a meeting of key executives, it is likely to serve as a coordinating body for policy decisions already made by executives.

Of the "outside" directors, substantial shareholders (or their representatives) typically hold about one out of five seats on the board. Prominent businessmen, financial counselors (bankers, investment brokers), and legal and other counselors also generally make up a large proportion of the outside directors. The actual situation would, of course, vary from company to company. When a corpora-

---

[1] R. A. Gordon, *Business Leadership in the Large Corporation* (Washington, D.C.: The Brookings Institution, 1945), pp. 343–344.

[2] National Industrial Conference Board, *The Corporate Directorship* (New York: National Industrial Conference Board, Inc., 1953), p. 7.

tion is undergoing rapid expansion and when a corporation is in financial difficulties, banking interests would tend to be somewhat more prominently represented on a corporation's board of directors or to have a bigger influence on executives' business control and decision making.[3]

Over-all direction and managerial control in most large corporations rests essentially with the *top executive group:* the president, key officers and vice-presidents, general managers, and full-time directors. Executives are the individuals responsible for the design of the over-all organization structure, selection of key personnel, top control of the operating organization, and implementation of general objectives and long-range plans. The top executive group establishes the organizational means and policy guides by which lower management makes operating decisions and carries out the productive tasks, and it provides the conscious and authoritative direction and coordination of the enterprise. Executives are thus identified in terms of their general functions and roles in the operating enterprise. The chief executive may be the officer who carries the title of president or chairman of the board of directors. Organizational arrangements and the division of managerial power at the top of the executive hierarchy would, of course, vary from firm to firm. By using appropriate organizational arrangements and control techniques to reduce the managerial burden (i.e., offset diminishing returns to management), business leaders are able to control effectively a large enterprise.

Hence, business leadership and managerial authority, rather than being exclusively centered in one individual, is often wielded by key officers who function as an executive group. Top leadership may be shared among executives in a number of different ways. In the formulation of company policies and plans, for instance, the chief executive is generally aided by, and works with, an executive group which usually functions as a formal (and sometimes informal) executive committee. The general executive committee (also designated by some such title as the "general management committee"), comprised of the chief executive and key executives, serves primarily as an over-all coordinating body and as a group that formulates or reviews long-range company plans and initiates decisions to be approved by the chief executive or it may, itself, serve as the

---

[3] The banker's role in corporation management has tended to decline as corporations rely more heavily on such internal financial sources as retained earnings and depreciation funds. The influence of insurance companies in corporate management tends to increase as these financial institutions become bigger suppliers of investment funds.

approving body.[4]   In the large firm both the upper and lower levels
of the executive hierarchy generally initiate and formulate decisions
for review and ultimate approval by the chief executive or by the
top executive group. The executive committee, for instance, frequently receives for review and approval plans and decisions ini-
tiated by one of several functional committees which deal with
engineering, manufacturing, marketing, and purchasing, among
other phases.[5]

The chief executive lightens his managerial load through delegation of authority along the lines of *functional specialization*. The
function of top management is divided and allocated to executives
(often designated "vice-presidents") along the usual lines of functional specialization (vice-presidents in charge of finance, purchasing, manufacturing or operations, sales, engineering, industrial
relations).

The task of the various executives is lightened through the *hierarchical organizational arrangement* whereby they delegate more or
less clearly defined managerial authority (power to make operating
decisions) down the line, for example, to department managers who
delegate to section heads who in turn delegate to supervisors. To
avoid overburdening an officer or a department head, the allocation
of related activities (i.e., the managerial assignment) is usually confined to a reasonably limited span of executive control. When the
activities, for instance, are more diverse or intricate, an executive
or head takes control over a smaller number of activities. If the
activities are closely related or are more routine, an executive takes
control over a larger number of activities.   Executives and line managers increase their effectiveness and lighten their burden through
the use of administrative secretaries, staff planners, and other staff
assistants and through the design and establishment of standard
procedures and systems which relieve the line authority of routine
duties.

Though functional specialization of management and business
operations improves efficiency through the division of labor, it increases the need for coordinating and integrating functions and
operating policies in the areas of finance, production, sales, expansion, etc. It is largely through executives, committees, and staff
specialists that company managers seek to achieve the desired
coordination of various specialized functions. Thus, in the large
corporation the process of managing and decision making (the en-

---

[4] P. H. Holden, *Top-Management Organization and Control* (Stanford University,
Calif.: Stanford University Press, 1941), p. 22.
[5] *Ibid.*, pp. 66–73.

trepreneurial function) is delegated and diffused throughout the organizational hierarchy of executive managers, staff specialists, and full-time directors.

OPTIMUM MANAGERIAL UNIT

Output must reach a certain minimum volume before managers can organize an optimum-production unit (an efficient-sized plant or multiple-plant grouping) that obtains economies through utilization of mass-production technology. When marketing is extensive and makes up a significant proportion of the selling price, economies stemming from large-scale marketing tend to determine the optimum-size business unit. With the continued expansion of a firm, economies from large-scale production, selling, procurement, and financing can become appreciable. Managerial economies in the large firm derive not only from employment of experts to cover specialized phases of the business (both in line functions and in staff functions) but from the full-time utilization of an expert's high-priced talents.

As a firm grows in size, executives maintain, and often increase, managerial efficiency by redesigning the organization and introducing a greater degree of managerial division of labor and decentralization of decision-making authority. This, of course, calls for the staffing of middle and lower managerial levels with more able and better trained men. The optimum managerial unit does not solely depend on size of organization. The *optimum-size managerial unit* depends primarily on the number of diverse managerial functions and variables found in the firm's business operations, rather than on mere size in terms of value added in production, number of people employed, or amount of capital controlled.

The task of coordinating specialized managerial functions would be less difficult in a large firm doing business in a narrow field or in a single industry than in a large firm engaged in diverse fields of business. Whatever the optimum managerial unit for a given firm, economies from the managerial division of labor must outweigh the extra cost of organizational arrangement and managerial effort necessary for coordination. The continued expansion of a firm nonetheless eventually leads to diseconomies from ill-coordination and inability of executive managers to comprehend adequately and control a wide range of diverse variables and special operating situations necessary for effective over-all direction and planning. The very big diversified firms, however, often obtain significant offsetting economies and profit-making potential from large-scale research and the use of sizable retained earnings and depreciation funds for investment. Profitability from quick exploitation of technological developments and rapid expansion into growing fields can often more than offset whatever diseconomies arise in large, unwieldy, bureaucratic firms doing business in diverse fields.

DEGREE OF MANAGERIAL DECENTRALIZATION

Centralized administration and decision making are found most often in smaller enterprises. Through centralized planning and direction the typical owner-manager feels that he can secure adequate performance and also avoid the need to employ additional supervisory or other higher-priced personnel. One-man managerial control thus tends to be imbedded in the nature of entrepreneurial ownership and in traditional practice. Moreover, since in the large corporation the chief executive (or the top executive group) is ultimately responsible for the successful operation of the enterprise, he is inclined to retain important areas of authority and control necessary to fulfill his responsibility and to delegate only limited authority and responsibility to lower managerial levels and local plant managers. An executive's power and status (and often income and job security) depend on the amount of authority he wields, the "unique and indispensable" ability he possesses, and the position he holds. The development of managerial-control methods, moreover, has tended to improve the effectiveness of centralized administration and further its adoption. An executive is able to manage and control a larger operation through the use of modern reporting and control techniques (operating ratios, statistical summaries, computers), systematized procedures, and staff assistants. Modern means of communication enable a chief executive to issue direct orders to distant operations and to control subordinates. Through centralized management a firm benefits from the unusual administrative ability and effective generalship of strong, talented executives. The foregoing forces and tendencies toward managerial centralization are somewhat offset by organizational arrangements and techniques that make managerial decentralization profitable.

Decentralization of managerial authority in the bigger firm is initially achieved through functional decentralization: the division of the top management function along the lines of functional specialization and the allocation and delegation of the key functions to technical and managerial experts (purchasing agent, sales manager, works manager, research director, personnel director, and the like). The top executive group generally assumes centralized authority and control over company policies, long-range programing, coordination of major functions, and the design of the organizational structure. Executives thus determine the degree and kind of decentralization logical for the various areas of management and business operation —i.e., what kinds of problems and decisions should be made by lower echelons and supervisory heads and what decisions should be reserved for executive action or review. The lower the organizational level to which decision-making authority is delegated, the greater the degree of decentralization.

The firm's staff experts on organizational design, guided by top policy, can ordinarily determine the degree of decentralization economical for the key phases and areas of the business. The sales and the purchasing functions may, for instance, warrant a greater degree of decentralization than that of finance and comptrollership. The decentralization plan must deal not only with the level at which a particular class of decisions is to be made but also with the manner whereby the decision is to be reviewed by higher administrative authority. Ideally, decision-making authority should be delegated as far down the organizational hierarchy as is practical and economical. Ordinarily, decision-making authority for short-term operational aspects and recurring problems can generally be delegated down the hierarchical structure to the level at which supervisory heads or technicians are sufficiently close to the problem that they can properly assess the pertinent facts and make appropriate decisions. Executive managers can outline general policies and procedures to guide lower supervisory heads for the desired or appropriate decisions on pertinent matters.

Executives would ordinarily require review and approval of only those decision-making problems that are of higher managerial significance and non-recurrent, involve high cost or expenditure of considerable sums, or must be coordinated with the functions of other departments or operating units. The delegation and delineation of decision-making authority must of course avoid costly duplication and overlapping of duties and the working at cross-purposes that result in friction.

Business leaders who employ a logical degree of managerial decentralization reap economic benefits through the concentration of top executive and managerial talent on essentials rather than on detailed operating problems, increased flexibility gained from timely decision making, greater organizational enthusiasm from a sense of participation in management, and through the development of supervisory ability which provides a supply of managerial talent for future years. The assignment of a given class of decisions to a lower level of authority should essentially be based on the marginal gain in efficiency and revenue over the additional cost of a larger supervisory staff.

Relatively greater economic advantages from decentralization can be expected for firms in expanding fields and in lines of business characterized by changing technology and shifts in market demand. The need for a greater degree of decentralization (delegation) of managerial authority and decision making also stems from such structural changes and trends as the growth in the size of business enterprise, regional dispersal of operations, diversification, an increased recognition of the efficiency to be derived from decentralization, and the need for greater managerial emphasis on long-range programing and development which requires that executives be relieved of some administrative responsibilities, particularly those of a routine nature.

A large firm cannot operate effectively with the same degree of managerial centralization that a smaller enterprise can. The larger the firm, the more general must be the executive decision-making function. With growth in the size of business, relatively more emphasis tends to be given to organizational design. Business leaders recognize that operational necessity and workability dictate that managerial decentralization must accompany size.

Decentralization of managerial authority has generally tended to follow rather than precede the physical or regional decentralization of an enterprise. Managers of geographically separated operating units are often burdened with the task of maintaining effective communication with the home office, and they often have managerial problems that call for local decision making. Multiple-plant firms with dispersed establishments and business operations therefore generally organize for a greater degree of managerial decentralization than do firms with geographically concentrated establishments. When the firm's branch establishments are duplicate units performing the same or similar operations and commercial transactions, managerial centralization is likely to be greater—a number of managerial offices may be set up to direct regional business operations. When branch establishments put out different products and carry out distinct business operations and transactions, a greater degree of managerial discretion over local operations is likely to exist. The very big or highly diversified firms generally decentralize by setting up major operating divisions specializing according to type of product or type of manufacturing process, and they usually assign a general manager (or a works manager) to take charge of the division's output and sale of a related group of products.

The firm's central administrative office is usually staffed with various types of specialists who provide services (finance, accounting, engineering, marketing) to dispersed establishments. Company-wide services may also be provided by regional offices or subsidiaries. The chief executive's administrative office generally maintains control over company-wide policies and handles such matters as contract negotiations with labor unions, the procurement of key materials in major markets, research and development, forecasting and sales promotion, etc. The chief executive's office often includes a number of general staffs assigned to attain coordination and over-all control through such means as budgets, audits, and field-controller units and to draw up long-range plans for top executives who review programs and allocate investment funds for expansion and development of the various phases of the enterprise.

EXECUTIVE ENTREPRENEURIAL FUNCTIONS AND GOALS

The productive nature and structure of a business enterprise determine the economic tasks and managerial activities that must be carried out to control and direct the development of the business. "Entrepreneurship" is the ultimate authority and responsibility for directing and controlling the over-all enterprise through the making (or approving) of decisions which determine the scope, structure, and operations of the business. Executives performing entrepreneurial functions are those in the managerial organization who formulate over-all objectives and policies and make or approve decisions that determine the long-run direction and development of the enterprise. The top executive group develops and controls the over-all organization structure, delegates authority and responsibility for major functions, and coordinates and directs the enterprise. From the structural standpoint short-run entrepreneurial functions can be distinguished from the long-run functions.

Executive Functions

Executive *short-run routine functions* are carried out within the existing structural framework of the enterprise. In the short run, executives control current business operations by the continuous exercise of ultimate authority and by assuring the coordination of various specialized functions and solutions to current business problems. Executives evaluate the current business situation and make operating adjustments to attain the desired level of profitability.

They direct and adjust current operations in line with shifts in market demand and the competitive situation, changes in selling prices and input prices, and changes in other external factors. Executives control current business operations by formulating (or approving) the operating budget which stipulates the plant units to be operated or shut down, the rate of output, the length of the workweek, inventory ratios, working capital ratios, and so on.

In carrying out their *long-range functions,* executives review, adjust, and develop the scope and structure of the enterprise for long-term profitability. They formulate (or receive for approval from lower echelons) long-range plans and investment projects which include changes or additions to the product line, development of distribution outlets, plant modernization and expansion, plant acquisitions and mergers, reallocation of production in the multiple-plant system, and changes in the firm's over-all organizational structure. In the formulation and implementation of their long-range plans, executives take into account the existing structure of the firm and the industry and the business environment and economic trends. Their long-range plans may be rationally designed on the basis of careful decision making, or they may be belatedly improvised to meet changing economic conditions and technological developments.

Executive Goals

As his primary motivation the businessman essentially strives for profits—for an increase in net worth through an excess of revenue over outlay. Producers in highly competitive industries are under constant pressure to maximize profits. Their drive for short-run profits is a competitive necessity, a condition of survival. Producers in oligopolistic and monopolistic industries are ordinarily not under the same pressure to maximize short-run profits. Instead, they generally aim to maximize long-run profits. The prevalence of imperfect competition in industry means that producers enjoy a degree of market control and a latitude in price-output policy which permit them to pursue goals other than short-run profit maximization. A desire to be the largest producer and to enjoy power and prestige, for instance, may induce businessmen to produce at a volume above the profit-maximizing level of output. When impediments to the entry of new firms into the industry are considerable, businessmen in protected fields can safely strive for objectives that deviate considerably from short-run profit maximization.

In an economy of constant change, moreover, a producer's market situation and strategy may be complex, and his actual business motivation and goals may differ over time. A producer may find himself in any one of a number of situations in which the immediate maximization of profits may be subordinated to other objectives. Business leaders generally design their competitive strategy (nonprice competitive practice) and strive for objectives (e.g., expansion into new fields or maintenance of market share) which they consider to be rationally consistent and effective means for attaining long-run profit maximization. Producers generally consider it to be of crucial importance to maintain a strong market position, that is, to hold or to increase their market share. The maintenance of a firm's market share at a sacrifice in short-run earnings may be the policy to attain long-run earnings. Though the maintenance of a dominant market position at a sacrifice of short-run earnings may promise continuity of income, technological change and adverse business developments may, however, forestall the actual realization of the long-run gains.

A firm's profit-seeking horizon is at times more or less conditioned by external influences which, to varying degrees, exercise control over the firm. Powerful outside influences may modify both the goals toward which business leaders strive and the manner whereby they seek to attain their objectives. External pressures may come from the big shareholder group, financial or banking group, potential competitors, government, suppliers, and customers. In seeking long-run maximum profits, a businessman may limit his short-run earnings in order to forestall entry of potential competitors, antitrust action, Congressional hearings on price levels, or union wage demands. A producer may, therefore, seek a satisfactory level of profits consistent with stable business relations with customers, rival firms, governmental bodies, or other pressure interests.

Executives in the well-managed firm may seek to stabilize business operations, rather than to maximize profits, by anticipating the impact of external factors and formulating plans to minimize their disruptive influence. A producer, for instance, may diversify his fields of business (at a sacrifice in an investment field which may reap quicker return) to stabilize sales volume and income over the business cycle or at least to minimize the cyclical contraction in income. Since temporary financial embarrassment or bankruptcy is always possible during periods of business adversity, conservation of the enterprise is obviously one of the key ends sought by executives. Producers in less stable industries or regional markets tend to hedge against the possibility of financial distress by striving for liquidity and the accumulation of financial reserves. When executives direct their business operations to strategy objectives other than current maximization of profits, economic interpretation based on marginal analysis for price-output, investment, and other business decisions does not adequately portray actual business operations and entrepreneurial behavior. The maintenance of company control by the management group may at times limit the drive for short-run earnings and the exploitation of profit opportunities. By adopting limited or conservative expansion plans, executives can maintain liquidity and avoid debt financing. Executives find that they can somewhat stabilize sales volume, improve long-term profitability, and control the firm's scope of business by developing the product line.

PRODUCT LINE AND MARKET

A firm's scope of business is its particular field and range of productive activities in the output and distribution of specific goods and services. Under a system of free enterprise, a firm is not limited to a definite field of business or types of commercial transactions. A firm may extend the scope of its activities into various fields of business and to different degrees, or it may restrict the scope to a single industry. A firm's "over-all scope of business" may be defined in terms of the range or breadth of its commercial activities and depth of its productive operations and in terms of the composition of its product line and the kind and size of markets in which it sells goods.

Range of Business Operations and Activities

A firm may own and operate the plants and establishments needed for the output and distribution of its line of products or services, or it may narrowly confine or limit the range of its direct production operations and fixed investment and rely on outside firms and suppliers for much of the required production and distribution activities. A firm may, for example, own and operate its plants, or it may lease all or part of the plant facilities it needs. It may fabricate many of its components and assembled units, or it may purchase these items. It may market the products through its own outlets, or it may market the goods through independent wholesalers and retailers. It may finance the sale of goods to customers, or it may sell on a cash basis.

Promoters or managers may initially have determined the basic scope and breadth of business operations when the enterprise was launched, or they may have developed them in stages over a number of years. During periods of comparatively stable economic conditions, much of the scope of business operations of most firms is relatively stable and long-lasting. Certain operating and product-line aspects of the enterprise are, of course, modified to meet changes in business conditions and shifts in the market.

The Product Line

A firm's product line is composed of a group of products that it turns out. The "product line" is a fundamental means of characterizing a firm's field of business and indicating its role and contribution in the economy. A firm's economic function is to produce efficiently goods or services of intrinsic value to consumers. The value of goods depends not only on their scarcity relative to the demand for them but on the utility offered by the product. The utility of products derives largely from the effectiveness with which technicians design products for consumer satisfaction. In their quest for profits, businessmen strive to attain a degree of price-fixing power by differentiating their products through distinctive design, styling, novel packaging, particularized services to customers, advertising and promotional campaigns, and exclusive sales outlets.

A firm's product line and volume of output determine the kind of processes and facilities required, material and labor inputs, location, the multiple-plant organization pattern, and other structural features. A firm's product line may have been improvised over the years (i.e., it may have evolved in piecemeal fashion) and may therefore have little inherent structural or economic logic, or it may have been wisely conceived through analysis and deliberate planning and design for rational consistency with production technology and efficiency in output, effective marketing, and ease of expansion and growth. More precisely, managers and engineers can design a structurally sound product line on the basis of a logical combination of the rational economic and technological foundations discussed below:

(1) The composition of the product line may consist of those *material-related products* that originate from the complete processing of a crude raw material through vertically integrated production facilities. (2) The product line may consist of a narrow group of *process-related products* which can be economically put out on highly specialized facilities intensively utilized to supply a large market, or it may consist of a wider aggregation of process-related items the total volume of which permits efficient utilization of a given type of processing technology and comparatively adaptable

facilities. (3) The product line may consist of those *demand-related products* which can be concentrated for efficient marketing of the "complete trade line" items through low-cost distribution channels to comparatively well-defined markets. (4) The product line may consist of *technically related products* that can best be developed for production and marketing by a large staff of engineers and technicians who function as a team of specialists in a given field of technology. (5) The product line may consist of *diversified products or unrelated products* (i.e., unrelated with respect to materials, process, or demand) that tend to stabilize sales and revenue, utilize available or excess capacity, or facilitate penetration of new markets or entry into growing industries. This business line may be construed as a rational, diversifiedly related product line. (6) The product line may consist of *exclusively marketed products* which achieve or maintain a dominant market position by virtue of ownership of scarce natural resources, patents, and technical knowledge, promotional (good-will) advantages, cartelization, or other means of securing market exclusiveness in the output, distribution, or servicing of goods.

Thus, a firm's product line is inherently logical (and a firm has greater prospects of profitable success) if it is based on a prudent combination of the foregoing rational product-line features applied to a logical degree. Many firms are multiple-product enterprises. The multiple product firm originates from the economic forces that give rise to a group of material-related, process-related, technically related, and demand-related products. Product multiplicity is extended by entrepreneurial efforts to diversify, and product diversification reflects business efforts to adapt to shifting markets, economic fluctuations, and secular change in the economy. Competitive conditions in multiple-product enterprises would obviously differ greatly from product to product.

We can discern the degree of economic logic that underlies a firm's product line through an analysis of its composition to ascertain the consistency and degree of rational relatedness in its structure. Each firm must be individually analyzed to ascertain the degree to which the composed design of the product line consists of an economically logical combination of material-related, process-related, technically related, and diversifiedly related products and the extent to which they are exclusively marketed products.[6]

---

[6] In establishing new industries underdeveloped countries must break down industries on a logical basis. A rational product line for each division of an industry would be a key consideration for setting up logical divisions for an industry.

We can elucidate and amplify the rational foundation for the design of a product line by outlining some typical product lines which are based on a dominant feature but also exemplify a combination of other product-line features that contribute to production, marketing, and managerial efficiency.

MATERIAL-RELATED PRODUCT LINE—PRODUCTS FROM VERTICALLY INTEGRATED PRODUCTION. The product line of firms involved in early-stage production generally consists of items that derive from the processing of crude materials through a series of vertically integrated facilities. Specialized plants set up in consecutive series are usually employed to process the primary material into specific products which are characterized as "joint-cost products." The processing of raw materials usually branches out into separate production lines and is continued until the full economic value is derived. The integrated nature of the vertically linked production system permits built-in coordination and effective planning which obtains operating economies. By concentrating their research and engineering effort primarily on material processing and product development, firms attain substantial technological advances from the employment of specialized technical talent in a comparatively narrow field.

The market for major material-related products must be of sufficient size to make large-scale operations economically feasible. The processing of a given crude material usually yields joint products in relatively fixed proportions. The processing of crude oil, bauxite, and certain agricultural products would yield primary products and also "spin off" certain secondary items or by-products. Firms in the same early-stage industries would ordinarily put out the same kind of goods; the parallelism in their product lines would make the firms more or less competitive in many items.

Economies in distribution are lessened to the extent that each product calls for a separate channel to reach its respective markets. Certain major products of many early-stage industries are, however, distributed to a limited number of large markets with the attendant economies. The composition of a product line originating from material-related production may, however, be such that no special marketing economies accrue. Though they tend to be variable in the long run, the proportions (product-mix) of joint products are relatively fixed in the short run. An increase in the demand for some joint products tends to raise the prices of these items but lowers the prices of other "overproduced" items. Since the products are put out in relatively fixed proportions, overproduced items may require special promotion or price cutting for disposal in the market.

PROCESS-RELATED PRODUCT LINE. A firm's product line may consist of a few process-related items that can be economically mass-produced on highly specialized facilities, or it may consist of a wider group of process-related items that can be turned out through given kinds of processes and facilities. The degree of plant specialization, of course, depends on the size of the market. A firm that concentrates on the output of a comparatively narrow product line attains its economic advantage from the efficiencies that accrue in the utilization of specialized talent and sometimes from economical distribution. Firms putting out a narrow product line are exemplified by producers of ball bearings, tin cans, cigarettes, and shoes. Firms can concentrate their research effort to obtain technological advances in a comparatively narrow field of production. Research and engineering tend to emphasize product improvement and the development of product designs which make for low-cost output.

A producer of one main kind of product (ships, television sets) may turn out many sizes, models, or varieties of the product on specialized, though somewhat adaptable, facilities. The range of models and sizes may be narrow or somewhat broader, depending partly on the degree of adaptability obtainable in facilities without excessive sacrifice of efficiency. By putting out a product in many varieties, a producer "horizontally" extends his product line. Since many components may be designed to go into the assembly of a number of models, economies of scale in fabrication are not sacrificed. If a firm in an industry of broad product coverage (e.g., machine-manufacturing industry) concentrates on the output of one kind of product, it essentially becomes a specialized producer and is, in a sense, a "divisional unit" of the industry. Its pre-eminence in a narrow field of production often means that it has few serious competitors, particularly in its regional market. If the product is expensive to ship, a specialized producer in the industry would obviously tend to have a strong competitive position in a regional market.

Some firms select and develop a comparatively broad product line comprised of items that are designed for output or are suited for output through given kinds of processes and facilities which are designed for the required adaptability. The output of a product line that has a certain common naturalness in production is exemplified by producers of drugs, baking products, and paints and varnishes. The aggregation of a line of process-related products permits the attainment of a large over-all volume of output that assures certain economies in the utilization of capital-intensive indivisible facilities. In many cases considerable use of mass-production methods of output is economically feasible. When a firm takes on products for output that require considerable tooling up, conversion of facilities, or the acquisition of specialized facilities, it begins to lose some of the advantages that inhere in the process-related product line.

Firms putting out a process-related product line can in some cases distribute much of their output through the same channels; in other cases distribution calls for a multiplicity of channels. Whether a firm's product line is economical to make depends on the diversity of products with respect to end use and the number of separate markets in which they sell. If, for instance, the product is of a technical nature (locomotives, special machinery) and of high unit value, direct distribution makes for economical marketing.

DEMAND-RELATED PRODUCT LINE. Some firms develop a more or less extensive demand-related product line in an endeavor to supply a substantial proportion of the product needs of a specific market. By specializing in a "complete trade needs" product line, a firm essentially gains economies in the distribution of the bulk of its output through certain major channels and market outlets and a competitive advantage in marketing and advertising. The market gain from handling a multiplicity of products is generally greater the more difficult it is to secure contact with buyers and consumers. Some producers, of course, do not attempt a complete trade line. They specialize in a given phase of the trade products. The "full-line program" often refers to a policy that calls for the output of the broad parallel line of products successfully sold by a rival firm.

The demand-related product line is particularly advantageous in those fields in which effective marketing is crucial. Producers of the demand-related product line are exemplified by those who turn out hardware items, building supplies, appliances, furniture, and farm implements. Quick delivery requires that a large diversified stock of finished goods be carried. Purchasing agents who buy many items enjoy the advantage of procuring a multitude of items in large sums from one supplier or producer of a complete trade line. Such firms often attain a considerable degree of mass-production output of fast-moving, large-volume items; they set up specialized production lines in their plants for such output.

Big producers gain advantages by employing research and engineering for the development and improvement of products that fit the trade needs of their market. Through research, firms strive to develop and add complementary products. Their long-term institutional advertising enables them to utilize their "brand-name carry-over" advantage to establish a new product in the market. Some large producers (soap and liquor), however, tend to enlarge their over-all sales volume by turning out two or more varieties of a product under different brand names for sale in the same market outlets. The lower-priced "off-brand" items are also distributed through alternative channels such as discount houses. The multiple-brand product policy is designed to increase (or at least to maintain) the company's share in the market by pre-empting "product choices" in the minds of consumers and pre-empting display space in retail outlets, thereby discouraging new entrants into the market.

DIVERSIFIED-PRODUCT LINE. A firm may add products or lines of products to diversify its scope of business in an effort to gain greater stability in sales and earnings, to put available idle capacity to profitable use, or to expand into growing markets. Hence, firms that adopt a policy of diversity are those experiencing a decline in the sale of major products or experiencing abrupt seasonal or cyclical fluctuations in sales, those that have idle capacity, or those intent on entering growing industries.

Firms experiencing seasonal slumps in sales strive to adopt complementary products that sell in the slack season or are at least comparatively stable in their annual sales pattern. Even though a firm puts out a narrow product line, it generally introduces de luxe models or high-priced items which sell well to people in the higher-income brackets, particularly in prosperity times, and it also introduces economy models or low-priced items which sell in comparatively large volume during recession times. Firms whose products undergo abrupt cyclical fluctuations in sales (e.g., consumer and producer durable goods) often strive to adopt products or acquire enterprises that are less sensitive to cyclical fluctuations.

Firms with idle production and distribution capacity strive to put the available capacity to profitable use by adopting suitable products. Excess capacity may be due, for example, to the secular decline in the demand for products, acquisition of facilities, and regional shifts in markets. Diversification tends to be induced by the fact that the incremental cost (e.g., the outlays for plant conversion) may be small relative to the addition to total revenue. A firm may purchase an enterprise or build a plant to sell products in growing markets; in this case diversification is a means of expanding into growing industries or penetrating new markets. Diversification through acquisition has been motivated by "loss carry-over" provisions in profit-tax levels. Tax incentives prompt some profitable businesses to acquire firms with substantial income losses as deduction offsets for high current profits.

Diversification is economically more rational and profitable when the acquired products or enterprises fit the firm's growth pattern or effectively dovetail with the firm's scope of business in terms of being process-related, technically related, or demand-related. The long-run benefits of diversification must, of course, be balanced against certain diseconomies that set in when top executives must cope with many "diversified" problems posed by the production and distribution of many unrelated products and services. Excessive diversification is essentially a trend away from the economies of scale and the benefits of specialized production, distribution, and research.

The Product-Mix and Market Outlets

A firm's product-mix is the proportionate shares that the various items in the product line contribute to total sales. Some items will be major products; other items, minor products. Each item in the firm's product line is generally sold in a number of market segments, that is, sold to different classes or types of consumers in the market.

The size of the market and the potential demand for a product depend on consumption habits and purchasing power, the closeness of substitute products, and the number of consumers in the market area. The geographical limits of a firm's market for each product are determined by the cost of shipping the product, the firm's competitive position, and the degree of plant dispersal in the industry. Some firms would be dominant producers in certain regions, while other firms would be dominant in other market regions. The firm's market share may be high for some products and in some markets and low in others. Changes in the firm's market share mean that sales in the various markets vary, and the product-mix also would vary. Firms with geographically dispersed plants may have a strong selling position in widely separate markets. Their product-mix and market segments in each region, however, would ordinarily differ.

A firm's product-mix in a given market area usually varies over time because seasonal and cyclical fluctuations in sales differ for products, because of shifts in consumer demand for particular products, and because of the relative ease or effectiveness in promoting sales for each product. Changes in the product-mix often create idle capacity in some production lines or facilities along with shortage of capacity in other facilities. The extent of capacity imbalance depends on the degree of adaptability of facilities. Some firms, of course, enjoy a comparatively stable product-mix in their various regional markets. A firm usually markets its products through a number of distribution outlets. The distribution channel used by a firm depends on the kind of product it handles and the kind of market (e.g., household market, industrial market, agricultural market) to which it sells.

The factors that determine or influence the kind of channels a firm selects are (1) the achievement of a profitable sales volume at low distribution costs, (2) maintenance of the firm's competitive position, and (3) the ease in promoting sales. A firm often employs the same distribution system used by rival producers in the industry. This is due to the fact that many industries have over time developed comparatively effective distribution channels and because an industry's established and typical outlets are familiar and habitual to the majority of the purchasers of a particular class of goods. A firm selling highly specialized or unique products may, of course, distribute through outlets that differ from those of the industry's.

In marketing products through its distribution channels (whether through wholesalers, retailers, or other channels), a firm may use (1) the general or widespread distribution method (sell to any interested middleman), (2) the restricted distribution method (sell to a limited number of middlemen), or (3) the integrated distribution method (sell through company-owned outlets).

The *general distribution method* is, for instance, used by firms producing widely purchased goods (e.g., groceries, drug items, industrial supplies). The *restricted distribution method* is employed by firms that strive for certain marketing and competitive advantages that may be obtained by selling to a limited number of the better outlets in each area (i.e., by selective distribution) or by selling to a single middleman in each area (i.e., by exclusive distribution). A firm that employs restricted (whether selective or exclusive) distribution may benefit from more desirable outlets, lower marketing costs, increased sales promotion effort by the middleman, ease of introducing new products, and better price maintenance. These benefits may be partially offset by certain disadvantages associated with the restricted distribution method. The firm's sales volume may be low because of incomplete or inadequate coverage of the market. The firm may have difficulty in selecting middlemen, or the middlemen may be reluctant to accept exclusive agency agreements. The firm may have difficulty in coordinating its promotional effort with the distributors' marketing program. Middlemen participating with restricted distribution methods may also be at a disadvantage: Because he is obliged to accept marketing policies stipulated by the producer, a middleman loses some independence in business discretion, or he may be compelled to relinquish the distribution of the product.

A firm will tend to use the *integrated distribution method* (i.e., establish its own outlets) when the available middlemen do not serve as suitable market outlets. A firm may find it profitable to expand into the marketing function (integrate forward) to varying degrees: It may perform the wholesaling function through its own branch offices and branch warehouses, or it may integrate all the way and carry out the retailing function through its own retail outlets. A firm may adopt fully integrated distribution when it is assured of the competitive advantages gained through better control over price, advertising and sales promotion, speed in introducing new products and penetrating new market regions, and provision of adequate consumer credit and customer servicing. The increased revenue derived from these advantages must be balanced against the additional outlay required for integrated distribution (i.e., the return on investment must be adequate) and compared to that of available alternative distribution methods. A firm's particular product line and volume of sales not only influence the extent to which the firm may profitably integrate forward into the distribution function but largely determine (as outlined in the next chapter) the type of processing technology and physical organization of production that is economical.

QUESTIONS FOR REVIEW AND APPLICATION

1. "The economic study and analysis of a representative firm in a given line of business is an extension of the study of an industry and its structural pattern." Explain.

2. How do the functions of executive management differ from those of operating management? Illustrate.

3. What are the goals of executive management? Distinguish between short-term profit maximization and long-term profit maximization.

4. How may holding-company pyramiding augment return to the shareholders of a parent company?

5. (a) Explain what is meant by "managerial decentralization." (b) What are the practical limits to managerial decentralization? (c) What kind of managerial-organization changes occur when a firm decentralizes?

6. "As the firm expands over time, structural changes in the organization of the managerial function and in the multiple-plant system tend to offset diseconomies to management." Explain.

7. "Diseconomies to management accrue more from the number of diverse variables that require top-level decision making and coordination rather than from the increase in the magnitude of production or output capacity per se." Explain.

8. Explain what is meant by a firm's scope of business. Illustrate.

9. Distinguish between the utility (functional) aspect and the production aspect in the design of a product or a line of product. Illustrate.

10. "A firm's particular product line and the scale of output largely determine the type of plant facilities and process that will be employed and the multiple-plant system that will be set up." Explain.

11. (a) What are the economic factors that underlie or give rise to the demand-related product line, the process-related product line, and the product line from vertical production? Explain why the demand-related product line derives from market aspects and behavior, while product line from vertical production derives from the nature of an industry's production technology. (b) What are the primary sources of economies that inhere in the above types of product line?

12. (a) What are the different patterns of (and approaches to) diversification of a firm's business? (b) What are the benefits that may be obtained from diversification? (c) Does overdiversification produce diseconomies in executive management? Explain.

CHAPTER 7

Structural Design: Production and Break-even Analysis

PLANT PRODUCTION: FACTOR PROPORTIONALITY; CAPACITY

Managers strive for the least-cost combination of productive factors in the design and development of plants for the output of products. To develop an efficient production system, managers must concentrate sufficient engineering effort on product design and production technology and must effectively apply the principles of specialization and standardization and the law of proportionality to the combination of productive factors. This means that in designing their production system they must use comparative-cost analysis and profit potential for the selection of the most effective product line, multiple-plant combination and locations, processing depth of each plant, production methods, and plant-layout schemes.

Logically designed multiple-plant systems make for a rational industry structure; the more rational the industry structure, the more productive can be the respective firms. A rational industry structure achieves increasing returns in production through output of a logical line of products, progressive division and specialization of plant production, and logically organized multiple-plant systems—effective vertical and horizontal integration of plants.

Multiple-Plant System

When managers select a process-related product line, engineers can design the product line for efficient output through a specialized plant or multiple-plant system. If business managers select an illogically diversified line of products with respect to production technology, engineers are unable to organize rationally specialized plant

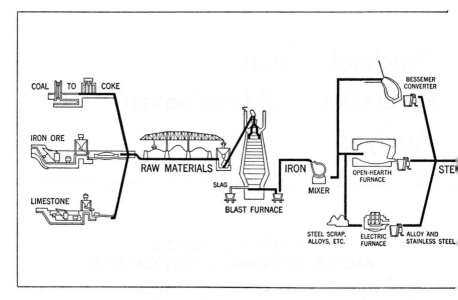

Fig. 7–1. A vertically integrated series of processes illustrated by flow chart of steelmaking. Raw materials are transferred into technically related finished

processes or a rational multiple-plant system because technically unrelated products will not permit an adequate degree of process specialization.

The larger the volume of output of uniform products, the greater the economies from scale and from division of labor, that is, from the vertical division and from the horizontal division and specialization of production. In a vertically integrated series of plants, specialized plants are set up for consecutive stages of production (e.g., mining and processing, fabrication, assembly of products, by-product output, warehousing, and distribution outlets) (Fig. 7–1). To the vertical production arrangement, managers may add specialized plants in the horizontal direction. The horizontal plants may be set up to produce different, though related, end products, or the horizontal branch plants may be geographically dispersed duplicate plants turning out the product for regional markets. A firm's plants may thus be geographically concentrated or dispersed, depending on the availability of markets, materials, labor, and other factors that determine the locations that attain low unit cost of production and distribution. Regional plants serving local markets often derive their economies by eliminating or reducing the need for transporting goods from geographically concentrated production centers and

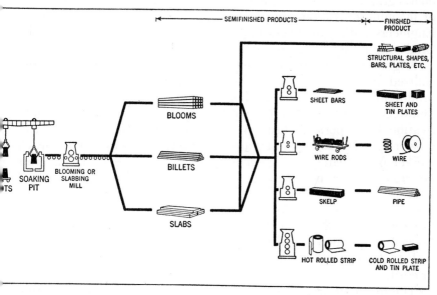

products. (United States Steel Corporation, *TNEC Papers.* New York: 1940, vol. II, pp. 190–191.)

sometimes by using low-price input factors available in scattered regional areas.[1]

The modern plant carries out the productive process through an organized system composed of integrated machines and other facilities that perform specialized operations in the output of goods. A

---

[1] The multiple-plant systems of big firms are often broken down into regional divisions comprised of clusters of plants (i.e., the works divisions). The localization of a number of divisions of various firms in one area constitutes an industrial center or an industrial complex. Various types of plants locate in a given area because they use similar kinds of material and labor inputs, supply the same market area, and because of their complementary nature. Well-developed industrial centers have many specialized service enterprises (some cooperatively owned) that give rise to external economies and contribute to increasing returns to industry. The service enterprises include utilities, suppliers of materials and parts, tool and die shops, engineering and construction firms, technical and trade schools, industrial hospitals, specialized financial institutions, and others.

factory's facilities (plant and equipment) may be classified according to functional specialization: production machines (rolling mills, lathes, presses), tools (jigs, fixtures, dies), inspection devices, handling equipment (belt conveyors, cranes), storage facilities, power plant—all sheltered by a specially designed building.

Engineers design the process and the layout of plant facilities through the preparation and use of process charts. The process charts graphically outline the required production sequence in terms of machine operations, inspection, movement of work, and so on. Engineers anticipate operating conditions and provide for the desired output capacity, productivity, and adaptability.

Engineers design the production process to employ efficient specialized facilities and labor. The labor input consists of specialized production workers (direct labor) and specialized service workers (indirect labor). Production workers operate the machines in fabrication lines, perform tasks in assembly lines, and perform tasks at work stations in an integrated production process. Thus, each worker participates as a specialist in a task or a craft (e.g., press operator, welder, machinist). In well-engineered plants the speed of work in process is ordinarily paced by a mechanized materials-handling system. The flow of work in the production line is facilitated by service workers: the work of production operators is aided by tool set-up men, inspectors, materials-handling men, dispatchers and stock clerks, and maintenance men, each a specialist in his task or craft.

The responsibility for managing the production or manufacturing phase of the business is delegated to line managers. A works manager is ordinarily in charge of a works division (a group of plants), and factory managers or superintendents are in charge of individual plants. The production phase is facilitated by various company-wide functionalized service departments—engineering, purchasing, sales, controllership, and so on. The degree of centralized home-office control in geographically dispersed enterprises depends on the nature of the business and the managerial philosophy of top executives.

Thus, we see that specialization in the firm is interrelated and occurs on a number of levels: (1) on the company-wide level specialization takes place according to major business functions (sales, purchasing, etc.); (2) on the plant level, according to process stages in vertical integration and according to end products in horizontal integration; (3) within the plant, according to factory departments (service and production departments); and (4) on the production line, according to individual operations or tasks.

Plant-operating Characteristics

In selecting or designing the processes and facilities, engineers coordinate and integrate production operations and service activities, that is, they achieve a certain measure of "built-in" technical and operating coordination in the plant. The degree of built-in coordination obtained depends on the nature of the process and the extent of specialization and mechanization of the process. In selecting processes and designing the layout of facilities, engineers strive to provide, within the technical limits permissible and without sacrifice of efficiency, the desired kind and amount of plant *adaptability*. The plant may be made adaptable with respect to the kind of operations performed and work processed, ease of varying (increasing or decreasing) the rate of production, ease of converting plant to the output of other types of products, and ease of expanding production capacity. Once the plant has been designed and erected, the plant's production technology takes on a certain "fixity," but within the limits of adaptability provided. Future plant revisions or expansion will require not only engineering effort and capital outlays but a certain lead-time to carry out the change. Each plant is characterized not only by (1) its types and degrees of adaptability, but is also characterized with respect to (2) level of modernity and efficiency, (3) amount of production bottlenecks, (4) production interval, (5) amount of technical control required, and (6) amount of plant maintenance needed.

Plants in the same industry often differ not only with reference to type of processes employed but with respect to *modernity*. A multiple-plant firm with duplicate branch plants will have some up-to-date plants and some old plants of varying vintage. Moreover, plants of the same vintage producing the same type of product may use different processes; they may nonetheless produce at comparable costs. A plant may be able to produce at a certain cost level because of its access to cheap power which enables it to employ a certain type of process, while another plant may produce at a comparable level of efficiency because of its accessibility to low-cost materials rather than to power. Thus, we see that a plant's processes and combination of productive factors are affected by its location.

A plant may have one or more bottleneck operations in the production process that tend to restrict or prevent output from exceeding a certain level. The *bottleneck* may be of a short-term nature in that it may be due to technical difficulties of a more or less temporary nature or to scarcity of certain skilled labor, or it may be of a long-run nature such as that of the inadequate provision of machine capacity at certain points in the process. The latter may be due to management's reluctance to purchase additional units of expensive, indivisible equipment (e.g., a heat-treating unit or a heavy-duty press). Output limitation due to some of the foregoing types of bottlenecks may be overcome by working the bottleneck operations on an overtime basis. But difficulties may arise should the plant inaugurate multiple-shift production. The output capacity of plants with a few bottlenecks can often be readily increased up to a certain level. The installation of additional machines at bottleneck points in the process would quickly expand the plant's output capacity to a level in line with that of the balance of the facilities of the plant.

Output among plants differs with respect to the *production interval*—the interval from raw materials to completion of the final product. Complex products made up of many components and of high unit value generally require a long production interval, particularly when the plant is not tooled up for volume output, as is ordinarily the case in job-order production. The longer the processing interval, the greater the quantity of goods in process and the time required to adjust finished-goods inventory levels to changes in sales volume.

Plant processes differ with respect to the amount of *technical control* needed for their operation on a production basis. The amount of technical control required by a process depends on the intricacy and the quality level of the product and the complexity and degree of standardization of the process. The production of antibiotics and medical equipment would, for instance, call for greater technical control than would the production of hardware items. The greater the technical control required, the larger the number of technicians needed to regulate the process at key points and to maintain the quality standard of the product.

Plants differ also with respect to *repair and maintenance needs*. The intensive utilization of highly mechanized and intricate facilities requires many man-hours for their upkeep, overhaul, and renewal. The uninterrupted operation of integrated processes is essential in keeping costs low and in maintaining the planned rate of output. When equipment is run down and in disrepair and is difficult to keep in proper adjustment, the quality of the product and the volume of output decline. It is sometimes difficult, however, to identify the dividing line between machine overhaul and renewal and machine replacement; substantial machine overhaul and renewal tend to shade into machine replacement in the extension of the operating life of productive processes.

Plant Capacity

The organization of productive factors and the operation of plants rest on a practical grasp of the nature of capacity. Plant capacity may be conceived as technical capacity, total economic capacity, rated capacity, optimum capacity, excess capacity, or long-run capacity. The concept of capacity selected depends on the purpose for which production capability is to be gauged and the aspect of industrial behavior to be analyzed.

Technical capacity is the physical output rate of a piece of equipment under continuous production and ideal operating conditions. Such capacity in plant machinery can be attained only if machines ideally operate at their designed capability and at a maximum flow of balanced production from machine to machine without interruption. Normal plant production cannot attain the output capability of the technical capacity of individual machines. Technical capacity cannot, therefore, be used to measure plant output under normal conditions of production.

Engineers nonetheless use technical capacity to specify or to select the desired machine size, to obtain adequate capacity-balance among machines for efficient processing, and for the layout of production facilities. When engineers select facilities, they specify the equipment in terms of technical capacity on the basis of the anticipated operating conditions and normal delays. They may, for example, specify a press of 20-ton capacity, a furnace of 36 cubic feet capacity, a crane of 40-ton capacity, and so on. Engineers may specify a higher technical capacity for certain pieces of equipment than would normally be needed in order to provide for stand-by capacity, for unanticipated seasonal peak production, and for ease of future plant expansion.

Managers can specify the size of plant in terms of total economic capacity or in terms of rated capacity. The *total economic capacity* is the plant output volume (or industry output volume) that can be attained by continuous round-the-clock utilization of plants seven days a week with an allowance for normal delays. In some plants the third shift may operate with a somewhat smaller production force since normal delays require that adequate time be provided for required equipment maintenance. The utilization of a plant's total economic capacity would require that production be scheduled on this basis. The labor force may, however, put in a 40-hour week (or some other workweek) on a staggered work-assignment basis.

Rated capacity (or the effective output potential) is plant (or industry) output attainable when plants operate on the basis of the standard or customary length of week and number of shifts (e.g., single shift, 40-hour week) with an allowance for normal delays. For plants that must, for technical reasons, operate continuously 24 hours 7 days a week (e.g., blast furnaces and certain chemical plants), rated capacity is identical with the total economic capacity. For any given industry the total economic capacity is obviously larger than the rated capacity.

Managers schedule production on the basis of the rated capacity of the plant. They balance production requirements for a given period against the available rated capacity for the period. From production schedules managers prepare the production budget which stipulates the weekly or monthly rates of output of the product-mix required to maintain adequate inventory levels to meet sales needs. The plant may, for example, be scheduled to operate at 70 per cent (or at 95 per cent) of rated capacity. Actual production is thus more volatile than capacity—output moves up or down with seasonal variations, cyclical changes, shifts in demand, the effectiveness with which managers solve production problems, etc. The current production volume can at times exceed the computed rated capacity. The postponement of equipment overhauls and renewals and longer production runs, for instance, provide an additional "temporary" capacity that can be used. On the other hand, current production may not reach the computed rated capacity because of smaller lot sizes, undue material shortages, abnormal absenteeism, or new-model changeovers.

Managers essentially compute rated capacity on the basis of a suitable unit for measuring physical output per week or month, allowance for normal delays, and length of workweek and number of shifts selected for plant operation. Rated capacity is computed from past performance, trial runs, or time study and other engineering data.

The physical capacity of a plant (or an industry) may be expressed in terms of certain common measures, such as tons of crude steel, barrels or gallons of liquid products, board feet of lumber, yards of textiles, and ton-miles. Capacity may also be expressed in product units for plants that turn out a single product or closely similar products. For plants (or firms) producing a product-mix of varied but related final products, capacity may be expressed in man-hours required to manufacture the main product, designated as the "output unit." The number of man-hours required to turn out a unit of each of the related products are converted to, and expressed in terms of, the main product or production unit.

In computing the effective physical capacity per week or month,

managers make an allowance for normal delays and shutdowns resulting from machine failure and equipment repair and renewal, job
setups and product changeovers, processing difficulties, absenteeism,
and the like. Since the causes for some plant idleness (machine
breakdowns and processing difficulties) can be eliminated during
the off-shift, the allowance for delays is smaller for single-shift operation than for the multiple-shift operation. Managers also make
allowance for normal spoilage and scrap (the shrinkage during processing) caused by substandard work and waste. Both the allowances for normal delays and for scrap (e.g., 18 per cent) are then
used to set the rated capacity for the length of week and number of
shifts of plant operation.

Within the limits of the total economic capacity of the plant,
managers determine the output capability they will use for short-run
or current production. The amount they elect to use is designated
"rated capacity." Rated capacity is essentially based on output obtainable from the selected time intensity in the utilization of facilities,
with intensity being determined by the length of workweek and
number of shifts. Managers elect (or accept) the standard length
of week and number of shifts that are adequate for the current and
projected (short-run) production requirements and suited to the
current and anticipated business and economic conditions.

The commercial utilization of an industry's production potential
takes into account the costs of production. High production costs in
a given plant, incidentally, may be due to uneconomical location of
plant (which makes for high input prices or high shipping costs),
obsolete facilities, inefficient organization of plant facilities, or in-
competent management. Periods of comparatively high demand
and prices permit the use of high-cost plants. An industry's rated
capacity (as well as its total economic capacity) is the combined
output of all the plants, except for the high-cost plants and facilities
that can be used only during periods of inordinately high prices.
Thus, only plants that can be operated more or less economically
are included in the computation of an industry's rated capacity for
a particular phase of the business cycle.

Though a certain length of workweek and number of shifts (i.e.,
the rated capacity) tend to become the standard or conventional
practice in a given industry and region, in many specific cases, business managers determine the time intensity of plant utilization and
the rated capacity they will adopt as standard for a plant on the
basis of a number of factors. Managers would tend to adopt a multiple-shift production intensity when investment in plant is high and
unit cost (as well as the initial investment outlay) can be lowered

through multiple-shift operation. They would tend to adopt a single shift when labor is a comparatively expensive factor, i.e., when straight-time and overtime wage rates and night-shift wage differentials are high. The time intensity selected for rated capacity would also tend to be influenced by wage and hour laws and by union contracts that call for severance pay and company unemployment insurance.

In selecting rated capacity managers also take into account whatever seasonal pattern in business volume that prevails. The method that managers adopt to deal with seasonal variations influences how much rated capacity they will provide for the various production periods of the year. Managers may select a year-round rated capacity for a steady, uniform output level which builds up the inventory stock during the period of slack sales so as to meet the needs of the following peak sales period. Managers may, on the other hand, select the multiple-shift plan for its rated capacity for periods of high sales volume and the single-shift plan for periods of low sales volume. Managers can avoid employee layoffs through a compromise plan: overtime work may meet the requirements of the peak sales period, while accumulated maintenance work and vacations scheduled for the slack sales period may avoid undue layoffs. (For discussion, see Chap. 8).

The above factors influencing the rated capacity selected operate within the framework of the business cycle as it affects an enterprise in a given industry. Industry tends to adopt a lower rated capacity for periods of recession and depression and a higher rated capacity for periods of prosperity. As a recession develops and demand declines, firms begin to operate at a lower percentage of rated capacity. They may lay off labor or spread employment by shortening the hours of work and staggering the work assignments. During depression times many industries gradually adopt a smaller rated capacity. Some use a 36-hour week, others a 4-day week. As prosperity and boom develop and demand and prices rise (or when a growth industry experiences a rapid increase in demand), managers adopt higher levels of rated capacity (e.g., a longer workweek or a multiple shift).

A plant's alternative levels of higher rated capacity can be graphically illustrated in terms of the short-run average unit cost curve for (1) single shift, (2) double shift, and (3) triple shift. The shifts may consist of a five- or six-day week.[2] (See Fig. 4–4.)

---

[2] During wartime or periods of high preparedness, defense industries expand, convert, and tool up facilities to the output of military goods, and many adopt the highest level of rated capacity—triple shift and overtime. Cost-plus pricing and price

During prosperous times, high-capacity operation leads to induced investment: when market demand continues high and plants operate at a high percentage of rated capacity, managers begin to expand existing plants or build new plants. Some firms tend to build ahead of demand in order that they may increase, or at least maintain, their market share. This is particularly true for industries that require a long lead-time for the expansion of plants or for the design and construction of new plants. As plants and industries expand, their rated capacity in absolute terms is revised upward. The competitive need to build ahead of demand and the business advantage derived from quick delivery to customers contribute to "excess" capacity. During prosperity times many industries operate at approximately 80 per cent of rated capacity, that is, with 20 per cent "excess" capacity. The excess capacity would obviously be greater if it were expressed in terms of total economic capacity.

In expanding plant (as in selecting the initial size of a plant) managers take into account long-run capacity, that is, the optimum or the most economical plant size. The most economical plant size is determined by the principle of diminishing returns applied to plant management as an input factor. An average plant superintendent can effectively manage a plant of a given size. In a rationally designed multiple-plant system, in which plants are broken down and specialized so that they may not exceed the optimum size, diminishing returns in the industry can, for all practical purposes, be largely offset. Except for rising input prices of materials and labor, in cases of their relative scarcity, the average unit cost at the optimum operating rate typically declines as an industry expands.

Proportionality in the Combination of Productive Factors

Engineers design and erect plants of a specific size for the required volume of output of products. Once a plant is erected, the plant size and the production technology cannot be quickly changed; the plant is thus a "fixed" productive factor in the short run. In a going concern the combination of factors can be altered only by varying the input of labor and materials, the variable factors. The

---

subsidies permit the use of high-cost (submarginal) plants and stand-by capacity, so that some plants and industries operate above total economic capacity. During wartime (as in peacetime) multiple-shift operating capacity must be engineered far in advance in order that production bottlenecks may be eliminated or minimized. Because of wartime imbalances and dislocations, shortages in tooling, materials, and skilled labor, and transportation bottlenecks, some plants fail to operate at close to 100 per cent of the highest rated capacity.

most economical (optimum) combination of productive agents is indicated by the *law of proportionality* or its variant, the law of diminishing returns, which may be stated as follows: As more and more inputs of labor and materials (the variable factors) are added to a plant (the fixed factor), the total output increases until it reaches the point of diminishing returns and then it decreases. Diminishing returns set in at a certain point primarily because when more units of labor are added, each has less and less equipment to work with.

The law can be stated in terms of additional units of output (i.e., in terms of marginal product): As additional equal inputs of productive factors (labor and material) are added to a fixed factor (a plant or a plot of farm land), there is an increasing output (an increasing marginal product) per input of variable factors until the point of diminishing returns, after which there is a decreasing output (decreasing marginal product) per input of variable factors. The law of proportionality is also reflected in the behavior of short-run average cost. In a going concern the average cost per unit of output declines as the rate of output reaches optimum capacity (the point of diminishing returns), then average cost per unit (the SRAC curve) rises as the rate of output is pushed beyond optimum capacity.

The point of maximum total profitability is the final entrepreneurial determinant in the combination of productive factors. This point depends on the selling price of the product and on the input prices of labor and materials. At high selling prices the businessman can profitably employ more of the variable factors; at low selling prices he finds it advantageous to employ less of the variable factors. Thus, when he adds variable factors, the businessman takes into account input prices—he economizes on the input factors which are scarce and have gone up in price. If wages rise, he can, within limits, use less labor; if wages decline, he generally finds it profitable to employ more labor.

Theoretically, in order to produce at the most profitable level, the businessman applies variable inputs to the point at which the addition to total costs (marginal cost) is equal to the addition to total output or to total revenue (equal to the marginal product). If he produces at a lower level (at an output level at which his marginal cost is not equal to the marginal revenue), his net revenue can be bigger. If, however, he pushes output beyond the point at which marginal cost equals marginal revenue, his net revenue declines.

Since, in the long run, all productive factors are variable, the law of proportionality applies to any combination of productive factors or to the use of any productive factor. It operates when increasing quantities of capital are applied to a fixed amount of land and labor, when increasing amounts of land are applied to a fixed amount of capital and labor, and so on. When they design and establish plants and other business units, production managers apply the law in a more sophisticated manner (as explained below) than is indicated in the foregoing discussion.

In the short run (when plant or land or other natural resource is fixed in size), the problem of combining productive factors is essentially one of varying the firm's rate of output or, more specifically, of varying the intensity in the utilization of plant by changing the input rate of variable factors. In the long run (when all factors are variable), the problem of combining productive factors occurs on a number of levels and in degrees of magnitude, from a minor revision of plant to a major production-development project involving the design and erection of a new plant for the output of a wholly new product.

In a going concern managers undertake long-run types of revisions of plant when they modify, to varying degrees, the combination of productive factors by redesigning products and adjusting processes to accommodate the change, by converting facilities (usually idle capacity) to the output of an additional product, by improving and more intensively mechanizing some high-cost operations, by modernizing and replacing facilities and improving the plant layout, by relocating some facilities, or by any combination of the foregoing. Thus, the long-run proportionality of productive factors in a going concern is often being revised to cut costs and to fit the needs of the estimated sales-mix.

A more involved long-run problem of process selection and combination of productive factors arises when firms must erect additional plants to expand output of their established products. In such cases, notably for the bigger firms, the economic and technical problem of selecting processes from among alternatives may not be too difficult. The problem is often largely one of improving upon, and designing an advanced version of, the firm's newest plant to include the latest technical advances in production processing. Since research and development laboratories are continually at work innovating new and improved production techniques, the design of new plants would obviously incorporate the latest technological advances ready for commercial exploitation.

If a firm is to erect a plant for the output of a new product, yet one similar to the products the firm is currently producing, the problem of process selection and combination of productive factors, though more complex, is essentially the same in nature as that of the erection of a new plant for the output of the firm's established products. Because of its long experience in a given field of production, a going concern ordinarily enjoys an advantage in technology as compared to new entrants into the industry.

Process selection and combination of productive factors, however, are most difficult and time-consuming when a wholly novel or distinctly new type of product is to be manufactured, particularly when its manufacture requires the development of new processing techniques. But such industrial projects are somewhat rare in the field of commercial production. New types of products (antibiotics) are first ordinarily produced on a small scale and on a semicommercial basis. This offers opportunities for trial runs, testing and improvement of product design and of processing.

In their long-term production projects managers essentially strive to attain an economical combination of a number of interrelated productive factors. In the development of their projects, managers endeavor to anticipate the future cost of productive factors, the trend in technological advances, long-run shifts in market demand, and so on. Managers and engineers generally provide for the desired kind and amount of plant adaptability through the types of processes and facilities they select. They appraise alternative approaches and methods for the design of products and processes and for plant adaptability on the basis of comparative costs and rate of return on investment. In establishing a new plant or in revising a plant, managers have a number of alternative methods for achieving an economical combination of productive factors. They consider all elements entering into the physical organization of a plant as mutually interdependent variable factors. Managers can, for instance, vary (1) the amount of research and engineering effort to be applied (i.e., the research input), (2) the product design in relation to volume of output, and (3) the kinds of production methods or processes to be used which in turn determine the combination and input of capital facilities, labor, and materials per unit of output.

RESEARCH AND ENGINEERING INPUT. The scientific and engineering effort devoted to the development of production technology is a crucial long-run factor in attaining an economical combination of productive factors for the output of quality products. Scientific and engineering manpower (the research and development input) is the first input and substitute for other productive factors to be combined in production. The role of research and technological progress cannot be omitted from the theory of production. The accumulated knowledge and techniques of basic science and industrial research are the technological heritage, and scientific and technical education and the supply of scientists and skilled labor are society's contribution to industrial progress.

Though society's contribution is somewhat generalized throughout the economy, some industries and larger firms generally reap bigger benefits from their research effort and the application of technological advances. A firm's research effort can, in part, be measured by the size of the research budget. But the quality of the research and engineering input depends on the contributions of university and government-sponsored research and on the education of scientists and engineers. A firm's scientific and research effort is generally directed to the high-cost aspects of production and to advances in products, materials, and processes that reduce the input of the productive factors. The greater the long-run input of research and development, the lower the cost of production and the greater the product utility. Products turned out in immense quantities can profitably absorb large inputs of research and development to the economic advantage of the firm and the consumer. The cost of research is often more than recouped through economies obtainable in production.

PRODUCT DESIGN AND THE VOLUME OF OUTPUT. Before engineers can effectively design products, they must ascertain the consumer-utility features, salability, and market-appeal features to be embodied in the design of the product. Through marketing experience, consumer-use studies, and laboratory and field tests, managers and engineers determine the utility features desired by consumers and the various "use conditions" to be met by the products. On the basis of such data, engineers select and develop the required product-design features, for example, durability, quality, performance, economy in operation and maintenance, and styling. Effective engineers attain the desired balance among the various features, and they achieve a balance in the wearability and durability among the various components of the product. Engineers will obviously temper their designs to incorporate features that derive from the custom, aesthetic tastes, and trade and legal prescriptions of the community.

Concurrent with the consumer-utility and salability phase of product engineering, technicians develop and adapt the product design for minimum-cost production processes for the selected or anticipated volume of output. Thus, when engineers initially determine the consumer-utility features to be embodied in the product, they take into account the production aspect (economical processing) and the volume to be produced (plant size). To attain economical production, engineers design products for the utilization of processes that minimize the input of scarce, high-priced factors. The reduction in the input of a single factor (e.g., labor through use of more mechanized processes) would, of course, involve a change in factor proportionality; other factors would be substituted for the factor minimized. Engineers strive to balance the consumer-utility and salability features with the features that make for low-cost production—they aim to design products for manufacture at a selected range of unit cost and for marketability at a selected range of prices. It is obvious that a simple economy-model product can often be manufactured through inexpensive processing at low unit cost, while a high-priced luxury product may call for manufacture at comparatively high cost.

The product-design specifications and the selected volume of output (size of plant) largely determine the kinds of production processes that can be economically employed. The processes adopted in turn determine the kind and amount of facilities, materials, and labor that will be combined at various rates of output. Engineers can often therefore design products to suit the kinds of processes they wish or plan to adopt. Since the determination of proportionality in the combination of productive factors obviously depends on and involves the design of the product, both the product design and the research inputs are the initial variable inputs in the organization of production for the output of given products.

The larger the volume of products to be put out, the greater the research and engineering inputs that can be economically applied to perfect the design of the product and the production technology. The more minute division of labor made possible by a large volume of output permits the utilization of advanced types of processes comprised of highly specialized automated facilities and elaborate tooling, inspection, and testing devices. The speed of output attainable through mass-production processes lowers the input of both capital and labor per unit of output.

Through various production and organizational approaches, firms can enlarge their volume of output and increase the size of the production run, thereby increasing the degree to which they can apply mass-production technology and obtain economical output. Firms putting out goods for which demand is relatively elastic can, for instance, design products for low-cost output so that the products can be priced low enough to obtain a large sales volume. To increase continuity and intensity in the utilization of specialized facilities, firms can also design products for maximum interchangeability of components. Firms that specialize in the output of products that can be economically shipped to a wide market can attain effective large-scale output by concentrating production at one or a few locations rather than by dispersing production to a number of regional plants. Firms in some industries have been able to specialize along comparatively narrow product lines, and as specialized producers in the industry, their concentrated output of standard products permits a more extensive utilization of mass-production processes. Small producers in an industry sometimes combine to gain a scale of output that permits the use of more specialized production technology.

Processes and Equipment

When managers and engineers combine the three categories of productive factors (capital, material resources, and labor), they combine them as various classes of specialized productive agents which make up the productive factors. The capital input, for instance, would be applied as production machines, tools, inspection devices, materials-handling equipment, and power plant; material resources would be applied as raw materials, goods in process, and fuel; and labor would be applied as machine operators, inspectors, clerks, supervisors, and engineers. Since there are many classes of capital, labor, and materials, each productive factor is not strictly homogeneous. The law of diminishing returns applies to each of the specialized productive agents. In applying any one agent (operators, supervisors, or engineers), a point is reached at which additional inputs will contribute less to total output of the product than previous inputs of the same agent.

Certain classes of capital and labor are complementary in use and would therefore be applied jointly as a complementary unit. Under the simplified assumption of variable proportions and price-induced substitutability, moderate changes in input price ratios lead to commensurate substitution among factors. But when complementary or fixed technical proportions of certain factors are required by the process, changes in the relative prices of the factors (within a certain range) have no effect on the proportion in which factors are combined. Hence, to a limited degree, input proportions are independent of price changes. But once critical points in relative price changes are passed, changes in factor proportionality are again possible, since ordinarily more than one process is available for attaining a given production objective.

Process and equipment selection involves both technical and economic considerations. In their appraisal and selection of processing methods and equipment, engineers take into account and solve pertinent managerial problems (many of which have been earlier noted) on the basis of economic analysis.

In their *procedure to set up plant,* engineers ordinarily begin by selecting the required production machines, that is, the machines which will perform the specific fabrication and assembly operations on the production lines. They then select the required service equipment (appropriate materials-handling devices, inspection devices, utilities) that facilitate the manufacturing activities on the production line. The product-design specifications to some extent permit the use of alternative processes for the manufacture of the goods. From among the available alternative production methods, engineers select the kind of processes and equipment that will turn out the required volume of goods at low cost and that will provide the desired type of production adaptability.

In choosing equipment engineers take into account the *required output capacity* because this determines the extent to which it would be economically feasible to subdivide the production process into individual operations and tasks and thereby to permit the adoption of more highly specialized technology (use of special-purpose equipment). Engineers also take into account the kind and amount of adaptability required in plant facilities (e.g., the extent to which general-purpose machines should be used) and the extent to which provision should be made for ease of plant convertibility and for ease of future expansion in capacity.

In order that they may select the appropriate production machines, engineers carefully study the *specifications of the product*— the data which stipulate the specific materials and the design of each component. From this study engineers outline (usually on process charts) the *sequence of operations needed to process the materials* or fabricate parts and to assemble the product. Engineers indicate on process charts where highly specialized operations and machines can be economically used and where general-purpose machines should be used. On the basis of the prepared sequence of operations, engineers select the production machines (e.g., metalworking machines) needed to carry out the manufacturing process and then select the appropriate service equipment that will effectively facilitate the production process.

In choosing equipment engineers appraise each machine or facility for its suitability in performing the required quality of work, its capacity, adaptability, reliability in operation, purchase price and cost of installation, and operating cost. Engineers select the best suited equipment on the basis of comparative cost. They arrange and integrate the facilities for over-all balanced output capacity among the production machines to assure a uniform flow of work at the desired rate of output. They strive to avoid the acquisition of machines with excess (unusable) capacity, and they also aim to avoid capacity shortages (bottlenecks) in machines anywhere on the production line or in the service activities. Managers usually provide for a certain amount of extra production capacity to meet the anticipated sales increases in the years immediately ahead, and they design the plant layout and provide for a certain amount of extra capacity in some of the service facilities (utilities, handling facilities, building space) which will make for ease of future expansion in plant capacity. Thus, by means of an appropriate development approach, future expansion of the plant will call for low incremental cost, a low capital-output ratio for capacity increments.

Engineers sometimes find it advantageous to employ the "pilot" plant as a device for developing new processes, equipment, and products and for testing the efficiency of the process and the quality of the product under controlled conditions. In the pilot-plant stage engineers can refine their developments and eliminate flaws in production (processing difficulties, machine failures, high scrap ratios) before the process is released for utilization on a production basis.

In the selection of processes and facilities and in the design of plants for economical production, managers and *engineers can vary factor proportionality in a number of ways.* They may use product- and process-design approaches, organizational approaches, as well as operational arrangements to achieve substitution among factors in order to minimize the input of high-price factors, whether capital, materials, or labor.

MINIMIZING THE INPUT OF CAPITAL. When capital (or any productive factor) is scarce and high-priced relative to other productive factors, managers can employ a number of approaches and methods to minimize the capital input (i.e., the capital-output ratio) while at the same time obtaining an economical combination of productive factors for the required volume of output. The basis for minimizing the input of capital, materials, and labor can be progressively established and implemented at various stages or phases in the over-all development of a production project—at the product development and design phase, at the process and equipment selection and development phase, at the plant-layout and physical-organizational phase, and at the distribution phase.

Managers and engineers can minimize and conserve capital input per unit of output by selecting an effective process-related product line, by designing products for economical processing (e.g., by omitting superfluous design features), by obtaining the maximum interchangeability of components among products in the line, or by adopting the "selective assembly" practice, whenever practical. Through concentrated engineering effort on product design and processing methods, technicians can therefore lower the input of capital (or other factors) and attain low-cost production while maintaining the fundamental utility features in the product. The total consumer utility would, of course, be enlarged, since at lower production costs and selling prices the market ordinarily absorbs and enjoys larger amounts of the product.

Engineers can often conserve capital by developing product designs adaptable to the use of processes that require a small input of capital. Such processes tend to employ labor-intensive production techniques. For example, the design of components and products so that they can be fabricated by welding processes calls for a comparatively small capital input in facilities, while, conversely, the use of large presses for fabricating parts requires a considerable capital input but a small labor input per unit of output.

Engineers can sometimes minimize the input of capital by selecting low-priced, general-purpose machines of standard make. Since these machines are adaptable for processing a certain variety of work, fewer machines are generally required to meet a given range of production requirements. Moreover, the installation of attachments (automatic feeding and timing devices) on some types of general-purpose machines enables them to fabricate at an efficiency level approaching that of some special-purpose machines.

Engineers can minimize the over-all input of capital and attain considerable productivity through a selective approach for equipping plant operations. They may equip the production line with high-speed specialized equipment and precision machines that can produce economically with a low labor input but specify manual methods and inexpensive facilities for the handling of materials, inspection, and other plant service activities. For example, handtrucks may be used in place of expensive mechanical handling equipment, and hand-gauging instruments may be used in place of elaborate inspection devices.

Through the foregoing product-design-and-processing approach and through the "freezing" of the product design for a reasonable period (i.e., avoiding frequent product restyling), managers increase the volume of components and products that are processed by capital facilities. This minimizes the capital input per unit of output, because it permits the use of highly specialized machines for the production line, longer production runs, and fewer production changeovers. Moreover, the resulting smaller over-all inventory requirements lower the material input.

In those lines of production in which manufacturing technology and productivity call for a capital-intensive plant, managers can, through a longer workweek and multiple-shift production, attain intensive use of facilities and thereby a low capital input per unit of output. Such intensive use of plant substantially lowers the capital-output ratio (i.e., the capital requirement for a given quantity of output). Moreover, the consumption and wearing out of capital facilities over a shorter time interval reduce their vulnerability to technological and market obsolescence.

Seasonal fluctuations in production give rise to idle facilities as well as to changes in factor proportionality. Hence, in cases in which output or sales are seasonal, managers can more or less offset fluctuations in output by adopting a complementary (process-related) product for output during the slack season. Capital would be conserved through the fuller utilization of plant.

Managers sometimes can advantageously reduce the investment required for the output of goods by leasing facilities or by procuring components from suppliers. Through the use of leased facilities, the firm attains a certain adaptability in factor proportionality and in capacity. During periods of low business volume, for instance, the firm need not carry idle facilities.

MINIMIZING THE INPUT OF MATERIALS. Through the appropriate design of products and selection of processes and facilities, engineers can minimize the input of materials. In the development of the product, engineers can emphasize those design approaches, techniques, and features that minimize the input of materials. Through careful analysis engineers can avoid overdesign of components and of structural sections of the product and thereby reduce the absorption of expensive materials. They can seek out cheaper grades of materials or develop inexpensive substitute materials that meet structural requirements.

Engineers can also select or develop processing techniques that conserve materials during the fabrication of the product. For example, the use of appropriate types of tooling (multiple-stage dies) absorbs smaller quantities of material in the fabrication of components. Production facilities can be designed for, or adapted to, the processing of cheaper (e.g., non-uniform) grades of materials. Effective inspection methods (e.g., statistical quality control) can cut down material waste in processing of work through the plant. Special facilities may be employed to salvage substandard products, to rework "process" scrap, or to turn waste material into by-products. Reduction in the input of materials per unit of output decreases the ratio of materials to capital input and the ratio of materials to labor input. But it does not directly affect the ratio of labor to capital input.

Capital and labor can be substituted for scarce materials in a more direct manner. The development of a special process to extract low-grade ores (e.g., the beneficiation of taconite iron ore) is, in a sense, a substitution of capital and labor for materials. The erection of plants to supply fertilizer, for instance, involves a substitution of capital for land.

MINIMIZING THE INPUT OF LABOR. Through appropriate design of products and processes, engineers can minimize the input of labor in the combination of productive factors. Engineers have been particularly effective in reducing the input of labor through the subdivision and standardization of processes and the development of mechanized facilities (including automation) for the output of standard products. Managers have found greater opportunities for the introduction of laborsaving methods through the breakdown of complex and skilled jobs into simpler tasks and the design of machines and work stations on the basis of motion-economy principles which minimize labor effort. The attainment of continuous, uninterrupted production reduces plant "down time." Worker idleness, too, can be minimized through the provision of stand-by facilities that are activated when production on regular facilities has been interrupted.

Labor input can be reduced not only through the intensive mechanization and automation of the production line but also through the mechanization of the plant auxiliary activities that serve and support the production line. This means mechanized handling of materials from receiving to the shipping of goods, mechanized inspection activities through the use of special gauging machines, and mechanized repairing of facilities which permits easier attainment of preventative maintenance and the continuity of production. Moreover, clerical work has been increasingly routinized so that laborsaving office machines can be adopted to advantage.

Imaginative engineers continually design novel devices and find opportunities for fitting available mechanisms into the existing pattern of production. The interrelatedness of capital facilities does not hinder the adoption of newly innovated devices. Thus, in a labor-scarce economy, technicians invariably apply considerable engineering ingenuity to the development of efficient methods and to the design of standard, laborsaving equipment for all repetitive and arduous tasks, particularly if the tasks are common to many industries. Engineers, for instance, have designed earth-moving equipment, manned by one operator, to do the work of several scores of men equipped with shovel and wheelbarrow.

The input of labor can also be minimized by effective selection, training, and placement of workers and by the adoption of well-designed wage-incentive systems. The conservation of labor and the law of proportionality likewise apply to organization and managerial systems. Ineffective organization and managerial systems (resulting in an ill-coordinated use of productive agents) waste manpower and capital, preventing the full attainment of the output potential, while excessive systemization and overorganization contribute less to total output than the extra expense involved in maintaining the overelaborate system. The total productive effort, in fact, would be stifled by excessive managerial control and bureaucratic red tape.

Labor Input and the Divisibility of Plant Facilities

Capital as a productive agent is considered to be divisible in plants where it can be applied in small increments as individual machines to establish or increase the capacity level. Highly divisible production facilities and output capacity are exemplified by those plants where a battery of identical (or duplicate) production machines perform the major operation in the fabrication of the product, as in the case of cigarette-making machines, tire-molding machines, and presses and die-casting machines. Because such machines (like many machines in industry) are usually designed to be manned by a single operator, they are considered to be unadaptable with respect to the input of labor. Thus, in their initial design, many plant processes (comprised of individual machines) are divisible with respect to capital input for production machines but are not adaptable with respect to labor input to man the machines. In such plants the rate of output can be varied by decreasing or increasing the employment of labor: to cut back the production rate, managers would shut down some of the duplicate production machines and lay off workers; to increase the rate of output, managers would hire workers to operate the machines that were idle.

Since each worker operates a single production machine (i.e., labor is combined with a given amount of capital), he ordinarily puts out the same quantity of product as the previous workers hired. Since the marginal product of each production worker would tend to be identical, the marginal productivity curve for labor would be represented by a comparatively straight line throughout much of the middle range of rated capacity, say, from 40 to 85 per cent of capacity. In cases in which the last workers added are assigned to operate the less productive machines (e.g., older machines or stand-by equipment), their contribution would be lower, with the result that the marginal-productivity curve would tend to decline as full rated capacity is approached. When the plant is operating at a low production rate, the marginal-productivity curve for labor would be below that of the middle range because of the comparative indivisibility and unadaptability of the plant's specialized service equipment (power plant, overhead bridge cranes, for example) and service departments (inspection, maintenance).

Capital inputs are essentially indivisible when a production process is carried out by a large internally integrated facility (e.g., a refinery or a rolling mill) or by an integrated fabrication line or an integrated assembly line comprised of special machine units and work stations arranged and coordinated in the sequential order of the operation necessary to fabricate a component or assemble a product. Since a certain minimum-sized unit is required for a power plant and for such specialized heavy-duty equipment as huge presses, furnaces, planing mills, and bridge cranes, these may also be considered indivisible facilities. Indivisible facilities can be employed economically only if they are continuously used so that their high-capital burden can be spread over many units of output.

To erect indivisible-type capacity would therefore call for capital inputs of large increments. A certain amount of capital input is necessary for the erection of an efficient minimum-sized plant. The capacity of a production line may be designed for the minimum economic level (i.e., for the minimum practical size) or for the maximum economic level. Duplicate production lines would have to be established if the capacity required were greater than that provided by the maximum-sized production line. If the production lines were housed in separate buildings, they would be identified as duplicate plants. Since a plant comprised of indivisible capacity ordinarily requires a certain complement of workers to man the various work stations and operate the facility, the plant is considered to be unadaptable with respect to varying the size of the labor input. The output rate of a plant or a production department comprised of indivisible and unadaptable capacity may be increased or decreased by varying the length of the workweek or the number of shifts.

A firm's over-all production process and capacity would ordinarily be comprised of both divisible and indivisible facilities, some of which would be adaptable and others unadaptable with respect to variation in labor input. Managers would vary the firm's rate of output through a combination of methods best suited to the processes and capacity of each plant or department. For example, the production rate of processes characterized by divisible and adaptable capacity may be varied by increasing or decreasing the labor input and the number of production machines operated, while the output rate of indivisible and unadaptable capacity may be adjusted by varying the length of the workweek. Whenever economically feasible, managers tend to apply a uniform plan so that the firm may operate as a unit.[3]

The divisibility of plant facilities as well as the optimum size for various specialized production functions is among the long-run factors (as outlined on the pages below) that determine the extent to which economies of scale will accrue in a given enterprise.

SIZE: SCALE ECONOMIES IN MULTIPLE-PLANT INTEGRATION

Bigger firms have a competitive advantage and can produce at lower costs than smaller firms because they achieve economies through the use of large-scale methods of production and of specialized professional and managerial experts and because they attain technological advances and profitability through large outlays for industrial research and development. "Economies of scale" refers to the ability to secure lower unit cost by increasing the size of the enterprise.

Large enterprises generally achieve economies in distribution as well as in production, particularly when they can employ a given production technology to put out a demand-related line of products. Big firms attain low unit-cost distribution through a large specialized selling organization, mass-marketing methods, and big outlays for advertising, sales promotion, and market research. A big enterprise can obtain economies in procurement of materials through the use of purchasing experts and through bargaining power

---

[3] The marginal-productivity curve for variable inputs would reflect the combined effect of the divisibility and adaptability of the firm's capacity in the various plants and departments and the plan adopted for varying the rate of output. In many cases the marginal-cost curve would be saucer-shaped, and the marginal-productivity curve for the variable inputs would take the shape of an inverted saucer.

and quantity discounts in bulk buying. Financing, too, is generally cheaper and easier for a large firm than for a small business. Because it has better access to money markets and large banks and because it borrows in larger amounts, a big firm can acquire loans at a lower rate of interest and can sell its securities more readily and at a better price. The "optimum firm" may be defined as a business unit that, in a given state of technology (including organizational and managerial practice), obtains the lowest average unit cost of production and distribution. "Optimum" also applies to a plant, a divisional unit or group of related plants, a retail outlet, or other constituent units that make up a firm.

When a firm grows beyond a certain size, diseconomies develop because of difficulty in coordinating specialized functions, the over-burdening of executives when they attempt to master the numerous variables of an unwieldy enterprise, and because of managerial inability to develop potential economies through the rational structuring of the enterprise.

Economies of Scale in Plant

The optimum-sized plant and the optimum firm differ for each industry. Among industries that tend to be comprised of large-scale plants (or multiple-plant units) are those employing continuous processes and other large indivisible facilities (pulp mills, metal rolling mills), those producing large products of high unit value (automobiles, farm machinery), those comprised of geographically concentrated plants turning out products of high unit value (business machines) which can be readily shipped and sold nationally and internationally, those that exploit geographically concentrated resources (mineral deposits), and those requiring a long processing interval.

Economies of scale do not derive from mere size or bigness per se but from the specialized organization of large-scale operations (from specialized plants and multiple-plant systems) designed for the exploitation of available advanced types of technology and efficient operational and managerial practice. If low-cost production of a given product (or a few closely related products) is to be attained, the volume of output must be sufficiently large to permit the erection and organization of an optimum (low-cost) plant or a multiple-plant unit. With increasing volume of output and plant size, at least up to moderate size, average costs of production decline as size increases, assuming that factor costs are constant. A larger volume of output permits a greater division of labor; the process can be subdivided into minute, simple operations which permit ease of mechanization of the production process. When automated facilities are introduced, a large transfer machine would perform a series of operations on the work or piece being processed, or an automated machine would simultaneously perform different operations on a component part. Automation tends to reverse the division of labor as far as the worker is concerned, and it favors larger plants in terms of output capacity.

The equipping of a production line with highly specialized, expensive machines and the use of mass-production processes increase the speed of output and lower the labor and capital cost per unit of output. The output requirements must be sufficiently large to permit engineers to balance machine capacities on the production line and achieve a uniform flow of work, avoiding bottlenecks at machine stations as well as minimizing unused machine capacity. Hence, a certain minimum volume of output (a certain minimum-sized plant) is necessary to employ large indivisible (lumpy) capital equipment or highly integrated, mechanized production lines to full capacity. The enlargement of the output capacity beyond the efficient minimum size (the optimum size) often calls for the installation of a duplicate production line, and if the line is housed in a separate structure, it would be designated as a duplicate plant. The plant (and output volume), too, should be of sufficient size to make it economical to install processing facilities for the conversion of any waste materials into by-products. The concept of optimum-sized plant also includes the economies gained from the full-time employment of plant managerial and technical specialists (metallurgists, production planners, plant engineers) and from the distribution over a large production volume of such plant overhead services as clerical activities, inventory control, planning, and utilities. When two or more plants are located on one site, certain auxiliary service plants (power plant, tool shop, maintenance shop) can be economically utilized. The optimum production unit would then refer to the cluster of interrelated plants.

In the long run, in many industries two *opposing trends influence the optimum-sized plant* or the optimum multiple-plant divisional unit. Advances in production technology, organizational and managerial practice, and gains in plant productivity increase the value added in production and thus enlarge the optimum plant. On the other hand, producers in many industries tend, over time, to the increasing purchase of standard materials, components and supplies rather than to the fabrication of these items. As industrial output grows, a greater variety of standard-type materials and components (electric motors, instruments, fittings) become available for purchase by industries producing assembled-type products. This enables producers to design more of their products in such a way as to incorporate standard components that can be purchased more cheaply than they can be specially turned out in the producers' own plants.

Since the numbers and types of subcontracting firms differ in each industrial region, the optimum plant or divisional unit (in terms of value-added) tends to differ between regions because of differences in the depth of plant production that is economically feasible. Though the optimum plant is a useful concept for guiding production managers and engineers in the designing of a plant on the basis of the latest production technology, the optimum plant is, in fact, often difficult to identify and measure for any given industry.

Economies in Multiple-Plant Operation

The limited demand in a given market area may make it uneconomic to erect an optimum plant—a plant of sufficient size to secure the lowest possible unit cost. A plant or a divisional unit may therefore not reach optimum size because of the limited size of the local market. A firm may nonetheless find it profitable to establish plants in each of several market areas. A horizontally combined multiple-plant firm may spread over a wide geographical area and enjoy managerial economies which would more than compensate for the inability to establish optimum plants in each of the market areas. On the other hand, the market size in a given area may exceed the optimum-sized plant, but it may not be big enough to absorb the output of two optimum plants. The firm would in this case operate on an overtime or a two-shift basis, or it may provide additional capacity (with some in excess) for operation on a single-shift basis. The excess capacity would await the growth of demand in the local market.

As a business grows and capacity expands, individual plants or a cluster of related plants (a "works" division) may expand to their optimum size. But this may be too large for efficient local plant management, that is, the plant optimum exceeds the managerial optimum under the original physical organization and division of production. The continued growth of capacity through machine additions and floor-space expansion under the same plant organizational arrangement often results in diseconomies in capital utilization and plant production which are compounded by the growing diseconomies in plant management. The overcoming or the forestalling of such tendencies calls for long-term planning (and the expenditure of replacement funds) for the reallocation of production through the physical division of the plant into separate producing units. The new, smaller (but optimum) plants may be organized and erected along process lines: the various production departments under the old plant arrangement (e.g., foundry, machining, pressing departments) and/or the easily separable production phases of the over-all process (e.g., certain fabrication lines, subassembly lines) set up as separate plants, each under a plant superintendent. If the firm is engaged in multiple-product output, the new, smaller plants may be organized and erected along product lines. Top managers may also find it economical and more profitable to set up plants smaller in depth of production, wherein plant operations would consist largely of assembly processes supplied with components procured from outside producers. The evolution and development of a multiple-plant system may involve the relocation of certain plants (usually assembly plants) in areas of expanding markets. The subdivision of the over-all production system into separate operating units would not only restore optimum plants (or the trend toward optimum plants) but provide operating flexibility with respect to ease of inaugurating multiple-shift or overtime operation in certain plants without difficulties in the material handling of work in process, and it would make for ease in cutting back production through curtailing the length of the workweek or shutting down the less efficient plants.

When management expands its multiple-plant combination through acquisitions and mergings, such plant additions may not be of the logical specialization with respect to process or product for the type of rational structure desired by the firm for its over-all system. A multiple-plant combination wholly or partly made up of plant acquisitions may not at the outset achieve the full potential economies until plants are reorganized and more appropriately equipped to fit the desired rational allocation of production.

In industries in which the size of the low-cost plant is relatively small (i.e., the plant optimum is considerably smaller than the managerial optimum), an optimum firm would consist of a chain of plants or a chain of retail or other types of establishments. Small firms with fewer plants would be at a cost disadvantage in marketing and distribution since they would be involved in duplicate crosshauling of freight in making sales. A large horizontal combination can operate efficiently because its chain of plants can be sufficiently large to permit realization of the optimum-sized firm with its attendant economies. Even though some local plants may not be up to the efficient size, savings in transportation cost may be sufficient to warrant plant dispersal rather than concentration. The location of branch plants at regional markets would not only attain savings through reduction in transportation but would also make possible more effective adjustments to shifts in local demand and greater stability in the over-all sales volume, since a drop in sales in one area may be offset by a sales gain in another. By permitting the shutting down of older or less efficient units, branch-plant systems also make for flexibility and economy in the reduction of output. Advantages also derive from the fact that the home office can economically provide a common selling organization and certain specialized managerial and technical services (procurement, forecasting, engineering) which would not otherwise be available at the same level of proficiency.

When marketing costs make up a large share of the selling price, a firm often finds it profitable to expand its product coverage to include a full line of demand-related goods that can be marketed through the same distribution channels and outlets. Since production costs are a smaller share of the selling price, the economies gained through large-scale selling will more than offset the less economical level of output of some of the products. Because of the limited size of certain local markets, some of the firm's distribution establishments may not be of the optimum size. But large-scale procurement, financing, advertising, and specialized management would produce significant economies that make for profitable operation.

Economies in Vertical Integration

Vertical integration is the process whereby a firm brings more and more sequentially related production stages and business activities under its managerial control. In a fully integrated enterprise the firm controls the sequential production stages from raw-material output to the final completion and distribution of the product. The degree of vertical integration is indicated by the share of value-added in sales and by the ratio of profits to sales. Return on investment in a vertically combined enterprise may, of course, be no larger than the return in a horizontally combined enterprise.

Vertical integration would obviously differ among industries. The extent to which vertical integration is economically advantageous depends on the nature and peculiarities of an industry's production technology and the pattern of the vertical structure of production. In certain industries production economies from vertical integration are obtainable through a greater degree of standardization and interchangeability of materials and components, specialization of sequential plants, elimination of some initial or terminal operations (inspection, packaging, heating or other preparatory operations), reduction in the level of over-all inventories, elimination of selling activities, and through the attainment of better or more uniform quality of materials and more reliable delivery.

A firm tends to expand vertically (either backward or forward) when the return on investment for earlier-stage plants or for distribution establishments is higher than the return on its alternative investment projects. Opportunities for vertical integration tend to grow out of the expansion of output, for example, when a firm expands in the direction of horizontal combination.

Items that were cheaper to buy than to make when they were procured in relatively small quantities often become cheaper to produce by the consuming firm when the items are absorbed in large quantity. When a firm's demand for certain purchased material or fabricated items is sufficiently large, the firm may find it profitable to erect or acquire an optimum-sized plant to supply the specialized needs of its plants. When it is economically feasible, vertical integration is encouraged if materials must be procured from monopolistic suppliers who make a high return on investment, and integration also tends to occur during periods when materials are relatively scarce and high priced. As earlier indicated, vertical integration is economically feasible in industries characterized by certain types of structural patterns. Metallurgical industries (steel, aluminum, copper) tend to be vertically integrated. A winery, for example, can integrate with a large vineyard, but a whiskey distillery cannot feasibly be integrated with grain production or a large meat-packing plant with cattle raising.

Many large corporations develop a *diversified combination pattern* consisting of horizontally linked, vertically linked, and complementarily linked establishments, as well as sideline establishments unrelated to their main fields of business. Some of the major divisional units or plant groupings would be structurally more rational than others. A firm's diversification pattern may be designed to achieve stability in the over-all volume of business, penetration into growing industries and markets, or other objectives discussed earlier in this chapter.

Though large highly diversified combinations, as compared to the more specialized combinations, lead to diminishing returns to top management, their offsetting economic advantages derive from large-scale research and development and the concentration of internal investment funds (particularly depreciation funds) which permit rapid mobility of capital into those fields of business in which market demand is growing and profit opportunities are un-covered. A highly diversified firm can quickly direct sufficient finan-cial resources to erect more new plants (i.e., achieve effective capital mobility) in any one of a large number of fields of business in which the firm has a foothold and experience. Managers can use break-even charts for estimating the profitability from capital out-lays for plant expansion, plant modernization, or other investment in productive capacity. Before they can effectively use such charts as an aid in decision making, managers must have an adequate grasp of the nature of break-even analysis.

BREAK-EVEN ANALYSIS: PROFITABILITY

A firm's potential profitability is indicated by its break-even chart which shows the output range at which the firm's total revenue is greater than its total cost. The break-even chart graphically portrays the relationship between total cost and total revenue for various volumes of output within the limits of capacity. Along its horizontal axis the break-even chart (Fig. 7–2; see also Fig. 4–1) shows the volume of output, and along its vertical axis it shows total cost for the various volumes of output and the total revenue from the sale of various volumes of output. The total-cost curve and the total-revenue curve in the chart represent a firm's short-run business operations so long as the firm's factor costs, prices, and long-run structure remain constant. The break-even chart serves as a measur-ing rod of profits (or losses) at various volumes of business. It ordinarily shows that the firm makes profits in the higher ranges of output, where total revenue is greater than total cost, and that the firm incurs losses in the lower ranges of output and sales. By studying the firm's break-even chart, a businessman can see at a glance the volumes of output at which he makes a profit or a loss and the volume of output at which the firm breaks even. In Figure 7–2, for instance, the firm breaks even at 70 per cent of rated capacity because at this point the total revenue covers total costs. Thus, the break-even point is the volume of business at which the firm starts to make a profit. The chart does not in itself forecast profits; it merely indicates what the firm's profit (or loss) would be for different volumes of business. However, by forecasting the sales volume, the businessman can, through the use of the break-even chart, forecast profits.

If an analyst draws up a break-even chart for a future period of business operation or for a given business situation but draws the chart with the assumption that the structure of the enterprise remains unchanged for the period (that the product line, capacity, production technology, and efficiency remain constant), the chart may be of limited value. The chart can meaningfully and appropri-

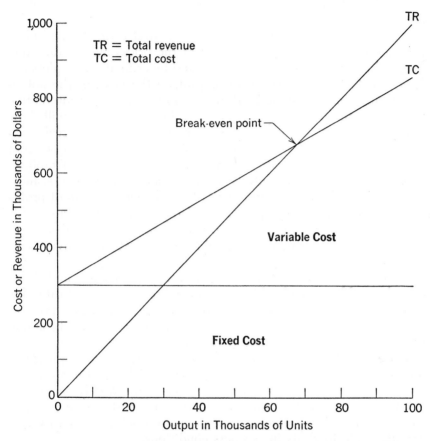

Fig. 7–2. Break-even chart prepared from annual revenue cost figures:

Volume of output	30,000	60,000	90,000
Fixed cost	$300,000	$300,000	$300,000
Variable cost	$150,000	$300,000	$450,000
Sales revenue	$300,000	$600,000	$900,000

ately relate total cost to total revenue for various volumes of output and show the profit potential for the business period ahead only if it is prepared on the basis of the product-mix and of selling prices and factor costs that actually prevail for the period. The analyst must therefore prepare his chart on the basis of estimated or anticipated wages, material costs, selling prices, and product-mix. If the firm is modernizing plant and expanding capacity for use during the future period, the analyst must prepare the break-even diagram for the anticipated capacity and productivity. The break-even chart essentially projects a firm's short-run business operations and profit potential within the firm's long-run structural framework.

In preparing a break-even chart, the analyst estimates and plots the total-revenue curve on the basis of the prices and product-mix that will prevail in the future period, and he estimates and plots the approximate total-cost curve for output on the basis of the anticipated costs for the period. If he prepares charts for alternative production and business programs, each break-even chart will show a different set of revenue, cost, and profit projections. Break-even analysis provides information that businessmen need in order that they may take appropriate action to maintain desired profitability; it aids executives in the analysis and appraisal of alternative business plans (particularly short-term plans) for selection of the most profitable program. For the preparation and appraisal of long-term investment programs, managers must supplement break-even analysis with long-range forecasts and estimates of the rate of return on investment from alternative capital projects.

Because firms differ with respect to scope of business and structure, the problems involved in preparing a break-even chart differ for each enterprise. A break-even chart for a single-plant firm producing a homogeneous product, for instance, would be relatively simple to prepare. The preparation of charts for break-even analysis becomes progressively more difficult and expensive when products, production technology, and scale vary appreciably in the span of a few short years, when raw materials that vary widely in market price make up a high proportion in the unit cost of the product, and when marketing practice and promotion outlays can vary and are adaptable to shifts in business conditions.

Construction of a Break-even Chart

The principles and the procedure for the design and preparation of a break-even chart provide insight into the dynamics of production and business operation and indicate the approaches for economic analysis of managerial problems. To prepare a break-even chart for a future period of business operation, an analyst must (1) determine the appropriate scope for break-even analysis (i.e., whether to prepare a chart for company-wide business operations or for a divisional unit), (2) select a suitable unit or index of output that will consistently measure production volume even though the prod-uct-mix varies, (3) estimate and plot the total-revenue curve on the basis of anticipated selling prices and product-mix, and (4) estimate and plot the total-cost curve (i.e., plot the appropriate fixed costs and variable costs for various levels of output) and note the break-even point.

SCOPE OF BREAK-EVEN CHARTING. In preparing a break-even chart for a multiple plant firm, the analyst must decide whether to construct a company-wide chart or a chart for each divisional unit or each branch plant. If a firm consists of a vertically integrated multiple-plant combination in which a series of plants sequentially carry out the over-all process for the output of goods for a given market (whether a regional market or a national market), the analyst would prepare a break-even chart on a company-wide basis, as he would for a single-plant firm.

In the case of a horizontal multiple-plant firm in which two or more divisional units or branch establishments (e.g., rubber-tire plants, breweries) turn out completed products for regional markets, the analyst would prepare a break-even chart for each divisional unit or plant. The analyst would find it difficult to prepare a valid company-wide chart for the latter case because shifts in regional demand and in production would result in different total costs for the firm even though the physical output and dollar sales volume are the same. This is because a horizontal multiple-plant combina-tion often includes plants of different size (and therefore of different economies of scale), of varying degrees of newness and levels of efficiency, and of different wage scales and material purchase prices.

MEASUREMENT OF OUTPUT. The analyst must select an appro-priate unit to measure production and plot output on the horizontal axis for which he plots total cost and total revenue. If the product is homogeneous, he can appropriately use physical units (tons, barrels, yardage, product unit) to measure output. If two or more products are put out (i.e., in multiple-product or heterogeneous out-put), production volume may be measured by a single index of output (e.g., physical unit, typical product) which converts on an appropriate basis (e.g., unit cost, labor input, material input) the various products into equivalents of the output unit or typical product. The output volume for the above types of production may be appropriately expressed in terms of percentage of rated capacity when production capability is properly computed and when avail-able capacity does not vary appreciably because of fluctuations in plant down time. The output unit or index selected or designed must correctly measure output, even though changes occur in product-mix, selling prices, wages, or cost of material purchases.

Output may be satisfactorily measured in terms of sales volume (in constant dollars) if a uniform percentage markup is used and if there is only a small lag between output and sales. Dollar sales volume as a measure of output would be unreliable if products differ in percentage markup (as is often the case) and if the product-mix varies. The measure of output in terms of dollar sales volume for a changing product-mix would not properly relate production cost to physical output or to sales volume. Costs, for instance, would be understated if sales shift to products of low-profit contribution margin.

TOTAL-REVENUE CURVE. Because selling prices are relatively stable (particularly in short-term business operations) in many imperfectly competitive industries wherein managerial price discretion exists, the analyst ordinarily assumes constant selling prices in the projection of the total-revenue curve. When a single-product firm sells a homogeneous product at a constant price, the analyst plots revenue as a linear total-revenue curve for a wide range of output. When a multiple-product firm sells a relatively stable product-mix at constant prices, the analyst also plots a single linear total-revenue curve.

In some cases a single linear total-revenue curve would not represent sales revenue because of variations in sales-mix and shifts in market demand. The sale of a given volume of products would yield different total-revenue figures when the contribution margin for products differs and the product-mix varies. A different total-revenue figure for a given volume of sales may also result from changes in the market-segment composition of sales when price discounts differ for each market segment or distribution channel.

For multiple-product firms the analyst must plot the total-revenue curve on the basis of anticipated prices and a carefully forecast product-mix and market-segment ratio. When the product-mix differs for different volumes of sales, the analyst may plot a total-revenue curve based on the revenue from the product-mix at each level of sales. A break-even chart may also be designed to project the total-revenue and total-cost curves for each alternative forecast of business volume and product-mix for a given period. A series of break-even charts (or a series of revenue and cost projections on a composite break-even chart) would show the firm's probable break-even points and profit potential for different sales-mixes and production programs anticipated in the future period.

TOTAL-COST CURVE—THE MEASUREMENT OF COST.. Since many firms build capacity in advance of demand, the analyst often finds that the short-run total-cost curve (the cost-output function) will be more or less linear for the range of capacity that is likely to be used. As indicated in Chapter 4, the shape of a firm's short-run total-cost curve for the full range of capacity is determined by such factors as the proportion of variable cost to fixed cost, divisibility of productive facilities, adaptability of productive facilities to

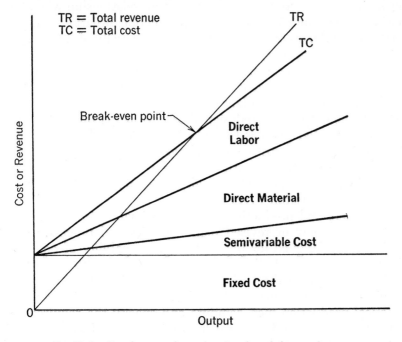

Fig. 7–3. Break-even chart showing breakdown of costs.

changes in the product-mix, the degree of production continuity and stability at various ranges of capacity, and higher wage rates for the overtime and multiple-shift range of production. The use of alternative methods for varying the rate of output will also influence the shape of the cost curve.

In preparing a break-even chart for a future period, the analyst estimates and plots the total-cost curve for the anticipated range of output (Fig. 7–3). He plots the total-cost curve for the firm's anticipated production organization and structure which he assumes will be constant for the future period of business operation, and he assumes for the period a constancy in products, technology, scale price of input factors, and level of managerial efficiency. His primary objective is to estimate on some practical basis the firm's costs for a future period, which estimate enables construction of an empirical approximation of the theoretical short-run cost function illustrated by the short-run cost curves presented in Chapter 4.

An analyst may use the accounting approach, statistical analysis, or the engineering approach for estimating the total-cost curve for a future period of business operation. He would use the *engineering approach* for estimating the cost-output relationship when future business operations involve a new production situation. Statistical analysis and the accounting approach are generally of little value for estimating the cost-output relationship when a firm's future production is to be based on improved processing technology to be provided by equipment replacement and modernization expenditures, when production facilities and plant layout are to be converted or changed over for the output of a redesigned or new-model product, or when a new automated plant is to replace an outmoded marginal plant. The projection of a cost-output relationship and rated capacity for such new production situations calls for an engineering estimate. Industrial engineers, in fact, typically design new plants or revise old plants for the desired rated capacity.

Engineers and production planners estimate rated capacity and unit cost for new or revised plant facilities and processes on the basis of the designed-for physical output capability of equipment, the output rates of similar processes, experience with normal plant performance, or on the basis of normalized time-study data which specify hourly performance for various types of machine operations. Practical production men compute and specify the required skills, man-hour inputs, and material inputs for different hourly physical outputs, and they apply the appropriate learning curve to determine the lead-time required for the plant to work up to the normal output performance. They estimate the cost-output relationship for the anticipated range of output by converting estimated physical inputs into labor and material costs and by converting physical outputs into the sales value of finished goods. Production planners in job-order firms, incidentally, take into account the cost-output relationship in their routine procedure for estimating the cost of new work to be put out to customers' specifications and for loading and scheduling diverse production orders on available plant capacity to meet delivery dates. The engineering approach for estimating the cost-output relationship is always an available supplement to the accounting and statistical approaches when historical costs are dated or obsolete.

Because of its economy and comparative simplicity, an analyst would, whenever possible, use the *accounting approach* and employ other methods as supplementary approaches. The accounting method for estimating the total-cost curve for break-even analysis is based on the costs compiled in accounting records. He would use the accounting cost data covering a recent period of sufficient duration which show the cost of production for different levels of output and over a sufficient range of capacity.

To facilitate the analysis and accumulation of cost, the analyst generally classifies expenses into categories of fixed costs, variable costs, and semivariable costs. In a simple cost-output function, generally characteristic of a single-plant firm producing a homogeneous product under stable conditions, a break-even chart (and the profit potential at different volumes) can be readily computed if all costs are classifiable into fixed costs or variable costs and if the latter costs vary with sales volume according to a fixed ratio.

In order that he may correctly indicate the cost-output relationship, the analyst compiles and matches the relevant costs applicable for each level of output. He generally finds it necessary to adjust and apportion certain cost items in order to accumulate more accurately the appropriate total cost for each selected level of output. For instance, the contribution or benefit derived from outlays for certain periodic activities, such as equipment overhaul and maintenance, product restyling, and special promotion campaigns, generally extends over a considerable time span of business. The analyst allocates only that portion of the cost of such outlays that is applicable to the output volume of a given period. In compiling fixed costs, the analyst would include the estimated economic depreciation charge based on replacement cost (rather than original cost) that most accurately reflects capital consumption, and he would include the appropriate input costs (interest on invested capital, for instance) if he is to project potential profits on the basis of economic costs.

The analyst may compile both variable costs and semivariable costs from accounting records. If wage rates and the purchase price of materials vary, the analyst compiles the cost of variable and semivariable input factors in terms of constant dollars for each level of output in order that he may properly indicate the cost-output relationship for the period. A firm's labor contract can sometimes serve as a basis for forecasting wages.

On the basis of his cost study and anticipated increase in net investment, the analyst plots on the break-even chart the estimated

fixed cost for the future periods; on the basis of his study and anticipated prices for input factors, he plots variable- and semivariable-
cost curves for the range of capacity. The analyst may plot more
than one variable-cost curve when alternative prices for input factors
are likely. The firm's future total-cost curve may be lower than the
past total-cost curve because of a gain in productivity. A forward-
looking replacement program may yield a big productivity gain
from adoption of facilities that achieve laborsaving and capital-
savings improvements which make for significant gains in productivity with no incremental increase in fixed costs.

Because the future total-cost curve is constructed on the basis
of the constancy of future factor prices, technology, scale, and other
factors, a firm's actual total-cost curve in a future period of business
operation will deviate from the plotted empirical approximation of
the theoretical short-run total-cost curve to the extent that dynamic
factors operate to modify the short-term cost function. For instance,
the adoption of a computer-based inventory system will lower
stock levels and increase rated capacity because of less machine
idleness from material shortages; operation at lower capacity levels
in some lines of business involves shorter production runs and
more frequent production changeovers as compared to higher-
capacity operation; the development of a slack labor market may
reduce labor turnover and improve labor performance; and products
may be redesigned to permit use of new materials that process
faster.

Managerial Application of Break-even Analysis

Managers may design break-even charts of varying degrees of
precision to analyze different business situations and problems. They
may, for instance, design charts and use break-even analysis (1) to
show the effect of changes in prices, product-mix, wages, and material costs on the break-even point and profit potential, (2) to
indicate the need for, and to aid in, the reduction of cost and the
break-even point, (3) to appraise alternative business programs and
plans, (4) to facilitate the forecasting of profits and sales volume,
and (5) to determine the amount of increase in capacity or in the
size of plant that will be profitable for the forecast volume of business
and rate of output.

Break-even analysis can show how business will be affected by
anticipated changes in capacity and changes in material costs, prices,
and other market conditions. Managers find specific uses for break-
even analysis when their firm possesses sufficient price-fixing power

to enable it to raise or lower prices within limits, when it periodically negotiates a wage contract or must adjust wages, and when it negotiates a materials-purchase contract or a lease of facilities on an annual or longer basis. Managers can project different cost and revenue curves on break-even charts to show the effect on business of alternative decisions and to compare the results of business operations under proposed or anticipated conditions with those under existing conditions. A firm's projected revenue curve for a future period of operations may be lower than that for a past period because of a decline in selling prices, changes in the product-mix, and changes in the market segment-mix.

The comparative inflexibility of prices during a business downturn in monopolistic and oligopolistic industries tends to result in a somewhat constant revenue curve, while cost cutting through the elimination of superfluous indirect labor and service activities lowers the cost curve. Though the decline in business volume and employment tends to be augmented by price rigidity, the lowering of the break-even point through a policy of austerity and cost-reduction measures somewhat slows the shrinkage in profits. If, with a lowered cost curve and break-even point, business rebounds and sales volume climbs, profits will exceed previous peak levels for the same volume of sales.

In the more competitive industries, price and market flexibility during a business downturn brings about a downward adjustment in the revenue and the cost curves: A decline in selling prices is followed (with a lag) by a decline in factor costs (e.g., lower material costs, salaries) and by cost-cutting measures. Thus, the break-even point in the more competitive enterprise often tends to be more or less constant because a drop in the level of the revenue curve (lower prices) is followed by a drop in the level of the cost curve. Because of a downward movement in selling prices, business volume and employment in the competitive non-durable-goods industries generally do not decline to the same magnitude as that of GNP.

A firm in a strong competitive position may be able to offset a possible decline in its revenue curve by shifting its marketing effort in the direction of increasing the sales volume of the profitable items in the product line. Managers can use break-even analysis to indicate how much reduction in costs and in the break-even point is necessary to attain profitable operations on the basis of the anticipated volume of business; and they can project cost reductions that are possible by alternative measures or approaches (Fig. 7-4). Costs are classifiable as fixed and variable costs on the basis of how they vary in total with output. The term "fixed costs" does not mean that certain costs are not susceptible to reduction. Many items included in overhead costs are essentially stand-by costs. A firm does not need to carry the same load of fixed overhead if it operates at a lower volume for any length of time. (See Fig. 8–5.) A firm may find that it can cut overhead and the break-even point by selling some of its facilities or by subletting part of its premises. Ex-

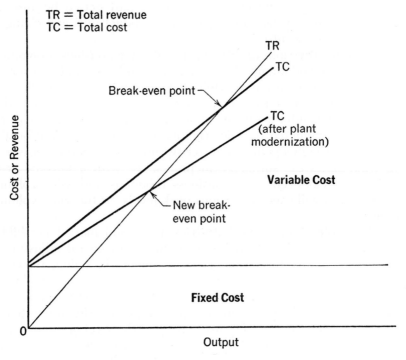

Fig. 7–4. Break-even chart showing cost reduction from plant modernization.

penditures can often be quickly curtailed for certain service activities in the plant, employee welfare, public relations, and front-office amenities. For the long run, costs can be lowered by such measures as employee training programs, adoption of properly designed wage-incentive plans, tighter production planning and supervision, closer budgetary control, the dropping of unprofitable items, and plant-layout studies and modernization of facilities.

Though capital outlays for plant mechanization and modernization may increase fixed costs, such capital outlays lower the input of labor and appreciably cut variable cost when wages are high.

The profit gain from cost-reduction projects calls for precision in estimating the return on investment and in comparing the income gain with the return from other competing investment opportunities within the company. By designing charts to show sets of revenue and cost projections for alternative business programs, managers can use break-even analysis to estimate the profitability of alternative business plans, particularly for the short run. But to appraise properly the worth and profit gain from various alternative investment projects and expansion programs, break-even analysis must be supplemented by capital productivity analysis, discussed in the capital-budgeting procedure in Chapter 11.

Managers use break-even analysis and demand forecasts as a basis for determining the incremental increase in capacity that will be profitable to hold in the future period of business operations. Because of the indivisibility of modern productive facilities and processing technology, capacity can be increased economically only in certain increments. Horizontally combined multiple-plant firms can often expand capacity in increments of optimum-sized plants— erecting new plants in expanding market areas and at more desirable sites, while abandoning old marginal plants of smaller capacity in less desirable locations. In this way they combine net capital formation, replacement, and mobility in a single plant-investment project. Managers try to avoid acquisition of undesired excess capacity. On the basis of break-even analysis, managers can determine the size of capacity that is profitable to hold in the light of anticipated demand.

The level of a firm's future short-run total-cost curve based on the proposed expansion of scale is typically lower than that of the past level largely because of new economies of scale and the utilization of the latest production technology. A break-even chart may be prepared for each of two or more proposed larger plants or scales of capacity that are likely to be selected. A chart indicates excess capacity and overinvestment (the selection of too large a scale) by showing that the anticipated sales volume is not sufficiently beyond the break-even point to yield an adequate profit. A profitable scale of capacity can then be determined by selecting the next smaller capacity scale or plant size (and lower fixed cost) until the anticipated sales volume is sufficiently beyond the break-even point to yield the desired profit and the available extra capacity is adequate to meet the projected increase in demand for the years immediately ahead.

To appraise the need for, and the profit gain from, plant expansion calls for a forecast of sales and production requirements. Break-even analysis can be used to forecast profits, but it is only one aspect of a systematic approach for forecasting business volume and profits. This approach involves a projection of general business conditions (the trend of industrial production, employment, national income, consumer-purchasing power), a forecast of industry demand, an estimate of the company share of the market, and a forecast of company profits on the basis of a break-even chart (or alternative charts) prepared for the future period of business operation. A break-even chart may encompass (or be supplemented by) a projection of a firm's income statement and/or its operating budget so as to forecast the profit for the immediate period of business operations, say, a six-month period. An operating budget (which estimates the cost of output for a period) is prepared from an estimate of sales volume based on a forecast of the product-mix and market-segment ratio.

For a given revenue curve, the relative magnitude of fixed cost and the ratio of fixed to variable cost determine the output rate at which a firm breaks even. Establishments or firms with high fixed costs (those that generally employ capital-intensive processes) tend to have a higher break-even point than firms with low fixed costs (those employing labor-intensive processes). For sales volume beyond the break-even point, profits increase at a faster rate in high fixed-cost firms than do profits in low fixed-cost firms, assuming a given total-revenue curve. Break-even analysis can thus be used to compare the cost structure, the break-even point, and profit potential between two firms as well as between a firm's various divisional units when they produce for separate markets. Break-even analysis, therefore, is a useful technique not only for estimating a firm's profitability but for gauging a firm's competitive position and, to some extent, its adaptability.

THE FIRM'S COMPETITIVE POSITION AND ADAPTABILITY

Firms in most lines of business differentiate their products in order to gain steady acceptance by buyers and thereby achieve some measure of control over selling price. Firms in industries in which sellers are few, particularly differentiated oligopolists, have considerable latitude in price setting. Thus, since selling price in imperfectly competitive industries is more or less determined by managerial discretion and price tends to be somewhat stabilized among firms, price reduction in many cases is removed as a primary means of competition among firms. Rather than relying on price cutting to gain sales volume, firms resort to non-price competition (market promotion, product improvement, and the like) to expand sales and improve their competitive position (Fig. 7–5).

A firm's competitiveness would be indicated by its ability to expand or hold its market share. A firm's competitive performance is, in the final analysis, reflected by the rate of return on its investment (by profitability). In economic terms, however, the per-

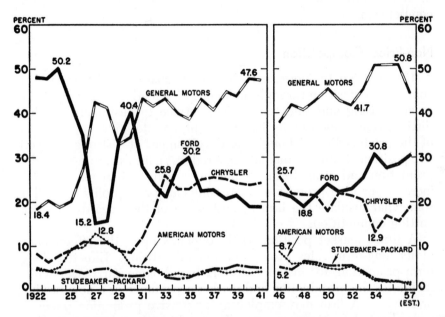

Fig. 7–5. Shifts in competitive position: Passenger-car market penetration by company, with registrations as percentage of industry.

The percentage of total passenger cars sold by each present producer in 1922–1957 is shown. The graphs plot the decline of Ford from 1924 to 1927, its temporary recovery, its decline again to 1933, another brief recovery, and then a slow decline to 1941, followed by postwar resurgence of the company. Chrysler rose suddenly in 1931–33, lost position in the postwar period, and recovered partially in 1957. American Motors had 12.8% of the business in 1927, declined to 1933, recovered, hit another high in 1946, and lost position drastically after 1952. Studebaker-Packard increased in relative volume in the thirties, did well in the early postwar period, and declined sharply after 1952. General Motors has had a relatively more stable history but had a setback in the late twenties, a substantial rise after 1952, and a sizable setback in 1957. Of firms able to survive at all, only General Motors has managed to avoid severe losses of position with real threats to its continued existence.

(U.S. Senate Subcommittee on Antitrust and Monopoly, Hearings, February, 1958, Washington, D.C.: Government Printing Office, 1958, p. 58.)

formance of an enterprise is indicated by the efficiency with which it employs scarce resources for the output of goods desired by consumers.

In modern industry firms improve their competitive position and market share (1) through greater adaptability of production and business operations to shifts in market conditions, (2) through cost reduction and concentration of economic resources for the development and promotion of the enterprise, and (3) through non-price competition.

Non-Price Competition

Firms strive to increase their market share and improve their competitive position through such non-price methods of competition as advertising and sales promotion, service to customers, product distinctiveness and quality improvement, and design or modification of the product line. Though the development of a strong competitive position at some immediate cost reduces a firm's earnings, market promotion and other forms of non-price competition may actually increase—or give promise of increasing—long-run profits as well as somewhat insulate the firm against some of the hazards of price-cutting competition.

A firm's market position partly depends upon the effectiveness of its long-term sales promotion and advertising. Effective long-term promotion, for instance, fosters brand-name carry-over which facilitates the introduction and market acceptance of a new product or service. A firm may employ an aggressive promotion policy or may play a defensive game, merely matching the advertising efforts of rival firms. A firm can sometimes promote sales and increase its market share by resorting to the principle of reciprocity whereby the firm uses its purchasing power to acquire as customers firms from which it buys materials, supplies, and transportation services, for example.

A firm may gain new customers and expand sales volume by providing such services as engineering surveys, freight allowance, appropriate packaging or crating, guarantee of product performance, and liberal credit terms, which are convertible in terms of price and have monetary value. Such customer servicing as the provision of quick delivery and the acceptance and shipment of small orders also involves higher cost to sellers but may not be viewed as price concessions by purchasers.

A firm can maintain an advantageous competitive position or expand sales through product improvement and periodic product remodeling. A firm sometimes enlarges its share of a growing market by continual product differentiation through frequent restyling. When a firm achieves style improvements that are highly distinctive and difficult to duplicate, it essentially acquires a greater measure of monopoly features in its goods. Where product improvements contribute to greater consumer utility and are readily measurable, they are in the nature of price concessions. Since product improvement and restyling are sometimes expensive to carry out, the larger, more profitable, or financially better situated firm has an advantage in this form of promotion because it can absorb the cost of these heavy outlays. The large firm in the field of consumer goods can sometimes quickly expand its market share by adopting as its market-promotion policy the practice of frequent or annual product restyling which places a financial burden on the smaller firm and on the larger one that is temporarily in a less favorable financial situation.

A firm's product line may include some inexpensive or low-priced goods that are primarily designed to compete on the basis of price, and it may also include some highly differentiated quality products in which the firm has a strong market position. A firm's products may have a good reputation in some market areas and less favorable acceptance in other areas.

A firm's competitive approach and marketing strategy may be based on a well-designed demand-related product line. By means of a demand-related product line, a firm may not only gain economies in distribution, but it also gains promotion and selling advantages because it can supply a large share of the product needs of certain consumers and market segments.

The design of a firm's product line depends, of course, on many factors that have been earlier discussed. A firm, for instance, may develop a diversified product line in order to stabilize its sales, and with steadier sales revenue it can more effectively promote the marketing of its goods. A multiple-product firm can sometimes advantageously put out a number of grades or brands of a given type of product in order to meet the challenge to its market position from aggressive rivals.

A firm's promotion and marketing strategy is sometimes based on forward integration. Through the availability of its own distribution outlets, a firm can often more effectively promote sales, service customers, meet price concessions, and manipulate price margins.

Oligopolies generally maintain their superior competitive position because of structural restrictions to entry of new firms into certain

industries. Restriction of entry of new firms into certain monopolistic fields derives from the fact that large well-established firms
in oligopolistic industries enjoy special advantages from economies
of scale in production, distribution, sales promotion, research and
product improvement, and from other factors.

Entry into an oligopolistic field of business may be costly and
risky because of the prevalence of large optimum-sized plants in
the industry and because oligopolies expand capacity ahead of
demand and hold reserve productive capability that can quickly
satisfy any new increase in demand. Long-established oligopolies
have generally attained market acceptance and buyer preference
of their well-known brands, and they may also have well-organized
distribution outlets.

Efficient low-cost business operations enlarge a firm's earnings
and provide it with financial resources with which it can improve
its competitive position through promotion, research, product improvement, and further cost reduction. Aside from economies of
scale, production efficiency stems from the use of technology appropriate to the production objective, modification of product design
to permit use of any newly available low-cost processing methods
or lower-priced materials, and from timely replacement of obsolescent facilities and adoption of improved production technology. A
progressive firm offsets rising material and labor costs and lowers
its break-even point through productivity gains which it achieves
through the above type of cost-reduction program and through the
adjustment and updating of its internal organization structure to
fit shifts in its scope of business operations.

Adaptability in Production and in Business Operations

A firm enjoys a stronger competitive position if its plants and
business operations can be quickly and economically adapted to
various market and technological changes. A firm's operating
adaptability is largely based on the cost and ease of varying the rate
of output (i.e., based on short-run production adaptability), ease of
revising and changing over plant to the output of new models and
new products (i.e., convertibility), and the incremental cost and
lead-time required for expanding productive capacity (long-run
expandability). The foregoing over-all adaptability contributes to
a firm's competitive position and profitability when it enables a
firm to adjust to changes in market and technological conditions
more quickly and at lower expense than rival firms.

Because of their smaller depth of production and smaller investment commitment, firms with low fixed costs obviously tend to have greater operating adaptability than firms with heavier investment in fixed plant. A firm initially gains adaptive capability when its organization and productive facilities have, at the outset, been designed or engineered for adaptability and when a procedural system is set up to forecast business and market trends sufficiently far in advance to provide ample time for planning operating adjustments.

A firm achieves *short-run production adaptability* (e.g., ease of increasing the rate of output) through such measures as the provision of stand-by capacity and prearranging and organizing plant layout for ease of inaugurating overtime and multiple-shift operations. A firm can, at some expense, always attain a degree of adaptive capability through contingency programs for anticipated alternative adjustments that may be required. Business adjustability would, for example, call for the creation of an adaptive managerial organization and the development of a versatile technical staff and work force. Production adaptability is furthered through the maintenance of adequate sources of supply and ready subcontractors for components that can be quickly procured and through the varying of the proportion of components procured from outside producers.

A firm's ease and cost of making product design and style changes and of adopting new products depend upon the "convertive" adaptability of its plant and equipment. In some cases an adequate amount of convertibility is possible through retooling. Plant convertibility is primarily based on the initial adaptability built into the plant layout and on the provision of a judicious amount of general-purpose machines.

Competitive position in terms of *long-run expandability of capacity* depends on the speed and the incremental capital-output ratio for plant expansion. Producers in such capital-intensive fields as the chemical and metal-producing industries, for instance, require a longer lead-time for expansion of capacity than producers in such less heavily capitalized fields of production as the food-processing and clothing industries. Producers in the technically more stable fields of production have the advantage of employing more or less standard equipment (e.g., textile and woodworking machinery) which is often available from the finished inventory stocks of machine manufacturers. Because of the relative divisibility of their production facilities, some producers are able economically to expand capacity in comparatively small increments.

A firm's competitive position with respect to long-run expansion depends on how effectively its productive facilities have been planned for speed of capacity enlargement at a low incremental capital-output ratio. Long-run expandability partly depends on the availability and cost of alternative processes and the different depths of production that are economically feasible in the industry. This would vary from area to area because of differences in the price of input factors and in the availability of suppliers. Industry differences in production technology influence competitiveness among producers in cases in which firms put out competing substitute products, as in the case of producers of fuels, building materials, and chemicals.

Because of long lead-time, capital-intensive enterprises must forecast their capacity requirements sufficiently far in advance to permit timely acquisition of capacity necessary to maintain their share of growing markets. Multiple-plant firms in capital-intensive fields of output, notably in cases in which vertically integrated and comparatively indivisible production processes are employed, find that they must make relatively large outlays for increases in capacity as well as expand sufficiently far in advance of the growth of demand. Miscalculation of capacity requirements can lead to acquisition of burdensome excess capacity or, on the other hand, to a shortage of capacity that puts the firm at a competitive disadvantage in capturing new business.

Large multiple-plant enterprises strive to maintain a strong competitive position through *long-term production adaptability* by means of capital mobility, both with respect to geographical location of plants and with respect to field of business or line of products put out. Through the use of replacement funds, big firms are often able to install new capacity in sufficiently large increments to permit erection of complete plants. Through long-range forecasting and outlay of their large replacement funds, big multiproduct enterprises can readily shift their productive capacity from marginal lines of business to the output of products with growing demand and to regions of expanding markets. The availability of large replacement funds thus enables big enterprises to achieve internal capital mobility on a scale that permits erection of optimum-sized or relatively efficient-sized plants embodying the latest production technology, thereby maintaining a high marginal productivity of capital. Because smaller enterprises must rely on limited replacement funds, they cannot achieve comparable capital mobility. Moreover, small producers employing comparatively indivisible facilities sometimes find it expensive and difficult to improve production technology on a piecemeal basis.

When large diversified enterprises use numerous and somewhat diverse channels of distribution, they gain flexibility in marketing. Because of their wide product coverage and breadth of business, such firms can quickly expand into growing fields of business by purchasing or leasing established productive facilities or by rapidly erecting plants, and by penetrating new markets through their extensive distribution system. Thus, diversified enterprises are often able to attain a somewhat more stable volume of business than the more specialized firms, particularly when the latter sell in regional rather than in national markets.

QUESTIONS FOR REVIEW AND APPLICATION

1. "A firm's multiple-plant system often includes plant specialization according to process and plant specialization according to product." Explain and illustrate.

2. Explain what is meant by *built-in coordination* in plant production and by the *production interval*. How does the length of the production interval affect short-run adaptability in varying the rate of output?

3. (*a*) How does the factor of divisibility in production facilities affect the adaptability of plant? (*b*) What are the principal types and sources of production adaptability?

4. (*a*) Explain how producers in a given industry determine rated capacity. (*b*) What kind of changes (e.g., the shortening of the workweek) revise the basis for computing rated capacity? (*c*) How does rated capacity differ from optimum capacity?

5. (*a*) State and explain the law of diminishing returns as applied to plant production. (*b*) Why is the problem of combining productive factors different in the short run from what it is in the long run?

6. "It is primarily through the design of the product and the type of production processes they select that engineers determine the proportion in which they combine productive factors for long-run operation." Explain.

7. (*a*) How does the relative scarcity of productive factors influence the proportion in which they are combined? How may indivisibility in capital limit the attainment of an efficient combination of factors? (*b*) Explain how, in the combining of productive factors for establishment of plant, (*i*) labor input may be minimized and (*ii*) capital input may be minimized.

8. Distinguish between the economies of scale to the firm and the economies of scale in production. Give several illustrations of each.

9. Distinguish between economies accruing from horizontal combination of producing units and economies accruing from vertical integration of producing units. Illustrate.

10. (*a*) How may expansion in output capacity of a given product (or a line of process-related products) create opportunities for greater economies from vertical integration? (*b*) Should the decision to buy or to make components be

periodically reviewed because of possible changes in production technology? Explain.

11. What types of cost savings may a large steel company obtain from an integrated multiple-plant system?

12. What are some of the factors that have contributed to the growth in size (in terms of output capacity) of plants and firms during the past fifty years? Explain.

13. "A firm obtains productivity gains from both internal economies and external economies that occur in a growing economy." Explain and illustrate.

14. Briefly describe the break-even chart and indicate what is meant by break-even analysis.

15. (a) Explain how such data as the anticipated product-mix, the comparative income statement, anticipated changes in plant facilities, estimated fixed and variable costs, standard costs, and anticipated price of input factors (e.g., wage rates) are used in the preparation of a break-even chart for a future period. (b) Does the above data serve as part of the basis for the preparation of a company operating budget?

16. (a) Prepare a break-even chart for a single-product plant (e.g., a cement mill) from the following data:

Fixed costs	$200,000
Variable costs per unit	$10
Selling price per unit	$40

(b) What is the break-even point in the above chart? (c) How would an anticipated 20 per cent increase in unit variable cost affect the break-even point? An anticipated 10 per cent drop in selling price?

17. (a) Explain the problem of matching cost with the relevant output in the preparation of a break-even chart for a future period. (b) What is the product-mix problem in break-even charting for a multiple-product firm?

18. Contrast the problem of preparing a break-even chart for a monopoly firm producing a single product with that of preparing break-even chart(s) for a multiple-product firm comprised of dispersed plants putting out final products for sale in competitive regional markets.

19. Discuss the principal managerial uses of the break-even chart.

20. How have labor unions used the break-even chart in wage bargaining with management?

21. (a) What are the factors (and sources) that make for adaptability in the firm? (b) How does enterprise adaptability contribute to profitability, notably during periods of rapid economic changes?

22. What are the different methods whereby a firm can improve or maintain its competitive position under various economic conditions?

CHAPTER 8

Short-Run Business Operation and Profit

Managers conduct business operations and make a wide range of short-term decisions within the framework of the firm's long-run structure. The structural framework within which managers plan current operations is comprised of a given product line, processes and plant capacity, operating adaptability, managerial organization, long-range plans and policies, and other factors. The firm's structural design is not, of course, absolutely rigid or fixed during short-run operations. Managers can, more or less concurrently with short-term business operations, modify the production process or reduce costs through such means as plant-layout improvements and adoption of more efficient procedures for production and inventory control. A business enterprise is thus readily amenable to modifications of varying degrees.

DECISION MAKING: PRICE-OUTPUT ADJUSTMENT

In order to operate at the most profitable level, the businessman in theory regulates his volume of output so as to produce at that rate at which marginal cost equals marginal revenue, i.e., at the cost-price equilibrium rate of output (see Fig. 5–1). He adds materials, labor, and other variable inputs to the plant so long as his marginal revenue is larger than marginal cost. In the theoretical model of the firm, therefore, the most profitable level of operations is at that volume at which sales revenue brings in the largest total profit. The actual structure and behavior of the firm differ from the theoretical model in a number of ways. The theoretical model assumes a single-product enterprise, knowledge of marginal cost and marginal revenue, smooth adjustment in the rate of output, and constancy of the short-run profit-maximization motive. The firm in the real business world, however, is generally a multiproduct enterprise; the business-man deals with a more complex situation and with many more variables and does not always seek to maximize short-run profits.

Multiple-product output complicates the cost and revenue computation for determining the theoretical cost-price equilibrium rate of output. The ideal policy in formulating price and output decisions in multiple-product output is to equate marginal revenue with marginal cost for each product. Though producers can generally allocate direct or traceable costs to the output of particular products, because of the difficulty involved they allocate common costs on a more or less arbitrary basis.

In the usual business situation managers forecast sales volume and use the *operating budget* to estimate total cost and total revenue and to plan the rate of output for the period ahead in order to maintain finished goods at levels adequate to make deliveries on a competitive basis. Since business managers produce for inventory and subsequent sale, they cannot readily determine the production rate at which marginal cost equals marginal revenue because of the problem of matching the cost of goods put out currently with the sales revenue from goods that are sold at a later period, sometimes months later as in the case of some seasonal lines of business.

During current operations the businessman is never really certain that he is maximizing profits. His plans and anticipations for future business developments may cause business operation to depart appreciably from the profit-maximizing level of output. For instance, in order to hold his market share, to capture new markets, or to discourage new entrants from getting a foothold in the industry, a businessman may produce at a rate beyond the point at which marginal cost equals marginal revenue. He generally produces beyond the cost-price equilibrium rate of output when demand is high and when he plans to expand output capacity. The businessman would likely, however, produce at the rate of output at which marginal cost equals marginal revenue if it were consistent with his competitive strategy and long-range plans, if it did not involve sacrifice of needed financial liquidity, or if it were possible for him to have accurate and relevant marginal-cost and marginal-revenue data.

Competitive strategy does not always permit selection of the most profitable rate of output or selection of the least-cost method for increasing the rate of output. Competitive strategy, for example, may call for the fastest plan for accelerating output. In order to gain new business, production may be stepped up through overtime operation and premium rates of pay rather than through the hiring of new workers to man idle machines. Business planning in competitive situations may demand the use of high-cost facilities in order to assure the capture of a market prior to the erection of new facilities; it may call for costly multiple-shift operation in anticipation of the opening up of a branch plant. The multiple origin of profits generally demands emphasis on long-term earnings, improvement in competitive position, and other strategic considerations which may involve sacrifice of short-run profit maximization.

Gardiner C. Means offers an explanation of the businessman's empirical price-output adjustment:

MR. MEANS. I was just describing, Senator Wiley, the fact that I formerly ran a small blanket business and am using that as the basis for bringing out what I think is a very important point, what I call a zone of relative price indifference, something that has I think been completely neglected by economists up to this time.

There was plenty of competition in the blanket business but my blankets were a specialty and within limits I was free to make my own price. The question was what price I should set.

Now traditional theory has a simple calculus by which a producer in my position can determine his most profitable price if he knows what his costs and the demand for his product will be. First he estimates how many units he could sell at a high price and how much it would cost to produce this quantity. He could sell more at a lower price so he estimates how much more it would cost to make additional units and how much more revenue he could obtain from their sale at the lower price.

At some price and quantity, the additional cost of producing one more unit would just equal the additional revenue. This is the price and quantity at which he will make the most profit. If he produces more he will have to lower his price to such an extent that his additional revenue will be less than his additional costs. And if he produces less he will forego some profit he might have made. This most profitable price I will refer to as the classical price.

What is important about this analysis is that, if the producer's objective is to make the maximum profit, the price is just as much determined by market forces as is the price of wheat or cotton.

In setting a price by this procedure, the price maker is only reacting to economic forces. He does the calculating, but the economic forces of demand and cost determine his price. If this were the whole story, the price maker would in effect, have no discretion, provided he sought to maximize his profit, and the particular significance of administered prices would disappear. The pattern of economic behavior would be set by Adam Smith's unseen hand of market forces.

Actually, this calculus covers up an important fact which I soon discovered when, as an economist, I tried to apply it to my own business. This fact is that there is likely to be a considerable area within which any one of several prices will produce about the same profit. I can bring this out by restating the above price calculation in terms of the total units I produced and the total revenue I could expect from them. [See Fig. 8–1.]

❋   ❋   ❋

The curved line shows the way my total revenue would increase as I produced and sold more blankets.

With larger quantities my total revenue would increase but not in proportion since I would have to lower my price to dispose of a larger quantity.

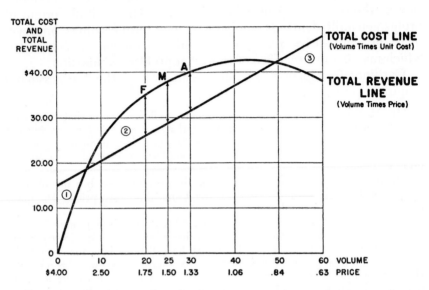

Fig. 8–1. Maximum profit calculations showing slight changes in profit with increased volume and lowered price *(A)* and with decreased volume and higher price *(F)*.

The straight line represents my total costs for different quantities. Once I was in production, my costs were almost constant; i. e., each additional unit cost the same additional amount to produce.

Now you can see that in the area (1) where the volume is small my total costs would be greater than my total revenue and if I had set one of the high prices included in this area, I would have suffered a loss.

Also in area (3), my total costs would have exceeded my revenue. Clearly I should not have my price too high or too low.

Area (2) is the area where I would make a profit, the amount of profit being represented by the distance between the two lines. I would make the most profit at the price and volume represented by *M* where the lines are furthest apart. This is the classical price and there is nothing wrong with the classical theory so far.

But consider for a minute the point on either side of *M*. Notice that my profit at *A* would be practically the same as at *M*. My maximum profit would be made at a price of $1.50 but if I set my price at $1.33, I would make practically the same total profit, but on a 20 per cent larger volume.

Or if I set my price at $1.75, my total profit would still be approximately the same, though on a 20 per cent smaller volume.

Tradition says the American producer is more likely to price on the right side of M—the high volume side, while the French producer is more likely to price on the left with a higher unit profit. What is important for us here is that in this example there is a price range of 28 per cent from $1.33 to $1.75 within which the total profit would be almost the same. And this price range corresponds with a 40 per cent range in production.

The presence of this range of almost as profitable prices would not prevent me from adopting the classical price if I actually knew what my costs and demand would be.

I would still select the price which yielded the most profits even though a higher or lower price would yield almost as much. Classical theory would be served. But as a practical matter, while I could estimate my costs pretty closely I really had very little idea of how much a difference in price would make on my volume of sales.

Instead of representing my total revenue by a sharp line, I had to represent it by a rough blurred zone, a zone within which I was uncertain as to what price was likely to be most profitable.

Thus I was faced both with a zone of uncertainty as to the most profitable price and a zone within which I could be sure that the total profit would be practically the same.

This gave me a zone of relative indifference. It is a zone within which I was not greatly concerned whether I set the price somewhat higher or somewhat lower.

Once I discovered this fact, it greatly simplified my pricing problem. I just went ahead and set my price somewhere in the middle of the zone, and left it constant. In one case I kept it constant for as long as 5 years even though my costs and demand were far from stable. I was a full-fledged price administrator.

I believe this zone of relative indifference is to a considerable extent responsible for the infrequency of changes in administered prices. Once I had set my price, there had to be a considerable change in demand or costs before it was worth my making a change. Suppose that I have set my price at $1.50 and this happens to be exactly the most profitable price—the classical price. But then suppose that demand rises so that the classical price would be $1.60. So long as this price lies within my zone of relative indifference, I would stick to my $1.50 price. If demand continued to rise, say enough to make the classical price $1.70, I might still not change my price.

But at some point, say where the classical price would be $1.75, my zone of indifference would have been exceeded and I would revise my price.

The same was true when demand fell as it did in the depression of the 1930's. Then it was not until late in 1930 that my zone of relative indifference was exceeded and I revised my prices downward. And even in this case, it was more the decline in the price of wool, my raw material, than in demand which led to my price reduction.

Senator WILEY. Did you create that phrase "the zone of relative indifference"?

Mr. MEANS. Yes, I did, sir.

Senator WILEY. That is your own?

Mr. MEANS. That is my own, as is the phrase "administered prices."

Senator WILEY. If you take your own figures from $1.50 to $1.60, in other words a 10-cent increase, would not have a sufficient appeal, but when you got $1.75, then you are in where you think you had better take some action; is that it?

Mr. MEANS. That is right.

Senator WILEY. All right; I am trying to get this.

                ❖   ❖   ❖

Mr. MEANS. You see, the classical economists assumed that there was no zone of relative indifference, and it is the difference between the classical and what we actually have that is fundamental.

I have described the zone of relative indifference in terms of my own direct experience, and my own case may have been an exaggerated one. However, it is clear that the phenomenon is widespread. Theoretical analysis indicates that, wherever a price can be administered, there is almost certain to be a zone of relative indifference within which various prices would produce practically the same profit, and observation supports this conclusion.

Also, it is important to notice that this zone of relative indifference and price administration itself does not depend on bigness or on having a monopoly.

That is why I chose my own concern.

The necessity of adjusting to price changes made by competitors can narrow the breadth of the zone or can make it a zone for an industry and not for just a single firm, but I believe that such a zone of indifference is a pervasive fact in industries which operate on the basis of administered prices.

Once we accept this idea of a zone of relative indifference, it must be clear that the individual producer who is in a position to adopt a policy of administered prices does have an area of discretion within which he can choose to set one price rather than another and within which the price he actually sets is not determined by market forces even though market forces set limits on the area of his choice.

But the zone of relative indifference is not the only factor creating an area of price discretion for the price administrator. A second influence is the opportunity to choose between maximizing profits in the short run or in the longer run. Once a company is in a position to administer prices, if it aims to maximize its profits, it may have to choose between higher immediate profits and higher profits over a longer period. And often it will forego immediate profits for future profits. This may well be what happened immediately after the recent war when the established automobile companies were faced with a demand for cars far in excess of what they could supply. Instead of raising their prices to the level that would have maximized their current profits, they kept prices well below what the traffic would bear. Clearly these companies were not required by market force to keep their prices so low. It may have been that long-run profit considerations overweighed the advantages of greater immediate profits.

But whatever the reasons, in this case, the opportunity to choose a longer or shorter period to aim at profit maximization adds a second dimension to the area of discretion.

And this dimension, like the first, is not a product of bigness or of being a monopoly.

A third dimension to the area of discretion does arise from bigness and also from monopoly. Whenever a company is large enough in relation to its market to be vulnerable to governmental action under our antitrust laws, it may well choose to set prices lower than the most profitable for fear of stimulating Government intervention. This can further widen the discrepancy between the classical price and the actual price set, representing a further widening of the area of discretion in pricing.

There are other factors which can contribute to the area of discretion, but I have already given enough to show that administered prices involve an area of pricing discretion which lies entirely outside of classical theory.

Within this area, prices are not dictated by market forces. Within this area Adam Smith's unseen hand fails to operate. I have mentioned here examples in which price discretion has or may be used in favor of lower prices. But it can also be used to raise prices. I have been unable to discover purely economic forces which will ensure that this discretion will be used in a manner that would serve the public interest. Within this area, the decision is as open as the difference between the American and French traditions of pricing.[1]

SHORT-TERM BUSINESS PLANNING: THE OPERATING BUDGET

Managers generally use the operating budget as a primary tool for short-term planning and control of business activity. The budget is primarily a short-period plan of operation in which management, on the basis of anticipated sales and revenue, determines the level of output and cost allowances and controls business volume for the immediate future period of operations. In the control of business volume and the required operating activities through the budget system, managers compare actual expenditures with planned (budgeted) expenditures and take corrective action to bring deviations in performance in line with predetermined levels of business activity. For planning and regulating current business operations, managers select an appropriate *short-term planning period* (e.g., six months) on the basis of such factors as the time span over which sales can be effectively forecast, seasonal variations in the given field of business, and the time interval for the production cycle and materials procurement. The short-term planning period is largely determined by the periodicity in business operations and the frequency with which important short-term operating decisions must be made.

In industries in which business volume is somewhat predictable, managers can, through progressive sales forecasting (i.e., by adding a future month of estimated sales, revenue, and costs to the budget),

[1] U.S. Senate Subcommittee on Antitrust and Monopoly, Hearings, Part I, *Administered Prices* (Washington, D.C.: Government Printing Office, 1957), pp. 77–78, 80–83, 90.

readily employ an operating budget. They generally find the *fixed-type budget* suitable to lines of business in which sales, revenue, and costs can be predicated with a reasonable degree of accuracy. They would generally use a *variable-type (flexible) budget* if the field of business is one in which demand is uncertain and forecasting more difficult. By estimating the revenue totals and expenditure totals for

OPERATING BUDGET

	Estimated Minimum	Estimated Maximum
Sales budget		
Product A sales	$4,000,000	$5,000,000
Product B sales	500,000	600,000
Product C sales	400,000	500,000
Total	$4,900,000	$6,100,000
Manufacturing budget		
Product A cost	2,400,000	3,000,000
Product B cost	320,000	390,000
Product C cost	280,000	350,000
Total	$3,000,000	$3,740,000
Estimated gross profits	$1,900,000	$2,360,000
Marketing budget		
Sales administration	100,000	110,000
Operation of sales districts	500,000	550,000
Advertising and promotion	200,000	250,000
Total	$ 800,000	$ 910,000
Administrative budget		
Administrative expense	300,000	310,000
Estimated net profit	$ 800,000	$1,140,000
Financial budget		
Taxes	$ 100,000	$ 180,000
Dividends	200,000	360,000
Reserve for expansion	300,000	300,000
Increase in surplus	200,000	300,000
Total	$ 800,000	$1,140,000
Plant and equipment budget		
Expansion and modernization	500,000	500,000
New stock issue	300,000	300,000
Balance from retained profits	$ 200,000	$ 200,000

Fig. 8–2. Operating budget for short-term planning.

two or more anticipated volumes of output (e.g., for intervals of 10 per cent change in business), managers can, through the flexible budget, plan to accommodate for possible changes in the volume of business (Fig. 8–2).

A firm's short-period operating budget, an operating plan which essentially translates policies and decisions into a coordinated program of business operations, is comprised of a number of separate departmental or functional budgets (sales, production or manufacturing, materials, and labor budgets) and a number of service budgets such as those for the employment office, controllership, and the engineering department. The constituent budgets are generally prepared by division and department heads on the basis of the production and sales program projected by top management. Department heads, on the basis of standard costs or estimated costs, compute the expenditure required to carry out properly their specialized activities at a level of performance necessary to achieve the over-all production and sales goal.

The sales budget is a marketing program based on the anticipated sales volume which is generally broken down into quotas for various market segments or districts. The sales-expense budget allocates and controls expenditures for salesmen's expense accounts, salaries, advertising, and other items. The manufacturing or production budget specifies the rate of output necessary to maintain finished inventories at desired levels; it stipulates the length of the workweek and the plant facilities to be used. In selecting a feasible or desired rate of output, managers balance the estimated production requirement against the available rated capacity for the short-term planning period. When expressed as a *percentage of rated capacity*, the stipulated rate of output indicates the extent to which the firm can increase output by taking up available capacity. The current volume of output can exceed 100 per cent rated capacity when production runs (lot sizes) are longer than usual, when the product-mix is comprised of a larger proportion of items with a shorter than average production interval, and when the maintenance and overhaul of key equipment are readily postponable. The current production volume may fall below the maximum rated-capacity level when output is comprised of smaller lot sizes and when plant down time is greater than normal because of high absenteeism or because of material shortages. The planned volume of output for the budget period, supply conditions, and purchase prices determine the material budget and procurement requirements. Managers establish the inventory-sales ratio at a level that they consider to be optimum for the specified rate of output and anticipated sales volume, anticipated prices for materials, procurement lead-time, and their need for liquidity. Because the procurement lead-time is relatively fixed at any given time, producers cannot always quickly alter the rate at which they receive materials; hence, changes in raw-material inventory levels often lag somewhat behind changes in the rate of output. The actual inventory-sales ratio for the short-term production period at times deviates from the desired ratio because of unanticipated changes in supply conditions and the firm's rate of production.

The labor budget specifies the manpower requirements (in man-hours or man-days) necessary to meet the rate of output stipulated by the over-all budget. Department and section heads determine manpower needs and the wage bill on the basis of the governing wage schedules, anticipated production rate, and the hourly output standard (time standard) based on past performance or on comprehensive time studies. When manpower needs are broken down by job grades, the employment office can project what grades of skilled and professional labor may be in short supply, and it can then determine the method for recruiting each grade of labor and for training labor in scarce supply.

Executive managers thus plan and regulate current business operations through a system that generally includes budgetary control, standard costs, financial and operating ratios, and other performance standards, such as allowable plant down time and allowable spoilage, that provide for detailed control. It is primarily through the short-term budget that executive managers gauge the effectiveness of operating managers in directing their spheres or areas of authority, whether plants, production departments, or service departments. Executive managers measure and control performance by comparing actual with planned expenditures and by taking corrective action to bring performance in line with predetermined standards. The design of an effective system for measurement and control of performance is based on the compilation of traceable costs and controllable costs for the respective divisional units, plants, departments, or other operating units to be measured for efficiency. *Traceable costs* are those that can be easily identified with, and allocated to, the operating unit to be controlled. Direct labor and direct materials, for instance, are cost items traceable to production processes or cost centers; and supervision, utilities, and maintenance can be traced and allocated to particular departments and sections. The foregoing cost items are separable from certain overhead or common cost items (e.g., personnel, public relations, and other service departments) which are not readily traceable on a practical basis to particular managerial or operating units. (Management also uses traceable costs for pricing products, selecting cost-reduction methods, and for deciding upon adding or dropping a product.) The practicability of budgetary control depends on the effectiveness with which traceable costs and controllable costs are compiled for the appropriate operating unit. *Controllable costs* are those that are susceptible to reduction or regulation. The controllability of some cost items depends, of course, on the level of managerial authority.

Managers can use *standard costs* to compile operating costs and to gauge and control the efficiency performance of certain specific activities or production departments. Standard costs are selected on the basis of the anticipated and lowest attainable cost under normal conditions for materials, labor, overhead, and other items. When actual costs deviate from standard costs, managers analyze the causes for the discrepancy and take remedial action.

CASH BUDGET			
Third Quarter		June 19___	
		Receipts	Disbursements
JUNE 1	Balance on hand	$1,100,500	
	Non-operating income	20,600	
	Accounts receivable (collections)	3,801,000	
	Materials		$1,500,100
	Payroll		850,500
	Rent		8,000
	Insurance and taxes		15,100
	Maintenance		18,300
	Utilities		20,000
	Factory expense (misc.)		25,400
	Selling expense		301,000
	Administrative expense		405,000
			$3,143,400
JUNE 30	Cash balance		$1,778,700

Fig. 8–3. Sample of a cash budget.

Managers use certain *financial and operating ratios* as tools for regulating and controlling business operations. Through various ratios (derived from financial and other records) that compare, against a selected standard, one phase or aspect of business operations with another aspect, managers can note trends and control business activities. Managers can gauge the firm's competitive position and performance by comparing the firm's operating ratios with those of rival firms. The ratio of investment to revenue (the capital turnover), for instance, measures the importance of capital cost for a given operating unit and measures the revenue-producing efficiency with which capital is employed. Managers may use ratios of operating expenses (materials, direct labor, maintenance, etc.) to compute operating revenue for a given period. They can show turn-over in finished stock by dividing the cost of goods sold by the average finished stock; they indicate over-all performance by such ratios as the percentage of gross profits on sales, the percentage of net profits on sales, and rate of return on investment.

Managers can indicate turnover in working capital by dividing sales by the difference between current assets and current liabilities. The number of times a firm's working capital turns over during the short-term planning period or during a year is a factor contributing to net earnings. Working capital (or circulating capital) flows from cash to production outlays, to inventory accumulation, to accounts receivable, and back to the cash budget (Fig. 8–3). A profitable firm will show more cash at the end of each operating cycle (the interval covering materials procurement, production, and sales) than at the beginning of the cycle.

When a firm's financial and operating ratios are computed quarterly and annually in constant dollars and plotted over a period of years and when they are projected on the basis of anticipated conditions, they indicate significant operating trends which may call for business adjustment to seasonal variations or to short-term increases or decreases in business volume.

BUSINESS ADJUSTMENT: ADAPTATION TO SEASONAL VARIATIONS

Short-term planning and regulation of business operations are more difficult when a firm's products and processes are less standardized, when demand varies appreciably and sales are difficult to forecast, and when the production interval and the lead-time for procurement of materials are long. Irregularity in operations sometimes stems from the business need to modify or revise the design of the product. Though radical changes in the design of the product often improve a firm's competitive position and increase sales volume, they typically require revision of processes and facilities and retooling of production lines. Irregularity in plant operations is sometimes caused by scarcity of certain types of materials or grades of labor and by machine failures or technical difficulties in newly installed equipment.

When managers effectively plan and control production, they lower the unit cost of output by maintaining a uniform flow of work in process with low idleness in machines and labor. The tighter the over-all processing cycle and the more effective the production-control system, the more rapid is the turnover of work in process and the higher the return on working capital. Poor production planning results in ineffective use of productive facilities and in the need for rush orders which call for extra machine setups or overtime work. Poor planning can also result in an overstocking of some finished products and a shortage in others.

Irregularity in production sometimes stems from changes in a firm's sales-mix caused by shifts in consumer demand. A firm's sales volume in one or more items of its product line is sometimes irregular because of the influence of cross-elasticity of demand: A temporary price drop of a competing substitute product would pull sales away from a firm, while a price drop of a complementary product put out by other producers would tend to expand the sale of a firm's related product. When a firm produces joint products in somewhat inelastic or fixed proportions, it may be plagued with the problem of market disposal of one or the other of the products because of differences in the behavior of market demand for the products and because the products differ in their seasonal sales pattern. The foregoing and other types of changes in a firm's sales-mix generally create an imbalance in the utilization of productive capacity —some production lines may be operating at high capacity, while other productive facilities may be operating at low capacity. When productive facilities are easily changed over or convertible to the output of related products, imbalances in productive capacity are, of course, lessened. Productive capacity is made adaptable not only through the use of general-purpose equipment and the provision of suitable tooling but through the design of a product line on the basis of maximum interchangeability of components and subassemblies.

Because of irregularity in current business operations and the lead-time required for the procurement of materials, a firm must hold a stock of raw materials sufficient to feed the production process without interruption and to enable replenishment of finished-goods inventory when sales temporarily surge upward. The holding of excess stocks of raw materials, on the other hand, results in a loss of liquidity and in the lowering of the return on working capital.

Managers determine their material reordering point (the stock level at which materials are to be replenished) on the basis of the amount of material necessary for uninterrupted production and on the basis of the length of the procurement lead-time. The procurement lead-time varies with supply conditions. Lead-time, for instance, is generally longer during periods of prosperity and during periods of possible work stoppage or other interruptions. Managers aim to maintain a certain desired or optimum material stock-output ratio (the quantity of raw materials for a given rate of output).

They find it necessary to adjust their stock-output ratio when material supply conditions and procurement prices change (e.g., when inflation develops), when they have a greater need for liquidity or a more profitable use for funds, and sometimes when the rate of interest changes.

Firms find it necessary to carry a stock of finished goods because sales and shipments to customers are irregular while finished goods flow off the production lines at a more or less predetermined rate of output. Managers find it necessary to hold larger stocks of finished goods when production becomes more irregular or when the sales volume or sales-mix becomes more irregular. Managers also find it necessary to adjust their finished-stock–sales ratio to changes in competitive conditions (e.g., the need to hold larger stock in order to make deliveries on short notice).

A firm's volume of business within a given year often fluctuates because of *seasonal variations.* Firms in most lines of economic activity exhibit a seasonal pattern in business operations to one degree or another (Fig. 8–4). Seasonal variations result from the yearly cycles in weather (or climatic seasons) and the traditional purchases of goods in the observance of social seasons such as year-end holidays. The seasonal factor may exert one or both of two influences on a business: seasonal variations in production and seasonal variations in sales.

The fluctuations in a firm's business operations within any given year may thus arise from both seasonal variations in the demand for its product and from seasonal variations in the supply of raw materials. Firms in the food-processing industries, for instance, are subject to seasonal variations in the supply of materials characteristic of agricultural output. Flour mills and cigarette-producting establishments must therefore accumulate large stocks of raw materials during the seasons when they are available. Firms that produce automobiles, petroleum products, and building materials, on the other hand, are subject to seasonal variations in the demand for their products. Cotton and woolen textile firms, however, experience seasonal variations in both the demand for their products and in the supply of the natural fiber. Firms that predominantly sell in a local or regional market tend to experience greater seasonability, particularly when they specialize in a comparatively narrow line of business. Depending on the degree of competition among sellers, prices in a given industry tend to fluctuate in an inverse fashion to the seasonal variations in the output of the product.

Businesses subject to strong seasonal variations in production may be confronted by acute problems of labor recruitment, layoffs, and

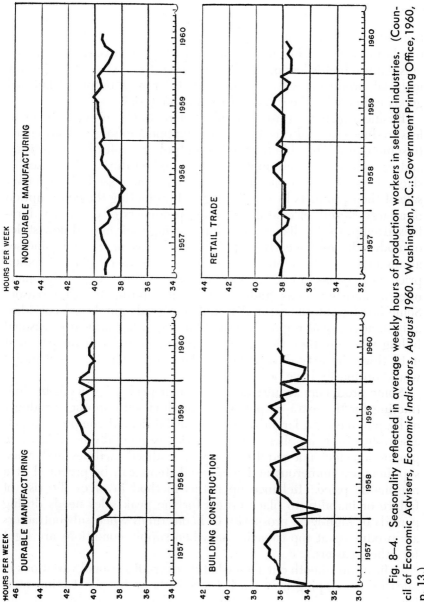

Fig. 8–4. Seasonality reflected in average weekly hours of production workers in selected industries. (Council of Economic Advisers, *Economic Indicators, August 1960.* Washington, D.C.: Government Printing Office, 1960, p. 13.)

the maintenance of a nucleus of key personnel. Difficulty in labor recruitment would vary with the tightness in the supply of labor during the period of expansion of output. Businesses subject to sharp variations in the supply of materials may be perennially confronted by the problem of estimating their large material needs and regulating material inventories or finished-goods inventories. If the finished product is less perishable or less costly to store than the raw material, producers will generally vary the rate of output of finished goods in line with the supply of the raw material.

Business managers use a number of methods to even out or at least reduce seasonal variations in production and sales. A firm may, to some degree, be able to stabilize output and sales by advertising and promoting the consumption of the product during the season of slack demand. Meat-packing houses have increased the summer sale of their products by developing and promoting the consumption of a large variety of cold cuts. Many producers of consumer durables attempt to stabilize sales by introducing their annual new styles or models during the early part of the slack season. Some businesses attain a more uniform physical volume of sales by offering off-season price concessions in one form or another. A firm may, for instance, offer a more generous trade-in allowance during the dull season. Some firms grant off-season discounts for goods purchased considerably in advance of regular seasonal buying; other firms use seasonal billing whereby they ship goods early but do not call for payment until thirty or sixty days after the date at which the merchandise would ordinarily have been shipped.

Some producers acquire goods for their peak sales needs by contracting for the extra output of the product with another producer or by purchasing a larger proportion of fabricated components and assemblies from suppliers. This practice is generally feasible when production does not require highly specialized facilities and when suppliers are numerous and purchased items can be procured at a reasonable price. Reliance upon this method involves the risk of failure or inability to place orders for the peak sales needs during periods of high-level prosperity or boom times when subcontractors are producing at top capacity, or when supply conditions are tight for other reasons.

A firm can smooth out somewhat its over-all seasonal variations in sales by developing new market segments or by penetrating markets in regions that have a different seasonal sales pattern. By appropriately widening and diversifying its market, a firm can thus dovetail the seasonal sales pattern in one market with that in another market. A firm may also stabilize its volume of business by adopting products that sell in the slack period and that can be produced on the same facilities. By developing an appropriately diversified product line, a firm can reduce its over-all seasonal fluctuation in business volume even though the sale of some products is subject to wide variations, provided the product line includes items with seasonal production and sales patterns that dovetail.

After a firm has somewhat stabilized its production or sales volume through the promotion of off-season purchases, introduction of new models early in the period of slack sales, offering some off-season price concessions, or through other methods outlined above, the firm then has the choice of producing at a uniform rate (and accumulating some finished goods for the period of peak sales) or producing at a fluctuating rate in line with the seasonal variation in sales. Managers must analyze the cost and the labor problems involved in the latter plans to determine which plan or combination of plans is most suitable and economical for its business. In *appraising plans and selecting their methods,* managers take into account the cost of storing finished goods or semifabricated goods, the incremental cost for extra productive capacity for peak periods, the problem of recruiting labor and the higher cost of using inexperienced workers, and the desirability of maintaining steadier employment and better employee morale.

Business managers may elect to gear the rate of production to seasonal variations in sales by scheduling overtime work for the peak production period and scheduling employee vacations and long-term plant-maintenance work for the slack period of production. This plan is feasible when the work force largely consists of semiskilled and unskilled workers readily available for hire on the labor market and when investment in plant is low and fixed costs are relatively small.

Business managers may elect to stabilize output by producing at a uniform rate the year round—accumulating finished goods during the period of slack sales and then drawing on the builtup finished stock to meet the needs of peak sales volume. This plan is feasible when style obsolescence and product spoilage are absent or low and storage costs are small and when investment in finished inventory is not excessive. The plan enjoys the advantages of lower investment in facilities, more efficient production planning and output, and steadier employment. Through the promotion of off-season purchases, a firm may, of course, shift the storage of some finished goods to distributors. If a businessman is to accumulate off-season stocks of finished goods, it is absolutely essential that he accurately forecast seasonal variations. Some producers may be reluctant to accumulate a large off-season finished stock without an adequate forecast of the cyclical trend for fear that their stock buildup may be timed with a cyclical downturn.

DECREASING THE RATE OF OUTPUT

If demand and sales decline over an extended period of time, managers find it necessary to liquidate inventory stocks, curtail production, and look for ways to cut costs. A decline in sales is first generally indicated by a rise in finished stock or by a shrinkage in the backlog of orders. A firm's sales may decline because of a shift in population, a shift in consumer tastes, emergence of a competing substitute product, or a decline in the firm's competitive position and market share. Sales may also drop because of a loss of an export market, an imposition of an excise tax, an increase in income taxes, or because of a general decline in business and consumer-purchasing power.

When sales decline, a producer may curtail his rate of output or cut prices, or he may do both—cut prices a bit and curtail output somewhat. An unanticipated drop in sales generally results in an accumulation of finished stock. A firm tends to accumulate finished goods for some time after sales have turned downward because it is not always able to forecast sales accurately and because it may be reluctant to curtail output or lower prices until it is certain that its volume of business is falling off. During a period of a declining volume of business, producers find that they must eventually cut the rate of output faster than the decline in sales if they are to liquidate excess inventories. When the price of raw materials drops and when the procurement lead-time is shortened, firms can generally cut their raw-materials stock appreciably, i.e., below the previous stock-output ratio.

As a decline in sales volume levels off, the rate of decrease in finished stock begins to diminish and eventually comes to an end. A producer sometimes finds that he cannot prudently cut his finished stock proportionate to the drop in sales (i.e., he must increase his stock-sales ratio) during a period of declining sales because he must compete on the basis of faster deliveries to customers who, because of an easier supply situation, have switched to hand-to-mouth buying after having accumulated stocks through forward buying in anticipation of a price hike or a work stoppage. During business contraction firms try to get into a more liquid financial position partly by liquidating inventories. With a contraction in business, firms can convert both inventories and accounts receivable into cash.

The method managers use to achieve a downward adjustment in output depends on the certainty and magnitude of the decline in sales. The method selected for curtailing output also depends on the cost of storing the product, divisibility of plant, the extent to which skilled labor is employed, and the cost reduction obtainable by alternative methods for curtailing output. Managers may use a combination of methods to cut successively the volume of output and liquidate excess inventory stocks.

If business managers are not certain that the shrinkage in demand will persist, they will generally eliminate overtime work or decrease the length of the workweek. The cutting back of working hours is generally the fastest and the most flexible method for adjusting labor input, and it minimizes the disruption of a trained work force. A cutback in labor input can also be achieved by not replacing men who retire or quit. A firm may cut excess finished inventories by shutting down its plants for a few days or a few weeks; whenever possible, it would schedule the cutback to coincide with holiday periods. A firm may accumulate orders while a plant is shut down and then start up production when it has acquired sufficient work. A firm may cut back its volume of output and maintain employment in its own plants by not renewing subcontract work and by pulling in outside work for processing in its plants. Whenever possible a firm would curtail production by shutting down leased facilities and not renewing the lease. A firm with declining sales may seek subcontract work or lease out its own facilities.

When a firm curtails production by laying off workers and shutting down a plant or a department, it reduces the "escapable" cost of doing business, but it must cover the "unavoidable" cost. *Escapable costs* include variable costs (direct labor and materials), some part of semivariable costs, and other costs associated with contraction in business activity. *Unavoidable costs* include fixed financial charges, rent, property taxes and other overhead, and cost items that must be met in doing a given volume of business. Some of the unavoidable cost can be eliminated by the sale of productive facilities and the use of leased facilities and by relying more heavily on outside suppliers for productive work.

Retrenchment in most businesses involves not merely a curtailment in the level of operations but some reallocation of work loads and activities among various operating units or plants. The reallocation of work and a rise in the cost of some units may partially offset the reduction of variable costs in the operating units that have been cut back to lower levels. It is therefore the net effect on the total cost of doing business that is relevant and not just the direct outlays avoided in the units shut down because of a contraction in business. Managers may plot on a break-even chart the comparative cost for the alternative methods for cutting back production in order that they may elect the most economical method for retrenchment.

Though sales revenue declines during a contraction in business volume, a firm gets some relief through an increase in its cash resources: a firm needs less working capital for a lower volume of busi-

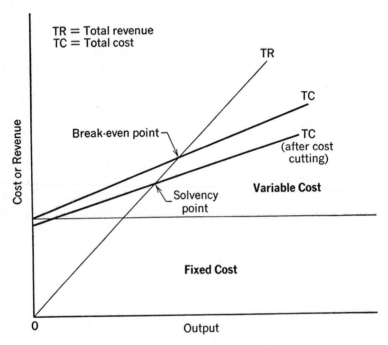

Fig. 8–5. Break-even chart showing how administrative cost cutting for a period of a smaller volume of business achieves a lower ("solvency") break-even point.

ness. A firm frees working capital because it makes smaller outlays for labor, materials, and indirect costs; it enlarges its cash balance by postponing the replacement of equipment, by liquidating inventories, and by trimming the advertising budget, promotion appropriations, and outlays for service departments. A firm can sometimes acquire cash for operating needs by selling non-operating property and securities. As a firm's sales decline, it loses revenue from business operations. Its losses in sales revenue may, moreover, be greater than the shrinkage in sales volume if consumer demand shifts to lower-priced items and economy models. The latter change in the product-mix together with any price cuts that are made will lower the level of the total-revenue curve and raise the break-even point. The firm, of course, makes a net loss for any rate of output less than the break-even point.

A firm can often operate somewhat below its break-even point for some time if its cash receipts cover its minimum current cash expenditures, i.e., its total paying-out costs which consist of total variable costs plus total paying-out indirect costs. Since the firm need not make payments on its imputed costs (interest on capital and rent on natural resources), its total paying-out cost curve is lower than its total-cost curve. Thus, its short-run solvency point is lower than its economic break-even point, as is indicated in Figure 8–5. If the firm operates below the short-run solvency point, it can do so only by making inroads into cash reserves or by borrowing funds. If the firm continues to operate at such a low volume of business, it will eventually fail.

If a firm with high overhead costs cuts prices substantially and maintains sales revenue at a level somewhat below its short-run solvency point, it can usually more than cover its current paying-out costs by postponing the replacement of equipment and using the available replacement funds for current operations. A firm with comparatively new facilities can, through effective repairs, maintain plant efficiency for a number of years. It may, in fact, be able to improve efficiency and lower unit costs through inexpensive modernization of plant. When machine manufacturers develop and offer new cost-reduction equipment which can lower the break-even point, a firm may improve its competitive position and increase its market share and rate of output.

INCREASING THE RATE OF OUTPUT

A firm in a growing industry or a firm that is expanding its market share is concerned with the problem of increasing its current rate of output. The method businessmen use to increase the rate of output partly depends on the origin and type of increase in demand. Some increase in a firm's sales obviously comes from secular growth in demand stemming from population growth and rising personal income—sales generally grow faster for products with high income elasticity of demand. Since economic growth is a more or less continuous process, the long-term increase in demand is reflected in short-run business operations. An increase in the demand for a firm's products may come from a cyclical upswing in business and the associated rise in consumer-purchasing power. Though a firm may expand capacity in large increments, it usually must step up its current rate of output somewhat gradually. A firm may increase sales through product improvement and the introduction of new items to its product line. It may also enjoy a larger sales volume because of a price reduction or because of the removal of an excise tax. A firm may also expand its sales by improving its competitive position through more effective promotion by means of distinctive product differentiation, advertising, and the extension of low credit terms. A firm sometimes experiences a short-term rise in demand because of purchasers' forward (or hedge) buying based on the anticipation of a price hike or a work stoppage or some other interruption in the supply of goods. A firm can more effectively capture a larger share of a new demand through speed in increasing its rate of output and fast-delivery capability.

A firm generally meets a sudden, unanticipated increase in demand for its stock of finished goods by stepping up its rate of output to replenish and maintain stocks at desired levels. Because of the difficulty or inability to predict accurately an increase in sales and to adjust instantaneously output, a firm may unintentionally liquidate its stock of finished goods for some time after sales have increased. The speed of building up finished stock depends on the time needed to increase output, length of the production interval, and the ability to maintain an adequate stock of raw materials. When sales successively increase, output generally increases at a faster rate because a firm must produce at a rate equal to sales plus its buildup of finished stock. Because of the procurement lead-time, the stock of raw materials initially tends to be drawn down, and the buildup of material stocks tends to lag behind unanticipated increases in output. When raw-material prices move upward and the procurement lead-time becomes longer, as is generally the case during periods of high-level business activity, producers tend to find it more difficult to build up their stock of raw materials.

The method managers use to increase the rate of output and the extent and rapidity with which a firm can increase its output depend on the availability of reserve capacity, the ease of forecasting sales, and the type of increase in demand. It is patent that managers can more readily vary the rate of output when forecasting is relatively easy, when the production interval is comparatively short, and when materials and labor are quickly available. To increase output, managers generally elect that combination of methods best suited to the firm's business situation and production technology. Many firms often find the inauguration of overtime the fastest and most flexible means for enlarging the input of labor and stepping up production.

In a tight labor-supply situation, overtime production is generally the only alternative to recruiting inexperienced and untrained workers. Moreover, when plant facilities are indivisible and unadaptable to small incremental increases of labor input through recruitment, the increase in the length of the workweek is generally the only immediately practical means for increasing volume. The ability of the firm to increase output appreciably may depend on the adaptability of plant facilities to changes in the product-mix. If a general upswing in demand promises to continue, managers usually increase the rate of output by hiring additional workers to operate facilities. To raise output rate beyond single-shift overtime operation, managers generally find that they must go into multiple-shift operations and recruit more labor. A firm sometimes finds that it can readily step up production through increased subcontracting of work.

When managers increase output through overtime and multiple-shift operations, greater input of labor, subcontracting, and leasing of facilities, they essentially increase *out-of-pocket costs*, which consist of the current payments for labor, materials, and rental on leased facilities. Since these productive resources are acquired and paid for on a current basis, they can be retired when not needed. When the cost of an increase in output can be met through out-of-pocket payments, managers meet a larger sales volume without need for long-term outlays for plant capacity whereby the investment becomes a "sunk" cost.

The shape of the short-run total-cost curve over the range of capacity utilized depends on the amount of reserve capacity, type of production technology used, and the method used to increase the rate of output. Since firms often build capacity in advance of demand, the short-run total-cost curve generally tends to be more or less linear for the range of capacity likely to be employed. The shape of the short-run total-cost curve for the full range of capacity is determined by the change in the proportion of fixed costs relative to variable costs, plant divisibility and adaptability, and the higher payment for wage differentials for overtime and multiple-shift operation. Average costs at higher levels of production tend to rise because of bigger outlays for plant maintenance, increase in spoilage, and an increase in production delays. Average costs may rise because of the use of marginal facilities and an increase in material procurement costs.

The firm's total-revenue curve depends on future price changes, product-mix, and contribution margins of various products. A firm can generally increase its total revenue by stepping up its turnover of inventory and working capital through a shorter production cycle and tighter control; it can also, of course, improve its cash position through the liquidation of excess inventories. A firm's profits from a given volume of sales may go up because of a shift to the sale of high-profit items or because of an increase in selling prices.

PROFITS OF BUSINESS ENTERPRISE

Though business profits partly stem from effective long-term planning, they are essentially realized in the short run. The net profits reported in accounting statements consist of the revenue that remains after the costs (i.e., the explicit costs) of operations have been covered. A firm computes such profits in order to record past business activity and to determine taxable income.

Measurement of Profit

Because accountants do not deduct implicit costs (e.g., interest on owner's capital) in the computation of net profits, their concept of profits is viewed by the economist as a somewhat "mixed" income category. Corporate profits include imputed interest and imputed rent on land owned, and the profits of individual proprietorships and partnerships, in addition, often include the wages of management. The economist defines profits in a less inclusive manner, as a narrower income category. He defines *profits* as residual income accruing to the owners of a business after all other factors are compensated—after implicit as well as explicit costs are met.

Profits may be expressed in a number of forms. In business usage it is customary to express profits as a percentage of net sales receipts. Because it ignores the annual turnover in sales, value-added in production, and the total investment in the business, this expression of profits is not a true measure of profitability. But percentage return on sales can roughly indicate the relative profitability of firms in a given industry. The expression of profits as a percentage of the total assets of a firm (excluding investments in securities and investment income) is a more adequate measure of a firm's profitability, and it can appropriately compare profitability among industries. Profitability to the owners of a business is best expressed as percentage return on equity capital—a firm's total assets minus debt.

Because producers in imperfectly competitive and in oligopolistic industries have some latitude in setting prices, they can set prices that aim for a certain level of profits. Such producers formulate profit policy on the basis of price policy. Business managers may seek to maximize long-run profits by maintaining lower prices and limiting short-run profits in order to discourage entry of potential competitors, maintain customer good will, restrain union wage demands, and discourage antitrust investigations. Business managers may, however, aim for a profit level that permits substantial plowback investment for expansion, plant modernization, and intensive research and development; or a profit level that permits dividend payments at a capital-attracting rate which enables expansion through external financing; or a level that enables the accumulation of sufficient liquidity as a hedge against recession.

If managers are to regulate operations and invest capital funds on an economically sound basis, they must correctly measure current earnings and realistically estimate anticipated return on planned capital expenditures. To compute properly the net profits earned by a firm's divisional units (or the profit contribution by various products), for instance, managers must compute profits on the basis of implicit costs as well as explicit costs, particularly if some divisional units (or production lines) employ highly capital-intensive processes; and to compare current business earnings with the earnings of past years, managers must express profits in the real terms of constant dollars (i.e., they must adjust income figures for changes in the general price level).

During inflation times accountants would overstate business net profits if they were to compute material costs on the basis of FIFO valuation of materials absorbed in production and compute depreciation charges on the basis of the original cost of equipment. The overstatement of business income may lead to excessive dividend payment which, because of the higher cost of inventory replenishment, would deplete working capital and, because of the higher cost of equipment replacement, would tend to undermine the fixed-assets stock. By computing profits on the basis of LIFO valuation of materials and on the basis of replacement-cost depreciation charges, managers can largely avoid overstatement of the current year's business net profit and can more correctly determine the amount of funds available for plow-back investments.

Since profits, in terms of economic function, serve as an inducement to undertake business activity, it is anticipated profit that is especially relevant for economic analysis and decision making: prospective profits essentially serve as an incentive to undertake business activity in the face of uncertainty and unpredictability. The prospect of earning profits provides the motive force for business operations.

Sources of Profits

Whether a firm makes profits or incurs losses (makes negative profits) depends on such factors as cyclical fluctuations, the firm's competitive position, its effectiveness in anticipating and adjusting to shifts in demand, and its effectiveness in long-range planning and introduction of successful innovations. Thus, there are a number of sources of profits: imperfect competition, shifts in demand and frictional change, innovations, and cyclical fluctuations.

During a cyclical upswing and expanding prosperity, the rise in sales volume for a wide sector of business enterprise increases sales revenue and lowers unit costs through high-capacity operation. If inflation develops during prosperity times, profit margins are widened to the extent that factor costs (particularly the costs of materials and labor) lag behind the rise in selling prices (Fig. 8–6). Conversely, during a cyclical downswing and recession, declining sales volume and revenue and rising unit cost, due to low-capacity operation, reduce profits and, in many instances, result in losses. Not all firms, however, are adversely affected by a general business recession. Firms in growing industries and firms in a strong competitive position that are able to increase their market share can generally maintain profitable operations. During a recession these firms can, in fact, sometimes increase their profit levels because of lower prices for input factors and the opportunity for increased efficiency from low-cost plant modernization and plant expansion.

Short-term shifts in demand are often difficult to forecast. Firms in a given industry may enjoy higher profits (or incur losses) because of unanticipated increases (or decreases) in sales volume and in selling prices. Similarly, the profit levels of firms in a given industry are also affected by unexpected increases or decreases in the price of materials, labor, or plant equipment. These changes in profit levels result from the existence of disequilibrium in the industry, that is, from the fact that producers cannot immediately adjust the scale of plant and production to changes in demand and to changes in the price of input factors. Industry disequilibrium is essentially due to the capital-intensive nature of production and the relative fixity of modern production technology. Frictional changes in the economy also influence profit levels. A rapid rise in demand and output in one industry bids up the prices of input factors for other industries, thereby shrinking their profits.

Market imperfections also influence profit levels. As compared to the more competitive industries (business fields in which entry is relatively easy), firms in oligopolistic industries can sometimes en-

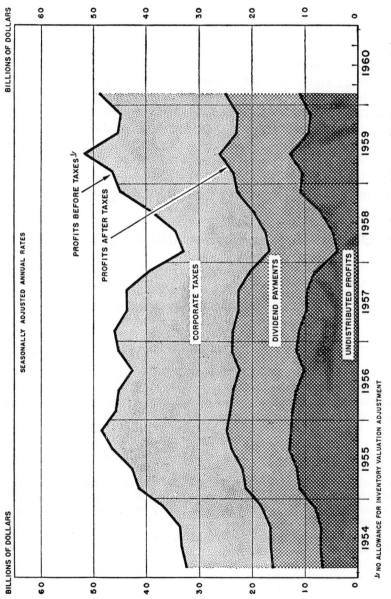

Fig. 8-6. Corporate profits during a period of prosperity and inflation. (Council of Economic Advisers, *Economic Indicators, August 1960.* Washington, D.C.: Government Printing Office, 1960, p. 8.)

large profits by restricting output and raising prices. Oligopolistic enterprises attain an exclusive market position wherever entry into the industry is difficult because of the existence of large firms which enjoy economies of scale in production or distribution, ownership of patents permitting use of efficient technology, and other advantages.

Profits generally accrue to firms that gain an increase in sales volume or a reduction in costs through adoption of successful innovations (e.g., a new product, a more effective marketing or promotion method, or an efficient processing method). Because successful innovations tend, in time, to be imitated by rival firms and the innovating firm's competitive advantage is often short-lived, a firm must continually innovate to maintain its differential earning capability. Profit making through innovation rests not only on the continual discovery of promising new ideas but on effective business forecasting and long-range planning of capital expenditures.

QUESTIONS FOR REVIEW AND APPLICATION

1. Graphically illustrate (draw a graph) and explain the short-run model of the firm for decision making concerned with price-output adjustment in the field of imperfect competition.

2. (a) Explain the value of the short-run model of the firm for theoretical analysis of industry equilibrium. (b) Can you formulate a more useful model for such theoretical analysis?

3. (a) Does the theoretical model of the firm assume short-run profit maximization? Explain. (b) What are some limitations of the theoretical model of the firm as a practical tool for managerial decision making for short-run operation in many fields of business.

4. Contrast short- and long-term planning (a) with respect to specific business objectives and (b) with respect to the framework of planning.

5. (a) What are some evidences of ineffective short-run business planning? (b) Identify and briefly explain the economic factors and operating characteristics in certain lines of business (industries) that make short-run business planning difficult.

6. (a) Explain how the preparation and use of a company operating budget give management a comprehensive picture of the firm's internal operating situation (e.g., available capacity, inventory levels, etc.) and serve as a primary device for short-term planning and over-all control of current business operations. (b) How is the budget device used to gauge and control plant (or departmental) performance?

7. (a) What are the factors that determine the length of a firm's budgetary period (i.e., the short-term planning period)? (b) Illustrate how the short-term planning period would differ among industries. Cite examples.

8. Why do many firms use a flexible type of budget rather than a fixed type?

9. How is the flexible (step-type) operating budget related to, or similar to, a break-even chart prepared for a future period?

10. (a) Identify the types (or sources) of operating irregularities that occur in short-run business operations. (b) Illustrate how in short-run operations irregularity and uncertainty that occur in different lines of business (industry) affect unit cost of output.

11. (a) Identify the principal sources of seasonal variation that take place in business. (b) Illustrate why and how the seasonal pattern in a given line of business may change over time. (c) How do seasonal variations in volume affect business operations, variable costs, and fixed costs? Illustrate.

12. Identify and explain four methods that businessmen may use for dealing with seasonal variations.

13. (a) Can changes in production technology and in processing methods serve to moderate seasonal variations in volume and to lower unit cost? Illustrate. (b) With respect to the food-canning industry, explain how the development of improved methods for storing freshly picked crops, the staggering of crop-planting dates, and greater product diversification have lessened seasonality in production and cut the unit cost of output.

14. (a) What may be the principal sources (causes) of a drop in demand (sales) for a firm? Explain. (b) Identify and explain the internal and external factors that may delay the effective cutback in a firm's rate of output.

15. (a) Explain the different methods that a firm may use to curtail its rate of output. (b) Distinguish between escapable costs and inescapable costs. (c) Explain how a multiple-plant firm would use these costs in deciding whether to cut the rate of output through reduction in the length of the work-week for all plants or through shutdown of its least-efficient duplicate plant.

16. (a) Explain why a producer might continue to operate at a loss even though he did not anticipate profits later. (b) Explain how firms are able to operate below their break-even points for some time without actual failure of the business.

17. (a) What may be the principal sources of an increase in the demand (sales) for a firm? (b) What are the different methods whereby a firm may step up its rate of output? Explain the cost impact of each method.

18. (a) How may a firm's production interval and procurement lead-time affect the speed with which it can actually accelerate its rate of output? Cite illustrations from different industries. (b) What cyclical or other external factors may affect the speed and cost at which a firm may step up output?

19. Explain (give several reasons) why a producer may push output beyond the point at which marginal cost equals marginal revenue.

20. (a) Evaluate "rate-of-return on investment" and "percentage return on gross sales" as yardsticks for gauging a firm's profitability. (b) Why would an industry's relative profitability be more adequately measured on the basis of rate of return on total assets employed rather than on the basis of total net worth?

21. (a) What is meant by the "going concern value" of an enterprise? (b) How may "going concern value" influence the investment base of a firm, particularly when some of the firm's operating units came from mergers and acquisitions?

22. What are the cost and profit concepts that are relevant in appraising the profit performance of semiautonomous branches or units? Illustrate.

23. (a) What is the effect of the FIFO method of evaluating inventories on reported profits during a period of inflation and during a period of deflation in the price level? (b) The LIFO method?

24. Distinguish between straight-line depreciation and accelerated depreciation. Indicate the profit-reporting consequences of each.

25. (a) Distinguish between replacement cost and original cost. (b) Explain the application of these cost concepts in determining the adequacy of a firm's profits.

26. How does the proportion of debt in a firm's financial structure affect the amount of profit shown in its income statements? Explain what is meant by "trading on the equity."

27. (a) Explain what is meant by "pure profits" (or economic profits). (b) Assume of two corporate firms that one has very low fixed costs and no debt and the other has high fixed costs and a large debt outstanding. In which of these two corporations is the difference between economic profits and accounting profits bigger? Explain.

28. (a) Distinguish between historical profits (accounting profits) and anticipated profits. Explain the business or managerial use of each. (b) Why does the theory of the firm as a going concern (particularly with reference to managerial decision making) focus on anticipated profits?

29. Identify several profit standards and explain and illustrate the conditions under which one or another profit standard may be the accepted policy.

30. Discuss the principal reasons why management may limit the size of the firm's profits. How may management limit profits? What are the possible income-distributive effects of profit limitation?

31. (a) Discuss the internal and external factors that give rise to business profits (or losses). (b) Explain and illustrate the innovation theory of profits.

References and Supplementary Readings for Part III

Business Leadership

*GORDON, R. A. *Business Leadership in the Large Corporation.* Washington, D.C.: The Brookings Institution, 1945.

*LAWRENCE, PAUL R. *The Changing Organizational Pattern; A Case Study of Decentralization.* Boston: Harvard University Graduate School of Business, 1958.

ROSE, THOMAS G., and FARR, D. E. *Higher Management Control.* New York: McGraw-Hill Book Co., Inc., 1957.

SELZNICK, PHILIP. *Leadership in Administration.* Evanston, Ill.: Row, Peterson & Co., 1957.

Production and Factor Proportionality

*COLBERG, MARSHALL R., BRADFORD, W. C., and ALT, R. M. *Business Economics; Principles and Cases.* Homewood, Ill.: Richard D. Irwin, Inc., 1957. Chaps. 8, 10.

*DOYLE, LEONARD A. *Economics of Business Enterprise.* New York: McGraw-Hill Book Co., Inc., 1952. Chaps. 8, 9.

Scale Economies and Integration

KAPLAN, A. D. H. *Big Enterprise in a Competitive System.* Washington, D.C.: The Brookings Institution, 1959.

ROBINSON, E. A. G. *The Structure of Competitive Industry.* Chicago: University of Chicago Press, 1958.

Theory of the Firm

BEACH, E. F. *Economic Models.* New York: John Wiley & Sons, Inc., 1957.

CADY, GEORGE. *Economics of Business Enterprise—A Study of the Firm in the Aggregate Economy.* New York: The Ronald Press Co., 1950.

*COPPOCK, JOSEPH D. *Economics of the Business Firm.* New York: McGraw-Hill Book Co., Inc., 1959.

DAHL, ROBERT A., HAIRE, MASON, and LAZARSFELD, PAUL F. *Social Science Research on Business: Product and Potential.* New York: Columbia University Press, 1959.

*HAIRE, MASON. *Modern Organization Theory.* New York: John Wiley & Sons, Inc., 1959.

PENROSE, EDITH T. *The Theory of the Growth of the Firm.* New York: John Wiley & Sons, Inc., 1959.

POPANDREOU, ANDREAS G. "Some Basic Problems in the Theory of the Firm." In B. F. Haley (ed.). *A Survey of Contemporary Economics* (American Economics Association). Homewood, Ill.: Richard D. Irwin, Inc., 1952, vol. II, chap. 5.

* Suggested reading.

Short-Run Business Operations

*ANDREWS, P. W. S. *Manufacturing Business.* London: Macmillan & Co., Ltd., 1949. Chaps. 2, 7.

BROWN, ROBERT G. *Statistical Forecasting for Inventory Control.* New York: McGraw-Hill Book Co., Inc., 1959.

*DOYLE, LEONARD A. *Economics of Business Enterprise.* New York: McGraw-Hill Book Co., Inc., 1952. Chap. 10.

HEISER, HERMAN C. *Budgeting—Principles and Practice.* New York: The Ronald Press Co., 1959.

KUZNETZ, SIMON S. *Seasonal Variations in Industry and Trade.* New York: National Bureau of Economic Research, Inc., 1933.

MARTING, ELIZABETH (ed.). *Top-Management Decision Simulation: The AMA Approach.* New York: American Management Association, Inc., 1957.

SASIENE, MAURICE, YASPAN, ARTHUR, and FRIEDMAN, LAWRENCE. *Operation Research, Methods and Problems.* New York: John Wiley & Sons, Inc., 1959.

SHUBIK, MARTIN. *Strategy and Market Structure.* New York: John Wiley & Sons, Inc., 1959.

SMITH, E. S. *Reducing Seasonal Unemployment; The Experience of American Manufacturing Concerns.* New York: McGraw-Hill Book Co., Inc., 1931.

Profits

*COLBERG, MARTIN R., BRADFORD, W. C., and ALT, R. M. *Business Economics; Principles and Cases.* Homewood, Ill.: Richard D. Irwin, Inc., 1957. Chap. 1: "Uncertainty and Profit."

*DEAN, JOEL, and Joel Dean Associates. *Managerial Economics.* Englewood Cliffs, N.J.: Prentice-Hall, Inc., 1951. Chap. 1: "Profits."

*GORDON, R. A. "Enterprise, Profits, and the Modern Corporation." In B. F. Haley and W. Fellner (eds.). *Readings in the Theory of Income Distribution* (American Economics Association). Homewood, Ill.: Richard D. Irwin, Inc., 1952. Chap. 29.

KNIGHT, FRANK H. *Risk, Uncertainty and Profit.* London: London School of Economics and Political Science, 1935. Chaps. 5-11.

*SPENCER, MILTON H., and SIEGELMAN, LOUIS. *Managerial Economics.* Homewood, Ill.: Richard D. Irwin, Inc., 1959. Chap. 4: "Profit Management."

*TERBORGH, GEORGE. *Corporate Profits in the Decade of 1947–1956.* Washington, D.C.: Machinery and Allied Product Institute, 1957.

* Suggested reading.

Part IV
FORECASTING AND LONG-TERM BUSINESS PLANNING

CHAPTER 9

Impact of Environment
on Business

RISK AND UNCERTAINTY

Executives conduct business and carry out operations and plans in an environment of risk and uncertainty stemming from economic change. Because executive managers make decisions, plans, and commitments in the face of risk and uncertainty of demand and costs (i.e., with an imperfect knowledge of the future), expected results may not be realized, and the best-laid plans must often be adjusted to changing business conditions. Executives make decisions in the face of uncertainty with the hope that they will be successful and rewarded by profit. *Profit prospects* constitute the motivating force for business operations and for the employment of productive factors which determine the direction of an enterprise and the course of business activity.

The economist draws a distinction between risk and uncertainty. *Risk* arises from changes and fluctuations that can be foreseen. The risk loss to business from certain kinds of events (fire and theft) can be quantitatively measured and predicted. When a given kind of event involving business risk occurs with reasonable regularity, the average behavior of a large number of such events is predictable and can be insured. By taking a large number of observations from a big group of firms, insurance companies use the probability curve to predict the loss for a given kind of risky event. Through the sale of policies, an insurance company consolidates and diffuses a given kind of risk and places a specific premium cost on covered firms. By insurance coverage of specific risks, an individual firm essentially substitutes a premium (a current expense which it includes as a cost of doing business) for a potential loss which is uncertain as to magnitude and time of occurrence. Outside insurance is not necessary when a large firm can self-insure certain internal risks by establishing the probable loss (bad debts and work spoilage) and including it as a cost of doing business.

Uncertainty arises from developments and fluctuations that cannot be sufficiently foreseen and adequately predicted, such as changes in consumer style tastes and unforeseeable product developments by rival firms. Since uncertainty is not insurable, it cannot be included in a firm's cost as can risk. Business losses from uncertainty result from unpredictability and imperfect knowledge of future economic and technological changes. Businessmen establish productive facilities and an operating organization to produce and sell specific products for a future market. Their long-term decisions involving a commitment of capital are based on *expected* demand, prices, and costs. The uncertainty and the possibility of loss result from the fact that production involves an outlay of fixed capital for specialized facilities, from the need to make payments for input factors in advance of production, and from unpredictable or unanticipated changes in market demand, costs, prices, competitive practices, and other external developments that affect the level of profits.

Uncertainty and potential loss largely stem from the fact that modern capital-intensive production generally involves a long-term commitment of resources, and losses occur when market demand, prices, and costs change adversely. Since organized productive capital is comparatively specialized and has a long life, often a score or more years, the fixity and longevity of sunk capital tend to confine productive establishments to the output of certain products and services. Uncertainty and the possibility of loss are greater the more capital-intensive the production and the more vertically integrated the process, that is, the higher the value-added per dollar of sales. The possibility of loss is greater when firms require longer lead-time for erection of plant capacity or for the development, production, and promotion of a new product or a new model. Technological advance also increases business uncertainty when it renders obsolete certain productive facilities and products or places a firm at a cost disadvantage or in a weaker competitive position. A firm can somewhat minimize the uncertainty inherent in the utilization of fixed productive capital by providing for greater production adaptability in terms of speed in expansion and in increasing the rate of output, and in terms of converting or changing over plant facilities to meet changes in the product-mix.

Business uncertainty and potential losses derive also from the need to accumulate an inventory of finished goods in advance of sales. The businessman makes financial outlays for the procurement of materials and labor for production and for the maintenance of the reserve inventory of finished goods before he can market his output and be certain that his sales proceeds will cover his costs and yield earnings sufficient for an adequate return on investment. The longer the time duration of the operating cycle (procurement, production, and marketing), the greater the uncertainty.

Potential business losses derive from the uncertainty of future demands and possible fluctuations in sales and revenue. Lying behind unpredictable changes in demand and market uncertainty are changes in consumer tastes, prices, competitive strategy of rival firms, and in consumer income. Businessmen are vulnerable to entrepreneurial risks and losses so long as periodic recessions and business contraction are possible. Uncertainty in demand is considerable in enterprises that sell style goods, particularly when firms must accumulate a large finished stock of fashion goods for a future peak seasonal sales period. Managerial miscalculations of style trends and current fashions and a firm's overproduction for a seasonal demand can result in severe losses from style obsolescence. Thus, business forecasting and a comparatively accurate estimate of demand are essential if short-term operations and long-range managerial planning are to be successful.

Potential operating losses stem from uncertainty in the level of future costs, that is, from unpredictable variations in the procurement cost of materials and labor. Lying behind unpredictable or unanticipated changes in costs are union wage demands, technological changes, discovery of new resource deposits, uncontrollable variations in the output of raw materials, and so forth. Firms that purchase certain types of raw materials (such commodities as cotton, copper, coffee, and rubber) for which there exist organized commodities exchanges can, through the practice of hedging, minimize potential inventory losses from unpredictable fluctuations in the price of raw materials. Costs can also become uncertain because of the unforeseeable impost of a new tax, government expenditures, inflation, and other external factors.

If firms responded to uncertainty as analyzed and predicted by traditional economic theory, they would tend to move in the same direction. Differences in businessmen's attitude toward uncertainty, however, tend to account for different rates of business adjustment to economic change. Moreover, because firms are situated differently with respect to product line, cost structure, competitive position and financial resources, and the fact that businessmen evaluate future events and uncertainty differently, firms sometimes move in different directions or, at least, do not adjust at the same speed or in the same way to a given widespread economic change.

Businessmen deal with risk and uncertainty in a number of ways, for instance, through insurance, hedging and long-term purchase and sales contracts, business and production adaptability, business research and forecasting, and, of course, through the assumption of risk and losses from economic uncertainty. Executives in well-managed firms make decisions and formulate long-range plans on the basis of economic analysis and emphasize business research and forecasting to gauge shifts in the economic environment and the impact of cyclical fluctuations, governmental tax programs, and union bargaining demands.

IMPACT OF LABOR UNIONS ON BUSINESS ENTERPRISE

Labor unions influence governmental legislation, the supply of labor, and business operation. Of particular importance to managers is the direct impact of unionism on business enterprise. The influence of unionism on business is partially indicated by the extent of union organizational coverage. The great majority of workers in manufacturing, mining, construction, and communication industries belong to labor unions. In the early 1960's union membership consisted of 18,500,000 workers—approximately one-fourth of the total labor force. Because labor unions differ with respect to the proportion of the workers who are members in a given industry and with respect to maturity, policies, and tactics, union influence differs from business to business. In ascertaining the impact of unionism, one must take into account the fact that there are all kinds of labor unions operating and bargaining under all kinds of industrial and business situations.

Labor unions are essentially pragmatic organizations that exist to advance the economic interests of their members. As is common with other social and economic organizations, trade unions strive for institutional survival and expansion and attempt to explain and rationalize their objectives in terms of public interest. Union expansion takes place through organizational campaigns that offer workers a prospect of higher income and other economic gains and through skillful use of economic pressure in bargaining with management. Though American trade unions typically do not seek ideological goals and their objectives and tactics change with changing economic circumstances, they nonetheless tend to advance welfarism in government policy and bring about important social changes. Union demands, of course, change with changing economic conditions and developments in industry. The extent and kind of union influence on a given business depend not only on the amount of bargaining power acquired by the unions but also on the characteristics of the industry with respect to labor intensiveness of production, the range of occupational skills employed, the pace of technological change, and the rate of growth of the industry.

The existence of unionism requires that management establish organizational arrangements to bargain with the trade unions and to deal with union representatives in the plant on a day-to-day basis. Managers generally centralize the formulation of company labor policies and personnel procedures in order that they may deal with the union and carry out contract provisions in a consistent manner. Collective bargaining is the joint determination of decisions dealing with wages and other related matters. Because such joint making of certain business decisions limits managerial unilateral action in some aspects of business, collective bargaining is a penetration of the domain of managerial prerogatives.

In bargaining with management, unions strive for such concrete and immediate goals as greater union security (maintenance of membership, union shop), job protection and economic security for members, a rise in income and living standards, and participation in managerial decisions dealing with employment and personnel matters. In collective bargaining the company and the union essentially negotiate the terms of employment and arrive at an agreement (a union contract) which stipulates employment conditions with respect to compensation, hours of work, rules covering promotion and layoff, and other conditions.

Labor unions seek to attain more or less uniform contract provisions covering wages and working conditions among employers in the same industry or in the same area. Certain large unions and large employers generally establish a wage pattern for other unions to demand of their employers. Such *pattern-setting bargains* influence negotiations and labor agreements in related industries. Unions strive to attain uniform agreements through separate negotiations with each firm or through industry-wide bargaining. National unions tend to favor industry-wide bargaining because of its administrative convenience, uniformity, and stability. Uniform contracts with employers place firms on a more equal competitive footing with respect to wage rates and other employment costs.

Union bargaining and contract agreements with management

influence (1) the assignment of manpower in the plants, (2) the adaptability of production operations and the ease with which managers can regulate output, (3) the size of financial outlays made to improve working conditions, and (4) the pace of capital investment and technological advance.

Union contract provisions usually protect employees against arbitrary discharge—the labor agreement generally stipulates the conditions and the kinds of behavior that shall be the basis for discharging employees. Seniority clauses in the contract usually govern employee transfers, layoffs, and re-employment; unions attempt to ensure that job vacancies and the availability of work are governed by seniority so that employment opportunities are shared. Contract provisions thus often limit management discretion in shifting workers to different jobs in the plant or the manner whereby workers are laid off. Though many of the initial union demands for improved working conditions tended to increase labor productivity, beyond a certain point the provision of pleasanter working conditions adds more to cost than to gain in production efficiency.

Union bargaining with management and union sponsoring of legislation are among the factors that have led to a gradual *reduction in the length of a workweek*. Union demands for overtime pay are generally intended to prevent overtime work and to spread the availability of jobs, as well as to secure additional earnings for workers. Though the long-term reduction in hours tended to increase output per man-hour, employers have generally been hesitant to reduce the length of the workweek; they have not been certain that an increase in man-hour output would offset the cutback in weekly hours and have felt they would be compelled to invest in plant expansion and to increase the size of the work force in order to maintain output levels.

In order to offset technological displacement of labor and to increase employment opportunities, unions sometimes seek to limit output per worker. They would, for instance, strive for joint determination of the speed of assembly lines. Unions at times seek to restrict the introduction of improved production technology which displaces labor, particularly when displaced skilled labor cannot be reabsorbed because of the slow growth of the industry. Unions can more effectively resist increased mechanization of work when it is of a piecemeal nature and when organized labor has sufficiently unionized the industry so that newly established firms cannot avoid unionization. In cases in which unions cannot long delay adoption of improved production technology, they may attempt to regulate the rate at which improved processing techniques are introduced and endeavor to get displaced workers compensated by a dismissal wage when they cannot be reabsorbed by the industry.

Though craft unions in some industries may somewhat limit the piecemeal type of mechanization (the adoption of more highly mechanized machines), unions in general cannot retard the pace of adoption of the more far-reaching types of technological improvements (including adoption of new materials and product designs) that appreciably reduce fabrication time and cost. Multiple-plant firms adopt the more extensive types of technological advances through their large-scale replacement and modernization of production capacity, which frequently involve the erection of new plants, often at new locations. Moreover, union bargains which appreciably push up wages tend to step up the pace of laborsaving (automation) types of technological advance and investment more quickly than would otherwise likely occur.

Among the factors that influence union demands for higher wages are the workers' desire for better living standards, the prevalence of some substandard wage levels (particularly in recently unionized plants), the wage increases already gained by other unions (pattern-setting bargains), and the level of profits earned by the firms in the industry. Depending on the phase of the business cycle and the economic circumstances surrounding the industry, *union bargaining strategy* formulates *wage demands* on the basis of the rise in the cost of living, wages paid in comparable occupations in other industries, the employers' ability to pay, the gain in labor productivity in the industry, and the need for more purchasing power to maintain consumer demand and thereby to maintain employment. Unions resist wage cuts during periods of business depression, arguing for the need to maintain purchasing power and employment. If there are non-union firms in the industry, union ability to raise the wages of unionized firms is sometimes limited by the competitive advantage that accrues to non-union firms when the latter do not grant comparable wage increases.

The over-all union-management *wage settlement* consists of an agreement usually covering the general wage level of the firm or the industry, the relative wage rates for different occupations, the time standards or piece rates that enter into incentive payments, the supplementary payments (overtime pay, vacation pay), as well as improved physical working conditions. To workers, wages are earnings; to employers, a cost. All the costs associated with recruiting and employing a work force do not, however, enter into worker income.

Union efforts to bargain over *occupational wage differentials* have tended to promote managerial rating of occupations (the application of a job-evaluation procedure) in an objective, consistent manner on the basis of explicit criteria (skill, effort, training, etc.) to determine the relative value of jobs for the purpose of establishing occupational wage differentials on a rational basis. Having rated jobs through an appropriate job-evaluation procedure, management can bargain with the union on the basis of more or less rationally determined wage rates for different occupations. Managers aim to maintain logical occupational wage differentials by adjusting the wage scale on the basis of uniform percentage changes in rates rather than on the basis of a given monetary sum. Unions generally press for the joint determination of occupational wage differentials, and they generally bargain for equal cents-per-hour increases (e.g., a fifteen-cent increase for all jobs) rather than for a given percentage increase. Such wage adjustments tend to narrow gradually the percentage spread in wage rates for skilled and unskilled workers. The increased mechanization of productive processes and its attendant reduction in the number of less-skilled jobs in industry have also, of course, narrowed wage differentials. After following a wage-leveling policy for a number of years, a union often changes its policy and demands a bigger wage increase for skilled jobs in order to restore appropriate occupational wage differentials.

In their bargaining over wage payment, unions demand higher *supplementary compensation*—paid vacations and holidays, group insurance, pensions, and so on. Some of the supplementary payments become new overhead-expense items, and once granted they are difficult to cut back. Because irregular production raises the costs of certain supplementary payments (overtime pay, minimum workweek, unemployment insurance, severance pay), such payments induce firms to stabilize production and thereby more effectively utilize labor. Supplementary unemployment insurance adversely affects industries whose production fluctuates cyclically, but it aids industries that are steadily expanding and those with little seasonal fluctuation in sales volume.

Unions seek to attain *greater uniformity in wage levels and in employment conditions among competing firms* in the industry and among firms in a given labor-market area. A wage bargain between the union and a dominant firm often establishes a pattern in the industry; unions emphasize the industry-wide bargaining approach to reduce wage differences among firms in the same industry. The union scale of pay and conditions of work spread with the unionization of formerly non-union fields of business.

Though union pressure tends to reduce geographical wage differentials in the industry, it does not eliminate them. To the extent that unions attain more uniform wages and raise the wage level throughout the industry, their initial effect is to lower profit levels and induce greater managerial efforts to improve efficiency and reduce waste. Union success in gaining wage increases tends, in the short run, to raise selling prices somewhat. Since a gradual rise in wages changes the relative cost of input factors and thus tends to induce more mechanization, the increased introduction of laborsaving technology works to more or less offset the rise in the unit cost of the product stemming from a rise in wages. Hence, in the long run unions cannot increase wages at the expense of profits so long as employers can adopt improved technology and change the proportion of input factors and so long as employers can adjust selling prices. In the more competitive industries, the relative rise in selling prices may occur through the elimination of the inefficient or marginal firms and the reduction in the supply of the industry's goods. In the oligopolistic industries a rise in labor costs leads, in time, to the upward adjustment of prices. An oligopolistic industry is in a better position to stand a higher wage level when its labor costs are a small proportion of the unit costs, when the demand for goods is relatively inelastic, and when new firms find entry into the industry difficult to achieve. But monopolistic profits gained through impediments to the entry of new firms or other restrictive practices may be limited by antitrust laws.

IMPACT OF ANTITRUST POLICIES

The popular attitude in the United States favors competitive enterprise and supports public policy in the form of antitrust laws to curb monopolistic tendencies in industry and to curb certain undesirable business practices. Popular sentiment against monopoly grew out of the recognition that monopolies are socially and economically undesirable. Monopolies, for instance, restrict economic opportunity by closing certain business fields to all except those who hold monopoly power. Because monopolies charge exorbitant prices, they lower the volume of output and consumption of monopolized goods and thus use resources less efficiently than would be the case in competitive industry. Such misallocation of resources results in a loss of real income. The price rigidity of monopoly industry, moreover, tends to accentuate cyclical fluctuations. Because monopolists maintain high prices and cut back output and employment in the face of shrinking demand resulting from a business downturn, monopoly industry makes economic recessions more extreme. The evils of monopoly in a dynamic economy, however, are somewhat less harmful than strictly static economic analysis would indicate.

Governmental programs to prevent monopoly and to maintain and encourage competition may be carried out not only through antitrust laws but through promotion of lower-cost transportation which widens the scope of markets and stimulates competition, reduction of tariffs and other restrictions on foreign trade so as to broaden the base of competition, aid to small business, and removal of financing difficulties and tax impediments, and the creation of favorable economic conditions that encourage the formation of new enterprises.

Scope of Antitrust and Fair-Trade Laws

A survey of antitrust legislation enacted to regulate monopolies outlines the scope of the problem and the nature of the difficulties in this area of public policy. The Sherman Act, passed in 1890 as a result of public pressure, gives the federal government responsibility for preventing monopoly in interstate commerce. The Act in Section 1 states: "Every contract, combination in the form of trust or otherwise, or conspiracy in restraint of trade or commerce among the several states, or with foreign nations, is hereby declared to be illegal." In Section 2 the Act states: "Every person who shall monopolize, or attempt to monopolize, or combine or conspire with any other person or persons to monopolize any part of the trade or commerce among the several states or with foreign nations, shall be deemed guilty of a misdemeanor." In an attempt to curb certain types of business practices by which monopoly could be achieved and to strengthen the Sherman Act, Congress passed the Clayton Act (1914) designed to impose limitations on interlocking directorates and to prohibit discrimination in selling, tying contracts, and exclusive-dealer contracts.

In addition, the Federal Trade Commission Act (1914) set up a commission principally to prevent business firms from using unfair methods of competition and to investigate and make public such violations. The passage of the Wheeler-Lea Amendment (1938) broadened the Commission's functions so that it can take action against false and misleading advertising and other unfair or deceptive practices damaging to the consumer. In the Robinson-Patman Act (1936), Congress sought to prevent certain price discrimination practices that would lessen competition or tend to create monopoly.

In order to further strengthen the antitrust laws, Congress passed the Antimerger Amendment (1950) to the Clayton Act which made it illegal for one corporation to acquire the assets of another when such merger would substantially lessen competition or tend to lead to monopoly power.

In the case-by-case *governmental enforcement of antitrust laws*, a firm may be required to comply with a "consent decree," wherein it agrees to abide by certain stipulated rules of business behavior but does not undergo a court trial; it may be required to face a private suit for damages pressed by an injured party (individual, corporation, or state); it may be required to comply with an injunction to refrain from certain unlawful practices; or it may be required to dissolve or to divest itself of certain business undertakings (e.g., acquisitions).

The problem of determining when monopolistic practices are excessive is a difficult one. The FTC and the courts follow a case-by-case approach. In determining whether monopoly exceeds legal limits, the government would likely take into account several relevant factors: the number of firms in the industry and their market shares, minimum size required for economies of scale, opportunity for entry of new firms into the industry, the degree of product homogeneity and the substitutability of products, the lessening of competition through the pre-emption of business opportunities, and price discrimination and unfair trade practices that tend to lead to monopoly.

Effect of Antitrust Laws on Business Structure and Practices

The meanings of antitrust and fair-trade laws were more or less determined by their application to particular business and economic situations through a long series of cases decided by the courts. The impact of antimonopoly laws on business can be outlined by analyzing their influence (1) on the structure of industry and business firms with respect to restrictive agreements and combinations and (2) on business operations with respect to discriminatory pricing and certain selling practices (e.g., exclusive and tying contracts).

CONTROL OF RESTRICTIVE AGREEMENTS AMONG FIRMS. Antitrust laws have probably curbed many loose combinations, overt price agreements, and other restraints on competition which would otherwise have occurred. Without the governmental antimonopoly program American industry might have become openly organized along cartel lines. Business firms are likely to be confronted by antimonopoly action and declared in violation of antitrust laws if they make direct or indirect, overt or implied agreements that result in the division or the sharing of the market, price fixing, restriction of output or of purchases, exclusion of competitors, and in the elimination of opportunity to compete. Firms that establish or use trade associations for overt price maintenance or limitation of output, for instance, would likely be confronted by rigorous invocation of antitrust laws.

Though stiff legal barriers against collusive agreements among independent firms have tended to curb overt price-fixing agreements and the formation of selling syndicates, the less stringent legal barriers against close-knit combinations (mergers) have not forestalled (and may have encouraged) the combining or merging of separate firms into single enterprises. Thus, paradoxically, though looser forms of restrictive combinations are illegal, firms may increase their size and market share by direct consolidation through mergers and acquisition, so long as they do not substantially lessen competition.

CONTROL OF MONOPOLISTIC FIRMS AND MONOPOLISTIC MERGERS. In the United States Steel case (1920), the Supreme Court decided that if a corporation does not attempt to monopolize, coerce, or employ exclusive tactics, the mere size of the corporation is no offense. A monopolistic firm or a near-monopoly firm must thus actually exert monopoly power, as evidenced by unfair market practices, if it is to be held in violation of the law. In its ruling in the Alcoa case (1945), however, the government reversed its position when it held that the size of the firm was considered to be of the essence of monopoly power. Even if it never abuses its monopolistic position, a giant firm with monopoly power may be declared illegal, particularly if it creates barriers to entry of new producers into the market.

Though the Clayton Act forbade interlocking directorates (a director on two or more boards) among competing corporations over a certain minimum size (i.e., when any one of them has capital, surplus, and undistributed dividends exceeding $1 million), antitrust enforcement against such interlocking directorates has not been vigorous. The existence of this statutory restriction, however, has probably somewhat forestalled the use of interlocking directorates for promoting monopoly.

The Clayton Act as amended by the Antimerger Amendment forbade a corporation's acquiring either the stock or assets of another corporation when the effect of such merger or control may substantially lessen competition or tend to create a monopoly in a given line of business or in a particular market area. Antitrusters consider mergers and acquisitions on an individual basis and use judgment to determine what acquisitions substantially lessen competition or tend to create a monopoly. When two small firms merge, the FTC generally holds that the merger does not tend to create a monopoly. But when a large firm buys out smaller enterprises in the same line of business or when two bigger firms in the same line of business merge, the FTC is likely to undertake antitrust action. The antitrust agencies, for instance, opposed the merger of Bethlehem Steel Company and Youngstown Sheet and Tube Company on the grounds that it would substantially lessen competition in certain market areas.

The government would also carefully scrutinize for antitrust violations mergers in which a big producer carries out backward integration (e.g., the control of a raw-material supplier who also sells to other firms) or forward integration when such mergers tend to lessen competition. The Supreme Court in 1957, for instance, held that the Du Pont Holding Company violated the Clayton Act when it used its 23 per cent holding of General Motors stock to attain a more or less exclusive market position in the sale of paints and certain other materials to General Motors.

When mergers or acquisitions do not substantially lessen competition, firms often find it advantageous to effect mergers or acquisitions as a means of quickly gaining additional productive or distributive capacity, assuring dependable supplies of materials at cost, penetrating new market areas, filling out their product lines, and adding new items for effective product diversification. On the other hand, a selling firm may find it advantageous to dispose of its facilities or organization because of the difficulty of keeping up with competition, desire to join with a larger firm, desire to reduce the load of key executives, or the desire of executives to retire.

CONTROL OF EXCLUSIVE AND TYING CONTRACTS. A firm can sometimes obtain or extend a position of monopoly by using exclusive-dealer contracts and tying contracts. Such arrangements serve to exclude competitors from gaining access to certain business buyers and markets, and they limit the activities of some middlemen in the purchase and distribution of certain types of goods. The Clayton Act forbade exclusive-dealer contracts and tying contracts in interstate commerce when such contracts substantially lessen competition. The use of exclusive-dealer arrangements, however, is difficult to eliminate because the same distributive arrangement can be attained indirectly by the refusal of producers or wholesalers to market through non-cooperating retailers.

Patents, essentially a means of granting temporary monopolies to inventors, are held to be socially desirable because they promote invention. But patent rights have sometimes been used as a device for apportioning markets, controlling output, and fixing the prices of an industry's products. Though cross-licensing and patent pooling are not considered illegal per se, they are likely to be held illegal when used as a method of eliminating competition among patent-owners and licensees. The courts have somewhat consistently declared illegal tying contracts that extend the scope of a patent monopoly beyond the limits of a patent grant.

CONTROL OF CERTAIN TYPES OF PRICE DISCRIMINATION. The Clayton Act was primarily designed to curb the effects of discriminatory pricing on competing sellers, while the Robinson-Patman Act was essentially designed to curb the effects of discriminatory pricing on competing buyers, particularly the buying advantages of chain stores and big distributors, but to permit it in favor of smaller distributors. The two acts, that is, the Clayton Act as amended by the Robinson-Patman Act, essentially forbid price discrimination and discounts that "substantially lessen competition or tend to create monopoly" and that may "injure, destroy or prevent competition . . ." They also forbid price discounts that exceed allowances based on differences in sales or delivery costs.

The FTC has generally held that it *is* lawful for sellers to grant different trade discounts for each functional type of distributor (e.g., bigger discounts to wholesalers than to retailers), so long as they are not in competition with one another. With respect to quantity discounts, the Commission's policy has been to permit discounts justified by savings in selling and shipping costs but not by the savings in manufacturing costs. However, if the Commission feels that certain discounts are injurious to competition, it may view such discriminatory pricing as illegal even if justified by savings in selling and distribution. A big distributor can, of course, circumvent limitations on the savings from the foregoing type of discounts by contracting to buy the entire output of a supplier or by manufacturing the product himself in a newly acquired plant.

The Commission holds price discrimination in the form of *brokerage allowances or payments* illegal when no brokerage function is involved, and it maintains that all sales allowances and services must be available to all customers on proportionally equal terms. *Geographical price differentials* (price discrimination arising from locational differences that exist between buyers and sellers) are important with respect to antitrust policy in industries when the cost of transportation makes up a significant proportion of the final delivered price. The FTC views basing-point systems (a geographical pricing method that results in identical delivered prices among sellers) as monopolistic and illegal, but it does not prohibit independent or sporadic freight absorption in delivered pricing when such pricing promotes competition.

Thus, sellers may grant price discounts on the basis of distributive function, differences in grade or quantity of the product sold, or differences in selling or transportation costs. They may also make price concessions (engage in price cutting) in good faith to meet competition in the sale of goods to consumers, whether private buyers or governmental buyers financed by tax revenue.

IMPACT OF PUBLIC EXPENDITURES AND TAXES ON BUSINESS

When the government's role in the American economy involves public revenue and expenditures approximating $100 billion a year (roughly 20 per cent of national income), it cannot but have a significant impact on business enterprise and the economy. Public expenditures include outlays for conservation of resources, agricultural aid, public facilities (highways, waterways), national defense, and education and other social services. For a breakdown of federal revenue, see Tables 9–1 and 9–2. In appraising the effects of govern-

TABLE 9-1
Internal Revenue Collections by Principal Sources, 1940-58
(in millions of dollars. For years ending June 30)

Year	Total Internal Revenue Collections	Income, Profits, and Employment Taxes			Estate and Gift Taxes	Alcohol Taxes	Tobacco Taxes	Manufacturers' Excise Taxes	All Other Taxes
		Total	Individual Income and Employment Taxes[1]	Corporation Income and Profits Taxes[2]					
1940	5,340	2,963	1,816	1,148	360	624	609	447	337
1945	43,800	36,841	20,813	16,027	643	2,310	932	783	2,292
1950	38,957	30,652	19,798	10,854	706	2,219	1,328	1,836	2,215
1955	66,289	56,134	37,870	18,265	936	2,743	1,571	2,885	2,019
1956	75,113	63,932	42,633	21,299	1,171	2,921	1,613	3,456	2,019
1957[3]	80,172	68,141	46,610	21,531	1,378	2,973	1,674	3,762	2,244
1958[3]	79,978	67,746	47,213	20,533	1,411	2,946	1,734	3,974	2,167

[1] Beginning January, 1951, withheld income taxes and social security employment taxes on employees and employers are paid into the Treasury in combined amounts without separation as to type of tax; figures for prior years have been combined accordingly in this table for purposes of comparison.
[2] Includes tax on business income of exempt organizations.
[3] Excludes $3,767,000 transferred to the Government of Guam ($3,363,000 from individual income and employment taxes and $404,000 from corporation income and profits taxes) in 1957 and $3,500,000 (all individual income and employment taxes) in 1958.
Source: U.S. Department of Commerce, Bureau of Census, Statistical Abstract of the United States, 1959 (Washington, D.C.: Government Printing Office, 1959), p. 369.

TABLE 9-2

Internal Revenue Collections by Detailed Sources, 1957 and 1958

(in thousands of dollars. For years ending June 30)

Type of Tax	1957	1958
TOTAL	80,171,971	79,978,476
Income and employment taxes	68,140,946	67,746,260
Individual income and employment	46,610,293	47,212,944
Withheld	33,481,192	34,785,274
Income and old-age insurance	32,865,172	34,209,992
Railroad retirement	616,020	575,282
Not withheld	12,799,067	12,091,789
Unemployment insurance	330,034	335,880
Corporation income tax	21,530,653	20,533,316
Misc. internal revenue	12,031,024	12,232,217
Estate tax	1,253,071	1,277,052
Gift tax	124,928	133,873
Alcohol taxes[1]	2,973,195	2,946,461
Distilled spirits	2,118,957	2,092,183
Imported, excise	290,297	307,338
Domestic, excise	1,788,715	1,745,317
Rectification tax	23,511	22,103
Other	16,436	17,425
Wines, cordials, etc.	88,672	91,617
Beer	765,565	762,660
Excise	760,520	757,598
Other	5,045	5,063
Misc. internal revenue—Cont.		
Mfrs.' excise taxes—Cont.		
Phonograph records	16,450	18,282
Musical instruments	14,781	14,635
Mechanical pencils, etc.	9,114	9,060
Refrigerators, freezers, air conditioners, etc.	46,894	39,379
Matches	5,865	5,111
Business and store machines	83,175	90,658
Cameras, lenses, and film	19,901	22,546
Sporting goods	14,614	16,250
Firearms, shells, cartridges	16,566	16,185
Retailers' excise taxes	336,081	341,621
Furs	29,494	28,544
Jewelry	156,604	156,134
Luggage	57,116	58,785
Toilet preparations	92,868	98,158
Miscellaneous excise taxes	1,718,509	1,741,327
Sugar	86,091	85,911
Long distance telephone, telegraph, cable, radio, etc., and leased wires	266,185	279,376
Local telephone service	347,024	370,810

Tobacco taxes[1]	1,674,050	1,734,021
Cigarettes	1,610,908	1,668,208
Cigars	44,859	47,247
Other	18,283	18,566
Documents, other instruments, and playing cards	107,546	109,452
Manufacturers' excise taxes	3,761,925	3,974,135
Lubricating oils	73,601	69,996
Gasoline, inc. floor tax	1,458,217	1,636,629
Tires and tubes	251,454	259,820
Trucks and buses, chassis, bodies, etc.	199,299	206,104
Passenger automobiles, chassis, bodies, etc.	1,144,233	1,170,003
Parts and accessories for automobiles, trucks, etc.	157,291	166,720
Electric, gas, and oil appliances	75,196	61,400
Electric light bulbs and tubes	26,080	24,936
Radio and telev. sets, phonographs, components, etc.	149,192	146,422
Transportation of—		
Oil by pipeline	37,159	35,143
Persons, seats, berths	222,158	225,809
Property	467,978	462,989
Use of safe deposit boxes	5,826	6,137
Club dues and initiation fees	54,236	60,338
Bowling alleys, pool tables, etc.	3,122	3,139
Coin-operated devices	15,044	17,513
Admissions	119,089	97,602
Theaters, concerts, etc.	75,847	54,682
Cabarets, roof gardens, etc.	43,241	42,919
Use tax on highway motor vehicles weighing over 26,000 pounds	27,163	33,117
Narcotics and marihuana	972	1,038
Coconut and other vegetable oils processed	19,652	9,383
Diesel fuel	39,454	46,061
Wagering	7,325	6,939
Other,[2] incl. repealed taxes	30	25
All other[2]	81,719	−25,725

[1] Includes taxes collected in Puerto Rico on tobacco and liquor manufactures coming into the United States.

[2] Includes undistributed depositary receipts and unclassified advance payments of excise taxes.

Source: U.S. Department of Commerce, Bureau of Census, Statistical Abstract of the United States, 1959 (Washington, D.C.: Government Printing Office, 1959), p. 370.

ment expenditures on industry and the use of productive resources, we must take into account not only the magnitude and direction of public expenditures but the methods of taxation and borrowing employed to finance governmental activity.

Impact of the Public Budget

Government revenue and public expenditures alter the distribution of income and consumption and influence the direction of production and allocation of resources and the stability of employment and national income. Government subsidy payments designed to support the prices of certain products (government support of agricultural prices), for instance, can influence the general price pattern beyond the magnitude of the expenditure involved. An increase in government expenditure generally has an expansive influence on the economy. When the economy is operating at less than full employment, public expenditures can directly and indirectly create employment and augment national income; a rise in public expenditures generally increases aggregate demand and exercises an expansive influence on the economy. In the absence of an offsetting expansion in one or more sectors of the economy, a decrease in government spending would generally result in a corresponding contractive effect.

The economic effects of public expenditure in terms of income and employment are greater when spending is financed by borrowing. A shift from balanced-budget financing to deficit financing may come about through an increase in expenditures while tax revenue remains the same, through a tax cut while expenditures remain the same, or through a combination of the two. When the government borrows from commercial banks during a period of underemployment, it brings into the market new buying power which may put into productive use industrial capacity and manpower that would otherwise be idle. Public expenditures may swell employment and consumption (i.e., expenditures can have a multiplier effect), and they may increase employment by inducing investment (i.e., expenditures can have an accelerator effect). Public expenditures designed to promote full employment may be outlays for programed public works, social relief, support of automatic economic stabilizers, and other programs.

Federal supplementary contributions to state funds for unemployment insurance benefits, for instance, will tend to offset a business contraction in areas of growing unemployment and thereby attain a measure of economic stability. But a substantial increase in public expenditures may have an uneven or an unanticipated impact on industry, labor markets, and prices. Government outlays for public works, for instance, may take up little of the production and employment slack in the consumer-goods industries that are experiencing a contraction. Moreover, because of the long lead-time involved in carrying out many types of public projects and because the level and direction of the over-all business activity can quickly shift, public expenditures can create tight markets for materials and labor and thereby promote an undesired increase in prices and contribute to an inflationary movement in the general price level.

Impact of Taxes

Because of the complex system of direct and indirect taxation in the economy and the heavy impact of taxes on business enterprise, changes in tax levies and the tax aspects of enterprise are crucial to business planning and decision making. The impact of taxes is greater on some industries than on others (Tables 9–1 and 9–2). An appraisal of the tax burden (business income tax, excise tax, payroll tax, property tax, etc.) and an analysis of the tax aspects of business must take into account such factors as (1) the form of business organization, (2) the capital intensiveness of production, (3) cyclical stability of income, (4) degree of competition in the industry, (5) elasticity of consumer demand, (6) flexibility of output, and (7) the elasticity of the supply of productive factors. The impact of various taxes on enterprise can influence its corporate structure, location, growth, method of expansion and long-run financing plans, and the type and magnitude of current business expenditures.

The personal income tax, for instance, affects personal savings and may affect the productive effort of individuals. Because of the very high marginal rates of tax, a progressive personal income tax would presumably affect the productive effort of some people in high-income brackets, and the shrinkage in personal savings is greater the more progressive the tax rate schedule. To the extent that the supply of labor is sensitive to changes in take-home pay, an increase in the personal income tax, particularly for the lower-income brackets, may reduce the aggregate supply of labor. The employers' *payroll tax* for the social security program (which is essentially a levy on labor input), for example, has an uneven impact on industry. The experience rating provision of the payroll tax relieves firms with relatively stable employment of part of the payroll tax and in this way tends to induce firms to stabilize employment.

The experience rating feature, however, tends to penalize inherently unstable or seasonal lines of business (e.g., the garment and construction industries), and the tax discriminates against labor-intensive industries.

EXCISE TAXES AND GENERAL SALES TAX. Consumption taxes are levies paid by buyers in the price of commodities or services they purchase. Such levies include excise taxes, general sales tax, gross income tax, and tariff duties. An excise tax is a consumption tax on a particular commodity. The manufacturers' excise tax is exemplified by levies on producers' sales of automobiles and liquor; the retail excise is exemplified by levies on the merchants' sales of jewelry and cosmetics. The federal government confines its consumption tax to the manufacturers' excise tax; state and local governments generally use the retail excise tax and the general sales tax.

The burden of the excise tax and other consumption taxes, as in the case of all indirect taxes, is generally the result of a number of forces that determine the tax incidence—the final resting place of the tax burden. A firm may be able to shift much of the tax burden forward toward the consumer in the form of a higher selling price, or it may be able to partially shift the tax backward toward raw-material producers and workers in the form of lower payments. The extent to which a firm or industry shifts the tax burden depends on the degree of the elasticity of the demand and supply of the taxed commodity and on the extent to which the firm has a monopoly position.

A firm can more readily shift the tax burden to buyers when consumer demand is inelastic, as in the case of the demand for cigarettes. When demand is inelastic, sellers, through a small reduction in output, raise the price appreciably, thus shifting much of the tax forward. When demand is relatively elastic, producers tend to absorb a large part of the tax because they cannot shift the tax burden forward in the form of a higher price without a substantial loss in sales volume.

When the supply of productive factors (particularly materials and labor) is inelastic and relatively immobile, a reduction in output permits a backward shifting of the tax burden. As the volume of output is cut back, producers shift the tax burden backward by paying lower procurement prices for materials and labor which have become redundant. The more elastic and mobile the supply of productive factors, the less, of course, will producers be able to shift the tax burden backward. Thus, it is largely through a reduction in production and capacity that a tax can be shifted either forward or backward. The long-run shifting of the tax burden is encouraged when the capital-output ratio is low (i.e., when production is more labor intensive), when capital facilities can be amortized for income tax purposes in a relatively few years, or when the production process is convertible to the output of untaxed goods. Because it takes time to shift productive resources to untaxed fields of production, the reduction in output is greater in the long run than in the short run; and the long-run forward shifting of the tax is greater the more competitive the industry.

In the more competitive industries, an excise tax tends to be shifted forward to consumers through the elimination of the highest-cost producers and the resulting curtailment in industry supply. A smaller supply will raise the price to cover all or most of the tax for firms remaining in the industry. The forward shifting of the tax in competitive industry is, of course, greater when consumer demand is inelastic and the producers' supply is relatively elastic. Monopolistic firms that maintain a profit-maximizing price (a price above cost) tend to absorb much of the tax when consumer demand is relatively elastic, shift much of the tax forward when demand is inelastic, and shift the tax backward to raw-material producers and workers when the supply of these and other productive factors is inelastic or the factors relatively immobile. The bargaining power of labor in unionized industry will, however, tend to maintain wages.

Excise taxes influence demand in that they more or less deter buyers from purchasing the taxed goods. The impact of an excise tax on a firm or an industry largely depends, in the final analysis, on the shiftability of the tax. An excise tax that cannot readily be shifted affects adversely a firm's volume of output and level of profits, size, and expansion.

Though a general sales tax can be levied at the manufacturing, wholesaling, or retailing level, it is usually levied on retail sales at 2 or 3 per cent of sales value. The so-called general sales taxes levied by many states do not apply to all commodities; certain major groups of commodities and services are often exempt. The effects of a uniform general sales tax differ from the effects of the excise tax on a single commodity. The initial impact of a general sales tax will depend on the elasticity of consumer demand for the products of different industries and on the degree of mobility of productive factors. In the long run a general sales tax is usually shifted to consumers. However, when there are neighboring cities in two states, only one of which levies a sales tax, the tax sometimes cannot be effectively shifted to consumers. In order to forestall the shift of buyers and a loss of business to a neighboring shopping area in the state that is free of the sales tax, retailers in the borderline city of the state levying the sales tax often find that they must absorb the tax. Some states impose a "use" tax which is a levy on the use or storage of certain goods within a state even though the goods have been purchased in another state. The use tax is difficult to administer for most goods. An unpaid use tax for an automobile is generally assessed when the vehicle is registered for its automobile license.

Because of the comparatively inelastic supply of productive factors (factor immobility) in certain industries or in certain areas, the initial imposition of a general sales tax may result in a partial backward shifting of the tax through the lowering of payments to productive factors. But public expenditures financed by revenue from consumption taxes maintain the aggregate demand for productive factors, and oligopolistic suppliers of materials (steel, aluminum, cement, chemicals, etc.) and organized labor tend to maintain the selling prices for the productive factors they supply.

An imposition of, or an increase in, a general sales tax during boom times, and the resultant absorption of consumer purchasing power accompanying a government budgetary surplus produce an anti-inflationary effect. A cut in the sales tax during a business decline, however, will ordinarily stimulate buying and raise the volume of business.

GENERAL EFFECTS OF CONSUMPTION TAXES ON BUSINESS. Since consumption taxes that are shifted forward to consumers would cause no reduction of profits, such levies would not adversely affect business incentives. A consumption tax levied on any early stage in processing or distributing, if it can be shifted forward, pyramids the tax burden for the ultimate consumer. This is likely to accumulate when businessmen use cost plus a percentage markup for setting selling prices. As such taxed goods pass through the distribution system, wholesalers, jobbers, and retailers, adding their customary percentage markup on taxed items, may cause the ultimate consumer to pay an inflated sales tax. The result may be that middlemen, in a sense, make a profit on the tax. The taxed goods of non-integrated industry, produced and distributed through a long series of stages involving a number of firms, tend to bear a heavier tax burden than the taxed goods of integrated industries.

Any tax levied on early stages which can be wholly or partially shifted forward may result in such pyramiding. This would include consumption taxes levied on business transactions (e.g., the turn-over tax and the gross income tax), for these, too, tend to induce vertical integration (both backward and forward) in industry. A firm in an economy honeycombed with indirect taxes can lower somewhat its cost of doing business through greater vertical integra-tion, thus lowering the over-all tax burden on final goods ready for sale to ultimate consumers. To the extent that indirect and some direct taxes in a given industry are shiftable forward and add to the operating costs of firms in later stages in the over-all production and distribution process, vertically integrated firms have a competi-tive advantage over non-integrated firms.

Consumption taxes, particularly excise taxes, can also lead in other ways to a reallocation of resources and a redistribution of income. Excise taxes on products with highly inelastic demand, for instance, increase consumer dollar outlays for the taxed items and reduce demand, prices, and business income for firms selling untaxed goods. In the short run, in addition, such levies lower the return on productive factors employed in producing untaxed items.

CORPORATE INCOME TAX. Both federal and state governments apply the personal income tax to the net income of unincorporated business. A high percentage of state governments tax corporate net income, usually at flat rates. In some cases a minimum levy is imposed, and a surtax is applied when income exceeds a certain sum.

The federal government levies a corporate income tax of 30 per cent on the first $25,000 and 52 per cent on the remainder; the bulk of corporate earnings are thus taxed at 52 per cent. In computing taxable income, corporations deduct from gross receipts (sales revenue) the cost of production, uncompensated losses, certain taxes, contributions, and other allowable deductions.

The shiftability of the burden of the business net income tax (and the tax incidence) must be analyzed in both their short-run and long-run contexts. Since the net income tax is assessed on net profits and does not affect the rate of output (short-run supply), the tax is considered not to be shiftable in the short run. But, as the tax lowers the return on investment in certain fields, it will tend to decrease the number of firms operating in these lines of business. This would reduce the industry supply, and the resulting higher prices would bring about a forward shifting of the tax. In the long run, therefore, it is likely that much of the tax will be shifted forward in the form of higher selling prices. This is because firms will not, in the long run, stay in a given line of business if the return after taxes does not yield a reasonable profit on the investment for the owners. The withdrawal of firms from unprofitable (after tax) industries will reduce supply, and the resultant higher (more profitable) prices will yield a higher profit after taxes for firms remaining in the industry. (A development similar to the foregoing is likely to obtain in the case of geographical differentials in tax levies. Lower over-all business taxes in neighboring states would induce the migration of business to those states.) Firms in monopolistic industries are likely to shift the tax burden by taking the initiative in raising prices. In a growing economy, however, the long-run forward shifting of business net income taxes is likely to come about through a growth of demand.

It is frequently held that the corporate income tax and the personal income tax impose a *double tax* on the dividend income of individuals. The corporation pays a tax on net income, and then shareholders must pay a personal income tax on dividends received. Double taxation is partially avoided to the extent that the corporation retains earnings and reinvests the funds. But as the successful investment of retained earnings increases corporate earning power and raises the market value of its stock, shareholders will be obliged to pay a 25 per cent capital gains tax when they sell their shares. In closely held corporations owner-officers sometimes reduce their tax burdens by having tax-free expense accounts and by sharing in employee benefit plans.

At a charge of an additional 2 per cent tax rate, the corporate income tax allows firms with affiliated companies to file *consolidated tax* returns and thereby offset the income loss of some operating units against the profits of other units. The 2 per cent penalty tax has induced some multiple-unit firms to eliminate the separate character of subsidiaries and thus simplify their over-all corporate structure. A smaller corporation, on the other hand, can avoid the higher (52 per cent) rate by dividing the enterprise into two or more legally separate corporations so that the net income of each approximates $25,000.

The corporate income tax tends to even out a firm's after-tax earnings in any given period of a few years through the *loss-carry-over provision* which allows losses to be carried back two years and forward five years as an offset against profits. A high corporate profit tax tends to reduce a net loss from an unsuccessful business project. The carry-forward privilege aids newly established firms which incur losses during the initial years of business. Since early losses are essentially a cost of launching a new enterprise, it is economically logical that such losses should be prorated over future years. Until tighter Internal Revenue Service rulings were put into effect, the loss-carry-over provision was, in some instances, a significant tax motive contributing to mergings with tax-loss firms (i.e., firms with unused tax losses).

Because it allows deduction of explicit interest but not implicit interest, the corporate income tax would presume to encourage debt financing. To the extent that the tax penalizes equity financing, it discourages venture capital and excessively encourages debt financing through bonds and mortgages. Because debt financing increases the fixed financial overhead, it makes for cyclical disadvantages by handicapping a firm in its ability to cut back over-all costs during periods of business contraction. But since many factors are involved in business financing plans, it is difficult to estimate the extent to which the corporate income tax actually promotes debt financing.

In computing its operating costs to determine taxable income, a firm can deduct depreciation of property but cannot deduct imputed interest on its investment. A firm can gain a substantial tax savings by changing from owner to renter of business property (e.g., industrial plant, office building, department store, and supermarket) and by deducting rental payments from business income. The corporate income tax thus tends in some cases to discourage the purchase of facilities and to encourage the leasing of productive facilities. In a sale-leaseback arrangement, for instance, a firm sells its principal business property to an investment group or to one of its subsidiaries and takes it back immediately for use on a long-term lease. Both the sale and leaseback are parts of a single transaction. The arrangement frees the firm's capital through the transfer of property while it remains in control of the business property as a tenant. The lease firm gains a tax benefit when the rental charge is reasonable, and it also acquires cash, formerly tied up in property, for use as working capital or for other investment purposes. It is easy to see how a tight money market can force a cash-short firm into sale-and-leaseback financing. The leaseback arrangement may raise more capital than if property had been mortgaged and mortgage bonds sold. The buyer of the business property (the lessor) also tends to benefit since he generally receives a higher and safer return on his investment than from many types of conventional securities and can take the allowed depreciation on the property, though the upkeep and repair are left to the lessee.

Heavy tax levies on net business income tend to encourage certain types of business expenditures, some of which may be considered extravagant. A high business income tax, for instance, may encourage a profitable firm to make larger than usual outlays (items chargeable to current income) for sales promotion, research, public relations, salesmen's expense accounts, and the like. To the extent that high corporation taxes encourage extravagant expenditures chargeable to current income, they lead to wastage or misallocation of resources and tend to contribute to inflation during periods of high employment.

An increase in the corporate income tax generally reduces the availability of internal business funds, particularly in the short run. The reduction of internal funds would be more appreciable during prosperity than during recession. The corporate income tax together with the personal income tax, moreover, tends to reduce the attractiveness of risk taking and thereby to impede business expansion, particularly in fields comprised of smaller firms. Even though the corporate income tax is wholly shiftable to consumers, the tax tends to reduce the incentive to invest in the same line of business because higher selling prices and lower effective demand reduce the need for productive capacity.

Incentive taxation in the form of various tax concessions has been proposed to encourage business investment, employment, and economic growth. To induce more stable employment some states provide lower unemployment insurance (payroll) tax rates on the basis of experience rating to firms that maintain steadier employment. Loss carryover in the computation of the tax liability on business income tends to contribute to business stability and efficiency. The designation of expenditures for industrial research (e.g., the development of new products from crude oil) as a cost against current income stimulates technological advance and gain in productivity. A generous *depletion allowance* on mineral resources (coal, sulfur, oil) induces mineral and oil firms to undertake costly and risky exploration and development of new deposits, the maintenance of a proved reserve for rapid economic growth, and an adequate domestic supply for national emergencies. An annual depletion allowance of 27.5 per cent of gross income from the output of oil wells, for instance, yields ample funds for prospecting and opening up of new wells. As oil companies develop and add new items to the product line, their enlarged gross income base yields a bigger depletion allowance. Accelerated depreciation of capital outlays would also presumably induce new investment and business expenditures for equipment replacement.

In computing taxable income the businessman deducts a depreciation charge on productive capital from gross revenue. The emergence of governmental tax levies on business income leads to the need for an adequate conceptualization of depreciation for computing taxable income. *Depreciation* (or capital consumption) is the expiration of the economic life of productive capital facilities resulting from wear, deterioration, and obsolescence. Unlike the materials or wage bill, depreciation is a non-paying-out charge that leads to the accumulation of funds for the replacement (capital maintenance) of man-made productive capital assets that have been retired (or relegated to stand-by or marginal use) because of physical deterioration, obsolescence, or inadequacy. In applying or writing off depreciation charges against annual gross income, most firms have generally used the straight-line method whereby they prorate over the life of the assets equal amounts of the original cost less the salvage value.

In an effort to provide an incentive and direct investment to new productive facilities, Congress in the Internal Revenue Act of 1954 permits firms to elect (as an alternative to straight-line depreciation) a faster write-off on new capital facilities. Firms may use certain specified *accelerated-depreciation formulas* (declining-balance or sum-of-the-years' digits methods) which apply a rate that does not exceed twice the straight-line charge and does not yield, during the first two-thirds life of the asset, an accumulation greater than that under straight-line depreciation. Accelerated depreciation provides a greater incentive to invest in new plants or to modernize plants and obtain a gain in productivity when taxes are high than when taxes are low. Since accelerated amortization applies only to firms that invest in depreciable productive assets, it is a *selective incentive* for investment in contrast to investment stimulus induced by reductions in interest rates or taxes. The rapid write-off provision offers a stronger stimulus to investment in relation to the decline in public tax revenue than would result from a cut in the business income tax.

Special provisions for fast write-off of productive facilities were employed as a means of expanding defense plant capacity. Through the acquisition of a "certificate of necessity," a firm could deduct for tax purposes the investment cost of a plant or other facility in five years instead of the twenty or more normally permitted. This meant much lower tax on gross earnings in the first five years of the use of the new facility.

Accelerated depreciation can substantially reduce taxable income (and the tax liability in early years), and it diminishes the relative importance of the over-all tax liability on the income derived from a given capital outlay. Rapid amortization would tend to induce firms to make larger investments and to replace old facilities earlier than they would otherwise. Rapid amortization essentially enables businessmen to recover the bulk of their capital outlay sooner (supplying funds for other profitable uses) and gain a permanent saving in interest; it lessens risk and uncertainty. The interest savings (the discount factor) are greater the longer the life of the asset and the higher the interest rate applied. Because accelerated depreciation shortens the period over which a large portion of an asset is written off, it serves to partially offset the adverse impact of inflation on the cost of replacing capital when it is amortized on the basis of the original cost. But if depreciation allowances are too high as compared to actual economic depreciation, conventional accounting practice would understate net income and net investment.

Whether a firm adopts the accelerated-depreciation method for computing tax liability depends on a number of factors. The investment stimulus of accelerated depreciation, for instance, is smaller to the extent that the liberal loss carry-over in computing taxable income reduces the impact of the income tax. Rapidly expanding enterprises, particularly those in capital-intensive industries, stand to gain more from the use of rapid write-off than the mature industries or those that are not capital intensive (e.g., personal-service, distributive, and financial lines of business). Firms that have a plenitude of high-yielding investment opportunities may be only slightly influenced by the rapid-amortization provision. Advantages from the adoption of accelerated depreciation are greater if businessmen have good reason to anticipate lower tax rates and higher earnings in the future or if they anticipate a marked inflationary trend generally associated with a cyclical upswing in business.

IMPACT OF CYCLICAL FLUCTUATIONS ON BUSINESS

Cyclical fluctuations in employment and output (in GNP) consist of recurring alterations in business contraction (recession) and business expansion (recovery). No two business cycles have been alike; they generally differ in duration and amplitude of movement. The level and fluctuation in total business activity (in GNP) are but a statistical aggregate of the industries making up the total. In the process of cyclical fluctuations, such major industry groups as consumer non-durable goods, capital goods, and construction industries usually differ with respect to timing and amplitude patterns (Figs. 9–1 and 9–2; Table 9–3). But because industries are inter-related, the various industry groups move more or less in unison in the over-all cyclical fluctuation.

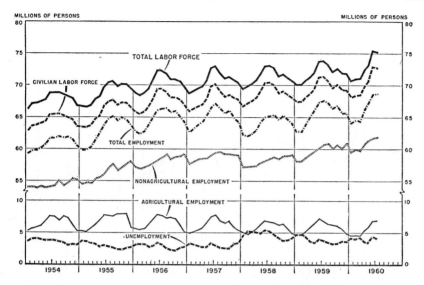

Fig. 9–1. Cyclical turns in employment and unemployment. (Council of Economic Advisers, *Economic Indicators, August 1960.* Washington, D.C.: Government Printing Office, 1960, p. 11.)

Cyclical Impact

The impact of the business cycle on a given firm and a firm's cyclical sensitivity thus depend somewhat on its line of business. A firm's cyclical behavior also depends on the economic characteristics of the geographical region in which it produces or sells its goods. Because regions differ in the rate of population growth, resources, and economic diversity or degree of industrial specialization, some regions experience steadier secular growth and enjoy greater economic stability than other regions. Though each industry's and firm's behavior and adjustment in the business cycle differ, certain more or less typical cumulative developments and changes portray a firm's cyclical contraction and expansion and indicate how the business cycle (including deflation and inflation) affects a firm's operations, structure, and financial organization.

Each business downswing and upswing persists in a given direction until certain developments in business and forces in the economy accumulate to reverse the direction. The cumulative movement in a business upswing usually consists of an increase in aggregate demand and rises in production, employment, prices, profits, and investment; the cumulative movement in a business downswing

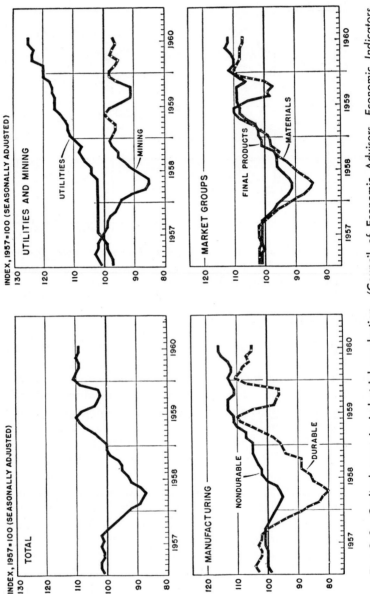

Fig. 9-2. Cyclical turns in industrial production. (Council of Economic Advisers, *Economic Indicators, August 1960.* Washington, D.C.: Government Printing Office, 1960, p. 16.)

TABLE 9–3
Cyclical Turns in Industrial Production
(1957 = 100, seasonally adjusted)

Period	Total Industrial Production	Industry					Market			
		Manufacturing			Mining	Utilities	Final Products			Materials
		Total	Durable	Non-durable			Total	Consumer Goods	Equipment	
1950	75	76	71	79	80	53	74	82	54	75
1951	81	82	80	82	87	60	79	81	75	82
1952	84	85	85	83	87	65	85	83	90	83
1953	91	92	96	87	89	71	91	88	96	91
1954	85	86	85	87	86	77	87	87	85	84
1955	96	97	98	95	95	85	95	97	91	97
1956	99	100	100	99	100	94	99	99	99	100
1957	100	100	100	100	100	100	100	100	100	100
1958	93	92	87	100	91	105	95	99	87	91
1959	105	105	102	110	95	115	107	110	100	104
1959: June	110	110	110	111	98	116	108	111	102	110
July	108	108	105	113	94	116	109	112	104	106
August	104	104	98	113	91	116	109	112	103	98
September	103	104	97	113	91	117	109	112	103	99
October	102	102	96	111	91	117	109	112	103	97
November	103	102	96	111	96	118	106	109	101	100
December	109	109	107	112	98	120	109	113	102	109
1960: January	111	112	111	113	98	120	112	116	103	110
February	110	110	109	112	96	121	110	113	102	109
March	109	110	108	112	95	124	110	113	104	108
April	109	109	106	113	98	124	111	115	102	108
May	110	110	107	115	97	123	113	117	105	108
June	109	110	105	116	96	125	112	116	104	107
July[1]	109	110	105	116	97	125	112	116	104	107

[1] Preliminary
Source: Council of Economic Advisers, Economic Indicators, August 1960 (Washington, D.C.: Government Printing Office, 1960), p. 16.

usually consists of a contraction in aggregate demand and a decline in output, prices, profits, and investment.

Businessmen sometimes are not aware of an economic downturn until a sufficient decline in over-all business activity has taken place. They generally become cautious, however, when their backlog of orders begins to decline or sales slip and finished stocks begin to rise; they become more anxious to reduce output when an unplanned accumulation of inventories continues. Manufacturers' inventories may rise for a time because producers are not always sure that sales will remain sluggish and they are often reluctant or not always able to adjust output to sales fast enough.

When a downturn continues and consumers become uncertain of their future incomes, they begin to shift their purchases to lower-priced brands and economy models and to curtail purchases of expensive durable goods such as dwellings, automobiles, and electrical appliances. Producers and sellers of non-durable goods, however, generally find that their physical volume of business does not decline appreciably. During the downturn, retailers and wholesalers are often quick to shift to hand-to-mouth buying as their business volume begins to slip and their stocks begin to mount. In the face of declining sales, producers start to cut back the volume of output. In general, production and employment tend to fall faster than the decline in retail sales and consumption.

In the more competitive industries, prices begin to decline because of shrinkage in demand and overextended capacity and supply. In the monopolistic industries the maintenance of prices in the face of declining demand produces a relatively sharp contraction in sales volume, with the result that earnings begin to drop because of a smaller volume of business and rising overhead costs per unit of output. The unfavorable cost-price relationship lowers the return on investments. With profits impaired, business expectations deteriorate. Though profits are cyclically very volatile, large corporations maintain comparatively stable dividend payments, and as a result retained earnings tend to fluctuate sharply.

A business downturn tends to become cumulative to the extent that profit expectations (and optimism) decline and businessmen curtail output and inventory stocks and hold back capital expenditures. When times are uncertain, businessmen strive for greater liquidity (an improved cash position) by reducing inventory levels, converting accounts receivable into cash, selling securities, postponing equipment replacement, and curtailing investment outlays. A deflationary trend, too, induces businessmen to scramble for greater liquidity. During a period of decline in the general price level, businessmen find that their interest payments and debt retirement become burdensome while the market value of their assets declines. As a hedge against deflation, businessmen sometimes sell company assets that are not necessary for business operation.

Self-correcting forces develop as business undergoes a cyclical contraction; certain economic developments begin to stimulate recovery. Through the postponement of equipment replacement, for instance, industry works off some excess capacity and brings productive capability into better alignment with demand. The forces of secular growth (increase in population and improved profit prospects from technological developments) and government stabilization and fiscal measures limit economic contraction and in time stimulate business recovery. Disposable income and consumption decline less sharply than GNP due to the fact that income tax payments decline more than earnings. Moreover, some individuals draw on personal savings, while others receive income (transfer payments) in the form of unemployment insurance and retirement benefits. As the stock of durable goods in the hands of consumers begins to wear out, producers find an increased replacement demand for durable goods. The cessation in the decline of consumer demand and increased business liquidity improve the position of firms. Profit margins begin to improve as the decline in selling prices levels off while the procurement prices of raw materials (particularly agricultural raw materials and minerals) and wages in general continue to fall for a time. Businessmen gradually slacken the pace at which they reduce inventories; their rate of inventory reduction begins to diminish and eventually comes to an end (Fig. 9–3). As the decline in material prices begins to level off, businessmen are less hesitant to hold larger inventory stocks. Because businessmen have more or less postponed purchases of equipment and can no longer prudently allow replacement needs to accumulate, they begin to increase outlays for productive facilities. The revival in gross investment stimulates expansion in the capital-goods industries.

As demand and sales increase and prices rise moderately, firms contribute to cumulative business expansion by building up inventories and hiring more labor. A rise in selling prices while material procurement prices and wages remain low increases profit margins. Unit costs decline and total profits rise as firms operate at a higher capacity. The business upswing gains momentum as employment rises and consumer demand grows, inventory levels (induced by higher production rates and rising material prices) are built up, out-

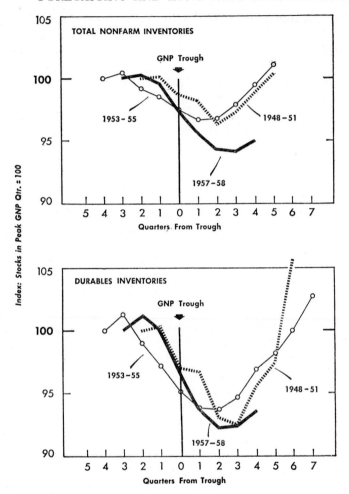

Fig. 9–3. Stock movements in three postwar cycles show similar timing patterns. (U.S. Department of Commerce, *Survey of Current Business*, vol. 39 [April, 1959]: p. 5.)

lays for plant modernization and expansion increase, and business expectations improve from investment opportunities growing out of technological advance and secular economic expansion (Fig. 9–4). With the increase in the volume of business, firms generate higher income and larger retained earnings for the exploitation of profitable investment opportunities. The continued rise in aggregate demand after full employment has been reached tends to bid up the market value of goods, and the increased demand tends to partially dissipate itself in higher prices or inflation.

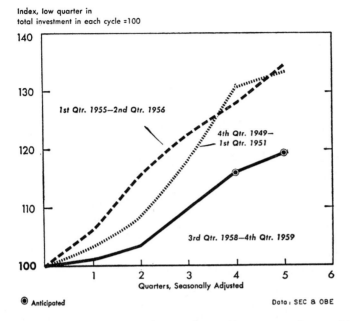

Index, low quarter in
total investment in each cycle =100

Fig. 9–4. Postwar upturns in plant and equipment expenditures. (U.S. Department of Commerce, *Survey of Current Business*, vol. 39 [April, 1959]: p. 5.)

Impact of Inflation

A rise in the general price level affects a firm's *financial structure* and the *level of profits* reported on income statements. Inflation increases the market value of physical assets but reduces the real burden of a firm's debts and liabilities. A firm finds a debtor status better than a creditor status—firms can meet interest payments and retire obligations with a cheaper dollar. But election of debt financing in place of equity financing involves other considerations as well.

Inflation affects profits by changing a firm's cost-price relationship. Because a rise in material prices and wages (particularly in non-unionized fields of business) lags behind the rise in selling prices, an inflationary trend widens profit margins. Prompted by rising prices, firms tend to engage in forward buying and build up material inventory stocks to higher than normal levels; firms purchase materials and labor at one price level and, after an interval of processing, sell finished goods at a higher price level. "Inventory profits" emerge because of a rise in the price level during the time period when a plant stores procured materials, converts the material in processing, and holds completed goods in final storage. Thus, inflation distorts the measurement of profits because the purchase cost of material is determined at one time but the selling price of converted goods is determined at a later time when the goods are sold.

Businessmen should therefore take into account the trend of prices before they select a method for determining the cost at which materials should be valued (costed) for computing the unit cost of the product. The first-in-first-out (FIFO) and the last-in-first-out (LIFO) methods have been used for valuating the cost of materials in determining taxable business income. Under the *FIFO method of valuation,* the cost of materials is based on the actual purchase price at which the given materials were originally procured. During a period of declining prices (deflation), the high-priced materials (as valuated by the FIFO method) that go into computing the cost of the product reduce the profit margin and show a smaller profit figure. During inflation, on the other hand, because FIFO takes the early, low purchase prices (i.e., when materials were initially procured) to compute the cost of goods, it reports a higher profit and a larger profit margin in the income statement. The consequent overstatement of net income (inflation of profits) exaggerates earnings, increases taxable income, and erodes working capital. Businessmen must add new funds to working capital in order to cover rising material prices.

In order to offset at least partially the overstatement of profits and tax liabilities resulting from inflation, businessmen have largely adopted the *LIFO method for valuating materials* in the computation of the unit cost of the product. Since under the LIFO method the price of the last material purchased is taken to compute the cost of the product, the LIFO method results in a lower profit figure during inflation than the FIFO method.

Though the LIFO method more closely approximates current material prices than FIFO, it does not altogether offset the change in the cost-price relationship resulting from inflation. If, during a period of inflation, a firm curtails the procurement of materials and works off its inventories, for instance, the LIFO method cannot avoid the resultant overstatement of profits.

During a period of rising prices, the *cost of replacing worn equipment* as well as the cost of replenishing inventories goes up. Depreciation charges based on original costs rather than on replacement cost overstate business income and the tax liability, and the rise in the price of equipment means that replacement funds cannot cover the cost of new equipment necessary to renew worn facilities. Funds from retained earnings and external sources must be added to replacement funds to cover the cost of price-inflated equipment. But when a firm modifies or improves its products and substantially alters its production processes, it becomes difficult to determine the appropriate replacement cost to use in place of the original cost for amortizing facilities that are no longer the same. A firm that pays a high price for equipment to replace old machines can, of course, use the appropriate rapid write-off method (e.g., the declining-balance method) to amortize the equipment on the basis of the high (inflated) purchase price.

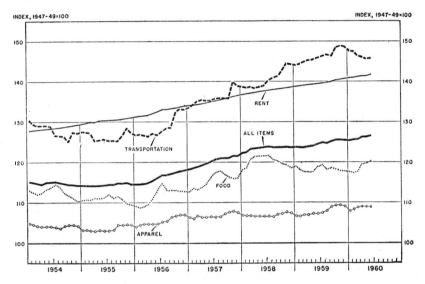

Fig. 9–5. Consumer price rises in inflationary periods can be used as a basis for increased wage demands. (Council of Economic Advisers, *Economic Indicators, August 1960.* Washington, D.C.: Government Printing Office, 1960, p. 23.)

Because they are largely computed on the basis of historical rather than current costs, accounting profits do not always serve as an adequate basis for long-term decision making. Managers must take into account the changes in the value of money if they are to measure business income in real terms. When company assets are valued at original cost, business income must be expressed in terms of the constant dollars of an earlier period, if a realistic rate of return on investment is to be reported and if investment decisions are to be made on a consistent basis.

Inflation also complicates *wage bargaining* between labor and management. To the extent that conventional accounting practice reports business income in inflated dollars and thus indicates a higher ability to pay, labor unions are induced to use the company's ability to pay as a basis for wage demands. In many highly unionized fields of business, organized labor has gained a cost-of-living provision in its labor contract which keeps wages in line with the rise in the price of consumer goods (Figs. 9–5 and 9–6).

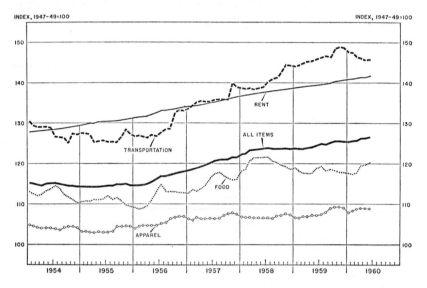

Fig. 9–6. During inflation consumer prices rise and affect higher-wage demands. (Council of Economic Advisers, *Economic Indicators, August 1960.* Washington, D.C.: Government Printing Office, 1960, p. 24.)

QUESTIONS FOR REVIEW AND APPLICATION

1. Define and illustrate business risk and uncertainty. What are the main sources of risk and uncertainty in business? Explain briefly.

2. (a) What are the methods whereby businessmen can deal with risk and uncertainty? Explain briefly. (b) Why do businessmen find it prudent to carry wider insurance coverage during a period of high taxes on profits than during a period of low taxes on profits?

3. Identify the lines of business that can practice hedging (i.e., hedge their purchases) to reduce inventory losses from unanticipated fluctuations in the prices of raw materials.

4. Compare the risk and uncertainty in an enterprise that employs highly specialized capital-intensive processes to produce stylized consumer durable goods with those of an enterprise that employs labor-intensive processes to produce a consumer non-durable staple good.

5. How does the minimum-investment approach for setting up a business establishment lessen the impact of risk and uncertainty in enterprise? What

are some offsetting disadvantages of such a policy (e.g., a policy of heavy reliance on suppliers)?

6. Identify and briefly explain the nature and scope of the various external influences or impacts on business enterprise.

7. Explain how union bargaining and labor-management agreements in the unionized industries influence non-union fields of business.

8. Explain the nature of the following problems relating to the influence of labor unions on business: (a) the occupational and geographical mobility of labor, (b) hours of work, (c) managerial prerogatives and the benefits of labor participation in the enterprise, (d) company wage policies and labor productivity, and (e) company competitive position.

9. (a) "Unions seek to standardize employment conditions and compensation among producers, thereby attaining more uniform competitive conditions in the industry." Explain and evaluate. (b) Explain when and how industry-wide collective bargaining may favorably or unfavorably influence a firm's competitive position.

10. (a) How do key wage bargains influence pending labor-management bargaining? (b) Analyze a representative union-management agreement in a given industry and show how the various clauses (grievance procedure, seniority, call-in pay, etc.) influence the management of manpower, the wage structure, and the cost pattern.

11. (a) Why do some unions prefer a flat wage rate to a wage-rate range as a method of compensation? (b) How do wage-rate increases in absolute amounts (as compared to percentage amounts) affect occupational-wage differentials and the rate of the long-term increases in the wage scale?

12. (a) How does a union-company unemployment insurance plan tend to induce greater managerial effort for the stabilization of short-term business volume? (b) Select a specific industry in the field of durable-goods output and analyze the problems of introducing the guaranteed annual wage in it.

13. Under what conditions (i.e., situations of cost structure, demand behavior, growth potential, etc.) can a producer adopt a high-wage policy (a wage level somewhat above the market level) without adversely affecting earning power? What may be some advantages of such a policy?

14. (a) What is the attitude of some unions toward technological displacement of labor? What compensation do some unions seek for displaced labor? (b) How would the price elasticity and the income elasticity of demand for an industry's products influence its capabilities for reabsorbing displaced labor? (c) Why is technological displacement less evident during a business upswing or during a period of an industry's steady growth?

15. What are the different policies or economic measures that federal and state governments can pursue to stimulate competition and forestall the emergence of monopolistic trends in business? Explain.

16. What factors would the antitrust agencies take into account in determining whether monopoly in a given enterprise or field of business exceeds legal limits? Explain.

17. Why does the FTC view the basing-point system of pricing as monopolistic and illegal?

18. Explain what is meant by tying contracts and exclusive-dealer contracts. When are such contracts illegal? Explain.

19. When is a merger, whether horizontal or vertical, likely to be held illegal by the antitrust agencies? Explain and illustrate.

20. (*a*) Enumerate the principal tax levies on business enterprise. (*b*) Explain and illustrate what is meant by the tax angle in business decision making. (*c*) How are investment decisions affected by a tax system that undergoes periodic revision as compared to a tax system that is somewhat stable over time?

21. Explain and illustrate the following: (*a*) the shifting of a tax, (*b*) the incidence of a tax, (*c*) the tax inducement of accelerated depreciation, and (*d*) the difference between evading and avoiding taxation.

22. Explain how a relatively high corporate income tax may affect management's willingness to make outlays for research, product remodeling, market promotion, and educational endowments.

23. (*a*) Explain how the ample depletion allowance permitted by the revenue laws in the computation of taxable income serves as a tax inducement to expand the capacity of crude oil production. (*b*) Why will capital-intensive industries characterized by rapidly changing technology benefit more from the use of the accelerated-depreciation method for computing taxable income than labor-intensive industries employing a comparatively stable technology?

24. Explain why high corporate income tax rates may encourage the merging of a parent company and its separately incorporated subsidiaries of different earning power into one over-all corporate structure comprised of branch units rather than subsidiaries.

25. What is the direction (on the buyer or the seller) of the short-run shifting of the excise tax on goods of elastic demand? Explain. On goods of inelastic demand?

26. Would an excise tax on goods of highly elastic demand result in a larger loss of short-run profits in a capital-intensive industry or in a labor-intensive industry? Explain.

27. What may be the effect of the inheritance tax on an unincorporated enterprise or on a "closely held" corporation?

28. (*a*) "Among the tests of a good change in taxation is whether it stimulates production and efficiency, preserves incentives, and avoids penalties on those who innovate or take risks." Explain. (*b*) What are the different requirements of a good tax system so far as business enterprise and industry are concerned? (*c*) Explain how the burden of business taxes (payroll tax, excises, corporate income tax) on a firm can be minimized or partially avoided by such measures as the stabilization of production and employment, greater vertical integration, sale-leaseback arrangement, and adoption of accelerated amortization.

29. Explain why the cyclical sensitivity of a firm in a given line of business depends on such factors as the magnitude of fixed costs, importance of inventories, the diversity of its product line, the elasticity of demand, and the geographical diversity of its market.

30. Explain how inflation affects a firm's profit margin, debt burden, replacement costs, and the market value of its property (land, buildings, inventories, securities). How does deflation affect the foregoing?

31. (*a*) With reference to the shifts in the business cycle that induce a change in business policies, explain cyclically induced policy changes dealing with inventories, consumer credit, equipment replacement, and the type of products that will be emphasized in the product line. (*b*) Describe the behavior of the firm (its decisions and policy changes) during the process of cumulative expansion associated with an upswing in business.

32. (*a*) How may the monetary policy of the Federal Reserve Bank influence the extent to which firms will draw on outside funds for working capital and long-term investment capital? (*b*) Under what cyclical conditions will a drop in the rate of interest have some influence on the level of business investment? (*c*) Will a governmental policy of credit stringency (a tight money policy) equally curb boomtime overexpansion of business (and its attendant inflationary pressure) in both the big corporation and the small firm? Explain.

33. How has governmental price support of raw cotton affected the competitive position of American cotton mills in both foreign and domestic markets?

34. How may currency devaluation affect a firm that produces for export? A firm that depends on imported raw materials?

CHAPTER **10**

Forecasting the Economy
and Business Outlook

Because decision making and policy formulation involve making assumptions regarding future economic developments, business firms as well as governmental bodies find it necessary to project economic trends and to forecast the course of general business activity. The federal government, for instance, attempts to forecast the turn in the business cycle and the trend of national income in order to estimate tax revenue and to formulate monetary and fiscal policy designed to maintain economic stability; state governments formulate programs for highways, education, resource development, and other purposes on the basis of a forecast of economic developments and future tax revenue and of the needs of the community.

Since managerial decisions rest on an estimate of the future, businessmen cannot avoid forecasting to one degree or another. Even when they make no estimate of what lies ahead, businessmen operate under an assumption or an implied forecast that economic conditions will not change enough to affect their business operations. Businessmen generally use short-term (year-to-year) forecasting of economic developments, market demand, and costs, to formulate their operating budget which stipulates the rate of output and projects the earnings for the period. Businessmen use long-range forecasts (projections of two or more years) of business activity and market demand to formulate investment plans for expansion of productive capacity, revision of the product line, and so on; and they project their income flow and appraise the money market in order to draw up their financing plans. In formulating their short- and long-range plans, businessmen thus find it necessary to forecast market demand, prices and costs, and monetary and fiscal policy.

Comprehensive business forecasting for managerial decision making consists of a long-range projection of the trend of the gross national product (GNP) and aggregate demand, a short-term forecast of business conditions (the turn in the cycle), a forecast of industry demand, and a forecast of the company share of the market.

PROJECTING THE LONG-TERM TREND OF GNP

The secular growth of GNP is sometimes projected by merely extrapolating the historical trend of economic growth. Since 1900 the average annual rate of growth in GNP in the American economy has approximated 3.5 per cent; and the average gain in productivity approximated 2 per cent a year. By extrapolating the historical trend, the secular growth of GNP would be projected at the annual rate of 3.5 per cent. A historical projection, however, rests on the assumption that the past trend and pattern of growth will continue. But the future necessarily involves structural changes in the economy and elements that did not exist in the past. The time span of a long-term projection is, of course, limited by our knowledge of the future.

The long-term growth of GNP can be more realistically projected on the basis of economic analysis and an appraisal of the causal factors. Such a secular-growth forecast would be based on an estimate of the growth rate of the labor force in terms of man-hours and on an estimate of the rate of increase in output per man-hour. The long-term trend of GNP would then be projected on the basis of the change in man-hours of employment times the change in productivity per man-hour. But the output per man-hour differs among economic sectors. The same total labor force can yield a different GNP total, depending on the composition of the economic sectors (the sector-mix). A realistic projection of a GNP total must thus be based on an estimate of the future composition of economic sectors (the future distribution of the labor force among the economic sectors). A projected GNP total must, therefore, be broken down into its components and checked for internal consistency.

Because of a high rate of capital formation and rising expenditures for research and technological progress, we may likely see a somewhat higher annual productivity gain (say 2.5 per cent) for the decade of the sixties as compared to the 2 per cent rate of increase in productivity per man-hour from 1900 to 1955.

A projection of the growth rate of the labor force beyond 15 years in the future must take into account the growth rate of population. A forecast of the growth rate of the labor force for a future period of 15 years or less is based on the survival of the existing population plus net immigration (Table 10–1). Thus the nearer term projection of the labor force is primarily based on the birth rate 15 to 20 years earlier. A projection of the size of the labor force must also

TABLE 10-1
Projected Total Labor Force, Annual Averages 1960-65

Age	Total Labor Force (thousands)					
	1960	1961	1962	1963	1964	1965
Total, 14 years and over	73,550	74,752	75,886	77,181	78,412	79,872
14-19 years.	6,215	6,637	6,873	7,114	7,401	7,930
14-17 years. . . .	3,180	3,297	3,430	3,791	4,091	3,997
18-19 years. . . .	3,035	3,340	3,443	3,323	3,310	3,933
20-24 years.	7,570	7,713	7,967	8,386	8,676	8,955
25 years and over. .	59,765	60,402	61,046	61,681	62,335	62,987

	Net Change (thousands)					
	1959-60	1960-61	1961-62	1962-63	1963-64	1964-65
Total, 14 years and over	945	1,202	1,134	1,295	1,231	1,460
14-19 years.	209	422	236	241	287	529
14-17 years. . . .	78	117	133	361	300	− 94
18-19 years. . . .	131	305	103	−120	−13	623
20-24 years.	78	143	254	419	290	279
25 years and over. .	658	637	644	635	654	652

Note: These projections indicate that the number of young workers 14-24 years old will increase by more than 4 million between 1955 and 1965 and by about 5 million in the following 10 years. This sharp rise will occur, despite a small decline in labor force participation rates, because of the large increase taking place during this period in the population of these ages.
Source: U.S. Department of Labor, Bureau of Labor Statistics.

take into account changes in the proportion of the population in the labor force; and a projection of the labor force in terms of man-hours must take into account the trend toward a shorter workweek. The working force in the population for the decade of the sixties, for instance, may be expected to increase at an annual rate of 1.4 per cent. And if we assume a .07 per cent annual reduction in the length of the workweek, this gives us a .07 per cent yearly increase in total man-hours. Thus, if we were to assume for the decade of the sixties a .07 per cent increase in labor force in terms of total man-hours and a 2.5 per cent increase in output per man-hour, the

GNP would rise secularly at an annual rate of 3.2 per cent for the decade. (See Tables 2–5 and 2–6.)

SHORT-TERM FORECASTING OF GNP AND THE BUSINESS OUTLOOK

Since most firms are affected by general business conditions, businessmen usually find it necessary to forecast economic conditions as reflected by the change in the GNP. Effective business planning and operations generally call for a year-to-year forecast of sales volume. The short-term forecast of GNP is usually projected for a year ahead, by quarters. Quarterly forecasts are expressed at annual rates with an adjustment to eliminate the influence of seasonal variations. Short-term forecasting is more valid when it is made within the analytic framework of a projected long-term trend of GNP. A projected trend of GNP aids short-term forecasting by indicating the upper limits of the GNP for the immediate years. The year-to-year forecast of the actual GNP (as distinct from the secular trend of GNP) essentially involves a forecast of the cyclical turn in business activity.

A comprehensive approach to short-term forecasting emphasizes cross-section analysis of the current business situation. Such forecasting uses national income data (essentially the income-expenditure approach) for appraising the current business situation and forecasting the GNP for the immediate year ahead. The estimates and breakdown of national income and output provide the most pertinent data for analyzing short-term business conditions. The national income approach, moreover, provides a framework of analysis for projecting the cyclical pattern of business. For a more complete measurement of economic activity, national-income data can be appropriately supplemented by additional statistical measures of economic activity.

Effective forecasting calls for flexibility and judgment in the use of available national-income data and economic indicators to aid in the analysis and projection of the business cycle (Table 10–2 and Figs. 10–1 and 10–2). Cross-section analysis and forecasting through the income-expenditure approach permit the study of factors influencing the major components of the GNP. Because it emphasizes the causal relations among economic sectors, cross-section analysis contributes to the development of a more accurate forecast of business conditions. The GNP, built up from the size of the labor force (in terms of man-hours) and the rise in productivity, can be broken down into estimates for various sectors of the economy. Cross-sec-

TABLE 10-2

The Nation's Income, Expenditure, and Saving

(billions of dollars)

Economic Group	1959 Year Receipts	1959 Year Expenditures	1959 Year Excess of Receipts (+) or Expenditures (−)	1959 Second Quarter Receipts	1959 Second Quarter Expenditures	1959 Second Quarter Excess of Receipts (+) or Expenditures (−)	1960 First Quarter Receipts	1960 First Quarter Expenditures	1960 First Quarter Excess of Receipts (+) or Expenditures (−)	1960 Second Quarter Receipts	1960 Second Quarter Expenditures	1960 Second Quarter Excess of Receipts (+) or Expenditures (−)
						Seasonally adjusted annual rates						
Consumers												
Disposable personal income	337.3	.....	.....	338.3	.....	.....	347.0	.....	.....	354.1	.....	.....
Personal consumption expenditures	.....	313.8	.....	.....	313.6	.....	.....	323.3	.....	.....	329.0	.....
Personal net saving (+)	.....	.....	23.4	.....	.....	24.8	.....	.....	23.7	.....	.....	25.2
Business												
Gross retained earnings	50.5	.....	.....	51.8	.....	.....	52.5	.....	.....	(1)	.....	.....
Gross private domestic investment	.....	72.0	.....	.....	78.9	.....	.....	79.3	.....	.....	75.5	.....
Excess of investment (−)	.....	.....	−21.6	.....	.....	−27.1	.....	.....	−26.8	.....	.....	(1)
International												
Foreign net transfers by government	1.5	.....	.....	1.4	.....	.....	1.6	.....	.....	1.7	.....	.....
Net exports of goods and services	.....	−1.0	.....	.....	−2.2	.....	.....	1.2	.....	.....	2.0	.....
Excess of transfers (+) or of net exports (−)	.....	.....	2.5	.....	.....	3.6	.....	.....	0.4	.....	.....	−0.3

Government (Federal, State, and local)				
Tax and non-tax receipts or accruals...............	129.1	131.3	137.3	(1)
Less: Transfers, interest, and subsidies (net)........	34.5	34.0	36.0	37.0
Net receipts............	94.6	97.3	101.3	(1)
Total government expenditures..............	131.6	131.7	133.5	135.6
Less: Transfers, interest, and subsidies (net)........	34.5	34.0	36.0	37.0
Purchases of goods and services.............	97.1	97.7	97.5	98.6
Surplus (+) or deficit (−) on income and product account..	−2.5	−0.4	3.9	(1)
Statistical discrepancy.........	−1.8	−1.0	−1.1	(1)
GROSS NATIONAL PRODUCT	482.1	487.9	501.3	505.0

1 Not available

Source: Council of Economic Advisers, Economic Indicators, August 1960 (Washington, D.C.: Government Printing Office, 1960), p. 1.

401

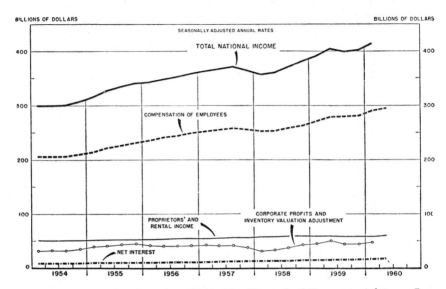

Fig. 10–1. National income, 1954–60. (Council of Economic Advisers, *Economic Indicators, August 1960.* Washington, D.C.: Government Printing Office, 1960, p. 3.)

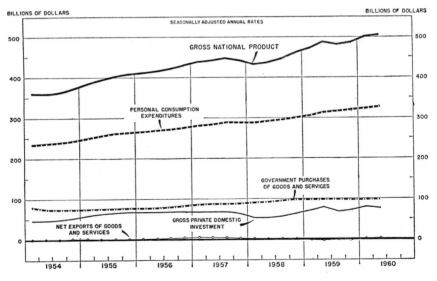

Fig. 10–2. Gross national product or expenditure, 1954–60. (Council of Economic Advisers, *Economic Indicators, August 1960.* Washington, D.C.: Government Printing Office, 1960, p. 2.)

tional income-expenditure analysis, moreover, offers a means of studying business behavior in its more aggregative form.

The national-income-and-product approach to forecasting enables identification of strategic factors (government expenditures, investment in productive facilities and inventories, consumer expenditures) and the derivative factors (profits, retained earnings, personal savings, tax revenues) that determine the level of GNP and affect the course of business. Hence, a forecast of GNP for a year ahead can be built up by estimating expenditures by government, business, foreign buyers, and consumers. A GNP forecast built up of estimates of expenditures by the several components can be cross-checked by a forecast of the future level of production and employment which yields estimates of income flows, including disposable income. In formulating his forecast, an analyst draws on economic data from publications and reports of the Department of Commerce, Department of Labor, the Federal Reserve Bank, Securities and Exchange Commission, National Bureau of Economic Research, National Industrial Conference Board, and other sources.

Governmental Expenditures

The government sector is a major and independent component of the nation's economy. Because governmental purchases are generally not directly related to business conditions, variations in public expenditures can have a significant impact on the level of business activity, particularly during periods of deficit financing. A forecaster must, therefore, estimate and appraise the impact of government expenditures in formulating his forecast of short-term business conditions. A forecaster generally projects annual public expenditures on the basis of the pending fiscal budget. But because some of the appropriations and expenditures are subject to change, a forecaster should break down the budget into logical segments and carefully appraise the larger and more volatile programs (foreign aid, agriculture, housing) for possible congressional revision. Since government outlays for agricultural aid, for instance, tend to be determined by the price level for agricultural products and the surplus disposal program in effect, expenditures for the farm program have been the most volatile phase of civilian spending. With respect to state and local government outlays, the forecaster must take into account the tendency of these public budgets to cut back outlays for public works when the national income is low and to increase expenditures when national income is high. An appraisal of the impact of public-works expenditures and other capital projects should be based on the appropriate lead time.

A forecaster must ascertain the extent to which the current level of business and employment will give rise to either new congressional spending programs or to reductions in taxation; and he must ascertain the extent to which a steady rise in national income and the accompanying automatic rise in tax revenue will lead to more public spending and the extent to which it will lead to a tax cut. A projection of the federal budget several years into the future, however, must be based on the long-term growth in national income, shifts in public notions of governmental responsibility, and the economic feasibility of possible programs. A forecaster gauges the economic impact (particularly the impact on the general price level or inflation) of government spending on the basis of the cash budget rather than the conventional budget. The *cash budget* consists of all receipts and payments to the public, particularly the income and outgo into trust funds of social security, unemployment insurance, highway aid program, veteran's life insurance, which are not reflected in the conventional budget.

Gross Private Domestic Investment

To forecast the short-term level of business, a forecaster must estimate the immediate year's volume of gross private domestic investment (comprised chiefly of outlays for residential construction, plant and equipment, and business inventories), a highly volatile component of the gross national product. (Government construction is included under public expenditures discussed earlier.) Because outlays for erection of plant structures and for producers' facilities stimulate demand for many types of materials and services, variations in gross private investment significantly influence the level of the gross national product and may induce prosperity or recession. Gross private investment influences the level of business and, in turn, is affected by the course of business (Figs. 10–3 and 10–4).

It is largely the interaction of supply and demand for housing which determines the volume of *residential construction*. The long-term demand and supply for housing are prime factors which must be studied in forecasting short-term changes in the volume of residential construction (Figs. 10–5 and 10–6). The existing supply of housing is indicated by the vacancy rate and geographical distribution of dwellings and the size of the adult population (individuals over twenty-one) relative to the number and regional location of dwellings. Among the key factors affecting the demand for dwellings are changes in the rate of family formation, the extent of internal migration, changes in the level of disposable personal income, changes in the intensity of the use of dwellings (the extent of "doubling"),

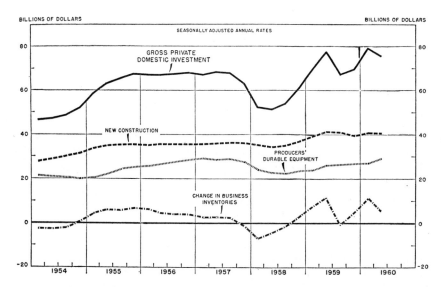

Fig. 10–3. Gross private domestic investment, 1954–60. (Council of Economic Advisers, *Economic Indicators, August 1960*. Washington, D.C.: Government Printing Office, 1960, p. 9.)

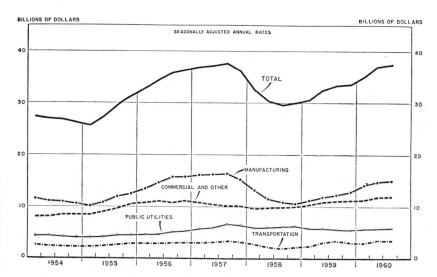

Fig. 10–4. Expenditures for new plant and equipment, 1954–60. (Council of Economic Advisers, *Economic Indicators, August 1960*. Washington, D.C.: Government Printing Office, 1960, p. 10.)

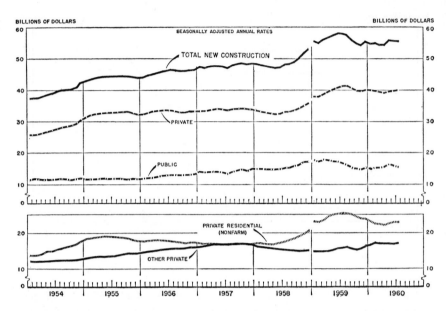

Fig. 10–5. New construction, 1954–60. (Council of Economic Advisers, *Economic Indicators, August 1960.* Washington, D.C.: Government Printing Office, 1960, p. 19.)

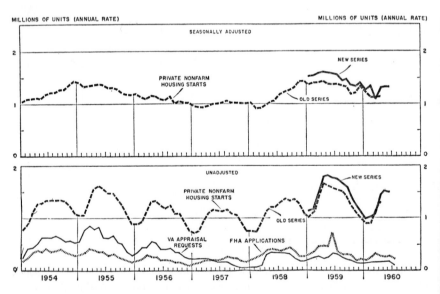

Fig. 10–6. Housing starts and applications for financing, 1954–60. (Council of Economic Advisers, *Economic Indicators, August 1960.* Washington, D.C.: Government Printing Office, 1960, p. 20.)

the cost and the market price of dwellings, and the availability of credit.

The progressive liberalization of credit terms on purchase of homes and a steady rise in disposable personal income stimulate the demand for new houses. For a given level of disposable income, important factors influencing the decision to buy homes are changes in FHA interest rates, size of down payments, and the length of mortgage permissible. Thus a forecast of the volume of residential construction can be made on the basis of a study of the supply and demand factors, including possible changes in the availability of credits, and estimates (building permits and contracts awarded) provided by various private and government publications. Since new construction of residential and business structures involves planning, estimates of the volume may be projected in advance of actual erection. Before housing starts can be more or less accurately forecast, building permit data must be adjusted for incomplete coverage, unused permits, understatement of costs, and so forth.

Business expenditures for productive facilities consist of outlays for plant structures, machinery, and other plant facilities. The long-term business demand for productive facilities is based on, and derives from, the trend of population growth, consumer disposable income, wage levels, innovations, and changes in the capital-output ratio. Within this framework of long-term growth in capital formation, business investment tends to fluctuate cyclically. Because, during a period of low business activity, businessmen tend to postpone equipment replacement and underestimate future demand, output capacity sometimes tends to be inadequate for the ensuing rise in business volume. During an upswing and prosperity, businessmen accelerate the pace of equipment replacement and plant expansion; and if capacity is overextended, businessmen curtail the pace of capital accumulation. A forecaster must therefore gauge the variations in the magnitude of business investment and its effect on the level of GNP and on the general price level.

In estimating the short-term volume of business expenditures, a forecaster must take into account the fact that past patterns in business investment are subject to modification by structural changes in the economy, and he must study any special peculiarities of the current business situation and the impact of government economic policy.

In the absence of a severe economic depression, business expenditures are likely to be somewhat more stable in the years ahead than they were in the past, because of a number of developments. Businessmen, for instance, are aware of the numerous stabilization measures that have been introduced and built into the economy, and they seem assured of the greater tendency of government to mitigate any appreciable drop in business. Bigger and more stable business outlays for industrial research make for a higher and steadier pace of expenditures for product improvement, introduction of new products, revision of productive facilities, and modernization of plant for cost reduction. As compared to past practice, businessmen are inclined to plan their capital outlays on a longer-term basis; their long-range investment programs tend to be somewhat less influenced by short-run changes in sales volume. A high level of business income over a span of a few years and a large annual flow of replacement funds, moreover, augment the volume of internal funds, and with larger cash reserves and improved business liquidity, managers are less prone to sharply cut capital outlays whenever sales drop. Outlays for productive facilities, if not for direct expansion of capacity, would nonetheless tend to be at higher levels because of somewhat greater shifts in the regional distribution of plants and in consumer tastes and because of changes in the product-mix prompted by the introduction of new types of goods.

Since outlays for plant and equipment must be planned in advance, estimates can be made of the volume of such expenditures. A forecaster can make his preliminary estimate on the basis of government and private surveys—surveys by the Department of Commerce, Securities and Exchange Commission, McGraw-Hill, and the National Industrial Conference Board. At the beginning of each year the surveys provide information of planned annual business expenditures which are followed by quarterly reports. The NICB surveys of large manufacturing firms provide data on capital "appropriations" which are more timely and tend to be more firm than "planned" expenditures. To his preliminary estimate of business expenditures, a forecaster adds an estimate of farm expenditures for agricultural machinery and equipment, which he projects on the basis of farm income and past purchases of equipment by farmers. A forecaster follows the development of general business conditions to ascertain realization of business plans for capital expenditures. Business plans for capital outlays are generally more firm for larger programs than for smaller projects. Anticipated expenditures of public utilities are likely to deviate less from actual outlays than the anticipated expenditures of manufacturers and railroads. A forecaster, in the light of his final appraisal of the business outlook, reviews his estimate of business investment. He may find it necessary to revise his figures for consistency with other current developments and his over-all forecast of business activity.

Because *inventory investment* is a highly volatile component of total private investment, it is the most difficult to forecast. Inventory stocks can rise and fall rapidly to accommodate a shift in business conditions (Fig. 10–7; see also Fig. 9–3). Inventory liquidation often accounts for a large part of the contraction in GNP in minor recessions. When businessmen begin to liquidate their inventories, production and employment can fall off markedly, even though final sales are maintained. But when firms add to their inventories, total production and employment rise even faster than total final sales. A forecaster must predict the movement of the over-all inventory level (particularly whether there will be heavy inventory liquidation or sharp inventory buildup) and its impact on the volume of business activity and on the level of GNP.

In deciding whether they will accumulate or liquidate inventory stocks, businessmen take into account the anticipated course of sales, the trend of the general price level, supply condition, need for liquidity, and the availability of credit and the level of interest rates. Thus, businessmen essentially take into account the current and anticipated business conditions in determining their optimum or desired stock-sales ratio.

An inventory imbalance exists when the stock-sales ratio is out of line (is too large or too small) relative to current or anticipated volume of sales. The anticipated course of sales and production largely determines whether businessmen build up or liquidate stocks. They tend, however, to accumulate finished stocks for some time after sales have turned down because they cannot always accurately estimate sales and because they are reluctant to curtail output until they are certain that business will actually fall off in the immediate months ahead. Thus, when inventory stocks become markedly out of balance with the volume and trend of sales, businessmen sooner or later adjust (liquidate or build up) inventory stocks.

An inventory liquidation process or an inventory accumulation process generally takes a number of months before the stock-sales ratio reaches the desired level. A cumulative decline in business volume can prolong an inventory adjustment process. Since an inventory movement lags a number of months (often as much as four months) behind the course of sales, an analyst can forecast the movement of inventories by studying the factors that influence the course of inventory stocks and lead to an eventual inventory correction. To estimate the magnitude of an inventory correction, a forecaster must determine the extent to which the current stock-sales ratio is out of line with a normal stock-sales ratio for the current and anticipated business volume. He does this by reviewing the size of

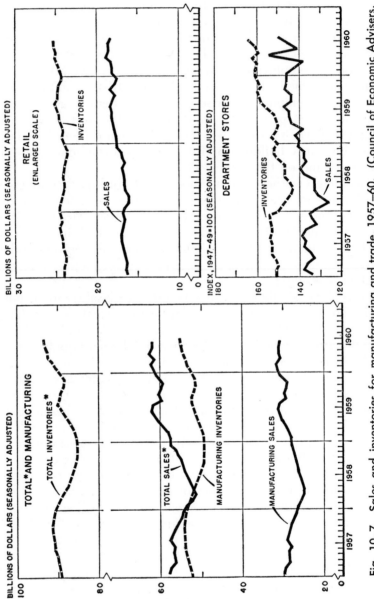

Fig. 10–7. Sales and inventories for manufacturing and trade, 1957–60. (Council of Economic Advisers, *Economic Indicators*, August 1960. Washington, D.C.: Government Printing Office, 1960, p. 21.)

unfilled orders and the probable course of sales, supply conditions, the trend of prices, the availability of bank credit, and so on. A forecaster cross-checks his estimate of the change in inventory investment for consistency with other economic developments on the horizon and with his final conclusions as to the short-term trend in the over-all level of business activity.

To his short-term forecast of gross private domestic investment, a forecaster must add an estimate of the nation's net *foreign investment*. This essentially involves a forecast of the net surplus of exports over imports. A forecaster must appraise and project the prospective changes in exports and imports, and changes in the level of foreign aid. Imports and exports may be projected from recent levels on the basis of an analysis of the factors that are likely to affect the level of prices and demand for items traded internationally. An upswing in business and an anticipated increase in the volume of domestic expenditures would, for example, generate an increase in imports. Exports may, for instance, be expected to decline from recent high levels because previously abnormally strong demand factors may have spent themselves. Exports of manufactured goods may be inclined to level off because of increasing price competition in international markets from countries that have devaluated their currencies or from efficient producers in expanding common-market areas. An anticipated export volume may also reflect changes in the terms of trade. Exports of merchandise, for instance, may begin to decline because of a rise in selling prices. The level of exports also depends on the amount of foreign exchange reserves and gold stocks available to overseas importing countries and their willingness to draw upon these reserves.

Personal Consumption Expenditures

Because consumer expenditures are more or less dependent on the level of over-all business activity, these expenditures are generally best forecast last. Wage and salary compensation (comprising approximately 70 per cent of personal income), is largely determined by the level of aggregate business activity or GNP (Figs. 10–1 and 10–2). A small percentage change in total personal consumption expenditures can have a favorable or an adverse effect upon the course of general business activity.

In projecting short-term consumer expenditures from recent levels, a forecaster ordinarily breaks down such spending into expenditures for durable goods, non-durable goods, and services, and he estimates each category separately. Some segments of consumer

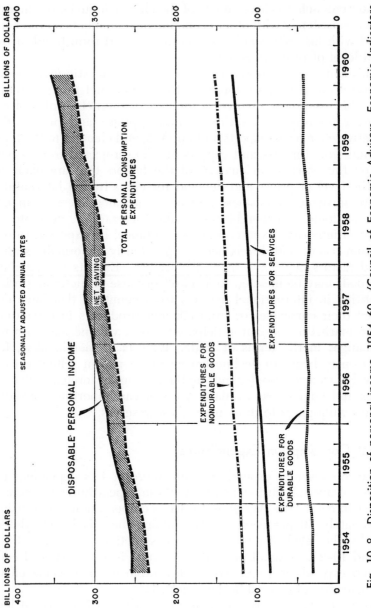

Fig. 10–8. Disposition of personal income, 1954–60. (Council of Economic Advisers, *Economic Indicators*, *August* 1960. Washington, D.C.: Government Printing Office, 1960, p. 6.)

expenditures are comparatively stable, while other segments vary over time. A drop in consumer spending for hard goods is often associated with a shift of expenditures for soft goods and services and for repayment of consumer installment indebtedness. In his estimate of personal consumption expenditures, an analyst should take into account progress made in *surveys of consumer intentions* to buy, such as those conducted by the Survey Research Center of the University of Michigan. Though an analyst may feel that consumer surveys have some predictive value, he will likely note that consumer purchasing behavior is generally affected by developments (employment, business downturn, tax changes, work stoppages) beyond the consumers' ability to foresee or control.

A forecaster may estimate aggregate, as well as each category of, consumer expenditures by projecting from recent levels and by relating spending to disposable income, current levels of and anticipated changes in installment credit, the volume of liquid assets in the hands of consumers, changes in the price level, possible tax cuts, anticipated level of employment, and so on. An economic analyst can forecast the level of transfer payments to individuals (unemployment insurance, old age benefits, and the like) for a given level of unemployment on the basis of the most recent levels, taking into account emergency congressional appropriations in support of social security payments to the public. Income of unincorporated firms and dividend, rental, and interest income to individuals may be initially projected from recent levels and adjusted on the basis of factors in the over-all economic situation that are likely to be influential. Farm-business income may be forecast on the basis of world agricultural output, movement of agricultural prices and farm operating costs, and governmental price support and aid in the agricultural program.

On the basis of the short-term projection of government expenditures, gross private investment, and personal consumption expenditures, a forecaster projects the preliminary forecast of GNP for a year or more.

Checking the Preliminary Short-Term Forecast

An analyst must employ a flexible approach and judgment in checking the accuracy of his preliminary forecast. Through economic analysis he identifies and gauges the impact of special factors in the developing business environment and economic trend. He uses appropriate economic indicators and the circular checking procedure to insure that estimates of the various components of GNP

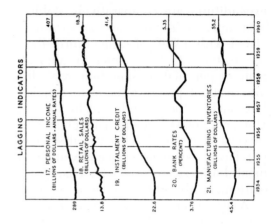

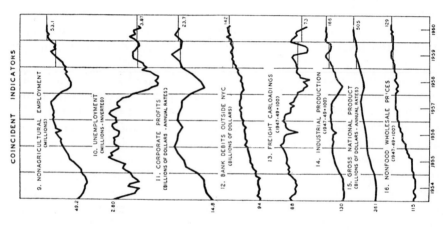

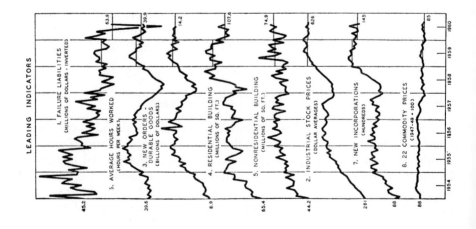

Fig. 10-9. (See next page for caption.)

are consistent with each other. In this process, the analyst essentially subdivides and traces the flow of GNP to check the plausibility of the relationship of his estimates for the various components. When the estimates for some components are out of alignment (too high or too low) with reference to other components, the analyst revises his estimates to arrive at an internally consistent short-term forecast of GNP, a forecast which is economically feasible in terms of the cyclical behavior of business activity and the secular trend of the economy. The analyst, for instance, checks whether the estimated investment for inventories is consistent with consumer expenditures, and whether the forecast outlay for plant and equipment is consistent with the level of unused capacity, level of retained earnings and depreciation funds, and the level of estimated GNP. An analyst can check his estimated consumer expenditures against the disposable personal income which he derives from the forecast GNP by subtracting capital consumption allowances, social security contributions, taxes, and by adding transfer payments and other items. A forecaster may also analyze and project the level of production and of employment in such highly cyclical industries as construction, consumer durables, and plant machinery and equipment to ascertain the impact on other components and on total GNP.

Since forecasting for business purposes involves periodic re-examination of short-term economic projections, business forecasting generally places emphasis on the direction of GNP rather than on the precise magnitude of change in national income. An analyst may check the direction of his estimated GNP by an over-all appraisal of the economic situation aided by economic indicators, including the "lead-lag" series of indicators selected by Geoffrey H. Moore of the National Bureau of Economic Research.

LEAD-LAG INDICATORS. Because they reflect leading, coincident, and lagging business activities in the economic process, the lead-lag indicators are respectively grouped into a *leading* series, a *coincident* series, and a *lagging* series (Fig. 10–9). The three groups of series

---

Fig. 10–9. Major economic indicators: leading, coincident, and lagging series, 1954–60. Except for indicators 2 and 20, all series are seasonally adjusted. Indicators 6, 9, and 16 are on an arithmetic scale because monthly percentage changes are too small to be seen on a ratio scale. All other indicators are on a ratio scale; thus, equal vertical distances measured in the same direction anywhere on the charts represent equal percentage changes. (Statistical Indicator Associates, report of August 31, 1960, North Egremont, Mass.)

are adjusted for seasonal variations. The leading series include new orders for durable goods, wholesale prices of industrial common stocks, number of new incorporations, and liabilities of industrial and commercial business failures. These leading series have historically tended to turn up or down in advance of the general level of business by a number of months. The leading series, however, omit the coverage of the non-durable goods and the service sectors, and they inadequately reflect important economic activities. The periodic occurrence of unusual economic situations and long-term structural changes in the economy, moreover, tend to render obsolete the reliability of the series for predictive purposes.

The leading series are not expected to lead with complete consistency. Changing economic conditions may give rise to erratic fluctuations of the group, and the series may likely point in different directions at the same time. An analyst may be able to tentatively spot the turning points of the leading series group only after a lapse of time. Unless the leading series move in a similar direction and in sufficient magnitude, a preliminary indication of a business turn would be difficult to identify.

The leading series group has tended in the past to point to a change in economic activities as a result of expectations regarding anticipated business conditions. On the basis of economic analysis of each item comprising the leading series, the series would logically be expected to indicate a turn in general business activity. The rate of flow of new orders for producers' durable goods, for instance, indicates the level of business spending for equipment and expansion of plant capacity and the expectations of businessmen regarding the future. The size of the backlog of new orders for aggregate durable goods indicates the movement of demand for these goods, the level of future production and employment in the respective industries, and whether producers in the line of business will build up or reduce their raw material stocks. The movement of wholesale prices for basic commodities is a sensitive indicator which reflects shifts in demand—the markets' estimate of the demand for basic commodities. But it can also partly reflect unanticipated increases in supply. The quantitative change in building contracts projects the level of construction activity in the months ahead and the level of demand for building materials. The impact of changes in demand and sales is often first reflected in the length of the workweek. The change in the average number of hours worked in the manufacturing sector indicates producers' adjustment to anticipated volume of sales and the probable change in the level of inventory stocks. Monthly data from the Department of Labor's Bureau of Labor Statistics on the volume of overtime and overtime as a proportion of average man-hours is an indicator of the course of business activity which con-tributes to the knowledge of cyclical variations in earnings and in-come flow.

Timed with total business activity are the roughly coincident series which are comprised of the GNP, freight carloading, industrial production, corporate profits, unemployment, non-agricultural em-ployment, non-food wholesale prices, and bank debits outside New York City. The lagging series are comprised of personal income, retail sales, manufacturers' inventories, consumer installment credit, and bank rates on business loans.

Because none of the individual series has consistently shown leads and lags in every business cycle, an analyst can achieve best results from a study of the whole series. An analyst should compare the timing of the three groups of series. By a study of the combined timing relationships, an analyst may avoid some of the confusion resulting from erratic movements. A business downturn may be indicated if the leading series begins to decline while the coincident and the lagging series are still rising. The business downturn may be confirmed after a few months if the leading series continues to fall and the coincident group also begins to decline.

FACTOR-LISTING AND OPINION POLLS. An analyst may find it use-ful to compile and check through a list of favorable and unfavorable factors to assure coverage of all relevant aspects in the economic situation that may affect the level of aggregate output, expenditures, and the movement of the general price level. In gauging the busi-ness outlook, he should take note of various private and public sur-veys and opinion polls of general business activity that are prepared on the basis of "expert" judgment of business people and others who make decisions regarding future business expectations. An analyst would periodically assess the reliability of the survey practice em-ployed before he would place much reliance on the results. An analyst would nonetheless find the "survey" business forecasts useful as indicators of psychological expectations.

ECONOMETRIC FORECASTING. The analyst should also follow the progress made in the econometric approach to business forecasting (i.e., in the use of formulas or models of the economic process). The econometric method aims to construct an equation or a system of equations that comprise the set of relationships which describe past economic activity and effectively explain the past movement of busi-ness activity. It uses current and anticipated data as variables in the mathematical model of the economic process to predict the future course of business activity in numerical terms. The econometric method of forecasting is handicapped by the difficulty of reducing the economy's complex operations to a limited number of variables, assumption that a past set of relationships will hold for the future, and inability of a formula to incorporate psychological and special economic factors that often characterize future economic conditions.

THE ROLE OF GOVERNMENTAL STABILIZATION MEASURES. In arriving at his final forecast of GNP and the business outlook, the analyst should gauge the impact of government measures, such as monetary and fiscal measures, economic stabilizers, and other likely programs, on the course of business activity. If his short-term projection points to a boom level of business, the effectiveness of monetary and fiscal measures in restraining excessive expansion should be appraised on the basis of economic and political plausibility. If his short-term projection points to a business downturn, the analyst should estimate the effect on GNP of automatic economic stabilizers, the liberalization of bank credit, and emergency measures to limit a business recession. Since a recession shrinks government revenues and produces a deficit, an analyst notes that a resultant economic stabilizer comes into effect because the government exacts less tax revenue and purchasing power out of the economy than it puts in through public expenditures.

Depending on the magnitude of a downturn, an analyst will anticipate varying degrees of action by the executive branch to accelerate authorized public works and to activate certain expenditure plans that can be started and completed quickly for the desired stimulus to business. Antirecession congressional measures may include temporary federal supplements to unemployment compensation and a federal tax adjustment designed to quickly stimulate business and employment. A "premature" tax cut may be resisted by some legislatures as potentially inflationary, on the grounds that it may sharply increase an existing budget deficit, result in such a sharp upturn in business as to generate excessive inflationary pressures, or be unnecessary for a business revival that will come after a normal inventory adjustment has been consummated. Those who may favor recovery measures other than a tax reduction will likely maintain that a tax cut is an irrevocable step; for, once taxes are reduced, it will be difficult to reimpose them. Thus an analyst will follow the political cross-currents and formulate his detailed short-term business forecast partly on the basis of playing by ear.

FORECASTING THE COMPANY OUTLOOK
AND SALES

Business forecasting provides pertinent economic information which improves the quality of executive judgment and decision making. Because cyclical change in the course of business affects the volume of sales, the cost of input factors, and the level of earnings in practically all lines of business, managers find economic forecasting essential for long- and short-range planning. When executives forecast business conditions and analyze economic developments to gauge the probable effect on sales and costs, they gain time to formulate sales plans and programs designed to minimize any adverse effect on their business should a general economic downturn develop and, conversely, to obtain the maximum sales volume and competitive advantage during periods of expanding business. The sales forecasting problem and the degree of accuracy attainable vary from industry to industry. The importance of business and sales forecasting to a particular firm depends on the nature of its products (e.g., whether consumer non-durables, consumer durables, producers' durable goods), the magnitude of cyclical fluctuations in demand, the extent of diversification, the firm's competitive position, and so on. Rapidly growing industries and firms would obviously find business forecasting crucial and essential for long-range planning.

Most firms find it useful to undertake both short- and long-term sales forecasting. Long-term sales forecasts project the trend of sales for one to five or more years into the future. Such forecasts serve as a basis for long-range investment planning for plant capacity, product innovation, market promotion, and so on. Long-term sales forecasts thus facilitate long-range planning by determining the probable sales revenue and projecting the amount of capital, labor, and materials required for the future level of output. Businessmen who undertake long-range forecasting of future markets can somewhat anticipate shifts in the trend of consumption and competitive conditions and they can formulate somewhat bolder investment programs than businessmen who are inordinately oriented to present markets.

Short-term sales forecasts generally estimate the volume of sales of a future period of three months to a year. Short-term changes in sales stem from seasonal and cyclical movements in demand, changes in the availability of credit, product improvement, advertising, and so on. Businessmen use short-term sales forecasts to prepare the operating budget, schedule production, adjust inventory levels, recruit labor, and estimate revenue.

An analyst typically uses the forecast of general business conditions (discussed earlier) as a first step in his sales-forecasting procedure which may include correlation analysis, an estimate of industry demand and company share, salesmen's estimate of demand, and an appraisal of special factors. These are presented below.

Forecasting Industry Sales

Because market factors and economic trends and indicators apply to the aggregate demand for each type of product, an analyst generally finds it easier first to forecast sales for the entire industry and then to forecast the sales share for his firm. The analyst thus derives an estimate of the firm's sales from a forecast of industry sales. Analysts often find that they can use an economic indicator of general business activity (GNP, personal income, industrial production) to project industry sales. Even though an industry puts out more than one product, an analyst may be able to estimate, on the basis of the forecast of general business activity, the sales of an industry's total product coverage, particularly when the same demand determinants apply more or less to all products. When the demand factors markedly differ for each of the industry's products, an analyst finds it useful to break down the industry's product coverage into homogeneous classes comprised of similar demand characteristics.

The analyst may also employ "end-use" analysis to subdivide the aggregate market for each product class into appropriate market segments. In his end-use analysis, the forecaster may, for instance, study the procurement and inventory practices of consuming industry groups (i.e., the market segments) and the demand determinants for the sales of those industry groups that absorb the product in the further fabrication and output of final products. The market segments for a given class of lumber, for instance, may consist of the demand by the construction industry segment (which may be correlated with building contracts and national income) and by the manufacturing-industry segment (which may be correlated with the industrial production index).

After having logically classified the industry's products into homogeneous groups for forecasting purposes, the analyst may use a statistical method of forecasting. He does this by seeking out a consistent pattern of relationship between the sales of a product class or between the industry's total output (the dependent variable) and one or more measures of aggregate economic activity (e.g., personal income) or an economic factor, such as population growth or family formation (the independent or controlling variable). (See "Consumption-Income Relations" appearing later in the chapter.) The analyst seeks to determine and isolate the factors with which sales of the product have been closely associated in the past and may reliably foretell sales in the future. In many cases several demand factors influence sales. For instance, the major factors that generally influence demand for consumer durable goods include the trend of disposable income, the trend of employment, terms for installment credit, the stock of durable goods in the hands of consumers, and the effectiveness of product improvement or remodeling. Thus by using an appropriate mathematical formula which relates future sales of a product class (or of the industry's total output) to a relevant factor in the national economy (e.g., personal income, freight carloadings, manufacturers' new orders), an analyst relates industry sales to changes in general business activity. The analyst sometimes finds that he can use data on income-elasticity of demand (i.e., the sensitivity of sales to disposable income) to estimate the change in sales.

As his statistical forecasting tool, the analyst thus uses correlation analysis (an estimating equation) to show the relationship between two or more factors. Through correlation analysis the forecaster determines the nature of the relationship between the dependent variable (sales) and one or more independent variables (e.g., economic indicators). For estimating industry sales through correlation analysis, the forecaster may, for example, relate the consumption of paper to population growth, clothing sales to consumer disposable income, the sale of construction materials to building contracts, and the consumption of electricity to residential construction and the index of industrial production.

When only one independent variable is involved, the analyst uses a simple correlation; when two or more variables are involved, the analyst uses multiple correlation. The relationship between two variables may be determined by graphing (which is easier and simpler to comprehend) or by statistical correlation analysis. The effectiveness of his estimating equation depends upon the degree of relationship and on the reliability of the relationship. After selecting the most relevant variable (e.g., an economic indicator) to forecast sales, the analyst can determine the nature of the relationship by the graphing technique or by statistical correlation analysis. The analyst determines the stability and usefulness of a selected relationship by studying the relevant qualitative factors of the past and the future. This may, for instance, involve an appraisal of the extent to which consumer buying habits in the immediate future years may deviate from the past pattern.

When there is considerable difficulty in forecasting the movement of the independent variable (e.g., the index of industrial production), regression analysis merely *shifts the forecasting problem* from the dependent variable (i.e., the forecasting of company sales) to the independent variable. Thus, sales forecasting may be ineffective not only because of a weak correlation but because one forecast depends on other forecasts, which may be equally difficult to make. The forecasting usefulness of an estimating equation (i.e., a given correlation) may be impaired over time by the introduction of new products, changes in consumption patterns, technological developments, and structural changes in the economy. In many cases, however, an analyst can discover a workable correlation for forecasting industry sales. When an analyst can safely use an independent variable (e.g., manufacturers' backlog of orders) that precedes fluctuations in the sale of his products, this lead-lag correlation is particularly useful for forecasting sales.

Forecasting Company Sales and Prospects

If a firm's sales are largely confined to one geographic area, or if a firm puts out highly specialized products, the analyst would find little value in attempting to forecast industry sales. The analyst would forecast company sales through correlation analysis, a study of factors that underlie regional growth in income and economic development and influence sales. When a firm's product line *is* comprised of products sold nationally and classed in two or more industries, the analyst would forecast the sales of the respective industries preliminary to estimating company sales. (Correlation analysis is, of course, not initially applicable for forecasting sales of new products introduced by a firm.)

The analyst forecasts the company share of industry sales by studying the share the firm obtained in past years and, with appropriate adjustments, projecting the trend into the future. He forecasts the company share by appraising possible changes in customer acceptance of the firm's products, the firm's competitive position, introduction of new products, price changes, and company sales policies. The analyst's share-of-the-industry forecast would indicate the ratio of company sales to that of the industry.

The analyst's forecast of the firm's sales may be cross-checked against an estimate of sales made by company salesmen. The latter survey may, in fact, be a well-designed sampling procedure of "customers intentions" conducted by salesmen who, with first-hand knowledge of the market, are able to seek out the needs and buying intentions of distributors, jobbers, and major outlets. Salesmen's estimates would be inadequate if their polling procedures differ, lack coverage, or if salesmen are not grounded in the elementary market factors that affect demand. Moreover, if sales quotas are derived from sales estimates, salesmen may be inclined to understate prospective markets. In compiling the salesmen's estimates of demand for their areas, regional and district managers can reappraise salesmen's polling practice and survey method.

The analyst would reconcile discrepancies in the over-all sales forecast before he submits the results to a top executive committee which reviews the forecast on the basis of their pooled judgment. The analyst's forecast, past trends, estimate of general business conditions, and other data on economic developments may be studied by the executive committee for a reappraisal of the forecast and possible revision on the basis of their knowledge of company plans and intentions, and their long-term familiarity with the peculiarities of the industry. In view of its planned marketing programs and promotion campaigns, the executive committee may recast the sales forecast into a sales goal, stipulating a rise in the company share of the market. The analyst traces current sales and business activity, seeks out the reasons for their deviation from his forecasts, and gauges future business conditions and economic developments in the formulation of his quarterly forecast.

Business managers sometimes find it useful to project a profit-and-loss estimate much in the same manner that they construct a break-even chart. They project total cost on the basis of standard costs, estimates of material prices, and wage rates specified in union contracts; and they project total sales revenue on the basis of anticipated prices, product-mix, and sales volume. Business managers can sometimes forecast sales volume on the basis of the impact of the change in consumer disposable income on the sales volume of a specific product, as is presented in the study below.

CONSUMPTION-INCOME RELATIONS [1]

The consumption-income relations will be viewed in this section through the use of correlation analysis. The relationships presented involve essentially an updating of similar materials published earlier in the *Survey*, particularly to incorporate the revisions which have recently been made in the basic data for the postwar period. Also

[1] Reprinted from: Louis J. Paradiso and Mabel A. Smith, "Consumer Purchasing and Income Patterns." U.S. Department of Commerce, *Survey of Current Business*, vol. 39 (March, 1959): 21–28.

TABLE 10–3

Sensitivity [1] of Personal Consumption Expenditures to Changes in Disposable Personal Income

Group	Prewar	Postwar [2]
Based on Constant (1957) Dollars		
Total personal consumption expenditures	0.8	1.0
Durable goods	2.1	1.2
Non-durable goods	.7	.9
Services	.5	1.0
Automobiles and parts	2.8	1.1
Furniture and household equipment	1.6	1.0
Clothing and shoes	0.9[3]	...
Food and alcoholic beverages	.8[4]	...
Gasoline and oil	.6[3]	...
Household operation	.9	1.5
Housing	.2	1.3
Transportation	1.0	.3
Based on Current Dollars		
Total personal consumption expenditures	0.9	1.0
Durable goods	1.6	1.1
Non-durable goods	.9	1.0
Services	.7	.9
Automobiles and parts	1.9	1.0
New cars and net purchases of used cars	2.1	1.2
Tires, tubes, accessories, and parts	1.3	.7
Furniture and household equipment	1.5	.8
Furniture	1.6	1.0
Kitchen and other household appliances	1.3	.8
China, glassware, tableware, and utensils	.7	.7
Other durable house furnishings	1.4	.4
Radio and television receivers, records and musical instruments	2.5	1.0
Other durable goods	1.4	1.2
Jewelry and watches	1.8	.8
Ophthalmic products and orthopedic appliances	.8	1.3
Books and maps	1.2	1.2
Wheel goods, durable toys, sport equipment, boats, and pleasure aircraft	1.5	1.5
Clothing and shoes	1.0	.5
Shoes and other footwear	.8	.4
Women's and children's clothing and accessories	1.1	.5
Men's and boys' clothing and accessories	1.1	.6
Food and alcoholic beverages	1.0	.8
Food (excluding alcoholic beverages)	1.0	.8
Gasoline and oil	.5	1.6
Tobacco products	.5	.8
Other non-durable goods	.7	1.0
Toilet articles and preparations	.8	1.0
Stationery and writing supplies	1.4	1.2
Fuel and ice	.6	.3
Drug preparations and sundries	.6	1.4
Magazines, newspapers, and sheet music	.5	.9
Non-durable toys and sport supplies	1.0	1.3
Flowers, seeds, and potted plants	1.6	1.0

TABLE 10–3 (*Continued*)

Group	Prewar	Postwar [2]
Household operation	0.6	1.4
Electricity	.2	1.8
Gas	.2	1.8
Water	.2	1.3
Telephone, telegraph, cable, and wireless	.5	1.6
Domestic service	1.3	.6
Other	.6	1.1
Housing	.5	1.4
Personal services	1.0	.6
Cleaning, dyeing, pressing, alteration, storage, and repair of garments (in shops) n.e.c.	1.2	.6
Laundering in establishments	.9	.1
Barber shops, beauty salons, and baths	.8	1.5
Recreation	.8	.9
Radio and television repair	1.1	2.2
Admissions to specified spectator amusements	.8	([5])
Transportation	.9	.9
Automobile repair, greasing, parking, storage, and rental	1.1	1.3
Automobile insurance premiums less claims paid	.6	1.0
Street and electric railway and local bus	.5	([6])
Railway and sleeping and parlor cars	1.4	([6])
Intercity bus	.7	([6])
Airline	n.a.	3.0
Other services	.7	1.5
Physicians	.8	1.1
Dentists	.9	1.4
Other professional services	.8	1.1
Privately controlled hospitals and sanitariums	.3	1.7
Funeral and burial expenses	.7	.7
Personal business	.8	1.7
Private education and research	.6	1.3
Religious and welfare activities	.4	1.0

[1] Based on least squares using equation $C = aI^{\alpha}(1 + r)^t$ for the period 1929–40 and $C = aI^{\alpha}$ for the postwar period where C = personal consumption expenditures, I = disposable personal income, and t = time. The exponent α derived from the data is an approximate measure of the income sensitivity of the expenditure items.

[2] In the case of total goods and services, durable goods, non-durable goods, and services, the sensitivity coefficients in this column were based on the twenties and the postwar period.

[3] Based on period 1929–40 and postwar years including income and time as factors. The postwar relations using income alone give a coefficient of 0.5 for clothing and 2.0 for gasoline.

[4] Based on period 1933–41 and postwar years.

[5] The relation to income was negative from 1947–53. Since then, these expenditures have tended to stabilize.

[6] The postwar relation to income has been negative. In the case of intercity bus transportation, there has been some tendency for the relation to be moderately positive in the most recent years.

SOURCE: U.S. Department of Commerce, Office of Business Economics.

analyses are presented involving Office of Business Economics' new data in constant prices.

Although the analyses will be considered in constant dollars, it should be noted that in certain instances there may be a significant difference from the current dollar relationships, which are of particular interest for marketing.[2] The income-sensitivity coefficients —that is, the response of demand to a 1 per cent change in disposable personal income—are shown in Table 10–3 for the prewar period 1929–40 and for the postwar period, in constant dollars for major groups and in current dollars for more detailed subgroups.

Some summary facts may first be noted:

1. In real terms, total consumer purchases over the long-run period of the twenties and postwar years have shown a close relationship to consumer income; a change of 10 per cent in real income was associated on the average with a change of approximately 10 per cent in real purchases. In periods of sharp cyclical changes in business, a variation of 10 per cent in real income was associated on the average with a change of 8 per cent in real purchases.

2. The response of the major groups—durables, non-durables, and services—to income change over the long-run period of course differs from what occurred in the 1930 depression. The secular tendency has been for real purchases of durable goods to show a moderate upward response relative to income, while for non-durable goods and services the response has been approximately equal—a 1 to 1 association. During swings in the business cycle, however, durable-goods purchases in real terms have responded more intensely, non-durable goods rather moderately, and services have been fairly insensitive to income changes.

3. By subgroups of expenditures, there is a wide diversity of income response in all periods. In addition, purchases of durable goods, particularly automobiles, have shown wide fluctuations, often not directly related to the income flow, in the postwar years.

Consumption-Income Patterns

A re-examination of past relationships provides the basis for some generalizations regarding the over-all consumption-income

---

[2] An important case in point is provided by the services area, where the unusually steep advance in the dollar value of expenditures in the postwar period has reflected primarily a catching-up of the prices of services, which were relatively low at the end of the war, with those of commodities; also noteworthy, long-run changes in consumer outlay for housing differ somewhat from those of other services generally, by reason of the lesser advance of rental rates than of most other service prices.

pattern. The first panel of Figure 10–10 shows this pattern for the years 1920–58 with total consumption and income both in real terms. So far as the entire period since World War I is concerned, expenditures in relation to income show noticeable shifts. Consequently, a single relation or simple expressions such as ratios or linear forms will not account for all of the changes.

The consumption response to income change is considerably different over long periods than during swings in the business cycle. The line of the chart represents a regression fitted to the high-level activity years of the twenties and the postwar years.[3] It may be seen that the points for these 22 years cluster closely about this line—the average departure being about 1 per cent. This relationship indicates that the secular response of consumption to income change in years of rising, high-level economic activity is such that a given per cent change in real income is associated with a closely similar percentage change in consumption.[4]

Two points may be made concerning this relation. First, in periods of brief and relatively small cyclical fluctuations, such as those of 1923–24, 1926–27, 1948–49, and 1953–54, the consumption-income pattern was approximately in line with the secular relationship shown on the chart.

Second, in the sharp cyclical swings of 1929–37 and 1937–38, with large-scale unemployment, the relationship shifted. Both in the pronounced downswing and in the subsequent recovery, consumer demand exhibited a marked lag relative to the income advance.

All three major groups of expenditures show significant differences between the secular and cyclical relationships of consumption to income. This may be seen from the other panels of the chart (Fig. 10–10).

As would be expected, the cyclical response to income change is sharply pronounced in the durable-goods group, much less so in the non-durables, and even less so in the services. The income coefficients are, respectively, 2.1, 0.7, and 0.5.[5]

In the case of durable goods, the cyclical response has been sharp even in periods of relatively small business fluctuations. Such

[3] The equation for this line and all other regressions referred to in subsequent sections are shown in Table 10–5.

[4] As detailed in the September, 1955, *Survey* article, the secular relations represent averages of changes in purchases associated with changes in incomes in periods when incomes were generally in the growth phase. Thus, these and other secular relations presented here are to be interpreted for periods of growth and should not be used to evaluate the response in periods of sizable cyclical movements.

[5] These imply that, other factors being constant, a given change in real income of, say, 10 per cent is associated with a change in the same direction for durables of 21 per cent, non-durables 7 per cent, and services 5 per cent.

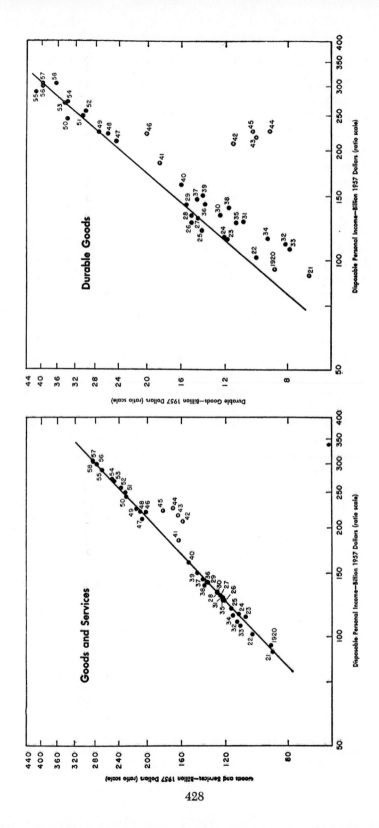

428

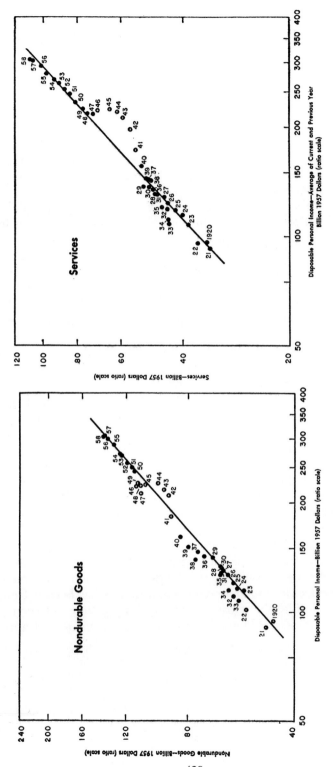

Fig. 10-10. Consumer purchases related to income in constant dollars, 1920-58. (U.S. Department of Commerce, Office of Business Economics.)

429

behavior results from the longer life of these goods and the flexibility of replacement, and from the use of credit as an important element of financing. Consumers are more willing to increase installment debt when income is rising and are more reluctant to incur additional indebtedness when income declines and prospects appear less favorable. Lenders are likewise more agreeable to the process of debt creation in good times. Purchases of non-durable goods and services—much less postponable—have shown a smaller reaction to cyclical changes in income.

Real durable-goods purchases show wide swings around the long-term relation, which at times are autonomous and quite independent of income changes. For example, the Korean war touched off a wave of durable-goods buying in 1950 which brought purchases to a point considerably above the long-term relationship. In the next two years, 1951 and 1952, despite rising incomes but with production restricted, such purchases were cut back severely. Again in 1955, the unusually favorable conditions for automobile purchasing resulted in a bulge in durable-goods buying. In 1956 and 1957, purchases fell back to the long-term line. Finally, they were reduced sharply under the adverse market conditions of 1958 to a point considerably below the long-term relation.

In contrast to the autonomous fluctuations in durable-goods spending, purchases of non-durable goods and services in constant dollars have been closely geared to income changes over the longer period.[6] This simply means that consumers spend a high proportion of their incomes at all times, but are able to supplement them by borrowing to a greater extent under certain conditions of general business than at other times.

In the case of non-durable goods, the most marked deviations from the line of relation occurred in the years 1946–48, which were temporarily high due to the making up of wartime shortages. In all the other years these purchases bore a close proportionate relation to income change. Similarly, the long-term relation between purchases of services and income in constant dollars has been extremely close. Considering the close degree of association between real purchases of non-durable goods and services and income, it appears

[6] For many groups of services, the consumer response to a change in income tends to lag. This is due to the reluctance on the part of consumers to change their habits or status with respect to these services immediately after the change in the income status. Statistically, this aspect of consumer behavior was indicated by obtaining "much closer fits" in the correlations when an average of the current and previous years' income was used as the independent variable (shown in the chart). This, in effect, approximates a 6 months' lag in income relative to current year's purchases.

that variations in such purchases are not sufficient to provide an offset to the wide swings in durable-goods purchases.

Analysis of Special Groups

Data for the 1920's are available only for the three major categories of consumption—durables, non-durables, and services. Therefore, analysis of the response of purchases of the more detailed categories of goods and services to income change under conditions of high level economic activity is confined to the experience of the postwar years alone. For many of these groups, the postwar responses to income change have varied significantly from those in the prewar years. In addition to the basic difference in cyclical characteristics between the two periods, there have been many special influences operating in the postwar years.

It should also be pointed out that there are difficulties involved in analyzing the nature of the postwar patterns since the usual methods utilized in deriving consumption-income relationships may be inapplicable. This arises in large part from the fact that the period has been characterized by a persistent upward movement in total economic activity with only three periods of relatively moderate decline interrupting the advance.

Thus, there is little or no basis for testing empirically the nature of the consumer response under conditions of pronounced cyclical changes. The difficulty is essentially a technical one, namely, that when the usual correlation techniques are applied to variables which have no pronounced cyclical movements, they are not likely to yield cyclical measures of sensitivity, but rather trend associations. Thus, these relationships are limited in their applications and considerable caution should be used in deriving generalizations from them.

The effect of the rather steady rise in the postwar period in consumption of most goods and services on the determination of their response to income change, may be brought out by introducing in the correlation time as a separate independent variable along with real income. The coefficients of income sensitivity thus obtained would be, in most cases, materially different from those derived without the use of the time variable, reflecting the influence of the strong intercorrelation between time and income. Taking into account limitations of the sensitivity coefficients based on income alone, it is, nevertheless, of interest to examine the response of consumption of some of the more important categories of goods and services to income changes.

TABLE 10–4

Real Personal Consumption Expenditures and Disposable Personal Income, 1920–58

(billions of 1957 dollars)

	Personal Consumption Expenditures				Disposable Personal Income
	Total	Durable Goods	Non-durable Goods	Services	
1920	88.9	8.7	46.0	34.2	94.3
1921	88.5	6.9	48.0	33.6	90.9
1922	100.7	9.8	54.7	36.2	101.8
1923	105.6	11.8	55.3	38.5	114.0
1924	110.1	12.1	57.9	40.1	115.7
1925	115.2	14.0	59.1	42.1	120.1
1926	120.8	15.0	61.7	44.1	126.3
1927	123.5	14.3	63.9	45.3	130.0
1928	126.9	15.0	64.1	47.8	132.2
1929	134.8	15.5	67.9	51.4	141.8
1930	126.6	12.4	64.5	49.7	132.8
1931	122.7	10.7	64.3	47.7	127.7
1932	111.6	8.1	59.2	44.3	110.1
1933	109.0	7.9	57.4	43.7	107.4
1934	114.7	9.1	61.2	44.4	114.7
1935	121.8	11.2	64.6	46.0	126.2
1936	134.2	13.7	72.0	48.5	142.1
1937	139.0	14.4	74.5	50.1	146.7
1938	136.6	11.7	75.8	49.1	138.9
1939	144.3	13.9	79.8	50.6	150.5
1940	152.1	16.0	83.5	52.6	160.8
1941	162.2	18.5	89.0	54.7	184.1
1942	158.5	11.4	90.8	56.3	207.6
1943	162.6	9.8	93.7	59.1	216.1
1944	168.4	9.0	97.7	61.7	225.1
1945	180.2	10.2	105.5	64.5	222.7
1946	202.2	20.3	111.9	70.0	220.6
1947	205.7	24.4	109.5	71.8	211.6
1948	209.6	25.7	109.3	74.6	222.4
1949	214.9	27.5	110.6	76.8	225.0
1950	228.1	33.6	113.6	80.9	242.9
1951	229.9	30.5	115.7	83.7	249.2
1952	235.9	29.8	119.6	86.5	256.1
1953	247.3	34.6	123.0	89.7	268.3
1954	250.4	33.9	124.1	92.4	270.4
1955	269.4	41.5	130.4	97.5	287.7
1956	277.5	39.7	135.4	102.4	299.1
1957	284.4	39.9	138.0	106.5	305.1
1958 [1]	283.9	36.5	138.8	108.6	304.3

[1] Preliminary.

SOURCE: U.S. Department of Commerce, Office of Business Economics.

TABLE 10–5

Equations for Consumption-Income Relationships

Major Groups	Long-Term (twenties and postwar)	Prewar (1929–40)
Based on Constant (1957) Dollars [1]		
Goods and services	$C = 1.108\ I^{.969}$	$C = 2.920\ (1.002)^t\ I^{.777}$
Durable goods	$C = 0.0407\ I^{1.203}$	$C = 0.000391\ (0.984)^t\ I^{2.094}$
Non-durable goods	$C = 0.723\ I^{.919}$	$C = 2.197\ (1.012)^t\ I^{.716}$
Services [2]	$C = 0.443\ I^{.956}$	$C = 3.019\ (0.997)^t\ I^{.565}$
Based on Current Dollars [3]		
Goods and services	$C = 1.048\ I^{.979}$	$C = 1.628\ I^{.874}$
Durable goods	$C = 0.0702\ I^{1.113}$	$C = 0.00721\ I^{1.608}$
Non-durable goods	$C = 0.446\ I^{1.013}$	$C = 0.735\ (1.010)^t\ I^{.914}$
Services [2]	$C = 0.538\ I^{.913}$	$C = 1.146\ (0.991)^t\ I^{.729}$

Selected Groups	Postwar	Prewar
Based on Constant (1957) Dollars [1]		
Automobiles and parts	$C = 0.0317\ I^{1.096}$	$C = 0.00000384\ (0.980)^t\ I^{2.819}$
Furniture and household equipment	$C = 0.0759\ I^{.951}$	$C = 0.00197\ (0.988)^t\ I^{1.639}$
Food (excluding alcoholic beverages) [4]	$C = 0.929\ I^{.743}$	....
Clothing and shoes [4]	$C = 0.192\ (0.987)^t\ I^{.887}$	....
Gasoline and oil [4]	$C = 0.198\ (1.031)^t\ I^{.594}$	....
Housing and household operation [3]	$C = 0.0224\ I^{1.354}$	$C = 2.123\ (1.002)^t\ I^{.464}$
All other services [3,4]	$C = 0.626\ I^{.781}$	....

[1] C is real personal consumption expenditures, I is real disposable personal income, both in billions of 1957 dollars, and t is time with 0 at 1940.

[2] In the case of services, the average of current and previous years' income was used.

[3] C is personal consumption expenditures, I is disposable personal income, both in billions of current dollars, and t is time with 0 at 1940.

[4] Both prewar and postwar years were used in this regression.

Analyses involving the use of one factor—consumer income—are not to be considered as complete since other variables affecting demand would have, in some cases, important effects on purchases. Such other factors would be, for example, relative prices of the items, population changes, and substitute and competitive products. Deviations from the income relationship would reflect not only possible shortcomings in the data, but also the effect of the omission of other variables.

Nevertheless, consumption-income relations yield useful—though incomplete—information on the impact of a change in the basic demand factor on consumption. This is so since income often represents by proxy, wholly or in part, the effects of other factors to which it is highly correlated.

AUTOMOBILES HIGHLY VOLATILE. Purchases of automobiles and parts are not closely correlated with short-run fluctuations in real income. Furthermore, in the prewar and postwar periods the responses differed as would be expected with different economic forces operating. In the 1929–40 period of depressed business, the response of purchases of automobiles and parts to a change in income in constant dollars was nearly 3 to 1. This sharp reaction is explained by the ready postponability of such purchases and the reluctance of consumers to buy them in periods of pronounced business declines, while in the subsequent period of upswing automobile purchases are stepped up sharply not only as a result of rising incomes and employment but with the associated willingness of consumers to incur debt.

In the postwar period, aside from the early years when cars were in relatively short supply, autos and parts purchases have shown only a moderate rise in relation to income. However, the year-to-year purchases in relation to income have shown wide swings due to temporary and unusual factors. For example, in 1950 purchases of autos and parts (in constant prices) increased 28 per cent from 1949 whereas the real income rise was only 1 per cent. This sharper rise in purchases of autos and parts reflected, of course, the heavy buying following the outbreak of Korean hostilities. In 1955, due to special factors relating to more favorable credit terms and markedly different styling of cars and other innovations, purchases of automobiles and parts again increased substantially relative to income. Finally, in the 1957–58 period, a drop in automobile purchases of 20 per cent occurred along with a decline in real income of less than 1 per cent.

FURNITURE AND HOUSEHOLD EQUIPMENT. Consumer purchases of furniture and household equipment in constant dollars have shown a closer degree of association with real purchasing power in both the prewar and postwar periods than has been the case with automobiles and parts. In the postwar period the income sensitivity of the furniture and household equipment group was less than in the prewar years of cyclical variability. Special factors affecting these purchases in the past decade or so included the making up of the large wartime deficits in houses, and hence furnishings, and the large increase in the birth rate and in family formation. Thus, it should not be concluded that the relation to income thus observed will persist in the future.

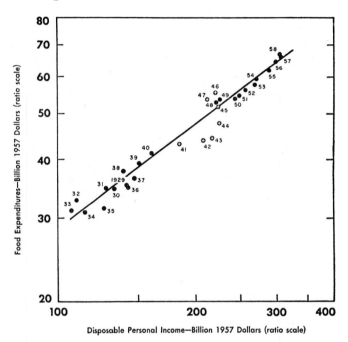

Fig. 10–11. Food expenditures (excluding alcoholic beverages) related to income in constant dollars. (U.S. Department of Commerce, Office of Business Economics.)

FOOD PURCHASES. Food purchases in the 1957–58 recession were maintained in high volume, and due to higher food prices, dollar expenditures for food reached new peaks. Figure 10–11 shows real food expenditures (excluding alcoholic beverages) tend to rise, over the long run, with increases in real incomes. However, in certain periods the income relation has been affected materially by the available supplies of food.

The positive relation shown by these purchases to income—on the average 7 per cent more real food purchases were made for every 10 per cent increase in real income [7]—is partly explained by the increasing consumer preference over the years for higher quality

[7] Approximately this same response holds when food purchases and real income are correlated on a per capita basis.

and more highly processed foods, including the frozen food lines. The question of what is a "real" change here as elsewhere is often a difficult one, and in fact has to be constantly borne in mind when speaking of changes in real consumption or real income over time.

Actually, consumer current-dollar expenditures for food as a per cent of income have tended to vary within a narrow range—22 to 24 per cent. The ratio fell outside this range only during the war and the period immediately thereafter. In the last 4 years the food expenditure-income ratio has been around 22 per cent.

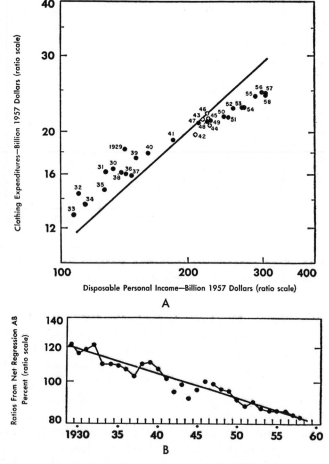

Fig. 10–12. Differential trends of consumer expenditures relative to income: clothing and shoes expenditures in constant dollars. (A) Expenditures are moderately sensitive to income change. (B) Even after allowance is made for income effects, the trend in clothing purchases is seen to have been declining. (U.S. Department of Commerce, Office of Business Economics.)

RELATIVE DECLINE IN CLOTHING AND SHOES. Clothing purchases relative to income have shown a persistent decline over a long period (Fig. 10–12). A relationship based on the experience from 1929 to 1958, excluding the war years, indicates that consumers purchase on the average 9 per cent more clothing and shoes for every 10 per cent increase in real income, other factors assumed unchanged. However, actual purchases have been lower than is implied by the income relation alone due to the effect of other factors which have produced a steadily declining trend in real clothing purchases relative to income.

This loss has averaged 1.3 per cent per year. The upper panel of the clothing chart shows the basic response of clothing expenditures to income change, expressed in constant dollars, while the lower panel shows the steady reduction in such purchases over the years, obtained after making allowance for the effect of real income on these purchases—i.e., dividing the actual purchases by the values from the income line of relationship.[8] The final variations shown about the trend line in the lower panel are relatively small —for the entire period of years, the average deviation from the total relationship being 2 per cent, with the largest deviation of less than 5 per cent occurring in 1937.

GASOLINE AND OIL UP. Purchases of gasoline and oil illustrate a tendency quite the reverse of that for clothing and shoes. Figure 10–13 portrays the basic relationship involved. As is shown in the left panel, there is a somewhat lower response of these purchases to income change than is the case for clothing. Here the relation indicates that, other factors being equal, for every 10 per cent change in real income there is associated a 6 per cent change in real purchases of gasoline and oil—a rather modest response.

However, other factors have resulted in a strong upward trend in these purchases, after taking into account the income influence. As shown in the right panel, the rate of increase in gasoline purchases has averaged 3 per cent per year, after allowance for income

[8] Note that this is a multiplicative relation. The lines on the chart represent the different parts of this formula. To obtain a calculated value of clothing and shoe purchases the corresponding readings from the two lines are to be multiplied.

The use of this relationship may be illustrated as follows: Real income increased 37 per cent from 1948 to 1958. As a result of this factor alone the relationship implies (indicated from the line in the upper panel) that clothing and shoe purchases should have increased 33 per cent. Over this 10-year period, however, factors which had a deterrent effect on the purchase of clothing and shoes resulted in a cumulative loss of 12 per cent (indicated from the line in the lower panel). Thus, combining these effects of the two factors yields an expected increase in purchases of 17 per cent. This compares with the increase of 15 per cent in actual purchases, the small difference being due to the error of estimate.

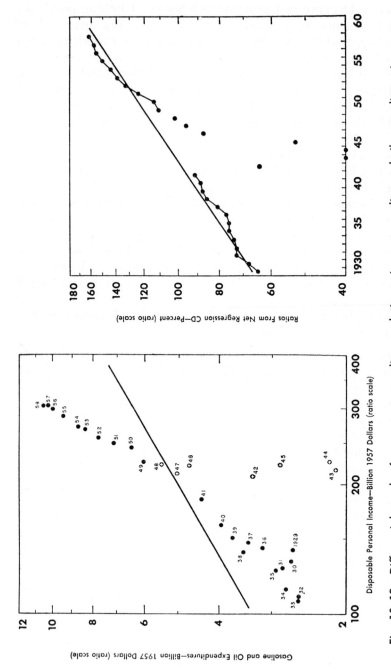

Fig. 10–13. Differential trends of consumer expenditures relative to income: gasoline and oil expenditures in constant dollars. (*Left*) Expenditures are not quite so sensitive to income change. (*Right*) The net trend in gasoline purchases is upward. (U.S. Department of Commerce, Office of Business Economics.)

change. It is this strong uptrend which has accounted for continued increases in purchases of gasoline and oil during recessionary periods of the postwar years as well as in the thirties—at times when incomes dropped. In the 1957–58 recession, for example, real purchases of gasoline and oil increased 3 per cent although real income declined fractionally.

HOUSING AND HOUSEHOLD OPERATION. As indicated earlier, consumer purchases of services in constant prices have comprised an approximately steady share of total real consumption over the long run. Because of price differentials between services and all consumer items, the relation is less close in current dollars. Within various groups, consumers have used considerable discretion in the types of services purchased, so that divergent trends are apparent.

Perhaps the most striking expansion in the major groups of services purchased occurred in the categories of housing and household operation as shown in Figure 10–14. In the 1929–40 depression period these services [9] showed only a moderate response to income change—for example, a 10 per cent change in real income was associated, on the average, with a 5 per cent change in real purchases.[10] The great expansion in population, the steady increase in number of families and households, the increasing tendency toward home ownership and other factors resulted in almost a basically new market in the postwar period. Since 1947 these purchases have increased on an average of 14 per cent for each 10 per cent rise in real income.

Within the household operation group, nearly all major components have shown strong growth. For example, in the past 10 years the average annual rate of increase of expenditures for utilities—electricity, gas, and telephone—has been in each case about 10 per cent. Purchases of these utilities have been accelerated by the large postwar growth in home electrical appliances, in the use of gas for heating, and the increase in the number of telephones. Purchases of domestic service have followed a contrary course, showing a general downdrift in the postwar period due in part to the easing of the burden of household work through the use of home appliances and in part to the limited availability of household help.

Since housing and household operation expenditures comprise almost half of the total purchases of services, they contribute im-

[9] These include the following major categories: Rental value of owner- and tenant-occupied dwellings, electricity, gas, water, telephone, domestic service, and radio and television repair.

[10] As in the case of total services, the average of the income of the previous and the current year was used to explain the demand for these services.

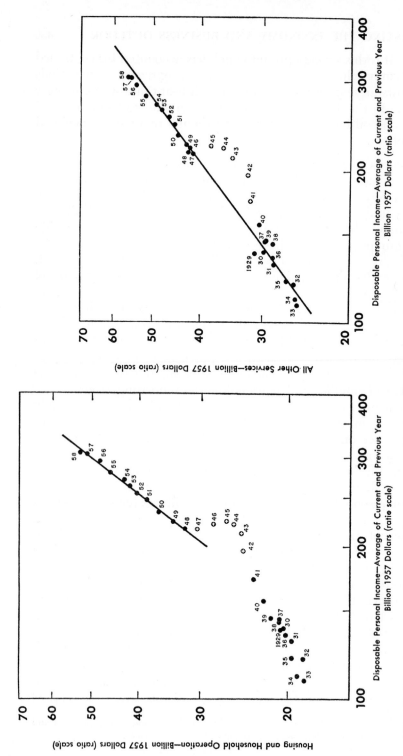

Fig. 10–14. Consumer expenditures for services in constant dollars related to income, 1929–58. (*Left*) Services purchased for housing and household operation in relation to income change have shown a marked shift from prewar to postwar. (*Right*) However, the purchase of all other services has shown a rather constant relation to income. (U.S. Department of Commerce, Office of Business Economics.)

portantly to the strong long-term growth of total services in the postwar period in line with the advance in income. When these two groups are excluded from the total services, the resulting series shows a notably stable relation to income in both the pre-war and postwar years. In both periods a change of 10 per cent in real income, for example, was accompanied on the average by a change of 8 per cent in purchases of services other than housing and household operation.

The movements within this "all other" services group, however, have reflected contrasting trends and differential responses to income changes. For example, real purchases of recreation services have fluctuated within a very narrow range in the postwar years. The fact that this group did not rise in line with income in the postwar period was due to sharp reductions in admissions to movies, theatres, and spectator sports. The decline in admissions has its counterpart in the substantial increase in consumer purchases of repairs of radio and television sets. Recreational services other than admissions maintained the same rising relationship to real income as in the prewar period.

QUESTIONS FOR REVIEW AND APPLICATION

1. What are the specific objectives of business forecasting?
2. Explain the general procedure for forecasting the business outlook and the industry and company outlook.
3. When (in what cyclical phase) will the projected trend of GNP be useful for forecasting actual GNP? Explain.
4. What is the income-expenditure approach for estimating the turn in GNP?
5. What is the distinction between the government's administrative budget and its cash budget?
6. Explain why business forecasting depends more on the direction of the change in GNP rather than on the level of GNP or on the actual change in the magnitude of GNP.
7. (a) Explain what is meant by lead-lag series in economic forecasting. (b) Illustrate how a lead-lag series may be used for forecasting industry sales. (c) When and how may correlation analysis be used in forecasting industry sales?
8. What are the weaknesses in the "factor-listing" approach to economic forecasting?
9. Contrast the problem of forecasting industry demand for early-stage producers with that of forecasting industry demand for final-stage producers.
10. Explain why a survey of intentions of business-buyers (survey of antici-pated capital expenditures) would tend to be more reliable than a survey of intentions of consumer-buyers of durable goods.
11. What are the factors that must be considered in forecasting the total demand for capital goods (i.e., in estimating business capital expenditures)?

12. In what industries (or lines of business) or under what conditions could historical data be of value in estimating sales? Explain.

13. In what industries and in what cyclical phase may industry sales move against (opposite to) the change in GNP?

14. What are the advantages of computing economic trends and comparisons in terms of per capita and deflated data? Illustrate.

15. (a) For what lines of business is a forecast of consumer disposable income particularly useful? (b) Explain what is meant by "income sensitivity of consumer expenditures." (c) Explain the arithmetic computation of the income sensitivity of consumer expenditures to show income-elasticity of demand.

16. Why is it more difficult to forecast sales of consumer durable goods than it is to forecast sales of consumer perishable goods?

17. Why will a firm's market-share forecast tend to be more accurate for a pure oligopoly than for a differentiated oligopoly?

18. When may estimated sales in certain regional markets depart from the anticipated change in over-all GNP?

19. Under what kind of market-demand conditions will a forecaster find it necessary to estimate sales by market segments? Illustrate.

20. In what way can opinion-polling of key executives improve a forecaster's estimate of company sales? For instance, will managerial plans for the marketing program and for price adjustments be a factor in estimating sales potential?

21. (a) Why is it necessary to forecast wage rates and the price of raw materials in order to forecast profits? (b) How may the break-even chart be used in forecasting profits? (c) Explain how and when a projected profit-and-loss statement may produce a good spot projection of earnings.

22. Why is a profit forecast and an estimate of the supply and cost of funds necessary for company long-range investment planning?

CHAPTER 11

Long-Range Planning
and Capital Budgeting

Economic growth essentially depends upon the development and expansion of business firms. Investment in productive and distributive facilities introduces the latest technological improvements and expands and adapts capacity to growth and shifts in demand. Because business investment expands capacity for the output of particular products and restructures productive enterprise, it determines the direction of capital formation and economic growth. It is primarily through long-range planning and adjustment of business enterprise to market forces that executive managers carry out their primary function of capital formation and development of productive establishments which determine the current and future use of resources in the output of goods and services. But long-range business planning is no simple undertaking. Executives find that there are certain inherent limitations to long-term planning—for instance, the basic uncertainty of the future, the human inability to forecast accurately, the tendency toward rigidity in the thinking of managerial personnel, and the time and expense required for developing long-term plans and programs.

When business managers do not formulate long-range plans to direct their enterprise, or when their planning approach is ineffective, the firm's development is uncertain and progress is impeded because of the absence of clearly defined managerial goals, the absence of adequate forecasting of business conditions, and the absence of well-conceived capital-expenditure programs whereby the enterprise is enlarged and adapted to changes and growth in market demand and shifts in technological developments. Failure to plan on a long-term basis means that current decisions would tend to be made within the context of short-term considerations.

Executives cannot avoid decision making that revises the long-term structural aspects of their enterprise. Managers cannot decide not to plan. The problem is essentially how to plan—through analysis and foresight or through improvisation under the pressure of temporary circumstances. By means of long-range planning, executives not only reduce the number of piecemeal, *ad hoc* solutions to business problems but insure that current decisions do not jeopardize the development of a desirable growth pattern for the enterprise. The growth and profitability of the firm largely depend upon the wisdom and effectiveness with which managers formulate long-term goals and plan and direct capital expenditures. Though businessmen find that they are forced to plan because of the uncertainty of the future, changing technology, and the need for profitable growth, the basic appeal of long-range planning itself partly accounts for its growing popularity.

PROCESS OF LONG-RANGE PLANNING AND DECISION MAKING

Long-range managerial planning essentially consists of the efforts of top executives to plan the firm's major moves three to five or more years in the future. In the process of planning, executives set goals, carefully determine the course of action, and then formulate a program designed to attain the goals. More precisely, long-range planning is the process whereby top management (1) selects an appropriate planning period, (2) determines its long-term goals, (3) clarifies the planning premises and compiles forecasting and other pertinent data, (4) develops the most profitable course of action and direction of the program and estimates the financial requirements, (5) seeks out alternative approaches or plans for attaining specific objectives, and (6) selects from among the alternatives those specific plans and capital projects which most profitably contribute to, and effectively integrate with, the over-all program.

The Planning Framework: Premises and Objectives

Executive managers develop their long-range program on the basis of certain planning premises or assumptions. To state it more fully, their *planning frame of reference* consists of a comprehensive knowledge of the structure and the economic behavior of the industry and the firm, a knowledge of the influence of external factors on their business, the recognition of the influence of past planning on the enterprise, a forecast of business conditions and clarification of desired business goals, and the application of appropriate economic concepts for analysis and formulation of the long-range program. These factors, which basically make up the framework of planning, warrant more precise definition.

If they are to effectively plan and guide the long-term development of their enterprise, top executives must have intimate knowledge of the structure of their industry and firm and insight into the behavior and role of their enterprise in the economy. Because of structural and behavioral differences among industries, the nature and magnitude of long-range planning obviously differ for each line of business. The relative ease (and success) in long-range planning partially depends on such factors as the complexity of the product and process, the pace of technological change, the volatility of demand, and the lead-time required for developing new products or remodeling old products and for expanding productive capacity.

Business planners must have a keen grasp of the external factors that bear on the long-range planning and operations of the company. The patent importance of this can readily be indicated: The industry's market structure and the plans and intentions of competitors influence the nature and direction of a firm's plans. Long-term shifts in market demand, too, influence the direction of company planning. Innovations in terms of new products, materials, and productive processes influence the pace of obsolescence and the extent to which innovations will be introduced. Governmental monetary and tax policies and union goals and policies likewise influence the direction of business planning and investment. For a comprehensive discussion, see Chapter 9, Impact of Environment on Business.

Executive managers well know that since long- and short-term plans are interdependent, the objectives of one tend to become the premises for the planning of the other and that past business planning influences the direction of future policy and programs. Because capital investments create built-in production and organization features that extend over many years, such projects influence the long-term pattern and future of the business. The results of past planning and investment thus tend to condition what the firm will do or can feasibly carry out in the future. Short-sighted past planning may have directed a firm into comparatively stagnant lines of business, whereas forward-looking past planning and investment would have put the firm into growing industries and supplied present managers with a sizable flow of earnings available for future growth. Because previous planning may have wisely emphasized long-run profit maximization (in contrast to immediate profit maximization), the firm may have gained a strategic economic and competitive position with respect to future growth and profit prospects.

Attainment of profitable capital expenditures depends on effective business forecasting for the formulation of the over-all program. In addition to forecasting sales volume, estimates must be made to determine market acceptance of new products, kind of processing technology to adopt, input prices of materials and labor, distribution methods that would be profitable to adopt, and competitive intentions of rival producers.

The initial step in the planning process is the determination and clarification of company objectives or business goals. In general, businessmen typically seek to maximize profits. But, at times, they forego realization of maximum profits when they strive to increase their market share and build business empires, or strive for company prestige or the maintenance of management's position. In order to protect their position of authority or income, for instance, managers at times follow a conservative path and pass up profit opportunities—that is, they are sometimes disinclined to assume even the normal risks involved in gaining a bigger increment to profits. For a presentation of a rational planning process, however, we must assume that the businessman always seeks to maximize long-run profits. This would seem generally to be the case for most firms most of the time.

To be meaningful, pragmatic planning must be directed toward certain definite and obtainable goals. Specific business objectives serve to indicate where emphasis is to be placed and stipulate what is to be accomplished. In concrete business terms, long-range planning involves the selection and stipulation of desired goals in such terms as the line of products to put out, sales volume or market share, target rate of return on investment (profit level), and the formulation of a detailed over-all program to reach these goals.

The Planning Period

Executive managers develop their long-range plan and investment program for a logical planning period. A firm's planning interval is basically the time span or horizon over which its major capital projects (those with the longest lead-time) can be formulated and brought to fruition. The factors that largely determine the lead-time required for major capital projects include the complexity of the product and process, the degree of specialization of facilities, and the capital intensiveness of production (i.e., the size of the capital commitment).

Executives elect an appropriate planning period for the preparation and implementation of their long-range programs not only on the basis of the lead-time required to prepare and implement their over-all program, but on the distance into the future they can forecast with a reasonable degree of reliability. The planning horizon for a firm in a given industry thus partly depends on the reliability with which managers can estimate future demand, prices, and costs. Though the future is always uncertain, the degree of uncertainty varies markedly for different fields of production, markets, and geographical areas. Periods of business instability or contraction tend to compel businessmen to assume a shorter planning period than they would like. Whenever feasible, planners design the main outlines of the firm's long-term development program to fit the broader trends (the secular pattern) rather than the shorter cyclic swings of business.

The investment-planning period obviously differs for each industry. Firms in the field of utilities, for instance, are often able to project and plan productive capacity five to ten years ahead because of the relative stability of their sales, the upward secular trend of demand, the regional stability of their market area, and the relative absence of competing substitute services or products. The investment-planning period for a firm in the chemical or metallurgical fields of business is typically longer than for a firm in the field of food processing or similar light manufacture. Firms in the latter fields or in the distributive fields can realistically and profitably plan for a shorter time span because they are able to more quickly erect plant and install equipment. At times, they can provide for additional capacity by purchasing standard makes of equipment and installing the facilities in plant acquired by lease.

Though the long-range planning period can be broken down into subperiods for the constituent plans in the over-all program (i.e., a different horizon for each type of project), all specific plans and capital projects must, nonetheless, be integrated and coordinated in the time horizon of the over-all long-range program.

Planners strive to project their programs as far into the future as it is useful to plan, but no further than it is possible to plan realistically with the desired degree of precision. Many firms are likely to find that they can plan three or more years in advance. Where a series of planning periods or horizons are feasible, the shorter periods would certainly permit a greater measure of clarity and precision. Executives will find it of little value to plan so far into the future when it will have little or no influence on nearer term decisions. Whereas planning far in advance becomes too nebulous for developing supporting plans (well-specified derivative plans related to major projects), an excessively short planning period comes too close to the needs of current business operations, does not allow sufficient time to seek out lucrative profit opportunities, and cramps adequate consideration of alternative plans and adequate evaluation of the over-all long-range program. A company's long-range program, incidentally, may be defined as a group of related specific plans and expenditure proposals covering a well-defined, integrated over-all plan designed to attain clearly specified long-term goals.

DEVELOPMENT AND DESIGN OF THE LONG-RANGE PROGRAM

Of all their managerial problems, businessmen find the problem of formulating a profitable program for long-term investment the most complex and time-consuming. Business investment is a crucial and difficult problem primarily because of its long-term nature. Capital outlays for specialized facilities and operating organization involve a long-term commitment of resources in a given direction for the output of specialized products, often in the face of an uncertain future. The direction of capital outlays and the choice of investment projections from among alternatives not only influence near-term profitability but determine the character of the firm's long-term business operations and competitive position.

On the basis of their long-term projection of business conditions, and on other premises, top executives determine the major course of action and formulate a long-range program comprised of specific plans and capital projects. When there are alternative projections of the business future and economic conditions, planners often can, within limits, prepare a flexible short-term plan which can be modified or converted into one of two or more long-term courses of action that best meet future business conditions. Because of the uncertainty of the future and the inability to reliably forecast long-term economic conditions for many lines of business, executives strive to prepare flexible plans and capital budgets in order to reduce risk in investment. The flexibility of a program, or plan, depends on the program's capacity to modify a course of action without sacrifice of an economical approach to investment or its capacity to change a plan without serious financial loss. The longer the lead-time required and the heavier the commitment of capital, usually the less flexible is the long-range program. Adaptability in programing is crucial, notably when specialized, capital-intensive facilities are involved, financing is an important consideration, and the amount of internal funds (retained earnings) that will be generated is difficult to predict with reliability. Executives can often shorten somewhat the lead-time of their development program and gain greater flexibility in planning through the use of an expeditious planning procedure and through the dovetailing or telescoping of projects—i.e., through the concurrent or simultaneous designing and implementation of a group of related projects.

Effective, adaptable long-range planning emphasizes open end or progressive planning, that is, one based on a moving forecast, say, four years in advance. As the long-range over-all plan unfolds and moves ahead into the next year or period, planners forecast an additional year and review and revise the program in the light of new developments and then again project a four-year plan. Thus, each year executives review the remaining three years of the over-all program and add a fourth year, so that a projected four-year plan is always available to direct long-term investment. Planners must periodically review their estimates of the future and re-examine and adjust their plans in the light of a fresh appraisal of the future. Unanticipated shifts in business conditions, for instance, may call for an acceleration of the program or, conversely, a stretchout and a cutback stipulating the elimination of some marginal projects; or business conditions may require the revision of specific plans and projects that call for a reallocation of funds.

The uncovering of profitable investment opportunities depends on the initiative and imagination not only of the top levels of management but on the individuals in other areas of company organization. Proposals and specific plans for profitable capital expenditures could come from research directors, market and sales analysts, production engineers, plant managers, and others. In the well-managed firms, lower echelons of the organization generally produce a steady flow of plans and investment proposals covering, for example, equipment replacement, elimination of production bottle-necks, and adoption of lower-priced materials. Because the fields and *opportunities for profitable investment differ among industries,* economic analysis for long-range planning must be directed and adapted to the development trends and problems that characterize each industry. Early-stage industries, for instance, generally uncover good profit opportunities through a search for cheaper types of materials and lower-cost processing techniques. Consumer-goods industries generally find good profit prospects in the field of product development and improvement and in the designing of a more efficient distribution system, as well as through production economies. Rapidly growing industries would tend to discover good profit opportunities in the development of low-cost capacity and in the steady transition to a more mass-production type of technology.

If they are to develop a profitable long-range program and improve their competitive position, executives must correctly determine the firm's areas of strength and areas of weakness; and they must take into account their competitors' areas of strength and weakness, as well as what their rivals are likely to do. Planners generally find that they must break down and analyze their over-all scope of business in order to seek out those factors that are central or strategic to the solution of the investment problem and the formulation of the over-all plan. Executives will generally find that they need not review every facet of the problem. The neglect of the less important aspects through oversight is less damaging than the risk involved in the delay of decision making and in the initiation of a specific plan of action. Since the central managerial problem is usually the need to provide adequate, more efficient productive capacity to put out the type of goods demanded by the market, the formulation of the long-range program generally evolves from an analysis of the product line, a market survey for the improvement or development of new products, a survey of opportunities to introduce laborsaving or capital-saving facilities, and so forth.

The core of a firm's over-all plan often includes two or more integrated major projects, coordinated in a long-range program. Interrelated plans must be consistent with each other as well as fundamentally contribute to the realization of the long-term goals. In developing the major course of action, executives carefully formulate short-term plans that effectively integrate within the scope of the long-range program, and they develop the necessary derivative plans to round out the program properly. In the hierarchy of plans that make up the over-all program, the more specific proposals and plans will be subordinate to and will develop within the limits of the broader controlling plans.

BUDGETING OF CAPITAL INVESTMENT

Executives increase earning power not only through the process of long-range planning but through the application of the economic principles and concepts that attain profitable capital investment in business. In well-managed firms, executives employ the capital budget to plan the investment of funds for maximum economic advantage in the fulfillment of their long-range program. Through capital budgeting executives allocate funds among competing investment proposals on the basis of relative profitability and contribution to the attainment of company goals. Capital budgeting, an integral part of long-range programing, essentially reflects the ability and logic of managerial planning. In the absence of capital budgeting, outlays for each capital project would be made at different times and without benefit of over-all review on the basis of comparative profitability of all investment opportunities for a given period, and often without review of outlays for consistency with long-term goals.

Process of Capital Budgeting

A sound capital-budgeting procedure compels those who propose investment projects not only to seek out profit opportunities but to make careful estimates of the relevant cost and revenue factors for the computation of a correct profit return on the capital required for a project. Such budgeting enables executives (1) to evaluate investment proposals against competing profit opportunities, (2) to assign priorities to capital projects in line with the firm's limited financial resources, and (3) to obtain over-all control on capital investments. Thus, when the budgeting of capital is based on a well-designed procedure for discovering profit opportunities and for marshaling, screening, and selecting investment projects, it serves as a primary means of directing the firm into lucrative fields of business.

Sound capital budgeting is primarily a product of forward-looking management. A firm under good management is constantly forecasting and reviewing its sales position by product lines and seeking ways to improve earnings, competitive position, and market share. As earlier indicated, the preparation of a capital budget for a future period begins with a compilation of investment proposals which originate in both upper and lower levels of management and in various parts of the company organization. Capital projects are generally conceived by individuals who are closest to and primarily interested in particular operations and investment fields. The discovery of good profit opportunities often involves a search for alternatives in the attainment of a specific goal—for example, cost reduction through plant modernization or through product simplification. In place of the search for the best alternative, management is sometimes compelled to seek a satisfactory alternative—one that achieves the desired objective while at the same time satisfying certain limiting conditions. Management, too, must consider the consequences that are attached to each alternative. The consequences of a given capital expenditure are sometimes so intangible as to make difficult an evaluation in terms of profitability.

The initial proposals for capital expenditures make up the ideas and raw data for analysis and evaluation. For effective development and appraisal of capital proposals, management draws on information from market and engineering research and from cost analysis. The beginning estimates may be rough approximations, but as investment proposals move up closer to ultimate managerial evaluation, estimates of outlay and return are computed closely. Investment proposals pass through a number of stages in the degree of refinement of estimates and computations as they move up through the managerial hierarchy for screening and approval on the basis of profit return or other acceptance criteria. Since many investment projects originate in the lower echelons and in the office of staff planners, much ultimate executive decision making tends to be selective rather than creative. In the large firm capital projects for plant facilities and expansion are first reviewed by plant managers and then, in turn, by division managers, top executives, and, often, by the board of directors.

If top management is to review adequately investment projects for approval, the *summary statement of the pertinent data on each project* must include the best available estimate of the capital required (e.g., the base cost of equipment, transportation and installation cost, additional working capital that may be needed, and taxes), the time of the year that funds will be needed, and the anticipated additional earnings or savings to be gained from adoption of the investment project (Fig. 11–1). A well-prepared investment proposal is essentially the result of a careful analysis of all relevant factors, supported by detail sufficient to substantiate the outlay required and the profit estimate. To achieve well-directed investment and profitable development of the enterprise, executives must review competing investment proposals in the light of the firm's financial situation and anticipated business conditions, and they must consistently keep in mind the goals of their long-range program in the selection and adoption of investment proposals for the coming planning period. In evaluating alternative proposals for the acquisition of needed capacity, for example, executives would compare the advisability and relative profitability of acquiring capacity through such measures as erection of a new plant, purchase of an existing plant, and leasing of facilities.

EQUIPMENT REPLACEMENT PROPOSAL
(Estimate of Outlay and Return)

Required Investment (Cost)
    Equipment purchase price .... $ _____
    Transportation and installation .... _____
    Cost to be capitalized .... _____
        Less: salvage value obsolete equipment .... _____
    Net capital outlay .... _____
        Plus: non-recurring expenses .... _____
        Total outlay .... $ _____

Profit Improvement (Annual Added Profit) .... $ _____

$$\frac{\text{Total outlay}}{\text{Annual added profit}} \quad \frac{\$ \text{_____}}{\$} \text{. Years of life of asset _____}$$

Cash payout period _____ years

COMPUTATION OF ANNUAL ADDED PROFIT

	Additional Expense	Savings or Additional Income
Net sales	$ _____	$ _____
Cost of sales		
Raw materials	_____	_____
Direct labor........................	_____	_____
Factory overhead	_____	_____
Administrative expense.................	_____	_____
Distribution expenses	_____	_____
Total	$ _____	$ _____
Added annual profit before depreciation and income taxes		$ _____
Added annual profit after depreciation and income taxes		$ _____

Fig. 11–1. Computations of capital layout, rate of return, and added profit.

Executive approval of a capital project does not generally mean approval to spend funds. The approval of expenditures and the appropriation of funds take place when management authorizes the implementation of a capital project. Executives generally call for periodic progress reports for each capital project, drawn up to show the amount of funds appropriated and the amount spent.

Executives, moreover, periodically (e.g., every quarter) review the over-all capital budget and program and make adjustments to meet shifts in the firm's business outlook. Management therefore sometimes finds it necessary to eliminate expenditures that are not absolutely necessary for efficient operations and to postpone (or stretch out) some of the capital projects. Funds allocated for projects and plans that are to be eliminated or cut back are made available for new investment projects and plans on the basis of relative profitability and contribution to the long-range program.

In summary, if they are to carry out capital budgeting and make profitable investment decisions effectively, executives must make a number of economic estimates and evaluations: (1) They must estimate the cost and availability of capital—that is, they must determine the amount of funds that can be raised internally from depreciation and retained earnings and the amount that can be obtained by outside financing. (2) They must estimate the amount of money the firm will need for investment purposes in the coming fiscal year (or planning period) and ascertain when during the year the funds will be spent. (3) They must select economically sound criteria for measuring the profitability or contribution of capital projects for the purpose of selecting those investment proposals that will maximize earnings. (4) Finally, they must determine the lowest level of profitability (rate of return) required for the acceptance of a capital project—that is, the cut-off point for investment by the firm.

Criteria for Selection and Measurement of Investment Proposals

Though a firm may allocate available funds to liquidate more quickly its long-term obligations or to meet the need for more working capital, profit opportunities discovered and developed by the firm usually make up the primary demand for funds. Top management generally appropriates a portion of its funds for certain types of investment proposals on the basis of their intrinsic value and strategic contribution to the long-run progress of the enterprise, rather than on the basis of a rigid rate-of-return estimate of earnings. In order to preserve or enhance the firm's over-all earning power, managers would, for instance, allocate a portion of the available funds for research, product improvement, long-term promotion, and other investment proposals that improve or maintain the firm's competitive position, even though the return on such outlays cannot readily or accurately be measured by the profitability yardstick—that is, on the basis of how much added profit will be produced from added investment. Management, on the basis of necessity, would also allocate some funds for projects that provide stand-by facilities or fulfill contingency plans to meet emergencies, projects needed to meet legal requirements (e.g., a waste-disposal plant), and projects stipulated by company personnel policy (e.g., enlargement of a cafeteria).

Some firms use *postponability* as one basis for allocating funds among investment plans. This means that management may pass up an investment proposal if it can be deferred to the future, even though it promises a high return in the present. The postponability standard is a weak basis for reviewing and passing on a profitable investment project, particularly when the availability of its profitability in the future is difficult to ascertain. The use of postponability as a standard for screening and acceptance would, moreover, tend to forestall the adoption of technological improvements and plant modernization.

The central problem in capital budgeting, therefore, is the selection of a standard to measure the profitability of investment proposals for the purpose of screening and selecting those that promise the highest rate of return consistent with long-range plans. Well-managed firms generally use the pay-out period and the rate of return on investment as the criteria for choosing the best proposals from among a number of alternatives.

Some firms choose their capital projects largely on the basis of the *pay-out period*—the rapidity with which an investment project will recoup the original outlay of funds. It is calculated by estimating the length of time required for cash earnings (earnings before depreciation or depletion) to return the original outlay of funds. The selection of projects with a short pay-out period seems to offer advantages. The pay-out period as a standard for acceptance is popular because it appears safer than the rate-of-return yardstick and is simpler to compute, since it does not call for an estimate of the economic life of the investment. Management tends to use the pay-out period as the criterion for screening and selection of projects when the future is uncertain and investment is risky and when funds are in short supply and outside financing is costly. The pay-out period as a guide for investment has a number of drawbacks or pitfalls. It tends to overemphasize the importance of liquidity as a business objective. Because it ignores the economic life of the investment (i.e., the aspect of capital wastage), the pay-out standard fails to take into account earnings from a capital project after the initial outlay of funds has been recouped.

Because the pay-out period for recouping the outlay essentially does not measure profitability in terms of return on capital, it is often not a sound criterion for screening and selecting investment proposals. For example, if management has the alternative of installing a materials-handling device A for $8,000, with an estimated cash savings from cost reduction of $2,000 for four years, or installing a handling device B for $8,000, with an estimated cash savings of $2,000 for seven years, both handling methods have the same pay-out period.

$$\text{Pay-out period} = \frac{\$8,000}{\$2,000 \text{ savings per year}} = 4 \text{ years}$$

Though these alternative capital projects have the same pay-out period, handling device A has no estimated useful life after the fourth year, while handling device B will continue to gain cost-reduction savings for three more years.

To determine its *demand for investment funds*, management must compile individual capital projects, estimate the anticipated profitability from each, and group the projects on the basis of their estimated profitability over the economic life of the capital project. When the foregoing investment proposals are arrayed on the basis of their rate of return, this makes up the firm's demand schedule for capital funds. The firm may, for instance, have three proposals with a prospective return exceeding 50 per cent on investment; it may have six projects promising a return of 40 per cent on investment, and so on down the scale of return on investment. Investment proposals that offer a comparatively low return (e.g., 10 per cent) may be considered too unprofitable for further consideration because their return is below the cost of external funds (the borrowing rate).

Thus, the firm's demand for funds is comprised of a number of investment opportunities differing in their estimated profitability. A well-managed firm in a growing industry will typically find many profitable investment outlets; and if the firm is riding the crest of boom-time business, it will obviously have a strong demand for funds. A firm in a comparatively static industry may have little demand for funds because of fewer investment opportunities. The amount of funds that a firm may invest internally may be based on considerations other than that of profitability. A firm with numerous, highly profitable investment projects may pass up projects promising a 30 per cent return because of management's aversion to external financing. A firm may, on the other hand, make outlays for investments within the company that promise a small return merely because it has considerable sums of retained earnings.

The screening and selection of the most profitable and otherwise economically desirable investment projects constitute the central problem in capital budgeting. A sound basis for selecting projects rests on the proper *computation of the rate of return on investment.* This means that each project must be appropriately computed for a realistic estimate of profitability. Estimates of costs must be carefully based on anticipated future costs of material, labor, facilities, etc., and the return on the investment must be based on a careful forecast of the revenue or savings to be obtained. Investments that involve two or more years for their development before they are ready for application are obviously computed with less precision than projects that could be in operation within a period of a year or so. The profitability of each project must be estimated on an individual basis. How a given project produces its revenue should be clearly identified so that the total amount of revenue can be ascertained. The anticipated savings from the revision of a product design undertaken to reduce the cost of processing, for instance, will produce savings from faster production. The cost involved for the revision must include all relevant costs—engineering time, retooling, revision of facilities, for example.

The estimate of profitability from a capital project should take into account the indirect effect that the proposal will make on other company activities. If it raises operating costs elsewhere in the firm's business operations, these should be charged against the earnings. The estimate of the total investment required for a given project should include not only the initial outlays but subsequent expenditures that may be needed, and the investment should be computed on the basis of the incremental cost rather than on any sunk cost basis. The operating costs of a project must, of course, be based on an estimate of future costs (anticipated wages, cost of material, etc.). The anticipated revenue should be based and computed on a carefully projected estimate of the appropriate activity, such as sales volume.

If managers are to compare correctly the profitability of mutually exclusive investment proposals, they must compute the rate of return on the capital outlay for each alternative project up to the terminal date of the longer-lived alternative. Though most investment outlays are written off in regular depreciation charges, some outlays (or portion of outlays) can be charged as a total to current cost for computation of taxable income. Earnings should, therefore, be stated after corporate income taxes (i.e., deflated for taxes), particularly since firms generally aim to pay dividends at least at a capital-attracting rate.

The estimate of earnings should take into account the *factor of uncertainty*. The greater the uncertainty, the greater the discount of future earnings. A project that promises somewhat uncertain earnings in the future would thus carry a heavy discount. When, for instance, an investment proposal calls for the adoption of a new product of uncertain sales volume and uncertain selling prices, the estimated profitability should obviously be considered a rough approximation. A large allowance would have to be made in the calculation of its anticipated profits.

In economic terms a firm's standard of minimum acceptability for adopting investment proposals should generally be based on its cost of capital. Thus, managers would adopt a project if the rate of return is greater than the firm's cost of capital. Managers, moreover, would likely obtain a more constant cutoff rate for internal investment if they used the firm's cost of capital as the cutoff rate than if they were to set their current volume of investment on the basis of the amount of funds the firm generates from internal sources. If the future is uncertain, however, managers may adopt a somewhat higher cutoff rate than that which is equal to that of the firm's cost of capital.[1]

Projects that do not fit into the company over-all field of business may be rejected even though they promise a comparatively high return. Since management appraises the desirability of capital projects on the basis of rate of return, projects are arrayed according to their rates of return. Available investment funds will be allocated to specific projects starting with those that promise the highest return and ending with those whose profitability approaches the cut-off point, say, 20 per cent return on investment.

SUPPLY OF FUNDS FOR THE FIRM

In planning capital investments, businessmen must take into account the supply of funds available to the firm as well as the demand for funds stemming from profitable investment proposals. In estimating the availability of funds from internal and external sources, they

[1] As a suitable substitute for the rate-of-return approach for identifying profitable projects, managers sometimes use the present-value method. This method discounts earnings to reflect the diminishing value of distant earnings. In the present-value approach, managers find the present value of the expected cash earnings for the project. They also find the present value of a capital outlay, using the cost of capital as a discount rate. Managers would then accept the project for consideration if the present value of earnings is greater than the present value of the outlay. To facilitate their calculation, as a practical matter managers can readily derive the present value of any given future sum or income from present-worth tables found in any financial handbook.

take into account the cost of capital to the firm from various sources. To meet their need for investment capital, managers can draw both on internal sources of funds and on the external sources of funds. A firm sometimes acquires internal funds by tapping the large cash accumulations of previous years, by selling non-operating property or unnecessary assets, or by selling operating assets (plant, office building) with a lease-back arrangement for the use of the facilities. For financing capital investment, most large firms rely primarily on internal sources—retained earnings and depreciation funds. (Table 11–1.)

Depreciation funds comprise an important share of internally generated funds available to the firm. A firm's annual depreciation charges generate internal funds which more or less approximate the value of productive assets which are used up in the process of production during the year. Theoretically, depreciation charges represent the attempt to compensate for the using up of productive assets. (The adequacy of depreciation funds for replacing worn facilities is discussed in Chapter 9.) The change over time in the proportion of depreciation cost in the unit cost of the product is an indicator of the trend in the size of depreciation funds in a given firm. Because depreciation accruals tend to show little cyclical fluctuation, the size of depreciation funds is a relatively stable component of internal funds as compared to retained earnings. Depreciation funds tend to increase over the years because of the growth of depreciable fixed assets owned by business. The amount of depreciation funds generated and available differs among industries and among firms in a given industry. The amount of depreciation funds available to a firm in a given year depends on the capital intensiveness of production, the amount of depreciable assets owned, the average useful life of the assets, and the formula (whether straight-line or accelerated) used for amortizing assets.

The profits that a firm earns and retains during a given year are an important source of funds generally available for investment. Retained earnings, however, are a highly unstable component of internal funds. They are highly variable because of year-to-year variations in sales revenue and profits and because of periodic changes in tax laws. A corporate firm establishes the amount of earnings it will retain by the dividend policy and the reinvestment (plow-back) practice it adopts.

The amount of earnings a firm retains depends on such factors as the amount of profits generated, dividend policy, need for funds to exploit profit opportunities, and the cost and desirability of external financing. Corporate retained earnings typically vary with the level of net income earned. Some corporate managers, nonetheless, con-

TABLE 11-1

Sources and Uses of Corporate Funds, 1948-59[1]

(billions of dollars)

Source or Use of Funds	1948	1949	1950	1951	1952	1953	1954	1955	1956	1957	1958	1959[2]
Total uses	27.0	16.8	36.5	36.8	27.3	28.2	24.0	45.1	39.5	38.6	31.2	46.0
Plant and equipment outlays	18.8	16.2	16.9	21.6	22.4	23.9	22.4	24.2	29.9	32.7	26.4	27.0
Inventories (book value)	4.2	-3.6	9.8	9.8	1.3	1.8	-1.6	6.7	7.6	2.7	-4.4	3.0
Customer net receivables[3]	2.8	0.9	5.0	2.0	3.1	0.7	2.4	6.4	3.3	4.0	4.1	6.0
Cash and U.S. Government securities	1.0	3.2	4.5	2.8	0.1	1.8	(4)	5.0	-4.3	-1.9	3.4	5.5
Other assets	0.2	(4)	0.3	0.6	0.4	(4)	0.8	2.8	3.0	1.1	1.7	4.5
Total sources	27.8	15.8	35.4	36.9	28.1	30.0	22.4	44.8	42.4	40.2	31.6	47.0
Internal sources	18.8	14.9	20.8	19.0	17.8	19.7	19.8	26.6	27.8	27.7	25.6	30.5
Retained profits and depletion allowances	12.6	7.8	13.0	10.0	7.4	7.9	6.3	10.9	10.5	9.0	6.0	10.0[5]
Depreciation and amortization allowances	6.2	7.1	7.8	9.0	10.4	11.8	13.5	15.7	17.3	18.7	19.6	20.5
External sources	9.0	0.9	14.6	17.9	10.3	10.3	2.6	18.2	14.6	12.5	6.0	16.5
Federal income tax liability	0.9	-2.2	7.3	4.3	-3.1	0.6	-3.1	3.8	-1.7	-1.9	-2.5	2.5
Other liabilities	0.4	0.5	1.0	1.9	2.4	2.2	0.4	2.1	3.0	2.2	0.1	2.0
Bank loans and mortgage loans	1.8	-2.3	2.6	5.4	3.1	0.4	-0.6	5.4	5.4	1.7	-1.1	4.0
Net new issues	5.9	4.9	3.7	6.3	7.9	7.1	5.9	6.9	7.9	10.5	9.5	8.0
Discrepancy (uses less sources)	-0.8	1.0	1.1	-0.1	-0.8	-1.8	1.6	0.3	-2.9	-1.6	-0.4	-1.0

[1] Excludes banks and insurance companies.

[2] Preliminary estimates.

[3] Receivables are net of payables, which are therefore not shown separately.

[4] Less than $50 million.

[5] Preliminary estimate by Council of Economic Advisers.

Note: Detail will not necessarily add to totals because of rounding.

Source: Economic Report of the President, 1960 (Washington, D.C.: Government Printing Office, 1960), p. 224.

sider the retention of fifty cents out of every dollar of net income a sound principle of corporate financial management. Many firms, however, annually pay a more or less stable rate of dividends, in line with the concept of the implicit interest charge on stockholders' investment. In order that they may pay dividends in less prosperous years and thereby maintain a comparatively stable dividend rate, managers may retain part of the earnings in profitable years even though the firm may have little need for investment funds. Dividends paid in preceding years generally tend to affect the amount of income retained in a current year. The amount of earnings retained is often determined by the firm's need for investment funds arising out of the pressure for expansion of capacity or out of the availability of highly profitable, internal-investment projects. Managers often retain income so long as the capital can be invested at a certain minimum rate of return, for example, at a return above the full cost of funds from external sources. Managers may, however, hold to the practice that a certain constant percentage of the profits should be retained for long-term growth and contingencies. If a firm reinvests too high a proportion of its earnings, it may depress the market value of its stock. This may be a significant factor if the firm contemplates resorting to substantial external financing.

Businessmen may draw on external sources of funds by resorting to equity financing or debt financing. The extent to which managers would rely on external financing partly depends on the cost of external funds. Managers generally determine the desirability of external financing by comparing the estimated earnings from internal investments with the cost of external funds. The borrowing rate of interest is often considered as the measure of the cost of capital for a firm. In sound capital budgeting, managers would use the cost of external funds as a basis for determining the cut-off point in the use and allocation of internal funds for company investment projects. But in estimating the rate of return from a given investment project for purposes of allocating funds among alternative uses, managers should also take into account the opportunity cost—the income foregone from alternative uses of the funds.

Financial officers estimate the cost of external funds from the sale of securities by computing the interest charge (in case of debt financing), the commission to underwriters for their services, and the expense of the flotation, as a ratio of the net proceeds derived. The cost of outside funds fluctuates with the firm's prospective earnings, the market level of securities, and the favorability for financing (Fig. 11–2). The cost of funds also depends on the firm's market reputation and the size of the issue. Business managers are sometimes reluctant to resort to external financing. Debt financing involves risk and carries a fixed financial cost; bank borrowings may involve restrictions on the use of funds and on future financing. Though equity financing carries fewer restrictions, it is sometimes a costly source of funds.

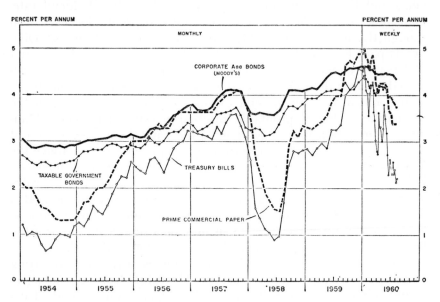

Fig. 11–2. Bond yields and interest rates, 1954–60. (Council of Economic Advisers, *Economic Indicators, August 1960*. Washington, D.C.: Government Printing Office, 1960, p. 29.)

QUESTIONS FOR REVIEW AND APPLICATION

1. What are the evidences of ineffective long-range business planning? What are the long-term consequences?

2. What are the human and other limitations to business planning?

3. Identify and briefly explain the external and internal factors that condition and influence company objectives and direction of investment—that is, the types of capital expenditures made.

4. What is the framework of long-range planning? Explain.

5. (*a*) Cite some lines of business in which the industry and firm structural aspects make long-range investment planning difficult. Explain. (*b*) Cite lines of business in which long-range planning is less difficult.

6. Identify the areas or aspects of business for which over-all policies must be explicitly formulated in order that company-wide planning may be properly directed toward desired goals.

7. Outline and briefly explain the process of long-range planning and decision making.

8. (*a*) Explain and illustrate the interdependence between short- and long-term plans. (*b*) Explain what is meant by the coordination of short- and long-term plans and capital projects.

9. (*a*) What are the factors that determine a firm's planning period? (*b*) Cite an industry that requires a long planning period. Explain. Cite an industry that requires a short planning period. (*c*) What pitfalls and disadvantages does management encounter when it selects an excessively long planning period?

10. (*a*) What are the methods whereby planners gain flexibility in long-range programing? Explain. (*b*) What are the economic benefits of flexibility in planning? For instance, how does flexibility lessen uncertainty?

11. Explain the components (or facets) of, and the managerial process for, capital budgeting.

12. Discuss the procedure through which a single investment proposal may pass from its initial conception to the point of top-executive screening for final acceptance.

13. (*a*) Classify capital expenditures as to type. (*b*) Explain what is meant by "capital projects compete for funds." Illustrate. (*c*) What are the different criteria that executives may use as a standard to screen, rank, and select capital projects for appropriation of funds?

14. What are the weaknesses in using postponability and pay-out as criteria for top-management screening and acceptance of investment proposals?

15. (*a*) Explain what is meant by the capital recovery period. (*b*) How does the capital recovery period differ from the long-range planning period?

16. Illustrate the procedure and explain the problems involved in computing the outlay required for a capital project and in estimating the rate of return on investment.

17. (*a*) Explain what is meant by the firm's internal demand for capital. (*b*) Illustrate a company's demand schedule for funds. (*c*) What may determine a firm's investment-cut-off point?

18. Explain how trading on the equity may increase earnings to stockholders. (*b*) What are the limits and pitfalls of such financing?

19. (*a*) How may the cost of external funds be estimated? (*b*) Why will the external cost of capital differ for firms?

20. What capital cost rate may executives impute to funds derived from retained earnings and depreciation allowances in their allocation of funds for competing investment projects? Explain.

21. (*a*) Explain the tendency toward debt aversion by some top executive groups—that is, explain why some executives prefer internal financing. (*b*) What is the effect of debt aversion on profit maximization?

22. How may emphasis on retained earnings (i.e., the forgoing of dividend payments to stockholders) for the financing of company capital expenditures benefit present stockholders?

CHAPTER 12

Long-Range Program and Policies

SCOPE OF LONG-RANGE PLANNING
AND PROGRAMING

A well-designed company over-all program is comprised of a group of related investment projects and capital expenditures which implement an integrated plan for developing the enterprise for a given period. To maximize long-term earnings, executive managers generally design the long-range program to improve their product line, to reduce the costs, and to expand sales volume and output capacity. Because it modifies and restructures the firm's scope of business and production organization, the company over-all program vitally affects the long-term future of the enterprise.

A firm's development program is generally characterized by a number of economic features. Some investment projects in the program will be designed to improve the firm's competitive position, others to achieve greater business adaptability, and still others to attain better business stability in the face of seasonal or cyclical fluctuations. Some investment projects will add to earnings through the expansion of sales volume and revenue, while other projects will add to earnings through cost reduction. Some types of investments are considered necessary or desirable without anticipation of immediate gain in earnings. The accuracy in gauging the profitability, moreover, differs for the various classes of investment outlays. The estimated gain in earnings from the replacement of obsolescent equipment, for instance, is generally more accurate than the estimated gain from the adoption of a new product.

464

The types of projects and capital expenditures that would generally make up a firm's over-all development program obviously depend on the firm's field of business. A *development program of a manufacturing firm,* for instance, would generally consist of projects and capital outlays for (1) industrial research and cost reduction, (2) development of the product line and distribution channels, (3) plant facilities involving expansion and modernization of output capacity and equipment replacement, (4) certain necessary investments (e.g., those designed to meet a geographical shift in the market), and (5) strategic investments, those which provide indirect benefits to the firm as a whole, such as the improvement of the firm's competitive position (e.g., through the redesign of packaging or the modernization of distribution outlets in order to move ahead of, or to match the plans of, rival firms) or the improvement of working conditions and welfare plans in order to maintain better labor recruitment standards.

INDUSTRIAL RESEARCH AND COST REDUCTION

Managers ward off technological obsolescence and improve the firm's profitability by establishing research programs to develop and introduce new and improved products and processes and to reduce costs. Managers generally orient the research function and channel the research effort to those fields of technology and science that are fairly directly related to the commercial interests of the firm. To assure profitable return on research expenditures, the company research effort must be somewhat guided. If the scope of company research is unrestricted, the firm's research laboratory would tend to undertake technological developments that, because they go beyond the firm's line of business and technology, cannot readily be exploited on a commercial basis.

Though business firms occasionally undertake some basic research (a search for new knowledge to enlarge the scope of scientific information), their primary emphasis is on applied industrial research consisting of both long- and short-term projects. Applied research is an organized search for new knowledge for a specific need and the translation of the findings of basic research into new or improved processes, materials, and products that can be commercially exploited. A firm's research program would ordinarily include some exploratory research—a broad search in areas of possible interest. Such research generally consists of long-term projects—those that take a number of years before they are ready and available for development and commercial exploitation. A research program would also include short-term projects—those that have a definite specific objective that can be attained in a limited time period.

Research directors and executive managers periodically review the progress of company research and they select "development" projects from among those projects that have progressed to the point at which they can be somewhat realistically appraised for commercial exploitation. Development projects are sometimes costly, particularly if they require design and output of new-type products, design and provision of facilities, and extensive market research and consumer tests. When a new product or process, because of its complexity, cannot be economically exploited directly on a commercial basis, it may require a pilot-plant stage for further development. In the pilot-plant stage of development, a product and process are improved and refined to a point at which the regular work force in a commercial plant can put out the item without prohibitive waste and costly interruption. Though it is somewhat costly, the development of new products and the improvement of processes and facilities on a pilot-plant (or semiworks) basis can reduce the overall lead time required to put out a product on a commercial or larger-scale basis.

Top executives can more or less guide and direct the firm's industrial research by the type of organizational plan (e.g., whether a centralized plan or a decentralized plan) they select for the research function, the types of objectives (e.g., creation of new products, cost reduction, or a search for new materials) they emphasize in the research program, and the amount of funds they allocate for the various types of research projects. Because of the long-term nature of many research projects, directors of research endeavor to secure funds for a sufficient time span to permit continuity of research activity regardless of short-term business conditions. When managers employ economic analysis to plan research, they determine the level of expenditures for research and development on the basis of opportunity cost (the anticipated return from other fields of investment), the amount rival firms are spending for research, the financial resources available, and the research director's judgment and estimate of the rate of return on expenditures for various research projects under consideration. Managers sometimes find it appropriate to budget an over-all annual (or a longer period) outlay for research and development and allow the research director to make detailed allocations.

The areas in business operations to which research effort will tend to be directed and the types of cost-reduction and profit-making opportunities that will be uncovered will vary for firms in different lines of business. Though improvements may come from a number of sources, firms sometimes find that outlays for research will yield their biggest returns in certain areas. Firms with wide distribution outlets marketing consumer goods, for instance, may find it profitable to emphasize the development and sale of new products. Firms in industries in which the cost of materials makes up a high proportion of the unit cost of the product would, of course, seek lower-cost materials and aim to reduce the quantity of materials going into a unit of the product. Firms processing and breaking down expensive raw materials can reduce material costs by converting waste materials into by-products and by discovering lower-cost, substitute materials. Firms producing final products can often reduce the input of scarce, costly materials by detailed analysis for the redesign of products. By adopting statistical quality control techniques and mechanized inspection devices, firms can reduce the amount of spoilage in production, attain a more uniform quality in the product, maintain a higher level of workmanship, as well as lower the cost of inspection itself.

Firms employing capital-intensive processes generally strive to develop capital-savings types of technological improvements. Capital savings per unit of output may be realized not only through the improvement of plant layout and the use of new fabrication techniques and chemical and electrochemical processes in place of mechanical processes that require bulky, expensive equipment but through the adoption of high-speed equipment (e.g., automated machinery and rapid mechanical-handling devices) and production-control techniques that achieve low capital cost per unit of output. Through the use of well-designed planning and control systems, plant managers eliminate production delays, quicken the pace of processing, and lower overhead cost per unit of output; and through the design and adoption of special-purpose inventory control systems, managers can hold inventory stocks at economical levels, assure an adequate turnover in stock, and centralize the responsibility and control over inventory and procurement Firms employing high-priced labor and labor-intensive processes strive to develop or adopt laborsaving types of technological improvements, processes, and production arrangements. Improvement of worker performance through time-and-motion studies and the adoption of incentive wage plans and labor-training programs are important means for attaining productivity gains on the plant level. Factory managers know that the provision of a desirable physical environment in the plant steps up output and morale and improves labor relations. Plans for stabilizing production and employment, effective recruitment and placement of new workers, and sound personnel practices reduce absenteeism and labor turnover.

The adoption of any cost-reduction plan or project should be based on carefully estimated savings to be obtained from the improvement proposals; and the net savings to be derived from an outlay for a given improvement should be compared to the gain that can be obtained from alternative opportunities that take a comparable expenditure of effort and investment. (For further discussion, see Research and Development, Section 17, in Gordon D. Carson's *Production Handbook.*)

DEVELOPMENT OF THE PRODUCT LINE

Managerial concern and preoccupation with the problems of the firm's product coverage are due to the fact that the development of the firm's product line is crucial to profitability and the fact that the product line determines the type of production processes and materials that the firm employs. Ideally, managers strive for an optimum product line—one that maximizes profits in the long run. Because of shifts in consumer demand and technological change in the economy, a profitable and economically logical product line is one that must change with the times. Effective product planning and development rest on a careful estimate of future demand and technological developments. Managers plan and control the product line through (1) periodic revision of the product line (addition of new products and product diversification), (2) simplification of the product line, (3) product modification for cost reduction, and (4) product improvement and periodic restyling. (See discussion in Chapter 6 for the initial design of a profitable product line.)

In adapting the product line for increased profitability, business managers are keen to the opportunities of introducing new products. Managers know that plans for revision of the product line must be coordinated with plans for production facilities and distribution and promotion practices. Hence, product-line changes frequently involve many of the other aspects of the business. In drawing up their program for introduction of new items to the firm's line of business, managers aim to enlarge profits. The adoption of new products, for instance, may put a firm's idle plant and other resources to productive use, improve the firm's market position, and often beneficially diversify the product line so as to minimize fluctuations in sales and stabilize revenue.

New-product ideas originate from a number of sources. Because salesmen are familiar with market needs and competitive products, they are often a prime source of new-product ideas. Their proposals, however, must be carefully screened, because salesmen sometimes misjudge potential market and are often unaware of the technical and economical obstacles that must be overcome in the introduction of some types of products. Valuable proposals for new products generally come from the research and engineering staff. Though their proposals take into account technical aspects in the adoption of new products, their suggestions of products sometimes reflect lack of familiarity with market needs and the salability features of products.

Most product proposals for company adoption consist of commercially established products. The evaluation of the desirability of adopting these types of products is not nearly so difficult to estimate as compared to wholly new types of products. The market potential and the cost of output may be extremely difficult to estimate for the latter class of products. Wholly new types of products may not only involve large capital outlays for their development and promotion, preliminary to commercial output, but they also often entail a considerable lead-time for their maturation before they can be profitably exploited.

The economic desirability of adopting a new item partly rests on the behavior of market demand. When the demand for the product is complementary to demand for other product items in the firm's line of output, the candidate product appropriately fits the pattern of the firm's product coverage. But when a proposed product is substitutive and tends to displace other products of the firm's line, its contribution to total revenue may be limited. The firm's marketing strategy, however, sometimes permits adoption of substitutive products because it improves a firm's over-all competitive position by preempting sales.

Managers often plan and develop the firm's product coverage for different types and degrees of *diversification*. A diversification plan may, for instance, call for the introduction of low-priced or economy models that sell well during recession times to balance high-priced items that sell well during prosperity times. Firms gain a measure of diversification by penetrating those new markets for products that promise a more stable sales volume. A firm may, for instance, wish to balance its sales in highly specialized geographical regions with sales in regions that are not so specialized. It may introduce consumer non-durable goods to balance its sales of consumer durables. When managers fail to obtain sufficient benefits from diversification, the firm's scattered business activities tend to enlarge the managerial problem unnecessarily.

Managers may adopt a policy of *product simplification,* including elimination of unprofitable or marginal items in the line. A product-simplification program undertakes a careful reappraisal of the total line of products and the current and estimated sales performance and contribution of each item to total earnings. On the basis of such a survey, managers may find opportunities to eliminate excess variety in the items sold in order to reduce waste and improve operating efficiency. A reduction in superfluous product variety obtains savings by lowering the level of inventory required, increasing the use of facilities through longer production runs, and permitting greater specialization of processes. Elimination of marginal products must take into account the need to meet the purchase requirements of customers, the sunk cost in facilities putting out these items, and the possible need for redesigning some related products.

Business managers find it most profitable to adopt those types of new products that they could put out and market at considerably lower cost than it would take for a newly established firm set up to produce and market the product. Firms that have excess production capacity and idle capacity in marketing and promotion or under-utilization in other types of resources, find that they can economically adopt a new product when they can utilize the current excess capacity. The introduction of such a new product would not require investment for the establishment of new facilities but would require outlays for the conversion and adaptation of existing processes and other business activities required to put out and market the product. The computation of the return on the investment would be based on the *incremental cost* required to introduce the product and the addition to total sales revenue. Managers adopt proposals for new product additions when the rate of return on investment is higher than that from available alternative uses for investment funds. Managerial estimate of the return from the adoption of new products in industries that emphasize new-product development must take into account the costs and losses from failures. The long-term gains from successful product innovations must more than offset the losses from product innovations that have misfired or have been aborted in the process of maturation.

Managers may diversify their business for both stability and growth. Managers diversify their business operations not only by adopting somewhat unrelated products but by entering new fields of business with the aim of stabilizing their income in the face of seasonal and cyclical variations in sales or in the event that sale of some of their products may decline for other reasons. A program of diversification may also aim to penetrate or obtain a foothold in industries that promise substantial future growth.

A firm's product program invariably includes revision or modification of products for the purpose of reducing costs of production. Product design may be revised to permit utilization of less expensive materials and of more economical processes and to reduce spoilage of work during processing. Products may also be redesigned to attain a greater degree of interchangeability of components. The gain from the foregoing types of economies must not only be balanced against the cost of making product and process revisions but against whatever losses may occur from a decline in the over-all marketability of the product line as a whole.

A firm's product-and-promotion program also, of course, stresses the improvement and better adaptation of products to market needs. Products, for instance, may be adapted to new uses and improved in quality and styling to meet competition. Producers of consumer durable goods often find that they can partially offset seasonal slumps in sales by introducing new models during the low sales period. Producers of consumer durables emphasize periodic or annual product restyling to step up the market's replacement demands. The gain from investment in product improvement and restyling must be computed on the basis of the outlay for product revisions (retooling, shutdown for changeover, disruption of production schedules) as compared to the increase in sales volume and income, or the investment may be merely balanced against the cost of maintaining competitive position.

Style and Design as Competitive Factors

The problem of estimating the funds required and the rate of return on the capital outlay for a style change in product models is often thorny because of the difficulty of gauging consumer tastes in style and forecasting company share of industry demand and because of the lead-time required by such capital investment projects. Managers are generally induced by competitive necessity to allocate funds for such purposes. This is exemplified by clothing, appliance, automobile, and other consumer goods industries, as discussed below in quotations from Senate hearings (see footnote 15).

Mr. Lawrence Crooks, automotive consultant for Consumers Union, explained the curious function that annual style changes played in the automobile industry. In his opinion, these changes have little effect upon the total number of cars sold, though they are crucial in determining which company obtains the business. As he put it:

"... styling plays a relatively minor role in increasing the total number of cars sold in the market in a given year. Now, perhaps, you have to qualify that to say provided somebody has some well-styled cars in the year.

"Of course, styling is a big factor, for good or for bad, in deciding which company is going to increase its sales at some other company's expense. The expense of the victory is, of course, borne by the consumer." [1]

STYLE VERSUS INNOVATION. In his testimony before the subcommittee, Mr. Richard S. Latham, industrial designer, drew a sharp distinction between style and innovation. One is related to superficial changes in appearance, designed to make the product seem new and different; the other reflects distinct advances in the art affecting both the product itself and its appearance. According to him, style changes are regarded as the easy way to newness; they can be measured and predicted with some exactness. But there are dangers:

"... The stylist cannot depart too radically from the over-all characteristics of the object, be it hat, dress, or automobile. It took literally years to eliminate fenders, and the symbol of the radiator cap and temperature gage is still with us, even though the instrument itself long ago went to the dashboard. The fact is that the stylist has a very limited palette. If the calendar of change is speeded up, he begins to run short of acceptable variations. Then, little by little, he is pushed into creating ridiculous changes. When people realize this at a mass level, however slowly, then styling ceases to motivate people to buy.

"There is another way out discovered by the designers who use style and function in almost equal quantities. Because it is based in the main on real progress, new looks and forms can generally be generated by functions that are new. But this approach never really works unless there is genuinely new technology behind it. When the designer attempts to instill a sense of newness into something which is in fact no different, the consumer is seldom taken in for long." [2]

In referring to the automobile as an instance of "style obsolescence" Mr. Latham contrasted automobiles with refrigerators. Both products are durable goods, with life spans of 12 years or longer. Both are subjected to the pressures of obsolescence by annual style changes. Yet, in the case of refrigerators, "statistics show that people want a new one every 12 years." [3] Here the drive to convert a durable good into a perishable item has run up against an impenetrable wall of consumer resistance.

According to Mr. Latham, frequent style changes have a place in some industries where the cost involved is not great and where consumers can exercise an option to reject the new style. As he put it:

"Now, there is nothing, to our mind, inherently wrong with the idea of style change per se, provided it is applied where it belongs. It works quite successfully in soft goods and women's clothing, for instance, where it is recognized that people like change when it is optional, inexpensive, or just plain fun." [4]

A different problem, however, is presented by the automobile where annual

---

[1] U.S. Senate Subcommittee on Antitrust and Monopoly, Hearings, 1st Session, 85th Congress, *Administered Prices—Automobiles* (Washington, D.C.: Government Printing Office, 1957), p. 3068.

[2] *Ibid.*, p. 3148.

[3] *Ibid.*, p. 3146.

[4] *Ibid.*, p. 2791.

style changes add substantially to production costs and the prices charged. In the early days of the industry, changes emerged from significant developments in technology; today they are largely superficial merchandising devices designed to enhance sales.

*   *   *

Once a styling race starts, the other contestants for the consumers' dollar, with one notable exception, feel that they are forced to enter it.[5] When the most powerful entrant runs as fast as he can, his competitors must run even faster than they are capable of running, safely, in order to cross the finish line at all. If the race lasts long enough, the weaker competitors fall by the wayside. And if the entry fees are high enough, there will be no new runners to take the place of those who drop out.

This is a very realistic prospect in the automobile industry. Dr. Ralph C. Epstein, writing 30 years ago, blamed rapid design changes for the heavy mortality rate which was even then transforming the automobile manufacturing from a highly competitive industry into one dominated by a few firms.[6] More recently a Ford executive stated that the failure of his company to change 1956 models drastically enough resulted in a loss of nearly 200,000 sales to Chevrolet.[7] It is hardly likely that Ford and Chrysler enjoy spending $350 million and $200 million a year, respectively, on style changes. A more probable explanation of this behavior is that the Ford and Chrysler managements believe that these sums are the least they can spend and still stay in business, in the light of General Motors' annual expenditures of some $500 million. The possible necessity of complete annual retooling for model changes, suggested by the new General Motors policy discussed above, will put even greater strains on the resources of the lesser members of the Big Three.

If Ford and Chrysler will be hard pressed to follow General Motors' leadership, the effects on any smaller companies which tried to compete on an annual model change basis could well be disastrous. . . .

*   *   *

Another factor of consequence is the time interval between design and market sales. This was discussed by Mr. Yntema. Speaking in early 1958, he remarked:

*   *   *

"The 4-year gestation period for new-model development (not counting engineering research) is, I believe, unique to the automobile industry in the consumer-goods field. Certainly, no other industry of comparable magnitude faces such a long product-planning cycle for all of its models in every year." [8]

In view of this situation, one can only wonder how the consumer may be expected to know what he will want 4 years from the time of his interview with the customer-research staff. Even with the best intentions in the world, he can

[5] The possibility of staying out of the race and utilizing the cost savings which would result from less frequent model changes to reduce prices appears to have been rejected as a competitive device by all of the major producers.

[6] Ralph C. Epstein, *The Automobile Industry* (New York: A. W. Shaw Co., 1928). Chap. 6.

[7] *Wall Street Journal,* December 10, 1957.

[8] U.S. Senate Subcommittee on Antitrust and Monopoly, Hearings, 1st Session, 85th Congress, *Administered Prices—Automobiles* (Washington, D.C.: Government Printing Office, 1957), p. 2731.

but express his immediate preferences. A significant development in technology, an economic depression, major changes in other automobiles may make his selection utterly irrelevant in the space of 4 years.

* * *

In the course of the hearings, Mr. Curtice expressed pride in the "styling leadership" of General Motors.

* * *

The enthusiasm of Ford for annual style changes was far less marked. Mr. Yntema, vice president, explained, however, that the company virtually had no choice: "When the competition comes out with a changed model, we find ourselves in trouble." He went on:

"In our own experience, we find when the model is not changed substantially, the customers do not buy it. Now not only we, but our competitors, have had the same experience, and this is a very, very unfortunate thing, from our point of view.

"We would like to have lower tooling costs; we would like to have people buy our models, but we find we have to make these changes if we are going to get an increasing share of the business." [9]

* * *

Mr. Yntema's testimony suggested that the role of the consumer—rather than dictator of style changes—is that of final arbiter on the offerings of the automobile companies. From his remarks, it would appear that the aim of the companies is to hit upon some novelty which will have especial appeal to an unpredictable and fickle public. At one point he remarked:

"The consumer is king. I mean we cannot sell automobiles that he does not want. This is very clear. And we have to try to guess what he wants . . . it is a very risky and a very uncertain business, but we cannot sell our cars unless we make the kind of cars the consumer wants, as we find to our sorrow when we do not." [10]

[9] *Ibid.,* p. 2657.
[10] *Ibid.,* p. 2696. Some of the industrial tension on this phase is indicated in an article in *Fortune,* September 1954, p. 195, relative to Ford in the late 1940's:
"Breech was convinced that Chevrolet would have model changes by the fall of 1947. If Chevy changed and Ford didn't, all the Jack Davises in the world wouldn't be able to sell the prewar Ford. It normally takes 3 years to style, engineer, and tool a completely new model for production. This meant that Ford would have nothing but the 1941 product until 1949 and would, as succeeding models of Chevrolet appeared, be at a greater and greater disadvantage.
"When the policy committee convened the morning after the Youngren report, Breech said: 'All right, we start from scratch. We don't spend time or money phonying up the old Ford because this organization will be judged by the market on the next car it produces, and it had better be new. So, we have a crash program, just like a war program. Any questions?' There were plenty. By throwing economy out the window and taking chances motorcar manufacturers should never take, they believed they could have a new car in production in 14 months. As it turned out, Chevy did not introduce a new model quickly. When the 1949 Ford came to market in June 1948, it was the first Big Three make that was completely new."

In view of this situation, one can only concur with him that the "risks in the automobile business are extraordinarily great" and that "a few wrong decisions can wreck a company." [11] Mr. Yntema stated:

"No manufacturer can guess right on these 100 percent of the time, especially when the guessing must start 4 years before the first sale. When it appears that his original guess is likely to be wrong, the producer has two alternatives:

"1. Rush last-minute product changes at great expense, and hope the second guess is right.

"2. If it is too late for that, or if the second guess is also wrong, take a licking in the market.

"Neither alternative is pleasant; yet no producer has been able to avoid at least an occasional year of wrong guessing." [12]

✻   ✻   ✻

STYLING COSTS. A significant portion of the automobile industry's overhead costs arises from an emphasis upon style, rather than price, competition. This has served to inflate general selling and administrative costs to an increasing extent over time, as the styling and engineering efforts devoted to model changes are general staff functions in each of the major companies. Since the tools and dies used in new models are charged against costs of production, manufacturing overhead is also affected by style changes.

Dr. Theodore O. Yntema, vice president of the Ford Motor Co., estimated to the subcommittee that major model changes in all of Ford's automotive lines would cost $440 million, or $189 per vehicle on the basis of 1957 output.[13] This figure covers styling, engineering, and the purchase of special commercial tools. It does not include any allowance for facilities expenditures and rearrangement costs for the model changeover, or any abnormal costs associated with the introduction of the Edsel line. Changes of this magnitude are seldom made in a single year. Therefore, Dr. Yntema indicated that Ford's normal expenditures for style changes total only $350 million a year, or about $150 a unit on an output of 2.34 million vehicles. If the costs of installing special tools and rearranging facilities to accommodate the new models were added to the figures above, it would be clear that the full cost of style changes is even higher than the level disclosed by Dr. Yntema.

Dr. Yntema's estimate understates, of course, the unit cost of style changes on the basis of current production. It appears that Dr. Yntema's $350 million estimate of normal annual styling costs will be spread over only 1.3 to 1.4 million vehicles in 1958.[14] At this level of output, the unit cost of style changes will fall between $250 and $270.

. . . In short, the 3 leading automobile producers are together spending well over $1 billion a year to convince buyers that last year's car models are obsolete.

Accurate information as to the extent to which styling costs have risen in the industry as a whole is not available. The Ford Motor Co., however, placed in the record a chart which illustrates the growth of that company's general tool amortization, engineering, and styling costs from 1948 to 1957.

[11] *Ibid.*, p. 2730.

[12] *Ibid.*, p. 2732.

[13] Letter from Ford Motor Co., dated March 10, 1958, in files of subcommittee.

[14] The Automotive News report (June 30, 1958) of January 1–June 29 production shows that Ford's output for this period was 58 per cent of its output for the comparable period in 1957.

The index of Ford's model-change costs shows that expenditures in 1957 were more than 6½ times the 1948 level. It is worth noting that these costs were stable from 1948 through 1951, a period in which there were no major model changes. Between 1951 and 1953, styling expenditures were roughly doubled, according to Fig. 12–1. Staggering increases have taken place since

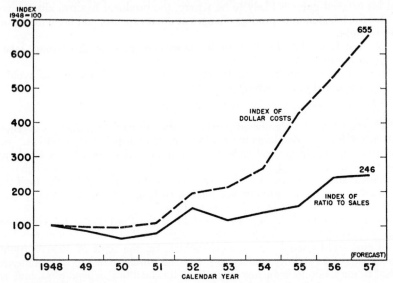

Fig. 12–1. Ford Motor Company's index of major model-change costs of 1948–57. (U.S. Senate Subcommittee on Antitrust and Monopoly, Hearings, *Administered Prices—Automobiles*. Washington, D.C.: Government Printing Office, 1958, p. 122.)

Indexes show the increase in the company's special tool amortization, engineering, and styling costs. These are the costs most directly related to model changes, although many product changes also involve piece-cost increases and significant expenditures for new facilities.

The top line shows the index of changes in dollar expenditures for tooling, engineering, and styling, with 1948 as a base of 100. Expenditures have risen every year since 1950; in 1957, they were more than 6½ times the base. The lower line shows an index of these expenses as a percentage of the company's annual dollar sales (excluding defense sales). In relation to sales, model-change costs are almost 2½ times as large as in 1948.

1954, when the current styling race began. By 1957, Ford's annual model-change costs were more than three times as high as in 1953. As annual dollar sales have risen much more slowly, the ratio of styling costs to sales—and by implication to total production costs—has more than doubled over the 10-year period.[15]

[15] Reprinted from: U.S. Senate Subcommittee on Antitrust and Monopoly, Hearings, 2d Session, 85th Congress, *Administered Prices—Automobiles* (Washington, D.C.: Government Printing Office, 1958), pp. 78–81, 86, 121–122.

PLANT EXPANSION: REPLACEMENT AND MODERNIZATION AND CAPITAL MOBILITY

Business managers expand the firm by increasing output capacity to handle a larger volume of business. Such expansion invariably involves an increase in the total assets that the firm will employ. Expansion usually means a change in the position and shape of the firm's cost and supply curve. Growth in this form often requires considerable investment for expansion projects (Table 12–1). Such projects are designed to create greater capacity for the output of the firm's existing products or for the output of new products. The economic justification for expansion lies in the anticipated sales and return on investment. Business managers determine the kind and amount of capacity that will be needed in the future on the basis of a careful estimate of the product-mix and long-term sales requirements.

Managers generally have a number of related economic and technical objectives in their expansion plans. They are, for instance, compelled to expand capacity when their plants have been operating at a high level of output, that is, when output has been pressing at the upper limits of capacity and a backlog of orders has been accumulating for some time. In a single expansion plan, the businessman may not only provide greater output capacity but may take the opportunity to revise his product line and improve or restyle his products to meet changes in consumer demand. The business manager always, of course, strives to adopt processes and facilities that are technically more advanced and that more extensively apply mass-production methods of output. The foregoing technical aims are usually based on the firm's research efforts which seek to reduce operating costs, achieve a greater measure of flexibility in the productive facilities, and introduce new or improved products. Plant expansion may also involve the relocation of productive facilities closer to expanding markets, richer resource deposits, or at areas that make for lower-cost production for other reasons. A businessman's expansion program sometimes seeks to improve the firm's competitive position. This often means "building ahead of demand" so that the firm may ward off new entrants, steal a march on rival firms when the demand increases sharply, and make quick delivery on rush orders. In the final analysis a firm's expansion program must be justified in economic terms. This essentially means that the increment in return must exceed the increment in cost. But because

TABLE 12-1

Expenditures for New Plant and Equipment, 1950-60

(billions of dollars)

Period	Total[1]	Manufacturing			Mining	Transportation		Public Utilities	Commercial and Other[2]
		Total	Durable Goods	Non-durable Goods		Railroads	Other		
1950	20.60	7.49	3.14	4.36	0.71	1.11	1.21	3.31	6.78
1951	25.64	10.85	5.17	5.68	0.93	1.47	1.49	3.66	7.24
1952	26.49	11.63	5.61	6.02	0.98	1.40	1.50	3.89	7.09
1953	28.32	11.91	5.65	6.26	0.99	1.31	1.56	4.55	8.00
1954	26.83	11.04	5.09	5.95	0.98	0.85	1.51	4.22	8.23
1955	28.70	11.44	5.44	6.00	0.96	0.92	1.60	4.31	9.47
1956	35.08	14.95	7.62	7.33	1.24	1.23	1.71	4.90	11.05
1957	36.96	15.96	8.02	7.94	1.24	1.40	1.77	6.20	10.40
1958	30.53	11.43	5.47	5.96	0.94	0.75	1.50	6.09	9.81
1959	32.54	12.07	5.77	6.29	0.99	0.92	2.02	5.67	10.88
1960[3]	36.85	14.90	7.47	7.43	1.07	1.06	2.14	5.85	11.82
			Seasonally Adjusted Annual Rates						
1958: Third quarter	29.61	10.86	5.16	5.70	0.88	0.63	1.29	6.10	9.85
Fourth quarter	29.97	10.58	4.86	5.72	0.97	0.58	1.62	6.26	9.96
1959: First quarter	30.60	11.20	5.25	5.95	0.95	0.65	1.70	5.80	10.35
Second quarter	32.50	11.80	5.75	6.05	0.95	1.00	2.10	5.80	10.85
Third quarter	33.35	12.25	5.85	6.40	1.00	1.30	2.15	5.60	11.05
Fourth quarter	33.60	12.85	6.15	6.70	1.05	0.85	2.15	5.50	11.20
1960: First quarter	35.15	14.10	7.15	6.95	1.00	1.00	2.00	5.75	11.35
Second quarter[3]	37.0	14.8	7.3	7.5	1.1	1.1	2.4	5.8	11.9
Third quarter[3]	37.5	15.1	7.6	7.6	1.1	1.2	2.3	5.9	12.0

[1] Excludes agriculture.

[2] Commercial and other includes trade, service, finance, communications, and construction.

[3] Estimates based on anticipated capital expenditures as reported by business in late April and May, 1960. Includes adjustments when necessary for systematic tendencies in anticipatory data.

Note: Quarterly anticipated data are rounded to nearest $100 million; beginning 1959 all other quarterly data rounded to nearest $50 million.

Annual total is the sum of unadjusted expenditures; it does not necessarily coincide with the average of seasonally adjusted figures.

These figures do not agree with the totals included in the GNP estimates of the Department of Commerce, principally because the latter cover agricultural investment and also certain equipment and construction outlays charged to current expense.

Source: Council of Economic Advisers, Economic Indicators, August 1960 (Washington, D.C.; Government Printing Office, 1960), p. 10.

of the uncertainty of future competitive conditions and markets, the added outlay for expansion can often be no more than the best estimate that can be made when expansion plans must be projected for several years into the future.

Expansion plans are often the manager's most difficult capital investment decisions, because productive facilities are typically highly specialized and a large commitment in fixed assets predetermines the direction of the firm's business for a score or more years into the future. Capacity expansion can also be undertaken on a somewhat modest basis, that is, in terms of piecemeal additions of specific pieces of equipment, enlargement of operating and service departments, removal of operating bottlenecks, and addition of distribution outlets. Because capacity is created for output of specific products, expansion plans, whether piecemeal or large scale, must be formulated on the basis of a careful appraisal of future demand and product-mix. It is the specific product-mix that a firm sells that essentially determines the kind and amount of output capacity that should be provided.

Businessmen provide capacity in a number of different ways. Expansion may involve the addition of new products to the firm's line of business, or it may involve expansion in the same line of business. Moreover, a firm may grow through internal expansion, that is, through the erection of new plants or through the creation of capacity by adoption of more productive facilities; or it may grow through external expansion, for instance, through an increase in subcontracting (procurement of components), through leasing of plants, or through mergings.

Expansion in terms of specific types of facilities is exemplified by erection of fabrication plants, assembly plants, power facilities, extraction plants at newly acquired raw-material reserves, warehouses, distribution outlets, and office or administration buildings. Planning expansion for the foregoing types of facilities calls for careful and detailed analysis, if the firm's over-all production system is to maintain an internally consistent operating design. This means that scattered activities must be effectively integrated and coordinated and that facilities must be set up with a provision for adaptability and expandability. Expansion by multiple-plant firms, because of the integrated nature of their operations, typically involves an over-all analysis of the company's operations, if large-scale expansion is to maintain economically balanced facilities. It is for this reason that investment projects dealing with a specific facility must take into account their effect on the firm's over-all multiple-plant system. The foregoing aspect of expansion also applies to external expansion, whether through the leasing of facilities or the acquisition of plants through mergings.

External Expansion—Mergings and Leasings

Capital investment for the enlargement of capacity through external expansion sometimes yields a higher rate of return than capital investment for internal expansion. A firm may enlarge its output capacity or volume of business through such forms of external expansion as the increased reliance on suppliers for the fabrication of components or the provision of service, through the leasing of production machines, hauling equipment, and, in fact, whole plants, and through merging with other establishments. The leasing of production facilities not only conserves investment funds but obtains tax savings. Imputed interest included in rental payments is an allowable expense in computing taxable income. Leasing, moreover, often achieves a measure of adaptability in that undesired or excess capacity can be quickly retired from production. (For further discussion of lease-or-buy decisions, see Special Cost Analyses, Section 19, in Robert I. Dickey's *Accountants' Cost Handbook*.)

Mergers and acquisitions as a form of expansion have long been an important feature of business. An important reason for mergers is the desire to gain capacity in manufacturing and marketing. Advantages in expansion through a merger often outweigh disadvantages. An acquisition of a going concern engaged in the same type of business offers a quick method for adding capacity. The acquired firm already has in its organization package the management personnel, plant, and all the groundwork entailed in expansion by the method of starting from scratch. Expansion by mergings may be desired for the diversification of company activities, so that such expansion essentially broadens the base of the business instead of merely adding capacity to an existing line of output. Mergers of this type are often vertical, horizontal, and conglomerate at the same time (Figs. 12–2 and 12–3).

Although the specific reasons for each merger vary, the motivating forces are essentially the same: (1) a desire to expand the economic base of the firm's operations to level off seasonal and cyclical fluctuation of business, (2) a desire to assure a steadier flow of income to the firm and to penetrate new markets and keep abreast of changes in the economy, (3) a desire to keep taxes low by spreading high profits of one division over all divisions, and (4) a desire to gain dependable sources of material supply and production economies by more completely utilizing the channels of distribution and plant capacity.

Some disadvantages of a merger include: the risk of key employees' leaving the firm, reluctance of personnel of the acquired firm to come under the control of an "outsider," loss of some specialization of the parent company due to ill-conceived diversification, and increased load on top management with resulting drop in managerial efficiency.

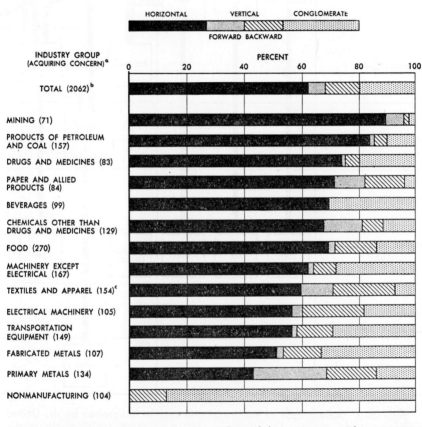

Fig. 12–2. Direction of expansion indicated by mergers and acquisitions of manufacturing and mining concerns (classified by industry of acquiring concern), 1940–47. [a]Figures in parentheses indicate the number of concerns acquired. [b]Includes groups not shown separately in the chart. [c]Does not include 388 acquisitions reported in *Textile World*. (Actions reported by Moody's *Investors Service* and Standard and Poor's *Corporation*.) (Federal Trade Commission, *The Merger Movement*. Washington, D.C.: Government Printing Office, 1948, p. 31.)

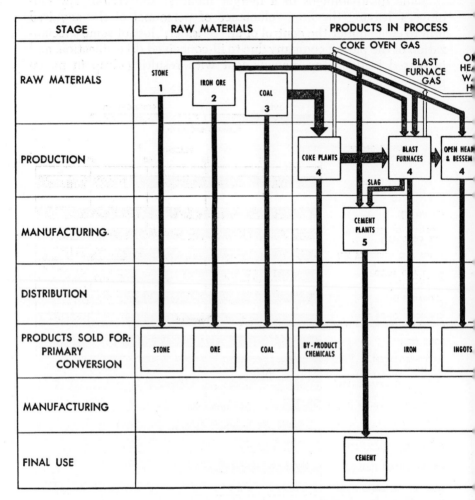

Fig. 12–3. An example of horizontal and vertical integration by the United States Steel Corporation. By illustrating the flow of steel in relation to the operations of subsidiary companies, the chart shows the corporation's combination of horizontal with vertical integration. Note evidence of conglomerate

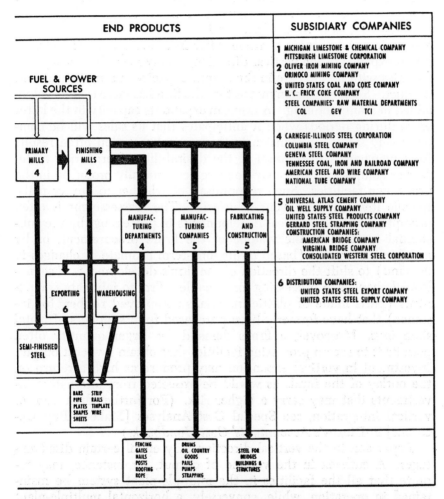

END PRODUCTS	SUBSIDIARY COMPANIES
	1 MICHIGAN LIMESTONE & CHEMICAL COMPANY PITTSBURGH LIMESTONE CORPORATION **2** OLIVER IRON MINING COMPANY ORINOCO MINING COMPANY **3** UNITED STATES COAL AND COKE COMPANY H. C. FRICK COKE COMPANY STEEL COMPANIES' RAW MATERIAL DEPARTMENTS COL GEV TCI

FUEL & POWER SOURCES

PRIMARY MILLS 4 → FINISHING MILLS 4

4 CARNEGIE-ILLINOIS STEEL CORPORATION
COLUMBIA STEEL COMPANY
GENEVA STEEL COMPANY
TENNESSEE COAL, IRON AND RAILROAD COMPANY
AMERICAN STEEL AND WIRE COMPANY
NATIONAL TUBE COMPANY

MANUFACTURING DEPARTMENTS 4 — MANUFACTURING COMPANIES 5 — FABRICATING AND CONSTRUCTION 5

5 UNIVERSAL ATLAS CEMENT COMPANY
OIL WELL SUPPLY COMPANY
UNITED STATES STEEL PRODUCTS COMPANY
GERRARD STEEL STRAPPING COMPANY
CONSTRUCTION COMPANIES:
    AMERICAN BRIDGE COMPANY
    VIRGINIA BRIDGE COMPANY
    CONSOLIDATED WESTERN STEEL CORPORATION

EXPORTING 6 — WAREHOUSING 6

6 DISTRIBUTION COMPANIES:
    UNITED STATES STEEL EXPORT COMPANY
    UNITED STATES STEEL SUPPLY COMPANY

SEMI-FINISHED STEEL

BARS STRIP
PIPE RAILS
PLATES TINPLATE
SHAPES WIRE
SHEETS

FENCING / GATES / NAILS / POSTS / ROOFING / ROPE

DRUMS / OIL COUNTRY GOODS / PAILS / PUMPS / STRAPPING

STEEL FOR BRIDGES BUILDINGS & STRUCTURES

("diagonal") integration in which by-product chemicals are concerned. (U.S. House of Representatives Subcommittee of Monopoly Power of the Committee on the Judiciary, Hearings, *Study of Monopoly Power.* Washington, D.C.: Government Printing Office, 1950, facing p. 600.)

Internal Expansion

In the long run most business enterprises grow largely through internal expansion. Expansion, whether internal or external, may be characterized as horizontal integration or vertical integration. The economic consequences of these differ in a number of respects. If a firm expands in the vertical direction, it may make big outlays for facilities with no increase in the output capacity in terms of the end product. Such expansion means that the firm has increased its value-added in manufacturing. A firm can expand its capacity in the latter sense during periods when it anticipates that its sales will be comparatively stable. Expansion in the vertical direction often results from managerial reappraisal of the desirability of procuring materials or components that may be more economically produced in the firm's own facilities. Such reappraisals of whether to buy or make specific items do not occur arbitrarily. The reassessment is often prompted by technological developments in processing, by the substantial increase in the volume of the firm's procurement, or by managerial decision (based on its long-term estimate of changes in demand) to shift the direction of the firm's development. Technological changes in processing may enable a firm to fabricate components (parts made of plastic material or improved rubber, for instance) that have formerly been purchased from suppliers of metal stampings. Moreover, a firm's demand for larger quantity often permits it to set up processing facilities that obtain low-cost output. Investment in vertical expansion may promise as high a return on the outlay of the funds as would be expected from alternative investments that may carry a higher risk. (For further discussion of vertical integration, see Special Cost Analyses [Make-or-Buy Decisions] in Dickey's *Accountants' Cost Handbook*.)

Expansion in the vertical direction may entail certain disadvantages. A cutback in the volume of output, for instance, may require that all the facilities in the multiple-plant system be maintained in operation, while, conversely, a horizontal multiple-plant system permits the shutdown of older or marginal plants and the concentration of production in the efficient newer plants. Loss of markets for the products put out by integrated facilities generally involves a greater loss in terms of capacity, particularly when the firm's products have been technologically displaced by new products. Whether a firm expands its capacity in the horizontal or the vertical direction or whether it expands internally or externally is not a decision based on the abstract virtues of each. Investment in a given expansion project should be appraised on the basis of the rate of return and consistency with the firm's long-range over-all program as compared with alternative competing investment projects.

The pattern of expansion by the firm may not only be characterized with respect to horizontal or vertical direction, but it may also be characterized with reference to changes in terms of addition of products and expansion in the scope of business activity. The internal pattern of expansion differs from that of external expansion with respect to frequency, suitability of the facilities for long-term output, and the degree of coordination and physical integration with the firm's multiple-plant system as a whole.

Internal expansion can occur on a number of levels. Piecemeal, month-to-month enlargement of capacity usually occurs through the normal plant-engineering method. Production bottlenecks can be removed at critical points in processing through methods analysis and retooling. Plant down time can be lowered through the introduction of an improved inventory-control system, streamlining operations, use of an appropriate wage-incentive system, and a worker-training program.

A somewhat more extensive expansion of capacity is provided through the enlargement of an existing plant. This generally entails expansion of the floor space, the extension of the building, the installation of new facilities, and their integration with existing facilities. The latter type of expansion program is generally coupled with the replacement of certain pieces of equipment in the existing processes. The expansion of capacity often raises the question of whether a new plant should be erected and located in another, perhaps more profitable, area. The latter problem is commoner in the larger, multiple-plant firms than in the smaller enterprises.

Expansion projects of a larger scope thus generally entail the erection of a complete plant, often in a new location. Expansions of this type usually permit the utilization of wholly new types of production processing methods. When a new plant is being established, it is generally planned and designed on the basis of a long-range projection of the need for capacity. Bigger plant expansion programs generally involve the establishment of several related plants in a new location. Such an enlargement of productive capacity is usually planned to meet the sales requirement of a regional market. The plants making up a regional division may be set up to put out a complete line of products (in the case of light manufacturing), or they may be set up to put out a certain specialized group of products that will meet the market requirements of a regional sales area, as well as supply some of the sales needs of the firm's national market. Plant expansion on the divisional level, too, calls for a forecast of company demand and the provision for future expansion of capacity to satisfy the sales requirements of the more distant years.

Internal expansion on the branch-plant level and on the divisional level requires *long-range planning of location*. In fact, the erection of a new plant or several plants in new areas may have been prompted by the disadvantages of an old location. An old location sometimes results in rising cost of operations because of a limited ground area and congestion, rising shipping and receiving costs because of the congestion in densely settled metropolitan areas, higher cost of transporting the product to distant market areas, or depletion of local material resources. Company managers may undertake a location study to resettle their plants in more favorable areas. Plant-location studies, moreover, are generally an integral part of large-scale plant expansion programs. In their search for new plant sites, industrial engineers seek an "ideal" location, one which promises the lowest unit cost of production and distribution for long-term business operation.

Plant-location planning invariably involves the problem of determining the degree of geographical decentralization that is economically desirable for the long pull. The internal migration of population, new resource discoveries, technological developments, expansion of highways, and the development of inland waterways are among the factors that tend to favor dispersal of plants. The foregoing factors indicate that plant-location studies typically involve an analysis of a large number of variables. The selection of a favorable location from among a number of alternatives sometimes comes down to a survey of the availability of subcontractors to supply components, the availability of certain scarce grades of labor, and a projection of the future size of the local sales potential. Decentralization may be favored by management because of personal notions with reference to the character of labor available in outlying areas and certain benefits that are to be derived from smaller-scale establishments. The location-planning aspect of investment in plant facilities is generally crucial for long-term development because it tends to predetermine the character of some of the facilities and, to some extent, the direction of an investment.

Capital investment in direct plant expansion generally involves the determination of the degree of production adaptability that is economically desirable. Facilities that are excessively adaptable may not attain as low a unit cost of output as more specialized facilities. But adaptability has a number of other facets aside from adaptability of production machinery. A plant, for instance, may, at the outset, be designed to utilize certain alternative processing methods and, at the same time, be designed for ease of expansion. Adaptability is best achieved through effective forecasting of market requirements so as to permit orderly and economical conversion of facilities to the output of other types of related products.

Equipment Replacement and Plant Modernization

Productive capacity, created through savings and capital accumulation, must be maintained through capital replacement if the productiveness of industry is to be preserved. Capital facilities depreciate during production—they are gradually used up by wear and tear and become obsolete over time. Obsolescence is the relative decline in the productiveness and value of capital facilities resulting from the development of more efficient capital facilities. Some capital facilities (trucks) have a short productive life, others have a longer productive life (locomotives and buildings). Depreciation is measured by the loss in value of productive facilities; it is, essentially, a value concept.

Obsolescence can be minimized and capital conserved through the utilization of facilities that are adaptable to more than one productive use, through the substitution of labor for capital wherever it is economically feasible, and through intensive (multiple-shift) utilization of facilities. The intermittent use or underemployment of capacity tends to waste productive facilities since it renders facilities more vulnerable to obsolescence and to depreciation because of a low rate of utilization over time.

During a period of depression, a producer may fail to replace capital adequately and to maintain his productive capacity. Such abnormal consumption of capital sometimes makes future equipment replacement costly—the stepped-up replacement of equipment generally takes place during periods of business upswing and prosperity. Equipment replacement costs (the price of equipment) may be high because the bunching up of business expenditure for facilities places heavy demands on industries supplying capital goods. This makes for higher costs in the manufacture of equipment and, because of delays and longer lead-time, higher costs for plant construction and installation of facilities.

Whereas the economist theoretically breaks down capital investment business expenditures into net capital formation, capital replacement (or capital maintenance), and capital mobility, the industrialist makes no such corresponding differentiation. His investment program does not neatly coincide with the theoretical processes of net capital formation, capital replacement, or capital mobility—an outlay for a single project may include elements of all three types of the foregoing classes of investment. Long-range business programs to revise or expand plant capacity often modify the scope of business in any manner that promises to reap a sufficient return on capital. Capital programs often are, therefore, designed to attain simultaneously two or more of the following goals: expansion of plant capacity, modernization and revision of plant for cost reduction, development of products, relocation of plants, and replacement of equipment. Some of the older facilities may be relegated for stand-by capacity, and the marginal, obsolete, or worn-out facilities may be discarded.

Plant modernization, for instance, may be carried out in conjunction with a plant revision (or conversion) for the output of new and improved products and it would also incorporate replacement of facilities and an expansion of capacity. Technological progress and gains in productivity are thus achieved through the purchase and adoption of advanced types of facilities. *Equipment replacement and geographical capital mobility* are attained through the use of replacement funds for an erection of an up-to-date plant in a new location. *Capital mobility* may also be attained through the expenditure of replacement funds for the conversion of a plant to the output of new products or through the erection of a new plant for the output of new types of goods, whether in a new location or at the old site.

Progressive management usually formulates some definite program for the replacement of equipment for individual plants. Plant and equipment budgets prepared for individual factories often include appropriations for the betterment of equipment and prolongation of its life, for the retirement of inefficient machinery and its replacement by more technologically advanced facilities, and for equipment additions other than replacement. By careful planning for production capacity, management can benefit by expanding and replacing facilities when market conditions are most favorable. Under such a planned budgetary practice not only is hasty, unwise expansion avoided, but expansion and replacement are undertaken so as to attain lower overhead charges. In the formulation of plant and equipment budgets, engineers generally study physical facilities as a whole so that funds for replacement and additions will be spent where they will make the best contribution to production requirements and give the highest return on investment. In such an approach, equipment fully depreciated on the books may not be replaced. The funds, instead, may be used for the purchase of some other, more desirable, equipment.

Retirement of equipment is a matter of degree. A machine may not actually be taken off the production floor; it may instead be relegated to the status of stand-by equipment and operated only during an emergency or for less exacting types of jobs. Old machines that are not fully worn out often become more expensive to operate because the product put out may no longer be up to standard due to loss of accuracy in the equipment; spoilage may be excessive, maintenance costs high, and workers may be unable to turn out the standard volume of output. Replacement would undoubtedly occur at a slower rate than it actually does were it not for the savings in costs and the improvements in production made possible by technological advance. The reasons for the purchase of equipment should be considered in connection with the profit objectives that lie behind equipment purchases. Among the more important factors that bear on decisions to purchase individual pieces of equipment for replacement are cost reduction, the need for increased machine capacity, and the need for revision of processes to put out remodeled or newly developed products.

Equipment for replacement is usually purchased when cost savings derived from the use of new equipment will repay the original cost long before the equipment is worn out. Before purchasing equipment, producers compute the amount of cost reduction necessary to justify the purchase. As a general practice, management will usually not purchase equipment for replacement unless the savings derived from the use of such equipment will recoup the purchase expenditure within a period of two to five years. Over the remaining life beyond repayment period, therefore, the equipment will be earning a profit. Replacement of equipment essentially involves keeping up with technological advance. When individual units of plant equipment are replaced, the new units are typically different from the old, invariably being of greater efficiency as well as of the type specifically designed to put out products currently in demand. Technological advance is, in fact, directly reflected in all purchases of plant equipment. Many new products and processes are introduced in industry with sufficient gradualness to permit conversion of plant primarily through the replacement process, thus minimizing obsolescence and the need for net capital formation.

Even the replacement of old machinery by new machinery of the same kind involves more than the simple substitution of a new unit for an old one. The new equipment invariably has many new features and improvements not found in the old equipment. The new unit may have greater operating capacity, may turn out better quality work, may be able to perform additional operations, may require less labor, and may occupy less floor space. The larger capacity of the new unit must be effectively integrated into the layout of the process in order that it may be productively tied in with existing machines. In cases in which the aim of equipment replacement is to expand capacity, a detailed capacity study must be made not only of the new units but also of the equipment with which the new unit is to be integrated. Full utilization of the capacity of new equipment may require revision and improvement of existing work centers so that they will not cause bottlenecks in the revised production line.

The substitution of new methods for older techniques often calls for some redesign of the product. An equipment replacement program may therefore require a product analysis and a redesign survey in conjunction with an equipment study. In fact, in order to reap the full cost reduction and quality improvement benefits of technological advance, a concerted program often consists of a product redesign study, a materials survey, and a production-processing survey. A comprehensive layout study frequently accompanies an equipment replacement program of the latter type. Such replacement and layout projects involve equipping to reorganize the manufacturing facilities. New and different kinds of equipment may therefore be integrated with existing machines, utilities, and building facilities. Before the decision to purchase new equipment or to employ new methods is made, a complete layout and facilities study is often made to ascertain what total expenditures will be required and what savings will be attained. (For further discussion of replacement analysis and policy, see Machinery and Equipment Economics, Section 22, in Carson's *Production Handbook.*)

COST SAVINGS FROM NEW PROCESSING METHOD. Improvements in steelmaking illustrate cost savings from the adoption of a new processing method, with required investment computed by the engineering method for estimating outlay costs:

In normal manufacturing operations, several questions arise concerning new processes, new developments, and new techniques. These questions deal with the economics of the process, with the technology of the process, and with the quality of the product in its effect on product marketability. From the standpoint of the oxygen converter, the latter two questions have been answered in recent trade journals and need no elaboration here. It is the purpose of this paper to investigate the comparative economics of the oxygen converter process. Briefly, the history and development of oxygen converted steel is as follows:

The economic and thermodynamic advantages of pneumatic conversion have been known since the advent of the Bessemer converter. However, the product from the Bessemer converter is limited in its use because of its properties as affected by the higher content of gases and metalloids as compared to open hearth product. To eliminate these difficulties and retain the advantages of pneumatic conversion, the oxygen converter was developed in Europe, reaching the commercial stage within the last few years. This process required more than fifteen years in transition from laboratory experiments through various size pilot plants to the size and scope as we know it today.

❊   ❊   ❊

Since the open hearth shop accounts for about 90 per cent of the ingot production in this country, it will be used as a standard for cost comparison. In addition, the quality of oxygen converter steel is comparable to the finest product of the open hearth furnace.

❊   ❊   ❊

The production cycle of a 35-ton oxygen converter is about 40 minutes, made up of 20 minutes blowing and 20 minutes idle. The idle time is consumed in skimming, testing, pouring, and charging. Thus, the production rate of an oxygen converter is 52 tons per hour or 450,000 tons per year. The addition of a second converter could be installed having its production cycle staggered

TABLE 12–2

Estimated Investment Required for Plant and Equipment for Alternative Production Methods

	450,000-ton Annual Capacity Oxygen Converter	525,000-ton Annual Capacity Open Hearth	900,000-ton Annual Capacity Oxygen Converter	1,050,000-ton Annual Capacity Open Hearth
1. Buildings	$ 900,000.00	$ 5,700,000.00	$ 1,200,000.00	$ 9,300,000.00
2. Equipment ..	1,900,000.00	10,000,000.00	2,400,000.00	19,200,000.00
3. Utilities	2,600,000.00	1,600,000.00	3,400,000.00	1,900,000.00
4. Air pollution control	1,500,000.00	1,500,000.00	2,000,000.00	3,000,000.00
5. Storage facilities ..	2,200,000.00	2,000,000.00	2,400,000.00	2,000,000.00
Total ...	$9,100,000.00	$20,800,000.00	$11,400,000.00	$35,400,000.00
Cost per annual ton	$20.22	$39.61	$12.67	$33.71

so that it would be blowing while the first converter was idle. *This procedure would double the capacity of the plant without materially increasing the size or quantity of auxiliary equipment, other than the oxygen plant* [italics mine]. Correspondingly, the production rate of a modern open-hearth furnace using hot metal is about 21 tons per hour. On the basis of 90 per cent furnace availability, the net production rate is 18 tons per hour or 160,000 tons per year. Clearly then, one oxygen converter has about the same production capacity as three open-hearth furnaces. The economic study will be based on two plant capacities of 500,000 and 1,000,000 annual tons corresponding to one or two converter vessels, and then to three or six open-hearth furnaces.

Table 12–2 shows the estimated construction costs for oxygen-converter shops and open-hearth shops of approximately 500,000 annual tons and 1,000,000 annual tons. "Buildings" include the open hearth building, stockhouse, teeming building, etc. "Equipment" includes furnaces, vessels, ladles, buckets, molds, stools, charging machine(s), cranes, mixer(s), etc. The open hearths chosen for this particular study was 275-ton capacity. The oxygen converter vessels chosen were two 35-ton capacity (one operating and one stand-by) and three 35-ton capacity (two operating in sequence and one stand-by). "Utilities" includes water piping, steam piping, electrical distribution system, wiring and, for the oxygen converter, an oxygen plant of suitable capacity. "Air pollution" includes waste heat boilers, filtration equipment, duct work, sludge piping, etc. "Storage facilities" include trackage, scrap yard, slag disposal, flux storage, etc.

The actual installed cost of a conversion shop is widely variable depending not only on the type and design of the equipment, but on the restrictions imposed by the particular plant site. Therefore, the figures below may vary from an actual installation cost, but the relative proportions will remain essentially the same. The wide variations in cost for an oxygen converter shop and an open hearth shop lie principally in buildings and in equipment. In view of the small size [space displacement] of the oxygen converter as compared to the

TABLE 12–3

Comparative Unit Cost of Material for Alternative Production Methods

	Oxygen Converter		Open Hearth	
	Pounds per Ton of Steel	Cost	Pounds per Ton of Steel	Cost
Steel scrap at $43 per gross ton	475	$ 9.03	438	$ 8.32
Hot metal at $33 per net ton	1,650	27.23	1,465	24.17
Iron ore at $14 per gross ton	....	....	380	2.38
Deoxidizers	....	.75	....	1.20
Scale	....	.40	....	.60
Total	....	$37.41	....	$36.67

open hearth, less building area is required. In addition, lighter live loads and dead loads [in the equipment] result in less expensive columns, beams, and floors, reducing the cost per unit area. The equipment costs are lower for an oxygen converter shop not only because of the lower cost of the vessel as compared to three open-hearth furnaces, but also because of the lighter cranes and other auxiliary equipment. The reason for the smaller rate of increase for the oxygen converter shop as the capacity increases from 500,000 to 1,000,000 tons per year is due to the fact that at the lower capacity, virtually 100 per cent stand-by equipment is required. With the increase in capacity, virtually all funds are allocated to productive equipment. This margin does not appear for the open hearth.

Table 12–3 shows the burden and materials cost per ton of tapped steel for the oxygen converter process and for the open-hearth furnace. For comparison purposes, the hot metal ratio of the open-hearth furnace has been increased to the same rate as the oxygen converter (78 per cent) although this ratio is higher than used in normal practice. In view of the fact that at this time hot metal is lower in cost than scrap, the increase in hot metal operates to the advantage of the open hearth. . . .

The materials cost per ton of tapped steel shows a cost advantage of only 74 cents per ton for the open-hearth furnace. The principal factor in this cost advantage is from the metallic iron reduced from the ore. This was obtained at an equivalent cost of about $20 per ton of iron. This apparent advantage is offset by fuel required to reduce the ore to metallic iron and these costs appear in "Cost above." If the conventional hot metal ratio of 60 per cent were used, the materials cost for an open-hearth furnace would be about $37.50 per ton or an increase of 83 cents per ton over the higher hot-metal ratio. At 50 per cent hot metal in the open-hearth furnace, the materials cost would be $38.18 per ton. As might be expected then, on the same basis, the materials costs for the two processes are relatively close together (within 2 per cent).

TABLE 12–4

Breakdown of "Cost Above" for Alternative Production Methods

	500,000 Tons		1,000,000 Tons	
	Oxygen Converter	Open Hearth	Oxygen Converter	Open Hearth
1. Fuel (60 cents per MM B.t.u.)	....	$1.98	....	$ 1.98
2. Fluxes	$1.17	.50	$1.17	.50
3. Furnace refractories	.30	.70	.30	.70
4. Ladle refractories	.15	.15	.15	.15
5. Furnace repair	.60	1.50	.60	1.50
6. Molds and stools	.65	.65	.65	.65
7. Production labor	.80	1.60	.80	1.60
8. Maintenance labor and materials	.42	.70	.33	.55
9. Oxygen	1.00	.20	1.00	.20
10. Supplies, tools, and lubricants	.16	.20	.16	.20
11. Water, steam, and power	.30	.30	.30	.30
12. Yard switching	.20	.20	.20	.20
13. Slag disposal	.30	.30	.30	.30
14. Indirect labor	.20	.20	.20	.20
15. Employee benefits	.30	.30	.30	.30
16. General expense	.40	.40	.40	.40
Subtotal	$6.95	$ 9.88	$6.86	$ 9.73
17. Fixed charges (at 12 per cent)	2.42	4.75	1.52	4.52
Total	$9.37	$14.63	$8.38	$14.25

Table 12–4 shows the cost above per ton of steel for the oxygen-converter process and for the open-hearth furnace. As the oxygen converter requires no external source of heat, one of the major savings in cost is fuel. The fuel cost, per ton of steel, does not change with increased shop [output] capacity and is affected only by the heat requirement of the open-hearth process, which is about 3.3 million B.t.u. per ton. If the oxygen required for the oxygen converter is deducted, the net fuel cost of the open-hearth furnace is $1.18 higher than for the oxygen converter. The cost of fluxes is considerably higher for the oxygen converter because it becomes advantageous to use principally burnt materials such as burnt lime instead of the raw stone. Part of the fuel costs shown above are dependent upon the calcination of the $CaCO_3$. Furnace refractories and furnace repair are less for an oxygen converter for several reasons. From the standpoint of durability, the lining life of existing oxygen converters is about 230 heats or about 8,000 tons. Present practice is to recover as much of the lining as possible for reuse in tar-pressed bricks and tamping clay. The net consumption of refractories is 30 pounds per ton for the oxygen converter, as

compared to 80 pounds per ton in an open-hearth furnace (4). It is assumed that the masonry labor will be directly proportional to the quantity of refractory. Production labor, developed from comparative force reports, shows that the labor cost of an oxygen-converter shop is about half of that of an open-hearth-furnace shop.   In view of the simplicity of the oxygen converter, maintenance labor and materials, supplies, tools, and lubricants will also be about 60 per cent of the cost of an open-hearth installation. The quantity of oxygen required for conversion is 0.08 per ton of steel, and since oxygen can be produced for about $10 per ton in the quantity required, the cost of oxygen will be $0.80 per ton of steel. To that must be added the cost of oxygen for the remainder of shop uses ($0.20 per ton), giving a total cost of $1 per ton. Employee benefits are related to total wages and have been so proportioned. The other elements of cost above are related to the total production and should not be affected appreciably by the specific conversion process. No credit has been taken for byproduct recovery, such as flue dust and steam, which could amount to about 60 cents per ton.   This is based on the average generation of 1,000 pounds of steam per ton of steel.

The cost studies presented here are perhaps theoretical to some degree. Where possible, they are based on the experience of the existing Austrian oxygen-converter shops with due allowance for conditions in this country.   In those cases where data is lacking, experience from Bessemer converter plants was used as a basis of cost estimation.   In the remainder of the cases, the knowledge of the requirements of the process as compared to an open-hearth furnace was used to develop the cost figures.

It is the opinion of the authors that the economic importance of the oxygen-converter process is so compelling that the process must be given detailed study and evaluation for any program involving plant modernization or involving an increase in ingot capacity.[16]

QUESTIONS FOR REVIEW AND APPLICATION

1. What are the factors that determine or influence the composition and emphasis of the company long-range program (i.e., the areas selected for profit gain) in a given field of business? For instance, how would the composition and emphasis of the long-range program tend to differ between a firm producing a consumer durable good and a firm producing a homogeneous material (lumber, pulp, or cement) for the industrial market?

2. How can management channelize and control its research effort so as to obtain an adequate flow of desired types of technological innovations?

3. (a) How do company long-term goals influence the scope and objectives of a firm's research effort? (b) Distinguish between a firm's long- and short-term technological goals.

4. Compare the problem of estimating the funds required and the rate of return for a technical innovation with that of equipment replacement.

5. (a) Identify the functions and areas of business operation that generally offer cost-reduction opportunities. (b) How are product improvement, equip-

[16] "Economic Aspects of the Oxygen Converter Process" by W. C. Rueckel and J. W. Irvin. Reprinted from: U.S. Senate Subcommittee on Antitrust and Monopoly, Hearings, *Administered Prices—Steel*, Part 4 (Washington, D.C.: Government Printing Office, 1958), pp. 1386–1390. (Presented at the A.I.S.E. Meeting in Cleveland, Ohio, September 28, 29, 30, and October 1, 1954.)

ment replacement, and plant modernization related to cost reduction? Illustrate.

6. (a) Discuss the problems involved in estimating the capital outlay required and the rate of return on investment for a company training program. (b) Will the fact that the outlay for the program can be expensed (rather than amortized) and thus yield a high after-tax return favor managerial acceptance of the program? (c) What are some of the intangible benefits that may favor managerial adoption of the training program?

7. (a) Explain the types and sources of excess capacity that may prompt the adoption of a new item to a firm's product line. (b) Explain the cost and profit concepts that would apply in estimating the rate of return from an outlay for the addition of an item to the product line.

8. Compare the problem of estimating the rate of return from the adoption of a product similar to one produced by other firms (i.e., a commercially established product) with the adoption of a wholly new product (one new to the consumers).

9. Explain the ways whereby diversification of the product line may stabilize sales revenue and augment long-term earnings.

10. (a) Explain how a product-simplification program can reduce the amount of inventory and productive capacity required for the output of a given volume of products. (b) Can a product be redesigned to lower costs through the reduction of spoilage in processing? Illustrate other ways whereby the redesigning of a product may increase earnings, that is, identify the typical sources of cost savings derived from the redesigning of a product and identify the typical offsetting costs involved in redesigning a product and in revising the process and readjusting inventories.

11. Under what conditions may a firm continue to put out and market a product from which the sales receipts do not cover the total cost of the output including a fair share of the overhead?

12. (a) What are the various reasons why a firm may drop an item from its line of products? (b) What evaluations should a firm make before dropping a product from its line?

13. (a) Identify and briefly explain the different ways whereby a firm can enlarge capacity and business volume through external expansion. (b) What are the various managerial motives for business expansion through mergers?

14. In what way can the practice of leasing plant equipment accelerate the introduction of technological improvements in production processing?

15. Make an analysis of whether management should buy or rent a certain piece of equipment. Make the necessary assumptions to carry out your analysis.

16. Explain the different degrees (or levels) in which a firm may enlarge capacity through internal expansion.

17. "Even though they forecast no increase in long-term sales volume, managers may find it profitable to expand capacity in terms of value-added (i.e., vertically)." Explain.

18. Identify and explain sources of economies (cost reductions) that may accrue when a firm expands vertically.

19. (a) What price reductions and savings to the buyer and cost savings to the seller may result from a long-term procurement contract for the provision of materials and components? (b) Are the economy gains to the buyer and seller akin to the benefits derived from backward integration? Explain.

20. "When an expanding producer, who has been buying power, needs additional steam in the plant for processing purposes, he may find it cheaper to produce power and use the waste steam from the power plant in the factory." Identify and explain the sources of cost savings in the above situation.

21. What are the benefits that may be derived from the use of a pilot plant in developing a new production process?

22. How can the break-even chart aid in the selection of the most profitable size for the erection of a new productive establishment?

23. Why must the selection of a productive process and equipment for replacement purposes be made in conjunction with a plant-layout study and sometimes in conjunction with a plant-location study?

24. "When alternative machine processes are available, the most economical process is always the one which takes the lowest initial investment for the purchase and installation of the facilities." True or false? Explain.

25. (a) When is a piece of equipment worn out in terms of operating and maintenance cost? (b) When is it obsolete in terms of operating cost and technical level of performance? (c) Can a machine be rendered obsolete by a shift in consumer tastes for a product? Explain.

26. Under what conditions will businessmen not replace particular productive facilities as they wear out?

27. "The purchase of equipment for replacement purposes during a period of stable prices often results in both capital-saving and laborsaving improvements which permit output of more goods per dollar invested in plant facilities and in working capital." Explain.

28. (a) Explain how the pace of capital replacement affects the pace of introduction of technological improvements. (b) Explain how the economy's over-all productivity can increase with no net capital formation in monetary terms.

29. Explain how a firm's large-scale replacement program may simultaneously encompass the goals of cost reduction through plant modernization, the need for additional capacity for the output of established products, and the need for capacity to put out new products being introduced.

30. (a) Discuss the methods whereby a firm can achieve greater flexibility and adaptability, including capital mobility. (b) Contrast short- and long-run adaptability and mobility of capital.

31. Explain how the annual availability of large depreciation funds in big diversified multiple-plant corporations contributes to capital mobility among industries and geographical areas and smoothes the process of frictional change in competitive industry.

32. Discuss the relevance of the acceleration principle (i.e., the direct relationship between the increase in the demand for consumer's goods and the increase in the demand for producer's goods) for industries that hold reserve capacity for competitive purposes, build ahead of demand, and use replacement funds for production innovations that markedly enlarge output capacity.

33. Identify and explain some of the structural features of the multiple-plant firm that impede the movement of the industry toward equilibrium.

34. Discuss the relevance of the Keynesian liquidity preference concept in an economy in which a large proportion of business investment expenditures are internally financed through the use of retained earnings and depreciation funds.

References and Supplementary Readings for Part IV

Risk and Uncertainty

JONES, HOWE MANLEY. *Executive Decision Making*. Homewood, Ill.: Richard D. Irwin, Inc., 1957. Chap. 10.

*SHACKLE, G. L. S. *Expectations in Economics*. Cambridge: Cambridge University Press, 1949. Chaps. 1, 2.

Unionism

*OWENS, RICHARD N. *Business Management and Public Policy*. Homewood, Ill.: Richard D. Irwin, Inc., 1958. Chap. 34.

REYNOLDS, L. G. *Labor Economics and Labor Relations*. Englewood Cliffs, N.J.: Prentice-Hall, Inc., 1959.

Taxation

WALD, HASKELL P., and FROOMKIN, J. N. (eds.). *Agricultural Taxation and Economic Development*. Cambridge: Harvard University Press, 1954.

Government Policy

*BAIN, JOE S. *Industrial Organization*. New York: John Wiley & Sons, Inc., 1959. Chaps. 3, 12–15.

*COLBERG, MARSHALL R., BRADFORD, W. C., and ALT, R. M. *Business Economics; Principles and Cases*. Homewood, Ill.: Richard D. Irwin, Inc., 1957. Chaps. 13–14.

FEDERAL TRADE COMMISSION. *Report on Corporate Mergers and Acquisitions*. Washington, D.C.: Government Printing Office, 1955.

KOONTZ, HAROLD, and GABB, T. W. *Public Control of Economic Enterprise*. New York: McGraw-Hill Book Co., Inc., 1956.

PEGRAM, R. F. *Public Regulation of Business*. Homewood, Ill.: Richard D. Irwin, Inc., 1959.

STOCKING, G., and WATKINS, M. *Monopoly and Free Enterprise*. New York: Twentieth Century Fund, 1951.

Business Cycles

DUESENBERRY, J. S. *Business Cycles and Economic Growth*. New York: McGraw-Hill Book Co., Inc., 1958.

GORDON, ROBERT A. *Business Fluctuation*. New York: Harper & Brothers, 1952.

LEE, MAURICE WENTWORTH. *Economic Fluctuations; Growth and Stability*. Homewood, Ill.: Richard D. Irwin, Inc., 1959.

* Suggested reading.

Forecasting

°BRATT, E. *Business Cycles and Forecasting.* 5th ed.; Homewood, Ill.: Richard D. Irwin, Inc., 1959.

BROWN, LYNDON O. *Marketing and Distribution Research.* 3d ed.; New York: The Ronald Press Co., 1955.

°BRY, GERHARD. *The Average Workweek as an Economic Indicator.* New York: National Bureau of Economic Research, Inc., 1959.

°COLBERG, MARSHALL R., BRADFORD, W. C., and ALT, R. M. *Business Economics; Principles and Cases.* Homewood, Ill.: Richard D. Irwin, Inc., 1957. Chap. 2.

FERBER, ROBERT. *Factors Influencing Durable Goods Purchases.* Urbana: University of Illinois Press, 1955.

°JONES, HOWE MANLEY. *Executive Decision Making.* Homewood, Ill.: Richard D. Irwin, Inc., 1957. Chap. 11.

KATONA, GEORGE. *Psychological Analysis of Economic Behavior.* New York: McGraw-Hill Book Co., Inc., 1951.

°LEWIS, JOHN PRIOR. *Business Conditions Analysis.* New York: McGraw-Hill Book Co., Inc., 1959.

MARSEL, SHERMAN J. *Fluctuations, Growth and Forecasting.* New York: John Wiley & Sons, Inc., 1959.

NATIONAL INDUSTRIAL CONFERENCE BOARD. *Forecasting in Industry; Case Studies.* New York: National Industrial Conference Board, 1955.

SNYDER, RICHARD M. *Measuring Business Changes.* New York: John Wiley & Sons, Inc., 1955.

Business Investment (Capital Budgeting)

°BAIN, JOE S. *Pricing, Distribution and Employment.* New York: Henry Holt & Co., Inc., 1948. Chap. 11.

°DEAN, JOEL, and Joel Dean Associates. *Managerial Economics.* Englewood Cliffs, N.J.: Prentice-Hall, Inc., 1951. Chap. 10.

°DOYLE, LEONARD A. *Economics of Business Enterprise.* New York: McGraw-Hill Book Co., Inc., 1952. Chap. 15.

°EISNER, R. *Determinants of Capital Expenditures.* University of Illinois Bulletin. Urbana: University of Illinois Press, 1956.

°NATIONAL INDUSTRIAL CONFERENCE BOARD. *Controlling Capital Expenditures and Case Studies.* Studies in Business Policy No. 62. New York: National Industrial Conference Board, Inc., 1953.

°SOLOMON, EZRA (ed.). *Capital Management.* Chicago: University of Chicago Press, 1959.

°SPENCER, MILTON H., and SIEGELMAN, LOUIS. *Managerial Economics.* Homewood, Ill.: Richard D. Irwin, Inc., 1959. Chaps. 10–11.

°WELSH, GREEN A. *Budgeting: Profit-Planning and Control.* Englewood Cliffs, N.J.: Prentice-Hall, Inc., 1957. Chap. 10.

Long-Range Planning

°EWING, DAVID W. (ed.). *Long-Range Planning for Management.* New York: Harper & Brothers, 1958. Chaps. 3–4, 6–7, 9–13, 19–20, 24, 31, 37–42.

°JONES, HOWE MANLEY. *Executive Decision Making.* Homewood, Ill.: Richard D. Irwin, Inc., 1957. Chaps. 1–3, 6, 12–14.

Supply of Capital and Investment

HICKS, J. R. *Value and Capital.* 2d ed.; London: Clarendon Press, 1946.

KERSTEAD, BURTON S. *Capital Investment and Profit.* New York: John Wiley & Sons, Inc., 1960.

* Suggested reading.

LUTZ, F. and V. *The Theory of Investment of the Firm*. Princeton: Princeton University Press, 1951.

MARTING, ELIZABETH (ed.). *Top-Management Decision Simulation: The AMA Approach*. New York: American Management Association, Inc., 1957.

MEYER, JOHN R., and KUH, EDWIN. *The Investment Decision: An Empirical Study*. Cambridge: Harvard University Press, 1957.

WASSERMAN, PAUL, and SILANDER, FRED S. *Decision Making: An Annotated Bibliography*. Ithaca, N.Y.: Cornell University Press, 1958.

The Long-Range Program

*CARSON, GORDON B. (ed.). *Production Handbook*. 2d ed.; New York: The Ronald Press Co., 1958. Secs. 17, 22.

*DEAN, JOEL, and Joel Dean Associates. *Managerial Economics*. Englewood Cliffs, N.J.: Prentice-Hall, Inc., 1951. Chaps. 3, 6.

*DICKEY, ROBERT I. (ed.). *Accountants' Cost Handbook*. 2d ed.; New York: The Ronald Press Co., 1960. Sec. 19, Special Cost Analyses.

*EWING, DAVID W. (ed.). *Long-Range Planning for Management*. New York: Harper & Brothers, 1958. Chaps. 22, 25–32, 43.

GINZBERG, ELI, and REILLEY, EWING W. *Effecting Change in Large Organizations*. New York: Columbia University Press, 1957.

JAMESON, CHARLES LASELLE. *Business Policy*. Englewood Cliffs, N.J.: Prentice-Hall, Inc., 1953.

McNICHOLS, T. J. *Policy Making and Executive Action; Cases in Business Policy*. New York: McGraw-Hill Book Co., Inc., 1959.

MELMAN, SEYMOUR. *Decision Making and Productivity*. New York: John Wiley & Sons, Inc., 1959.

*OWENS, RICHARD N. *Business Management and Public Policy*. Homewood, Ill.: Richard D. Irwin, Inc., 1958. Chap. 13.

QUINN, JAMES BRIAN. *Industrial Research Evaluation*. New York: The Ronald Press Co., 1959.

* Suggested reading.

APPENDIX

Outline for Industry Study

A comprehensive outline for an industry study (including a survey of the representative firm) is presented as a guide for those who want to undertake a study of a specific industry. This outline of readings on the analysis of the composite industry and the firm will provide approaches that lead to deeper insight into the development and behavior of an industry and will minimize the risk of overlooking important aspects of the structure and functioning of an industry. The outline is sufficiently broad to permit an analyst to determine the scope and emphasis he desires in his study. The nature of the information an analyst compiles in his study will depend not only on the specific objectives of his survey but also on the type and nature of the industry being studied and the particular factors and circumstances influencing the industry's development.

In addition to the references listed in the text, an analyst conducting an industry study will generally use the following sources of information: economic studies of the industry available from past research, trade directories and trade association publications, annual reports of individual firms, financial journals, government statistical reports, and statistical and other publications of international agencies.

For detail and adaptation, see Index entry "Industry study, aspects of."

501

Index